The Bristol and Gloucestershire Archaeological Society
Gloucestershire Record Series

Hon. General Editor
Dr J D Hodsdon

Volume 29

The Religious Census of Bristol and Gloucestershire, 1851

THE RELIGIOUS CENSUS OF BRISTOL AND GLOUCESTERSHIRE 1851

Edited by Alan Munden

The Bristol and Gloucestershire Archaeological Society

2015

The Bristol and Gloucestershire Archaeological Society
Gloucestershire Record Series

© The Bristol and Gloucestershire Archaeological Society 2015

ISBN 978 0 900197 88 8

British Library Cataloguing in Publication Data
A catalogue entry for this book is available from the British Library

Produced for the Society
by 4word Ltd, Bristol
Printed in Great Britain

CONTENTS

ACKNOWLEDGEMENTS

I have much appreciated the invitation of the Bristol and Gloucestershire Archaeological Society to produce an edition of the 1851 Religious Census for the city and county. This publication provides a comprehensive record of about 900 places of worship in Bristol and Gloucestershire.

I have valued the comments and observations of Joseph Bettey on the places of worship in Bristol, and of the many other individuals who have answered my questions. In the south I have greatly appreciated the assistance of the staff of the Gloucestershire Archives and, in the north, of the staff of the Newcastle Literary and Philosophical Society Library. Finally, I record my thanks to the series editor, James Hodsdon, for his assistance in bringing the edition to its present form.

Alan Munden

Newcastle upon Tyne, July 2015

ABBREVIATIONS

AV	*Authorised Version* (King James Version)
BQ	*Baptist Quarterly*
CERC	Church of England Record Centre
CLHS	Cheltenham Local History Society
CMS	Church Missionary Society [now the Church Mission Society]
CPAS	Church Pastoral Aid Society
ECE	Ecclesiastical Commissioners for England
ECU	English Church Union
EQ	*Evangelical Quarterly*
GA	Gloucestershire Archives
GNQ	*Gloucestershire Notes and Queries*
Journal	*The Journal of the Rev John Wesley*
ODNB	*Oxford Dictionary of National Biography*
OPE	Other Permanent Endowment
National Society	National Society for the promotion of the education of the poor in the principles of the established church
QAB	Queen Anne's Bounty
SS	Sunday scholars
TBGAS	*Transactions of the Bristol and Gloucestershire Archaeological Society*
VCH	*Victoria County History* (of Gloucestershire, unless stated otherwise)
Venn	J. Venn and J. A. Venn, *Alumni Cantabrigienses*
WHS	Wesley Historical Society

BIBLIOGRAPHY

Online sources
www.archaeologydataservice.ac.uk, for Foyle, A., *Identity and the City: a History of Ethnic Minorities in Bristol, 1002–2001*, 2007
www.britishlistedbuildings.co.uk
www.cmhrc.co.uk, for report of Children's Employment Commission, 1842
www.theclergydatabase.org.uk
www.surman.english.qmul.ac.uk (Surman index of Congregational ministers)

Church of England Record Centre (CERC)
ECE 7/1/50193 St Bartholomew, Oakridge
ECE 7/1/1444 Christ Church, Chalford
ECE 7/1/3575 St Nicholas, Kemerton
ECE 7/1/20815; 20817 Holy Trinity, Slad

Gloucestershire Archives (GA)
GDR/F1/4 Faculty and consecration papers
GDR/A2/1–6 Surveys of the diocese 1831–63
GDR/Y Gloucester Diocesan Kalendar
GDR/P124 IN 3/2 Memorial of Henry Vizard
GDR/P284 IN 1/2 All Saints, Selsley, Register of Services
GDR/R63 4GS Annual Reports of the House of Mercy at Bussage
GDR/D1392 Sheepscombe Chapel
GDR/P288 IN 1/1/1 Sheepscombe Baptismal Register

Theses
Isherwood, D. O., The Churches of S. S. Teulon, M.Phil. NAA (Thames Polytechnic) 1986
Munden, A. F., The Church of England in Cheltenham 1826–1856 with particular reference to Rev Francis Close, M. Litt. (University of Birmingham) 1980

Printed sources
An Inventory of Nonconformist Chapels and Meeting-Houses in Central England. Gloucestershire (London) 1986
An Inventory of Nonconformist Chapels and Meeting-Houses in Central England. Herefordshire, Warwickshire and Worcestershire (London) 1986
The Bristol Mercury
Census of Great Britain, 1851. Religious Worship in England and Wales. Report and Tables (London) 1853. Reprinted in the Irish University Press series of *British Parliamentary Papers*. Population, vol. 10, 1970
CPAS. Report of the Committee read at the 17th Annual Meeting, on the 11 May 1852
CPAS. Abstract of Report and Speeches at the 18th Annual Meeting of the CPAS, 10 May 1853
The Clergy List for 1852 (London) 1852 [and other editions]
Crockford's Clerical Directory for 1860 (London) 1860 [and other editions]
Edwards's New Cheltenham Directory for 1851 (Cheltenham) 1851
Gloucestershire Notes and Queries (London) 1881–1905 (10 vols.)

Hardwick's Annual Biography for 1856 (London) 1857

Hunt and Co's Directory and Topography for the City of Bristol [etc.], London, 1850

Matthew's Annual Bristol and Clifton Directory and Almanac 1851 (Bristol) 1851

Oxford Dictionary of National Biography (Oxford) 2004 (60 vols.)

Post Office Directory of Gloucestershire, with Bath and Bristol (London) 1856

Religious Census of Bristol, Western Daily Press (Bristol) 1881

Anon, *A History of Baptist Christians and the Baptist Church, Hanham, Bristol from 1690* (Bristol) n.d.

Anon, Ashleworth Ecclesiastical Records, *TBGAS,* 1926, vol. 48, 275–86

Anon, Buildings in Bristol of architectural or historical interest damaged or destroyed by enemy action, 1940–42, *TBGAS*, 1944, vol. 65, 167–74

Aitken, J., (ed.) *Census of Religious Worship, 1851. The Returns for Worcestershire* (Worcester) 2000

Aldred, D. H., *A History of Bishop's Cleeve and Woodmancote* (Stroud) 2009

Aldred, D., Rev Dr Andrew Morton Brown and a Welsh Connection, CLHS, 2012, *Journal 28*, 53–60.

Baker, E. P., *Bishop [Samuel] Wilberforce's Visitation Returns for the Archdeaconry of Oxford in the year 1854* (Oxford) 1954

Baddeley, St C., *History of the church of St Mary at Painswick* (Exeter) 1902

Baddeley, St C., Avening Church, *TBGAS*, 1921, vol. 43, 181–90

Barlow, M., *The Life of William Hagger Barlow DD,* (London) 1910

Baker, W. J., 'Henry Ryder of Gloucester 1815–1824: England's first Evangelical Bishop', *TBGAS,* 1971, vol. 89, 130–44

Bell, G. K. A., *Randall Davidson. Archbishop of Canterbury* (Oxford) 1935, 2 vols.

Bendall, D. J., *The Parish Church of Clifton 1154–1954* (Gloucester) 1954 (supp. 1970)

Best, G. F. A., *Temporal Pillars. Queen Anne's Bounty, the Ecclesiastical Commissioners and the Church of England* (Cambridge) 1964.

Betjeman, J., *John Betjeman Collected Poems* (London) 2003

Bettey, J., *Historic Churches and Church Life in Bristol* (Bristol) 2001

Blake, S. T., *Cheltenham's Churches and Chapels AD 773–1883* (Cheltenham) 1979

Bond, F., *Dedications and patron Saints of English Churches* (Oxford) 1914

Boore, E. J., The Church of St Augustine the Less: an interim statement, *TBGAS*, 1986, vol. 104, 211–4

Baddeley, St C., Avening Church, *TBGAS*, 1921, vol. 43, 181–90

Bridgman, I., *Remarks on the reply of the Rev H. Berkin AM, to a candid appeal to the religious public, occasioned by the dismissal of the Rev Isaac Bridgman AB, from the curacy of Trinity Church, in the Forest of Dean, Gloucestershire* (London) 1823

Briggs, A., *1851* (London) 1951

Brooks, A. and Pevsner, N., *The Buildings of England. Worcestershire* (London) 2007

Brown, C. G., *The Death of Christian Britain* (London) 2001

Butler, D. M., *The Quaker Meeting Houses of Britain* (London) 1999 (2 vols.)

Butler, R. F., Brimpsfield Church History, *TBGAS,* 1962, vol. 81, 73–97

Carter, G., *Anglican Evangelicals. Protestant Secessions from the Via Media c.1800–1850* (Oxford) 2001

Carter, T. T., *A Memoir of John Armstrong* (Oxford) 1857

Chatfield, M., *Churches the Victorians Forgot* (Ashbourne) 1979

Chilcott, J., *Descriptive History of Bristol* (Bristol) 1851

Church, R. W., *The Oxford Movement twelve years 1833–1845* (London) 1891

Clark, G. K., *The Making of Victorian England* (London) 1965

Clarke, B. F. L., *The Building of the Eighteenth-century Church* (London) 1963

Close, F., *The 'Restoration of Churches' is the Restoration of Popery ... a sermon preached in the Parish Church, Cheltenham, on Tuesday, 5 November 1844* (London) 1845

Close, F., *Three Lectures on 'The Present State of Parties in the Church of England'* (Cheltenham) 1847

Cobb, P. G., *The Oxford Movement in Nineteenth Century Bristol* (Bristol) 1988

Coleridge, J. T., *A Memoir of the Rev John Keble* (Oxford) 1869 (2 vols.)

Conybeare, W. J., 'Church Parties' [1853] and republished in *Essays Ecclesiastical and Social* (London) 1855

Cripps, H. W., *A Practical Treatise on the Law relating to the Church and Clergy* (London) seventh edition, 1921

Crossley Evans, M. J. (ed) *'A Grand City' – 'Life, Movement and Work'. Bristol in the eighteenth and nineteenth centuries,* (Bristol) 2010

Currie, C. R. J. and Lewis, C. P., *A Guide to English County Histories* (Stroud) 1997

Curtis, S. J., *History of Education in Great Britain* (London) 1965

Dale, J. M., *The Clergyman's Legal Handbook and Churchwarden's Guide* (London) 1898

Dancey, C. H., The Crypt Church, Gloucester, sometimes called St Mary of South Gate, *TBGAS,* 1903, vol. 26, 293–307

Davie, G., *Religion in Britain since 1945. Believing without Belonging* (Oxford) 2000

Davies, G. C. B., *The First Evangelical Bishop* (London) 1957

Davies, R., and Rupp, G. (eds), *A History of Methodism in Great Britain* (London) 1965–88 (4 vols.)

Ellacombe, H. T., *The History of the Parish of Bitton, in the County of Gloucestershire* (Exeter) 1881

Evans, W., Bishop Monk and the Horfield Question, *TBGAS,* 2014, vol. 114, 201–16

Fennemore, E. P., *A History of Randwick* (Stroud) 1893

Foster, J., *Alumni Oxonienses 1715–1886* (Oxford) 1887–8 (4 vols.)

Foyle, A. and Pevsner, N., *The Buildings of England. Somerset: North and Bristol* (London) 2011

Gardiner, R. B., *The Registers of Wadham College, Oxford* (London) 1895

Gasquet, A., *The Order of the Visitation. Its spirit and its growth in England* (London) n.d. [c.1900]

Gay, J. D., *The Geography of Religion in England* (London) 1971

Gill, R., *The Myth of the Empty Church* (London) 1993

Gilbert, E., Deerhurst Priory Church revisited, *TBGAS,* 1954, vol. 73, 73–114

Gibson, W., Somerset Evangelical Clergy, *The Proceedings of the Somerset Archaeological and Natural History Society,* 1985–86, vol. 130, 135–40

[Glover, R.], *The Golden Decade of a Favoured Town* (London) 1884

Gracie, H. S., St Peter's Church, Frocester, and an underlying Roman building, *TBGAS,* 1958, vol. 77, 23–30.

Gracie, H. S., St Peter's Church, Frocester, *TBGAS,* 1963, vol. 82, 148–67

Gray, I. and Ralph, E., *Guide to the Parish Records of the City of Bristol and the County of Gloucestershire* (Bristol) 1963

Greenhalf, H., *A Glimpse of Heaven* (London) nd.

Hall, J. M., Haresfield: Manors and Church, *TBGAS,* 1894–5, vol. 19, 279–373

Hamlin, G., The Pithay Chapel, Bristol, *BQ,* 1954, vol. 15, 378–9

Hamlin, A. G., The Bristol Baptist Itinerant Society, *BQ,* 1965–6, vol. 21 (N. S.), 321–4

Harding, J. A., *The Diocese of Clifton 1850–2000* (Bristol) 1999

Harrison, J. F. C., *The Second Coming. Popular Millenarianism 1780–1850* (London) 1979

Heasman, K., *Evangelicals in Action* (London) 1962)

Herbert, N. M., 'Archdeacon Thorp and the rebuilding of Kemerton Church', *TGBAS*, 1971, vol. 90, 192–215

Higgins, G. L., Unity Chapel, St Philip's, Bristol (1850–1946), *EQ*, 1963, vol. 35, 223–235

Hill, A.W., *Henry Nicholson Ellacombe* (London) 1919

Hill, R., *A candid appeal to the religious public, in a letter addressed to the inhabitants of the Forest of Dean, Gloucestershire, occasioned by the dismissal of the Rev Isaac Bridgman AB* (Ross on Wye) 1823

Hobson, C., *The Clergymen of the Church of St Mary the Virgin, Fairford* (Fairford) 2011

Hodder, E., *The Life and Work of the Seventh Earl of Shaftesbury* (London) 1887 (3 vols.)

Hodsdon, J., *An Historical Gazetteer of Cheltenham* (Stroud) 1997

Howes, R., The rise and fall of Joseph Pitt, in *Glos. Historical Studies* 8 (1977)

Huddleston, C. R., Non-resident clergy of Bristol and Gloucestershire, *TBGAS*, 1978, vol. 96, 2–8

Jacques, N., The influence of the Oxford Movement on parish life: St Cry's, Stinchcombe, *TBGAS*, 1980, vol. 98, 155–170

Jones, A. E., Protestant dissent in Gloucestershire: a comparison between 1676 and 1735, *TBGAS*, 1983, vol.101, 131–45

Jones, O. W., *Isaac Williams and his Circle* (London) 1971

Jones, R. T., *Congregationalism in England 1662–1962* (London) 1962

Jordan, S., *Origin and History of the Baptist Church, Cinderford* [Cinderford] 1907

Kelly, B. W., *Historical Notes on English Catholic Missions* (London) 1907

Kendall, H. B., *The Origin and History of the Primitive Methodist Church* (London) 1906 (2 vols.)

Kirk-Smith, H., *William Thomson, Archbishop of York. His life and Times 1819–90* (London) 1958

Kitchin, G. W., *Edward Harold Browne* (London) 1895

Knowles, W. H., Elkstone Church, Gloucestershire, *TBGAS*, 1930, vol. 52, 187–200

Lambert, M. D., and Shipman, J., *The Unknown Cotswold Village: Eastcombe 1500–1980* (Eastcombe) 1981

Lander, J., Tent Methodism 1814–1832, *WHS*, 2002, vol. 53, 141–56

Latham, J. E. M., *Search for a New Eden. John Pierrepont Greaves (1777–1842): The Sacred Socialist and his Followers* (Madison, USA) 1999

Latimer, J., *The Annals of Bristol in the Eighteenth Century* (Bristol) 1893

Latimer, J., *The Annals of Bristol in the Nineteenth Century* (Bristol) 1887

Lawrence, A. T., *The Law Relating to the Church and Clergy* (London) 1921

Leech, J., *Rural Rides of the Bristol Churchgoer* [1843–45] (Stroud) 2004

[Leech, J.], *The Church Goer. Rural Rides. Calls at Country Churches* (Bristol) 1847

Lewis, V., *Satan's Mistress* [Joanna Southcott] (Shepperton) 1997

Lineham, P. J., The Origins of the New Jerusalem Church in the 1780s, *Bulletin of the John Rylands Library*, 1988, vol. 70, 109–22

Lloyd, E. W., Bromesberrow, *TBGAS*, 1923, vol. 45, 95–153

Lock, W., *John Keble. A Biography* (London) 1893

McLachlan, H., *English Education under the Test Acts* (Manchester) 1931

Medland, W. H., St Nicholas' Church, Gloucester, *TBGAS*, 1900, vol. 23, 109–28

Mercier, J. J., A History of Kemerton, *TBGAS*, 1894–95, vol. 19, 24–40

Munden, A., Evangelical in the Shadows: Charles Jervis of Cheltenham, *Churchman*, 1982, vol. 96, 142–50

Munden, A., Early Anglican Evangelicals in mid-Warwickshire, *Warwickshire History*, 1991–92, vol. 8, 118–30

Munden, A., *The History of St John's College, Nottingham* (Nottingham) 1995

Munden, A., *A Cheltenham Gamaliel. Dean Close of Cheltenham* (Cheltenham) 1997

Munden, A., Highbuy College, Islington, 1826–1951, *The Journal of the United Reformed Church History Society,* November 1999, vol. 6, 321–7

Munden, A., *Wearing the Giant's Armour. Edward Walker (1823–1872)* (Cheltenham) 2003

Munden, A., *A History of St Luke's Cheltenham 1854–2004* (Cheltenham) 2004

Munden, A., The Religious Census of Cheltenham, CLHS, 2005, *Journal 21*, 36–50

Munden, A., Thomas Snow and the Western Schism, CLHS, 2009, *Journal 25,* 57–63

Munden, A., The Religious Census 1851. Northumberland and County Durham, *Surtees Society,* vol. 216, 2012

Munden, A., Lord Dartmouth, 'the one who wears an coronet and prays' and the 18th-centrury religious revival in Cheltenham, CLHS, 2015, *Journal 31,* 31-4

Murch, J., *A History of the Presbyterian and General Baptist Churches in the West of England; with memoirs of some of their pastors* (London) 1835

Mumm, S., *Stolen Daughters, Virgin Mothers* (London) 1999

Myles, W., *A Chronological History of the People called Methodists* (London) 1813

Nicholls, H. G., *The Forest of Dean: An Historical and Descriptive Account* (London) 1858

Nicholls, H. G., *The Personalities of the Forest of Dean* (London) 1863

Noake, J., *The Rambler in Worcestershire* (Worcester) 1848

Nockles, P. B., *The Oxford Movement in Context. Anglican High Churchmanship, 1760–1857* (Cambridge)1994

O'Connor, D., Charles Cooke Higgs – an Eccentric Benefactor, 5–16; Holy Apostles – in the Bishop's Hands, 24–26 in *Charlton Kings Local History Society. Research Bulletin 60,* Spring 2014

Parker, A. J., *Music at the Bristol Chapel of the Countess of Huntingdon's Connexion,* in Crossley Evans 2010, 98–111

Parry, C., A Survey of St James's Church, Lancaut, Gloucestershire, *TBGAS,* 1980, vol. 108, 53–103

Perry, J., Natton Seventh Day Baptist Chapel, Ashchurch, *TBGAS,* 1996, vol. 114, 105–29

Petit, J. L., Tewkesbury Abbey Church, *TBGAS*, 1880–81, vol. 5, 70–85

Phillips, H. T., *The History of the Old Private Lunatic Asylum at Fishponds, Bristol 1740–1859* (Bristol) 1973

Platt, F., Charles Wesley's House in Bristol, *WHS, 1932,* vol. 18, 137–42

Playne, A. T., *A History of the Parishes of Minchinhampton and Avening* (Gloucester) 1915

Port, M. H., *Six Hundred New Churches. The Church Building Commission 1818–1856* (Reading) 2006

Power, J. C., *The Rise and Progress of Sunday Schools. A biography of Robert Raikes and William Fox* (New York) 1863)

Pym, R. (ed.), *Memoirs of the late Rev William Nunn* (London) 1842

Ralph, E. and Cobb, P., *New Anglican Churches in Nineteenth Century Bristol* (Bristol) 1991

Read, L. A., 'Nailsworth Tabernacle Church', *BQ*, 1949, vol. 13, 81–4

Redford, G., and James, J. A., (eds.) *The Autobiography of William Jay* [1854] (London) 1974

Reynolds, J. S., *The Evangelicals at Oxford 1735–1871* (Appleford) 1975

Ritchie, J. E., *The Religious Life of London* (London) 1870, 159–66

Roud, S., *The English Year* (London) 2008

Rowdon, H. H., 'Secession from the Established Church in the early Nineteenth Century', *Vox Evangelica*, 1964, vol. 3, 76–88

Rowdon, H. H., *The Origins of the Brethren 1825–1850* (London) 1967

Royce, D., The church of St Mary, Nether Swell, *TBGAS,* 1882–3, vol. 7, 45–55

Rudd, M. A., *Historical Records of Bisley with Lypiatt* [1937] (Stroud) 2008

Ryder, H., *A Charge delivered to the Clergy of the Diocese of Gloucester at the Primary*

Visitation of that Diocese, in the year 1816 (Gloucester) 1816

[Seymour, A. C. H.], *The Life and Times of Selina Countess of Huntingdon* (London) 1844 (2 vols.)

Shaw, J., *Octavia Daughter of God. The story of a female Messiah and her followers* (London) 2011

Sheppard, G. W., *Sunshine in the Workhouse* (London) 1860

Sidney, E., *The Life of the Rev Rowland Hill* (London) 1861

Skinner, E., *Sheepscombe: One Thousand Years in This Gloucestershire Valley* (Sheepscombe) 2005

Smith, T., *Memoirs of the Rev John Wesley Etheridge* (London) 1871

Smyth, C., *Simeon and Church Order* (Cambridge) 1940

Snell, K. D. M. and Ell, P. S., *Rival Jerusalems. The Geography of Victorian Religion* (Cambridge) 2000

Snell, K. D. M., *Parish and Belonging. Community, Identity and Welfare in England and Wales 1700–1950* (Cambridge) 2006

Solly, H., *'These Eighty Years', or, the Story of an Unfinished Life* (London) 1898 (2 vols.)

Spittal, C. J., Three Generations of the Exley Family in Bristol Education and Methodism 1800–1901, *TBGAS*, 1993, vol. 111, 201–13

Stapleton, B., *Three Oxfordshire Parishes. A History of Kidlington, Yarnton and Begworth* (Oxford) 1893

Stock, E., *The History of the Church Missionary Society* (London) 1899 (3 vols.)

[Stowell, H.], *The Peaceful Valley or, The Influence of Religion. A Narrative of Facts* (Wellington) 1825

Stunt, T. C. F., Leonard Strong: the motives and experiences of early missionary work in British Guiana, *Christian Brethren Review*, 1983, vol. 34, 95-105

Tayler, W. E. (ed.) *Passages from the Diary and Letters of Henry Craik of Bristol* (London) 1866

Thomson, D. P., *Lady Glenorchy and her Churches* (Crieff) 1967

Thompson, A. H., Notes on the ecclesiastical history of the parish of Henbury, *TBGAS*, 1915, vol. 38, 99–186

Thorp, J. D., Rectors of Cotes or Coats, *TBGAS*, 1926, vol. 48, 301–24

Tucker, H. W., *Memoir of the Life and Episcopate of Edward Field, Bishop of Newfoundland 1844–1876* (London) 1877

Torode, B., *The Hebrew Community of Cheltenham, Gloucester and Stroud* (Cheltenham) 1989

Tyerman, L., *The Life of the Rev George Whitefield* (London) 1890 (2 vols.)

Tyerman, L. *The Life and Times of the Rev John Wesley* (London) 1890 (3 vols.)

Urdank, A. M., *Religion and Society in a Cotswold Vale. Nailsworth, Gloucestershire, 1780–1865* (California) 1990

Venn, J. and Venn, J. A., *Alumni Cantabrigienses* (Cambridge) 1922–54 (10 vols.)

Verey, D., *Cotswold Churches* (London) 1976

Verey, D., *The Diary of a Cotswold Parson* (Gloucester) 1980

Verey, D. and Brooks, A., *The Buildings of England. Gloucestershire: 1 The Cotswolds* (London) 1999

Verey, D. and Brooks, A., *The Buildings of England. Gloucestershire: 2 The Vale and the Forest of Dean* (London) 2002

Vickers, J. A. (ed.) *A Dictionary of Methodism in Britain and Ireland* (Peterborough) 2000

Victoria County History. A History of the County of Gloucester
    Vol. 4, N. M. Herbert (ed.), London, 1988
    Vol. 5, C. R. J. Currie (ed.) London, 1996
    Vol. 6, R. B. Pugh (ed.) London, 1965

Vol. 7, C. R. Elrington (ed.) London, 1981
Vol. 8, C. R. Elrington (ed.), London, 1968
Vol. 9, N. M. Herbert (ed.), London, 2001
Vol. 10, R. B. Pugh (ed.), London, 1972
Vol. 11, N. M. Herbert (ed.), London, 1976
Vol. 12, A. R. J. Juřica, (ed.) London, 2010

Victoria County History. A History of Wiltshire
Vol. 3, R. B. Pugh and E. Crittall (eds.), London, 1965

Victoria County History. A History of Worcestershire
Vol. 3, J. W. Willis-Bund (ed.), London, 1913
Vol. 4, J. W. Willis-Bund (ed.), London 1924

Waller, J., *A Chronology of Nonconformity and Dissent in Cheltenham* (Cheltenham) 2007

Waters, T., Thornbury Church, *TBGAS*, 1883–4, vol. 8, 79–88

Welsford, J. and A., *Cirencester a History and Guide* (Stroud) 2010)

Wesley, J., *The Journal of the Rev John Wesley* (London, Dent edition) 1906 (4 vols.)

White, J. F., *The Cambridge Movement. The Ecclesiologists and the Gothic Revival* (Cambridge) 1962

[Whitefield, G.], *George Whitefield's Journals (1738–41)* (London) 1960

Whitley, W. T., Seventh-Day Baptists in England, *BQ*, 1947, vol.12, 252–8.

Williams, I., *A Short Memoir of the Rev Robert Suckling* (London) 1852

Wilson, R., 'The Industrial Archaeology of Leckhampton Hill', *The Gloucestershire Society for Industrial Archaeology Journal*, 2001, 35–46

[Wilson, J.] *Memoir of the life and character of Thomas Wilson* (London) 1849

Wood, J. G., The church and parish of Lancaut, *TBGAS*, 1936, vol. 58, 207–18

Yates, N., *Anglican Ritualism in Victorian Britain 1830–1910* (Oxford) 1999

Yates, N., *Buildings, Faith and Worship. The Liturgical arrangements of Anglican Churches 1600–1900* (Oxford) 2000

INTRODUCTION

Historically, 1851 was 'a year of national festival, the climax of early Victorian England, the turning point of the century. It was also a year of political uncertainty and ministerial instability.'[1] In that year the Crystal Palace was opened in Hyde Park, the window tax was abolished; and on the religious front the Protestant Alliance was founded, the Anglican archdeacon Henry Manning became a Roman Catholic, as did four clergy from Leeds, prompting Lord Shaftesbury to comment, 'Lord, purge the church of those men, who, while their hearts are in the Vatican, still eat the bread of the establishment and undermine her!'[2] Under the Ecclesiastical Titles Act, Roman Catholics (already having been permitted to establish the hierarchy) were not allowed to use ancient see titles for their bishoprics – for example, there could be Clifton but not Bristol, Plymouth but not Exeter, Southwark but not Canterbury, and Westminster but not London.

In 1851 three national censuses were conducted – the Civil Census, the Educational Census and the Religious Census.[3] The first recorded that the population of England and Wales was 17,927,609, and the third found that of that number only 7,261,032 had attended a place of worship on the day of the Census, Sunday 30 March 1851 (or the previous day for Jews). After allowances made for children, the sick, domestic servants and public employees, it was calculated that 5,288,294 people had chosen not to attend one of the 34,467 places of worship. However, even with the vast amount of statistical information that came to light from the Religious Census, 'the number of habitual non-attenders cannot be precisely stated'[4] for some individuals might have attended irregularly or intermittently.

The returns indicate that on Census day many people were absent from a place of worship due to the bad weather, outbreaks of influenza and measles, and because it was Mothering Sunday (in mid-Lent) when it was customary for individuals to visit their families and to absent themselves from their usual place of worship. Some of those employed as servants had a few hours off work, while those at the Swan Inn at Wotton-under-Edge, were given a glass of wine.[5] Other traditions on Mothering Sunday included giving presents and baking a simnel cake covered with white and pink icing.[6] Whatever the reasons for their absence it was believed that on 30 March fewer persons than usual were present in a place of worship. At Berkeley parish church it was calculated that the mid-Lent Sunday

---

[1] Briggs, 3.
[2] Hodder, 2, 338.
[3] Officially reported in the style 'Census of Great Britain 1851: Religious Worship in England and Wales', but in this edition usually simply 'the Religious Census'.
[4] *Census Report*, cliii.
[5] *GNQ* 4, 158–9; Roud, 105–8.
[6] For a description of a Mothering Sunday cake, see Leech 1847, 208–9.

attendance had been reduced by as much as a third (**4.39**).[1]

Sometimes worship was not conducted every Sunday, as where an Anglican incumbent was responsible for two or more parishes and within Methodism where there were a number of chapels within a circuit. Of course during the day of the Census individuals might have attended more than once, though where some explanation is given in the returns that number appears to have been quite small. Nevertheless, to allow for this a rough and ready calculation was devised that was based on the number of worshippers attending in the morning, together with half in the afternoon and a third in the evening. But this reckoning was not wholly reliable and was open to criticism. Generally the Church of England had larger congregations in the morning, fewer in the afternoon and fewest in the evening; while nonconformists had more in the evening, fewer in the morning and least in the afternoon. There is some evidence to suggest that the custom was for some people to attend their parish church in the morning, and a nonconformist chapel in the evening, the consequence being 'that the church itself is half Wesleyanized.'[2] Obviously the attendance figures have to be interpreted with some care but they do give some indication of the number of worshippers on a given day in the middle of the 19th century.

In their book *Rival Jerusalems: The Geography of Victorian Religion* (2000), K.D.M. Snell and P.S. Ell have provided a comprehensive study of the background and context of the Religious Census, including a detailed analysis of 15 counties. Though Gloucestershire was not one of these the book paints a broader perspective of the relative strengths and weaknesses of the various denominations. An earlier study by J. Gay, *The Geography of Religion in England* (1971), included a clear and useful summary of the nation and 'of the varied state of institutional Christianity'. From the Census it became clear that 'there were two distinct areas of high religious practice; first, the whole of the west country extending east into Gloucestershire, Berkshire and Hampshire; and secondly a large group of counties to the south of the Wash where both Nonconformists and Church of England attendances were at their highest.'[3] On the other hand there were a number of areas of the country where the lowest numbers were recorded: in London and in the four northern counties of Cumberland, Durham, Lancashire and Northumberland. That Gloucestershire was included in the group of high attendance counties should help us to interpret the relative strengths and weaknesses of the different denominations within the county. The comparatively large attendance figures given in the Census reveal just how far the nation has moved away from being a church-going, faith-based society. But there are some notable exceptions. Today, Holy Trinity, Cheltenham (**16.17**) is one of the largest Anglican churches in England, and with a congregation of 2,000 is much larger than it was in 1851.

The Census was concerned with Sunday *attendance* but not with religious *profession*. Today sociologists of religion speak of people 'believing without

---

[1] Bold references in brackets thus are to the entry headings in the main body of this edition.
[2] *VCH* Wilts. 3, 61.
[3] Gay, 57.

belonging'[1] to a place of worship but in the middle of the 19th century it was more a case of 'belonging without believing' through social convention, the presence of the local landowner (**8.8**) or a sense of occasion (at an assize sermon - **8.18**, **20**, **22**, **41**) or hearing a well-known preacher (**2.1**, **3**). Merely attending a place of worship did not necessarily imply a believing, saving faith, rather it was more an expression of an allegiance to a particular religious denomination. But this is not to dismiss the sincere faith of the many as evidenced in the care and education of the poor and in the improvement in the lot of the many. Throughout the nation the Christian faith was significant factor in the life of believers, as evidenced by the erection and restoration of churches and chapels, the publication of volumes of sermons, the lengthy biographies of Christian leaders, the composition of hymns and in the detailed reports of religious and philanthropic activity in local newspapers. Christians were active in urban and rural communities at home and in the promotion of the Christian faith overseas.

THE RELIGIOUS CENSUS OF 1851

The individual responsible for conducting the Religious Census was the young barrister Horace Mann, who in 1855 became the registrar, and 20 years later the secretary, of the Civil Service Commission.[2] Conveniently England and Wales were already divided into 30,610 districts and these were adopted as the administrative basis for the Censuses. This means that the information in the Civil Census may be easily placed alongside that of the Religious Census. The 2,190 registrars of births and deaths had overall charge of the local enumerators who were responsible for collecting the data. On Sunday 30 March, a week before the Census took place, the enumerators had to identify places of worship and the names and addresses of the leaders of the various denominations within their area. It would have been a straightforward task to contact the Anglican clergy, but much harder to locate and identify any small group of Christians who worshipped in an isolated house or cottage. Those completing the forms were given a sheet of instructions (reproduced at Appendix 6).

There were three main forms. First, for the Church of England (printed in black on pale blue paper); second, for other religious bodies (printed in red on pale blue paper) and third, for the Society of Friends (printed in black on white paper). However, this apparently simple scheme was not foolproof and sometimes mistakes were made (**4.12b**; **7.29**, **31**; **14.33**); in one case an Education Census paper was wrongly distributed and completed (**5.10**). There were a number of instances where two returns were completed: by Anglicans (**9.8**; **11.1**; **13.41**; **14.9**, **23**; **16.16**; **17.1**) and by Wesleyan Methodists (**4.8**, **29**; **7.25**; **14.20**, **27**, **32**). In addition to the main forms there were simplified forms for the Church of England and for other denominations. In the week after the Census forms had been completed the enumerators collected them and presented them to the local registrars who returned them to the Census office in London. The 34,000 or so forms were then numbered, and examined by the statisticians. Those who

[1] Davie, *passim*.
[2] *ODNB*, 'Horace Mann (1823–1917)'.

had not completed their returns were then issued with a replacement and if this failed to elicit a response then the local registrar was responsible for obtaining the necessary information. The details were then recorded on a summary form. As late as September 1852 this further information was still being obtained (**18.47**). The use of different forms accounts for the uneven presentation of some of the information recorded in this edition. In some cases the information is very detailed, with a covering letter (**4.48**; **10.74**; **13.21**) but in other instances it was very sparse (**2.57**; **3.2**; **4.3**; **5.5**; **12.10, 13, 37, 56**; **65**; **15.27, 34**; **17.37**; **19.4**; **20.8, 36**).

The Census of Religious Worship in England and Wales was published as a parliamentary paper in December 1853 and the findings were widely reviewed in the national and regional press. This was the only official religious census ever conducted: the experiment was never repeated in England and Wales. The published report was very detailed and included both commentary and summaries of the returns for larger towns, registration districts, counties and Anglican dioceses, but did not give the details of individual places of worship. It is this more detailed information that is given in this edition, the preparation of which has identified slight discrepancies between the numbers given in the printed summaries and what appears in the actual returns. All of the Religious Census returns for the city of Bristol (and made up of the five sub-districts of St Mary Redcliffe, Castle Precincts, St Paul, St James and St Augustine) are missing but the places of worship have been identified for this edition, and appropriate notes provided from other sources.

The published Census consisted of a detailed consideration of 35 denominations followed by a section on 'spiritual provision and destitution'. In his overview, Horace Mann recommended that it should be possible for 58% of the population to be accommodated in a place of worship. Out of 74 large towns that were listed only two from Gloucestershire were recorded – Bristol, which could accommodate 52.8%, and Cheltenham with 56.5%. This meant that Bristol needed another 7,134 sittings, and Cheltenham only 511. Of course in many places, particularly in rural Gloucestershire, it was possible to accommodate all who wished to attend, but it was not possible to provide sufficient sittings in the towns and cities. Mann discovered that 66.5% of the population could be accommodated in rural parishes but only 46.0% in urban communities. He found that there were 'widely varying condition[s] of particular localities: some fortunately basking in excess of spiritual privileges, other absolutely "perishing for lack of knowledge".'[1] For Mann the solution was obvious. More places of worship were required particularly in the larger towns, 'for relieving such deplorable deficiency.'[2] The cities and towns were the obvious places of need, but across Gloucestershire more church accommodation was required. Throughout the county in the 20 years 1836–55 some 40 Anglican churches were consecrated before the Census was conducted and 20 afterwards. In addition there were also a few places of worship that were licensed but not consecrated (**8.42**) and at the same time numerous Nonconformist chapels were erected or enlarged.

---

[1] *Census Reoprt*, cxxvii.
[2] Ibid., cxxx.

While Mann calculated that nationally some 2,000 more places of worship were required, he suggested that there could be other ways of accommodating more worshippers. Churches and chapels were largely underused and in many instances only one service was held on a Sunday. But additional services could take place on Sunday and during the week. Where people were indifferent and even hostile to clergy then lay agents could be employed, and street preaching should be adopted by the Church of England, and with greater use of schoolrooms in which to hold services. Of course these suggestions raised practical issues over the number of clergy and ministers who were trained and available, and much more contentious within the Church of England was the use of laymen to conduct worship. While Anglican readers were introduced in the late 1860s (**9.7**) they were not permitted to preach from a pulpit until 1945.

Mann was forthright in his observations. He noted that more money was devoted to overseas mission than to support church-building at home. He believed that new churches were often erected in middle-class areas where the population had 'not only the desire to have, but also the ability to get, an adequate provision for religious culture.'[1] Religion had become 'regarded as a purely middle-class propriety or luxury.'[2] Moreover society was deeply divided, and the working classes were absent due 'to a genuine repugnance to religion itself.'[3] Even where churches and chapels were opened and sermons preached, 'the masses of the population, careless or opposed, will not frequent them'[4] and the buildings remained half empty. But Mann commended both the Methodists and the Mormons for their obvious success in their evangelistic endeavours.

Before the Religious Census took place Samuel Wilberforce, the bishop of Oxford, was a determined opponent of the very idea, objecting to nearly all of the questions, and was highly critical of the findings when published. One of his objections concerned the reliability of those enumerators who were dissenters, the implication being that they would not be impartial, favouring nonconformity over the established church. In his visitation of 1854 Wilberforce asked a loaded question about 'the correctness of the numbers given in the recent Census.'[5] Only a few incumbents (and it was a few) believed that the numbers attending dissenting places of worship were exaggerated, and sometimes they were actually encouraged to attend a place of worship on Census day. In only one instance, in the parish of Great Tew, Oxon., 'a dissenter was employed to make the returns.'[6] The situation was much the same in Gloucestershire. There was one instance where an enumerator was a Wesleyan Methodist (**3.41**) and another where Henry Dodd was a Wesleyan Reformer preacher and the local enumerator (**4.8b, 11**). George Chute, the vicar of Frampton-on-Severn was highly critical of a local chapel. 'No reliance can be placed on the return from the dissenting place of worship in this parish. More than half of the congregation are collected from the

[1] Ibid., cl.
[2] Ibid., clix.
[3] Ibid., clxi.
[4] Ibid., clxi.
[5] Baker, 2.
[6] Ibid., 151.

parishes of Saul, Fretherne etc. and the very same persons attend elsewhere on the very same Census day to swell the ranks of dissent in other parishes' (**9.17**). In fact his accusation was unfounded since on the 30 March the chapel in question had a smaller than usual congregation. (**9.18**).

THE RELIGIOUS CENSUS IN BRISTOL AND GLOUCESTERSHIRE

The Civil Census found that in 1851 the combined population of Gloucestershire and Bristol was 469,308. There were three main urban centres – the cathedral cities of Bristol and Gloucester, and the spa town of Cheltenham – with populations of 137,328, 17,572 and 35,051 respectively. A number of smaller towns had populations ranging from 4,000 to 9,000, namely Bisley, Cirencester, Minchinhampton, Stroud and Tewkesbury. Smaller still there were about 20 other towns with populations of between 1,500 and 2,000, and then a large number of villages and hamlets. Some communities were quite isolated and therefore excluded from the mainstream and most if not all would have been reasonably self-sufficient, and with a high proportion of the population involved in agriculture. The Civil Census of 1851 recorded that throughout the area there were 4,216 farmers, 21,524 agricultural labourers, 1,846 farm servants and 2,300 gardeners. Occasionally the Civil Census recorded an increase of population due to the construction of the railways, and then a decrease after the construction workers had left the district. The development of the railway system reduced the sense of isolation and facilitated the movement of people, the expansion of farming and in the development of trade and commerce. In the area immediately to the east of Bristol and in the Forest of Dean many people were involved in coal mining and other industries. In Gloucestershire there were 1,486 male and six female coal miners. In some urban communities the population was rapidly increasing, but where the woollen industry had declined the population was much reduced, many being forced to move away to find employment (**5.1, 3,7,14 16, 18, 20, 24–5**). But those who remained were desperately poor. At Oakridge (**10.26**) the incumbent reported that 'the greater part of [the parish] are in such a state of abject poverty, in consequence of the failure of work in the factories in the neighbourhood, that day after day, they are compelled to beg at my door for a piece of bread.'[1] At nearby Chalford (**10.27**) the situation was much the same where the minister referred to his 'afflicted and destitute people, whose sufferings and poverty are severe almost beyond parallel.'[2] The decline of the cloth industry was recorded in sveral places (**10.25, 62, 70, 77**), with only one instance of an increase (**10.40**). Yet even after the removals there were still 6,230 individuals in the county who were involved in the manufacture of cloth. Cheltenham had many seasonal visitors and much of the local population was engaged in service industries, a large number being domestic servants. Labour was cheap and throughout the county there were 13,500 domestic servants, 4,853 washerwomen, 1,296 cooks, 1,080 housekeepers and 1,058 housemaids.

While the Religious Census identified Anglican clergy and nonconformist

---

[1] CERC, ECE 7/1/50193: letter of H. H. B. Farmar, 19 Nov. 1849.
[2] CERC, ECE 7/1/1444: letter of S. Compertz, 12 Oct. 1842.

ministers by name, the Civil Census only provided overall numbers. Thus in Gloucestershire there were 605 Anglican clergy, 165 Protestant ministers and 67 other religious teachers. Alongside them, but socially apart, there were 431 schoolmasters, 1,035 schoolmistresses, 653 governesses and 118 other women teachers. In rural parishes the clergy were regarded as minor gentry and, as a character in Anthony Trollope's novel *Dr Thorne* remarked, 'clergymen – particularly the rectors and vicars of country parishes – do become privileged above other professional men.'[1] Certainly as 'gentlemen' the clergy were socially separate from the majority of their mostly working class parishioners. The incumbent of Berkeley was a 'fox-hunting parson' (**4.39**), and 'Jumping Jones' of Charfield was 'a fine horseman' (**4.48**). Some clergy supplemented their income by taking pupils (**8.4**; **10.6**) but without a resident landlord and other professional residents life in a small Victorian parish would have been dull and and unrewarding. The freehold of the living gave security of tenure for life but unless the incumbent had private means, retirement was impossible (**10.21**) and many clergy remained trapped in their parishes for many years. Extreme examples were Henry Goodwin, incumbent of Twyning (**17.37**) for 70 years, and John Elliott, at Randwick (**10.6**) for 72 years, and who died in post aged 100. Very occasionally clergy were suspended from their livings as at Lower Guiting (**15.6–7**). No details are given for this suspension but it could have been for irregularity in duty, heresy, insolvency or drunkenness. In the case of William George it was for immorality (**11.13**) and of Lewis Clutterbuck for bankruptcy (**3.21**). While a suspension was a temporary measure it could lead to a permanent deprivation.

Anciently the county of Gloucestershire was part of the diocese of Worcester, but at the Reformation two new dioceses were created - Gloucester in 1541 and Bristol in 1542. The diocesan and county boundaries were not identical and some parishes in the Gloucester diocese are located in neighbouring counties. During the administrative reforms of the early 19th century various changes were implemented. Once Dorset was transferred to the diocese of Salisbury from the diocese of Bristol, then what to do with such a small diocese? The first unworkable proposal was to link it with Llandaff on the other side of the Bristol Channel, but it was more sensible to merge it with the neighbouring diocese of Gloucester. This took place in 1836 and with the bishop of Gloucester and Bristol living in Gloucester. In 1897 the two dioceses were reinstated and each with their own bishop. During the period 1836 to 1897 there were four diocesan bishops – James Henry Monk 1836–56 (who had already been in post for six years as bishop of Gloucester); Charles Baring 1856–61; William Thomson 1861–3, and Charles John Ellicott 1863–97. After only a brief time in Gloucestershire two of these men (both Evangelicals) were translated to bishoprics in the northern province – Baring to Durham, and Thomson to York. During the course of the twenty-year episcopate of bishop Monk some 60 new churches were consecrated and over 75 during the episcopate of bishop Ellicott. Some of the churches had been rebuilt but others were entirely new.[2]

[1] A. Trollope, *Dr Thorne* (1858) ch. 38.
[2] See Appendix 7.

In the mid-19th century the diocese of Gloucester and Bristol consisted of about 350 parishes and chapelries and some 30 'Peel' districts (created under The New Parishes Act, 6 and 7 Vict. c.37, of 1843). The two archdeaconries were sub-divided into deaneries - Bristol (consisted of the deaneries of Bristol, Cirencester, Cricklade, Fairford, Hawkesbury and Malmesbury) and Gloucester (consisted of the deaneries of Blockley, Dursley, Forest, Gloucester, Stonehouse, Stowe and Winchcombe). In turn each deanery comprised a number of parishes.

All information in the surviving returns is given in full in this edition; this does not mean they are all complete, as a few Anglican clergy (**2.16, 20**; **8.6–7**; **12.4**; **15.4, 27, 34**; **15.34**; **20.28**) and occasionally a nonconformist official (**4.8b**) adamantly refused to provide any or all of the information that was requested, or reluctantly answered only some of the questions (**3.17–18**; **13.9**). The High Churchman, George Prevost, who was to become the archdeacon of Gloucester, protested that he had 'not been authorised by the bishop' to complete the form (**5.24**) but Henry Knox 'made the returns requested from a feeling of deference to church power' (**12.66**). Henry Cooper said that although by law he was not compelled to make a return, he did so 'hoping it may have been sent for a good purpose' (**19.37**). Francis Bayly protested against being forced to answer the questions, but he did so voluntarily (**8.48**; **9.4**), and John Bellingham criticised 'this confusing document' (**13.12**).

When the clergyman was absent from his parish through illness (**6.36, 38**; **8.39**; **15.18**), insanity (**13.2**) or death (**6.40**; **17.15**) the form was completed by a layperson such as a churchwarden (**2.19**; **6.33**; **7.20**; **9.8b**; **12.33–34, 60**; **17.14–15**; **18.50**; **19.5**), a chapel warden (**13.41a**), a parish clerk (**10.25**), a 'sextoness' (**2.20**; **20.35**) or a Sunday school teacher (**17.18**). Women signed the returns for chapels at Hanham Green (**20.8**), Hook's Mills (**2.17**), Slimbridge (**5.30**) and Tetbury (**11.18**). The Methodist returns were invariably made by the minister or a layman usually described as a steward or trustee, and sometimes by a local preacher (**10.18**; **17.13**) or prayer leader (**9.9**). If the forms were not returned to the enumerator, or when the incumbent refused to make a return it was the responsibility of the local registrar to try to obtain the necessary information (**2.37–38**; **6.38**). At Brockworth a local farmer provided what was required (**8.46**) but at Charfield the person appointed by the registrar to help him failed to distinguish between adults and children (**4.48**). Gathering the information could take some time and between June and September 1852 information was still being sought (**2.76**; **8.2, 5–7**; **10.43**; **12.54**; **14.14**; **18.47**). There were at least nine missing returns for Anglican places of worship which meant that the returns were lost, or that the incumbent refused to complete them or that the local registrar gave up after making several unsuccessful attempts to obtain the necessary information. The precise number of nonconformist places of worship not included in the Census[1] is more difficult to determine.

Some congregations met in schoolrooms (**2.7, 32, 48**; **3.37**; **4.47**; **6.31**; **7.3**; **10.61**; **11.19**; **13.26, 37, 45**; **18.2, 24, 27, 35, 37–38, 40**; **20.14, 19, 48**); others in private houses (**2.42, 50, 53, 81, 86**; **4.6, 11**; **6.19, 22**; **9.9, 13, 19**; **10.9, 54, 55**,

[1] See Appendix 5.

69; **11.20**; **12.13**, **40**; **13.26**, **37**, **45**; **14.2**, **15**, **30**; **16.14**, **34**; **18.33**; **19.12**, **17**, **40**; **20**, **8**, **10**, **20**) and of these venues some would have been overlooked or even ignored by the enumerators (**5.14**, **9.13**). Less conducive for worship must have been the magistrates' room used by some Wesleyan Methodists (**18.31**), while others met in a room in a public house (**7.18**); other Baptists worshipped in the chapel of a lunatic asylum (**2.81**). Many of these congregations would have been small, but as they grew and raised sufficient funds then they were in a position to erect a modest chapel, which might in time be enlarged or rebuilt. It was not uncommon for there to be a considerable interval between the commencement of outdoor preaching to the erection of a chapel: at Withington it took 25 years (**13.29**).

How many people actually attended a place of worship and how reliable were the returns? The printed summaries for Gloucestershire recorded that out of a population of 458,805, there were 135,634 people in a place of worship in the morning; 75,367 in the afternoon; and 89,766 in the evening. In all, there were 928 places of worship and 280,746 sittings available to them.[1] Where the figures were rounded up (*up* rather than *down*) and imprecise there may well have been a certain amount of guesswork and coupled with this a reluctance to make the effort to count each person. On principle Thomas Browne stated that 'I never count the attendance at church: guessing would be worse than nothing' (**9.3**, **7**) and archdeacon Thomas Thorp was adamant that 'we are not in the habit of counting our congregations' (**17.21**) and so what he gave was an approximation. At English Bicknor the incumbent admitted that 'the numbers attending are merely guessed at. They have not been counted' (**18.49**) and for Joseph Baker 'no return can be made with accuracy' (**4.17**). Henry Knox believed that the figures relating to attendance 'must be fallacious' (**12.66**). Frederick Aston made it clear that 'I had no time or opportunity for enumerating' (**13.9**) and maintained that it was the responsibility of the churchwardens to count the congregation and not the clergy, and that is precisely what happened at Cinderford (**6.8**). In the diocese of Oxford the churchwardens at Hook Norton stood at the doors and counted the congregation as they left the building, and so 'the number at church therefore was accurately returned' and at Chipping Norton 'our own people were accurately counted by seven or eight persons specially ordered to do so.'[2] In Gloucestershire there are a number of instances where we can be certain that precise numbers were recorded (**6.2**; **15.16**; **16.3**, **17**). At Chedworth the incumbent was so meticulous that he checked the number of sittings three times (**13.21**), and at Tetbury the exact numbers of men, women and children were recorded (**11.14–15**). At Painswick 'the afternoon congregation exceeds the average of the morning congregation by 200, but the congregations do not consist of entirely different persons' (**10.13**). At Norton 'only seven of the attendants in the afternoon attended also in the morning' and six children only attended once (**8.8**) and at Ashleworth of the 150 adults who attended during the course of the day, only ten adults had attended twice (**8.4**), but at Gorsley over 100 persons attended the evening service (**7.3**). In the chapel at Leckhampton the minister reported that

---

[1] *Census Report*, ccv. See too Appendices 2, 3 and 4.
[2] Baker, 36, 76

'some members of this congregation attend other churches' in the evening (**16.6**). Those responsible for the returns at Berkeley and Tortworth recorded the numbers for the following Sunday (6 April) since on Census Sunday it was believed that the attendance was reduced by as much as a third (**4.39, 46**). At Moreton-in-Marsh the 'services [were] attended by one half of the population' of 1,512 people (**19.22**), and a similar proportion was at Bourton-on-the-Hill (**19.20**). At Twigworth the River Severn sometimes flooded and this could affect the attendance (**8.11**). Seasonal farmwork reduced the number of men and boys (**16.12**). When the landowner was absent the congregation would be lower (**8.8**) and where the incumbent suffered from ill-health there were fewer worshippers (**6.40**). Fewer people attended services in the winter and during bad weather. Generally heating was not provided (**3.3**) but there were some exceptions (**4.46**) and at Berkeley Joseph Leech sat in 'a pew in the central aisle close by a great roaring fire, and immediately in front of the pulpit and reading desk.'[1]

The Anglican clergy commented on the limited accommodation for their parishioners (**10.1**) and of churches being inconveniently situated so that the worshippers had to travel some distance (**7.17, 29**; **9.5**) and this discouraged them from attending twice on Sunday (**3.47**). The new churches opened at Hucclecote (**8.13**), Oddington (**14.21**) and Wick (**3.18**) were more conveniently located for the parishioners, and after Marshfield church reopened, more of the poor could be accommodated (**3.23**). But often the pews were unsuitable and uncomfortable and could be 'awkward' (**18.11**) or 'too large and very inconvenient' (**4.40**). At the Anglican chapel in Leckhampton 'many of the sittings are inconvenient and practically useless' (**16.6**). The social divisions in society were replicated inside the church and were indicated by their seating location. Even in the Northleach House of Correction social distinctions were maintained. There were 'two pews for the governor and matron, three seats for the turnkeys and fixed forms for the prisoners' (**13.43**). The middle classes paid for their sittings (more if they occupied a prominent position) but the poor had to sit on benches in the central aisle or in less favourable parts of the building (**5.7**). Children might sit on benches (**8.8**; **12.51**; **14.23, 26**;**16.11**) in the chancel (**8.48**; **10.70**; **12.3**; **17.3**; **18.11**; **19.13, 25**),[2] the aisles (**5.7**; **10.56**), the galleries (**2.35**; **3.5**; **5.1, 20**; **12.28**; **14.36**; **18.28**; **19.11**), the vestry (**18.20**) or belfry (**17.5, 9**). At Haresfield the 50 seats 'originally intended for the school children in the gallery behind the organ are not now used' (**9.6**). At Mickleton there were three galleries – one for the boys, another for the girls and the third for the men and singers (**19.11**). At Bitton (**20.1**) Joseph Leech found that the sexes were segregated and that the poor men sat apart from the poor women[3] and when he attended a service at Holy Trinity, St Philip's (**2.35**), he had to sit in the gallery with the poor children, 'watched

---

[1] Leech 1847, 213.

[2] At Kemerton (**17.21**) the chancel contained pews for the rector and his family and servants, 'a most offensive black stove, with a long funnel' and was separated from the nave 'by an ugly screen of unpainted deal and a green baize curtain and was only used for a Sunday school.' CERC, ECE 7/1/3575: printed letter 'to the parishioners of Kemerton', 1 Sept. 1846.

[3] Leech 2004, 264.

over by two masters, a mistress, and the old beadle.'[1] Pews were regarded as the
freehold property of the owners and sometimes these rights were attached to
particular houses (**3.34**; **10.56**). At Dursley parish church (**5.20**) many of the pews
were appropriated to the houses of dissenters, 'who neither occupy them
themselves not promote their occupation by others, so that the pews are many of
them unoccupied.'[2] When the owner-families were absent their pews were not
available to other churchgoers. At Longborough the north transept was a family
pew and burial vault (**14.36**) and at Avening to provide more free sittings the
incumbent paid an annual rental to the owner of the south transept (**10.70**).

THE CONTEXT FOR THE RELIGIOUS CENSUS
Competing convictions
After the Church in England separated from the Roman Catholic church in the
16th century, Protestantism developed into various factions. Doctrinal
convictions created dissent and provided the pathway for the creation of
numerous denominations, many of them represented in the returns edited here.
Nationally 35 separate denominations were identified in the Census, the majority
of which subscribed to a *Trinitarian* faith (Church of England, Presbyterian,
Independents or Congregational, Baptist, Moravian, Methodist, Countess of
Huntingdon's Connexion, Christian Brethren and Roman Catholic) and a
minority to a *non-Trinitarian* faith (Unitarian, Swedenborgian [or New Jerusalem
Church] and the Latter-day Saints [or Mormons]) and somewhere in between the
non-creedal, non-ministerial Society of Friends (or Quakers).

In the mid-19th century the divisions between the denominations were
theological, with clear distinctions between Anglican and nonconformist,
Episcopalian and Presbyterian, Protestant and Roman Catholic, and between the
majority who practised infant baptism and the minority who only baptised
believers following their personal profession of faith. Unusual for the time there
are a few examples of united congregations of Independents and Baptists at
(Bristol (**2.42**), Oldbury-on-the-Hill (**11.8**) and Coln Rogers (**13.19**), and where in
Gloucester the two denominations briefly shared a chapel (**8.26**). But the spirit of
ecumenical co-operations was not yet strong, and much more common was an
intense denominational rivalry. In the parish of Meysey Hampton there was an
uneasy relationship between the Anglican church and the Baptist chapel. William
Thomas, the Baptist minister, referred to 'the overbearing and unscrupulous
restraints imposed upon the people by certain individuals of the established sect'.
Moreover, without an evening service at the parish church there was 'the abuse
and general desecration of the Sabbath evening and in the increased drunkenness,
bad neighbourhood, and general disorder of the people' (**12.55**). The schools of
the Independent chapel at Hewelsfield had closed, and the children had
transferred to the church school (**18.17**). At Adsett there was a reduction the
number of children attending the Independent Sunday school through the

---

[1] Ibid., 119.
[2] Memorial of Henry Vizard of Dursley to H. M. Commissioners for Building New Churches,
Nov. 1844, GA, P124 IN 3/2.

insistence of the clergy of the parish church at Westbury-on-Severn that the children who attended the National School in the week had to attend the parish church on Sunday (**6.30**). At Poole Keynes the children had to attend both Sunday services (**12.28**). The situation at Welford-on-Avon was unique. The Church of England minister preached an annual sermon after which a collection was taken to pay the Wesleyan Methodists to teach the children the Anglican catechism and on Sundays to take them to the parish church (**19.6**).

Outside the larger centres of Bristol, Cheltenham, Gloucester and Stroud, there were pockets of a strong and vibrant nonconformity which challenged the monopoly of the Church of England. As early as 1794 an Anglican chapel was opened at Nailsworth to counteract the activity of the local nonconformists (**10.71**). In 1829 the incumbent of Painswick was anxious to erect a chapel of ease at The Slad (**10.15**) because 'dissenters of all kinds occupy the ground.'[1] In 1838 it had been calculated that two-thirds of the inhabitants of Gotherington were nonconformists and to counter this, the bishop was keen to open an Anglican chapel in the village.[2] A similar situation occurred at Horsley (**10.77**) where the parish church was rebuilt to accommodate 1,052 parishioners (though under half of that number actually attended the church) in order to counteract the strong nonconformist presence in the area. The Independents were particularly numerous at Wotton-under-Edge (**5.8**); and at Nailsworth the Independents (**10.72**) and the Baptists (**10.74**); the Calvinistic Methodists at Rodborough (**10.60**); and near Bishops Cleeve there were three Countess of Huntingdon's chapels (**15.37–39**).

In addition to the major parting of the Church of England from Roman Catholicism at the Reformation, other denominations referred to as 'old dissent' arose in the 16th and 17th centuries (Presbyterian, Unitarian, Independent, Baptist and Society of Friends), and 'new dissent' in the 18th century (Moravian, Methodism, Countess of Huntingdon's Connexion and Swedenborgian). In the 19th century Methodism divided into many competing factions; from the 1830s the Christian Brethren emerged as a new Protestant body; and the Mormons arrived from the United States. In addition to the 35 Christian denominations identified in the Census the only other faith to be included were the Jews. There were members of other world faiths living in England at the time but they were widely scattered and in insufficient numbers to have their own places of worship. It was not until the late 1960s that mosques and temples were opened in Bristol.

Old Dissent

Protestant nonconformity emerged during the 16th century as an alternative to the doctrine, teaching, control and direction of the Church of England. In 1603 there were only 183 dissenters in 32 Gloucestershire parishes, but by 1676 there had been a considerable increase brought about by the greater openness made possible during the Protectorate and the lifting of heavy-handed restrictions imposed during the Restoration. Under the Act of Uniformity those who had not been

[1] CERC, ECE 7/1/20815: letter of Robert Strong, 2 June 1829.
[2] *The Bristol Mercury,* 16 Dec. 1837.

episcopally ordained were ejected from their parishes and academic posts. In all 1,760 men were displaced including 56 from Gloucestershire who were ejected in 1660 and 1662. A minority of ministers were prepared to conform and were re-ordained by an Anglican bishop, but the rest suffered terrible deprivations and imprisonments and became Presbyterian or Independent ministers.

In 1676 nearly half of the population of Tewkesbury and Bourton-on-the-Water were no longer associated with the Church of England. 'In Tewkesbury the church had declined still further, claiming only a quarter of townsfolk as members'[1] and in other parts of the county about one-fifth of the population were dissenters. The passing of the Toleration Act of 1689 permitted nonconformist congregations to develop without the imposition of harsh penalties. In 1708 a nonconformist academy opened in Gloucester, and four years later it moved to larger premises in Tewkesbury where it remained until 1724.[2] By 1717 some 6% of the county were dissenters and with a claimed 10,000 attending nonconformist places of worship. Over the next 20 years Bourton-on-the-Water, Cirencester, Horsley and Wotton-under-Edge became significant centres of nonconformity and with the Presbyterians as the largest body of dissenters. But by the early years of the 18th century, it was evident 'that dissent was not a very large factor in the religious life of Gloucestershire.'[3] However old dissent became invigorated by the evangelical revival and in time Methodism eclipsed the number of adherents in the older Protestant denominations.

John Biddle,[4] the so-called father of Unitarianism, who was born in Wotton-under-Edge in 1615, was educated at the local grammar school and Oxford, and in 1641 became headmaster of the Crypt School, Gloucester. Because of his unorthodoxy in rejecting the Trinity he was imprisoned first in Gloucester and then in London. During the 18th century a minority of Presbyterian and Baptist ministers followed the same path and rejected the doctrine of the Trinity and became Unitarians. The principles of the new denomination were shaped by the enlightenment and of a faith based on human reason rather than a creedal confession. By 1851 there were Unitarian congregations in Bristol (**1.55**), Cheltenham (**16.40**), Clifton (**2.87**), Cirencester (**12.44**), Gloucester (**8.27**) and Marshfield (**3.27**).

In Gloucestershire Presbyterianism declined, and by the time of the Religious Census there were no places of worship connected with that denomination. However the Independents (by the mid-19th century they were becoming known as Congregationalists) were a larger body of dissenters with 84 places of worship in the county. Independent chapels had some of the largest nonconformist congregations, with 800–900 at Kingswood Tabernacle, Oldland (**20.11**); 700–800 at Hope Chapel, Clifton (**2.6**); 650–750 at Highbury Chapel, Cheltenham (**16.23**); 600–700 at The Tabernacle, Wotton-under-Edge (**5.8**) and The Tabernacle, Dursley (**5.22**); 550 at Southgate Chapel, Gloucester (**8.35**); 500–600

---

[1] A. E. Jones, 133.
[2] McLachlan, 126–31.
[3] A. E. Jones, 138.
[4] *ODNB*, 'John Biddle (1615–1662)'.

at Anvil Street Chapel, St Phillips, Clifton (**2.39**); 500 at Bradley (**5.5**); 400–500 at two chapels in Stroud (**10.44, 47**) and at Tewkesbury (**17.34**). In 1811 the Independents founded the Bristol Itinerant Society in order to establish and then to provide pastoral support for about 14 chapels that included Knowle (**20.40**), Mangotsfield (**20.29**), Marshfield (**3.24**), Oldland (**20.4**), Rodford (**3.4**) and Wick (**3.19**).

As the name suggests the Independents were independent of any central direction until the Congregation Union was formed in 1831. Nationwide, 'in 1875 the Congregationalists church had 2,980 churches, branch churches and preaching stations' and 'at the beginning of the 20th century [it] was a denomination of small churches.'[1] The larger churches were situated mostly in the cities and towns and the majority had a membership of fewer than one hundred members. In 1972 the Presbyterian and Congregational churches merged and became the United Reformed Church.

The Baptists emerged in the 16th century as separatists who baptised by full immersion only those who professed the Christian faith for themselves. In 1640 a Baptist church was founded at King's Stanley (**10.52**) and the first congregation of Baptists assembled at a house in Broad Street, Bristol. By the end of the 17th century Broadmead (**1.32**) and Pithay (**1.35**) chapels had been erected. In Tewkesbury the Barton Street congregation (**17.35**) began in the 1650s. In the following century the Baptist community divided into two distinct bodies – the General Baptists (who were largely Arminian in their theology and believed in a general atonement) and the Particular Baptists (who were Calvinistic by conviction and believed in divine election and in a limited atonement). The former group declined but the latter provided the origins of the modern Baptist denomination. Another smaller group, the Strict Baptists (**13.37**) were distinguished by their strict policy of only admitting to communion those who had been fully immersed in baptism, while the rest had an 'open table' policy.

One of the largest Baptist congregations in England was at Shortwood, Nailsworth (**10.80**) where there was a congregation of over 1,000, of whom 500 were communicant members. This chapel provided support for chapels at Leighterton (**11.6**) and a preaching room (with a congregation of upwards of 300) at Nailsworth (**10.74**). Even smaller Baptist chapels established additional places of worship. Thornbury (**4.27**) seeded congregations at Lower Morton (**4.28**); and at Woodford and Tytherington (**4.34**); Coleford (**18.26**) established preaching stations at Lane End (**18.27**), Little Drybrook (**18.28**) and Milkwall (**18.39**); the Baptist chapel at Gloucester (**8.26**) established congregations at Barton End, Longhope (**6.41**), Little Witcombe and Matson; and Coberley chapel (**16.8**) had oversight over several other meeting places in the area. In the Religious Census in Gloucestershire there were 103 Baptist congregations subdivided into General Baptists, Particular Baptists, Strict Baptists, Welsh Baptists and Seventh-Day Baptists. As early as 1737 a Seventh-Day Baptist was preaching at Naunton (**14.11**) but by the time of the Census there were only two Seventh-Day Baptist

---

[1] R. T. Jones, 319–21.

chapels at Mill Yard, East London and at Natton, Gloucestershire (**17.29**).[1] While the Seventh-Day Baptists were always a tiny denomination in the United Kingdom it had many adherents in the USA, where it still thrives.

In 1824 the Bristol Baptist Itinerant Society was founded to work within the city and in the surrounding villages mostly in Somerset at Barrow Gurney, Blackwell, Blagdon, Breech Hill, Cheddar, Chew Magna, Dundry, Nempnett, Rickford, Ridgehill and Winford and also in Hallen (**2.65**). On the Sunday morning two men (often students from the Bristol Baptist College) would teach children to read, then conduct a service and in the afternoon visit from house to house. In time after a chapel had been erected a lay pastor was appointed to give oversight to the congregation and to administer a monthly communion service.[2] A later development was the Gloucestershire Christian Union of Baptist and Independents founded c.1840. It too evangelised by open-air preaching.

The Society of Friends was founded by George Fox[3] and represented a more radical aspect of English Puritanism. The discernment of the mystical 'inner light' was normative, and creeds, sacraments, ceremonies and ministerial hierarchies were all dismissed. Never a large denomination (there were only 11 meeting houses in Gloucestershire) the Quakers had some of the smallest congregations in the county, with three worshippers at Chipping Sodbury (**3.11**) and five or six at Nailsworth (**10.81**).

New dissent and the 18th-century revival
In 1739 Methodism took root in Gloucestershire. It began with the field-preaching of George Whitefield and was then adopted by the brothers John and Charles Wesley.[4] After Whitefield, an important figure in the county was the itinerant Rowland Hill. 'Methodism' was not a uniform movement and included diverse theological convictions and different attitudes towards ministry and church order. Nationally there were some 300 to 500 Anglican Evangelical clergy (also known as 'Methodists'), mostly committed to working within their parish boundaries, though some became itinerants, in order to preach the good news. There were significant doctrinal differences between the High Church Arminianism of the Wesley brothers and the Calvinism of the Countess of Huntingdon, George Whitefield and Rowland Hill, and each faction established their own places of worship.

George Whitefield,[5] who was born in the Bell Inn, Gloucester, attended the grammar school at St Mary de Crypt, and after graduating from Oxford, was ordained in Gloucester cathedral in June 1736. He preached his first sermon to a packed congregation at St Mary de Crypt on 'the necessity and benefit of religious society'. It was the first of the estimated 18,000 sermons he preached during his ministry throughout the United Kingdom and in the American

---

[1] Ritchie, 159–66; Whitley, 252–8; Perry, 105–29.
[2] Hamlin, 321–4.
[3] *ODNB*, 'George Fox (1624–1691)'.
[4] *ODNB*, 'John Wesley (1703–1791)'; 'Charles Wesley (1707–1781)'.
[5] *ODNB*, 'George Whitefield (1714–1770)'.

colonies. In the words of a contemporary, 'Mr Whitefield preached like a lion',[1] his powerful voice could be heard some distance away and it was said that sometimes his open-air congregations consisted of over 20,000 people.[2] Benjamin Franklin calculated that it was nearer 30,000; even if these figures are exaggerated Whitefield clearly could make himself heard by thousands. Unlike John Wesley, Whitefield did not purposely create a new denomination, but with the encouragement of Selina, Countess of Huntingdon, his followers generally became Calvinistic Methodists, members of the Countess of Huntingdon's Connexion or (and without the approval of Selina), Independents. Though they held similar theological convictions 'the connexions of the Countess, and [George] Whitefield and [Rowland] Hill ... never properly met in council and acted in concert, to say nothing of the numerous congregations, unattached to either of these communities.'[3] This sense of a common identity was much more evident within the rigid structures of Wesleyan Methodism, but following the death of John Wesley and for the next 50 years, that unity and common purpose was fractured.

In the spring of 1739 Whitefield preached in several parish churches in Bristol, and was urged by his supporters to remain in the city, but he moved on to Bath, Gloucester, Oxford and then to London, where he again preached to huge congregations. His fervent evangelical message had its critics, and as time went on he had fewer invitations to preach in Anglican churches, apart from where there were sympathetic ministers like Sampson Harris of Stonehouse who permitted Whitefield to preach. The result there was that more people started to attend the parish church and soon it became necessary to erect a new aisle to accommodate them. At Randwick 'the church was quite full, and about 2,000 were in the churchyard, who, by taking down the window behind the pulpit, had the convenience of hearing.'[4] Whitefield's message was clear, simple and biblical and consisted of 'the doctrine of the new birth and justification by faith in Jesus Christ' and which 'made its way like lightning into the hearers' consciences.'[5] Though he was an immensely popular preacher throughout the United Kingdom, Whitefield was determined to go to the American colony of Georgia and to establish an orphanage. His gospel preaching and fund-raising for the project went hand in hand. Many people at the time asked the obvious question, why go overseas to preach? Whitefield noted in his *Journal*: 'Some urged that, if I had a mind to convert Indians, I might go amongst the Kingswood colliers, and find Indians enough there. But none of these things moved me. Having put my hand to the plough, I was determined, through divine grace, not to look back.'[6] Clearly he was not going to be diverted and in all Whitefield crossed the Atlantic 13 times. He died of asthma in America in September 1770.

Whitefield preached to all classes in society to the very poor and the very rich,

[1] Seymour, 2. 355.
[2] Certainly the case when he preached on Minchinhampton Common, 1 July 1739: Tyerman, 256.
[3] Seymour, 2, xiii.
[4] Tyerman, vol. 1, 256.
[5] Whitefield, 81.
[6] Ibid., 81–2.

and on a number of occasions he preached throughout his native Gloucestershire - in Burford, Cirencester, Chalford, Cheltenham, Dursley, Fairford, Gloucester, King's Stanley, Minchinhampton, Oxenhall, Painswick, Pitchcombe, Randwick, Stonehouse, Stroud, Tewkesbury and Thornbury, as well as in Bristol. In the county the main centres of his ministry were Kingswood (**20.11**) and Rodborough (**10.60**). The violent mob were particularly active in Michinhampton[1] and Wickwar[2] and the evangelist John Cennick remarked that 'I met with much opposition in Gloucestershire.'[3] In the spring of 1743 Whitefield preached to 12,000 people at Stroud and then to a similar number on Minchinhampton Common, which in time became known as 'Whitefield's Tump'.[4] In less favourable circumstances, but at which large crowds would gather, he preached on at least two occasions to condemned men about to be executed on the commons at Minchinhampton and Gloucester.

A monument was erected on Hanham Mount, Bristol, now surrounded by modern housing, to commemorate the place where Whitefield and Wesley preached to many thousands of people. In July 1839, to mark the centenary of the beginning of the revival, a large gathering of 100 ministers and 20,000 people assembled on Stinchcombe Hill, near Stroud, and though the weather was poor their spirits were high. Later at a meeting in Bristol it was resolved to erect a statue of George Whitefield on Stinchcombe Hill. But the enthusiasm of those present was short-lived and no statue was ever erected.

George Whitefield began what became a characteristic feature of the 18th century revival – open air or 'field preaching' – which first took place in February 1739 when Whitefield preached to the miners at Kingswood Hill, near Bristol. The following month it was reported that 'he has preached in other parts of Kingswood, among the colliers; and thousands come – horsemen, coaches chaises, etc. Thus the gospel spreads round the country, for divers come from far – some twenty miles ... the harvest is great, and great encouragement there is to spend and be spent for the good of souls.'[5] Whitefield's biographer observed that 'Kingswood was the rough cradle in which Methodism was first rocked and nursed.'[6] At first the Wesley brothers were reluctant to get involved, but soon they too adopted the practice of field preaching, and took every opportunity to 'offer Christ' to all and sundry in the open air, in all weathers, throughout the United Kingdom. Those who were converted met weekly or fortnightly in 'societies' and on Sunday either worshipped with an existing congregation or raised funds to convert a suitable building as a place of worship, and when sufficient funds were available, to erect a new chapel. The sequence of open air preaching, meeting in a barn or cottage, building a small chapel and then replacing it with a larger one is found throughout Gloucestershire.

[1] Tyerman, 2, 63–7.
[2] Ibid., 111–2.
[3] Ibid., 112.
[4] Ibid., 54.
[5] Ibid., 1, 187.
[6] Ibid., 191.

A prominent figure in the revival was Selina, the Countess of Huntingdon.[1] After her evangelical conversion she appointed her own chaplains (one of whom was Whitefield) and opened chapels in which her Calvinistic convictions were proclaimed. In 1768 she opened a theological college at Trevecca, Talgarth, South Wales, and where most of the 212 students became dissenting ministers.[2] In 1779 on being forced to register her chapels as dissenting places of worship, her Anglican chaplains promptly resigned from her service. The 60 or so chapels directly associated with her became part of the network known as the Countess of Huntingdon's Connexion. By the time of the Religious Census there were eight such chapels in Gloucestershire - at Bishop's Cleeve (**15.39**), Bristol (**1.45**), Cheltenham (**16.37**), Ebley (**10.7**), Gloucester (**8.21**), Gotherington (**15.38**), Randwick (**10.8**) and Woodmancote (**15.37**). The former Countess of Huntingdon's chapel at Bristol was rented to the Christian Brethren (**1.47**), Birdwood chapel was sold to the Wesleyan Methodists (**6.37**) and at Coleford the former chapel became a school (**18.35**). Less well known than the Countess, but from a similar social background and holding an identical theology, was Lady Willielma Glenorchy,[3] who opened a number of chapels[4] and was involved with Hope Chapel, Clifton (**2.6**) named after her co-founder Lady Henrietta Hope (c.1750–1786).

Independent of George Whitefield was Rowland Hill[5]; unlike Whitefield he was socially well-connected being the sixth son of a baronet. He had experienced an evangelical conversion through his older brother and began an itinerant ministry even before he left Cambridge University. He had every expectation of being ordained into the Anglican ministry, but he was only made a deacon since, because of his itinerant preaching no bishop would ordain him as a priest, so he went through life as he described it 'wearing only one ecclesiastical boot.'[6] But this restriction did not hamper his ministry and throughout his life he worked alongside sympathetic Church of England clergy and nonconformist ministers. Theologically he was a Calvinist and identified himself most closely with the Calvinistic Methodists. This group was the strongest in Wales and had congragations at Broadmead, Bristol (**1.43**), Cromhall (**4.36**) and Rodborough (**10.60–61**). Hill was from the next generation of evangelical revivalists following on from Whitefield (with whom he corresponded but never met), a contemporary of Charles Simeon of Cambridge, and active in Cheltenham before the arrival of the Evangelical Charles Jervis at the parish church. Church order became a contentious issue among Anglican Evangelicals, and Hill was influenced more by John Berridge, the itinerant vicar of Everton, and John Hensman of Clifton and Francis Close of Cheltenham by the more cautious Simeon, in deliberately not straying outside their parish boundaries.

---

[1] *ODNB*, 'Selina, Countess of Huntingdon (1707–1791)'.
[2] The College moved to Hertford in 1792 and to Cambridge in 1904.
[3] *ODNB*, 'Willielma Campbell, Viscountess Glenorchy (1741–1786)'.
[4] Two of her chapels were in Scotland (Edinburgh and Strathfillan, Perthshire) and five in England (Carlisle, Exmouth, Matlock, Newton Burhill and Workington): Thomson, *passim*.
[5] *ODNB*, 'Rowland Hill (1744–1833)'.
[6] Smyth, 179, footnote 5.

Hill made a considerable impact in Gloucestershire. He settled in Wotton-under-Edge and in 1771 opened his own chapel (**5.8**) in which he used the *Book of Common Prayer* of the Church of England, and welcomed evangelical preachers of any denomination. Apart from at Wotton-under-Edge, Hill opened three other chapels with which he was particularly involved at Surrey Chapel, Blackfriars, London (in 1783), Cheltenham Chapel (in 1809) (**16.24**) and in 1832 he bought Mill Street Chapel, Leamington Spa.[1] It was his custom to spend the summer months based at Wotton-under-Edge, and made what he called his 'episcopal visitation' to Cheltenham and during the rest of the year he was based at Surrey Chapel. He wanted to be known as 'the apostle of the common people'[2] and throughout his life, and until he was well into his eighties, he went on extensive preaching tours throughout the United Kingdom. His self-designation was that he was the 'rector of Surrey Chapel, vicar of Wotton-under-Edge and curate of all the fields, commons etc. throughout England and Wales.'[3] Apart from Saturday he preached throughout the week – occasionally in a parish church, frequently in a nonconformist chapel and invariably in the open air – and which made the Countess of Huntingdon describe Hill as the 'second Whitefield.'[4] In Gloucestershire much of Hill's itinerant ministry took place on a line between Bristol and Cheltenham, and centred on Wotton-under-Edge, with regular preaching at Dursley, Nibley, Painswick, Rodborough, Stroud, Uley and Wickwar. He also preached in the Forest of Dean and raised funds for the erection of the Tabernacle at Blakeney (**6.3**), and preached at the opening of the chapels at Cromhall (**4.36**), Cheltenham (**16.24**), Dursley (**5.22**), Winterbourne (**2.78**) and probably at Frampton (**9.18**). Living in Gloucestershire, Hill met up with Dr Edward Jenner; he became a keen advocate of vaccination (claiming to have personally vaccinated 10,000 people) and published a tract on the subject.

John Wesley's Methodism spread throughout the United Kingdom by the two Wesley brothers and by those clergy and lay preachers who identified themselves by their Arminian theology. Wesleyan Methodism centred around London, Bristol and Newcastle upon Tyne and as Wesley travelled the length and breadth of England, Wales and Scotland, he extended his ministry well beyond the confines of those towns and cities. In Kingswood he supervised the school that Whitefield had established and frequently preached throughout Gloucestershire. Some of his earliest chapels were opened in the county and he invariably made return visits to his followers to preach and to encourage them in their evangelical faith. Charles Wesley was less peripatetic than his brother, and from 1749–71 lived at 4 Charles Street, Stokes Croft, Bristol, and confined most of his preaching to Bristol and London. Eight of his children were born in the house and the majority of his many thousands of hymns were composed there.

Following Wesley's death in March 1791, Wesleyan Methodism fragmented and various rival sub-sets of the movement developed. First, the Methodist New

[1] Munden 1991–92, 124–6.
[2] Redford and James, 352.
[3] Sidney, 215.
[4] Seymour, 1, 211.

Connexion in 1797; the Primitive Methodists (also known as 'Ranters') in 1811; the Bible Christians in 1816 and the Wesleyan Association in 1834. Of these groups, there were no New Connexion Methodists in Gloucestershire; the Bible Christians had six in the chapels in the Forest of Dean (**6.13–15**; **7.19**; **18.9, 52**) and at Bedminster (**20.47**), Tirley (**17.7**) and in 1856 they acquired the former Wesleyan chapel at Mitcheldean (**6.27**). The small Wesleyan Association had one chapel in St George's, Clifton (**2.31**) and two in Cheltenham (**16.35–36**).

Between 1814 and 1832 a minority group, the Tent Methodists, was active in Gloucestershire, its members frequently preaching at Bedminster, and outside Bristol 'to the north of the city from the River Severn in the west, to the edge of the Cotswolds to the east, and as far north as Dursley.'[1] In Gloucestershire they are known to have been particularly active in the poorer parts of Bristol (and were based at Pithay Chapel (**1.35**) and at Coalpit Heath, Dursley, Kingswood, Tetbury (**11.18**), Wotton-under-Edge and at Frampton Cotterell where they opened a chapel (**3.50**). Soon the Tent Methodists were preaching in the neighbouring counties, and as far away as London, Manchester, Liverpool, south Wales and the Isle of Wight. Never a large denomination, by the end of 1825 the Tent Methodists numbered about 3,500 members, and though their presence was unrecorded in the Religious Census their followers remained actively involved within other branches of Methodism and Congregationalism.

Though only 31 Primitive Methodist chapels are recorded in the Religious Census in Bristol and Gloucestershire it does not mean that they were inactive elsewhere. For example, in the Bristol area the first Primitive Methodist chapel was built in Kingswood in 1841 and at Bedminster Down and Fishponds. The Bristol circuit was formed in 1835, and by 1843 there were two preachers and 284 members.[2] In Westbury-on-Trym Joseph Leech noted that there were 'half a dozen private Ranting rooms'[3] and in Gloucester the Primitive Methodists were known to have been active from 1837 to 1854. Preaching took place in the open air and by 1856 there were 21 adherents. Preaching rooms were obtained in Grove Street and Ryecroft Street and in 1858 a chapel was opened in Barton Street (replaced by a larger chapel in 1882).[4] Much the same story was true of Cheltenham. There were Primitive Methodists active in the town in the early 1840s. By the 1850s there were a handful of supporters who were involved with other denominations, open air preaching took place in Winchcombe Street and a cottage was rented for services - and where the first member was Mary Ducker. In the winter of 1856–57 they met outdoors and held prayer meetings in the cottage of a chimney sweep until an empty chapel off Winchcombe Street (in an area known as Mount Pleasant) was rented for their use.[5]

Sometimes chapels were transferred to other denominations. The Primitive Methodist chapel at Eastington, erected in 1824 was sold to the Baptists in 1831

---

[1] Lander, 144. The Tent Methodists first erected a tent in Dursley in May 1819 and soon there were 450 converts. They opened a chapel in 1821; it was closed by 1830.
[2] Kendall, 2, 350.
[3] Leech 2004, 216.
[4] Kendall, 2, 414.
[5] ibid., 415–6.

(**9.21**). In 1859 the former Baptist chapel in King Street, Cheltenham (**16.28**) was bought by the Primitive Methodists for £300.

The ongoing tensions within Methodism became more apparent in the schisms of 1827 and 1835 and particularly in 1849. This last secession was the most serious, causing havoc among the membership and drastically reducing the size of Wesleyan Methodist congregations. From 1844 a number of anonymous tracts started to appear and known collectively as 'Fly Sheets'. They attacked the leaders and the metropolitan elites but an investigation failed to identify the individuals behind the pamphlets. The outcome was the formation of the Wesleyan Reformers in 1849 and within two years many of the Wesleyan congregations had been decimated. Numerous Methodists had become disillusioned with the heavy-handedness of the Wesleyan Conference, which was described as being 'overbearing and tyrannical' (**2.33**), 'oppressive' (**6.34**) or, quite bluntly, simply 'unrighteous' (**20.24**). Five months before the Census was conducted the Wesleyan congregation at Saul was flourishing. But 'the conduct of the Wesleyan Conference preachers has been the means of dividing nearly all the congregation away from the chapel ... those who formerly worshipped here hold religious meetings in houses etc.' (**9.13**). The Reformers either took over a Wesleyan chapel (**8.23**) or, more commonly, left their previous place of worship and established a new congregation elsewhere (**2.11, 12, 32; 4.6**). Some had only recently opened (**20.19, 20**). Some Wesleyan chapels were forced to close (**2.28; 20.6, 33**) while others lost many of their members (**2.27, 45; 6.34; 20.17, 44, 46**) and in Gloucester some formed themselves into assemblies of Christian Brethren (**8.15, 31, 38**). Yet these divisions were not evident in all parts of the county: Cheltenham was untouched by the Reformers, while in south Gloucestershire, Clifton and Hanham there were some of the highest concentrations of Reformers' congregations in England. For Charles Clay, one of the Wesleyan ministers in the Kingswood circuit, it must have been disheartening for him to report that few if any were attending the local chapels (**20.6, 7, 16, 17, 33**). In the Bristol circuit the superintendent minister, Corbett Cooke, who became the subject of 'the ire of the party who were then spreading disaffection among the people' would have appreciated the support he received from John Etheridge, the minister of the Portland Street Chapel (**2.58**).[1]

Gradually the deep divisions within Methodism were healed through a series of amalgamations, first in 1857 with the formation of the United Methodist Free Churches, then in 1907 the United Methodist Church and finally in 1932 as the United Methodist Church of Great Britain. Amalgamation meant that fewer chapels were required and from the 1960s, with the steady decline in chapel-going, many were forced to close and the buildings converted to secular uses.

Older than Methodism, and a group that had a considerable impact upon John Wesley's conversion, spirituality, theology and early ministry, were the Church of the United Brethren, usually known as the Moravians, established in Bohemia in the early 18th century. The group was strongly evangelical in its doctrines and episcopal in its polity and initially more of a missionary movement than a distinct

[1] Smith, 121.

denomination. Never a large group in England and Wales, on Census day in 1851 there were only 32 Moravian places of worship with 7,768 worshippers. Locally there were three Moravian chapels, two in Bristol (**1.44**; **20.21**), and one at Brockweir (**18.8**). Two other Moravian chapels at Apperley (**17.13**) and at Broom's Green (**7.19**) had by 1851 been transferred to the Wesleyan Methodists.

Sunday schools

The earliest schools for the children of the poor began in the 17th century, and Sunday schools in the early 18th century. In Gloucester, the incumbent of St John's, Thomas Stock opened the first Sunday school in the city, but it was due to his friend the lay philanthropist and proprietor of the *Gloucester Journal*, Robert Raikes[1] that the movement received widespread publicity.[2] On 3 November 1783, Raikes published an article on the subject. 'Some of the clergy in different parts of this county, bent upon attempting a reform among the children of the lower classes, are establishing Sunday schools for rendering the Lord's Day subservient to the ends of instruction, which has hitherto been prostituted to bad purposes. Farmers and other inhabitants of the towns and villages, complain that they receive more injury in their property on the Sabbath than all the week besides; this in a great measure proceeds from the lawless state of the younger class, who are allowed to run wild on that day, free from every restraint. To remedy this evil, persons duly qualified are employed to instruct those that cannot read - and those that may have learned to read, are taught the catechism and conducted to church.'[3] Very soon Sunday schools were established by all denominations throughout the country. John Wesley noted that 'I find these schools springing up wherever I go. Perhaps God may have a deeper end therein than men are aware of. Who knows but some of these schools may become nurseries for Christians?'[4] In September 1786 a service was held at Painswick parish church. In the churchyard 331 children from various Sunday schools in the town assembled and after the service the large congregation gave £57 to support the work of the local Sunday schools.[5] More widely 'the Sunday school movement of the 18th century owes its importance not so much to what it actually achieved, as to the ideal towards which it strove, namely universal popular education.'[6] Nationally the movement made rapid progress so that in England and Wales the percentages of those aged under 15 attending Sunday school were as follows: 1818 (11.5%), 1851 (38%), 1901 (52.6%) - and then a steady decline throughout the 20th century so that by 1989 it was only 2.5%.[7]

By 1851 most denominations held a what was called a Sabbath or Sunday

---

[1] *ODNB*, 'Robert Raikes (1736–1811)'.

[2] In the church of St Mary de Crypt the epitaph to Robert Raikes commends him as the one 'by whom Sabbath schools were first instituted in this place and were also by his successful exertion and assiduity recommended to others.': Power, 200.

[3] Ibid., 85.

[4] Wesley, *Journal,* 18 July 1784.

[5] Power, 138–9.

[6] Curtis, 201.

[7] Gill, 24, 216.

school with large numbers of children in attendance. The work in the Sunday school could flourish even when there was no longer an adult congregation (**2.28**). Learning could be extended when there was a library (**2.24**) and at the Independent chapel in Thornbury in addition to the Sunday school there was 'also an evening school for [about 40] men and lads, and monthly lectures on scientific subjects' (**4.25**). At Westonbirt the incumbent 'kept a night school for 60 years' (**11.10**). But at Rangeworthy there was no Sunday school, 'there being no schoolroom, nor funds for the support of teachers, moreover a very poor parish. No residents to aid in the support of a Sunday school' (**4.22**). Illness could affect attendance: in the Wesleyan Methodist chapel at Berkeley 'many of the children have not attended for the last three weeks in consequence of the illness and absence of two of the teachers' (**4.44**).

Mystic alternatives
Two groups, though they had their origins in the 18th century, were totally unconnected with the Evangelical Revival. They were unorthodox in their teaching and led by charismatic but delusional leaders. The mystic Emmanuel Swedenborg (1688–1772) was a Swedish scientist, philosopher and theologian who created his own version of the Christian faith, but quite unconnected with orthodox teaching. 'Swedenborgianism was anything but a popular belief of English people: it was millenarian, theosophical, anti-enlightenment and foreign.'[1] John Wesley strongly condemned Swedenborg's teaching as heretical ('contradictory to scripture [and] to reason') and his views as 'brain sick.'[2] 'He is one of the most ingenious, lively, entertaining madmen, that ever set pen to paper. But his waking dreams are so wild, so far remote both from scripture and common sense, that one might as easily swallow the stories of Tom Thumb, or Jack the giant-killer.'[3] Fifteen years after Swedenborg's death his followers established the New Church or New Jerusalem Church in order to propagate his teaching, and by 1851 there were 50 chapels and 2,308 worshippers. In Gloucestershire there were two New Jerusalem Church congregations in Bristol (**1.54**) and in Chalford (**10.39**). The Swedenborgian, Samuel Wilderspin[4] who nationally promoted infant education became known to Francis Close of Cheltenham, and opened an infant school in St James Square in July 1830.

The other mystical movement was led by Joanna Southcott,[5] a self-styled prophetess whose confused utterances surprisingly attracted thousands of followers from all classes of society, including some Anglican clergy.[6] Her brother Joseph was one of 60 to 70 believers in Bristol in the early 19th century. Her 'revelations' were sealed in a special box that was only to be opened in the presence of 24 Anglican bishops.[7] Before finally settling in London, Southcott

---

[1] Lineham, 122.
[2] Wesley, *Journal*, 22 Apr. 1779.
[3] Ibid., 28 February 1770.
[4] *ODNB*, 'Samuel Wilderspin (1791–1866)'.
[5] *ODNB*, 'Joanna Southcott (1750–1814)'.
[6] For the wider context of the Southcottians, see Harrison, passim.
[7] Between 1915 and 1927 the Archbishop of Canterbury received repeated requests to open a

had lived in Exeter, Bristol and 'within the cosy seclusion of Rock Cottage',[1] Blockley, in the north of Gloucestershire, where she sewed a patchwork quilt and, so it was believed, conceived by miraculous impregnation the holy child known as Shiloh. But she died, bloated and childless, surrounded by a group of pipe-smoking sympathisers who awaited her imminent resurrection. When this failed to take place she was buried in north London as 'Mrs Goddard', the name by which she had been known in Blockley. Across the country in 1851 there were four places of worship connected with the sect, with about 200 adherents. The only known gathering of Southcottians was in Small Street, Bristol, but it was short-lived and by 1840 had closed.[2] In Gloucestershire there were a few followers who infiltrated the meeting of the Society of Friends at Painswick (**10.19**).[3] Today the handful of devotees are connected with the Panacea Society of Bedford.[4]

Roman Catholicism
In the late 18th century there were some 500 Roman Catholics in Bristol, Clifton, Westbury-on-Severn and Winterbourne, but comparatively few adherents across Gloucestershire. In 1851 there were only 14 places of worship, one of which, the church of the Holy Apostles, Clifton (**2.15**) also served as the pro-cathedral for the diocese of Clifton 1850–1973. Chipping Sodbury and six local villages had a Catholic community of 110 and a Sunday congregation 30 to 35 (**3.10**) and at Cheltenham the number of visitors increased the size of the Roman Catholic community to between 800 to 1,000 and with 250–400 worshippers in attendance at Mass (**16.38**). But some congregations were very small. At Nympsfield in 1847 a handful of Roman Catholics met in a cottage and at the chapel at Hartpury the Mass was only held four times a year in the presence of six people (**7.31**); in 1850 a house was rented in Bedminster, and at Westbury-on-Trym the convent chapel was private and not even open to the public (**2.63**).

Two 19th-century innovations
In the early 19th century two religious movements emerged, one representing an orthodox Christian position (the Christian Brethren) and the other a reworking of Christianity that developed alongside but never became part of any recognised Christian confession (the Church of Jesus Christ of Latter-day Saints, usually known as the Mormons).

The Christian Brethren movement traced its origins to Dublin and Plymouth, where a number of its leaders had seceded from the established church, while in

---

box. It proving impossible to convene 24 bishops and 2,000 maidens dressed in white, a box was opened on 11 July 1927 in the presence of the Bishop of Grantham. It contained a lady's nightcap, a novel, a lottery ticket, a calendar of the French Court, a medal, a pistol, a dice-box and a few coins. A further request was made in 1935 to open what was believed to be the true box of revelations: Bell, 1199–01. Today the allegedly true box is kept in Bedford and has yet to be opened.

[1] Lewis, 167.
[2] *GNQ*, 1884, 2, 409–10.
[3] *VCH*, 11, 83.
[4] Shaw, *passim*.

Bristol the two main leaders were nonconformists. Henry Craik[1] and George Müller[2] first met in Teignmouth and came to Bristol in 1832. Craik was called first to preach at Gideon Chapel (**1.26**) and through his ministry together with that of Müller, hundreds of people began to attend. Initially the congregation was regarded by outsiders as Baptist, and in time Craik became the Hebrew examiner to the Baptist Academy (later College). In 1832 Craik and Müller had contact with John Nelson Darby,[3] the leading light of the Dublin Brethren, and in the same year they took charge of Bethesda Chapel (**1.46**) and Salem Chapel (**1.47**).

In 1837 the two chapels were united and adopted a recognisably Brethren ecclesiology of biblical preaching, a weekly Breaking of Bread (restricted to those who had been fully immersed in baptism), no ordained ministers and a strictly regulated church discipline. In 1840 the two congregations divided. Gideon Chapel closed and in 1842 Salem Chapel (formerly belonging to the Countess of Huntingdon's Connexion) was rented for the former Gideon Chapel congregation. Craik and Müller became the undisputed leaders of the Bristol Brethren, Craik the accomplished biblical scholar and Müller the philanthropist who opened numerous homes for orphans. The Bristol Brethren became known for their conservative biblical outlook, their practical ministry to the poor (especially to orphans), their ministrations during the cholera outbreaks of 1832, 1849 and 1854, and their overseas mission.

By 1844 the total membership of Bethesda and Salem Chapels was 1,050, but after a crisis in the movement in 1846 Darby led his followers into what became known as the 'Exclusive Brethren' and Craik and Müller to the 'Open Brethren'. By 1851 Bethesda had lost over 250 members. In time the Bristol Brethren recovered and continued to grow. Unity Chapel had begun in 1850 with nine members meeting in a house in Unity Street; the chapel, opened in 1855, was replaced by a larger building in Midland Road, with an increasing membership of 303 (in 1864), 390 (in 1876) and 520 (in 1895).[4] The local Bristol Census of October 1881 identified eight places of worship conducted by the Christian Brethren, with a combined morning attendance of 1,855 and an evening attendance of 1,808.

The Religious Census of 1851 revealed that outside Bristol there were Brethren meetings at Clifton (**2.50**, **51**), Churchdown (**8.15**), King's Stanley (**10.55**), Nailsworth (**10.76**) and most probably Tetbury (**11.19**). After the Methodist schism of 1849 some members formed Brethren assemblies in Gloucester (**8.23**, **31**, **38**) and at Saul some people held 'religious meetings in houses etc.' (**9.13**) that were Brethren in all but name. Some of the non-denominational places of worship may also have embodied Brethren principles (**3.26**; **8.12**; **9.19**; **12.10**).

The Church of Jesus Christ of Latter-day Saints (or Mormons) were, and remain, an unorthodox religious body that claimed to supplement the canonical

---

[1] Henry Craik (1805–1866).
[2] *ODNB*, 'George Müller (1805–1898)'.
[3] *ODNB*, 'John Nelson Darby (1800–1882)'.
[4] Higgins, 223–35.

scriptures by additional revelations given to Joseph Smith (1805–1844) in New York State. His teaching was contained in *The Book of Mormon* (1830) and *A Book of Commandments* (1833). In the summer of 1837 the English mission began in Preston, Lancs., and gradually spread throughout the country initially by open-air meetings and then by providing places of worship. The movement soon became an attractive creed for the working classes but was condemned by clergy like Francis Close who, when he addressed the annual meeting of the CPAS in London in 1853, referred to Mormonism as 'one of the most abominable inventions of Satan that ever disgraced the moral world. I have read their books. I was led to do so in consequence of the attempts they made to spread their pestiferous doctrines in my parish, and which attempts have been promptly and strongly met.'[1]

In April 1840 the Mormon mission began in Gloucestershire and where the evangelist Wilford Woodruff experienced considerable opposition. At Leigh he was about to baptise ten converts when a mob of about 100 people tried to prevent the ceremony from taking place. At Gadfield Elm, Redmarley D'Abitot a United Brethren Chapel (a breakaway group from Primitive Methodism) had opened in 1836, but by June 1840 (through the preaching of Woodruff) all but one member had converted to Mormonism. The chapel was sold in 1842 and the proceeds were used to fund emigration to the USA.[2] Many of the early Mormons were encouraged to emigrate and by 1851 it was calculated that as many as 20,000 had settled in the Great Salt Lake area of Utah. In his 'progress of religious opinions' in England, Horace Mann, who produced the report on the Religious Census, commended the Mormons, not so much for their theology but for their zeal, and it was recorded that throughout the country there were 222 places of worship and as many as 30,000 adherents within the Mormon community. In Gloucester the first Mormon missionary preached in Worcester Street in 1841, but it was not until 1856 that a place of worship was registered. More widely across the county the Census recorded Mormon congregations in Bristol (**2.53**), Cheltenham (**16.42**), Compton Abdale (**13.26**), Minchinhampton (**10.69**), Sheepscombe (**10.20**), Tetbury (**11.20**) and Welford-on-Avon (**19.9**).

Church of England - Evangelicalism

By the close of the 18th century there were an estimated 300 to 500 Evangelical clergy in the Church of England.[3] While a minority were high-profile individuals, many spent their entire ministries in relative obscurity in rural parishes. Those in Gloucestershire known to have been in sympathy with evangelical revival included Sampson Harris, the incumbent of Stonehouse 1728–63, William Weston, of Chipping Campden 1743–91 and Samuel Taylor of Quinton 1738–72. By the mid-18th century there were eight 'serious' (i.e. Evangelical) clergy in Bristol. A succession of Evangelicals served at the Temple church, at St Werburgh's (where Rowland Hill had preached his first sermon) and at St

[1] *Abstract of Report and Speeches at the 18th Annual Meeting of the CPAS,* 10 May 1853, p.19.
[2] In 1994 the derelict chapel was bought by the Mormons, opening as a museum in 2004.
[3] Walsh, *Methodism at the end of the 18th century*, in Davies and Rupp, 291.

George's, Kingswood where Richard Hart was the incumbent 1759–1808. Bridging the two centuries Thomas Tregenna Biddulph[1] was the incumbent of St James 1799–1838. John Hensman was one of the longest-serving of the Bristol Evangelicals. He had been Charles Simeon's curate in Cambridge, and then served curacies at Wraxhall, Som., and Clifton, and finally as the incumbent of St Andrew's, Clifton 1847–64. 'By then he was considered to be one of the wisest and oldest members of the Evangelical clergy' in Bristol.[2]

Evangelicals were keen to provide modest financial support for young men intending to be ordained into the Church of England. To this end the Elland Society (founded 1777) provided assistance in Yorkshire; in Northamptonshire the short-lived Creaton Clerical Education Society; the Bristol Clerical Education Society (founded 1795) and the London Clerical Education Society (founded 1813). In December 1810 William Nunn (who served a brief curacy at Newland) applied for a £25 grant, and armed with four clerical references was interviewed by Biddulph, the secretary of the Bristol Society. 'After stating to me the importance of the trust reposed in the Society, he wished me to state my views of the gospel, my reason for going to Cambridge, and why I entered, without a prospect of being able to support myself there.'[3]

In 1815, at the end of the Napoleonic Wars, Henry Ryder,[4] regarded as 'the first Evangelical bishop'[5] was appointed to the see of Gloucester and served there until 1824 when he was translated to the larger and more lucrative diocese of Lichfield and Coventry). During his episcopate Ryder was active throughout his diocese and quietly won over those who initially had been critical of his evangelicalism. He consecrated ten churches, three of which were in the Forest of Dean – Christ Church (**18.37**), Holy Trinity (**6.6**) and St Paul (**18.36**) – and through his aristocratic connections was able to secure financial support from some of the leading Evangelicals of the day.[6] The Forest of Dean was a particularly deprived area of the diocese and before Holy Trinity was erected the inhabitants neglected their 'moral and religious duties. Few have been used to observe the Sabbath, still fewer to attend the churches on the borders.'[7] Henry Berkin, of Holy Trinity, Harrow Hill (**6.6**) believed that the morals of the area were injured by the numerous number of beer shops. He had see boys as young as twelve years old 'staggering drunk.'[8] Early in his episcopate bishop Ryder, supported by Anglican clergy and nonconformist ministers provided cheap Bibles for those who lived in the Forest. The other mining district in the diocese was Kingswood and it too suffered from considerable deprivation and was known for its immorality and barbarity. 'The wickedness and gross immorality of the

---

[1] *ODNB*, 'Thomas Tregenna Biddulph (1763–1838)'.
[2] *ODNB*, 'John Hensman (1780–1864)'.
[3] Pym, 64.
[4] *ODNB,* 'Henry Ryder (1777–1836)'
[5] G. C. B. Davies, *The First Evangelical Bishop* (London) 1957. W. J. Baker, Henry Ryder of Gloucester 1815–1824: England's First Evangelical Bishop, *TBGAS,* 1971, 89, 130–44.
[6] Nicholls 1858, 161, 166, 168.
[7] Nicholls 1863, 134.
[8] Children's Employment Commission 1842.

inhabitants of Kingswood Forest, have been for years proverbially notorious. It has been a matter of much surprise, that within so short a distance of the two populous towns of Bath and Bristol, a people should exist very little removed from a state of barbarianism.'[1] Members of the notorious 'Cock Road Gang' included the family of Benjamin Cains. Four of his sons were transported and two executed; the husbands of three of his daughters were transported or executed; and two grandsons were transported and another executed.[2] Ryder laid the foundation stone of St Matthew, Kingsdown (**2.18**) and returned, after his translation to Lichfield and Coventry, to consecrate the building. Kingswood was a particularly needy area and he had already laid the foundation stone and consecrated Holy Trinity (**20.27**). The first minister of Holy Trinity, the Evangelical Joseph Ditcher, went on to become the vicar of South Brent, Somerset 1841–75 and was involved in a high-profile court case brought against the Anglo-Catholic archdeacon of Taunton, George Anthony Denison,[3] for teaching the doctrine of the real presence in the Eucharist.

During Ryder's episcopate there were a number of Evangelicals in the Gloucester diocese. In the Forest of Dean two of the clergy had been converted through the ministry of Thomas Tregenna Biddulph, the incumbent of St James, Bristol - Henry Berkin of Holy Trinity, Harrow Hill (**6.6**) and Henry Poole of St James, Bream (**18.22**) and St Paul, Parkend (**18.36**). A third Evangelical in the Forest was Payler Matthew Procter the incumbent of Newland (**18.20**).[4] In Gloucester John Kempthorne (1775–1838) was the incumbent of St Michael and St Mary de Grace, Gloucester 1825–38 and a chaplain to bishop Ryder. Francis William Rice was the long-standing incumbent of Fairford 1828–78 (**12.60**); Strickland Charles Edward Neville, the curate in charge of Painswick, and the first minister of Sheepscombe 1820–27 (**10.14**) and Charles Jervis and Francis Close, covering 40 years in Cheltenham, 1816–56.

In 1816 Charles Jervis[5] was appointed as the perpetual curate of Cheltenham, and during the course of the next ten years he established the town as an Evangelical centre and provided the foundation for his illustrious successor Francis Close.[6] In 1824 Jervis had appointed the 27 year-old Close to the curacy of the chapel of ease of Holy Trinity where he remained for two years. Following Jervis' sudden death in 1826, Charles Simeon, the patron of the parish church, appointed Close to succeed him. During the course of the next 30 years Francis Close exercised a high profile ministry in Cheltenham where he erected churches, established schools and colleges, and his powerful preaching attracted large congregations of residents and visitors to the parish church so that the building which seated 1,600 people (together with others who stood) was 'always full and

---

[1] *The Christian Remembrancer*, January 1822, 4, no. 37, 8.

[2] Ellacombe, 212, footnote 2.

[3] *ODNB*, 'George Anthony Denison (1805–1896)'.

[4] William Nunn, a follower of Charles Simeon, was briefly the curate at Newland, 1814–5: Pym, 76–8. Nunn served another brief curacy at Foleshill, Coventry, 1816–7, and became the minister of St Clement, Manchester 1817–42.

[5] Munden 1982, 142–50.

[6] *ODNB*, 'Francis Close (1797–1882)'.

crowded' (**16.16a**). During Close's ministry Cheltenham parish church had the largest congregation in the county.

All Evangelicals were highly critical of the Oxford Movement (and later Anglo-Catholicism) and in this Close was no different. In Cheltenham most of the Anglican clergy, apart from the minister of St John's church, held similar theological convictions to him. As long as Francis Close remained in post at the parish church and with John Browne as his co-worker at Holy Trinity the schools and colleges in the town maintained an Evangelical outlook. In 1856 Close became the the dean of Carlisle where he remained until he resigned in 1881, a year before his death. In Cheltenham his name was commemorated in two educational institutions - the Dean Close Memorial School opened in 1886 and in 1997 when the St Paul's College buildings were renamed the Francis Close Hall.

By the mid-19th century Close calculated that there were between 4,000 to 5,000 Evangelical clergy in the Church of England, nearly 3,000 of whom were prepared to be identified with the leading Evangelical societies[1] eg. CMS and CPAS. In the Gloucester diocese about 80 clergy supported CPAS.[2] There are two contemporary observations about them. It was said that bishop Monk favoured the high-church party, 'rather than to the Evangelical party, whose influence at Bristol, Clifton and Cheltenham, and other places in his diocese occasionally proved to him a source of discomfort.'[3] Though Joseph Leech observed that Cheltenham and Clifton were 'very convenient retreats for clergymen who were not born with a talent or taste for rural life'[4] it is clear that those who ministered there were able and capable of exercising leadership in the church - Archibald Boyd became the dean of Exeter 1867–83,[5] Charles Bromby the bishop of Tasmania 1864–82[6] and Francis Close the dean of Carlisle 1856–81.

Gloucestershire was not untouched by what is known as the 'Western Schism'. In the early part of the 19th century some members of the Church of England (both clergy and laity) adopted a strict Calvinistic theology and were re-baptised by total immersion, and which by this action severed their connection with the Church of England. In his primary charge (1816) bishop Ryder referred to those in neighbouring dioceses who had seceded from the Church a of England and 'to the few who may yet remain in it, but who adopt, in some measure, their opinions and practice. Their charge against their brethren is, that we do not preach Christ freely and fully; that we detract from the all-sufficiency of faith, and promulgate an imperfect, and even another gospel.'[7] These accusations Ryder challenged by referring the schismatics to the teaching of the New Testament and to the Anglican Homily on Faith. 'Beware, then' he said, 'of this error ... in well-intentioned and pious persons, is, we must fear, but a snare of the devil, and an

---

[1] Close 1847, 32.
[2] CPAS, *Report of the Committee read at the 17th Annual Meeting, 11 May 1852* (London) 1852.
[3] *Hardwick's Annual Biography for 1856* (London) 1857, 116.
[4] Leech 2004, 306.
[5] *ODNB* 'Archibald Boyd (1803–1883)'.
[6] *ODNB*, 'Charles Bromby (1814–1907)'.
[7] Ryder, 15.

awful wresting of scripture, to the destruction of those who hear.'[1] Ryder had good reason to be concerned about these individuals for in the same year Thomas Snow and his family moved to Cheltenham. On becoming the incumbent of two parishes near Winchester, Snow came under the influenced of his patron, Sir Thomas Baring. His sister Harriet Wall exercised a powerful influence over other people and it was she who erected a chapel in Grosvenor Street, Cheltenham (**16.23**) where Snow served as minister 1818–22. Snow then became disillusioned with dissent, and for the next four years ate humble pie, re-aligning himself with the Church of England. In 1826 Snow assured the Bishop of Bristol that he had been in error, and was re-admitted to the Anglican ministry. Subsequently as a London incumbent he was involved in establishing the CPAS.[2]

Another person caught up in the Western Schism was Thomas Connolly Cowan, who from 1815 was the curate of St Thomas', Bristol and within two years his licence had been revoked by the bishop. Increasingly Cowan had become dissatisfied with the practice of infant baptism, being expected to administer holy communion to unbelievers and to the indiscriminate use of the burial service. Cowan adopted strict views on baptism and following his re-baptism briefly officiated in Bristol at Gideon Chapel (**1.26**) until 1819 when he acquired Bethesda Chapel (**1.46**) later to become the centre for the ministries of Henry Craik and George Müller.[3]

Though not directly associated with the Schism, Isaac Bridgman was forced to leave the Church of England. He was a curate at Mitcheldean and became the first minister of Holy Trinity, Harrow Hill (**6.6**) and was dismissed for irregularity in his ministry. He was accused of insulting the incumbent (Henry Berkin), instigating a riot, associating with the lower classes, being too anecdotal and controversial in his preaching and in adding words of explanation to the liturgy which brought contempt to the Anglican service. He asked if bishop Ryder would permit him to continue preaching at a Friday evening service at Ruardean, but this he refused unless he was first reconciled to Berkin. In 1822 the bishop revoked Bridgman's license which meant that he could no longer officiate in any Anglican church in the diocese. But in a petition he had the support of 691 individuals who wanted a chapel to be erected for him. At the same time, his friend Rowland Hill, who already wanted to open chapels at Lydbrook, Littledean Hill and Blakeney became involved, and he began to collect subscriptions for them. Soon one was opened at Blakeney Hill (**6.3**) and Bridgman became the first minister. Following the usual practice in Hill's chapels, Sunday worship followed the order of the *Book of Common Prayer* but in 1825 members of the chapel opted to become an Independent congregation and the use of the liturgy was discontinued.[4]

[1] Ibid., 17.
[2] Munden 2009, 57–63.
[3] G. Carter, 111, 118–9, 131–2.
[4] *The British Review*, August 1832, 27–52; Bridgman, *passim*; R. Hill, *passim*.

Church of England - The Oxford Movement and Anglo-Catholicism

In 1853 William Conybeare published an essay on the 'Church Parties' within the Church of England in which he identified three groups: low (including Evangelicals), high (including Tractarians), and broad (a minority liberal group).[1] Though imprecise, these groupings proved useful markers for the different factions within the established church. Since just under two-thirds of the Gloucestershire clergy had graduated from Oxford their churchmanship reflected the high church tradition of that university. Though high churchmen formed a distinct group set apart from the outlook of the Tractarians in time many would have been hard pressed to distinguish between them. From the 1830s a revived version of the pre-Reformation church in England was created in Oxford. It was pietistic and romantic, elitist and clerical, and stressed the catholic identity of the church, and adopted convictions about ordained ministry and the sacraments that were more in line with the medieval church than with the Church of England as established during the Reformation. The Oxford Movement spread its ideas by networking and through the publication of 90 *Tracts for the Times*. These tracts (ranging from a few pages to several hundred) were avidly read in country parsonages and discussed at clerical meetings. 'For all its variations, "Tractarianism" had specific points of ideological reference which bestowed a certain cohesion on the principles of its adherents. A common identity was provided by both the philosophical and ethical, and moral and spiritual dimensions of the Movement. These dimensions extended support for the Tractarians among those who had reservations on particular doctrinal points.'[2] The leaders of the Movement (all of whom were tract writers) were Edward Pusey,[3] John Henry Newman[4] and John Keble who had served curacies in several Gloucestershire parishes.

Gradually a number of Bristol and Gloucestershire clergy were drawn into the Movement. They included James Henry Scudamore Burr of Tidenham (**18.1**), William Lionel Darell of Fretherne (**9.16**), James Davies of Abenhall (**6.24**), Henry Eland of Bedminster (**20.37**), Henry Thomas Ellacombe[5] of Bitton (**20.1**), Edward Field of English Bicknor (**18.49**), Charles Fuge Lowder of Tetbury (**11.14**), William Frederick Powell of Cirencester (**12.37**), Henry Richards of Horfield (**2.20**) and Thomas Thorp[6] of Kemerton (**17.21**). At Ruardean, (**18.50**) Henry Formby became unpopular with his parishioners and resigned from his living, and soon after his friend John Henry Newman left the Church of England, he too was received into the Church of Rome. Others who seceded were Edgar Edmund Estcourt,[7] who had been a curate of Cirencester 1842–5, and Jonathan Henry Woodward, incumbent of St James, Bristol (**1.7**) who took with him two of his curates. The wealthy layman William Leigh (who became a Roman Catholic *c*.1844) founded the church and monastery at Woodchester (**10.58**).

[1] Conybeare, 57–164.
[2] Nockles, 39.
[3] *ODNB*, 'Edward Bouverie Pusey (1800–1882)'.
[4] *ODNB*, 'John Henry Newman (1801–1890)'.
[5] *ODNB*, 'Henry Thomas Ellacombe (1790–1885)'.
[6] *ODNB*, 'Thomas Thorp (1791–1877)'.
[7] *ODNB*, 'Edgar Edmund Estcourt (1816–1884)'.

The two Keble brothers made a significant contribution to the Oxford Movement. Thomas Keble[1] who was the vicar of Bisley (**10.25**) 1827–73 became the acknowledged leader of what was known as the 'Bisley-Fairford school'[2] that provided a catalyst for those conservative high churchmen who were committed to personal devotions, a pattern of daily services, weekly communion and the observance of saint's days. Thomas Keble influenced those who served as his curates – George Prevost,[3] Isaac Williams,[4] Robert Gregory[5] and Robert Suckling. Two of these men later received preferment. Prevost (the brother-in-law of Isaac Williams) became the vicar of Stinchcombe (**5.24**) and archdeacon of Gloucester 1865–81, and Gregory became dean of St Paul's cathedral 1891–1911. Technically only a curate, Isaac Williams, a university academic, poet and author of three of the Tracts, left Oxford in 1842 and settled first at Bisley and then from 1848 at Stinchcombe.

Geographically Bisley was a large parish and as the incumbent Thomas Keble was responsible for the erection of churches at Oakridge (**10.26**), Bussage (**10.28**) and France Lynch, and with the restoration of the 18th century chapel at Chalford (**10.27**). Keble's friends contributed towards Oakridge church, and 20 members of the University of Oxford contributed towards the new church at Bussage, with every expectation that it would become 'a model Tractarian parish.'[6] Robert Suckling, the first minister of Bussage, was also the chaplain to the Union workhouse at Stroud (**10.43**) where he ministered to the poor and to the six to eight prostitutes confined to what was known as the 'Black Ward'.

From the late 1840s 'Penitentiaries' or 'Magdalens'[7] were established to rescue and redeem fallen women. A pioneer in this movement was John Armstrong, incumbent of Tidenham (**18.1**) who supported the raising of funds for two penitentiaries in the south-east attached to the Anglican sisterhoods at Clewer, near Windsor and at Wantage. From 1850 he became directly involved with Robert Suckling in establishing a penitentiary at Bussage called the House of Refuge that opened in April 1851. Three years later a south aisle was added to Bussage church to accommodate the women. Initially Kirby's Cottage (owned by Suckling) housed five former prostitutes under the direction of Grace Anne Poole of nearby Brownshill House. Later the cottage was replaced by a new building to accommodate 25 women under Poole's direction; she was given the title of Mother Superior of the Community of St Michael and All Angels.[8]

John Keble,[9] like his younger brother Thomas, was born in Court House (now Keble House), the family home at Fairford. Their father was the vicar of Coln St

---

[1] *ODNB*, 'Thomas Keble (1793–1875)'.

[2] The term 'the Bisley and Fairford school' was coined by Isaac Williams: Church, 64.

[3] *ODNB*, 'George Prevost (1804–1893)'.

[4] *ODNB*, 'Isaac Williams (1802–1865)'.

[5] *ODNB*, 'Robert Gregory (1819–1911)'.

[6] O. W. Jones, 116.

[7] After Mary Magdalene, Luke 8:2; Mark 16:9.

[8] In 1900 the Bussage House of Mercy (as it became known) was taken over by the Community of St Mary the Virgin, Wantage, and remained under its direction until 1948.

[9] *ODNB*, 'John Keble (1792–1866)'.

Aldwyns from 1782 to 1835 (**13.13**) and educated his sons at home. After graduation and ordination to a college title John Keble during the summer vacation assisted at the two small neighbouring churches of Eastleach Martin (**13.2**) and Eastleach Turville (**13.3**). Keble rode from Oxford (where he was a tutor at Oriel College), officiated at one or other of the churches, and had his lunch in a cottage. He was instrumental in starting a Sunday school at Eastleach Turville. In 1823 he became the curate of Southrop (**13.1**) where he lived in the vicarage until he was succeeded by his brother Thomas who remained there until he was appointed to Bisley. After a brief curacy at Hursley, Hants., John Keble returned to live in the family home at Fairford and was his father's curate at Coln St Aldwyns until the latter's death in 1835.

From 1819 John Keble composed over 100 poems based on the church's liturgical year,[1] probably most of which were written in rural Gloucestershire. He confessed, 'I get fonder and fonder of the country and of poetry and of such things every year of my life.'[2] In June 1827 the poems were published anonymously as *The Christian Year* and which Edward Pusey believed to have been the inspiration for the Oxford Movement. The work caught the mood of the day and became an immensely popular devotional manual and which during Keble's lifetime went through nearly one hundred editions. Keble resumed his career at Oxford where he became the Professor of Poetry 1832–41; on 14 July 1833 preached the assize sermon that John Henry Newman regarded as the beginning of the Oxford Movement; and wrote seven of the *Tracts for the Times*. In 1836 he became the incumbent of Hursley where he died in 1866; Keble College, Oxford, founded in his memory, opened in 1870.

In 1834 George Prevost, who became the incumbent of Stinchcombe (**5.24**) and remained in post until his death in 1881, served also as rural dean of Dursley from 1852, and as archdeacon of Gloucester from 1865. He was the author of Tract 84 (with a conclusion by Thomas Keble). Prevost rebuilt the parish church and on the day on which it was consecrated (26 July 1855), John Keble preached in the morning and Samuel Wilberforce (bishop of Oxford) in the afternoon. In the late 1860s Prevost introduced a weekly communion service, and the records show that in 1867 there were 674 communicants at 31 services and in the following year 833 communicants at 51 services. During the course of the year 1867–68, Morning Prayer was said daily, and Evening Prayer on Wednesdays, Fridays and Saturdays. On Good Friday 1868 there were 150 in the congregation (including 17 communicants) and 80 present at Evening Prayer.[3]

The activities of the clergy sympathetic to the Oxford Movement, and later the ritualism introduced by the Anglo-Catholics did not pass unnoticed. From the mid-century there was much rancour between the different church parties, numerous court cases and even an Act of Parliament (The Public Worship Regulation Act, 37 and 38 Vict. c.85, 1874) designed to curb the extreme ritualists. But earlier Joseph Leech had noted that this sort of action could be

---

[1] The hymns and their dates of composition (1819–28) are listed in Lock, 239–41.
[2] Ibid., 15.
[3] Jacques, 155–70.

counter-productive. He made the point that John Clifford, 'the incumbent of St Matthew's [Kingsdown] (**2.18**), is, I believe, ranked amongst the extreme anti-high church party, as he seems to deem it, and I have no doubt sincerely, an imperative duty to introduce the subject into nearly all his sermons. For my part, though, I have as strong a disrelish and dread of the errors of Rome as any Reformer in England, yet I question the wisdom and utility of churchmen constantly harping on "the heresies of Oxford".'[1]

Architecture, pluralism and non-residence

During the 18th century many Anglican churches increased their seating capacity by erecting galleries. This was a far cheaper way of accommodating more people than by the enlargement of the existing building by erecting a a new aisle. The galleries, often located at the west end of the church, were intended for the musicians and singers, for the poor and for children. Where people sat in church and upon what they sat, is referred to in the Religious Census, and frequently Joseph Leech in his visits to churches referred to the galleries, orchestras and singers.[2] In Thomas Hardy's novel, *Under the Greenwood Tree* (1872), the new reforming, high-church vicar removed the galleried singers and players and replaced them with a robed choir in the chancel. The introduction of an organ deprived the congregation of the talented abilities of the musicians who invariably left the Anglican church and joined a nonconformist chapel. As to the galleries they were mostly removed during the Victorian 'restorations' and throughout Gloucestershire their erection and destruction is recorded in the *VCH*.

In Holy Trinity, Michinhampton (**10.62**) the interior of the church was described as having 'ugly galleries running along three sides of the nave. The organ and choir were located in a huge gallery, which blocked up the whole west end of the church. There was the inevitable "three decker" [pulpit], the rector preaching in a black gown, below him the curate facing the congregation in the reading desk, and below the curate again the clerk, who said the responses and gave out the hymns.'[3] In the 1870s the galleries were removed and the organ placed in the north transept. At St Mary's, Bitton (**20.1**) there were successive destructions, and the incumbent Henry Nicholson Ellacombe recorded that 'in the last century, or at the end of the eighteenth, the churchwardens destroyed the rood screen, the old seats, and the old roof and put up an elaborate Tuscan reredos, very ugly, as we would say, but costly and well worked. My father [Henry Thomas Ellacombe], in 1820, destroyed all their work as far as he could, and did some excellent work in the fashion of the day. Most of his work I destroyed, and received his thanks and approval for so doing.'[4] Ellacombe believed that in this he was no different from earlier generations of clergy. 'I should consider that I was not walking in the steps of the vicars of mediaeval times if I tied myself down to such an admiration of their work that I would limit the capabilities of the

[1] Leech 2004, 117.
[2] Ibid., 243, 278, 289, 303–306, 314.
[3] Playne, 55–6.
[4] A. W. Hill, 48–9, 289.

church to the requirements of their times when the requirements of my own called for something very different.'[1] When the rebuilding, repairs or restoration took place the parish church was closed, and the congregation met elsewhere such as in the schoolroom (**17.4**).

The medievalising viewpoint, looking back to an imagined pre-Reformation purity whether in what the church taught or what was expressed in the architectural style of the buildings, was widely debated. Francis Close of Cheltenham regarded the restoration of churches as being a contributory factor towards the restoration of popery. In a spirited attack on the Cambridge Camden Society he clearly stated his belief that 'Romanism is taught *analytically* at Oxford, [and] it is taught *artistically* at Cambridge – that it is inculcated theoretically, in tracts, at one university, and it is *sculptured, painted,* and *graven* at the other. The Cambridge Camdenians build churches and furnish symbolic vessels, by which the Oxford Tractarians may carry out their principles – in a word, that the "*Ecclesiologist*" of Cambridge is identical in doctrine with the Oxford Tracts for the Times.'[2]

In Trollope's *Dr Thorne*, the vicar of Greshamsbury was the high churchman, Caleb Oriel.[3] At Oxford he 'had become inoculated there with very high-church principles, and had gone into orders influenced by a feeling of enthusiastic love for the priesthood ... He delighted in lecterns and credence-tables, in services at dark hours of winter mornings when no one would attend, in high waistcoats and narrow white neckties, in chanted services and intoned prayers ... He eschewed matrimony, imagining that it became him as a priest to do so; he fasted rigorously on Fridays, and the neighbours declared that he scourged himself.'[4] Though fictional this impression was not far from the truth.

Close was convinced that 'an ecclesiastical mania [had] taken possession of men's minds, and that which was enacted on a small scale first at Oxford, has spread itself over the whole land. Every class of society is in some measure affected by it … all are touched and tinged with this Gothic taste, and this passion for everything connected with the middle ages. In fact we are completely gothicised.'[5] Certainly during the course of the 19th century many of the churches of Gloucestershire were restored or rebuilt by their over-enthusiastic clergy. Admittedly by that time much of the fabric of many of the buildings was in poor condition and badly needed attention, but the zeal of the restorers often destroyed important architectural features that were not consistent with their medieval world view. Sometimes a wealthy Tractarian incumbent, patron or landowner erected a new church that would embody the principles and secure the approval of the ecclesiologists as at Bussage (**10.28**), Fretherne (**9.16**), Highnam (**6.36**) and St Saviour's, Tetbury (**11.15**). James Russell Woodford, the high-church protégé of archdeacon Thomas Thorp (the secretary of the Bristol and West of England Architectural Society), erected two churches that embodied the principles of the

[1] Ibid., 285.
[2] Close 1845, 4.
[3] Oriel College was at the heart of Tractarian Oxford.
[4] A. Trollope, *Dr Thorne* (1858), ch. 32.
[5] Close 1847, 43–4.

ecclesiologists at Coalpit Heath (**3.3**) and St Mark's, Lower Easton, Bristol (**1.10**) where he introduced a chanted service and a surpliced choir. Thomas Thorp, who was the president of the Cambridge Camden Society from 1839–59, the incumbent of Kemerton (**17.21**) and archdeacon of Bristol 1836–73, was often at odds with Francis Close over doctrine, architecture and education, and Close was the formidable opponent of the Cambridge Camden Society.[1]

Pluralism and non-residence was an issue that was common in the 18th century and in the early part of the following century (e.g. **12.18**). Both were justified where there was no parsonage or where it was unsuitable and where the benefice income was insufficient. 'Ill-heath, infirmity and old age provide a fruitful crop of non-residence licences.'[2] This was certainly the case for poorer clergy who lacked private means to retire, and some could be absent when they or members of their family suffered from ill-health and it was considered expedient that they all lived elsewhere. In the absence of the incumbent the parishes were served by assistant curates, often on a modest stipend, and who, in the absence of the incumbent, often invariably lived in the benefice house. Under the Pluralities Act (1 and 2 Vict. c.106, 1838) clergy could only hold two benefices if they were within ten miles of each other. There were exceptions, an archdeacon could hold one or two benefices, or a cathedral canon, but, 'no one could hold a benefice with a population of over 3,000 with one of over 5,000, not two livings if their total value exceeded £1,000.'[3] In 1831 of the 286 Gloucestershire parishes only 116 had a resident incumbent, and half of these had no parsonage. 'In Bristol diocese in 1831 out of 252 incumbents only 113 were resident, 59 living at other benefices, 17 infirm and 23 having no parsonage houses,'[4] and poor housing was referred to in bishop Monk's primary charge of 1832. By 1851 there were still a few incumbents who held two or more parishes, but in all instances they had already served in the diocese for some time. With an increased stipend and the provision of a suitable parsonage clergy were more satisfied with the income from a single benefice.

Reviewing the period 1830–60 bishop Charles Baring recorded that 65 new churches had been erected, 136 had been rebuilt or renewed, 99 glebe houses had been built, and 278 new schools had been erected. But there were still 63 parishes without suitable schools for the poor, and 111 churches that needed to be enlarged or reseated to accommodate the poor. While the majority of parishes consisted of poor people, the majority of seating in the churches was more for the rich than the poor. As to the worship in the churches, there were 47 churches in which Holy Communion was only administered once a quarter, and 26 where there was only one Sunday sermon. However 'the returns also showed that the increased attendances at church were much larger than could be accounted for by any increase in population, and that the number of communicants had more than doubled.'[5]

---

[1] White, 139–44.
[2] Huddleston, 5.
[3] Ibid., p.3.
[4] Ibid., p.3.
[5] The triennial visitation of bishop Charles Baring, 1860: *The Bristol Mercury,* 29 Sept. 1860.

CONCLUSION

Writing to *The Times* in July 1861, Horace Mann said that the Religious Census of 1851 had never intended to 'attempt to enumerate the adherents to each denomination' but it was to ascertain, first, 'the amount of provision for public worship available throughout the land', and, second, 'the extent to which this available provision was made use of ... The Census was a census of religious worship, and the compiler therefore confined himself strictly to a statement of the provision for worship, and the number of worshippers on a given day'. Mann believed the Census was 'both accurate and complete within its professed scope' and that any accusations of falsehood and deliberate misrepresentation were ludicrous. It remained 'a faithful representation of the religious condition of the people, so far that can be represented by attendance upon public worship'.[1] His observations are noteworthy, and suggest that the Census remains today a generally sound basis of factual information, compiled in good faith by people on the spot.

We must however be cautious in using the Census findings to compare attendance at a place of worship then and now. On the face of it more people were in their churches and chapels than we find today. Then, many more children attended Sunday school than the very small number now involved. But we are not comparing like with like. Then church and chapel attendance were often more a matter of custom and conformity. Today church and chapel-going attendance is more closely connected with what individuals believe. Looking through the returns challenges the popular myth that 'the churches were always full'. That was far from the case; indeed the Census makes it clear that many churches and chapels were half empty (or should that be half full). Churches and chapels were built for potential rather than actual congregations, and in the expectation that providing a building would attract a worshippers. But this expectation was not often realised. Robin Gill, writing in 1993, concluded that the Church of England had been in continuous decline since the Religious Census of 1851, and similarly nonconformity had been in continuous decline since the 1880s.[2] Moving on a hundred years from the Census, Callum Brown made it clear that 'from 1956 all indices of religiosity in Britain start to decline, and from 1963 most enter free fall ... the result has been that the generation that grew up in the sixties was more dissimilar to the generation of its parents than in any previous century.'[3]

Taking a long view, the findings of the Census 'raise an important question. England has always claimed to be a Christian country; the phrase is of course ambiguous, it might mean a variety of things, but there is one rather obvious meaning which might be appropriate to it. A Christian country might mean a country of at least nominal Christians. If that is so, however, it is not clear how far the title might be claimed by a country in which there were a number of people with no contact with any Christian church and no knowledge of the rudiments of the Christian faith.'[4] If that was true of the nation in 1851, then it is even more the situation today.

[1] *The Times*, 11 July 1861.
[2] Gill, 76.
[3] Brown, 188, 190.
[4] Clark, 150–1.

TERMINOLOGY AND GENERAL NOTES

Church Building Acts

Between 1818 and 1856 over 20 Church Building Acts were passed, 'forming an almost impenetrable jungle of laws and orders.'[1] Under the first of these, 58 Geo. III, c.45, 1818, 'An Act for building and promoting the building of additional churches in populous parishes', the government set aside £1,000,000, and in 1824 a further £500,000, to erect new churches. Locally, two churches received grants from the first of these sums - St George, Bristol (£9,263) (**1.6**) and Holy Trinity, Kingswood (£2,457) (**20.27**). From the second, grants were made to: St Paul, Bedminster (£6,607) (**20.37**), Holy Trinity, St Philip's, Bristol (£6,031) (**2.35**), St Clement, Bristol (£100) (**1.16**), St Jude the Apostle (£275) (**2.38**), St Luke (£500) (**2.36**), St Michael (£250) (**1.14**), St Simon the Apostle (£300) (**2.37**), St Paul, Cheltenham (£3,626) (**16.18**), St Luke, Cheltenham (£250) (**16.16a**), Holy Jesus, Lydbrook £100) (**18.38**), Holy Trinity, Stroud (£1,142) (**10.41**) and St Paul, Stroud (£400) (**10.42**).[2]

Of most relevance to the Religious Census was 'An Act to make better provision for the spiritual care of populous parishes' (6 and 7 Vict. c.37, 1843). The Act, popularly known as Peel's Act, after Robert Peel (prime minister 1841–6), enabled clergy to be appointed to newly-created districts where an existing building (invariably the National school) was licensed by the bishop for worship in anticipation of a new church being erected. On their appointment the clergy received a fixed stipend of £130, raised to £150 on the church being endowed, consecrated and opened. On a new parish being created, the minister of the district became the perpetual curate of the new parish.

Church dedications

Nationally, and from the Middle Ages, the most popular dedications for parish churches were to St Mary (2,335), All Saints (1,255), and St Peter (1,140). These were followed by St Michael and All Angels (687), St Andrew (637), St John the Baptist (500), St Nicholas (437), St James (414), St Paul (326) and Holy Trinity (297). In the 19th century many newly built churches were dedicated to Holy Trinity or Christ Church. Surprisingly the Census revealed that some Anglican clergy were unaware of the dedication of their churches (**3.14**, **12.18**) and seemingly not particularly interested in finding out (**2.75**; **4.39**; **6.28**; **7.23**; **14.35**, **38**; **19.28**). Probably more confusing for us today is that over the centuries some dedications were changed (**2.71**; **4.16**, **46**; **5.20**, **27**; **7.22**; **12.65**; **13.12**; **14.16**; **17.5**; **19.34**).[3]

Church of England churches and chapels

Nationally there are parish churches, and then within parishes various types of chapel – private chapels, proprietary chapels, episcopal chapels and chapels of ease. A private chapel, located in or near to a private house, was not necessarily consecrated, and was outside the direction and control of the incumbent of the parish. Similarly a proprietary chapel was not always consecrated, and was independent of the parish in which it was situated. There were proprietary chapels in Gloucester (**8.40**) and Cheltenham (**16.6**, **17**,

---

[1] Best, 355. The Acts are conveniently listed in Port, 363.
[2] Port, 326, 333.
[3] Bond, 17.

19–20). The income received from pew rents paid the stipend of the minister (and other officials like vergers and organists), and a proportion of the income went to the proprietors. A popular preacher would both attract a congregation and provide a sufficient income for the proprietors. Chapels of ease, some of which were licensed but not consecrated, were directly regulated by the incumbent of the parish in which they were situated, and all services, apart from marriages, could be conducted there. Often, but not always, chapels of ease were later consecrated and became separate parishes with their own incumbent.

No new parish church could be consecrated until there was a sufficient endowment, and there might be a gap of some years before a building was opened and licensed for worship, and consecrated by the bishop. Technically, if a church was rebuilt on the same site, reconsecration was not essential.

Church of England clergy
The incumbent of an Anglican parish is known as a 'rector' (entitled to receive the great tithes); a 'vicar' was a deputy to a rector but unable to receive those tithes, and a 'perpetual curate' could only be removed from office by his licence being revoked. Generally clergy appointed to newly-created parishes were called perpetual curates and under the Incumbents Act (31 and 32 Vict. c.117, 1868) they too were known as vicars. Some Anglican clergy referred to themselves simply as 'minister'. Other clergy were chaplains to the army and navy, to workhouses (**10.43**), prisons (**8.17**; **13.43**) and in large urban communities to cemeteries. Every incumbent has 'the cure of souls' and is technically 'the curate' (**13.38**) of the parish, but usually the term 'curate' refers to the individual who assisted the incumbent as a stipendary curate who was licensed by the bishop. The stipend of the assistant curate was proportionate to the population of the parish. Where the incumbent was non-resident the assistant curate conducted the affairs of the parish. In this edition the term 'incumbent' is used to refer to parochial clergy (rectors, vicars and perpetual curates).

Under the Pluralities Act (1 and 2 Vict. c.106, 1838) no two benefices could be held unless they were within 10 miles of each other, and the annual income of one of them did not exceed £200. If the population of one exceeded 3,000, another could not be held with a population of more than 500. Clergy appointed before 1838 could legally hold two or more benefices at the same time. In addition to clerical rectors, there were also lay rectors (**12.33**), both types being responsible for the maintenance and repair of the chancel.

Church of England clerical income
In the mid-19th century the archbishop of Canterbury received an annual stipend of £15,000 and the bishop of Gloucester and Bristol £3,700. But the annual income of parochial clergy was well below this and varied nationally from under £100 to the remarkable £4,848 enjoyed by the incumbent of Stanhope in County Durham. Disparity was also evident locally. Some incumbents had received well below £100 a year, but at the upper end, some 20 incumbents had incomes between £504 at Naunton (**14.10**) and £1,574 at Bishops Cleeve (**15.35**).[1] Clergy of newly-erected churches received a fixed stipend of £150 from the Ecclesiastical Commissioners.

Clerical income came from various sources – glebe (held by clergy as quasi-tenants), and from land, tithes and the rental from buildings. Other sources included pew rents, surplice fees (**11.21**, **18.37**) (for prayers after childbirth, marriages and burials), voluntary Easter offering (roughly calculated at 2d a head, or 4d from each household). Some

[1] At Bredon, Worcs. (**17.24**), it was £1,498.

parishes received financial assistance from Queen Anne's Bounty, a fund set up in 1704 principally to augment the income of poorer clergy. By the 19th century the fund was also used to erect and repair parsonage houses. In 1948 the Queen Anne's Bounty and the Ecclesiastical Commissioners (founded in 1835) were united and formed the Church Commissioners.

Clerk

Technically a clergyman is a 'clerk in holy orders', and that is how Francis Bayly (**9.4**), Thomas Jones (**8.39**) and Henry Branckner (**20.25**) described themselves. But there were other 'clerks' who were laymen and in 1851 there were a total of 69 parish clerks in Gloucestershire. The parish clerk was appointed by the clergyman and assisted him in leading the services by making the responses and in announcing the hymns. At Slimbridge the parish clerk led the singing (**5.29**), at Bisley he completed the Census return (**10.25**), and at Brimpsfield (**12.8**) and Cranham (**10.21**) he was given the Easter offerings. The parish clerk had to be at least 20 years old and 'to be of honest conversation, and sufficient for his reading and writing and also singing, if it may be.' (Canon 91). Parish clerks could serve for some time. At St Mary's Bitton (**20.1**) 'Charles Ship was born in the year 1788; appointed parish clerk of the mother church of Bitton in 1823; and died 20 November 1853'.[1]

Sexton

The sexton could also be the parish clerk. The duties were various and included keeping the church clean, digging graves, provide the lighting, the bread and wine for communion, water for baptising, opening the doors of the pews, to assist the churchwardens in keeping order. Women could be sextons and in one instance completed the Census return (**2.20**). In 1851 there were 47 female church officers in Gloucestershire.

Names of nonconformist chapels

Often a nonconformist chapel did not have a name, apart from its identification by denomination ('Wesleyan Chapel') or location ('Langton Street Chapel' (**20.45**)), but in a number of instances a name was taken from a biblical text or allusion. Of such chapel names, the most popular were Ebenezer and Tabernacle.

Bethany (a village, the place of Jesus' anointing - Mark 14:3–9)
Cheltenham (**16.35**, **36**).

Bethel ('House of God' - Genesis 31:13)
Brockhampton Quarry (**13.34**), Chalford Hill (**10.37**), Cheltenham (**16.27**), Downend (**20.31**). Drybrook (**6.14**), Frampton Cotterell (**3.50**) and Rangeworthy (**4.26**).

Bethesda ('House of Mercy' - John 5:2)
Bristol (**1.46**), Cheltenham (**16.33**), Coaley (**5.15**), Hawkesbury Upton (**3.38**), Uley (**5.18**) and Westbury-on-Trym (**2.59**).

Ebenezer ('stone of help' - 1 Samuel 7:12)
Acton Turville (**3.31**), Adsett (**6.30**), Arlingham (**9.15**), Aston on Carrant (**17.30**), Bedminster (**20.46**), Bristol (**1.37**, **40**, **47**), Chalford (**10.35**), Cheltenham (**16.28**), Childswickham (**19.39**), Coberley (**16.8**), Easter Compton (**2.68**), Kingswood Hill

---

[1] A. W. Hill, 56.

(**20.20**), Lydbrook (**18.44**), Lydney (**18.15**), Maugersbury (**14.31**), Olveston (**4.10**), Painswick (**10.18**), Rangeworthy (**4.31**), Ruardean (**18.52**), Ryecroft (**8.38**), St George (**2.30**), Warmley (**20.24**), Wick (**3.20**), Winterbourne (**2.86**) and Withington (**13.29**).

Gideon ('mighty warrior' - Judges 6–8)
Bristol (**1.26**).

Hebron ('confederacy' - a town in the hills south of Jerusalem).
Bedminster (**20.48**).

Moriah ('the teaching place' or 'the place of fear' - 2 Chronicles 3:1)
Birdlip (**12.9**) and Cowley (**16.10**).

Providence is the unceasing activity of God the creator, whereby in 'general providence' he upholds the natural order, and in 'special providence' refers to his intervention in the life of Christian believers.
Cheltenham (**16.29**) and Stapleton (**2.73**).

Salem ('safe, at peace'; an earlier name of the city of Jerusalem - Genesis 14:18)
Bristol (**1.47**; **2.25**), Brockhampton (**13.33**), Cheltenham (**16.30**) and Winterbourne (**2.84**).

Tabernacle (the 'Tent of Meeting', a provisional and portable place of worship for the people of God - Exodus 33:7–10). George Whitefield's earliest Tabernacle in London was a wooden structure opened in 1741, and replaced in 1756 by a permanent chapel in Tottenham Court Road. In Gloucestershire there were at least four Tabernacles associated with his ministry - at Bristol (**1.24**), Dursley (**5.22**), Kingswood (**20.11**) and Rodborough (**10.60**). Other Tabernacles were at Blakeney Hill (**6.3**), Cheltenham (**16.42**), Dyrham (appropriately, a wooden building) (**3.16**), North Nibley (**5.4**), Oldland Common (**20.4**), Oldland (**20.12**), Westerleigh (**3.4**), Wick (**3.19**) and Wotton-under-Edge (**5.8**).

Zion ('eminence', the city of David (or Jerusalem) and also refers to the company of the people of God)
Bedminster (**1.30**), East Dean (**6.15**), Frampton Cotterell (**3.49**), Hewelsfield (**18.17**), Horfield (**2.21**), Longhope (**6.41**) and St Peter's (**2.50**).

Zoar (one of the cities of the plain - Genesis 14.2)
Cheltenham (**16.27**).

Pews

Legally all parishioners were entitled to be seated in their parish church but not to a particular pew (**6.16**). There would be paid pews for families and their servants (not necessarily situated near to each other), for the minister, his family and servants (often in the chancel), and also free pews (in the nave, aisles or gallery) or portable benches in the aisles for the poor and for visitors. In Anglican churches, churchwardens were legally responsible for the allocation of seats (**17.12**).

There were also pews in nonconformist chapels where many, but not all, were free. At the Wesleyan Methodist chapel at Pilning Street the seating had been free but a limited number of pews rents were being introduced to pay for chapel maintenancel (**4.10**).

Pew rents were the means by which the Anglican incumbent or nonconformist minister received some or all of his stipend. Pews were bought and sold as real estate and were subject to a scale of fees, the most expensive being in more prominent positions. Pews could be bought and sold and were advertised as such in local newspapers, and the rents had to be paid for in advance. The right to certain pews was sometimes attached to a house and were the freehold property of the owner (**3.34**, **10.56**). From 1856 at least half of the pews in new churches had to be free and for the rest there was a scale of charges approved by the Ecclesiastical Commissioners. In the mid 19th century there was a move to ensure that all church seating was free though in some cases pew rents were still being paid in the 1950s.

Sabbath

In the mid-19th century Sunday, the first day of the week, was often referred to as the Sabbath, a title that was derived from the Ten Commandments (Exodus 20:8–11; Deuteronomy 6:12–15). For Jews Friday/Saturday was the Sabbath and for Christians Sunday was the day for worship. There was however one exception at Natton (**17.29**) where there was a Baptist chapel associated with the Seventh-Day, one of only two such congregations in the whole of England and Wales. Obviously for the Jews their returns were made when their worship took place on Saturday, 29 March 1851 (**1.56**; **16.41**).

Schools

Sunday schools mostly date back to the 18th century and were associated with Thomas Stock and Robert Raikes of Gloucester. The education provided by the mostly unpaid teachers was very basic and consisted of Bible teaching, and the three Rs. Gradually as the denominations opened day schools and with the passing of the Elementary Education Act in 1870 it was no longer necessary for Sunday schools to provide basic numeracy and literacy, and so Bible and denominational teaching came to the fore.

Denominational education was mostly provided for by two bodies, the Royal Lancasterian School Society (f. 1808) and soon renamed the British and Foreign School Society (supported by nonconformists); and the National Society for promoting the education of the poor in the principles of the established church (f. 1811 and generally known as the National Society) and supported, as the name suggests, by Anglicans. In Gloucestershire there were 102 National schools (educating 10,317 boys and girls); 37 British schools (educating 5,317 boys and girls); and 8 Roman Catholic schools (educating 701 boys and girls). In the returns there are instances where services were held in licensed Anglican schoolrooms (**3.37**; **18.2**, **24**, **37–38**) and for nonconformists in British schoolrooms (**6.31**; **10.61**; **18.35**; **20.19**, **48**). In the National schools the children were taught the Bible and the catechism, and this could create tensions with the nonconformists when it was insisted that their children attend the Anglican Sunday school (**6.30**). There were wider issues too over the High Church stance of the National Society and in 1853 a number of Evangelicals left the National Society and formed the Church of England Education Society.

Throughout the county the level of literacy was reasonable, and there was only one example of a return where an individual (John Steel) made his mark instead of signing his own name (**19.35**). There was however poor spelling on the returns from Wesleyan and Primitive Methodists – 'lokel preacher' (**10.54**), there was a Wesleyan Methodist 'suppertendant' (**2.27**) and several individuals struggled with the spelling of 'chapel' and one Wesleyan put 'whas' instead of was (**15.29**). The Baptist William Cole, a 'clark' recorded that his congregation assembled for worship in a 'scool' (**18.40**).

Service times

Many churches and chapels held Sunday services in the morning, afternoon and evening. Generally the evidence suggests that the Anglicans had larger congregations in the morning and the nonconformists in the evening. In the 18th century Methodists were at first encouraged to attend services in their parish church and Wesleyan worship was not held at the same time as Anglican services. When an Evangelical minister was appointed to Wotton-under-Edge parish church, Rowland Hill closed his chapel and the congregation was encouraged to attend the parish church.

From the 1820s the introduction of gas lighting meant that evening services could be illuminated, and this, together with the general decline in church and chapel attendance, meant that Sunday afternoon services were phased out.

In the mid-19th century there were few Holy Communion services in Anglican churches. In the *Book of Common Prayer* the rubric specified that communion was to be administered at least three times a year, though in practice it was often held four times a year, and in cities and towns once a month (**5.21**) was becoming more common. Weekly communion services were favoured by Anglo-Catholic clergy, and became for them the norm during in the latter half of the century. When these services were accompanied by ritual, the wearing of vestments, the lighting of candles and the use of incense, then tensions might arise between clergy and parishioners. Evangelicals held communion services in the evening and continued the tradition of celebrating communion on Good Friday. Both traditions began to promote early Sunday morning communion services. For Evangelicals this was for practical reasons, while Anglo-Catholic clergy were keen to promote fasting before receiving communion.

EDITORIAL ARRANGEMENT OF RETURNS FOR DISTRICTS AND SUB-DISTRICTS

The Religious Census Returns of 1851 are held in series HO 129 at the National Archives.[1] The TNA piece number (given in brackets in the listing below) consists of HO 129 followed by three digits indicating the District number assigned by the census staff, with subsequent single digits indicating the sub-district and then the parish. In this edition the returns have been grouped into sections, largely following the numerical order of Districts, and re-numbered in bold from **1** to **20**, as in the left-hand column below.

Sections **2–17** are, with minor reordering, exact transcriptions of the returns. Sections **18–20** serve as a convenient way of grouping most of the Gloucestershire parishes included in returns for neighbouring counties. Lechlade, enumerated in the sub-district of Faringdon, Berks., is included in Section **12** with the returns for the Fairford sub-district.

Though the detailed returns for the five Bristol city sub-districts are lost, relevant information for their places of worship has been reconstructed from the Civil Census of 1851, city and county directories, the *Clergy List*, and *Crockford's Clerical Directory*. These sources do not however give attendance information, and to fill this gap, the attendance figures quoted are from a local census of religious attendance conducted on 30 Oct. 1881 and published in the *Western Daily Press* on 2 Nov. 1881. These figures serve to indicate the relative size of the city congregations, and are likely to approximate the 1851 attendance. For the returns covering what might be described as 'greater Bristol' see Sections **2** and **20**. The official summary statistics for Bristol are given at Appendix 1.

1   Bristol   (HO 129/329)   *Returns missing*
    1 St Mary Redcliffe
    2 Castle Precincts
    3 St Paul
    4 St James
    5 St Augustine

2   Clifton (HO 129/330)
    1 Clifton
    2 Ashley
    3 St George
    4 St Philip and St Jacob
    5 Westbury
    6 Stapleton

3   Chipping Sodbury (HO 129/331)
    1 Chipping Sodbury
    2 Marshfield
    3 Hawkesbury
    4 Iron Acton

4   Thornbury (HO 129/332)

---

[1] Copies of the material are now downloadable from *www.nationalarchives.gov.uk* without charge.

14   Stow-on-the-Wold (HO 129/342)
1 Bourton-on-the-Water
2 Stow-on-the-Wold

15   Winchcombe (HO 129/343)
1 Guiting
2 Cleeve

16   Cheltenham (HO 129/344)
1 Charlton Kings
2 Cheltenham

17   Tewkesbury (HO 129/345)
1 Deerhurst
2 Overbury
3 Tewkesbury

18   'Forest of Dean'
    (HO 129/576, 577, 347)
Chepstow (HO 129/576.1)
Lydney (HO 129/576.3)
Coleford (HO 129/577.1)
Ross (HO 129/347 2)

Returned   under   Monmouthshire   and Herefordshire

19   'North Gloucestershire'
    (HO 129/404, 406, 389)
Stratford on Avon (HO 129/404.3)
Old Stratford (HO 129/404.4)
Campden (HO 129/406.1)
Moreton (HO 129/406.2)
Shipston-on-Stour (HO 129/406.3)
Evesham (HO 129/389.1)
Broadway (HO 129/389.2)

Returned   under   Warwickshire   and Worcestershire

20   'South Bristol' (HO 129/327, 328)
Britton (HO 129/327.1)
Oldland (HO 129/327.2)
Bedminster (HO 129/328.1)

Returned under Somerset

ARRANGEMENT OF INDIVIDUAL ENTRIES

To find a place of worship calendared in this edition, see the Index of Places. See also Appendix 5 for some 45 places of worship not listed in census returns.

Structure of a typical return:

331.1.2 Parish of Pucklechurch   [331 = district; 1 = sub-district; 2 = parish]
Area 2,428 acres; 189 inhabited houses, 4 uninhabited. Population 931.

Information about the area of the parish, the number of inhabited and uninhabited houses, and the population is taken from the Civil Census of 1851, as is further information about the parish (eg. tithings, hamlets), the presence of a workhouse etc.

3.5 (4)   Church of England, St Thomas a Becket, Pucklechurch

3.5 is the reference number assigned in this edition for this place of worship, the number in brackets (**4**) referring to the original page number on the Census return.

Church of England, St Thomas a Becket, Pucklechurch: the denomination and heading have been supplied by the editor. In the original returns the order of denominations within each parish is quite arbitrary, and they are here presented in a standard sequence: Church of England, Independent, Baptist, Methodist, Moravian, Christian Brethren, Roman Catholic, Society of Friends etc. To find places of worship of a particular denomination, see Appendices.

In some instances a place of worship was originally misplaced and has been restored to its correct place (**13.43**; **14.16**). There are also a few duplicate returns: some appear to be accidental (**16.16**) while in other instances returns were made both by the Methodist minister of the circuit and the local chapel official (**4.8, 29**; **7.25**; **14.20, 27, 32**).

The notes attached to many of the entries refer to the appropriate volumes of the *Victoria County History*; to *Gloucestershire Notes and Queries;* to the *Pevsner Architectural Guides to the Buildings of England*; and in the case of Anglican churches in and around Bristol, to *Rural Rides of the Bristol Churchgoer* (Joseph Leech), giving a snapshot of the church and clergy only six years before the Census; and to the amount of the endowment within brackets { } taken from the *Clergy List* of 1852 (some clergy were clearly reluctant to reveal the benefice income in their own returns). Where known, the full names of clergy and ministers are given, together with their years of service. To locate a place geographically, users are advised to consult the clear maps in the appropriate *Buildings of England* volume.

An ellipse ... indicates unreadable handwriting. Square brackets [ ] indicate information or clarification supplied by the editor. Round brackets ( ) indicate material that has been slightly rearranged within the return. Occasionally the period of average attendance is less than 12 months, and is given in the form 3m (i.e., three months). Single quotation marks enclose selected idiosyncratic spellings.

TRANSFERRED PARISHES

As a general rule, this edition treats only those Gloucestershire parishes within the county in 1851 (for exceptions, see next paragraph); accordingly, the statistical summaries in the Appendices relate to the county as it was in 1851. However, for convenience a note is here made of the transfers *out* of Gloucestershire which took place in 1844, shortly before the Census year, and of other adjustments made between 1897 and 1935.

Note also that between 1834–1911 the territory of England and Wales was divided into Poor Law Unions (each cluster of 12 or so parishes being served by a single Union workhouse) and it was this administrative unit that was adopted for registration purposes for the three national Censuses of 1851. Poor Law Unions did not always respect county boundaries, with the effect in Gloucestershire that 50 or 60 parishes were enumerated under neighbouring counties. Conversely within the 'Gloucestershire' returns there are several parishes properly in Wiltshire (**11.22–23**; **12.26–32, 56**) and Worcestershire (**14.22, 24–25**; **15.1–2**; **17.8–10, 18.20, 24–27**). Some of these strays were in fact subsequently transferred to Gloucestershire, and for simplicity and to reflect fully the content of the original HO returns, they are all included in this edition. Returns for places *never* in Gloucestershire are given wholly in *italics*.

Transfers made in 1844
To Herefordshire:
>   Part of Lea
>   Lea Bailey

To Oxfordshire:
>   Widford
>   Shenington

To Warwickshire:
>   Little Compton
>   Sutton under Brailes

To Wiltshire:
>   Minety

From Berkshire:
>   Part of Great Barrington (HO 129/342.1.2) (**3.32**)

From Wiltshire:
>   Kingswood, Wotton-under-Edge (HO 129/333.1.1) (**5.1–2**)
>   Poulton (HO 129/340.3.5) (**12.53**)

From Worcestershire
>   Icomb (HO 129/342.1.12) (**14.17**)
>   Overbury (includes the hamlets of Little Washbourne and Alston)
>   (HO 129/343.2.8–9 and 345.2.3–5) (**17.18**)

Transfers made in 1897
From Wiltshire:
        Kemble (HO 129/340.2.5) (**12.26–27**)
        Poole Keynes (HO 129/340.2.6) (**12.28–29**)
        Shorncote (HO 129/340.2.8) (**12.32**)
        Somerford Keynes (HO 129/340/2.7) (**12.30–31**)

Transfers made in 1930
From Wiltshire:
        Ashley (HO 129/339.2.7) (**11.23**)
        Long Newton (HO 129/339.2.6) (**11.22**)

Transfers made in 1931
From Worcestershire:
        Blockley (HO 129/406.2.10)
        Chaceley (HO 129/345.1.6) (**17.8**)
        Cutsdean (HO 129/343.1.1) (**15.1–2**)
        Daylesford (HO 129/342.2.2) (**14.22**)
        Evenlode (HO 129/342.2.4) (**14.24–25**)
        Redmarley D'Abitot (HO 129/335.2.5) (**7.24–25**)
        Staunton, near Newent (HO 129/335.2.6) (**7.26**)
        Teddington (HO 129/345.2.3–5) (**17.19–20**)

To Worcestershire:
        Ashton under Hill (HO 129/389.1.1) (**19.26–27**)
        Aston Somerville (HO 129/389.1.4) (**19.29**)
        Beckford (HO 129/343.2.7) (**15.31**)
        Childswickham (HO 129/389.2.16) (**19.38–40**)
        Cow Honeybourne (HO 129/389.2.10) (**19.32**)
        Hinton-on-the-Green (HO 129/389.1.3) (**19.28**)
        Kemerton (HO 129/345.2.6) (**17.17.21–23**)
        Pebworth (HO 129/389.2.1) (19.30–31) (**19.30–31**)

To Warwickshire:
        Clifford Chambers (HO 129/404.3.3) (**19.1**)
        Dorsington (HO 129/404.4.5–6) (**19.5**)
        Marston Sicca (HO 129/404.4.1) (**19.3–4**)
        Preston-on-Stour (HO 129/404.4.3–5) (**19.2**)
        Welford-on-Avon (HO 129/404.4.5–6) (**19.6–9**)
        Weston-on-Avon (HO 129/404.4.3–4) (No return)

Transfer made in 1935
To Warwickshire:
        Quinton (HO 129/406.1.1) (**19.10**)

Census of Great Britain, 1851.

(13 and 14 Victoriæ, Cap. 53.)

A RETURN

18

several Particulars to be inquired into respecting the undermentioned CHURCH or CHAPEL in England, belonging to the United Church of England and Ireland.

Return (*mutatis mutandis,*) will be obtained with respect to Churches belonging to the Established Church in and, and the Episcopal Church there, and also from Roman Catholic Priests, and from the Ministers of every other Religious Denomination throughout Great Britain, with respect to their Places of Worship.]

NAME and DESCRIPTION of CHURCH or CHAPEL.

The parish Church of Frampton on Severn, dedicated to St Mary in July 1315 by Walter de Maydenstone, then Bishop of Worcester

WHERE SITUATED.	Parish, Ecclesiastical Division or District, Township or Place	Superintendent Registrar's District	County and Diocese
	Frampton on Severn archdeaconry of Gloucester	Wheatenhurst	Gloucester County & Gloucester Diocese

WHEN CONSECRATED OR LICENSED	— Under what Circumstances CONSECRATED or LICENSED
Consecrated before 1800	Consecrated before 1800

In the case of a CHURCH or CHAPEL CONSECRATED or LICENSED since the 1st January, 1800; state

HOW OR BY WHOM ERECTED	COST. how Defrayed
	By Parliamentary Grant..................
	„ Parochial Rate ....
	„ Private Benefaction, or Subscription, or from other Sources......
	Total Cost......£

V. HOW ENDOWED.	VI. SPACE AVAILABLE FOR PUBLIC WORSHIP
ndowment for church – The Clergy	Free Sittings 135
Pew Rents	Other Sittings 363
Fees	
Dues................	Total Sittings... 498
Permanent Easter Offerings	
...ment...} Other Sources	
income about £200 a year (net)	

Estimated Number of Persons attending Divine Service on Sunday, March 30, 1851.				AVERAGE NUMBER OF ATTENDANTS during 12 Months next preceding March 30, 1851. (See Instruction VII.)			
	Morning	Afternoon	Evening		Morning	Afternoon	Evening
General Congregation }	120	270	No service	General Congregation }	150	300	No service
Sunday Scholars	83	82	There are few at Frampton in the Evening	Sunday Scholars	90	90	There are few at Frampton in the Evening
Total..	203	352		Total...	240	390	

REMARKS No reliance can be placed on the return from the dissenting place of worship in this parish, more than half the congregation is collected from the parishes of Saul, Fretherne &c and the very same persons attend elsewhere on the very same Census day & swell the ranks of dissent in other parishes

I certify the foregoing to be a true and correct Return to the best of my belief.

...ess my hand this Thirty first day of March 1851.

IX. (Signature) George Chute

(Official Character) Vicar of the above named parish Church

(Address by Post) Frampton on Severn Dursley

Fig. 1: Example of Church of England form : Frampton-on-Severn (entry **9.17**)

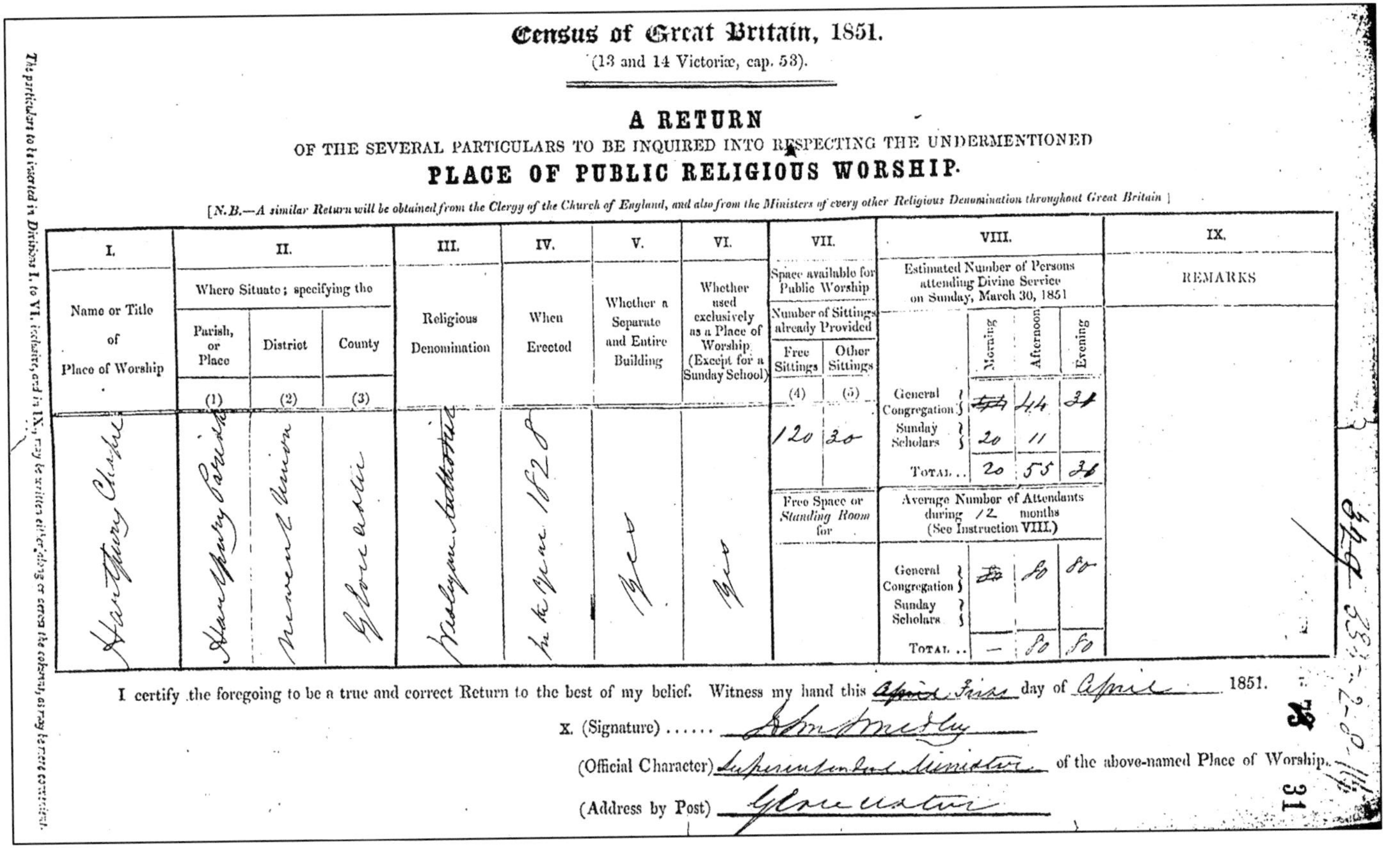

Fig. 2: Example of Other Demominations form: Wesleyan Methodist chapel at Hartpury (entry 7.30)

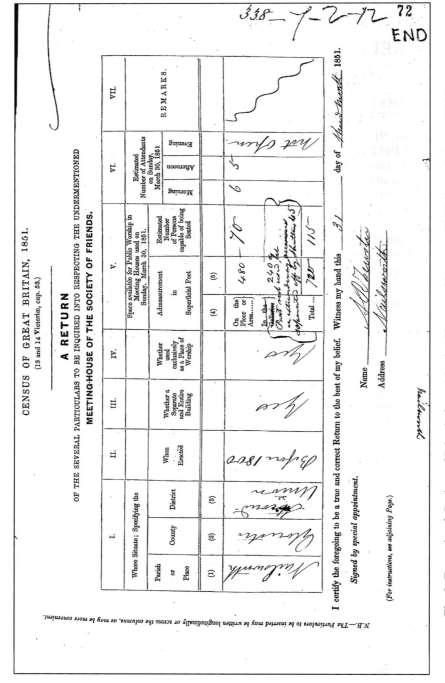

Fig. 3: Example of Society of Friends form: Meeting House at Chestnut Hill, Nailsworth (entry **10.81**)

THE RELIGIOUS CENSUS OF BRISTOL AND GLOUCESTERSHIRE, 1851

1. **HO 129/329 BRISTOL DISTRICT:** 56 places of worship

329.1	**ST MARY, REDCLIFFE SUB-DISTRICT**	Population 14,380
329.2	**CASTLE PRECINCTS SUB-DISTRICT**	Population 11,076
329.3	**ST PAUL SUB-DISTRICT**	Population 15,280
329.4	**ST JAMES SUB-DISTRICT**	Population 10,658
325.5	**ST AUGUSTINE SUB-DISTRICT**	Population 14,322

As noted above (p. 44), the returns of March 1851 for these five sub-districts are missing; the attendance figures given refer to the local census conducted on 30 Oct. 1881. The clergy and ministers are those who were in post in March 1851.

1.1	**Church of England, Cathedral, College Green**
Name	The Church of the Holy and Undivided Trinity
Erected	Restoration 1840; nave constructed 1867–77, further work completed 1887–8, and further restoration 1890–1900
Endowment	-
Sittings	-
Attendance	Morning 528
(30 Oct. 1881)	Afternoon 834
	Total 1,362
Dean	Gilbert Elliot 1850–91
	The Deanery, College Green

[The 12th-century abbey church had become a 'new foundation' cathedral in 1542: Leech 2004, 28–9. The estranged wife of dean Elliot was the already-divorced author Frances Minto Elliot: Bettey, 196–201.]

1.2	**Church of England, All Saints', Corn Street**
Name	All Saints (also known as All Hallows)
Erected	Rebuilt 1712 and completed 1716–7; restored 1853–4 and 1905–6.
Endowment	Total £154
Sittings	-
Attendance	Morning 53
(30 Oct. 1881)	Evening 157
	Total 210
Incumbent	Robert Llewellyn Caley, vicar 1848–61
	17 Mall, Clifton

[Caley was also precentor of Bristol cathedral 1837–61 and chaplain of the Bristol cemetery. Joseph Leech noted that the hymn book used at All Saints was called *Collections of Hymns and Psalms* and that visitors were 'request[ed] that this book be not removed from the pew': Leech 2004, 97.]

1.3	**Church of England, Blind Asylum Chapel, Park Street**
Name	School of Industry for the Blind
Consecration	20 November 1838, as a chapel of ease to St Michael (**1.13**)
Erected	1838
Endowment	-

Sittings	-
Attendance	Morning 225
(30 Oct. 1881)	Evening 227
	Total 452
	(About 80 below the average)
Incumbent	William Knight 1816–75
	9 Buckingham Villas, Richmond Park Road

[The Blind Asylum was founded in 1792 and until 1838 was located in Callowhill. William Knight was the incumbent of St Michael on the Mount (**1.13**).]

1.4   Church of England, Christ Church, Broad Street

Name	Christ Church
Erected	Rebuilt 1786–90; restored 1881–3
Endowment	Total £390
Sittings	-
Attendance	Morning 91
(30 Oct. 1881)	Evening 303
	Total 394
Incumbent	John Strickland, minister 1842–55
	4 Great George Street, Park Street

[In 1787 the nearby church of St Ewen was demolished and the benefice was united as Christ Church with St Ewen: Crossley Evans, 73–97; Leech 2004, 112–4.]

1.5   Church of England, St Augustine the Less, College Green

Name	St Augustine the Less
Consecration	-
Erected	Enlarged 1708
Endowment	Total £345
Sittings	-
Attendance	Morning 299
(30 Oct. 1881)	Evening 374
	Total 673
Incumbent	Robert Bateman Paul 1848–51
	1 Park Place, Clifton

[Boore, 211–4; Leech 2004, 72–4.]

1.6   Church of England, St George, Great George Street

Name	St George
Consecration	23 September 1823; restored 1871–6
Erected	Cost £10,000
Endowment	Total £285
Sittings	Free 920. Other 496. Total 1,416
Attendance	Morning 458
(30 Oct. 1881)	Evening 252
	Total 710
Incumbent	Ralph Lambton Hopper, vicar 1844–70
	24 Caledonia Place, Clifton

[Erected as a chapel of ease to St Augustine (**1.5**); became a separate parish in 1832. Within St George's parish, St Matthew, Moorfields was consecrated 28 Jan. 1873: Leech 2004, 134–7.]

1.7   Church of England, St James, Whitson Street

Name	St James [Since 1996 a Roman Catholic church dedicated to The Little

Brothers of Nazareth]

Consecration	[a former Benedictine priory, established in 1137]
Erected	Restored 1846, enlarged October 1864 (north aisle)
Endowment	Total £551
Sittings	-
Attendance	Morning 452
(30 Oct. 1881)	Afternoon 615
	Evening 434
	Total 1,501
Incumbent	Jonathan Henry Woodward 1839–51
	21 Somerset Street, Kingsdown

[Woodward's predecessor was Thomas Tregenna Biddulph who, from 1799–1838, was incumbent of both St James, Bristol and Durston, Som. He was 'a determined Calvinist', the leading Anglican Evangelical in the city, 'virtually the Bishop of Bristol'. He was a founding member of the Bristol Church Missionary Association; clerical secretary of the auxiliary of the Bristol British and Foreign Bible Society; and presided at the inaugural meeting of CPAS. He was the first secretary of the Bristol Clerical Education Society: *ODNB*, 'Thomas Tregenna Biddulph (1763–1838)'; tablet, 'The pastoral duties of which he discharged with irreproachable zeal, faithfulness and ability'. Within the parish four churches were erected: St Paul, consecrated 1794 (**1.16**); St Matthew, Kingsdown (**2.18**) consecrated 1835; St Bartholomew, Union Street, consecrated 1861 and St James the Less, Maudlin Street, consecrated 1868. After Biddulph's death the Evangelical tradition was lost, and Woodward resigned in May 1851; he and his two curates were received into the Church of Rome. A later curate of St James (1858–61) was William Hagger Barlow, later the first incumbent of St Bartholomew's 1861–73 and then the incumbent of St Mary, Islington and Dean of Peterborough: *ODNB* 'William Hagger Barlow (1833–1908)'; Barlow, 12–23; Leech 2004, 51–5.]

1.8	**Church of England, St John the Baptist, Broad Street**
Name	St John the Baptist
Consecration	-
Erected	Alterations 1827–8
Endowment	Total £150
Sittings	-
Attendance	Morning 102
(30 Oct. 1881)	Evening 78
	Total 180
Incumbent	George Neale Barrow 1834–55
	36 St James' Place, Kingsdown

[From 1580 the benefice was St John with St Lawrence. Barrow was also the incumbent of St Nicholas (**1.15**). Joseph Leech observed that 'the congregation of St John's are the simplest and humblest, as well as the most attentive I have yet seen at any church within the boundaries of Bristol': Leech 2004, 58. The church is now under the care of the Churches Conservation Trust.]

1.9	**Church of England, St Mark, College Green**
Name	St Mark (the Lord Mayor's Chapel)
Consecration	-
Erected	Reopened after restoration 31 Oct. 1830; restored again, 1889–90
Endowment	-
Sittings	-
Attendance	Morning 139
(30 Oct. 1881)	Evening 115
	Total 254
Chaplain	Samuel Emery Day, chaplain

32 Portland Square
[Day was the incumbent of St Philip and St Jacob (**1.18**). In 1687 the chapel was used by French Huguenots until in 1727 they moved to Orchard Street (known as the French Chapel) and vacated it in 1825. From 1722 St Mark's became the official place of worship for the mayor and corporation. From 1788 John Wesley was permitted to preach in the chapel after he was banned from preaching in other Anglican churches in the city. Leech 2004, 60–4.]

1.10	**Church of England, St Mark, Lower Easton**
Name	St Mark
Consecration	18 May 1848
Erected	Cost £2,500
Endowment	-
Sittings	Free 443. Other 73. Total 516
Attendance	Morning 245
(30 Oct. 1881)	Evening 239
	Total 484
Remarks	There was also a Holy Communion service at 8.00am and a children's service in the afternoon.
Incumbent	James Russell Woodford 1848–55
	Lower Easton

[Woodford, known as 'the Lion of St Mark's', established the first Anglo-Catholic church in the city. He became incumbent of Kempsford (**12.57**), vicar of Leeds 1868–73 and bishop of Ely 1873–85: *ODNB*, 'James Russell Woodford (1820–1885)'. He was the joint editor, with Greville Phillimore (**12.54**) and Hyde Wyndham Beadon, of *The Parish Hymn Book* (1863).]

1.11	**Church of England, St Mary le Port, Castle Park**
Name	St Mary-le-Port
Consecration	-
Erected	Tower restored 1859 and the rest of the building in 1876
Endowment	Total £150
Sittings	-
Attendance	Morning 126
(30 Oct. 1881)	Afternoon 133
	Evening 169
	Total 428
Incumbent	John Packer 1847–51
	5 Lower Park Row

[Leech 2004, 30–3.]

1.12	**Church of England, St Mary the Virgin, Redcliffe Street**
Name	St Mary the Virgin
Consecration	-
Erected	Restored 1846–7 and 1870–2
Endowment	Total £400
Sittings	-
Attendance	Morning 709
(30 Oct. 1881)	Evening 897
	Total 1,606
Incumbent	Martin Richard Whish, minister 1806–52
	The Vicarage, Redcliffe

[The benefice consisted of St John, Bedminster (**20.37**) with St Mary, Redcliffe, St Thomas (**1.20**) and Abbots Leigh. Joseph Leech found Whish a 'singular and eccentric' preacher, whose sermon notes were 'written on fly leaves of letters, backs of circulars and Christmas bills.' He employed too few curates and so Sunday duty was conducted by numerous clergy unknown to the congregations: Leech 2004, 244.]

1.13	**Church of England, St Michael on the Mount, St Michael's Hill**
Name	St Michael
Consecration	-
Erected	Apart from the tower, rebuilt 1775–7; reopened June 1777
Endowment	Total £372
Sittings	Free 408. Other 100. Total 508
Attendance	Morning 494
(30 Oct. 1881)	Evening 420
	Total 914
Incumbent	William Knight 1816–75
	9 Buckingham Villas, Richmond Park Road

[Knight was also chaplain to the Blind Asylum Chapel (**1.3**). His son, also William, served as his curate and from 1851–61 as secretary of CMS, and the examining chaplain to bishop (later archbishop) Archibald Campbell Tait 1856–82. Leech 2004, 98–102.]

1.14	**Church of England, St Michael the Archangel, Two Mile Hill**
Name	St Michael
Consecration	22 Aug. 1848
Erected	Cost £2,033
Endowment	Total £150
Sittings	Free 408. Other 100. Total 508
Attendance	Morning 494
(30 Oct. 1881)	Evening 420
	Total 914
Incumbent	John Brimble Riddle 1848–52
	2 Richmond Place, Kingswood

1.15	**Church of England, St Nicholas, St Nicholas Street**
Name	St Nicholas
Consecration	-
Erected	Rebuilt 1762–9, and restored 1882–3
Endowment	Total £253
Sittings	-
Attendance	Morning 192. 'The morning congregation was about 25 less than
(30 Oct. 1881)	usual, probably owing to the mayor being at St Philip's'
	Afternoon 182
	Evening 296
	Total 488
Incumbent	George Neale Barrow 1841–55
	36 St James' Place, Kingsdown

[The benefice consisted of St Nicholas with St Leonard's and St Giles. Barrow was also the incumbent of St John the Baptist (**1.8**). 'The pews are arranged amphitheatre-like, so that the inmates look point blank down on every person that enters': Leech 2004, 48.]

1.16	**Church of England, St Paul, Portland Square**
Name	St Paul
Consecration	25 Jan. 1794
Erected	1789–94
Endowment	Total £513

Sittings	-
Attendance	Morning 372
(30 Oct. 1881)	Evening 579
	Total 951
Incumbent	Aaron Rogers, perpetual curate 1849–67
	Cotham New Road

[Within the parish St Clements was consecrated on 24 April 1855. The church is now under the care of the Churches Conservation Trust. Leech 2004, 125–8.]

1.17   **Church of England, St Peter, Castle Park**

Name	St Peter
Consecration	-
Erected	Repaired 1795
Endowment	Total £239
Sittings	-
Attendance	Morning 167
(30 Oct. 1881)	Evening 254
	Total 421
Incumbent	Henry Crane Brice 1829–67
	5 Richmond Hill, Clifton

[Brice was the brother of Edward Cowell Brice, incumbent of Newnham (**6.5**); as a preacher, Joseph Leech found him 'friendly, affectionate and cordial, and his voice soft and agreeable': Leech 2004, 81.]

1.18 (see also 330.4)   **Church of England, St Philip and St Jacob, Jacob Street**

Name	St Philip and St Jacob
Consecration	-
Erected	Partial rebuilding 1837–41
Endowment	Total £440
Sittings	-
Attendance	Morning 612. In the morning the mayor and corporation were present.
(30 Oct. 1881)	Evening 687
	Total 1,299
Incumbent	Samuel Emery Day, vicar 1832–64
	32 Portland Square

[Day was also the chaplain of St Mark, the Lord Mayor's Chapel (**1.8**). Joseph Leech observed that St Philip's and St Jacob's 'is an exceedingly poor and populous parish; circumstances which impose on the pastor and his curates, an enormous degree of labour, both as religious instructors and charitable almoners': Leech 2004, 68.]

1.19   **Church of England, St Stephen, St Stephen's Avenue**

Name	St Stephen
Consecration	-
Erected	Restored 1862, chancel 1875
Endowment	Total £292
Sittings	-
Attendance	Morning 163
(30 Oct. 1881)	Evening 241
	Total 404
Incumbent	Charles Buck 1830–58
	51 Queen Square

[Joseph Leech found that 'there is much taste combined with earnestness in the style, manner, and delivery of Mr Buck which is most pleasing': Leech 2004, 90.]

1.20	**Church of England, St Thomas the Martyr, Thomas Street**
Name	St Thomas the Martyr
Consecration	-
Erected	Erected 1789–93 and restored 1878
Endowment	-
Sittings	-
Attendance	Morning 120
(30 Oct. 1881)	Evening 280
	Total 400
Incumbent	Martin Richard Whish, perpetual curate
	The Vicarage, Redcliffe

[The benefice consisted of St John, Bedminster (**20.37**) with St Mary, Redcliffe (**1.12**), St Thomas and Abbots Leigh. St Thomas was a chapel of ease until Whish's death in 1852, and is now in the care of the Churches Conservation Trust. Joseph Leech noted that 'St Thomas's church is well attended, and the congregation, with few exceptions, may be ranked under the class called "comfortable" ... the services are well performed, and the edifice kept in excellent order, but the arrangement of the pews, which set people looking in each other's faces, imparts a certain appearance of irregularity I think to the whole': Leech 2004, 77. J. H. Bettey, *The Church of St Thomas the Martyr: Demolition and Rebuilding 1786–1793*, in Crossley Evans, 156–67.]

1.21	**Church of England, St Werburgh, Corn Street**
Name	St Werburgh
Consecration	30 Sept. 1879
Erected	[Rebuilt and opened in 1761. Closed, demolished and replaced by a new church in Mina Road, Baptist Mills, with the tower from the original church]
Endowment	Total £70
Sittings	-
Attendance	Morning 618 (also includes 42 children from Hooks Mills and about
(30 Oct. 1881)	60 from the St Werburgh's SS)
	Evening 479 (Evening services usually twice as many)
	Total 1,097
Incumbent	John Hall, rector 1832–71
	10 York Place, Clifton

[Hall's preaching was plain and pious, 'his manner and matter are both marked by an impressive simplicity, and the great truths of religion are urged in a tone of earnest directness to the heart.' His sermon notes were 'all written in shorthand, which he reads with considerable facility': Leech 2004, 85.]

1.22	**Church of England, Temple Church, Temple Street**
Name	Temple Church or Holy Cross
Consecration	-
Erected	-
Endowment	Total £387
Sittings	-
Attendance	Morning 318
(30 Oct. 1881)	Evening 26 (There were also another 70 in the mission room)
	Total 579
Incumbent	Fountain Elwin 1816–69
	Walcot Parade, Bath

[Elwin, 'a prominent Evangelical clergyman' and 'the energetic [joint] secretary of the great Bristol Association', had been one of the founders in 1813 of the Bristol Association of the CMS; in 1824 he preached the annual CMS sermon at St Bride's church, London: Stock, 1, 130, 248. Joseph Leech remarked that 'the vicar of Temple is an absentee, through indisposition; and on the curate alone devolves the entire work of a populous and poor parish. The former resides in Bath, where he at present preaches to one of the many silk stocking congregations of that city': Leech 2004, 108. The church is now under the care of English Heritage.]

1.23	**Independent, Bridge Street, Barton Hill**
Name	Bridge Street Chapel
Erected	1631. Chapel opened 24 Aug. 1786; replaced by a chapel on Clifton Down, opened 11 Nov. 1868.
Building	-
Sittings	-
Attendance	Morning 60
(30 Oct. 1881)	Evening 80
	Total 140
Minister	Henry Isaac Roper 1836–70
	Royal Fort, St Michael's Hill

[Adjacent to the chapel was St Mary le Port (**1.11**) where, during Bible readings, the loud organ music and singing disturbed the Anglican worshippers. Joseph Leech believed that for the working classes 'constant singing' was one of the attractions of nonconformity, and it had 'an exciting influence on rugged and undisciplined natures': Leech 2004, 32.]

1.24	**Independent, Penn Street**
Name	The Bristol Tabernacle
Erected	Foundation stone laid by George Whitefield 13 July 1753, the chapel opening the following 25 Nov.
Building	-
Sittings	-
Attendance	Morning 277
(30 Oct. 1881)	Evening 337
	Total 614. There were also 135 at the Bible Class Mission in Callowhill St.
Minister	Various ministers

[The Bristol Tabernacle opened chapels in Anvil Street (**2.39**), Highbury (**1.29**) and Kingsland (**2.40**). Initially the tradition was Calvinistic Methodist but by 1855 the chapel was served by Independent ministers. On its demolition in 1957 some fixtures and fittings from Penn Street went to the Whitefield Memorial Tabernacle, Muller Road, Horfield.]

1.25	**Independent, Castle Green**
Name	Castle Green Chapel
Erected	c1679; enlarged twice in the 18th century and rebuilt in 1815
Building	-
Sittings	1,000
Attendance	Morning 114
(30 Oct. 1881)	Evening 123
	Total 237
Minister	John Jack 1834–54
	7 Catherine Place, Cheltenham Road

1.26	**Independent, Newfoundland Street**
Name	Gideon Chapel
Erected	1809–10 and rebuilt in 1848
Building	-
Sittings	-
Attendance	Morning 200

(30 Oct. 1881)   Evening 360

Total 560

Minister   Charles Brake 1848–53

13 Wilson Street, St Paul's

[From 1832–40 Henry Craik and George Müller (**1.46–7**) preached here.]

1.27   **Independent, Lower Castle Street**

Name   Welsh Chapel

Erected   1822

Building   Opened 8 Jan. 1823

Sittings   -

Attendance   Morning 20

(30 Oct. 1881)   Evening 53

Total 73

Minister   Various ministers.

[Services were conducted in Welsh at 10.30am and 6.00pm and in English at 2.30pm.]

1.28   **Independent, Brunswick Square**

Name   Brunswick Chapel

Erected   Foundation stone laid 25 June 1834 and the chapel opened 6 May 1835

Building   Cost £5,000

Sittings   -

Attendance   Morning 324

(30 Oct. 1881)   Evening 276

Total 600

Minister   John Timothy Beighton 1850–5

Sydenham Road

[The chapel was formed by 40 seceders from Castle Green Chapel (**1.25**). It was the first Nonconformist chapel in Bristol registered for marriages: *London Gazette*, 7 July 1837.]

1.29   **Independent, Cotham Road**

Name   Highbury Chapel

Erected   Opened 6 July 1843, the sermon being preached by William Jay of Bath. Enlarged 1863 and 1893

Building   Cost £3,000 (much of it given by members of the Wills family)

Sittings   700, of which 300–400 were free

Attendance   Morning 621. (Together with 138 children)

(30 Oct. 1881)   Evening 426

Total 1,047

Minister   David Thomas 1844–75

4 King's Parade, Durdham Down

[The chapel was opened under the superintendence of the Bristol Tabernacle (**1.24**) and was built on the site where five Protestant martyrs were burned to death 1555–7 (commemorative tablet inside the church). Closed in 1972, it was later acquired by the Church of England and became the parish church of St Saviour and St Mary, Cotham.]

1.30   **Independent, Guinea Street**

Name   Wycliffe Chapel

Erected   -

Building   -

Sittings   -

Attendance   Morning 51

(30 Oct. 1881)   Evening 91

Total 142

Minister   Thomas Porter 1848–52

6 Guinea Street

1.31   **Independent, King Street**
Name   Coopers' Hall Chapel
Erected   1743–4
Building   -
Sittings   -
Attendance   Morning -
(30 Oct. 1881)   Evening -
Total -
Minister   James Panton Ham 1849–54
16 Hampton Terrace, Cotham Hill

[In Bristol, Ham was a Congregational minister, but his theological position changed and he became the Unitarian minister of the Cross Street Chapel, Manchester 1855–59, then of the Essex Street Chapel, London 1859–83.]

1.32   **Baptist, Broadmead, Union Street**
Name   Broadmead Baptist Chapel
Erected   Built 1695, enlarged 1764–5, 1791, 1871–2 and 1875
Building   -
Sittings   -
Attendance   Morning 933
(30 Oct. 1881)   Evening 1,388
Total 2,321
Ministers   Thomas Steffe Crisp [1818–]
Baptist College, Stokescroft
Nathaniel Haycroft
Apsley Villa, Upper Montpellier

[Until the late 19th century the ministers of the chapel were also on the staff of the Bristol Baptist Academy (the origins of which went back to 1679).]

1.33   **Baptist, Old King Street**
Name   Old King Street Chapel
Erected   Built 1699, rebuilt 1791–2; new chapel erected in Old King Street opened 2 Apr. 1817; restored and altered 1895
Building   -
Sittings   1,060
Attendance   Morning 232
(30 Oct. 1881)   Evening 247
Total 479
Minister   George Henry Davis 1841–
2 Sydenham Villa, Sydenham Road

[Previously the congregation had assembled at Pithay Chapel (**1.35**).]

1.34   **Baptist, Counterslip, Bath Street**
Name   Counterslip Chapel
Erected   Founded November 1804 following a schism within the congregation at Pithay Chapel (**1.35**) this chapel opened in 1810. After a further division in 1834 the dissidents returned to Pithay Chapel.

Building	-
Sittings	1,250
Attendance	Morning 304
(30 Oct. 1881)	Evening 466. (In the evening there were an additional 155 children from the Ragged School. At a separate service for children there were 94 children.)
	Total 770
Minister	Thomas Winter 1823–60
	15 Harford Place, New Cut

[In 1832 members of the congregation had opened the Thrissell Street Baptist chapel (**2.43**).]

1.35	**Baptist, Pithay**
Name	Pithay Chapel
Erected	1650, rebuilt 1791–2; in 1817 the enlarged congregation moved to Old King Street
Building	-
Sittings	-
Attendance	Morning 405
(30 Oct. 1881)	Evening 440
	Total 845
Minister	Evan Probert minister 1834–67
	12 Kingsdown Parade

[From 1817 Pithay Chapel was occupied by other denominations (Tent Methodists and then Congregationalists); in 1834 a group of Baptists returned to Pithay from Counterslip Chapel (**1.34**). On Probert see *The Baptist Magazine*, July 1867; Hamlin 1954, 378–9.]

1.36	**Welsh Baptist, Upper Maudlin Street**
Name	Upper Maudlin Chapel
Erected	Founded 1820 and chapel erected in 1840
Building	-
Sittings	300 sittings
Attendance	Morning 15
(30 Oct. 1881)	Evening 49
	Total 64
Minister	Thomas Jenkins
	Blackfriars

[There were services in Welsh at 10.30am and 6.00pm and in English at 3.00pm.]

1.37	**Wesleyan Methodist, Old King Street**
Name	Ebenezer Chapel
Erected	1795. Repaired 1854, renovated 1869.
Building	-
Sittings	1,000
Attendance	Morning 343
(30 Oct. 1881)	Evening 309
	Total 652
Minister	John Carey Pengelly
	4 The Polygon, Clifton.

[Pengelly was also the minister of Clifton (**2.10**) and Hotwells (**2.13**). Ebenezer Chapel was opened in 1795 following a secession from the nearby New Room (**1.43**).]

1.38   **Wesleyan Methodist, Old Market**
Name   Old Market Street Chapel
Erected   Opened 26 Aug. 1817; extended 1865 as the Central Hall, and replaced
                      by a new Central Hall in 1924
Building   -
Sittings   -
Attendance   Morning 340
(30 Oct. 1881)   Evening 490
                      Total 830
Minister   -

1.39   **Wesleyan Methodist, Lower Ashley Road**
Name   Baptist Mills Chapel
Erected   1800. New chapel opened 22 November 1837
Building   -
Sittings   -
Attendance   Morning 712
(30 Oct. 1881)   Evening 882
                      Total 1,594
Minister   -

[John Wesley recorded that 'I could scarcely reconcile myself at first to this strange way of preaching in the fields ... At Baptist Mills ... I offered the grace of God to above 1,500 persons': *Journal*, 29 Mar. and 4 Apr. 1739. 'Near the spot on which the chapel is erected the Rev John Wesley preached his first [*actually his second*] sermon in the open air, the stone on which he stood has been used as the foundation of the present building': Chilcott, 233–4.]

1.40   **Primitive Methodist, Orchard Street, St Philips**
Name   Ebenezer Chapel
Erected   Opened 1849
Building   -
Sittings   250
Attendance   Morning 240
(30 Oct. 1881)   Evening 241
                      Total 481
Minister   Charles T. Harris

1.41   **Primitive Methodist**
Name   Lower Easton Chapel
Erected   -
Building   -
Sittings   -
Attendance   -
(30 Oct. 1881)
Minister   -

1.42   **Wesleyan Reformers**
Name   Tyler's Fields Chapel
Erected   -
Building   -
Sittings   -
Attendance   Morning 125
(30 Oct. 1881)   Evening 140

Total 265

Minister -

1.43   **Calvinistic Methodist, Broadmead**

Name   The New Room

Erected   Foundation stone laid by John Wesley, 12 May 1739 (tablet); rebuilt and enlarged in 1748; restored 1929–30

Building   -

Sittings   -

Attendance   Morning 39

(30 Oct. 1881)   Evening 60

     Total 99

Minister   -

['We took possession of a piece of ground, near St James's churchyard, in the Horse Fair, where it was designed to build a room, large enough to contain both the societies of Nicholas and Baldwin Street ...and on Saturday, 12th, the first stone was laid, with the voice of praise and thanksgiving': Wesley, *Journal*, 12 May 1739. The building, the oldest Methodist Chapel, was opened as the New Room in June 1739. After Wesley's death a division took place in the congregation and in 1795 those who left opened Old King Street chapel (**1.37**). In 1808 the New Room was sold to the Welsh Calvinistic Methodists, and it was owned by them until 1929 when it returned to the Wesleyan Methodists and restored and reopened on 13 Feb. 1930.]

1.44   **Church of the United Brethren, Upper Maudlin Street**

Name   Moravian Chapel

Erected   Opened 25 June 1757; rebuilt 1896–7

Building   -

Sittings   -

Attendance   Morning 122

(30 Oct. 1881)   Evening 165

     Total 287

Minister   John Pearce

     Upper Maudlin Street

1.45   **Countess of Huntingdon's Connexion, Lodge Street**

Name   Lodge Street Chapel

Erected   Opened 17 August 1831

Building   Cost £4,500

Sittings   1,100–1,200

Attendance   Morning 293

(30 Oct. 1881)   Evening 512

     Total 805

Minister   John Spencer Pearsall, minister 1850–5

     Great George Street, Park Street

[The previous Countess of Huntingdon's chapel opened in St Augustine's Place in Aug. 1775 was sold to the Christian Brethren in 1831 (**1.47**). The new chapel in Lodge Street was much larger: 'The additions to the congregation have been very encouraging since the opening of this place of worship: the number of communicants has considerably increased, and there is reason to hope that good has been effected through the preaching of the Word': Seymour, 2, 395.]

1.46   **Christian Brethren, Great George Street, Park Street**

Name   Bethesda Chapel

Erected   1819

Building   Rented by the Christian Brethren from July 1832 and in June 1857 purchased by Conrad William Finzil and presented to Henry Craik and George Müller

Sittings	-
Attendance	Morning 606
(30 Oct. 1881)	Evening 421
	Total 1,027
Leaders	Henry Craik
	19 Paul Street, Kingsdown
	George Müller
	21 Paul Street, Kingsdown

[Craik (1805–66) was 'eminently a man of prayer and a man given to the study of the Word of God': Tayler, xvii. Müller founded the Müller Homes for Children, the first opened in Bristol in April 1836. He was 'a man of great energy and vision ... one of the most remarkable religious figures of the Victorian era': *ODNB*, 'George Müller (1805–98)'. In 1850, John Victor, a member of Bethesda Chapel, began preaching in a small house in Goat Alley, Unity Street. Two years later the ministry was taken over by a former army major, R. S. Tireman who in 1855 opened Unity Chapel in Unity Street and in 1862 a larger chapel in Midland Road. There was a dramatic increase in membership from nine in 1855; 303 in 1864; and 520 in 1895: Higgins, 223–35.]

1.47   **Christian Brethren, St Augustine's Place**

Name	Salem Chapel
Erected	1775; opened for Brethren worship in 1831
Building	-
Sittings	-
Attendance	-
(30 Oct. 1881)	
Leaders	Henry Craik
	19 Paul Street, Kingsdown
	George Müller
	21 Paul Street, Kingsdown

[In 1775 a former assembly room had been acquired by the Countess of Huntingdon for £800 and adapted as a chapel; for about ten years many leading Anglican Evangelicals preached there. In 1831 the building was sold to the Christian Brethren: Parker, 98–111.]

1.48   **Bristol City Mission**

Name	The interdenominational Bristol City Mission was founded in 1826.
Erected	-
Building	-
Sittings	-
Attendance	-
(30 Oct. 1881)	
Leader	-

[In 1851 there were eight Bristol City Mission places of worship (including **2.8, 41–2**; **20.41–2**).]

1.49   **Seamen's Floating Chapel, The Grove, Broad Quay**

Name	Seamen's Floating Chapel
Opened	-
Sittings	-
Attendance	Morning 67
(30 Oct. 1881)	Evening 200
	Total 267
Chaplain	-

[There were three Sunday services (10.30am, 2.30pm and 6.00pm) and on Monday, Wednesday, Thursday and Friday at 7.00pm: M. J. Crossley Evans, *Christian Missionary Work among the Seamen and Dock Workers of Bristol 1820–1914*, in Bettey, 162–95.]

1.50	**Roman Catholic, St Joseph, Trenchard Street**
Name	St Joseph
Erected	Opened on 27 June 1790; in 1843 the congregation moved to St Mary on the Quay (**1.51**), and services continued at St Joseph's until 1861 when it became a school.
Building	-
Sittings	-
Attendance (30 Oct. 1881)	-
Minister	William Johnston 1849–60

1.51	**Roman Catholic, St Mary on the Quay, Colston Avenue**
Name	-
Erected	Opened in 1840 for the Catholic Apostolic Church and sold to the Roman Catholic Church for £5,000 and consecrated for their use on 7 July 1843. In 1861 it became the parish church.
Building	Cost £15,000
Sittings	600
Attendance (30 Oct. 1881)	Morning 500 Evening 522 Total 1,022
Minister	Patrick O'Farrell 1843–57

[Edward Irving was a minister in the Church of Scotland until 1833; in 1834 his followers formed the Catholic Apostolic Church, which included revivalism and millennialism under the leadership of apostles, prophets, evangelists, pastors and teachers. Their colourful worship and liturgy was strongly catholic and eccentric: *ODNB* 'Edward Irving (1792–1834)'.]

1.52	**Roman Catholic Chapel, Redcliffe Parade**
Name	-
Erected	Opened in a private house *c*.1850
Building	-
Sittings	-
Attendance (30 Oct. 1881)	-
Minister	W. Cullinan

1.53	**Society of Friends, Rosemary Street, Broadmead**
Name	Cutlers Hall; known as the Quaker Friars (built on site of a Dominican priory)
Erected	1747–9
Building	-
Sittings	-
Attendance (30 Oct. 1881)	Morning 250. In the morning there was also a children's service at which there were twelve adults and 85 children. Evening 96 Total 346
Secretary	-

1.54   **New Jerusalem Church, Lodge Street**
Name   New Church
Erected   Opened 1792; new chapel 1819; replaced by a larger chapel in Terrell
                       Street opened 7 Apr. 1878
Building   -
Sittings   -
Attendance   Morning 28
(30 Oct. 1881)   Evening 29
                       Total 57
Minister   -

[The New Jerusalem Church, which was founded in May 1787, was based on the mystical and theosophical writings of Emanuel Swedenborg (1688–1772): see Introduction, 23.]

1.55   **Unitarian, Lewin's Mead**
Name   -
Erected   1705; replaced by a new chapel in 1787–91
Building   -
Sittings   1,000
Attendance   Morning 339
(30 Oct. 1881)   Evening 488
                       Total 827
Minister   George Armstrong [1840s–57]
                       11 Clifton Vale, Clifton
                       William James [1842–76]
                       4 Montague Avenue, Kingsdown

[In Dec. 1817 the chapel was the first public building in Bristol to be lit by gas, enabling evening services to held. Those attending were reputed to be 'Bristol's wealthiest Nonconformist congregation': Foyle and Pevsner, 271). The congregation seeded another Unitarian Chapel which opened in Lower Montague Street on 12 July 1861. Armstrong had formerly been an Anglican incumbent in Bangor, Co. Down.]

1.56   **Synagogue, Temple Street**
Name   -
Erected   On 15 Sept. 1786 a first synagogue opened in the Weavers' Hall, Temple
                       Street; on 18 Aug. 1842 a former Quaker meeting house was consecrated
                       as a synagogue in Temple Street. It was replaced by new premises in Park
                       Row, opened 8 Sept. 1871.
Building   -
Sittings   -
Attendance   Morning 102
(30 Oct. 1881)   Total 102
Leader   Aaron Levy Green 1838–51
Reader   Joseph Benjamin

---

2. HO 129/330 CLIFTON DISTRICT: 88 places of worship

330.1 CLIFTON SUB-DISTRICT

330.2.1 Parish of Clifton
Area 740 acres; 2,498 inhabited houses, 162 uninhabited. Population 17,634.

2.1 (1)	**Church of England, St Andrew, Clifton**
Name	Parish church of Clifton
Consecration	[12 Aug. 1822]
Erected	[Rebuilt 1654, enlarged 1716 and 1768, rebuilt 1820–1]
Endowment	{Total £782}
Sittings	Free 800. Other 1,200. Total 2,000
Attend'ce 30 Mar.	Morning 1,200 + 250 SS. Total 1,450
Avge attendance	[Not given]
Remarks	The above number of 1,450 is returned as an average. The actual number present in the church on the evening of 30 March is supposed to have been about 2,500, by reason of a very popular preacher having been announced. [For his identity see (**2.3**)]
Dated	31 March 1851
Signed	John Hensman, incumbent [1847–64]
	[Clifton Grove, Clifton Hill], Clifton

[The benefice consisted of Clifton with Dowry Chapel (**2.2**). Locally, Hensman was the leading Anglican Evangelical. Ordained to a college fellowship, he first assisted Charles Simeon, the incumbent of Holy Trinity, Cambridge 1802–3. The remainder of his career was in the west of England, as curate of Wraxall, Som. 1803–9; curate of St Andrew, Clifton 1809–22, and curate in charge of Dowry Chapel 1822–30. Holy Trinity, Hotwells (**2.35**) was erected for him by his friends; he was incumbent there 1831–44. He then became the first incumbent of Christ Church, Clifton 1844–7 and finally the incumbent of St Andrew's, Clifton 1847–64. He was responsible for the erection of St Paul's (consecrated 8 Nov. 1854), St Peter's (a former Methodist church opened in Nov. 1833 and consecrated 10 Aug. 1855; rebuilt and consecrated 26 Sept. 1882). The chapel of ease, St James the Apostle (consecrated 23 Dec. 1862) became known as the Hensman Memorial Church: *ODNB* 'John Hensman (1780–1864)'; Leech 2004, 34–8.]

2.2 (3)	**Church of England, Dowry Chapel, Dowry Square**
Name	Dowry Chapel
Consecration	Neither consecrated nor licensed [Chapel of ease to Clifton]
Erected	[1744]
Endowment	[See Clifton (**2.1**)]
Sittings	Free 250. Other 350. Total 600
Attend'ce 30 Mar.	Morning 200 + 200 SS. Total [400]
Avge attendance	[Not given]
Dated	31 March 1851
Signed	John Hensman, incumbent [1847–64]
	[Clifton Grove, Clifton Hill], Clifton

[The benefice consisted of Clifton (**2.1**) with Dowry Square Chapel, which had opened as a chapel of ease to St Andrew's, Clifton in 1744. Demolished in 1872, it was replaced by St Andrew the Less, consecrated 24 Sept. 1873.]

2.3 (2) **Church of England, Holy Trinity, Hotwells Road**

Name The Holy Trinity has no district attached was built under the
Act called the 'Forty years Act'. [5 Geo. IV, c.103 (1824)]

Consecration [10 Nov.] 1830, as an additional church in the parish on account of the
great increase of population

Erected By private subscription. Private and other sources £10,186 15s 2d.
Total cost £10,186 15s 2d

Endowment All outgoings are paid out the pew rents which produce £410
Pew rents £410

Sittings Free 800. Other 800. Total 1,600

Attend'ce 30 Mar. Morning 1,000 + 140 SS. Total 1,140
Evening 700. Total 700

Ave. attendance Morning 1,000 + 140 SS. Total 1,140
Evening 1,300. Total 1,300

Remarks On Sunday, 30 Mar 1851, a very popular preacher the Rev Hugh Stowell
of Manchester preached at the parish church which very near   Trinity,
and some hundreds of my usual congregation attended there.

Dated 31 March 1851

Signed Humphrey Allen, incumbent [1845–68]
[19 Royal York Crescent], Clifton, Bristol

[Stowell, the influential incumbent of Christ Church, Salford 1831–65, had begun his ministry at
Sheepscombe (**10.14**): *ODNB* 'Hugh Stowell (1799–1865)'. Joseph Leech noted that 'the
congregation of Trinity, Hotwells, is of a particular character, being principally composed of
persons of that complexion in the Church [of England] commonly called "Evangelical" ... The
congregation on the whole were very decorous and attentive, and there was quite a devotional
character about them ... The ladies had a large majority, being I should think at least ten to one ...
The service was carefully performed, but the singing, both chaunting and psalms, though correct,
was, I thought, feeble': Leech 2004, 44, 45, 46.]

2.4 (5) **Church of England, St John the Evangelist, Apsley Road**

Name St John the Evangelist. District church, near Durdham Down,
and a perpetual curacy (1 and 2 Will. IV, c.38 [1831])
Patronage vested in the bishop of the diocese, Glouc[ester] and Bristol.

Consecration 27 April 1841. A considerable population in the adjoining outskirts of
Clifton and Westbury parishes, insufficiently provided with church
accommodation

Erected By the Diocesan Church Building Association, with grants from their own
funds; and of the Incorp. Church Building Society in London; and sundry
local and private benefactions, of the amount I am not sure, but I believe
between £3,000 and £4,000. Private sources less than £4,000. I believe
total cost was under £4,000.
[Enlarged 1864]

Endowment Land and tithe none. Glebe house and small garden. OPE £33. Pew
rents, fees, Easter offerings uncertain and precarious. {Total £120}

Sittings Free 315. Other 300. Total 615

Attend'ce 30 Mar. Morning 500 + 90 SS. Total 590
Afternoon less [than 500] + 90 SS
Evening less [than 500]

Avge attendance Much the same as foregoing [for morning, afternoon and evening]

Remarks Our present number of scholars necessarily limited by the unsuitable
smallness of our school house, a rented cottage. By mid-summer next

we hope to open our new school house (with residence for teacher attached) providing accommodation for between 300 and 400 children (boys, girls and infants schools).

Dated   31 March 1851
Signed   Henry George Walsh, MA, perpetual curate [1841–88]
                   [St John's] Parsonage, Durdham Down, Bristol

[Walsh was 'a high churchman of the pre-Tractarian type.' (Cobb, 17; Leech 2004, 121–4.]

2.5 (4)   **Church of England, Christ Church, Clifton Park**
Name   Christ Church district, created under the provisions of 1 and 2 Will. IV, c.38 [1831]
Consecration   8 October 1844, consecrated as an additional church
Erected   By private subscriptions £12,000. Total cost £12,000 [Enlarged 1857 and 1884–5]
Endowment   Glebe house cost £1,000. Pew rents £570. Fees very trifling and uncertain. No marriages or funerals
Sittings   Free 350 (one third of the whole). Other 680. Total 1,030
Attend'ce 30 Mar. Morning church full + 40 SS. Total 1,030
                   Afternoon see average
                   Evening see average
Avge attendance Morning full + 40 SS. Total 1,030
                   Afternoon about ¾
                   Evening about ¾
Dated   31 March 1851
Signed   James Marshall, perpetual curate [1847–55]
                   [19 Vyvyan Terrace], Clifton, Bristol

[Before being appointed as the incumbent of St Mary le Port 1842–7, Marshall had been a Presbyterian minister: Leech 2004, 32–3. After the wartime destruction of St Andrew's (Clifton's parish church – **2.1**), Christ Church became the parish church in 1951. 'A ritualist should be inducted here and want to put up altars. He would find the radiators inconvenient. Our only ritual here is with the plate; I think we make it dignified enough': Betjeman, 57.]

2.6 (13)   **Independent, Hope Chapel Hill, Hotwells**
Name   Hope Chapel
Erected   Before 1800 and rebuilt in 1838 on a larger scale
                   [Opened 31 Aug. 1788]
Building   Yes [separate and entire] Yes [exclusively as a place of worship]
Sittings   Free about 300. Other about 800. Total [1,100]
Attend'ce 30 Mar. [Not given]
Avge attendance Morning from 600 to 700 + 213 SS. Total [813–913]
                   Evening from 700 to 800. Total [700–800]
Dated   31 March 1851
Signed   William Gregory, minister of Hope Chapel [1831–53]
                   11 Polygon, Clifton, Bristol

[The chapel was founded by Lady Willielma Glenorchy and Lady Henrietta Hope (c.1750–86) who left £2,500 to erect a chapel: *ODNB* 'Willielma Campbell, Viscountess Glenorchy (1741–1786)'. The project was completed by their friend Lady Darcy Maxwell (1742–1810) who named it Hope Chapel. By 1820 it was an Independent congregation.]

2.7 (14)   **Independent, Clifton**
Name   Highbury School used also as a chapel.
Erected   1850

Building   Yes [separate and entire] No day school also.
Sittings   Free 300. Total [300]
Attend'ce 30 Mar. Evening 100 + 45 SS. Total [145]
Avge attendance   [Not given]
Dated   31 March 1851
Signed   James Garraway, manager
                    Durdham Down Nursery, Bristol

2.8 (16)   **Independent, Holywell Road**
Name   [Bristol] City Mission Station.
Erected   [Not given]
Building   No [not separate and entire] Yes [exclusively as a place of worship]
Sittings   Free 40. Total [40]
Attend'ce 30 Mar. Afternoon 20. Total [20]
Avge attendance   [Not given]
Remarks   In the above room there are two week evening services held. Average
                    of attending from 30 to 40.
Dated   31 March 1851
Signed   John Jewelton, minister
                    2 Frances Place, Ninetree Hill, Bristol
[Jewelton was also the minister of the Bristol City Mission Station in George Street (**2.41**). In 1851
there were eight Bristol City Mission (**1.48**) places of worship (including **2.8, 41–42**; **20.41–42**).]

2.9 (10)   **Particular Baptist, Buckingham Place, Queen's Road**
Name   Buckingham Chapel.
Erected   [Opened 2] June 1847 [Restored 1890]
Building   Yes [separate and entire] Yes [exclusively as a place of worship]
Sittings   Free 200. Other 600. Total [800]
Attend'ce 30 Mar. Morning 160. Total [160]
                    Afternoon 50. Total [50]
                    Evening 200. Total [200]
Avge attendance   Morning 250. Total [250]
                    Afternoon 80. Total [80]
                    SS no school
Remarks   On the given day to take the attendance there was a very unusually thin
                    congregation in consequence of an epidemic prevailing.
Dated   31 March 1851
Signed   Richard Morris, minister [1849–58]
                    11 Buckingham Place, Clifton

2.10a (7)   **Wesleyan Methodist, Clifton**
Name   Original Hotwell House or Rock Chapel.
Erected   Before 1801, but appropriated as a chapel in 1849
Building   Yes [separate and entire] Yes [exclusively as a place of worship]
Sittings   Free 65. Total [65]
Attend'ce 30 Mar. Evening 21. Total 21
Avge attendance   [Not given]
Remarks   This place is provided for the religious accommodation of the poor
                    persons/quarrymen and their families, who may be unable to attend
                    public worship in Clifton.
Dated   31 March 1851

Signed   John Carey Pengelly, Wesleyan minister of King St chapel, Bristol [1850–2]
                  4 Polygon, Clifton

[Pengelly was also the minister of Old King Street, Bristol (**1.37**) and and Hotwells (**2.13**).]

2.10b (9)   Wesleyan Methodist, Clifton
Name   Original Hotwell House or Rock Chapel
Erected   Before 1801, but appropriated as a chapel in 1849
Building   Yes [separate and entire] Yes [exclusively as a place of worship]
Sittings   Free 65. Total [65]
Attend'ce 30 Mar. Evening 21. Total 21
Avge attendance [Not given]
Remarks   This place is intended for the religious accommodation of the poor
                   persons, quarrymen and their families, residing in the neighbourhood,
                   who may be unable to attend public worship in Clifton.
Dated   31 March 1851
Signed   John Carey Pengelly, Wesleyan minister of King St chapel, Bristol [1850–2]
                   4 Polygon, Clifton

2.11 (6)   Wesleyan Methodist, Hotwell Road
Name   Hotwell Road Chapel
Erected   1833
Building   Yes [separate and entire] Yes [exclusively as a place of worship]
Sittings   Free 290. Other 310. Total [600]
Attend'ce 30 Mar. Morning 45 + 15 SS. Total 60
                   Evening 60. Total 60
Avge attendance Morning 300 + 40 SS. Total 340
                   Evening 350. Total 350
Remarks   A secession from the Wesleyan body has lately taken place, and the party
                   seceding has fitted up a place in the neighbourhood for public worship.
Dated   31 March 1851
Signed   William Withers, steward
                   Under the Bank, St Augustine's, Bristol

2.12 (15)   Wesleyan Methodist, Durdham Down
Name   Wesley Chapel
Erected   1835
Building   Yes [separate and entire] Yes [exclusively as a place of worship]
Sittings   Free 72. Other 156. Total [228] Standing room for 50
Attend'ce 30 Mar. Morning 37 + 39 SS. Total 76
                   Evening 34 + 17 SS. Total 51
Avge attendance Morning 80 + 50 SS. Total 130
                   Evening 120. Total 120
Remarks   'A seccession of sevaral persons from this congregation took place about
                   six months scence; they have assembeled in a nother place of worship.'
Dated   30 March 1851
Signed   William Henry Bould, chapel steward
                   Durdham Cottage, [Durdham Down] (gardener)

2.13 (8)   Wesleyan Methodist, Oldfield Place, Hotwells
Name   Grenville Place Chapel
Erected   1839 [Opened 23 June 1839]
Building   Yes [separate and entire] Yes [exclusively as a place of worship]

Sittings   Free 458. Other 257. Total [715] Standing room for 100
Attend'ce 30 Mar. Morning 130 + 60 SS. Total 190
                      Evening 150 Total 150
Avge attendance   Morning 200 + 60 SS. Total 260
                      Evening 250. Total 250
Remarks   The anniversary services of some popular institutions were held on Sunday
                      30 Mar. in the neighbourhood and the number attending divine service
                      was less than usual.
Dated   31 March 1851
Signed   John Carey Pengelly, minister of King St Chapel in Bristol [1850–2]
                      4 Polygon, Clifton
[Pengelly was also the minister of Old King Street, Bristol (**1.37**) and Clifton (**2.10**).]

2.14 (12)   **Roman Catholic, Meridian Place**
Name   St Catherine's Chapel [Convent of St Catherine of Siena]
Erected   1840
Building   Yes [separate and entire] Yes [exclusively as a place of worship]
Sittings   Free 120. Other 20.* Total [140] Standing room for 20
Attend'ce 30 Mar. Morning 40. Total [40]
                      Afternoon 120. Total [120]
Avge attendance   [Not given]
Remarks   * This is a gallery for the inmates of the house.
Dated   31 March 1851
Signed   Frederick Neve, chaplain
                      Bishop's House, Clifton

2.15 (11)   **Roman Catholic, Park Place**
Name   Church of the Holy Apostles
Erected   Opened in 1848 [21 September 1848]
Building   Yes [separate and entire] Yes exclusively [as a place of worship]
Sittings   Free 500. Other 650. Total 1,150. Standing room for 500
Attend'ce 30 Mar. Morning 752 + 70 SS. Total 822
                      Afternoon 120 + 70 SS. Total 190
                      Evening 550. Total 550
Avge attendance   Morning 900 + 70 SS. Total 970
                      Afternoon 200 + 70 SS. Total 270
                      Evening 600. Total 600
Remarks   31 March 1851
Dated   William Joseph Vaughan, residential clergyman
Signed   Bishops House, Clifton
[From 1850 the church was the pro-cathedral of the diocese of Clifton. It was replaced by the cathedral dedicated to St Peter and St Paul, consecrated 29 June 1973. Later Vaughan was bishop of Plymouth 1855–1902.]

330.2   ASHLEY SUB-DISTRICT

330.2.1 Parish of St James and St Paul
Area 490 aces, with 1,408 inhabited houses, 79 uninhabited. Population 7,935.

2.16 (17)   **Church of England, St Andrew, Montpelier**
(Summary form)
Name   St Andrew's, Montpelier
[*Consecration*   31 Jan. 1845. New chancel 11 Oct. 1878]

Erected	January 1845 [Cost £2,428]
[Endowment	Total £150]
Sittings	Free 688. Total 688
Usual attend'ce	Morning 250 to 300 + 70 SS. Total [320–370]
	Afternoon no service
	Evening upwards of 300. Total [300]
Remarks	Information refused by minister
Signed	John Lockhart, parish clerk
[Incumbent	Charles Evanson, perpetual curate 1845–74]

[Within the parish St Bartholomew, Union Street, was consecrated 22 Jan. 1861.]

2.17 (19)   Church of England, Orphan Asylum Chapel, Ashley Hill, Hook's Mills
(Summary form)

Name	Orphan Asylum chapel attached to asylum
Erected	Can't say but asylum instituted 1795. [The chapel was built in 1791]
Sittings	Free 120. Other 153. Total 273
Usual attend'ce	Morning full
	Evening half full
Signed	Mrs Britton, matron
[Chaplain	Henry Samuel Livius, minister [1844–69]

[The Blue Maids' Orphanage was founded in 1795, and closed in 1930: Leech 2004, 138–9.]

2.18 (21)   Church of England, St Matthew, Cotham Side, Kingsdown

Name	St Matthew. 1 and 2 Will. IV, c.38 [1831] No district assigned
Consecration	[23] April 1835. Deficiency of accommodation in the parish church.
Erected	By private subscriptions [for] £8,000. Total cost £8,000
Endowment	OPE £30 (odd). Pew rents £360
Sittings	Free 426. Other 840. Total 1,266
Attend'ce 30 Mar.	Morning 900 + 150 SS. Total 1,050
	Evening 1,000. Total 1,000
Avge attendance	Morning 1,000 + 150 SS. Total 1,150
	Evening 1,200. Total 1,200
Dated	31 March 1851
Signed	John Bryant Clifford, minister [1837–79]
	1 Highbury Place, Bristol

[Before becoming incumbent, Clifford was the curate, 1836–7. He was a committed Protestant. Joseph Leech remarked that Clifford, 'whose popularity amongst his own congregation is very great ... is, I believe, ranked amongst the extreme anti-High-Church party, as he seems to deem it, and I have no doubt sincerely, an imperative duty to introduce the subject into nearly all his sermons.': Leech 2004, 117. The church was founded by Thomas Tregenna Biddulph, the incumbent of St James', Bristol (**1.7**), and when he preached at the laying of the foundation stone 26 Aug. 1833 an estimated 15,000 were present. The first minister was his son Theophilus Biddulph 1835–7.]

2.19 (20)   Church of England, St Barnabas, Ashley Road
(Summary form)

Name	St Barnabas, Ashley Road
[Consecration	12 September 1843]
Erected	1843
[Endowment	Total £150]
Sittings	Free 500. Other 420. Total 920
Usual attend'ce	Morning 60 to 100 (SS none). Total [60–100]
	Afternoon no service

	Evening 60 to 80. Total [60–80]
Remarks	Minister out of town
Signed	John Holmes, churchwarden
[*Incumbent*	John Jefferis Coles 1843–70]

[Coles was 'understood to hold Tractarian or Puseyite principles': *Bristol Mercury*, 16 Sept. 1843; Leech 2004, 91–3.]

330.2.2 Parish of Horfield

Area 1,287, with 160 inhabited houses, 4 uninhabited. Population 998.
The population of Horfield was increasing due to being near Bristol, and the building of a barracks (1845–6), and a prison (1847, replacing Bristol Prison, burnt down in 1831).

2.20 (18)	**Church of England, Holy Trinity, Horfield**
(Summary form)	
Name	Holy Trinity, Horfield
[*Consecration*	22 December 1847]
Erected	About 600 years [Apart from the tower, mostly rebuilt in 1831]
	Enlarged 1846–7 (to accommodate the soldiers) [and 1891–3]
[*Endowment*	£91. In lieu of tithes the rent charge at Horfield was assigned to augment poor livings in the diocese, to pay the stipends of curates to elderly and infirm incumbents and to provide for the endowment of St Michael and All Angels, Bishopston]
Sittings	Free 382. Other 18. Total 400
Usual attend'ce	Morning 400 (including the soldiers from the barracks) + 40 SS
	Total [440]
	Afternoon very few
	Evening no service
Remarks	Information refused by the minister, the Rev Henry Richards who desired me to ask the reg. general if he was the archbishop of Canterbury.
Signed	Mrs Grey, sextoness
[*Incumbent*	Henry Richards, perpetual curate [1828–64]

[Leech 2004, 289–96. Richards, a friend of Edward Pusey (who preached at the opening of the chancel, 14 Feb. 1847), introduced daily services and weekly communion services making it the first church in Bristol associated with the Oxford Movement.Richards' role in the dispute with bishop Monk over the Horfield manor estate is discussed by W. Evans. The Civil Census recorded 320 men and women in Horfield barracks. Within the parish St Michael and All Angels, Bishopston was consecrated 28 Feb. 1862.]

2.21 (22)	**Wesleyan Reformers, Horfield**
Name	Mount Zion
Erected	1846
Building	Separate [and entire] Yes [exclusively as a place of worship]
Sittings	Free 80. Other 30. Total [110] Standing room for 30
Attend'ce 30 Mar.	Morning 30. Total [30]
	Evening 40. Total [40]
Avge attendance	Morning 40 + 19 SS. Total 59
	Afternoon 20 SS. Total 20
	Evening 90. Total 90
Dated	30 March 1851
Signed	Henry Hodges, chapel steward [farmer of 80 acres, employing eight labourers]
	14 Elton Terrace, Horfield, near Bristol

330.3 ST GEORGE SUB-DISTRICT

330.3.1 Parish of St George
Area 1,831 acres; 1,768 inhabited houses, 125 uninhabited. Population 8,905.

2.22 (23)	**Church of England, St George, St George**
Name	St George. Separated by Act of Parliament from the parish of St Philip and St Jacob, in the city of Bristol (**2.35**)
Consecration	[Erected] 1752 [Consecrated 6 Sept. 1756]
Erected	[Foundation stone laid 3 Mar. 1752. Church demolished 1845; new church opened 1846, burnt down 1878. Further new church opened 8 May 1880.]
Endowment	{Total £530}
Sittings	Free 645. Other 204. Total 849
Attend'ce 30 Mar.	Morning 135 + 60 SS. Total 195
	Afternoon 185 + 85 SS. Total 270
Avge attendance	[Not given]
Dated	31 March 1851
Signed	George Salt, vicar [1842–57]
	[Summerhill], St George, near Bristol

[Within the parish St Mark was consecrated 18 May 1848 (**1.14**) and St Michael, Two Mile Hill (**1.14**), on 22 Aug. 1848.]

2.23 (26)	**Independent, St George**
Name	Barton Hill Chapel
Erected	1844
Building	Yes [separate and entire] Yes [exclusively as a place of worship]
Sittings	Free 132. Other 80. Total [212] Stand[ing] room for 50
Attend'ce 30 Mar.	Morning 65 + 36 SS. Total 101
	Afternoon 40 SS. Total 40
	Evening 63. Total 63
Avge attendance	Morning 70 + 35 SS. Total 105
	Afternoon 40 SS. Total 40
	Evening 80. Total 80
Dated	31 March 1851
Signed	John Yalland, deacon
	34 Sussex Street, St Philips, Bristol

2.24 (27)	**Baptist, St George**
Name	Baptist Chapel Newchurch
Erected	1831
Building	Separate [and entire] Yes [exclusively as a place of worship]
Sittings	Free 160. Other 85. Total [245] Standing room for 100
Attend'ce 30 Mar.	Morning 35 + 71 SS. Total 106
	Afternoon 166 SS. Total 166
	Evening 125. Total 125
Avge attendance	[Not given]
Remarks	Average attendance Sabbath mornings including children 130; of children Sabbath afternoons 170; of congregation Sabbath evenings 150. Prayer meeting Monday evenings 20. Preaching* Wednesday evenings 25. There is a library well appreciated by the scholars.
	*Also on Sabbath mornings before breakfast.
Dated	30 March 1851

Signed   Charles Waring Wood, pastor
                     Redfield House Lodge, Redfield, St Georges

2.25 (28)   Wesleyan Methodist, St George
Name   Clay Hill Chapel [Salem Chapel]
Erected   1813 [Rebuilt 1867]
Building   Yes separate [and entire] Yes and Sunday school
Sittings   All free 100. Total [100] Standing room for 40
Attend'ce 30 Mar. Morning 70 SS. Total [70]
                     Afternoon 70 SS. Total [70]
                     Evening 60. Total [60]
Avge attendance   [Not given]
Dated   31 March 1851
Signed   George Hobbs, superintendent of Sunday school [plumber]
                     Clay Hill, St Georges

2.26 (24)   Wesleyan Methodist, St George
Name   Redfield Chapel
Erected   1815 [Replaced by a new chapel opened 8 April 1884]
Building   Yes [separate and entire] Yes [exclusively as a place of worship]
Sittings   Free 200. Other 246. Total [446]
Attend'ce 30 Mar. Morning 80 + 57 SS. Total [137]
                     Evening 102. Total [102]
Avge attendance   Morning 150 + 60 SS. Total [210]
Dated   30 March 1851
Signed   Charles Clay, minister [1850–1]
                     Kingswood, near Bristol
[Clay was also the minister of Bitton (**20.6**), Hanham Street (**20.7**), Cock Road (**20.14**), Kingswood (**20.16**), Longwell Green (**20.17**) and Soundwell (**20.33**).]

2.27 (29)   Wesleyan Methodist, White Way, St George
Name   Wesleyan Methodist Chapel
Erected   [Not given]
Building   Yes [separate and entire] Yes [exclusively as a place of worship]
Sittings   Free 150. Total [150]
Attend'ce 30 Mar. Morning 120 SS. Total 120
                     Afternoon 40. Total 40
                     Evening 19. Total 19
Avge attendance   Morning 220 SS. Total 220
                     Afternoon 110. Total 110
                     Evening 110. Total 110
Remarks   The present number of hearers and scholars is below the average in
                     consequence of a secession.
Dated   7 April 1851
Signed   William Rossiter, 'suppertendant'
                     St Georges Hill

2.28 (32)   Wesleyan Methodist, Crew's Hole, St George
Name   Wesleyan Chapel
Erected   [Not given]
Building   Yes [exclusively as a place of worship]
Sittings   [Not given]

Attend'ce 30 Mar.	Morning, afternoon and evening none [no adult congregation]
	Morning 100 SS. Total [100]
Avge attendance	[Not given]
Remarks	The chapel have been closed this last four months in consequence of the numerous expulsions in the Wesleyan connexion but the Sunday school is still held in the chapel.
Dated	31 March 1851
Signed	Edward Lawrence, steward [quarryman manager]
	Crew's Hole, St George, Bristol

[Lawrence also made the return for the Wesleyan Reformers (**2.34**).]

2.29 (25)   Primitive Methodist, Lower Easton, St George

Name	None
Erected	1808
Building	Yes [separate and entire] Yes [exclusively as a place of worship]
Sittings	Free 100. Other 96. Total [196] Standing room for 40
Attend'ce 30 Mar.	Morning 40. Total [40]
	Evening 60. Total [60]
Avge attendance	[Not given]
Dated	31 March 1851
Signed	Edward Forsey, minister
	Upper Easton, Bristol, Gloucestershire

[Forsey was also the minister of Orchard Street (**2.47**).]

2.30 (34)   Primitive Methodist, Two Mile Hill, St George

Name	Ebenezer
Erected	1841
Building	Yes [separate and entire] Yes [exclusively as a place of worship]
Sittings	Free 130. Other 48. Total [178]
Attend'ce 30 Mar.	Morning 200. Total 200
	Afternoon 90. Total 90
	Evening 120. Total 120
Avge attendance	[Not given]
Dated	30 March 1851
Signed	John Butcher, minister [Primitive Methodist preacher]
	42 Edward Street, St Philip's, Bristol

2.31 (35)   Wesleyan Methodist Association, St George

Name	None
Erected	1819
Building	No [not separate and entire] No [not exclusively as a place of worship]
Sittings	Free 40. Other none. Total [40] Standing room none
Attend'ce 30 Mar.	Morning 20. SS none. Total 20
	Afternoon 35. SS none. Total 35
	Evening 30. SS none. Total 30
Avge attendance	[Not given]
Dated	31 March 1851
Signed	Ira Miller, minister
	5 Kingsmead Terrace, Bath.

2.32 (33)   Wesleyan Reformers, Two Mile Hill, St George
Name   Day school rooms at Two Mile Hill (Wesleyan Methodists expelled)
Erected   1839
Building   Yes [separate and entire] For public worship and day and Sunday schools.
Sittings   Free 300. Other 50. Total [350] Standing room for 100
Attend'ce 30 Mar. Morning 250 + 82 SS. Total [332]
                Afternoon (none). 165 SS. Total [165]
                Evening 300. Total [300]
Avge attendance Morning 310 + 173 SS. Total 473
Remarks   Religious services are held morning and evening, and Sabbath school in
                the afternoon
Dated   31 March 1851
Signed   John Hook, steward
                School House, Kingswood Hill, near Bristol

2.33 (30)   Wesleyan Reformers,* Whiteway, St George
Name   None
Erected   Dec[ember] 1850
Building   Separate [and entire] Yes [exclusively as a place of worship]
Sittings   Free about 80. Other 32. Total [112] Standing room none
Attend'ce 30 Mar. Morning 50. Total 50
                Afternoon 120. Total 120
                Evening 120. Total 120
Avge attendance [Not given]
Remarks   *The term Wesleyan Reform is given to this denomination to distinguish
                them from the Conference Methodists. The former having separated
                themselves from the latter through their overbearing and 'tyranical'
                acts, and strictly adheres to the original rules laid down by their
                venerable founder, John Wesley.
Dated   31 March 1851
Signed   Edwin Weight, steward [seal (?) maker]
                St Georges, near Bristol

2.34 (31)   Wesleyan Reformers, St George
Name   White House Chapel, Crew's Hole
Erected   [Not given]
Building   Yes [exclusively as a place of worship]
Sittings   Free 250. Total [250]
Attend'ce 30 Mar. Afternoon 200. Total [200]
                Evening 200. Total [200]
Avge attend'ce (4m) Morning 200. Total [200]
Dated   31 March 1851
Signed   Edward Lawrence, chapel steward [manager of stone quarry]
                Crew's Hole, St George, Bristol
[Lawrence also made the return for the Wesleyan Methodists (**2.28**).]

330.4   ST PHILIP AND ST JACOB SUB-DISTRICT

330.4.1 Parish of St Philip and St Jacob (out parish)
Area 310 acres; 4,215 inhabited houses, 432 uninhabited. Population 24,961.

2.35 (36)	**Church of England, Holy Trinity, Trinity Road, St Philip's**
Name	Church of the Holy Trinity, generally called Trinity, St Philip's, Bristol.
Consecration	17 February 1832, [as] an additional church
Erected	By parliamentary grant (of £6,000) and by private subscription (of £3,020 19s 4d). Total cost £9,020 19s 4d
Endowment	{Total £400}
Sittings	Free 1,500. Other 700. Total 2,200
Attend'ce 30 Mar.	Morning 1,300 + 228 SS. Total 1,528
	Afternoon 300. Total 300
	Evening 1,800. Total 1,800
Avge attend'ce (6m)	Morning 1,400 + 220 SS. Total 1,620
	Afternoon 300. Total 300
	Evening 1,900. Total 1,900
Remarks	From the fact of church miss[ionar]y sermons being preached in an adjoining church, our attendance morning and ev[enin]g has been smaller than usual.
Dated	31 March 1851
Signed	David Cooper, perpetual curate [1850–90]
	[Redfield House], Ashley Hill, Bristol

[Visiting the church, Joseph Leech had to sit in the gallery with the poor children who were under the supervision of 'two masters, a mistress and the old beadle' who used his stick to maintain discipline during the service: Leech 2004, 118–20.]

2.36 (37)	**Church of England, St Luke, Avondale Road, Barton Hill**
Name	St Luke, in the parish of St Philip and [St] Jacob in Bristol. A district chapelry in the patronage of the vicar of St Philip and [St] Jacob. Built before Sir R Peel's Act passed [6 & 7 Vict. c.37 (1843)]
Consecration	[20 September] 1843, as an additional church
Erected	Erected by grant from ..., partly by voluntary contributions. Total cost abt £3,000. [£1,000 of which was given by the nearby Great Western Cotton Works]
Endowment	By Eccl[esiastical] Comm[issioners] ... £150. {Total £400}
Sittings	Free for 1,000 people. Other five pews for about five each [25] Total abt 1,025
Attend'ce 30 Mar.	Morning 89 SS. Total [89]
	Afternoon 97 SS. Total [97]
Avge attendance	[Not given]
Remarks	Unable to give the number. Congregation so very fluctuative. Tolerably good in summer especially in the afternoon.
Dated	31 March 1851
Signed	Charles Grant, perpetual curate [1850–61]
	13 Somerset Square, Bristol

[The preacher at the consecration was John Hensman (**2.1**) whose sermon was 'chaste, solemn and appropriate': *Bristol Mercury*, 23 Sept. 1843. Beneath the church were schools for 700 children. Within the parish Christ Church, Barton Hill was consecrated 12 Nov. 1885]

2.37 (41)   **Church of England, St Simon the Apostle, Baptist Mills**
(Summary form)
Name   St Simons
[Consecration   21 December 1847]
Erected   [Not given]
[Endowment   Total £150]
Sittings   [Free 500. Other 200] Total 700
Usual attend'ce   Average 200
Dated   26 Dec. 1851
Signed   From registrar's letter
[Incumbent   Thomas Lathbury, perpetual curate 1848–65]
[There were protests in the church over ritualism in May 1883 and Nov. 1898. It closed in 1956, reopening on 16 Mar. 1960 as the Greek Orthodox Church of St Peter and St Paul.]

2.38 (44)   **Church of England, St Jude the Apostle, Poyntz Pool, The Dings**
(Summary form)
Name   St Jude
[Consecration   31 June 1849]
Erected   [Not given]
[Endowment   Total £150]
Sittings   Total 450
Usual attend'ce   Morning thin
                    Evening tolerably well
Dated   26 Dec. 1851
Signed   From registrar's letter
[Incumbent   Alfred Oliver Wellstead 1850–64]

2.39 (52)   **Independent, Anvil Street, St Philips**
Name   Anvil St Chapel
Erected   1834 [Subsequently twice enlarged]
Building   Yes [separate and entire] Yes [exclusively as a place of worship]
Sittings   Free 400. Other 350. Total [750] Standing room none
Attend'ce 30 Mar. Morning 400 + 60 SS. Total 460
                    Evening 490 + 20 SS. Total 510
Avge attendance   Morning 500 + 60 SS. Total 560
                    Evening 600 + 40 SS. Total 640
Dated   31 March 1851
Signed   James Taylor, minister [1834–64]
                    Penstone Cottage, Stapleton, Road, Bristol
[The chapel was opened under the superintendence of the Bristol Tabernacle (**1.24**).]

2.40 (50)   **Independent, Kingsland Road, The Dings**
Name   Kingsland Chapel
Erected   1836 [Opened 1 Dec. 1836]
Building   Yes [separate and entire] Yes [exclusively as a place of worship]
Sittings   Free 250. Other 414.* Total [664]
Attend'ce 30 Mar. Morning 299 + 80 SS. Total 379**
                    Evening 420. Total [420]
Avge attend'ce (11m) Morning 200 + 70 SS. Total 270
                    Evening 350. Total 350
Remarks   * The sittings are let at 2s, 1s 6d and 1s per quarter.
                    ** Some of the younger children remain in the schoolroom.

The chapel has been closed for one month during the year.
We have been without a pastor during the year till our new pastor entered upon his duties this day.

Dated	30 March 1851
Signed	James Wade, deacon [brush and bellows maker]
	4 King Square Avenue, Bristol

[Chapel opened under superintendence of Bristol Tabernacle (**1.24**). By 1847 there were 147 members.]

2.41 (39)   Independent, George Street

Name	City Mission Station
Erected	[Not given]
Building	No [not separate and entire] No [not exclusively as a place of worship]
Sittings	Free 44. Total [44]
Attend'ce 30 Mar.	Evening 28. Total [28]
Avge attendance	[Not given]
Dated	31 March 1851
Signed	John Jewelton, minister
	2 Frances Place, [Nine Tree Hill], Bristol

[Jewelton was also the minister of the Bristol City Mission Station in Holywell Road (**2.8**). In 1851 there were eight Bristol City Mission (**1.48**) places of worship (including **2.8, 41–42**; **20.41–42**).]

2.42 (42)   Independent and Baptist (united), Queen Street

Name	Bristol City Mission School and Preaching Station
Erected	Opened for worship 1848
Building	The whole house. Yes [exclusively as a place of worship]
Sittings	All free 135. Total [135] Room in which the worship is performed 20 ft by 12½
Attend'ce 30 Mar.	Afternoon 56 SS. Total 56
	Evening 34. Total 34
Avge attendance	Evening 50 + 60 SS. Total 110
Dated	31 March 1851
Signed	George Kovachich, regular preacher [city missionary]
	Lawrence Hill, Bristol

[See preceding note]

2.43 (47)   Baptist, Thrissell Street, Easton

Name	Baptist Chapel
Erected	1830 [Destroyed by fire 1854, re-opened 1855. It was replaced by Kensington Chapel, Stapleton Road, which was opened by Charles Spurgeon the Baptist leader in 1888]
Building	Yes [separate and entire] Yes [exclusively as a place of worship]
Sittings	Free 200. Other 380. Total [580]
Attend'ce 30 Mar.	Morning 170 + 75 SS. Total 145
	Evening 280 + 42 SS. Total 322
Avge attendance	[Not given]
Dated	30 March 1851
Signed	Robert Tubbs, minister
	Stapleton Road, Bristol

[The chapel was seeded from Counterslip Chapel (**1.34**).]

2.44 (43)   Baptist, Brick Street

Name	Brick Street Meeting Ho[use]

Erected	About the year 1842
Building	Yes [separate and entire] Yes [exclusively as a place of worship] No school
Sittings	Free about 180. Total [180]
Attend'ce 30 Mar.	Afternoon 75. Total 75
	Evening 120. Total 120
Avge attendance	Afternoon 75. Total [75]
	Evening 140. Total [140]
Remarks	This is a mission station belonging to the Broadmead Baptist Church (**1.32**). The ministers are the students of the Baptist College, Bristol.
Dated	31 March 1851
Signed	Edward H. Phillips, manager North Street, Bristol

2.45 (45)   **Wesleyan Methodist, St Philip and St Jacob**

Name	Wesley Chapel
Erected	1837
Building	Yes [separate and entire] Yes [exclusively as a place of worship]
Sittings	Free 325. Other 325. Total [650]
Attend'ce 30 Mar.	Morning 70 + 30 SS. Total 100
	Afternoon 54 SS. Total [54]
	Evening 92. Total 92
Avge attendance	Morning 250 + 200 SS. Total [450]
	Afternoon 50. Total [50]
	Evening 300. Total [300]
Remarks	The great difference between the average congregation for the last twelve months, and the numbers attending the chapel on 30 March attributable to a considerable secession which has lately taken place. [Probably to Barton Hill Chapel (**2.48**)]
Dated	31 March 1851
Signed	William Hunt, Wesleyan minister 2 Paul Street, Portland Square, Bristol

2.46 (48)   **Wesleyan Methodist, Lawrence Hill**

Name	Lawrence Hill Chapel
Erected	About the year 1850
Building	Separate [and entire] Yes [exclusively as a place of worship]
Sittings	Free 130. Other 24. Total [154] Standing room none
Attend'ce 30 Mar.	[Not given]
Avge attendance	(6m) Morning 110. Total 110
	Evening 154. Total 154
Dated	31 March 1851
Signed	Samuel Baldwin, chapel steward [brick maker] Lawrence Hill, Bristol

2.47 (51)   **Primitive Methodist, Orchard Street**

Name	Ebenezer
Erected	1849
Building	Yes [separate and entire] Yes [exclusively as a place of worship]
Sittings	Free 335. Other 134. Total [469] Standing room for 100
Attend'ce 30 Mar.	Morning 250. Total [250]

Evening 400. Total [400]

Avge attendance	[Not given]
Dated	31 March 1851
Signed	Edward Forsey, minister
	Upper Easton, Bristol, Gloucestershire

[Forsey was also the minister of Lower Easton (**2.29**).]

2.48 (49)   Wesleyan Reformers, Barton Hill

Name	Barton Hill Chapel
Erected	Commenced April 1840 [1849?]
Building	Yes [separate and entire] Yes [exclusively as a place of worship]
Sittings	Free 150. Total [150]
Attend'ce 30 Mar.	Morning 42 + 77 SS. Total 119
	Afternoon 90 SS. Total 90
	Evening 52. Total 52
Avge attendance	[Not given]
Remarks	The building in which worship is performed is an old dwelling house erected AD 1658, and rented by me for that purpose in connection with a Sunday school. Sidney Sprod
Dated	31 March 1851
Signed	Sidney Sprod [bed and mattress maker]
	55 Castle Street, Bristol

2.49 (40)   Methodist Reformers, Baptist Mills

Name	Baptist Mills Chapel
Erected	1850
Building	Yes [separate and entire] Yes [exclusively as a place of worship]
Sittings	Free 140. Other 60. Total [200]
Attend'ce 30 Mar.	Morning 159. Total [159]
	Afternoon 60. Total [60]
	Evening 180. Total [180]
Avge attendance	[Not given]
Dated	[Not given]
Signed	Edward Millard, chapel steward
	6 Parade, St James' Church Yard, Bristol

2.50 (38)   Christian Brethren, St Peter's [sic]

Name	Zion Chapel.
Erected	1849
Building	Yes [separate and entire] Yes [exclusively as a place of worship]
Sittings	Free 100. Other none. Total [100] Standing room none
Attend'ce 30 Mar.	Morning 70. SS none. Total 70
	Evening 100. Total 100
Avge attendance	Morning 100. SS none. Total 100
	Evening 100. Total [100]
Remarks	All the sittings are moveable forms. The place is connected with a house, yet used exclusively for public worship.
Dated	11 April 1851
Signed	James Ben Smith, minister
	5 New Street, St Philip's

2.51 (53)   **Christian Brethren, Narrow Plain**
Denomination   By no particular denomination, but by those who meet simply in the
                   name of the Lord Jesus Christ. [In pencil *Society of Christians*]
Name   Church Alley preaching room
Erected   Before the yr 1800
Building   Yes [separate and entire] Yes [exclusively as a place of worship]
Sittings   Free 200. Other none. Total [200]
Attend'ce 30 Mar. Evening 81. Total 81
Avge attendance (4m) Evening 150. Total 150
Remarks   The preaching room enlarged four months since from this date
Dated   31 March 1851
Signed   John Victor, minister of the gospel
                   6 Kington Buildings, Kingsdown, Bristol
[In 1855 Victor became the first pastor of Unity Chapel (**1.46**).]

2.52 (46)   **Roman Catholic, Lawford's Gate, St Philip's**
Name   St Nicholas' Church [St Nicholas of Tolentino]
Erected   In 1850 [Enlarged 1861 and 1872–3]
Building   Yes [separate and entire] Yes [exclusively as a place of worship]
Sittings   Free 84. Other 130. Total [214] Standing room for 100
Attend'ce 30 Mar. Morning 360. Total [360]
                   Afternoon 80 SS. Total [80]
                   Evening 230. Total [230]
Avge attendance (3m) Morning 420 + 80 SS. Total 500
Remarks   We have two services in the morning, at each of which the church is nearly
                   full. The afternoon service is confined to the Sunday school scholars.
Dated   31 March 1851
Signed   Nicholas O'Donnell, pastor [1849–53]
                   3 Thrissell Street, Bristol

2.53 (54)   **Church of Jesus Christ of Latter-day Saints, Broad Street**
Name   Broad Street Chapel
Erected   Part of dwelling house converted to a chapel about 1820
Building   Separate [and entire] No [not exclusively as a place of worship]
Sittings   Free about 260. Other none. Total [260] Standing room none
Attend'ce 30 Mar. Morning 250. Total [250]   } SS
                   Afternoon 150. Total [150]   } none.
                   Evening 260. Total [260]   }
Avge attendance Morning 200. Total [200]   } SS
                   Afternoon 200. Total [200]   } none.
                   Evening 200. Total [200]   }
Remarks   The lower part of the building is used as a chapel, and the upper part
                   as a dwelling
Dated   31 March 1851
Signed   Joseph G. Manning, presiding elder
                   Broad Street Chapel, Broad Street, Bristol

330.5   **WESTBURY SUB-DISTRICT**

330.5.1–3 Parish of Westbury-on-Trym

Area 5,456 acres; 1,141 inhabited houses, 38 uninhabited. Population 6,728.
The parish includes the tithings of Stoke Bishop and Shirehampton (an ecclesiastical district).

2.54 (57)	**Church of England, Holy Trinity, Westbury-on-Trym**
Name	Westbury on Trym
Consecration	[Not given]
Erected	[Restored 1851–60]
Endowment	Land £35 [crossed out] Tithe £10. Glebe £35. OPE £38. Fees and Easter offerings uncertain. {Total £630}
Sittings	[Not given]
Attend'ce 30 Mar.	Morning 400 + 90 SS. Total 490
	Afternoon 300 + 80 SS. Total 380
Avge attendance	[Not given]
Remarks	The income of the above as an average I believe to be about £183.
Dated	31 March 1851
Signed	William Cartwright, incumbent [1847–1900]
	Redland [Parade], Bristol

[The benefice consisted of Westbury-on-Trym with Redland Chapel (**2.55**). Joseph Leech noted within the parish 'a Baptist chapel, a Methodist chapel, a Popish chapel, half a dozen private Ranting rooms [i.e. Primitive Methodist places of worship] and about twelve beer shops!': Leech 2004, 216.]

2.55 (56)	**Church of England, Redland Chapel, Green Road**
Name	Redland Chapel
Consecration	Opened 5 October 1743. Consecrated [12 November] 1790
Erected	[By John Cossins, a] private benefactor [as a private chapel to Redland Court] Total cost not known [Restored 1859]
Endowment	OPE two houses [See above, **2.54**]
Sittings	Total 150
Attend'ce 30 Mar.	Morning 120. Total 120
	Afternoon 80. Total 80
Avge attendance	[Not given]
Remarks	The income of the above is uncertain arising partly from Easter dues and fees and houses which are not always tenanted
Dated	30 March 1851
Signed	William Cartwright, incumbent [1847–1900]
	[Redland Parade], near Bristol

[The benefice consisted of Westbury-on-Trym with Redland Chapel (**2.55**). In 1942 Redland Chapel became a parish church.]

2.56 (64)	**Church of England, St Mary, High Street, Shirehampton**
Name	Shirehampton Church.
Consecration	Before 1800 [15 Jan. 1930]
Erected	[Rebuilt 1727 and 1827; destroyed by fire 15 Jan. 1928, rebuilt 1929–30]
Endowment	Land £30. Fees £8. Easter offerings £32. Other £5. [See above, **2.54**]
Sittings	Free 145. Other 220. Total 365
Attend'ce 30 Mar.	Morning 255 + 70 SS. Total 325
	Afternoon 245 + 70 SS. Total 315
Avge attendance	[Not given]
Remarks	Shirehampton was an ancient chapelry attached to Westbury uponTrym;

in 1844 it was made a distinct benefice, but the church, endowment and boundaries remained as before the division.

Dated   31 March 1851
Signed   Henry Samuel Sayce, incumbent [1844–58]
                   Near Bristol

2.57 (62)   Baptist, Trym Road
Name   Baptist Chapel
Erected   1846
Building   Separate and entire. Used as a place of worship. No school
Sittings   Free 120. Other 110. Total [230]
Attend'ce 30 Mar. Abt 200
Avge attendance [Not given]
Dated   [Not given]
Signed   [Not given]
                   [In pencil, John Howell, enumerator]

2.58 (58)   Wesleyan Methodist, Portland Street, Kingdown
Name   Portland Street Chapel
Erected   About 1792 [Opened 26 April 1792. Enlarged 1872]
Building   Separate [and entire] Exclusively for worship
Sittings   Free 150. Other 350. Total [500]
Attend'ce 30 Mar. Morning 320 + 60 SS. Total 380
                   Afternoon 100. Total 100
                   Evening 350 + 60 SS. Total 411 [*sic*]
Avge attendance Morning 280 + 60 SS. Total 240 [*sic*]
                   Afternoon 50. Total 50
                   Evening 300 + 30 SS. Total 330
Dated   31 March 1851
Signed   John Wesley Etheridge (DD), minister [1849–51]
                   Royal Fort, Bristol

[Etheridge's doctorate was awarded by Heidelberg University in 1847, for studies in Hebrew and Syriac: *ODNB*, 'John Wesley Etheridge (1804–1866)'. 'Kingsdown was a citadel of serious, pious, intellectual endeavour and the home of many locally esteemed dissenters': Spittal, 203.]

2.59 (60)   Wesleyan Methodist, Westbury-on-Trym
Name   Bethesda Chapel
Erected   1810 [Replaced by a new chapel 1889–90]
Building   Yes [separate and entire] Yes [exclusively as a place of worship]
Sittings   Free 100. Other 130. Total [230]
Attend'ce 30 Mar. Morning 18. Total [18]
                   Evening 20. Total [20]
Avge attendance [Not given]
Dated   31 March 1851
Signed   James Ford, steward [blacksmith]
                   Henbury, Gloucestershire

2.60 (65)   Wesleyan Methodist, Shirehampton
Name   Wesleyan Chapel
Erected   1823
Building   Yes [separate and entire] Yes [exclusively as a place of worship]
Sittings   Free 85. Total [85]

Attend'ce 30 Mar.	[Not given]
Avge attendance	Evening 60. Total [60]
Dated	31 March 1851
Signed	Robert Edbrooke, manager [black]smith
	Shirehampton, near Bristol

2.61 (59)   Wesleyan Reformers, Westbury-on-Trym

Name	None
Erected	[Not given]
Building	No [not separate and entire] Yes [exclusively as a place of worship]
Sittings	Free 50. Other 30. Total [80] Standing room none
Attend'ce 30 Mar.	Morning 60 + 30 SS. Total [90]
	Evening 80 + 30 SS. Total [110]
Avge attendance	Morning 70 + 30 SS. Total 100.
Dated	31 March 1851
Signed	Joseph Brookes, steward
	Westbury-on-Trym

2.62 (63)   Wesleyan Reformers, Westbury-on-Trym

Name	No name
Erected	1800
Building	Separate [and entire] Yes [exclusively as a place of worship]
Sittings	Free 60. Other 60. Total [120] Standing room none
Attend'ce 30 Mar.	Morning 60. Total [60]
	Evening 160. Total [160]
Avge attendance	Afternoon 110. Total 110
Dated	31 March 1851
Signed	James Giles, chapel steward [gardener]
	Slo Cottage, Techland, near Bristol

2.63 (61)   Roman Catholic, Sales House, Convent chapel of the Order of the Visitation of the Blessed Virgin Mary, Westbury-on-Trym

There is not any place of public religious worship in the place in which I reside, but there is a private chapel belonging to the house used by the inmates who are a society of ladies living in a community, to whom I am chaplain.

Dated	[Not given]
Signed	Lewis Maes BD

[The Order, first located at Shepton Mallet 1810–31, was at Westbury-on-Trym 1831–96 (buildings opened 1834), and then at Sudbury Grove, Harrow on the Hill, Middx. By 1900 it had 175 convents worldwide.]

330.5.4–9 Parish of Henbury

Area 9,892 acres; 400 inhabited houses, 7 uninhabited. Population 2,053.
The parish includes the tithings of King's Weston, Lawrence Weston, Henbury, Stowick, Compton and Charlton. The remainder of the parish is in the Almondsbury sub-district (332.1.10–1).

2.64 (67)   Church of England, St Mary the Virgin, Henbury

Name	Henbury, a very ancient parish church
Consecration	[Not given]
Erected	[Restored 1834–5 and 1875–8]
Endowment	Tithe £40. Glebe two acres. OPE vicarage house. Fees £25. {Total £700}.
Sittings	Free 250. Other 430. Total 680

Attend'ce 30 Mar.	Morning 348 + 188 SS. Total 536
	Evening 300. Total [300]
Avge attendance	Morning 400 + 200 SS. Total 600
	Evening 350. Total [350]
Dated	31 March 1851
Signed	Henry Hugh Way, minister [1830–60]
	Henbury, Bristol

[The benefice consisted of Henbury, with Aust (**4.14**) and Northwick (**4.13**). After Way resigned in 1860 he was succeeded by his son, John Hugh Way 1860–1906 and then Charles Parry Way 1906–27. Within the parish St John the Evangelist, Hallen was consecrated 25 Sept. 1854: Thompson, 99–186. The only criticism that Joseph Leech had of the congregation was 'a want of *heartiness* in the performance of their part of the service; in other respects, for so large a number, I never saw a better ordered or more attentive congregation in my life': Leech 2004, 187.]

2.65 (68)   Baptist, Hallen

Name	Baptist Chapel
Erected	1828
Building	Separate and entire. Exclusively as a place of worship and Sunday school.
Sittings	Free 80. Other 40. Total [120] Standing room none
Attend'ce 30 Mar.	Morning 27. Total 27
	Afternoon 29 SS. Total 29
	Evening 45. Total 45
Avge attendance	Morning 30. Total 30
	Afternoon 30 SS. Total 30
	Evening 60. Total 60
Remarks	Building belonging to the Bristol Baptist Itinerant Society
Dated	30 March 1851
Signed	Thomas Redwood, 'chapple keeper' [shoemaker]
	Hallen, nr Henbury

[While the Bristol Itinerant Society supported small Independent chapels on the Glos. side of Bristol, the Bristol Baptist Itinerant Society supported small Baptist chapels mostly on the Somerset side.]

2.66 (66)   Society of Friends, Lawrence Weston

Erected	Before 1800
Building	Yes [separate and entire] Yes [exclusively as a place of worship]
Sittings	Total 134. Ground floor 693 [square feet] No gallery
Attend'ce 30 Mar.	Morning 14. Total [14]
Remarks	The persons attending this meeting all reside at considerable distances, consequently there is a but one meeting in the day. The average attendance for the preceding twelve months has been about 17.
Dated	31st day of 3rd month (March) 1851
Signed	Joseph Davis
	Westbury upon Trym, near Bristol

330.5.10   Parish of Compton Greenfield

Area 650 acres; 10 inhabited houses. Population 64.

2.67 (70)   Church of England, All Saints, Compton Greenfield

Name	Compton Greenfield. Ancient parish church
Consecration	[Not given]
Erected	[Apart from the tower rebuilt 1851–2; restored 1896 and 1924–5]
Endowment	{Total £144}
Sittings	Free 40. Other 75. Total 115. (See letter)

Attend'ce 30 Mar.	Morning from 40 to 50. Total [40–50]
	Evening from 30 to 40. Total [30–40]
Avge attendance	[Not given]
Dated	31 March 1851
Signed	John Thomas Ludlow, rector [1846–73]
	[Compton Greenfield], Bristol

2.68 (69)   **Wesleyan Methodist, Easter Compton**

Name	Chapel
Erected	1819 [Rebuilt 1869. Tablet, 'Ebenezer, UMC, 1869']
Building	Yes [separate and entire] Yes [exclusively as a place of worship]
Sittings	Free 50. Other 70. Total [120]
Attend'ce 30 Mar.	Morning 20 + 13 SS. Total 33
	Afternoon 19 SS. Total 19
	Evening 27. Total 27
Avge attendance	Morning 24. Total [24]
	Evening 24. Total [24]
Dated	31 March 1851
Signed	Mark Prosser, leader and steward [farmer of 140 acres]
	[Dyers Farm], Compton Greenfield, near Bristol

330.6   **STAPLETON SUB-DISTRICT**

330.6.1 Parish of Filton

Area 1,030 acres; 54 inhabited houses, 6 uninhabited. Population 245.

2.69 (71)   **Church of England, St Peter, Filton**

Name	St Peter's, commonly called 'Fylton' church.
Consecration	Before 1800
Erected	[Apart from the tower, rebuilt and enlarged 1844–5; enlarged 1960–1]
Endowment	Tithe £145 6s 8d. Glebe £95. Fees £1. {Total £242}
Sittings	Free 90. Other 60. Total 150
Attend'ce 30 Mar.	Morning 57 + 12 SS. Total 57 [*sic*]
	Afternoon 58 + 15 SS. Total 58 [*sic*]
Avge attendance	Morning 30 + 15 SS. Total 45
	Afternoon 50 + 20 SS. Total 70
Dated	31 March 1851
Signed	James Bedford Poulden, rector [1832–76]
	Fylton rectory, Bristol

2.70 (83)   **Wesleyan Methodist, Filton**

Name	None
Erected	1833 [New chapel 1852]
Building	Yes [separate and entire] Yes [exclusively as a place of worship]
Sittings	Free 100. Other 20. Total [120]
Attend'ce 30 Mar.	Evening 40. Total 40
Avge attendance	[Not given]
Remarks	A comfortable chapel the gift of the late Mr Stratton of Bristol.
	Praise the Lord.
Dated	31 March 1851
Signed	John Holder, steward [servant]
	Fylton, near Bristol

330.6.2 Parish of Stapleton

Area 2,554 acres; 709 inhabited houses, 29 uninhabited. Population 4,840.
The Union workhouse situated within the parish had 658 inmates, and the asylum for the poor of Bristol had 729. Also within the parish was the palace of the Bishop of Gloucester and Bristol (1840–58 and then sold to Colston's School), and the Gloucester and Bristol Diocesan Training Institution for Schoolmistresses, opened 10 Sept. 1853).

No return	**Church of England, Holy Trinity, Stapleton**
[Erected	Rebuilt and consecrated 15 April 1857]
[Endowment	Total £160]
[Incumbent	Joseph Henry Butterworth, incumbent 1846–70]

[The sole benefactor of Holy Trinity was Bishop James Henry Monk: Leech 2004, 190–5.]

2.71 (72)	**Church of England, St Mary the Virgin, Fishponds**
Name	Fishponds Church
Consecration	In 1821 [31 Aug.], because the parish church [of Stapleton] was too small for the increased population
Erected	By John Kaye DD, the then bishop of Bristol [1820–27] Built by subscription and a payment from the Church Building Society. Total cost, say £1,200 [New chancel 1871–3, additional aisle 1901–2]
Endowment	Land, tithe and glebe none. OPE £45. Pew rents £25
Sittings	Free 574. Other 126. Total 700. (See letter)
Attend'ce 30 Mar.	Morning 200 + 232 SS. Total [432]
	Afternoon 300 + 21 SS. Total [321]
Avge attendance	Morning 200 + 250 SS. Total [450]
	Afternoon 350 + 25 SS. Total [375]
Remarks	Divine service is performed by the incumbent of the parish church in the evening and I have no means of ascertaining the number that attend.
Dated	31 March 1851
Signed	William Squire Mirehouse, perpetual curate [1820–64]
	Hambrook Grove, nr Bristol

[Mirehouse was also the incumbent of Colsterworth, Lincs. 1826–64, and was followed there by his son, John Mirehouse, who had been the curate of Fishponds 1862–4. On entering the church, Joseph Leech observed that the pews were 'devoted to the poor and the stranger', and he counted only 'about sixteen pews, which, being placed closely together, at the east end, accommodated the *elite* of Fishponds – yes, *elite*, for poor as Fishponds is, it cannot be without its elite. The rest of the building is occupied by the non-elite of the place and the pauper children and the old women of Stapleton workhouse. It was one of the simplest and humblest congregations (with the exception of the sixteen pews) I have ever seen': Leech 2004, 199–200. As a chapel of ease it was dedicated to Holy Trinity; on becoming a parish church in Dec. 1869 it was dedicated to St Mary the Virgin.]

2.72 (73)	**Wesleyan Methodist, Fishponds**
Name	Fishponds Chapel
Erected	1831
Building	Separate building. Worship and Sabb[ath] school
Sittings	Free 145. Other 130. Total [275]
Attend'ce 30 Mar.	Morning 105. Total [105]
	Evening 109. Total [109]
Avge attendance	Morning 180. Total [180]
Dated	30 March 1851
Signed	William Roberts, society steward
	Fishponds, near Bristol

2.73 (74)   **Primitive Methodist, Stapleton**
Name   Providence
Erected   1814
Building   Yes [separate and entire] Yes [exclusively as a place of worship]
Sittings   Free 90. Other 60. Total [150] Standing room none
Attend'ce 30 Mar.   Morning 125 SS. Total [125]
     Afternoon 140. Total [140]
     Evening 160. Total [160]
Avge attendance   Morning 125 SS. Total 125
     Evening 300. Total 300
Dated   31 March 1851
Signed   Isaac Smart, steward
     Fishponds, nr Bristol, Gloucestershire

2.74 (75)   **Wesleyan Reformers, Freeland Buildings, Stapleton**
Name   Wesleyan Methodist (Reform)
Erected   1840
Building   Yes [separate and entire] Yes [exclusively as a place of worship]
Sittings   Free 150. Other 24. Total [174]
Attend'ce 30 Mar.   Morning 10 + 28 SS. Total 38
     Evening 40. Total 40
Avge attendance   Morning 20 + 50 SS. Total 70
     Evening 40. Total [40]
Dated   30 March 1851
Signed   Edward Mullen, class leader
     6 St James Parade, Churchyard, Bristol

330.6.3 Parish of Stoke Gifford

Area 2,065 acres; 95 inhabited houses, 2 uninhabited. Population 488.

2.75 (82)   **Church of England, St Michael, Stoke Gifford.**
Name   Antient parish church. St Mary's, I think
Consecration   In the 13th century
Erected   [Restored 1894–7]
Endowment   Tithe £25. Fees £3. Total £60. {Total £60}.
Sittings   Free 120. Other 150. Total 270
Attend'ce 30 Mar.   Morning 150. Total [150]
     Evening 250. Total [250]
Avge attendance   [Not given]
Remarks   Sunday school returned on the other paper
Dated   31 March 1851
Signed   Edward Parker, vicar [1833–56]
     [St James's Place], Kingsdown, Bristol

[Joseph Leech observed that 'the Rev Mr Parker lived at Kingsdown, and contracted with a flyman to carry himself and a written sermon, once a week, to a parish six miles off, to the spiritual supervision of which he is supposed to attend': Leech 2004, 256.]

330.6.4–5 Parish of Winterbourne

Area 3,170 acres; 652 inhabited houses, 46 uninhabited. Population 2,876.
The parish includes the township of Winterbourne and the tithings of Frenchay and Hambrook. In 1834 the parish was divided into two districts, Winterbourne with the hamlet of Watley's End, and St John the Baptist, Frenchay with the hamlet of Hambrook.

Since 1841 the population of Winterbourne township had decreased by 520.

2.76 (76)   Church of England, St Michael the Archangel, Winterbourne

Request for information. Will you be so good as to furnish the following information as early as you conveniently can. Congregations including Sunday scholars.

[*Erected*	Partial rebuilding 1843–7 and alterations 1877–80]
[*Endowment*	Total £1,037]
Morning	200
Afternoon	180
Sittings	Free 200. Other 120. Total 320
Dated	30 June 1852
Signed	Edwin Day
[*Incumbent*	William Birkett Allen 1835–62]

[Within the parish St John the Baptist, Frenchay (**2.77**) was consecrated 21 Aug. 1834; All Saints, Winterbourne Down 1 Nov. 1861 and St Michael's Church Room (a chapel of ease) dedicated 18 Apr. 1888. Sitting in the churchwarden's pew Joseph Leech found Bibles in French, Italian, Latin and Greek. 'This must be a detachment from the Bodleian Library, said I to myself: one would think that the tower of Babel was in the neighbourhood, and that this was the family pew for it – a sort of Polyglot seat, as one might say, where a man might be accommodated in every language but the one he understands': Leech 2004, 175.]

2.77 (79)   Church of England, St John the Baptist, Frenchay

(Summary form)

Name	Frenchay
[*Consecration*	21 August 1834, as chapel of ease to Winterbourne]
Erected	1834
[*Endowment*	Total £500]
Sittings	Free 500. Other 300. Total 800
Usual attend'ce	Morning 200. Total [200]
	Afternoon 250. Total [250]
Signed	Edwin Day
[*Incumbent*	John Carter, rector 1840–75]

[On 27 May 1836 Frenchay became a separate parish and because of lack of clarity concerning the division of the mother parish of Winterbourne (**2.76**) the matter was clarified by 'An Act to remove doubts as to the division of the parish of Winterbourne in the County of Gloucester, into two parishes' (4 and 5 Vict, c.42, 1841).]

2.78 (77)   Independent, Whiteshill, Winterbourne

Name	Whites Free Chapel
Erected	1816
Building	Yes [separate and entire] Yes [exclusively as a place of worship]
Sittings	[Not given]
Attend'ce 30 Mar.	Morning 120. Total [120]
	Evening 200. Total [200]
Avge attendance	[Not given]
Dated	16 November 1851
Signed	Moses Young, deacon [farmer of 11 acres with two labourers; and a carrier employing a man and two apprentices]
	[Page torn] Hambrook, nr Bristol

[At the opening service, 28 Aug. 1816, the preacher was Rowland Hill (**5.8**).]

2.79 (88)   Independent, Winterbourne

Name	None

Erected	[Not given]
Building	No [not separate and entire] No [not exclusively as a place of worship]
Sittings	Free 50. Other none. Total [50]
Attend'ce 30 Mar.	Afternoon 25. Total 25
Avge attendance	[Not given]
Dated	31 March 1851
Signed	Robert Payne Thatcher, minister [1843–64]
	Frampton Cotterill, nr Bristol

[Thatcher was also the minister of Frampton Cotterell (**3.49**).]

2.80 (80)   Baptist, Broom Hill, Stapleton

Name	Baptist 'Chapple'
Erected	1833 [Enlarged 1905–6]
Building	[Not given]
Sittings	Free 200. Total [200]
Attend'ce 30 Mar.	Morning 80. Total [80]
	Evening 80. Total [80]
Avge attendance	[Not given]
Dated	31 March 1851
Signed	Enos Sparks, deacon
	Stapleton, Gloucestershire

2.81 (81)   Baptist, Stapleton

Name	None. A room in Dr [George Joseph] Bompas' private house, [Upper Fishponds House]
Erected	[Not given]
Building	No [not separate and entire] No [not exclusively as a place of worship]
Sittings	The room will accommodate about 85. Total [85]
Attend'ce 30 Mar.	Morning 55. Total 55.
	Evening 50. Total 50.
Avge attendance	(10m) Congregation about 60.
Remarks	The use of this room for public worship is only a temporary arrangement. Till lately this congregation worshipped in a chapel attached to the Fishponds Asylum and used by a Baptist congregation for nearly a century. In May last we were removed from it by order of the visiting magistrates. The average attendance for the last four years was about 100 [unclear] A new chapel is being built to be ready about mid-summer. No of sittings (without galleries) about 480. There has been no settled minister since May 1850 [when George Thomas left to go to Islington] One is now engaged whose duties will commence in June.
Dated	[Not given]
Signed	George Joseph Bompas MD, deacon
	Fishponds, near Bristol

[Upper Fishponds House (renamed Beechwood in 1861) was a temporary annex to the lunatic asylum and was used as a school 1844–55. Having moved first to Clifton, then to Redland, it closed in 1859. Between 1817–51 members of the Bompas family were superintendents of the asylum. In 1848 a magistrates' enquiry took place following complaints and allegations over the administration of the asylum; presumably as an outcome of this, the chapel congregation had to leave the premises. Before May 1841 the Bompas family had been members of the Downend Baptist chapel (**20.30**) and they were the principal donors to the Fishponds Baptist chapel (no return): Phillips, 1973.]

2.82 (89)   **Wesleyan Methodist, Winterbourne**
Name   None
Erected   Before 1800
Building   Yes [separate and entire] Yes [exclusively as a place of worship]
Sittings   Free 84. Total [84] Standing room for 20
Attend'ce 30 Mar. Evening 56 Total [56]
Avge attendance   Morning 50. Total [50]
Dated   31 March 1851
Signed   Robert Johnson, steward
                    Frenchay, nr Bristol

2.83 (84)   **Wesleyan Methodist, Winterbourne**
Name   Winterdown Room
Erected   Before 1840
Building   [Separate and] entire. Also for an infant school.
Sittings   Free 150. Other none. Total [150]
Attend'ce 30 Mar. Morning none
                    Afternoon none
                    Evening 50. Total 50
Avge attendance   Evening 50. Total 50
Dated   31 March 1851
Signed   John Amos, chapel steward
                    Winterbourne Down, near Bristol

2.84 (86)   **Wesleyan Reformers, Watleys End, Winterbourne**
Name   Wesleyan Chapel [Salem]
Erected   About 1786 [1787 enlarged 1792]
Building   Separate and entire. Yes [exclusively as a place of worship]
Sittings   Free 150. Other 200. Total [350]
Attend'ce 30 Mar. Morning 140 + 90 SS. Total 230
                    Afternoon 90 SS. Total 90
                    Evening 180. Total 180
Avge attendance   Morning 140 + 90 SS. Total 230
                    Afternoon 90. Total 90
                    Evening 180. Total 180
Dated   31 March 1851
Signed   Isaac Budgett, chapel steward [merchant]
                    Winterbourne, near Bristol

[Wesley recorded that 'I preached at Winterbourne, on the foundation of a new preaching house. There was much rain before I began, and a violent wind all the time I was preaching': *Journal*, 17 Sept. 1787.]

2.85 (78)   **Wesleyan Reformers, Fishponds**
Name   None
Erected   November 1850
Building   Yes [separate and entire] Yes [exclusively as a place of worship]
Sittings   Free 74. Other 43. Total [117]
Attend'ce 30 Mar. Morning 70. Total [70]
                    Afternoon S[abbath] School
                    Evening 110. Total [110]
Avge attendance   [Not given]
Dated   30 March 1851

Signed	Joseph Ball, steward
	Fishponds, nr Bristol, Glo'shire

2.86 (87) **Wesleyan Reformers, Watleys End Road, Winterbourne**

Name	'Ebenezar'
Erected	Previously a dwelling house [belonging to John Lewis], but converted into a chapel in the year 1851. [Replaced by the United Methodist Chapel. Tablet: 'Ebenezer Chapel, 1868']
Building	Yes [separate and entire] Yes [exclusively as a place of worship]
Sittings	Free 72. Other 36. Total [108] Standing room none
Attend'ce 30 Mar.	Morning 56. Total [56]
	Evening 100. Total [100]
Avge attendance	[Not given]
Dated	31 March 1851
Signed	George Lewton, chapel steward (clock maker)
	Winterbourne, near Bristol

2.87 (85) **Unitarian, Frenchay Common**

Denomination	Unitarian Christians
Name	English Presbyterian Meeting House or Chapel [Frenchay Chapel]
Erected	Before AD 1800 [c.1720. Restored 1800–1]
Building	A separate and entire building. Exclusively for divine worship (34 feet square)
Sittings	Free 100. Other 90. Standing room for 40 persons
Attend'ce 30 Mar.	Morning 50 + 44 SS. Total 94
	Afternoon none
	Evening 76. Total 76
Avge attendance	Morning 65 + 55 SS. Total 120
	Evening 110. Total 110
Dated	31 March 1851
Signed	Samuel Walker, minister
	Cotham New Road, Bristol

2.88 (90) **Society of Friends, Beckspool Road, Frenchay**

Erected	Before 1800 [1673 replaced by a new meeting house 1808–9]
Building	Yes [separate and entire] Yes [exclusively as a place of worship]
Sittings	Free 200. Ground floor 1,066 [sq ft] } Total 284 sittings
	Free 84. Gallery 468 [sq ft] } Total 1,534 [sq ft]
Attend'ce 30 Mar.	Morning 34. Total [34]
	Afternoon none
	Evening none
Dated	2nd day of the 4th mo. 1851
Signed	Philip Debell Tuckett [farmer]
	Frenchay, near Bristol

---

3.   HO 129/331 CHIPPING SODBURY DISTRICT: 53 places of worship

---

331.1   CHIPPING SODBURY SUB-DISTRICT

331.1.1 Parish of Westerleigh
Area 4,009 acres; 347 inhabited houses, 5 uninhabited. Population 1,679.
The parish includes Coalpit Heath, Henfield, Kendalshire, Mays Hill and Nibley.

Request for information. Will you be so good as to furnish the following information at your earliest convenience. Congregation including Sunday scholars.

3.1 (3)	**Church of England, St James the Great, Westerleigh**
[*Erected*	Chancel rebuilt 1879–81; restored 1895–6]
[*Endowment*	See Pucklechurch (**3.5**)]
Attendance	Morning 65. Total [65]
	Afternoon 110. Total [110]
	Evening no service
Sittings	Free sittings 250. Total [250]
[*Incumbent*	Thomas Boucher Coney, vicar 1839–84]

[The benefice consisted of Pucklechurch (**3.5**) with Abson, Wick (**3.17–18**) and Westerleigh.]

3.2 (3)	**Independent, Codrington**
Attendance	Morning no service
	Afternoon no service
	Evening abt 60. Total [60]
Sittings	Free 80. Other none. Total [80]
Dated	4 July 1852
Signed	John Godwin, registrar

3.3 (1)	**Church of England, St Saviour, Coalpit Heath**
Name	St Saviour's, Coalpit Heath. A new parish under Sir R Peel's Act. [6 and 7 Vict. c.37 (1843)]
Consecration	9 Oct. 1845, as an additional church [in the parish of Westerleigh]
Erected	Chiefly by the Lords of the Manor of Westerleigh Parliamentary grant £300. Private sources £2,200. Total cost £2,500 [Restored 1907]
Endowment	Fees £50. Other sources £150 per ann. from Ecclesiastical Commissioners. {Total £150}
Sittings	All free. Total 511
Attend'ce 30 Mar.	Morning 49 + 66 SS. Total 115
	Afternoon 78 + 58 SS. Total 136
Avge attendance (6m)	30 March a fair average
Remarks	The congregation during the winter months is bad in consequence of the church being damp and no means of warming it. In summer months the church fills well.
Dated	30 March 1851
Signed	William Robert Lawrence, curate [1850–4] St Saviour's, Coalpit Heath, Bristol
[*Incumbent*	Charles Henry Johnston 1848–74]

[The previous incumbent, James Russell Woodford, was later bishop of Ely - see **1.10**.]

3.4 (2)   **Independent, Rodford, Westerleigh**

Name   Tabernacle
Erected   1844
Building   Yes [separate and entire] Yes [exclusively as a place of worship]
Sittings   Free 200. Other 40. Total [240]
Attend'ce 30 Mar. Morning 55 + 49 SS. Total 104
                   Afternoon 49 SS. Total 49
                   Evening 110. Total 110
Avge attendance Morning 55 + 47 SS. Total 102
                   Afternoon 47 SS. Total 47
                   Evening 100. Total 100
Remarks   This chapel, with about 14 others within 12 miles of the city of Bristol,
                   is under the management of a society called the Bristol Itinerant Society,
                   all in connection with the Independent churches of the city. The whole
                   of the agents acting gratuitously.
Dated   31 March 1851
Signed   James M. Humberstone, superintendent
                   1 Fremantle Villa, Nine Tree Hill, Bristol

[The Bristol Itinerant Society provided pastoral support for about 14 Independent chapels that included Knowle (**20.40**), Mangotsfield (**20.29**), Marshfield (**3.24**), Oldland (**20.4**), Rodford (**3.4**) and Wick (**3.19**).]

331.1.2 Parish of Pucklechurch

Area 2,428 acres; 189 inhabited houses, 4 uninhabited. Population 931.

3.5 (4)   **Church of England, St Thomas à Becket, Pucklechurch**

Name   St Thomas. Ancient parish church.
Consecration   Before 1800
Erected   [Windows restored 1846–56 and 1889]
Endowment   {Total £765}
Sittings   Free (including a gallery for the school children and organ loft) 220.
                   Other 180. Total 400
Attend'ce 30 Mar. [Not given]
Avge attendance [Not given]
Remarks   It being considered that only inaccurate and partial information can be
                   obtained by replying to some of the inquiries here instituted, the blanks are
                   not filled in.
Dated   31 March 1851
Signed   Thomas Boucher Coney, vicar [1839–84]
                   Pucklechurch, Bristol

[The benefice consisted of Pucklechurch with Abson, Wick (**3.17–8**) and Westerleigh (**3.1**).]

3.6 (6)   **Independent, Pucklechurch**

Name   Independent Chapel
Erected   1845 [Opened Oct. 1845]
Building   Separate and entire building. Yes [exclusively as a place of worship]
Sittings   Free 100. Other 50. Total 150
Attend'ce 30 Mar. Morning 60 + 40 SS. Total [100]
                   Afternoon 40 SS. Total [40]
                   Evening 110. Total [110]
Avge attendance [Not given]
Dated   30 March 1851

Signed	Joseph Jefferies, deacon [blacksmith]
	Pucklechurch, Bristol

3.7 (5)   **Primitive Methodist, Pucklechurch**

Name	None
Erected	[Rebuilt 1909]
Building	No [not separate and entire] No [not exclusively as a place of worship]
Sittings	Free 40. Total [40]
Attend'ce 30 Mar.	Evening 40. Total 40
Avge attendance	Evening 40. Total 40
Remarks	The congregation is often fifty or more.
Dated	31 March 1851
Signed	Hugh Bennetts, manager [shopkeeper]
	Pucklechurch, Gloucestershire

331.1.3 Parish of Wapley cum Codrington
Area 2,448 acres; 68 inhabited houses. Population 305.

No return   **Church of England, St Peter, Wapley**

[*Erected*	Restored 1862]
[*Endowment*	Total £400]
[*Incumbent*	Charles Richard Ward 1825–58]

331.1.4 Parish of Chipping Sodbury
Area 120 acres; 253 inhabited houses, 22 uninhabited. Population 1,195.

3.8 (7)   **Church of England, St John the Baptist, Chipping Sodbury**

Name	St John the Baptist. Anciently a chapel of ease to Old Sodbury
	In 1822 under the Bounty Act was created a separate district under a
	perpetual curate [and it remained a chapel of ease until 1856]
Consecration	Before 1800
Erected	[Restored 1868–9]
Endowment	OPE £85. Dues and Easter offerings £15. Other £30. {Total £126}
Sittings	Free 30. Other 622. Total 652
Attend'ce 30 Mar.	Morning 96 + 91 SS. Total 187
	Afternoon 186 + 95 SS. Total 281
	Evening 90. Total 90
Avge attendance	Morning 130 + 100 SS. Total 230
	Afternoon 226 + 100 SS. Total 326
	Evening 100. Total 100
Remarks	Unusually small
Dated	31 March 1851
Signed	Thomas Smith, perpetual curate [1822–]
	Chipping Sodbury, Chippenham.
Counter-signed	James George Edward Hasluck, curate [1847–51]

[Hasluck was about to become the incumbent of Little Sodbury (**3.33**).]

3.9 (8)   **Baptist, Hounds Road**

Name	Baptist Chapel
Erected	Before 1800 [1735. Tablet: 'Rebuilt 1819'. New chapel in High Street, 1886]
Building	Yes [separate and entire] Yes [exclusively as a place of worship]
Sittings	Free 150. Other 150. Total [300]

Attend'ce 30 Mar.	Morning 100 + 50 SS. Total 150
	Evening 160. Total 160
Avge attendance	Morning 120 + 50 SS. Total 170
	Evening 200. Total 200
Dated	31 March 1851
Signed	Francis Hammond Roleston, minister [1850–69]
	Chipping Sodbury, Gloucestershire

3.10 (9)   **Roman Catholic, St Lawrence, Chipping Sodbury**

Name	Catholic Chapel
Erected	1836
Building	Yes [separate and entire] Yes [exclusively as a place of worship]
Sittings	Partly free for 120 persons
Attend'ce 30 Mar.	Morning 35. Total [35]
	Afternoon 30. Total [30]
Avge attend'ce (6m)	Morning 30. Total [30]
	Afternoon 30. Total [30]
Remarks	The number of Catholics in this and six other adjacent villages amounts to 110.
Dated	31 March 1851
Signed	Ralph Maurus Cooper, Catholic clergyman [1846–69]
	[Broad Street], Chipping Sodbury, Gloucestershire

[The presbytery was originally the Swan Inn; the chapel in the courtyard had been the stables and brewhouse. In 1858, 68 Roman Catholic families lived the area, 12 of them in Chipping Sodbury.]

3.11 (10)   **Society of Friends, Brook Street**

Name	Brook Street, Chipping Sodbury
Erected	Before 1800 [Dated 1692, enlarged 1892]
Building	Yes [separate and entire] Yes [exclusively as a place of worship]
Floor area	512 square feet
Sittings	Free 120. Total [120]
Attend'ce 30 Mar.	Morning 3. Total [3]
Dated	31 day of the 3rd month 1851
Signed	William Strange
	Yate, Gloucestershire

331.1.5 Parish of Old Sodbury

Area 3,637 acres; 161 inhabited houses, 2 uninhabited. Population 820.

3.12 (11)   **Church of England, St John the Baptist, Old Sodbury**

Name	The parish church of 'Old Sodbury'
Consecration	Before AD 1800
Erected	[Restored 1857–9]
Endowment	The benefice is a vicarage. Tithe vicarial or commutation, rent charge. {Total £490}
Sittings	Free about 120. Other about 280. Total about 400
Attend'ce 30 Mar.	Morning 60 + 50 SS. Total about 110
	Afternoon 100 + 50 SS. Total about 150
Avge attendance	[Not given]
Dated	31 March 1851
Signed	James Cadwallader, officiating minister [1851–2 (at Chipping Sodbury (**3.8**) 1852–3), 1853–6]

Old Sodbury, Wotton-under-Edge
[*Incumbent*   Robert Napier Raikes 1837–51 (died 22 March 1851)]
[Raikes had also been the incumbent of Longhope (**6.40**).]

3.13 (12)   **Baptist, Old Sodbury**

Denomination	Baptist with open communion
Name	Old Sodbury Chapel [Tyndale Baptist Chapel]
Erected	1835
Building	Yes [separate and entire] Yes [exclusively as a place of worship]
Sittings	Free 126. Other 24. Total [150] Standing room none but the aisles
Attend'ce 30 Mar.	Morning 20 + 40 teachers. Total 60
	Evening 60 + 8 teachers. Total 68
Avge attendance	Morning 18 + 35 teachers. Total 53
	Evening 70 + 7 teachers. Total 77
Remarks	The doctrines inculcated at this little chapel is Christ the only hope of salvation, and the children are instructed in the holy scriptures.
Dated	30 March 1851
Signed	George Smith, deacon [farmer]
	Old Sodbury

331.1.6 Parish of Dodington

Area 1,473 acres; 22 inhabited houses, 1 uninhabited. Population 135.

3.14 (13)   **Church of England, St Mary, Dodington**

Name	I know of no distinctive name belonging to the parish church of Dodington. It is the church of a distinct and separate parish. The old church was dedicated to St Mary.
Consecration	5 Decr 1805, in lieu of a previously existing church
Erected	[Rebuilt 1800–5 and connected to Dodington Park]
Endowment	Tithe commuted at £24 5s. Glebe £35. Fees under 10s. {Total £199}
Sittings	Free about 90. Other about 62. Total 152
Attend'ce 30 Mar.	Morning 31 + 29 SS. Total 60
	Afternoon 44 + 26 SS. Total 70
Avge attendance	[Not given]
Remarks	I consider the number of persons attending divine service on Sunday, 30 March 1851, to be about 10 or 12 below the usual average. Perhaps the deficiency may be attributed to the communication being made on mid-Lent Sunday, on which day family visiting generally obtains.
Dated	31 March 1851
Signed	Francis Drake Foster, rector [1827–72]
	Dodington, Chippenham

331.2   MARSHFIELD SUB-DISTRICT

331.2.1 Parish of Dyrham and Hinton

Area 3,005 acres; 96 inhabited houses, 3 uninhabited. Population 474.

3.15 (14)   **Church of England, St Peter, Dyrham**

Name	St Peter's. An ancient parish church
Consecration	Before 1800
Erected	[Restored 1877–8]
Endowment	Tithe £530. Glebe £100. Fees about £1. {Total £501}
Sittings	Free 83. Other 123. Total 206

Attend'ce 30 Mar. Morning 64 + 36 SS. Total 100
Afternoon 84 + 35 SS. Total 119
Avge attendance [Not given]
Remarks The tithe is commuted under the late Act. [An Act for the commutation of tithes in England and Wales, 6 & 7, Will. IV, c.71 (1836)]
Dated 31 March 1851
Signed William Scott Robinson, rector [1828–75]
'Dirham' rectory, Cross Hands, near Chippenham
[Robinson, the fourth son of Sir George Abercrombie Robinson (a director of the East India Company 1808–29, MP 1812–8), was also the incumbent of Farleigh Hungerford, Som. 1832–75. The church adjoins Dyrham Park House and is now under the care of the National Trust.]

3.16 (15)   Independent, Dyrham
Name Tabernacle. Wooden Chapel
Erected 1847
Building Yes separate [and entire] Yes [exclusively as a place of worship]
Sittings Free 100. Total [100] All free sittings
Attend'ce 30 Mar. Morning 40. Total [40]
Afternoon 30 SS. Total [30]
Evening 80. Total [80]
Avge attendance [Not given]
Dated 31 March 1851
Signed William Anstel, Sunday school teacher [grocer]
Hinton

331.2.2 Parish of Abson and Wick
Area 2,315 acres; 179 inhabited houses, 4 uninhabited. Population 826.
The parish includes the villages of Holbrook and Bridge Gate.

3.17 (16)   Church of England, St James the Great, Abson
Name Abson parish church
Consecration [Not given]
Erected [Restored 1873–4 and 1900–1]
Endowment [See Pucklechurch (**3.5**)]
Sittings Total 270.
Attend'ce 30 Mar. [Not given]
Avge attendance [Not given]
Remarks It being considered that only partial and incorrect information can be obtained by replying to the queries in this form, the blanks are not filled in.
Dated 4 April 1851
Signed Thomas Coney, curate of Wick and Abson [1850–56]
Pucklechurch vicarage, Bristol
[*Incumbent* Thomas Boucher Coney 1839–84]
[The benefice consisted of Pucklechurch (**3.5**) with Abson, Wick (**3.18**) and Westerleigh (**3.1**).]

3.18 (17)   Church of England, St Bartholomew, Wick
Name Wick chapel of ease. St Bartholomew
Consecration The parish church of Abson being at so great a distance from the bulk of the population a new church was needed. [Consecrated 3 Apr.1850]
Erected By voluntary contributions and by a private benefaction
Endowment [See Pucklechurch (**3.5**)]
Sittings Total 320. Almost all are free sittings. Total [320]

Attend'ce 30 Mar. [Not given]
Avge attendance [Not given]
Remarks It being considered that only very partial and incorrect information can possibly be obtained by replying to the other questions in this form, the blanks are not filled in
Dated 4 April 1851
Signed Thomas Coney, curate of Wick and Abson [1850–6]
Pucklechurch vicarage, Bristol
[*Incumbent* Thomas Boucher Coney 1839–84]
[The benefice consisted of Pucklechurch (**3.5**) with Abson (**3.17**), Wick and Westerleigh (**3.1**).]

3.19 (18)   Independent, Wick
Name Wick Tabernacle
Erected 1837 [Tablet: 'Wick Tabernacle 1837']
Building Yes [separate and entire] Yes [exclusively as a place of worship]
Sittings Free 117. Other 42. Total [159]
Attend'ce 30 Mar. Morning 18 + 14 SS. Total 32
Evening 110. Total 110
Avge attendance Morning 40 + 22 SS. Total 62
Evening 140. Total 140
Remarks This place of worship is under the care of the 'Bristol Itinerant Society', a society connected with the Independent churches of Bristol from which its teachers and preachers are supplied, all of whom labour gratuitously. The individual expenses are defrayed by voluntary contributions. The congregation is liable to fluctuations from various causes. On the Sunday of this date a funeral in the morning in the village drew away several.
Dated 30 March 1851
Signed William Spencer, minister (for the day)
30 North Street, Bristol
[The Bristol Itinerant Society provided pastoral support for about 14 Independent chapels, including Knowle (**20.40**), Mangotsfield (**20.29**), Marshfield (**3.24**), Oldland (**20.4**), Rodford (**3.4**) and Wick.]

3.20a (20)   Wesleyan Methodist, Bridgegate, Wick
Name Ebenezer
Erected 1810
Building Separate and entire. Yes [exclusively as a place of worship]
Sittings Free 170. Other 70. Total 240
Attend'ce 30 Mar. [Not given]
Avge attendance Afternoon 100. Total 100
Dated 31 March 1851
Signed James Meadmore, minister [1850–1]
Downend, nr Bristol
[Meadmore was also the minister of Downend (**20.31**), Iron Acton (**3.53**), Mangotsfield (**20.32**), Oldland (**20.15**), and Rangeworthy (**4.31**).]

3.20b (19)   Wesleyan Methodist, Bridgegate, Wick
Name Ebenezer
Erected 1810
Building Yes [separate and entire] Yes [exclusively as a place of worship]
Sittings Free 200. Other 50. Total [250]
Attend'ce 30 Mar. Afternoon no service
Avge attendance Afternoon 150. Total 150

Dated   1 April 1851
Signed   William Truebody, steward [shoemaker]
                     Bridgegate

331.2.3 Parish of Doynton
Area 1,703 acres; 91 inhabited houses, 2 uninhabited. Population 499.

3.21 (21)   Church of England, Holy Trinity, Doynton
Name   The church of the Holy Trinity. An ancient parish church
Consecration   Before 1800
Erected   [Nave rebuilt 1865–6 and chancel rebuilt 1893]
Endowment   Land none. Tithe £340. Glebe £140. OPE none. Pew rents none.
                     Fees £2. Dues, Easter offerings, other sources none. {Total £433}
Sittings   Free 48 (and a gallery) 40. Other 270. Total 358
Attend'ce 30 Mar. Morning 200 + 80 SS. Total 280
                     Afternoon 230 + 78 SS. Total 308
Avge attendance   Morning 210 + 75 SS. Total 285
                     Afternoon 240 + 75 SS. Total 315
Remarks   The tithe is commuted
Dated   30 March 1851
Signed   Lewis Balfour Clutterbuck, rector [1847–71]
                     Doynton rectory, Bath
[Though from a wealthy background, Clutterbuck was declared bankrupt. He had to resign the living in 1871 and died the following year.]

331.2.4 Parish of Cold Ashton
Area 2,300 acres; 93 inhabited houses, 4 uninhabited. Population 479.
The parish includes the village of Pennsylvania.

3.22 (22)   Church of England, Holy Trinity, Cold Ashton
Name   Ancient parish church
Consecration   Before 1800
Erected   [Restored 1894]
Endowment   Tithe £470. Glebe £200. Total £670. {Total £492}
Sittings   Free 132. Other 80. Total 212
Attend'ce 30 Mar. Morning 45 + 26 SS. Total 71
                     Afternoon 103 + 18 SS. Total 121
Avge attendance   [Not given]
Remarks   Having no Sunday school, it is to be understood that the Sunday scholars
                     belong to the parish school.
Dated   31 March 1851
Signed   Edward Sayres, rector [1851–88]
                     Cold Ashton, Marshfield

331.2.5 Parish of Marshfield
Area 5,845 acres; 365 inhabited houses, 12 uninhabited. Population 1,846.
The parish includes the villages of Becks, Rocks and Weston Town.

3.23 (23)   Church of England, St Mary the Virgin, Marshfield
Name   Parish church. Dedicated to St Mary. None other
Consecration   [Not given]
Erected   [Restored 1859–60 and 1902–3]
Endowment   Must be answered by the vicar. {Total £409}

Sittings   Free 200. Other 600. Total [800]
                      Accommodation might be given to all the parish by re-pewing the church.
Attend'ce 30 Mar.   Morning 300 + 120 SS. Total [420]
                      Afternoon 500 + 120 SS. Total [620]
Avge attendance   This I cannot answer. T. J. R.
Remarks   The accommodation for [the] poor exceedingly limited. At this time
                      the attendance is below the average number in consequence of much
                      sicknesss in the place.
Dated   31 March 1851
Signed   Thomas James Robinson, curate [1850–2]
                      The vicarage, Marshfield
[Incumbent   George Sherer 1822–58]

3.24 (24)   **Independent, High Street**
Name   Independent Chapel
Erected   [Founded 1799] 1847
Building   Yes [separate and entire] Yes [exclusively as a place of worship]
Sittings   Free 200. Other 200. Total [400] Standing room not any
Attend'ce 30 Mar.   Morning 100 + 90 SS. Total 190
                      Evening 250. Total [250]
Avge attendance   Morning 150 + 105 SS. Total 255
                      Afternoon 105 SS. Total 105
                      Evening 350. Total 350
Remarks   We are supplied by the Bristol Itinerant Society.
Dated   31 March 1851
Signed   James Bond, deacon [linen and wool draper]
                      Marshfield, Gloucestershire

[The Bristol Itinerant Society provided pastoral support for about 14 Independent chapels including Knowle (**20.40**), Mangotsfield (**20.29**), Marshfield, Oldland (**20.4**), Rodford (**3.4**) and Wick (**3.19**).]

3.25 (27)   **Primitive Methodist, High Street**
Name   Primitive Methodist Chapel
Erected   Before 1800
Building   Yes [separate and entire] Yes [exclusively as a place of worship]
Sittings   Free 84. Other 36. Total [100]
Attend'ce 30 Mar.   Afternoon 45. Total [45]
                      Evening 83. Total [83]
                      Total [for the day] 128
Avge attendance   120.
Dated   30 March 1851
Signed   Martin Palmer, local preacher [agricultural labourer]
                      [Main Street], Marshfield, Gloucestershire

3.26 (26)   **Non-denominational, Marshfield**
Name   None
Erected   [Not given]
Building   Yes [separate and entire] Yes [exclusively as a place of worship]
Sittings   Free 20. Total [20]
Attend'ce 30 Mar.   Morning 3. Total [3]
                      Afternoon 13. [Total 13]
                      Evening 16. Total [16]

Avge attendance	[Not given]
Dated	31 March 1851
Signed	John Jones, cordwainer [shoemaker]
	Marshfield, Glou're

3.27 (25) **Unitarian, High Street**

Name	Presbyterian Chapel [Old Meeting House]
Erected	[1699] 1751 [Foundation stone: 16 Oct. 1752; tablet: 1752]
Building	Separate and entire. Exclusively for divine worship
Sittings	All free 25. Other [125] Total [150]
Attend'ce 30 Mar.	Afternoon 20. Total 20
Avge attendance	Afternoon 20. Total 20
Remarks	The chapel will hold 150 persons.
Dated	30 March 1851
Signed	James Jeffrey, minister
	15 Grange Grove, Bath, Somerset

[William Hazlitt, minister of the chapel 1765–70, was the father of the essayist: *ODNB* 'William Hazlitt (1778–1830)'.]

331.2.6 Parish of West Littleton

Area 1,009 acres; 23 inhabited houses, 1 uninhabited. Population 161.

3.28 (28) **Church of England, St James, West Littleton**

Name	1. Parish church of West Littleton
	2. Church of an ancient chapelry
Consecration	Before 1800
Erected	[Mostly rebuilt 1855–6]
Endowment	Tithe £220 [See Tormarton (**3.29**)]
Sittings	Free 50. Other 36. Total 86
Attend'ce 30 Mar.	Morning 33 + 24 SS. Total 57
	Afternoon 58 + 24 SS. Total 82
Avge attendance	About the same
Dated	31 March 1851
Signed	Francis William Fowler, curate [1849–53]
	West Littleton, Marshfield, Chippenham
[*Incumbent*	James Stuart Murray Anderson 1851–69]

[Anderson was a chaplain to the queen 1836, and preacher at Lincoln's Inn 1844–58. The benefice consisted of Tormarton (**3.29**) with Acton Turville (**3.30**) and West Littleton.]

331.3 HAWKESBURY SUB-DISTRICT

331.3.1 Parish of Tormarton

Area 2,645 acres; 93 inhabited houses, 4 uninhabited. Population 463.

3.29 (29) **Church of England, St Mary Magdalene, Tormarton**

Name	St Mary's, Tormarton. Old parish church
Consecration	[Not given]
Erected	[Restored 1853–4]
Endowment	* {Total £800}
Sittings	Free 93. Other 85. Total 178
Attend'ce 30 Mar.	Morning 72 + 64 SS. Total 136
	Afternoon 118 + 58 SS. Total 176
Avge attendance	**[Not given]

Remarks   * As curate, I am not able to give definite information about the endowment.
                   ** The average attendance in summer is larger.
Dated   31 March 1851
Signed   Hugh Hinleath, curate [1847–]
                   Tormarton rectory, Chippenham
[*Incumbent*   James Stuart Murray Anderson 1851–69]
[On Anderson, see note at **3.28** above.]

331.3.2 Parish of Acton Turville
Area 1,009 acres; 70 inhabited houses, 2 uninhabited. Population 323.

3.30 (30)   **Church of England, St Mary, Acton Turville**
Name   Acton Turville parish church
Consecration   Before 1800
Erected   [Restored 1853 and 1912]
Endowment   Land £30. Tithe £50. Glebe £9 [See Tormarton (**3.29**)]
Sittings   Free 60. Other 45. Total 105
Attend'ce 30 Mar.   Morning 46 + 25 SS. Total 71
                       Afternoon 78 + 28 SS. Total 116
Avge attendance   Morning 50 + 30 SS. Total 80
                       Afternoon 100 + 30 SS. Total 130
Dated   31 March 1851
Signed   Nicholas Howard MacGachen, curate [1849–]
                       Acton Turville, Chippenham, Wiltshire
[*Incumbent*   James Stuart Murray Anderson 1851–69]
[On Anderson, see note at **3.28** above.]

3.31 (31)   **Baptist, Luckington Road**
Name   Ebenezer
Erected   1838
Building   Yes [separate and entire] Yes [exclusively as a place of worship]
Sittings   ~~Free 80. Other 40~~ Free 8. Other 10. Standing room for 30.
Attend'ce 30 Mar.   Morning 57. Total [57]
                       Evening 62. Total [62]
Avge attendance   Morning 70. Total [70]
Dated   30 March 1851
Signed   William Cam, deacon [boot and shoemaker]
                       Acton Turville, Chippenham

331.3.3 Parish of Great Badminton [part transferred to Gloucestershire, 1844]
Area 1,735 acres; 108 inhabited houses, 1 uninhabited. Population 521.

3.32 (32)   **Church of England, St Michael and All Angels, Great Badminton**
(Summary form)
Name   St Michael
Erected   About 60 years ago [Rebuilt 1783–5 and replaced a nearby medieval
                       church; chancel and apse added 1874–5]
[*Endowment*   Total £30]
Sittings   Free 150. Other 260. Total 410
Usual attend'ce   Morning about 100 + about 60 SS. Total [160]
                       Afternoon about 80 + about 60 SS. Total [140]
                       Evening no service

Signed   Ebenezer Bletchley, registrar
[Incumbent   Joseph Buckley 1840–80]

331.3.4 Parish of Little Sodbury
Area 1,071 acres; 28 inhabited houses, 1 uninhabited. Population 128.

3.33 (33)	**Church of England, St Adeline, Little Sodbury**
Name	St Adeline's. Ancient parish church
Consecration	Before 1800 [20 July 1859]
Erected	[Rebuilt 1859]
Endowment	[Tithe £200. Glebe 30 acres] [Total] about £240 net {Total £235}
Sittings	Free 68. Other 65. Total 133
	An equal proportion more than ample for the parishioners
Attend'ce 30 Mar.	Morning 16. Total [16]
	Afternoon 16. Total [16]
Avge attendance	Morning 16 + 10 SS. Total 26
	Afternoon 25 + 10 SS. Total 35
Remarks	Having only recently been presented to this living and not yet resident I am unable to afford more accurate information.
Dated	31 March 1851
Signed	James George Edward Hasluck, rector [1851–1901]
	Chipping Sodbury, Chippenham

[Hasluck had previously been curate of Chipping Sodbury (**3.8**). Little Sodbury is the only parish church in England dedicated to St Adeline.]

331.3.5 Parish of Horton
Area 3,540 acres; 99 inhabited houses, 2 uninhabited. Population 461.

3.34 (34)	**Church of England, St James the Elder, Horton**
Name	The parish church. St James
Consecration	Before 1800
Erected	[Restored 1864–5]
Endowment	Tithe £600. Glebe £50. Fees £1. {Total £657}
Sittings	Total 200 (appropriated to respective houses)
Attend'ce 30 Mar.	Morning 40 + 15 SS. Total [55]
	Afternoon 60 + 15 SS. Total [75]
Avge attendance	Morning 30 + 30 SS. Total [60]
	Afternoon 70 + 30 SS. Total [100]
Dated	30 March 1851
Signed	John Blackburn, rector [1848–94]
	Wotton-under-Edge, Gloucestershire

331.3.6–11 Parish of Hawkesbury
Area 9,770 acres; 477 inhabited houses, 19 uninhabited. Population 2,185.
The parish includes the tithings of Hawkesbury, Little Badminton, Upton, Saddlewood with Tresham and Killcott, and Hillesley.

3.35 (35)	**Church of England, St Mary the Virgin, Hawkesbury**
Name	Hawkesbury Church. An ancient parish church
Consecration	Before 1800
Erected	[Restored 1882–5]
Endowment	Tithe £350. Glebe £5. Fees £5. {Total £300}
Sittings	Free 220. Children's sittings 60. Total 280

Attend'ce 30 Mar.	Morning 104 + 21 SS. Total 125
	Afternoon no service
Avge attendance	[Not given]
Remarks	No afternoon service because the vicar has to perform a service at Tresham chapel (**3.36**) and a service at Hawkesbury National Schools (**3.37**).
Dated	30 March 1851
Signed	William Henry Boothby, vicar [1849–92]
	Hawkesbury, Wotton-under-Edge, Gloucestershire

[The benefice consisted of Hawkesbury with Tresham (**3.36**) and Hillesley. St Giles, Hillesley replaced an earlier dilapidated chapel and was consecrated 27 Nov. 1851. The chapel of ease, St Michael and All Angels, Little Badminton, was demolished 1750. *GNQ* 3, 181–3; 5, 189, 499–501.]

3.36 (42)   Church of England (no dedication), **Tresham**

Name	Chapel of ease to Hawkesbury
Consecration	Before 1800
Erected	[Rebuilt 1854–5; restored 1908]
Endowment	[See Hawkesbury (**3.35**)]
Sittings	Free 80. Total 80
Attend'ce 30 Mar.	Afternoon 25 + 18 SS. Total 43
Avge attendance	[Not given]
Dated	30 March 1851
Signed	William Henry Boothby, vicar [1849–92]
	Hawkesbury, Wotton-under-Edge, Gloucestershire

3.37 (38)   Church of England, National School, Hawkesbury Upton

Name	Hawkesbury National School
Licensed	November 1850 in consequence of a petition to the bishop from the vicar, churchwardens etc.
Erected	[1845–6] by subscriptions and parliamentary grant
	Total cost about £700
Sittings	Free 200. Total 200
Attend'ce 30 Mar.	Evening 141. Total 141
Avge attendance	[Not given]
Dated	30 March 1851
Signed	William Henry Boothby, vicar [1849–92]
	Hawkesbury, Wotton-under-Edge, Gloucestershire

3.38 (39)   Independent, Hawkesbury Upton

Name	Bethesda Chapel
Erected	1845 [1844]
Building	Yes [separate and entire] Yes [exclusively as a place of worship]
Sittings	Free 160. Other 40. Total [200]
Attend'ce 30 Mar.	[Not given]
Avge attendance	[Not given]
Dated	31 March 1851
Signed	Ebenezer Bletchley, deacon [surgeon]
	Hawkesbury, Wotton-under-Edge, Gloucestershire

3.39 (36)   Baptist, Hillesley

Name	Baptist Chapel
Erected	Before 1800 [1730, rebuilt 1823]
Building	A separate and entire building. Used exclusively as a place of worship

Sittings   Free 150. Other 300. Total [450] Standing room none.
Attend'ce 30 Mar. Morning 120 + 60 SS. Total 180
                     Afternoon 150 + 70 SS. Total 220
                     Evening 80 (SS none). Total 80
Avge attendance   About the same as above
Dated   31 March 1851
Signed   George Smith, minister
                     Hillesley, near Wotton-under-Edge, Gloucestershire
[During the ministry of William Hitchman 1764–1802 there was some association with the Seventh Day Baptists. For that denomination see Norton Chapel (**17.29**).]

3.40 (41)   Particular Baptist, Hawkesbury Upton

Name   Calvinistic Particular Baptist Chapel
Erected   1828
Building   Separate building. Exclusively for a place of worship
Sittings   Free 122. Other 65. Total [187]
Attend'ce 30 Mar. Morning 52 + 14 SS. Total [66]
                     Evening 94. Total [94]
Avge attendance   [Not given]
Dated   31 March 1851
Signed   John Osborne, minister [schoolmaster]
                     Hawkesbury Upton, Gloucestershire

3.41 (37)   Wesleyan Methodist, Hawkesbury

Name   Wesleyan Chapel
Erected   1836
Building   Yes [separate and entire] Yes [exclusively as a place of worship]
Sittings   Free 86. Total [86]
Attend'ce 30 Mar. Morning 36. Total [36]
                     Evening 12. Total [12]
Avge attendance   [Not given]
Dated   31 March 1851
Signed   Thomas Limbrick, enumerator [farmer]
                     [Lower] Chalkley [Farm], Hawkesbury Upton, Wotton-under-Edge

3.42 (40)   Primitive Methodist, Hawkesbury Upton

Name   None
Erected   Before 1800 [Later chapel dated 1860]
Building   Yes [separate and entire] Yes [exclusively as a place of worship]
Sittings   Free 60. Other 60. Total [120] Standing room none
Attend'ce 30 Mar. Afternoon 87. Total [87]
                     Evening 78. Total [78]
Avge attendance   Afternoon 100. Total [100]
                     Evening 90. Total [90]
Remarks   The above building was erected before the year 1800 but was not used
                     for Christian worship till the year 1843.
Dated   31 March 1851
Signed   Daniel Mossop, minister
                     Hawkesbury Upton, Gloucestershire
[In the 1851 Civil Census Mossop is described as a Wesleyan minister.]

331.3.12   Parish of Alderley

Area 898 acres; 27 inhabited houses, 4 uninhabited. Population 145.

3.43 (43)   **Church of England, St Kenelm, Alderley**

Name	Saint Kenelm
Consecration	Body of the church rebuilt about 1803. Original church built about 1458. Tower standing.
Erected	Private benefaction [Restored 1905–6]
Endowment	Tithe £160. Glebe £45. {Total £200}
Sittings	Free 40. Other 140. Total 180
Attend'ce 30 Mar.	[Not given]
Avge attendance	[Not given]
Remarks	The church has accommodation for more than the population of the parish. Always good congregations. Sunday and day schools supported by private individuals, and always well attended.
Dated	31 March 1851
Signed	Martin Henry Whish, rector [1847–1904] Alderley, Wotton-under-Edge

[Whish was the son of Martin Richard Whish, the incumbent of St John, Bedminster (**20.37**) with St Mary, Redcliffe (**1.12**), St Thomas (**1.20**) and Abbots Leigh.]

331.4   IRON ACTON SUB-DISTRICT

331.4.1 Parish of Wickwar

Area 2,307 acres; 214 inhabited houses, 14 uninhabited. Population 966.
In 1841 the population was 1,125, including labourers on the Gloucester and Bristol railway.

3.44 (44)   **Church of England, Holy Trinity, Wickwar**

Name	Wickwar parish church
Consecration	Before the year 1800, I believe
Erected	[Restored 1749 and 1880–1]
Endowment	{Total £392}
Sittings	Free 160. Other 276. Total 436
Attend'ce 30 Mar.	Morning 121 + 88 SS. Total 209 Afternoon 190 + 89 SS. Total 279
Avge attendance	Morning from 150 to 160. Total 150–160] Afternoon from 150 to 230. Total [150–160]
Remarks	I have not filled up [the question on endowment] having received permission from the Registrar General to withdraw it, as this [is] not easy to understand whether the net or gross income is meant, and ... no information of any value could believe, in consequence of the fluctuation in the ...
Dated	30 March 1851
Signed	Thomas Roupell Everest, rector [1830–55] Wickwar, Gloucestershire

[Everest (1801–55) was a pioneer in the homeopathic movement and had interests in mesmerism, hypnosis and clairvoyance. He was a victim of influenza and had lived in Poissy, France 1837–47; during his absence the parish was served by curates.]

3.45 (45)   **Independent, High Street**

Name	Independent Chapel [Lowder Chapel]
Erected	1815 [Tablet: 'Built 1817 restored 1919']
Building	Separate and entire. Exclusively [as a place of worship]

332.1.2–7 Parish of Almondsbury
Area 6,927 acres; 345 inhabited houses, 16 uninhabited. Population 6,770.
The parish includes the tithings of Almondsbury, Gaunts-Earthcott, Lea, Hempton and
Patchway, Over, and Lower Tockington.

4.4 (7)	**Church of England, St Mary the Virgin, Almondsbury**
Name	St Mary, Almondsbury, Thornbury
Consecration	Before 1800
Erected	[Alterations 1814–6; remodelled 1836–7]
Endowment	Land none. Tithe none for parish at present. Glebe and OPE none. Pew rents none. Fees £5. {Total £523}
Sittings	Free about 550. Total 550
Attend'ce 30 Mar.	Morning about 120. Total [120] } Depends on Afternoon about 130. Total [130] } weather and roads.
Avge attendance	[Not given]
Remarks	The parish is very scattered and it is impossible to state with any degree of accuracy the average number of the congregation. The services too are during the rest of the year increased in number, besides daily services during Lent.
Dated	31 March 1851
Signed	Henry Gray, clergyman [1831–64] Almondsbury, Bristol

[Gray was the son of Robert Gray, bishop of Bristol 1827–34, and the brother of Robert Gray, first
bishop of Cape Town 1847–72: *ODNB* 'Robert Gray (1809–1872)'. Leech 2004, 270–4. Within the
parish St Peter, Pilning was consecrated 9 Aug. 1855.]

4.5 (6)	**Wesleyan Methodist, Almondsbury**
Name	Almondsbury Chapel
Erected	About 1810
Building	Yes [separate and entire] Yes [exclusively as a place of worship]
Sittings	Free 160. Other 40. Total [200]
Attend'ce 30 Mar.	Morning 60 + 20 SS. Total 80 Afternoon 29 SS. Total 29 Evening 150. Total 150
Avge attendance	[Not given]
Dated	31 March 1851
Signed	William Powell, minister [1850–2] Thornbury, nr Bristol, Gloucestershire

[Powell was also the minister of Alveston (**4.2**), Littleton-on-Severn, (**4.18**), Milbury Heath (**4.32**),
Oldbury-on-Severn (**4.30**), Olveston (**4.8**) and Thornbury (**4.29**).]

4.6 (10)	**Methodist Reformers, Patchway**
Name	None
Erected	[Not given]
Building	Part of a common dwelling house. No [not exclusively a place of worship]
Sittings	Free 35. Total [35]
Attend'ce 30 Mar.	Evening 30. Total 30
Avge attendance (6m)	Evening 30. Total 30
Remarks	The meeting house referred to, has been established for a short time, in consequence of the division with Wesleyan body.
Dated	1 April 1851
Signed	George Hunt, in whose house the meeting is held [agricultural labourer] Patchway, Almondsbury, Bristol

332.1.8–9 Parish of Olveston
Area 4,787 acres; 344 inhabited houses, 17 uninhabited. Population 1,669.
The parish includes the tithings of Upper Tockington, Olveston and Cote.

4.7 (8)	**Church of England, St Mary the Virgin, Olveston**
(Summary form)	
Dedication	St Mary's
Erected	About 1400 or thereabouts [Enlarged and chancel rebuilt 1840–1; restored 1888–9]
[*Endowment*	Total £799]
Sittings	Free and other 760 persons. Total [760]
Avge attendance	Average about 500. Average about 80 SS. Total [about 580] Morning 11 o'clock. Afternoon 3 o'clock
Dated	[Not given]
Signed	James Addis, parish clerk, Olveston
[*Incumbent*	Henry Harvey 1850–5]

4.8a (40) (332.2.9)	**Wesleyan Methodist, Olveston**
Name	Olveston Chapel
Erected	1820
Building	Yes [separate and entire] Yes [exclusively as a place of worship]
Sittings	Free 240. Other 60. Total [300]
Attend'ce 30 Mar.	Morning 40 + 50 SS. Total 90
	Afternoon 90 SS. Total 90
	Evening 140. Total 140
Avge attendance	[Not given]
Dated	31 March 1851
Signed	William Powell, minister 1850–2]
	Thornbury nr Bristol, Gloucestershire

[Powell was also the minister of Almondsbury (**4.5**), Alveston (**4.2**), Littleton-on-Severn (**4.18**), Milbury Heath (**4.32**), Oldbury-on-Severn (**4.30**) and Thornbury (**4.29**).]

4.8b (2)	**Wesleyan Methodist, Olveston**
Name	Olveston Chapel
Erected	Date 1820 on the front of building
Building	Yes [separate and entire] Yes [exclusively as a place of worship]
Sittings	Free 100. Other 60. Total 160. Standing room about 40
Attend'ce 30 Mar.	[Not given]
Avge attendance	[Not given]
Remarks	The steward of the above place of worship refuses to give any returns for the following reason, that the returns will be given by Wm Powell, Wesleyan minister, Thornbury, direct to London. Steward's address. Daniel Sage, Olverston, nr Bristol
Dated	[Not given]
Signed	Henry James Dodd, enumerator of district [shopkeeper] Olveston, nr Bristol

['Wesleyan chapel return refused since particular interest by enumerator': Census return]

4.9 (11)	**Wesleyan Methodist, Cross Hands**
Name	Wesleyan 'Chappell'
Erected	1832
Building	[Separate and] entire [building] Yes [exclusively used for worship]

Sittings	Free 125. Total [125] Standing room for 200
Attend'ce 30 Mar.	Morning 40. Total [40]
	Afternoon [100] Total 100
	Evening 60. Total [60]
Avge attendance	Morning 80 + 25 SS. Total 125
Dated	April 1851
Signed	John Hopkins [agricultural labourer]
	[Olveston]

4.10 (14)   **Wesleyan Methodist, Pilning Street**

Name	Ebenezer Chapel
Erected	1850
Building	Yes [separate and entire] Yes [exclusively as a place of worship]
Sittings	Free 100. Other none. Total [100]
Attend'ce 30 Mar.	Morning 20. Total 20
	Afternoon no service
	Evening 28. Total 28
Avge attendance	[Not given]
Remarks	The sittings in this chapel are at present all free but it is intended that a few of them shall be reserved as private sittings and the rent of which to be applied to the use of the chapel for cleaning, etc.
Dated	31 March 1851
Signed	Isaac Sargent one of the trustees [retired farmer]
	Pilning, Olveston, nr Bristol

4.11 (3)   **Wesleyan Reformers, How Lane**

Name	Wesleyan Methodist (Reformers)
Erected	[Not given]
Building	Part of a house. Yes [exclusively used as a place of worship]
Sittings	Will hold about one hundred. All free. Total [100]
Attend'ce 30 Mar.	Morning 30. Total [30]
	Evening 40. Total [40]
	General congregation about 60
Avge attendance	[Not given]
Remarks	[None]
Dated	3 April 1851
Signed	Henry James Dodd, an unpaid preacher (shopkeeper)
	Olveston, nr Bristol

4.12a (12)   **Society of Friends, The Green**

Erected	Before 1800 [1696, repaired 1782]
Building	Yes [separate and entire] Yes [exclusively used for worship]
Sittings	[Ground floor] 1,154 [sq. ft] 215. [Galleries] 465 [sq. ft] 25. Total [240]
Attend'ce 30 Mar.	Morning 22
	Afternoon none
	Evening none
Dated	Second day of the 4th month 1851
Signed	Edward Sturge [landed proprietor; farmer of 65 acres]
	[Chester Green], Olveston, near Bristol

[Sturge was a member of a prominent Quaker family found across Glos., Bristol and Birmingham.]

4.12b (13)   Society of Friends, The Green

(On a nonconformist form)

Name	Friends Meeting House
Erected	Before 1800
Building	Yes [separate and entire] Yes [exclusively as a place of worship]
Sittings	Free 240. Other none. Total [240]
Attend'ce 30 Mar.	Morning 22. Total 22
	Afternoon no meeting
	Evening no meeting
Avge attendance	[Not given]
Remarks	Particulars similar to the adjoining have been inserted by the undersigned in one of the returns specially provided for places of worship belonging to the Society of Friends, and which will be forwarded with similar return to the Central office in London.
Dated	31st day of the 3rd month 1851
Signed	Edward Sturge, appointed to the cure
	[Chester Green,] Olveston, nr Bristol.

332.1.10–1   Parish of Henbury

Area 5,517 acres; 90 inhabited houses, 4 uninhabited. Population 472.
The parish (most of which is in the Westbury sub-district [330.5.4–9]) includes the tithings of Northwick, Redwick and Aust.

[For the parish church of St Mary the Virgin, Henbury see (**2.64**)]

4.13 (15)   Church of England, Northwick Episcopal Chapel

Name	Northwick Episcopal Chapel [St Thomas]
Consecration	1 March 1842, on the site of the old one, erected and consecrated
Erected	By the vicar of Henbury. Architect [John] Hicks of Bristol
Cost	Partly (parochial rate) chiefly (private sources) £800
Endowment	[See Henbury (**2.64**)]
Sittings	Free 270. Other 100. Total 370
Attend'ce 30 Mar.	Morning 28 + 67 SS. Total 95
	Afternoon 62 + 21 SS. Total 83
Avge attendance	Morning 70 + 100 SS. Total 170
	Afternoon 200 + 50 SS. Total 250
Remarks	Attached to Henbury. Morning and afternoon services alternately with Aust
Dated	31 March 1851
Signed	Henry Littlejohn Master Walters, curate
	Aust parsonage, Bristol
[*Incumbent*	Henry Hugh Way 1830–60]

[The benefice consisted of Henbury (**2.64**) with Aust (**4.14**) and Northwick.]

4.14 (17)   Church of England, St John, Aust

Name	Aust Tithing church
Consecration	Before 1800
Erected	[Restored 1865–6]
Endowment	[See Henbury (**2.64**)]
Sittings	Free 50. Other 100. Total 150
Attend'ce 30 Mar.	Afternoon 110. Total 110
Avge attendance	[Not given]

Remarks	Attached as chapelry to Henbury. Morning and afternoon services alternately
Dated	31 March 1851
Signed	Henry Littlejohn Master Walters, curate [1845–]
	Aust parsonage, Bristol
[*Incumbent*	Henry Hugh Way 1830–60]

[The benefice consisted of Henbury (**2.64**) with Aust and Northwick (**4.13**).]

4.15 (16)   Wesleyan Reformers, Redwick

Name	Wesleyan Reform Preaching Room
Erected	[Not given]
Building	No [not separate and entire] Yes [exclusively as a place of worship]
Sittings	Free 100. Total [100]
Attend'ce 30 Mar.	Morning 16 + 14 SS. Total 30
	Afternoon 20 SS. Total 20
	Evening 40 SS. Total 40
Avge attendance (5m)	Morning 27 + 14 SS. Total 41
	Afternoon 20 SS. Total 20
	Evening 90. Total 90
Dated	31 March 1851
Signed	John Norris, manager [grocer]
	Redwick

332.1.12   Parish of Elberton

Area 1,673 acres; 38 inhabited houses. Population 204.

4.16 (18)   Church of England, St John, Elberton

Name	Ancient parish church
Consecration	Before 1800
Erected	[Restored 1857–8 and 1901]
Endowment	Land £175. Tithe (commuted) £204. {Total £226}
Sittings	Free about 103. Other about 64. Total 167
Attend'ce 30 Mar.	Morning 53. Total [53]
	Afternoon 65. Total [65]
Avge attendance	[Not given]
Remarks	The children of this parish attend the National Society and Sunday school of the adjoining parish of Olveston (**4.7**).
Dated	31 March 1851
Signed	John Kynaston Charleton, vicar [1828–72]
	Elberton, Bristol

332.1.13   Parish of Littleton-on-Severn

Area 1,665 acres; 39 inhabited houses. Population 190.

4.17 (19)   Church of England, St Mary of Malmesbury, Littleton-on-Severn

Name	Parish church of Littleton-on-Severn
Consecration	Before 1800
Erected	[Restored 1877–8]
Endowment	Pew rents none. {Total £52}
Sittings	Free 150. Total 150 (sufficient)
Attend'ce 30 Mar.	Evening*
Avge attendance	Evening*
Remarks	Glebe and sundry other small payments: amount variable

*No return can be made with accuracy

Dated 29 March 1851
Signed Joseph Baker, clerk MA, rector [1849–55]
Littleton-on-Severn, near Thornbury

4.18 (20)   Wesleyan Methodist, Littleton-on-Severn

Name Littleton Preaching Place
Erected 1844
Building No [not separate and entire] It is used also for a day school.
Sittings Free 80. Total [80]
Attend'ce 30 Mar. Evening 80. Total 80
Avge attendance [Not given]
Dated 31 March 1851
Signed William Powell, minister [1850–2]
Thornbury nr Bristol, Gloucestershire

[Powell was also the minister of Almondsbury (**4.5**), Alveston (**4.2**), Milbury Heath (**4.32**), Oldbury-on-Severn (**4.30**), Olveston (**4.8**) and Thornbury (**4.29**).]

332.2   THORNBURY SUB-DISTRICT

332.2.1 Parish of Thornbury

Area 15,732 acres; 963 inhabited houses, 57 uninhabited. Population 4,614.
The parish includes the borough of Thornbury (population 1,470) and the tithings of Kington, Oldbury-on-Severn, Falfield and Morton and the chapelry of Rangeworthy. The Union workhouse situated at Kington had 89 inmates.

4.19 (21)   Church of England, St Mary the Virgin, Thornbury

Name St Mary's. Ancient parish church
Consecration [Not given]
Erected [Restored 1848–9]
Endowment {Total £500}
Sittings Free 398. Other 404. Total 802
Attend'ce 30 Mar. Morning 500. Total 500
Evening 500. Total 500
Avge attendance Morning 500. Total 500
Evening 500. Total 500
Dated 31 March 1851
Signed Maurice Fitzgerald Townsend (Stephens), vicar [1823–72]
Thornbury

[The benefice included Thornbury with Falfield (**4.20**) and Oldbury (**4.21**). Joseph Leech attended the Christmas morning service with mayor and corporation present. The vicar preached 'in a distinct and sonorous voice, and with a clearness and correctness of enunciation which must have made the discourse plain and distinct to everyone within the church. He had other advantages, too, which are seldom thrown away, even amongst more Evangelical ministers and hearers – a good head and shoulders, and he stood something like six feet, honest measure, in his shoes. His sermon, whether a holiday one or not, was a good one ... he was exceedingly popular amongst his parishioners': Leech 2004, 209. From Jan. 1827 Townsend adopted Stephens as his surname: Waters, 79–88. *GNQ* 4, 511–2.]

4.20 (31)   Church of England, St George, Falfield

Name Chapel of ease
Consecration [31 July 1860]
Erected [Rebuilt 1859–60]
Endowment [See Thornbury (**4.19**)]

Sittings	Total 70
Attend'ce 30 Mar.	Morning 35. Total 35
	Evening 35. Total 35
Avge attendance	Morning 35. Total 35
	Evening 35. Total 35
Dated	31 March 1851
Signed	Maurice Fitzgerald Townsend (Stephens), vicar [1823–72]
	Thornbury, Gloucestershire

[The benefice included Thornbury (**4.19**) with Falfield and Oldbury (**4.21**).]

4.21 (29)   Church of England, St Arilda, Oldbury-on-Severn

Name	Parochial chapel
Consecrated	[14 September 1899]
Erected	[Restored 1885–6 and rebuilt after a fire, 1898–9]
Endowment	[See Thornbury (**4.19**)]
Sittings	Total 220
Attend'ce 30 Mar.	Morning 120 + 70 SS. Total 190
	Evening 120 + 70 SS. Total 190
Avge attendance	Morning 120 + 70 SS. Total 190
	Evening 120 + 70 SS. Total 190
Dated	31 March 1851
Signed	Maurice Fitzgerald Townsend (Stephens), vicar [1823–72]
	Thornbury, Gloucestershire

[The benefice included Thornbury (**4.19**) with Falfield (**4.31**) and Oldbury. In 1863 Oldbury became a separate parish.]

4.22 (32)   Church of England, Holy Trinity, Rangeworthy

(Summary form)

Name	The Holy Trinity (originally a chapel to Thornbury)
Consecration	[Not given]
Erected	Not known. It has been lately (in the year 1849) restored and enlarged. The original chapel supposed to be from 400 to 600 years old
Endowment	{Total £80}
Sittings	Free about 200. Other some legally but only as a matter of present accommodation. Total 200
Usual attend'ce	Variable and uncertain
	Morning from 20 to 25. Total [20–25]
	Afternoon from 25 to 40 or 50. Total [25–50]
	Evening. There is no evening service.
Remarks	S[unday] S[chool] - none. There being no schoolroom, nor funds for the support of teachers, moreover a very poor parish. No residents to aid in the support of a Sunday school.
Signed	John Champion Hicks, incumbent [1834–55]

[In 1847 Rangeworthy became a separate parish. Hicks was the father of the architect John Hicks (1815–1869) who had practices in Bristol and from c.1850 in Dorchester; he built Northwick Episcopal chapel (**4.13**) and restored 27 churches.]

4.23 (27)   Independent or Congregational, Chapel Street, Thornbury

Name	Formerly a Presbyterian, but now an Independent chapel, sometimes called 'The New Meeting'
Erected	In the year 1826
Building	Yes [separate and entire] Yes [exclusively as a place of worship]

Sittings	Free 200. Other 200. Total [400] Standing room none
Attend'ce 30 Mar.	Morning 60 + 60 SS. Total 120
	Afternoon 100 SS. Total 100
	Evening 150. Total 150
Avge attendance	[Not given]
Remarks	I was from home 30 March 1851, but believe the fore-going statement to be tolerably accurate. I cannot state the average attendance for the last ... months.
Dated	2 April 1851
Signed	James Alsop, minister [1848–51]
	Thornbury, Gloucestershire

4.24 (22)   **Independent, Thornbury**

Name	Crossway Chapel
Erected	1837
Building	Yes [separate and entire] Yes [exclusively as a place of worship]
Sittings	All free. Other none. Total 100. Standing room none
Attend'ce 30 Mar.	Afternoon 40 + 37 SS. Total 77
Avge attendance	[Not given]
Dated	31 March 1851
Signed	George King, manager [agricultural labourer]
	Sibland, nr Thornbury, Gloucestershire

4.25 (24)   **Independent, Falfield**

Name	Mount Pleasant Chapel
Erected	About 1823. Rebuilt in 1843 [Tablet: 'Mount Pleasant Union Church, 1813'. Enlarged 1848]
Building	Separate [and entire] building. Yes [exclusively as a place of worship]
Sittings	Free 205. Other 45. Total [250] Standing room none
Attend'ce 30 Mar.	Morning 90 + 95 SS. Total 185
	Afternoon 110 SS. Total 110
	Evening 140 + 30 SS. Total 170
Avge attendance	[Not given]
Remarks	We have also an evening school for men and lads, and monthly lectures on scientific subjects. The number attending the week evening chapel is about 40.
Dated	31 March 1851
Signed	William Dove, minister [1843–55]
	[Falfield House], Falfield, near Berkeley, Gloucestershire

[Dove, previously minister of Thornbury 1831–43, was also the minister of Tortworth (**4.47**).]

4.26 (34)   **Independent, Rangeworthy**

Name	Bethel Chapel
Erected	Before 1800 [1726]
Building	Yes [separate and entire] Yes [exclusively as a place of worship]
Sittings	Free 170. Other 80. Total [250]
Attend'ce 30 Mar.	Morning 44 + 31 SS. Total 75
	Afternoon 43 SS. Total 43
	Evening 60. Total 60
Avge attendance	Morning 50 + 30 SS. Total 80
	Afternoon 48 SS. Total 48
	Evening 110. Total 110

Dated	31 March 1851
Signed	John Brain Taylor, minister [1851–3]
	Rangeworthy, Glo'shire

4.27 (26)   **Baptist, Gillingstool, Thornbury**

Name	Baptist Chapel
Erected	About 1790 [1789, enlarged 1806 and 1834]
Building	Separate and entire. Yes [exclusively as a place of worship]
Sittings	Free 100. Other 200. Total [300]
Attend'ce 30 Mar.	Morning 200 + 63 SS. Total 263
	Evening 260 + 12 SS. Total 272
Avge attendance	[Not given]
Remarks	There is an afternoon service for children and teachers.
Dated	31 March 1851
Signed	John Eyres, minister [1845–52]
	Thornbury, Gloucestershire

[Eyres was also minister of Lower Morton (**4.28**) and Tytherington (**4.34**). Thornbury Baptist chapel had seeded congregations at Lower Morton (1834), Woodford near Berkeley (1835) and Tytherington (1840).]

4.28 (28)   **Baptist, Lower Morton, Thornbury**

Name	Baptist Chapel
Erected	In the year 1834
Building	Separate and entire. Yes [exclusively as a place of worship]
Sittings	Free 100. Other 24. Total [124]
Attend'ce 30 Mar.	Morning 23 SS. Total 23
	Afternoon 50 + 12 SS. Total 62
Avge attendance	Morning 30 SS. Total 30
	Afternoon 65 + 19 SS. Total 75
Remarks	The children are instructed in the morning and afternoon.
Dated	31 March 1851
Signed	John Eyres, minister [1845–52]
	Thornbury, Gloucestershire

[Eyres was also the minister of Thornbury (**4.27**) and Tytherington (**4.34**).]

4.29a (23)   **Wesleyan Methodist, Thornbury**

Name	Thornbury Chapel [From 1888 called Cossham Hall]
Erected	About 1800 [1789; enlarged 1835. Replaced by new chapel in High Street 1877]
Building	Yes [separate and entire] Yes [exclusively as a place of worship]
Sittings	Free 130. Other 100. Total [230]
Attend'ce 30 Mar.	Morning 35. Total 35
	Evening 50. Total 50
Avge attendance	[Not given]
Dated	31 March 1851
Signed	William Powell, minister [1850–2]
	Thornbury nr Bristol, Gloucestershire

[Powell was also the minister of Almondsbury (**4.5**), Alveston (**4.2**), Littleton-on-Severn (**4.18**), Milbury Heath (**4.32**), Oldbury-on-Severn (**4.30**) and Olveston (**4.8**). John Wesley recorded, 'I went over to Thornbury, where we preached near fifty years, and hardly saw any fruit. But whom can we despair of? Now at length it seems that God's time is come. A few men of substance in the town have built a neat and commodious preaching house. It was filled within and without with serious hearers; and they did not hear in vain': *Journal*, 10 Sept. 1789.]

4.29b (25)   **Wesleyan Methodist, Thornbury**
Name   Thornbury Chapel
Erected   Before 1800
Building   Yes [separate and entire] Yes [exclusively as a place of worship]
Sittings   Free 150. Other 70. Total [220]
Attend'ce 30 Mar. Morning 35. Total 35
                     Evening 60. Total 60
Avge attendance   [Not given]
Dated   4 April 1851
Signed   James Clutterbuck, chapel steward [perfumer]
                     Thornbury, Gloucestershire

4.30 (30)   **Wesleyan Methodist, Oldbury-on-Severn**
Name   Oldbury Chapel
Erected   About 1835
Building   Yes [separate and entire] Yes [exclusively as a place of worship]
Sittings   Free 120. Other 30. Total [150]
Attend'ce 30 Mar. Afternoon 70. Total 70
                     Evening 150. Total 150
Avge attendance   [Not given]
Dated   31 March 1851
Signed   William Powell, minister [1850–2]
                     Thornbury nr Bristol, Gloucestershire

[Powell was also the minister of Almondsbury (**4.5**), Alveston (**4.2**), Littleton-on-Severn (**4.18**), Milbury Heath (**4.32**), Olveston (**4.8**), and Thornbury (**4.29**).]

4.31 (33)   **Wesleyan Methodist, Rangeworthy**
Name   Ebenezer
Erected   1820 [Replaced by a nearby chapel, 1874]
Building   Separate and entire. Yes [exclusively as a place of worship]
Sittings   Free 130. Other 20. Total [150]
Attend'ce 30 Mar. Afternoon 130 + 60 SS. Total 190
                     Evening 130. Total 130
Avge attendance   Afternoon 140 + 48 SS. Total 188
Dated   30 March 1851
Signed   James Meadmore, minister [1850–1]
                     Downend nr Bristol

[Meadmore was also the minister of Downend (**20.31**), Iron Acton (**3.53**), Mangotsfield (**20.32**), Oldland (**20.15**) and Wick (**3.20**).]

4.32 (9) (332.8–9) Wesleyan Methodist, Milbury Heath, Thornbury
Name   Milbury Heath Chapel
Erected   1839
Building   Yes [separate and entire] Yes [exclusively as a place of worship]
Sittings   Free 150. Total [150]
Attend'ce 30 Mar. Morning 25 SS. Total 25
                     Afternoon 90 + 25 SS. Total 115
                     Evening 60. Total 60
Avge attendance   [Not given]
Dated   31 March 1851
Signed   William Powell, minister [1850–2]
                     Thornbury, Gloucestershire

[Powell was also the minister of Almondsbury (**4.5**), Alveston (**4.2**), Littleton-on-Severn (**4.18**), Oldbury-on-Severn (**4.30**), Olveston (**4.8**) and Thornbury (**4.29**).]

332.2.6–7 Parish of Tytherington

Area 2,100 acres; 90 inhabited houses, 7 uninhabited. Population 465.
The parish includes the hamlet of Itchington.

4.33 (35)   **Church of England, St James, Tytherington**
(Summary form)

Name	St James
Consecration	[Restored 1891]
Erected	I cannot ascertain. [Chancel rebuilt 1779; restored 1883–4]
[*Endowment*	Total £300]
Sittings	Free 100. Other 150. Total 250
Usual attend'ce	Morning 50 + 25 SS (about 12 boys [and] 13 girls). [Total 75]
	Afternoon 100 + 25 SS. [Total 125]
Signed	William Henry Moncrieff Roberson, vicar [1830–81]

[*GNQ* 3, 198–200].]

4.34 (36)   **Baptist, Tytherington**
(Summary form)

Name	[Not given]
Erected	1840 [Opened July 1842, replaced by a chapel opened in May 1885]
Sittings	[Not given]
Usual attend'ce	Morning 55 + 45 SS. Total 100
Signed	[Not given]
[*Minister*	John Eyres 1845–52]

[Eyres was also the minister of Thornbury (**4.27**) and Lower Morton (**4.28**). Before 1840 the Baptists met in cottages.]

332.2.8 Parish of Cromhall Abbots

Area 2,579 acres; 154 inhabited houses, 8 uninhabited. Population 766.
The parish includes the tithing of Cromhall Lygon. The population of Cromhall Abbots had increased after the opening of a coal mine.

4.35 (37)   **Church of England, St Andrew, Cromhall**

Name	Church of St Andrew, commonly called 'Cromhall Church'
	An ancient parish church
Consecration	Before 1800. Was existing temp. Ric II
Erected	See above [Restored 1852–3]
Endowment	Tithe £452. Glebe £128. Lecture £3 [Total] £583. Fees about 30s
	Dues and Easter offerings none. {Total £468}
Sittings	Free 95. Other 185. Total 280
Attend'ce 30 Mar.	[Not given]
Avge attendance	Morning 70 + 80 SS. Total 150
	Afternoon 170 + 80 SS. Total 250
Remarks	The average attendance on Sundays is given. There are occasional weekly evg services.

1. The two tithings of Cromhall Lygon and C. Abbots are not distinct for any ecclesiastical purpose, nor parochial, except in the highway rate.
2. Scattered population
3. The rectorial income given in the gross. For nett say £485

Dated   27 March 1851
Signed   William James Copleston, rector [1839–74]
                 Cromhall, Chipping Sodbury
[Copleston was the nephew and biographer of Edward Copleston, bishop of Llandaff 1827–49.]

4.36 (39)   Calvinistic Methodist, Cromhall
Name   Cromhall Chapel
Erected   1821
Building   No [not separate and entire] Yes [exclusively as a place of worship]
Sittings   Free all
Attend'ce 30 Mar. Morning 40 + 45 SS. Total 85
                 Afternoon 27 + 51 SS. Total 78
                 Evening 120. Total [120]
Avge attendance Morning 50 + 50 SS. Total 100
                 Afternoon 30 + 60 SS. Total 90
                 Evening 180. Total 180
Remarks   Gallery holding 50 persons
Dated   30 March 1851
Signed   Christopher Keeling, deacon [coal mines proprietor]
                 Cromhall, Chipping Sodbury, Gloucestershire
[Keeling, with Samuel Long, had founded the chapel, which was opened by Rowland Hill (**5.8**).]

332.2.9 Parish of Rockhampton
Area 1,206 acres; 46 inhabited houses, 3 uninhabited. Population 235.

4.37 (38)   Church of England, St Oswald, Rockhampton
Name   [Not given]
Consecration   [Not given]
Erected   [Rebuilt 1861–2 (nave), and 1866 (chancel)]
Endowment   {Total £249}
Sittings   Free 70. Other 90. Total 160
Attend'ce 30 Mar. Morning 40 + 18 SS. Total 58
                 Afternoon 39 + 17 SS. Total 56
Avge attendance [Not given]
Remarks   My parish is a very small one with a population of 208 last Census [1841]
Dated   31 March 1851
Signed   Thomas Charles Hyde Leaver, rector [1848–59]
                 Thornbury, Gloucestershire

332.3   BERKELEY SUB-DISTRICT

332.3.1 Parish of Hill
Area 2,476 acres; 43 inhabited houses. Population 216.

4.38 (41)   Church of England, St Michael, Hill
Name   Hill Church dedicated at consecration to St Michael. An ancient parish church
Consecration   Before 1800
Erected   [Nave rebuilt 1759 and restored 1910]
Endowment   Land, tithe, glebe (house and garden) £250, rent charge, but reduced by
                 corn averages and taxes etc. to about £213 6s 6d. OPE none. Fees and
                 dues average £1 per anm. {Total £162}
Sittings   Free 111. Other 17. Total 128

Attend'ce 30 Mar.	Morning 57 + 19 SS. Total 76
Avge attendance	Morning 80 + 24 SS. Total 104
Remarks	NB. Mid-Lent Sunday, or, as it is commonly called Mothering Sunday, being a kind of lean day, does not offer a fair opportunity of returning the number of the congregation usually in attendance, so many being out visiting their friends or staying at home to receive them.
Dated	31 March 1851
Signed	Sir Edward Harry Vaughan Colt, [6th] bart, vicar [1839–82]
	Berkeley, Gloucestershire

[Colt succeeded to the baronetcy on 9 June 1849.]

332.3.2–8 Parish of Berkeley

Area 15,740 acres; 872 inhabited houses, 40 uninhabited. Population 4,344.
The parish includes the borough of Berkeley and the tithings of Hamfallow (includes the hamlets of Halmore and Wanswell), Hinton (includes the hamlet of Purton), Breadstone, Alkington, Ham and the chapelry of Stone. In 1831 the population of Hinton declined to 162 on completion of the Gloucester and Berkeley canal, but increased to 539 (1841) and 579 (1851) through greater traffic on the canal. The 1851 return included 90 living on barges.

4.39 (42) Church of England, St Mary the Virgin, Berkeley

Name	The parish church of Berkeley. The name given to it on consecration not known, nor the date thereof. It is an ancient parish church.
Consecration	Before 1800
Erected	[Tower rebuilt 1750–3; church restored 1865–6]
Endowment	Land, vicarage house and land £40. Tithe commuted at £750. Glebe £8. Pew rents nil. Fees and dues £60. Easter offerings nil. Other sources £878.
Sittings	Free 400. Other 100. Total 500
	A minority make a sort of claim to a few pews, else they are indiscriminately used.
Attend'ce 30 Mar.	Morning 165. SS not known. Total 165
	Afternoon 132. SS not known. Total 132
Avge attendance	Morning 247. Total [247]
	Afternoon 199. Total [199]
Remarks	On Sunday, 6th of April, the number, apart from the Sunday school children, were in the morning 247 [and in the] afternoon 199. Mid-Lent Sunday in this church has reduced the attendance ⅓, it may be assumed therefore to influence Berkeley to this extent.
Dated	17 April 1851
Signed	Thomas Orton, surgeon [registrar]
	Berkeley, Gloucestershire
[*Incumbent*	John Seton-Karr 1839–84]

[Joseph Leech observed that the vicar 'is what is emphatically called a fox hunting parson' and rode with the hounds two or three times a week, and 'is one of the most zealous and forward members of that hunt.' In church he read well and his sermon was 'delivered with an elegance of style, action and intonation which I have seldom or ever seen surpassed.': Leech 1847, 215, 218. An earlier incumbent, Samuel Jenner 1729–55, was the father of Edward Jenner, the vaccination pioneer.]

4.40 (43) Church of England, All Saints, Stone

Name	All Saints. It is the church of an antient chapelry.
Consecration	Before 1800
Erected	[Alterations 1831, 1846 and 1893–4]

Endowment	Land £27 1s. OPE £48 11s 6d. Fees (average) £5. {Total £80}
Sittings	Free about 80. Other 130. Total 210
Attend'ce 30 Mar.	Morning 70 + 30 SS. Total 100
	Afternoon 115 + 34 SS. Total 149
Avge attendance	[Not given]
Remarks	The pews which are only 25 in number, are too large and very inconvenient.
Dated	30 March 1851
Signed	Charles Cripps, perpetual curate [1848–97]
	Stone nr Berkeley, Gloucestershire

[Cripps (1819–1897) was 'vicar of this parish for 49 years and 7 months': tombstone.]

4.41 (45)   Independent, Salter Street, Berkeley

Name	Union Chapel
Erected	1835 [Foundation stone laid 3 May 1835, opened for worship 3 May 1836]
Building	A separate and entire building. Exclusively as a place of worship and Sunday school.
Sittings	Free 170. Other 130. Total [300]
Attend'ce 30 Mar.	Morning 140 + 73 SS. Total 213
	Afternoon 73 SS. Total 73
	Evening 170. Total 170
Avge attendance	Morning 120 + 70 SS. Total 190
	Afternoon 70 SS. Total 70
	Evening 250. Total 250
Remarks	The general average of the number of hearers including morning and evening congregations. The evening including the morning will average 250 exclusive of children.
Dated	31 March 1851
Signed	John Slatterie, Independent minister [1848–59]
	Berkeley, Gloucestershire

4.42 (47)   Independent, Newport

Name	Newport Chapel
Erected	1710 [Tablet: 'Built 1710, rebuilt 1825']
Building	[Separate and] entire. Yes [exclusively as a place of worship]
Sittings	Free 130. Other 182. Total [312] Standing room none
Attend'ce 30 Mar.	Morning 64 + 60 SS. Total 124
	Afternoon 69 SS. Total 69
	Evening 165. Total 165
Avge attendance	Morning 975 + 416 SS. Total 1,391
	Afternoon 494 SS. Total 494
	Evening 2,340. Total [2,340]
Remarks	The aforesaid place of worship was rebuilt in the year 1825. Each Sabbath morning service averages 75. Evening services 180. (General congregation). Scholars morning 32. Scholars afternoon 38.
Dated	31 March 1851
Signed	John Jones, secretary (saddler)
	Newport, nr Berkeley, Gloucestershire

[Occasional preachers were Rowland Hill of Wooton under Edge (**5.8**) and William Jay of Bath.]

4.43 (48)   **Independent, Ham**
Name   Berrington Chapel
Erected   1846
Building   Yes [separate and entire] Yes [exclusively as a place of worship]
Sittings   Free 60. Other 60. Total [120]
Attend'ce 30 Mar.   Morning 30 + 20 SS. Total [50]
                        Evening 50. Total [50]
Avge attendance   Morning 30 + 30 SS. Total [60]
                        Evening 70. Total [70]
Remarks   Middle Lent Sunday affects the congregations and the Sabbath school.
Dated   31 March 1851
Signed   Daniel Palser, minister
                        Clapton nr Berkeley, Glo'shire

4.44 (44)   **Wesleyan Methodist, Canonbury Street, Berkeley**
Name   Berkeley Wesleyan Chapel
Erected   1805
Building   It is both separate and entire. Yes [exclusively as a place of worship]
Sittings   Free 168. Other 153. Total [321]
Attend'ce 30 Mar.   Morning 43 SS. Total [43]
                        Afternoon no service. 23 SS. Total [23]
Avge attendance (6m) Afternoon 60. Total [60]
                        Evening 150. Total [150]
Remarks   The preacher did not come appointed for the 30 March in consequence
                        of severe indisposition. Many of the children have not attended for the last
                        three weeks in consequence of the illness and absence of two of the teachers.
Dated   31 March 1851
Signed   Francis Hands, chapel steward and trustee (surgeon)
                        [Salter Street], Berkeley, Gloucestershire

4.45 (46)   **Wesleyan Methodist, Halmore**
Name   Halmore Wesleyan Chapel
Erected   1829
Building   Separate and entire. Yes [exclusively as a place of worship]
Sittings   Free 78. Other 56. Total 134]
Attend'ce 30 Mar.   Morning 20 + 31 SS. Total 51
                        Afternoon 34 SS. Total 34
                        Evening 44. Total 44
Avge attendance (6m) Morning 30 + 40 SS. Total 70
                        Afternoon 46 SS. Total 46
                        Evening 60. Total 60
Dated   31 March 1851
Signed   Robert Hopton, trustee and chapel steward [farmer of 53 acres]
                        Halmore nr Berkeley, Gloucestershire

332.3.9 Parish of Tortworth
Area 1,551 acres; 44 inhabited houses, 3 uninhabited. Population 237.

4.46 (51)   **Church of England, St Peter, Tortworth**
Name   St Peter, Tortworth. An antient parish church
Consecration   Before 1800
Erected   [Rebuilt 1870–2; chancel restored 1885–6]

Endowment   Land and rectory £50. Tithe £500. Glebe £70. Pew rents nil
Fees £20. {Total £428}
Sittings   Free 30. Other 150. Total 180
Attend'ce 30 Mar.   Morning 34. SS none. Total 34
Afternoon 24. SS none. Total 24
Avge attendance   [Not given]
Remarks   Attendants at church on Sunday 6 April in the morning 50. Making a deduction of ⅓ for the 30 March according to the deficit of the churches on that day to estimate numbers ...
Dated   21 April 1851
Signed   Thomas Orton, surgeon [registrar]
Berkeley, Gloucestershire
[Incumbent   Clement Greswell 1840–82]
['The church contains a fine old font, of the early kind, and is warmed by two stoves, erected in 1852, chiefly at the expense of the tenant farmers. There is at present an organ and choir, maintained by the rector': *Post Office Directory*, 1856, 378. The church is now dedicated to St Leonard.]

4.47 (49)   Independent, Tortworth
Name   Tortworth School Room
Erected   In 1844
Building   Separate [and entire] building. A place of worship and day schoolroom
Sittings   All free. No other. Standing room no space but the passage
Attend'ce 30 Mar.   Morning 70 + 55 SS. Total 125
Evening 80. Total 80
Avge attend'ce (9m)   Morning 80 + 60 SS. Total 140
Evening 89. Total 89
Dated   30 March 1851
Signed   William Dove, minister [1843–55]
[Falfield House], Falfield near Berkeley
[Dove was also the minister of Falfield (**4.25**).]

332.3.10 Parish of Charfield
Area 1,369 acres; 113 inhabited houses, 4 uninhabited. Population 515.

4.48 (50)   Church of England, St James, Charfield
Name   St James, Charfield. An antient parish church
Consecration   Before 1800
Erected   [Unrestored, repaired 1858]
Endowment   Land and rectory £50. Tithe £313 13s 6d. Glebe £30. Fees £10 {Total £351}
Sittings   Free 30. Other 150. Total 180
Attend'ce 30 Mar.   [Not given]
Avge attendance   [Not given]
Dated   31 April 1851
Signed   Thomas Orton, surgeon [registrar]
Berkeley, Gloucestershire
[Incumbent   Richard Pranknard Jones rector 1816–53]
[Jones was also incumbent of Compton, Berks. 1829–53. 'He was also a fine horseman, and widely known as "Jumping Jones" being thus distinguished from two clerical neighbours of the same name': Gardiner, 249. The church is now under the care of the Churches Conservation Trust. In the nearby village, St John the Evangelist was consecrated 20 Apr. 1882.]

An attached letter addressed to Horace Mann Esq. (**4.49a**)

Berkeley
24 April 1851

Sir

Agreeably with the request of the Registrar General, I am now enabled to make a return for the parish church of Charfield with a slight omission to which I beg to solicit your attention.

I employed a person on Sunday, the 6 April to attend and count the numbers of all persons who were present at divine worship, distinguishing the general congregation from the Sunday school children. The party employed however neglected this latter particular, through where over I am enabled only to state the aggregate, including adults and children. Yet, as the return for the Sunday school has been sent to the Census office, I am happy to learn that the deduction necessary to be correct accordingly can be made in London under your inspection or, if deemed requisite, by myself. I may observe that the day on which these observations were made was 'fine' as respects the weather, to which therefore can be no objection, as an average; the same remark applying to the other churches under my cognisance.

As respects, in particular, the church at Charfield, with your permission, I may observe there is only one service on a Sunday, sometimes in the morning, at others in the afternoon. The numbers, including the children attending on the 6 April, were 67. I furnish the form filled up as far as I am able. If necessary that all should to be in my writing, in learning the numbers of the children, I shall have the pleasure to comply.
I beg to remain, sir, your most humble servant.
Thomas Orton
[Registrar]

4.49 (52)   **Independent, Charfield Green**

Name	Charfield Chapel
Erected	1846
Building	[Separate and] entire. Part of a day school on the British and Foreign School system
Sittings	Free 170. Other 65. Total [235]
Attend'ce 30 Mar.	Morning 110 + 55 SS. Total 165
	Afternoon 60 + 55 SS. Total 115
	Evening 190. Total 190
Avge attendance	Morning 120 + 60 SS. Total 180
	Afternoon 65 + 60 SS. Total 125
	Evening 200. SS none. Total 200
Remarks	The cause of congregation being rather less today is because it is mid-Lent. People went to see their friends. This is about the average attendance for the last 12 months.
Dated	30 March 1851
Signed	Stephen Miller, deacon
	Charfield Mill, near Wotton-under-Edge, Gloucestershire

---

5.   HO 129/333 DURSLEY DISTRICT: 32 places of worship

333.1   WOTTON-UNDER-EDGE SUB-DISTRICT

333.1.1 Parish of Kingswood [transferred from Wiltshire, October 1844]
Area 2,350 acres; 297 inhabited houses, 20 uninhabited. Population 1,227.
Since 1841 the population had dropped by 94 due to depression in the woollen cloth industry.

5.1 (1)	**Church of England, St Mary, Kingswood**
Name	St Mary's, Kingswood. The present church built in 1723 in place of the dilapidated church previously existing formerly connected with the Abbey of Kingswood. A very ancient parish, originally a rectory, now a perpetual curacy, as the tithes were changed with a money payment in the reign of Charles II.
Consecration	Before 1800
Erected	[1722–3, restored 1872]
Endowment	Land £32. Tithe and glebe money payment from the time of Charles II, £27 11s. OPE (Queen Anne's Bounty) £33 18s. Fees £6. Easter offerings £3. Other (lecture) £3 12s [Total] £106 1s. {Total £99}
Sittings	Free 350. Other 260. Total 610 Besides a gallery for Sunday school scholars
Attend'ce 30 Mar.	[Not given]
Avge attendance	Morning 110 + 72 SS. Total 182 Afternoon 350 + 72 SS. Total 422
Remarks	The above money payment of £27 11s as 'Minister's Money' made in the reign of Charles II, in lieu of tithe was so made under very disadvantageous circumstances for all future incumbents. The whole land in the parish, about 2,200 acres, being tithe free now.
Dated	31 March 1851
Signed	George Strochlin Weidemann, perpetual curate [1846–56] Kingswood, nr Wotton-under-Edge
5.2 (2)	**Independent or Congregational, Kingswood**
Name	Kingswood Chapel
Erected	Before 1800 [1702]
Building	Yes [separate and entire] Yes [exclusively as a place of worship]
Sittings	Free 250. Other 200. Total [450]
Attend'ce 30 Mar.	Morning 204 + 128 SS. Total 332 Afternoon 121 + 100 SS. Total 221 Evening 330. Total 330
Avge attendance	Morning 230 + 120 SS. Total 350 Afternoon 121 + 120 SS. Total 241 Evening 350. Total 350
Remarks	Note. The afternoon service is held in the schoolroom after the teaching is closed to save time and trouble etc. in remov[in]g children to the chapel.
Dated	30 March 1851
Signed	Benjamin Opie Bendall, minister [1843–53] Kingswood near Wotton-under-Edge

333.1.2 Parish of North Nibley
Area 3,245 acres; 260 inhabited houses, 19 uninhabited. Population 1,133.
Since 1841 the population had declined by 174 due to depression in the woollen cloth industry.

5.3 (3)	**Church of England, St Martin of Tours, North Nibley**
Name	St Martin of Tours, North Nibley
Consecration	Very ancient. Consecrated before 1800
Erected	[Restored 1859–60, 1873 and 1891]
Endowment	{Total £95}
Sittings	Free 185. Other 205. Total 390
Attend'ce 30 Mar.	Morning 75 + 46 SS. Total 121
	Afternoon 118 + 50 SS. Total 168
Avge attendance	Morning 120 + 60 SS. Total 180
	Afternoon 180 to 200 + 65 SS. Total 245
Remarks	The tithes are leased to Wm. Lea Ireton Esq. of Cadogan Place, London, by the Dean and Chapter of Ch[ris]t Ch[urch], Oxford and various small payments to lay societies endowed, but may be ascertained by applying to the perpetual change accounts in making about £96 per annum.
	A stipend for leases £20 10s. Rent etc. from land £30 per annum. From Parliamentary grants £36 2s ...
Dated	31 March 1851
Signed	Thomas Le Quesne Jones MA, perpetual curate [1828–56]
	North Nibley, Wotton-under-Edge, Gloucestershire

5.4 (4)	**Independent, North Nibley**
Name	Tabernacle
Erected	About 1800 [1815]
Building	Separate [and entire] building. Exclusively [as a place of worship]
Sittings	Free 140. Other 200. Total [340]
Attend'ce 30 Mar.	Morning 100 + 50 SS. Total 150
	Afternoon 40 SS. Total 40
	Evening 260. Total 260
Avge attendance	Morning 120 + 50 SS. Total 170
	Afternoon 60 SS. Total 60
	Evening 270. Total 270
Dated	30 March 1851
Signed	Robert Ivey Osborne, minister [1843–60]
	Uley, Gloucestershire

5.5 (5)	**Independent, Bradley Green**
(Summary form)	
Name	[Not given]
Erected	[Not given]
Building	[Not given]
Sittings	[Not given]
Usual attend'ce	Morning [500] Total 500
Dated	[Not given]
Signed	[Not given]

5.6 (7)	**Wesleyan Methodist, North Nibley**
Name	Wesleyan Chapel
Erected	About 1805 [1804]

Building   Yes [separate and entire] Yes [exclusively as a place of worship]
Sittings   Free 106. Other 36. Total [142]
Attend'ce 30 Mar. Afternoon 42. Total [42]
                  Evening 67. Total [67]
Avge attendance (6m) Afternoon 40. Total 40
                  Evening 68. Total 68
Dated   31 March 1851
Signed   William Davies, Wesleyan Minister [1850–2 and 1858–9]
                  [Woodlane House], Dursley
[Davies was also the minister of Dursley (**5.23**) and Uley (**5.19**).]

333.1.3 Parish of Wotton-under-Edge

Area 4,880 acres; 1,058 inhabited houses, 105 uninhabited. Population 4,224.
The parish of Wotton-under-Edge includes the borough of Wotton-under-Edge and the tithings of Huntingford, Sinwell and Bradley, Symonds Hall and Combe, and Wortley. Since 1841 the population had declined by 478 due to depression in the woollen cloth industry.

5.7 (6)   **Church of England, St Mary the Virgin, Wotton-under-Edge**
Name   Parish Church of St Mary the Virgin
Consecration   600 years or more ago
Erected   [Enlarged 1838 and restored 1882–5]
Endowment   By [all but pew rents and dues] {Total £112}
Sittings   Free 1,000. Other 750. Total 1,750
Attend'ce 30 Mar. Morning 700 + 200 SS. Total 900
                  Afternoon 750 + 200. Total 950
                  Evening 800. Total 800
Avge attendance Morning 700 + 220 SS. Total 920
                  Afternoon 800 + 220 SS. Total 1,020
                  Evening 800. Total 800
Remarks   It is impossible to state with any degree of accuracy from conjecture the average number of persons attending at the several services on the Sunday. On particular occasions many more are present than the church is estimated to hold as benches are then placed in the aisles, chancel and other parts. On unfavourable days there may not be more than 500 present.
Dated   31 March 1851
Signed   Benjamin Roberts Perkins, vicar [1829–81]
                  Wotton-under-Edge, Gloucestershire

5.8 (8)   **Independent or Congregational, Tabernacle Place**
Name   [The] Tabernacle
Erected   1771 [Rebuilt 1852]
Building   Yes [separate and entire] Yes [exclusively as a place of worship]
Sittings   Free 370. Other 280. Total [550]
Attend'ce 30 Mar. Morning 502 + 199 SS. Total 701
                  Evening 657. Total 657
Avge attendance [Not given]
Dated   31 March 1851
Signed   John Tyeth Feaston, minister [1848–55]
                  [Tabernacle Place], Wotton-under-Edge, Gloucestershire
[Tablet: 'Erected AD 1852 on the site of The Tabernacle built by Revd. Rowland Hill AD 1771. Henry Masters, architect'. During Feaston's ministry, 'the Tabernacle has been rebuilt, and the cause greatly prospered': Redford and James, 349.]

5.9 (9)   **Particular Baptist, Rope Walk**

Name	Baptist Chapel
Erected	1818 in lieu of one which existed before 1800
Building	Yes [separate and entire] Yes [exclusively as a place of worship]
Sittings	Free 234. Other 274. Total [508]
Attend'ce 30 Mar.	Morning 230 + 79 SS. Total 309
	Afternoon 79 [SS] Total [79]
	No afternoon service except for the Sunday school
	Evening 186. Total 186
Avge attendance	[Not given]
Remarks	Our congregations were considerably less than usual in consequence of mid-Lent Sunday, especially in the evening. Our average evening congregation would be about 250.
Dated	31 March 1851
Signed	John Watts, Baptist minister [1830–58]
	Wotton-under-Edge

5.10 (10)   **Wesleyan Methodist, Haw Street**

(Completed on form for Sunday Schools. 'Chapel' written in place of 'Sunday School')

Name	Haw Street
Denomination	Wesleyan
Established	1805 [Replaced by a new chapel in Bradley Street in 1898]
Where conducted	Meeting house
SS on 30 March	Total 8
Expenses	Collection at the door
Remarks	[I was] informed by one of the members of the meeting. Congregation at that time may be estimated at 100.
Signed	John Rogers, registrar
	Wotton[-under-]Edge

333.2   ULEY SUB-DISTRICT

333.2.1 Parish of Owlpen

Area 720 acres; 21 inhabited houses, 4 uninhabited. Population 82.
Since 1841 the population had declined by 12 following the demolition of cottages.

5.11 (11)   **Church of England, Holy Cross, Owlpen**

Name	Owlpen chapel annexed to Newington Bagpath
Consecration	Before 1800 [19 February 1875]
Erected	[Rebuilt 1828–30 and altered 1874–5; tower rebuilt 1911–2]
Endowment	Tithe rent charge £150. Glebe rented at £4 17s 6d. [See Newington Bagpath (**11.2**)]
Sittings	Free 153. Other 110. Total 263
Attend'ce 30 Mar.	Afternoon 63 + 23 SS. Total 86
Avge attendance	Morning 60 + 18 SS. Total 78
	Afternoon 70 + 20 SS. Total 90
Dated	30 March 1851
Signed	Francis Joseph Leigh, curate [1844–52]
	Kingswood [?], Wotton-under-Edge
[Incumbent	Alan Gardner Cornwall 1827–72]

[The benefice consisted of Newington Bagpath (**11.2**) with Owlpen. Cornwall was also the incumbent of Beverstone (**11.12**) with Kingscote (**11.1**).]

333.2.2   **Parish of Nympsfield**
Area 1,472 acres; 84 inhabited houses, 2 uninhabited. Population 417.

5.12 (12)   **Church of England, St Bartholomew, Nympsfield**
Name   Nympsfield parish church
Consecration   Before 1800 [23 July 1863]
Erected   [Rebuilt 1861–3]
Endowment   {Total £223}
Sittings   Free 80. Other 170. Total 250
Attend'ce 30 Mar. Morning 61 + 44 SS. Total 105
                    Afternoon 105 + 40 SS. Total 145
Avge attendance   [Not given]
Dated   31 March 1851
Signed   George Christopher Hayward, rector [1833–60]
                    Nympsfield, nr Stroud, Gloucestershire
[Members of the Hayward family were incumbents 1754–1860. *GNQ* 5, 361–5.]

5.13 (13)   **Baptist, Nympsfield**
Name   Nympsfield Baptist Chapel
Erected   1813
Building   Yes [separate and entire] Yes [exclusively as a place of worship]
Sittings   Free 120. All free except 5. Total [125] Standing room none
                    (Space 30 feet by 24 [feet])
Attend'ce 30 Mar. Evening 95 + 25 SS. Total 120
Avge attendance   Morning 24 SS. Total [24] } Total
                    Evening 35. Total [35]   } 59
Dated   31 March 1851
Signed   John Shelton, manager (draper)
                    Nympsfield, nr Nailsworth, Gloucestershire

333.2.3 Parish of Coaley
Area 2,463 acres; 186 inhabited houses, 16 uninhabited. Population 788.
Since 1831 the population had declined by 336. Locally the woollen cloth industry had
ceased and many of the inhabitants had moved away.

5.14 (14)   **Church of England, St Bartholomew, Coaley**
Name   Coaley near Dursley, Gloucestershire
Consecration   Is an antient building [14 April 1858]
Erected   [Apart from the tower, rebuilt 1856–8]
Endowment   Tithe rent charge £300. Glebe house and garden. Fees about £3
                    {Total £158}
Sittings   Near all free 270. Total 270
Attend'ce 30 Mar. Morning 66 + 17 SS. Total 83
                    Afternoon 99 + 16 SS. Total 115
Avge attendance   [Not given]
Remarks   There are many Wesleyans with a meeting house and a Sabbath school,
                    also Independent and Baptist dissenters.
Dated   31 March 1851
Signed   Charles Robert Fanshawe, vicar [1835–59]
                    Coaley Vicarage, Dursley, Gloucestershire
[Fanshawe was also incumbent rector of St Margaret, Morton on the Hill, Norfolk 1826–59.]

5.15 (15)   **Wesleyan Methodist, Coaley**

Name	Bethesda
Erected	1807
Building	Yes [separate and entire] Yes [exclusively as a place of worship]
Sittings	Free 70. Other 124. Total 194
Attend'ce 30 Mar.	Afternoon 58. Total [58]
	Evening 55. Total [55]
Avge attendance	[Not given]
Dated	30 March 1851
Signed	Thomas Wilkins, steward [butcher]
	Coaley, nr Dursley, Gloucest'shire

333.2.4 Parish of Uley

Area 1,492 acres; 352 inhabited houses, 43 uninhabited. Population 1,327.
Since 1821 the population had declined by 1,328. Locally the woollen cloth industry had ceased and many inhabitants had moved away.

5.16 (16)   **Church of England, St Giles, Uley**

Name	Antient parish church, dedicated to St Giles, in the patronage of the Lord Chancellor
Consecration	Before 1800 [28 September 1858]
Erected	[Rebuilt 1857–8]
Endowment	Land none. Tithe rent charge £237. Glebe £39. OPE none. Pew rents £2 15s. Fees and dues £3. Easter offerings £3. Other sources none. {Total £157}
Sittings	Free 200. Other 300. Total 500
Attend'ce 30 Mar.	Morning 150 + 108 SS. Total 258
	Afternoon 300 + 100 SS. Total 400
Avge attendance	Morning 150 + 108 SS. Total 158 [*recte* 258]
	Afternoon 300 + 100 SS. Total 400
Remarks	It may be necessary to remark that the above is a statement of the gross value of the endowment, without reference to the deductions.
	Additional note. The deduction affecting the incumbent of the rector of Uley, arising from parochial and other taxes, amount on an average [to] £68 per annum, reducing the net value of the living to about £200.
Dated	31 March 1851
Signed	Marlow Watts Wilkinson, rector [1823–67]
	Uley, Gloucestershire

[Wilkinson was also the incumbent of Harescombe (**9.5**) with Pitchcombe (**10.11**). 'He is said to have been the best scholar in a local clerical society; but the type of parochial clergyman to which he belonged, is now almost, if not quite extinct.': *GNQ* 2, 162–8, 399–401; 5, 103–5.]

5.17 (18)   **Independent, Fop Street**

Name	Whitecourt Chapel [Union Chapel]
Erected	Before 1800 [1790]
Building	Yes [separate and entire] Yes [exclusively as a place of worship]
Sittings	Free 66. Other 252. Total [318] Standing room none appropriated
Attend'ce 30 Mar.	Morning 159. Total 159
	Evening 219. Total 219
Avge attendance	Morning about 200 + about 90 SS. Total 290
	Afternoon 100 SS. Total 100
	Evening about 300. Total 300

Dated	31 March 1851
Signed	Henry Jones, minister [1849–70]
	Uley, nr Dursley, Gloucester[shire]

5.18 (17)   Baptist, Down South Street

Name	Bethesda
Erected	1821 [Opened 11 November 1821]
Building	Yes [separate and entire] Yes [exclusively as a place of worship]
Sittings	Free 50. Other 400. Total [450] Standing room for 100
Attend'ce 30 Mar.	Morning 130 + 40 SS. Total 170
	Afternoon 50 + 60 SS. Total 110
	Evening 200. Total 200
Avge attendance	[Not given]
Remarks	The congregation at Bethesda Chapel, Uley has been considerably decreased by emigration and also the removal of the clothing manufacture.
Dated	31 March 1851
Signed	Robert George Le Maine, minister
	Chapel House, Uley, Gloucestershire

5.19 (19)   Wesleyan Methodist, Uley

Name	Wesleyan Methodist Chapel
Erected	[1808]
Building	Separate [and entire] Yes [exclusively as a place of worship]
Sittings	Free 48. Other 72. Total [120]
Attend'ce 30 Mar.	Afternoon 25. Total 25
	Evening 30. Total 30
Avge attendance	Afternoon 25. Total 25
	Evening 30. Total 30
Dated	13 November 1851
Signed	William Davies, Wesleyan Minister [1850–2 and 1858–9]
	[Woodlane House], Dursley

[Davies was also the minister of Dursley (**5.23**) and North Nibley (**5.6**).]

333.3   DURSLEY SUB-DISTRICT

333.3.1 Parish of Dursley
Area 1,059 acres; 581 inhabited houses, 61 uninhabited. Population 2,752.
Since 1831 the population had decreased by 474 due to depression in the cloth industry.
In 1851 the local Union workhouse situated within the parish had 103 inmates.

5.20 (21)   Church of England, St James the Great, Dursley

Name	Holy Trinity. An ancient parish church
Consecration	Before 1800 [16 April 1868]
Erected	[Restored and enlarged 1867–8 and 1888–9]
Endowment	{Total £228}
Sittings	Not recorded and only to be ascertained by actual measurement. [There were 123 pews, 109 of which were private pews for families of gentlemen and tradesmen, and 14 for the poor (for no more than 150, and with a further 150 seats for children in the gallery). Many of the pews were attached to the houses of dissenters.]
Attend'ce 30 Mar.	Morning about 400 + 187 SS. Total [587]
	Afternoon about 300 + 192 SS. Total [492]

Avge attendance	Larger than the numbers stated for 30 March 1851
Remarks	The rector is non-resident, and I am unable unable to give the particulars of the endowment correctly, neither am I acquainted with the number of free sittings from the changes in the appropriation of pews etc.
Dated	31 March 1851
Signed	Henry Minniken, curate [1847–]
	Kingshill, Dursley
[Incumbent	John Timbrill 1825–65]

[Sometimes called Holy Trinity and sometimes (as today) St James; previously the south aisle was dedicated to Holy Trinity and the north to St Mary the Virgin. Timbrill (who later altered his name to Trimbrell) was the incumbent of Dursley with Woodmancote (**5.21**), of Beckford (**15.31**) with Ashton under Hill (**19.26**) and of Bretforton, Worcs. 1816–65. Timbrill was the last archdeacon and incumbent of Dursley, a linkage which had begun in 1475. For this he received a stipend of £232): GA P124, IN 3/2 (Memorial of Henry Vizard, Nov. 1844).]

5.21 (22)   **Church of England, St Mark, Woodmancote**

Name	St Mark's Chapel. Chapel of ease
Consecration	16 April 1844, as an additional church
Erected	By a grant from the Incorporated Society for Building Churches and Chapels and by private subscriptions [of] about £1,200. Total cost about £1,200. [Enlarged 1859]
Endowment	Land and cottages £38 per ann[um] out of which £4 yearly is paid to a repair fund for the church ... which, with insurance, income tax [and] repairs, makes the endowment for the ministers about £30 per ann[um] [See Dursley (**5.20**)]
Sittings	Free 350. Total 350
Attend'ce 30 Mar.	Morning once a month for Holy Communion
	Evening filled
Avge attendance	Evening generally full to inconvenience
Remarks	I believe the above returns to be correct with the exception of the particulars, how the sum for the erection and endowment was raised, for which no suitable columns of inquiry are here provided.
Dated	31 March 1851
Signed	Henry Minniken, sen'r curate of the parish church who officiates with the assist[ant] curate of the above named chapel of ease
	Kingshill, Dursley
[Incumbent	John Timbrill 1825–65]

[The benefice consisted of Dursley (**5.20**) with Woodmancote. In 1844 the chapel was 'well attended, particularly at the 6.00pm evening service when it is crowded', but the morning service held at 9.00am was not well attended. 'The poor are much pleased with it and call it their church.' Henry Vizard was prepared to provide £1,000 towards the endowment on condition that a service was held on Wednesday evenings to draw people away from the week night services held in the nonconformist chapels: GA P124, IN 3/2 (Memorial of Henry Vizard, Nov. 1844).]

5.22 (24)   **Independent, Parsonage Street**

Name	The Tabernacle
Erected	1808 [Opened opposite earlier chapel of 1760 on 22 August 1809]
Building	Yes [separate and entire] Yes [exclusively as a place of worship]
Sittings	Free 350 (seats for the poor or free). Other 400. Total [750]
Attend'ce 30 Mar.	Morning 500 + 115 SS. Total 615
	Evening 550. Total 550

Avge attendance   Morning 560 + 130 SS. Total 690
                    Evening 700. Total 700
Remarks   A considerable decrease in the attendance during Feb. and March in
                    consequence of influenza etc.
Dated   31 March 1851
Signed   Eliakim Lloyd Shadrack, minister [1835–56]
                    Tabernacle House, Dursley, Gloucestershire
[Early in his ministry George Whitefield preached to thousands in the Dursley area, and those
sympathetic to his message opened the Independent chapel. Later Rowland Hill (**5.8**) was also in
the area, preaching at the opening of the Tabernacle in 1809.]

5.23 (25)   **Wesleyan Methodist, Castle Street**
Name   Methodist Chapel
Erected   1802 [New chapel opened 1 June 1864]
Building   Separate [and entire] Yes [exclusively as a place of worship]
Sittings   Free 220. Other 320. Total [540]
Attend'ce 30 Mar. Morning 160 + 50 SS. Total 210
                    Afternoon 60 + 68 SS. Total 128
                    Evening 220. Total 220
Avge attendance (6m) Morning 200. Total [200]
                    Afternoon 80. Total [80]
                    Evening 300. Total [300]
Dated   31 March 1851
Signed   William Davies, Wesleyan Minister [1850–2 and 1858–9]
                    [Woodlane House], Dursley
[Davies was also the minister of North Nibley (**5.6**) and Uley (**5.19**).]

333.3.3 Parish of Stinchombe
Area 1,464 acres; 77 inhabited houses, 2 uninhabited. Population 354.
Since 1821 the population had declined by 78 due to depression in the cloth industry.

5.24 (23)   **Church of England, St Cyr, Stinchcombe**
(Summary form)
Name   Stinchcombe
Erected   1632 [Rebuilt 1854–5, and consecrated 26 July 1855]
[Endowment   Total £65]
Sittings   Free 80. Other 48. Total 128
Usual attend'ce   Morning 100 + 27 male and 28 female SS. Total [155]
                    Afternoon 120 + 55 SS. Total [175]
                    Evening none
Remarks   Additional note
                    Sir, I beg to inform the Reg. General that I have had a great deal of
                    trouble in obtaining information from Stinchcombe. The Rev and Sir Geo.
                    Prevost refusing to give me the slightest information on the subject
                    because he has not been authorised by the bishop to do so.
                    I am, Sir, your ob[t] ser[t],
                    George Leonard
Signed   George Leonard [registrar]
                    [Parsonage Street], Dursley
[Incumbent   Sir George Prevost 1834–81]

[Prevost had succeeded his father as the second baronet in 1816, aged 12. He was the curate of Thomas Keble at Bisley (**10.25**) 1828–34 and became closely associated with John Keble (**13.2**), an early supporter of the Oxford Movement and a founder member of the Bisley-Fairford school. From 1848–65 his brother-in-law Isaac Williams served as his curate at Stinchcombe. Prevost was the archdeacon of Gloucester 1865–81. *ODNB* 'George Prevost (1804–1893)'; *GNQ* 2, 107–9. On the day the church was consecrated, Samuel Wilberforce (bishop of Oxford) preached in the morning and John Keble in the afternoon: Jacques, 155–69.]

333.3.3 Parish of Cam

Area 2,946 acres; 391 inhabited houses, 44 uninhabited. Population 1,640.
Since 1831 the population had declined by 431 due to depression in the cloth industry.

5.25 (26)	**Church of England, St George, Upper Cam**
Name	St George's church. Ancient parish church
Consecration	Before 1800
Erected	[Chancel rebuilt 1845; restored 1889–1901]
Endowment	This is without any deductions whatever, for mortgage, taxes etc. Land £19 3s 9d. OPE £97 12s 4d. Fees £8. Other sources £36. {Total £150}
Sittings	Free 323. Other 73. Total 396
Attend'ce 30 Mar.	Morning* 169 SS
	Afternoon 159 SS
Avge attendance	Morning** 190 SS
	Afternoon 190 SS
Remarks	*I had no opportunity of counting the congregation.
	**The parish is large, and the population scattered, and the attendance at church varies very much according to the weather and time of year. I cannot tell the average number.
Dated	31 March 1851
Signed	George Maden, vicar [1838–52]
	Cam, Dursley

[The benefice consisted of Upper Cam and Lower Cam (**5.26**).]

5.26 (27)	**Church of England, St Bartholomew, Lower Cam**
Name	St Bartholomew's chapel. Chapel of ease
Consecration	24 August 1844, as an additional church
Erected	By private benefactions with aid from Church Building Societies [for] £3,529 8s 6d. Total cost £3,529 8s 6d
Endowment	Land, tithe, glebe and OPE none. Fees about 10s. [See Upper Cam (**5.25**)]
Sittings	Free 411. Total 411
Attend'ce 30 Mar.	Morning* SS none
	Evening 12 SS
Avge attendance	Morning** SS none
	Evening 12 SS
Remarks	*I had no opportunity of counting the congregation.
	**The parish is large and the population scattered, and the attendance at the chapel varies very much according to the weather and time of year. I cannot tell the average number.
Dated	31 March 1851
Signed	George Maden, vicar [1838–52]
	Cam, Dursley

[The benefice consisted of Upper Cam (**5.25**) and Lower Cam.]

5.27 (28)   **Independent, Upper Cam**
Name   Cam Meeting House
Erected   Before 1800 [c.1702, altered 1817–8]
Building   Yes [separate and entire] Yes [exclusively as a place of worship]
Sittings   Free 100. Other 370. Total [470]
Attend'ce 30 Mar.   Morning 123 + 31 SS. Total 144
                       Afternoon 200 + 31 SS. Total 231
Avge attendance   [Not given]
Dated   30 March 1851
Signed   Charles Thomas [1841–61] and Andrew Gazard [1842–69], ministers
                       Cam, Glo'shire
[*GNQ* 5, 71–2, 156–7.]

5.28 (29)   **Wesleyan Methodist, Lower Cam**
Name   Lower Cam Wesleyan Chapel
Erected   1825 [Opened 24 March 1826. Tablet, 'Enlarged 1838']
Building   [Separate and] entire. A place of worship and Sunday school
Sittings   Free 200. Other 200. Total [400] Standing room for 600
Attend'ce 30 Mar.   Morning 54 SS. Total 54
                       Afternoon 100 + 50 SS. Total 150
                       Evening 130. Total 130
Avge attendance   Morning 200 + 60 SS. Total 260
Dated   31 March 1851
Signed   Thomas Tyrell, trustee steward
                       Lower Cam, nr Dursley, Gloucestershire

333.3.4 Parish of Slimbridge
Area 4,430 acres; 179 inhabited houses, 5 uninhabited. Population 859.

5.29 (30)   **Church of England, St John the Evangelist, Slimbridge**
Name   Ancient parish church
Consecration   Before AD 1800
Erected   [Restored 1844–6]
Endowment   {Total £601}
Sittings   Free 300. Total 300
Attend'ce 30 Mar.   Morning 49 + 34 SS. Total 83
                       Afternoon 73 + 37 SS. Total 110
                       Evening no service
Avge attendance   [Not given]
Remarks   The account having been kept of the number of persons attending divine
                       service previous to 30 March, the average number of attendants for any
                       time previous to that date cannot be ascertained. [The] return to the best
                       of my belief, so far as regards the written answers.
Dated   March 1851
Signed   Robert Meadows White, rector [1846–65]
                       Rectory, Slimbridge, Dursley, Gloucestershire
[White had been a professor of Anglo-Saxon at Oxford 1834–9. As a visitor Joseph Leech sat in the
chancel, joining the small congregation. 'The singing consisted of a solo from the [parish] clerk, to
which the congregation listened with breathless attention. I tried to join him, but being at such a
distance our voices did not blend, and I gave it up; and indeed he did not seem to want any
assistance, for he warbled away as happy and independent as a bird': Leech 2004, 230–3.]

5.30 (31)   **Independent, Cambridge**
Name   Union Chapel
Erected   1807 [Enlarged 1876]
Building   Separate building. Used only as a place of worship and school.
Sittings   Free 100. Other 50. Total [150]
Attend'ce 30 Mar.   Morning 1,040 [*sic*] + 47 SS
    Afternoon 100. Total [100]
    Evening 1,040 [*sic*]
Avge attendance   [Not given]
Dated   31 March 1851
Signed   (Mrs) Mary Ann Lees, manager
    Cambridge, near Dursley, Gloucestershire

5.31 (33)   **Baptist, Slimbridge**
Name   Gossington Chapel
Erected   1834 [Rebuilt 1877]
Building   Yes [separate and entire] Sunday and day school, yes
Sittings   Free 60. Other 30. Total [90]
Attend'ce 30 Mar.   Morning 40 + 44 SS. Total 84
    Evening 75. Total 75
Avge attendance   Morning from 75 to 80 + 58 SS. Total 90 morning [*sic*] [133–138]
Dated   31 March 1851
Signed   George Foxwell [farm manager]
    Samuel Colborn [agricultural labourer], deacons
    Slimbridge, Dursley, Gloucestershire

5.32 (32)   **Wesleyan Methodist, Cambridge**
Name   Cambridge Wesleyan Methodist Preaching Room
Erected   Converted into a preaching place in 1847
Building   Not separate [and entire] Yes. Since November 1850 before which period
    as day school was reb[uil]t
Sittings   Free 70. Other none. Total [70]
Attend'ce 30 Mar.   Morning 60. Total [60]
Avge attendance   [Not given]
Remarks   There is no worship at this place in afternoon or evening on account of
    worship being afforded at a dissenting chapel near this place in after-
    noon and evening (**5.30**). The male scholars of the Sunday school of
    this dissenting place of worship generally attend [the] sermon at this
    place in the morning, to the number of 15 scholars.
Dated   30 March 1851
Signed   Joseph L. Hadley, local preacher and leader [grocer]
    Cambridge nr Dursley, Gloucestershire

6. HO 129/334 WESTBURY-ON-SEVERN DISTRICT: 41 places of worship

334.1   NEWNHAM SUB-DISTRICT

334.1.1 Parish of Awre
Area 6,115 acres; 276 inhabited houses, 6 uninhabited. Population 1,512.
The parish includes the tithings of Awre, Bledisloe, Hagloe, Etloe and Blakeney.
VCH 5, 14–46.

6.1 (1)	**Church of England, St Andrew, Awre**
Name	Awre Church. An ancient parish church. The church is a distinct and separate parish.
Consecration	Before 1800
Erected	[Restored 1875]
Endowment	[Total] £560 4s 1d. {Total £530}
Sittings	Free [none] Other 460. Total 460
Attend'ce 30 Mar.	Morning 33. Total [33]
	Afternoon 60. Total [60]
Avge attendance	Morning 40 + 35 SS. Total 75
	Afternoon 60 + 35 SS. Total 95
Remarks	A small congregation always on mid-Lent Sunday
Dated	31 March 1851
Signed	Joseph Henry Malpas, minister [1826–76]
	Awre vicarage, near Newnham, Gloucestershire

6.2 (2)	**Church of England, All Saints, Blakeney**
Name	All Saint's chapel of ease to the mother church at Awre (**6.1**)
Consecration	Before 1800, but enlarged and consecrated in 1820 [7 Aug. 1820]
Erected	[Restored 1895–6]
Endowment	There is no endowment. {Total £232}
Sittings	Free 410. Other 224. Total 634
Attend'ce 30 Mar.	Morning 106 + 105 SS. Total 211
	Afternoon 146 + 85 SS. Total 231
Avge attendance	[Not given]
Remarks	The return which I have made of the number of persons who attended divine service on 30 March 1851 is accurate. But I am unable to state whether that number represents the average or usual number of attendants.
Dated	31 March 1851
Signed	Charles Brooksbank, minister [1843–72]
	Blakeney, near Newnham, Gloucestershire

6.3 (4)	**Independent, Blakeney Hill**
Name	[Blakeney] Tabernacle
Erected	1823 [Replaced by a new chapel on a different site 1849]
Building	Yes [separate and entire] Yes [exclusively as a place of worship]
Sittings	Free 84. Other 196. Total [280] Standing room for 50
Attend'ce 30 Mar.	Morning 133 + 63 SS. Total [196]
	Afternoon 79 SS. Total [79]
	Evening 180. Total [180]

Avge attendance Morning 180 + 85 SS. Total [265]
Afternoon 85 SS. Total [85]
Evening 205. Total [205]
Dated 31 March 1851
Signed Thomas Young, minister [1849–55]
Blakeney, Gloucestershire

[Isaac Bridgman, the first curate of Holy Trinity, Harrow Hill (**6.6**), having been forced to leave the Church of England, became an itinerant minister. In 1823, with the support and encouragement of Rowland Hill (**5.8**), he opened a chapel at Brain's Green, Blakeney where he remained in post until c.1828. At first the Anglican liturgy was used, but from 1825 the chapel adopted Independent principles. In 1849 the congregation erected a new chapel in Blakeney village.]

6.4 (3) **Baptist, Blakeney**
Name Baptist Chapel (Baptists in the practice of open communion)
Erected [Opened 12 June] 1833 [Rebuilt 1874]
Building Separate and entire. Exclusively [as a place of worship] (S[unday] school adjoining)
Sittings Free 72. Other 214. Total [286] Standing room none
Attend'ce 30 Mar. Morning 141 + 57 SS. Total 198
Evening 110. Total [110]
Avge attendance Morning 170 + 80 SS. Total 250
Evening 170. Total 170
Remarks Dimensions of the chapel 48 by 32 feet. S[unday] schoolroom adjoining 32 by 21 feet
Dated [Not given]
Signed William Copley, minister
Blakeney, nr Newnham, Gloucestershire

334.1.2–6 Parish of Newnham
Area 12,487 acres; 1,506 inhabited houses, 36 uninhabited. Population 7,482.
In 1842 under the Dean Forest Ecclesiastical Districts Act (5 and 6 Vict. c.65) the Forest was divided into four ecclesiastical districts, departing from the previous division into the townships of East and West Dean (577.5–8). The four churches were: Christ Church, Berry Hill (**18.37**), Holy Trinity, Harrow Hill (**6.6**), St Paul, Parkend (**18.36**) and St John the Evangelist, Cinderford (**6.8**). [For the creation of parishes in the Forest of Dean see Snell 2006, 448–51]
VCH 10, 29–50

6.5 (5) **Church of England, St Peter, Newnham**
Name Ancient parish church (of Newnham, county of Gloucester)
Consecration [Not given]
Erected [Restored and enlarged 1874–5; burnt down 1881 and then rebuilt]
Endowment Glebe £15. OPE £95. Fees £20. Easter offerings £10. {Total £140}
Sittings Free 140. Other 270. Total 410
Attend'ce 30 Mar. Morning 214 + 60 SS. Total 274
Evening 176 + 40 SS. Total 216
Avge attendance Morning 244 + 70 to 80 SS. Total 314 to 324
Evening 215 + 30 to 40 SS. Total 235 to 245 [*recte* 245–255]
Remarks In consequence of the 30 March being mid-Lent Sunday, many families were visiting elsewhere.
Dated 31 March 1851

Signed   Edward Cowell Brice, perpetual curate [1847–81]
                      Parsonage, Newnham, nr Gloucester
[Brice was the brother of Henry Crane Brice, incumbent of St Peter's, Bristol (**1.17**).]

6.6 (10)   **Church of England, Holy Trinity, Harrow Hill**
Name   Holy Trinity church. It is a church of a distinct parish [known as the
                      Forest Church]
Consecration   In 1818 [26 June 1817. Altered 1853–4]
Erected   By voluntary contributions. By Parliamentary grant not known.
Endowment   [£2,200 from] Queen Anne's Bounty and Parliamentary grant £150.
                      {Total £150}
Sittings   Free 632. Other 18. Total 650
Attend'ce 30 Mar.   Morning 100 + 80 SS. Total 180
                      Afternoon 200 + 80 SS. Total 280
Avge attendance   Morning 100 + 80 SS. Total 180
                      Afternoon 250 + 80 SS. Total 330
Dated   30 March 1851
Signed   Henry George Nicholls, minister [1847–67]
                      Mitcheldean, Gloucester
[Nicholls was the only son of Sir George Nicholls, poor law reformer and administrator: *ODNB*
'George Nicholls (1781–1865)'. Subscribers to the erection of the church included the well-known
Evangelicals Thomas Baring, Nicholas Vansittart and William Wilberforce. It was erected under the
direct supervision of Henry Berkin (the first minister 1817–47) and the preacher at the opening
ceremony on 5 Feb. 1817 was Thomas Tregenna Biddulph the incumbent of St James, Bristol (**1.7**).
The first curate, who left the Church of England, was Isaac Bridgman (**6.3**); a later curate was John
Chell 1827–44: Nicholls 1863, 141–4. Under the Dean Forest Ecclesiastical Districts Act (Act 5 and
6 Vict. c.65) a parish was created in 1844. *VCH* 5, 392–3.]

6.7 (9)   **Church of England, room in the parish of Holy Trinity, Harrow Hill**
Name   Not consecrated, but licensed, and called 'The Mill'
Licensed   September 1849, [and] licensed as an additional place of evening worship.
Erected   Erected, originally, for manufacturing purposes, [by] private subscription
                      [for] £50. Total cost £50
Sittings   Free 100. Total 100
Attend'ce 30 Mar.   Evening 55. Total [55]
Avge attendance   Evening 60. Total [60]
Dated   30 March 1851
Signed   Henry George Nicholls, minister [1847–67]
                      Mitcheldean, Gloucester
[On Nicholls, see preceding entry.]

6.8 (11)   **Church of England, St John the Evangelist, Cinderford**
Name   Saint John the Evangelist [Sometimes called St John the Apostle]
Consecration   22 October 1844 under the Act of Parliament (30 July 1842) for dividing
                      the Forest of Dean in the County of Gloucestershire into ecclesiastical
                      districts.
Erected   Partly by private subscriptions, and partly by the aid of Her Majesty's
                      Commiss[ioners] of Woods, Forests etc. [Altered 1873–4]
Endowed   From such investment in Queen Anne's Bounty such income does not
                      exceed £130 per ann. {Total £150}
Sittings   Free 600. Other 50. Total 650

Attend'ce 30 Mar. Morning 348 + 80 SS. Total 428

Afternoon 379 + 83 SS. Total 460 [462]

Avge attendance The number counted by the churchwardens on the 30 inst[ant] exceeds the usual average. The Sunday scholars in attendance last year were 90 girls and 70 boys.

Remarks The minister will be under the painful necessity of fund-raising, the Sunday school not having any means of supporting it in future in consequence of the subscription viz. £15 per ann. hitherto received from the Crown having been entirely withdrawn by the Comm[issioner]s of Woods etc.

Dated 31 March 1851

Signed Thomas Gosselin Smythies, incumbent [1844–71]

Newnham, Gloucestershire

[*VCH* 5, 393–4. Within the parish St Stephen's was consecrated 29 May 1890.]

6.9 (6)   Independent, Littledean Road, Newnham

Name Newnham Chapel

Erected 1826 [Nearby chapel built 1859]

Building Yes [separate and entire] Yes [exclusively as a place of worship]

Sittings Free 30. Other 170. Total [200] Standing room none

Attend'ce 30 Mar. Morning 42 + 52 SS. Total 94

Evening 54 + 15 SS. Total 69

Avge attendance [Not given]

Dated 31 March 1851

Signed William Rhead, minister [1850–3]

Newnham, Gloucestershire

6.10 (17)   Baptist, Woodside, Cinderford

Name Woodside Baptist Chapel.

Erected 1843 [Opened 9 Nov. 1843; replaced by larger chapel, opened 31 July 1860]

Building Yes [separate and entire] Yes [exclusively as a place of worship]

Sittings Free 200. Other 140. Total [340] Standing room none

Attend'ce 30 Mar. Morning 170 + 170 SS. Total 340

Afternoon none school

Evening 280. Total 280.

Avge attendance (3m) As above

Remarks [unclear notes of Jan. and Feb. dates, possibly jottings by Census official]

Dated 31 March 1851

Signed Henry Webley, Baptist minister [1851–6]

Woodside, near Newnham, Gloucestershire

[The congregation 'became by far the largest Baptist meeting in the Forest and supported missionary work in several places': *VCH* 5, 397]

6.11 (7)   Wesleyan Methodist, Newnham

Name None

Erected Before 1800

Building No [not separate and entire] No [not exclusively as a place of worship]

Sittings Free 50. Total [50]

Attend'ce 30 Mar. Morning 18. Total [18]

Evening 23. Total [23]

Avge attendance [Not given]

Dated 31 March 1851

Signed   Samuel Wesley, minister
              Little Dean, Woodside, Newnham, Gloucestershire
[Wesley was also the minister of Coleford (**18.31**), Flaxley (**6.22**), Joyford (**18.43**), Lydbrook (**18.41**) and Mitcheldean (**6.27**).]

6.12 (13)   Wesleyan Methodist, Lea Bailey
Name   Wesleyan Chapel
Erected   1836
Building   Yes [separate and entire] Yes [exclusively as a place of worship]
Sittings   Free 87. Other 10. Total [97]
              Standing room only the aisle which is 18 feet by 3
Attend'ce 30 Mar. Afternoon 41 + 9 SS. Total 50
              Evening 27. Total 27
Avge attendance Afternoon 50 + 14 SS. Total 64
              Evening 30. Total 30
Remarks   In entering the sittings I have put single sittings not whole seats.
Dated   31 March 1851
Signed   Thomas Palmer, trustee, class leader and local preacher [farmer's son]
              New House, [Upper] Lea, Herefordshire

6.13 (14)   Bible Christian, Quarry Hill, Drybrook
Name   None
Erected   Before 1800
Building   No [not separate and entire] No [not exclusively as a place of worship]
Sittings   Free 56. Minister 4. Other 60. Total [120]
Attend'ce 30 Mar. Morning 14. Total [14]
Avge attendance [Not given]
Dated   30 March 1851
Signed   James Brooks, minister
              Drybrook, Mitcheldean, Gloucestershire
[Brooks was also minister of Broom's Green (**7.19**), Drybrook (**6.14**) and Ruardean (**18.52**).]

6.14 (12)   Bible Christian, Drybrook
Name   Bethel
Erected   In 1836 [Replaced in 1860 by the larger Providence Chapel]
Building   Yes [separate and entire] Yes [exclusively as a place of worship]
Sittings   Free 80. Other 20. Total [100]
Attend'ce 30 Mar. Morning 11 + 50 SS. Total [61]
              Afternoon 78. Total [78]
              Evening 110. Total [110]
Avge attendance [Not given]
Dated   30 March 1851
Signed   James Brooks, minister
              Drybrook, Mitcheldean, Gloucestershire
[On Brooks, see preceding entry.]

6.15 (8)   Bible Christian, Bradley Hill
Name   Zion Chapel
Erected   1846
Building   A separate building. Used exclusively for public worship and Sunday school
Sittings   Free 45. Other 35. Total [80]

Attend'ce 30 Mar.	Morning 57 + 30 SS. Total 87
	Afternoon 37 SS. Total 37
	Evening 65. Total 65
Avge attendance	[Not given]
Dated	31 March 1851
Signed	Thomas Wood, steward
	Sandley, near Blakeney, Gloucestershire

334.1.7 Parish of Littledean

Area 510 acres; 168 inhabited houses, 5 uninhabited. Population 947.
VCH 5, 159–73.

6.16 (18)   Church of England, St Ethelbert, Littledean

Name	Littledean. An ancient parish church
Consecration	[Not given]
Erected	[Restored 1863–4 and 1876–7]
Endowment	Tithe turnover [see below] {Total £90}
Sittings	Free about 350. Other (numbers). Total 350
Attend'ce 30 Mar.	Morning about 75 + about 55 SS. Total about 130
	Afternoon about 120 + about 55 SS. Total about 175
Avge attendance	Morning about 70 + about 55 SS. Total about 125
	Afternoon about 170 + about 55 SS. Total about 225
Remarks	Additional note. Whether the church is endowed or not, I cannot say. There are, however, tithes obtained from land in the parish amounting to about £115 a year. The Trustees of St Bartholomew's Hospital, Gloucester, who are the patrons of the living collect them, give me £70 a year out of them and apply the rest, I believe, to the hospital above named. [...] Many of the parishioners claim particular sittings. I believe they are not legally entitled to them. Henry Mark Willis
Dated	31 March 1851
Signed	Henry Mark Willis, perpetual curate [1847–57]
	Littledean, Newnham, Gloucestershire

[In 1849 'the church was described as in bad order, dirty and ill-kept': *VCH*, 5, 171.]

6.17 (20)   Independent, Broad Street, Littledean

Name	Littledean Chapel
Erected	The present chapel was erected in the the year 1821. Enlarged 1847
Building	It is a separate and entire building. It is used exclusively as a place of worship. No school except the Sab[ba]th school is kept in it.
Sittings	Free 211. Other 149. Total [360] Standing room for 79
Attend'ce 30 Mar.	Morning 150 + 84 SS. Total 234
	Evening 260. Total 260
Avge attendance	Morning 150 + 82 SS. Total 232
	Evening 300. Total 300
Dated	28 March 1851
Signed	Benjamin Jenkyn, minister [1842–54]
	Littledean, Gloucestershire

[Jenkyn was also the minister of the chapels at Pope's Hill (**6.18**) and Harrow Hill (**6.19**).]

6.18 (16)   Independent, Pope's Hill, Littledean

Name	Pope's Hill Chapel

Erected   1844 [Enlarged c.1870]
Building   It is a separate building. It is used exclusively as a place of worship,
                    except S[unday] school.
Sittings   All free 96. Total [96] Standing room space available for 112 persons
Attend'ce 30 Mar. Morning 24 SS. Total 24
                    Afternoon 70 + 24 SS. Total 94
Avge attendance (6m) Morning 24 SS. Total 24
                    Afternoon 70 + 24 SS. Total 94
Remarks   The entries of the numbers have been made according to the average
                    attendance of the last six months.
Dated   27 March 1851
Signed   Benjamin Jenkyn, minister [1842–54]
                    Littledean, Gloucestershire
[Jenkyn was also the minister of Littledean chapel (**6.17**) and Harrow Hill (**6.19**).]

6.19 (15)   **Independent, Harrow Hill, Littledean**
Name   Samuel Stephen's house, Harley Hill
Erected   [Not given]
Building   Dwelling house
Sittings   [Not given]
Attend'ce 30 Mar. [Not given]
Avge attendance (6m) Evening 15. Total [15]
Remarks   NB. I have taken notice of the provisions for Sabbath evening in the
                    circulars that I have fill up simply because I have thought that the last
                    six months attendance is the best.
Dated   27 March 1851
Signed   Benjamin Jenkyn, minister [1842–54]
                    Littledean, Gloucestershire
[Jenkyn was also the minister of Littledean chapel (**6.17**) and Pope's Hill (**6.18**).]

6.20 (19)   **Wesleyan Reformers, Cinderford**
Name   None except 'The Iron Works'
Erected   1841
Building   Yes [separate and entire] Yes [exclusively as a place of worship]
Sittings   All free. It will seat 250 persons. Total [250]
Attend'ce 30 Mar. Morning 90 + 70 SS. Total 160
                    Afternoon none
                    Evening 150. Total [150]
Avge attendance   [Not given]
Dated   31 March 1851
Signed   John Hirst, minister
                    Cinderford, Glo'ster
[Hirst was also the minister of Flaxley (**6.23**).]

334.1.8 Parish of Flaxley
Area 1,375 acres; 40 inhabited houses, 2 uninhabited. Population 242.
VCH 5, 138–150.

6.21 (21)   **Church of England, St Mary the Virgin, Flaxley**
Name   Not certainly known. But as the abbey to which it belongs is dedicated
                    to St Mary the Virgin, it is probable that the church is so likewise.

Consecration	Cannot ascertain if consecrated before 1800. It was originally the chapel to Flaxley Abbey and the appointment of the clergyman in the owner's hands.
Erected	[Replaced by a new church consecrated 18 Sept. 1856]
Endowment	OPE £8. {Total £104}
Sittings	Sittings all the private property of the patron. Total 130
Attend'ce 30 Mar.	Morning 70 + 80 SS. Total 150
	Afternoon 81 + 80 SS. Total 161
Avge attendance	[Not given]
Remarks	Flaxley is a peculiar and until recently was a district. The chief remuneration of the clergyman arises from a bequest made by Mr [Thomas Crawley-]Boevey, and to the present patron amounting to £115 per annum but it is left under conditions and if they are unfulfilled may be ... .
Dated	31 March 1851
Signed	Richard Lewis Daubeny, perpetual curate [1850–2]
	Flaxley Cottage, Gloucester

6.22 (22)   Wesleyan Methodist, Flaxley

Name	Ansterley Cottage
Erected	1850
Building	No [not separate and entire] No [not exclusively as a place of worship]
Sittings	Free 50. Total [50]
Attend'ce 30 Mar.	Morning 17. Total [17]
	Afternoon 25. Total [25]
Avge attendance	[Not given]
Dated	31 March 1851
Signed	Samuel Wesley, minister
	Littledean, Woodside, Newnham, Gloucestershire

[Wesley was also the minister of Coleford (**18.31**), Joyford (**18.43**), Lydbrook (**18.41**), Newnham (**6.11**) and Mitcheldean (**6.27**).]

6.23 (23)   Wesleyan Reformers, Flaxley

Name	Wesley Chapel
Erected	June 1850
Building	Yes [separate and entire] Yes [exclusively as a place of worship]
Sittings	Free 250. Other 350. Total [600]
Attend'ce 30 Mar.	Morning 300 + 200 SS. Total 500
	Evening 500. Total [500]
Avge attendance (9m)	[Not given]
Dated	2 April 1851
Signed	John Hirst, Wesleyan Reform minister
	Cinderford area, Newnham, Glo'ster

[Hirst was also minster of the congregation meeting at the Cinderford Iron Works (**6.20**).]

334.1.9   Parish of Abenhall (or Abinghall)

Area 751 acres; 47 inhabited houses, 1 uninhabited. Population 224.
Within the parish is the hamlet of Gunn's Mills.
VCH 5, 93–101.

6.24 (24)   Church of England, St Michael, Abenhall

Name	St Michael. An ancient parish church

Consecration	Before 1800
Erected	[Restored 1873–4 and 1879]
Endowment	Tithe £118. Glebe £25. {Total £142}
Sittings	Free 10. Other 200 or thereabouts. Total 210
Attend'ce 30 Mar.	Morning 100. Total [100]
	Afternoon 60. Total [60]
Avge attendance (6m)	Morning 70. Total [70]
	Afternoon 60. Total [60]
Remarks	Twenty girls sit together and attend the church, but they receive no instruction as Sunday scholars, nor do they go to or come from a school.
Dated	31 March 1851
Signed	James Davies, rector [1837–73]
	Mitcheldean

[Davies was a High Churchman and 'a firm if moderate supporter of the Tractarians. He was also an inveterate gossip and kept Isaac Williams informed on a host of matters, including the activities of the younger men who sometimes gave cause for amusement and sometimes for distress': Jones, 123.]

334.1.10 Parish of Mitcheldean
Area 680 acres; 147 inhabited houses, 9 uninhabited. Population 662.
VCH 5, 173–95. *GNQ* 1, 346–347.

6.25 (25)   St Michael and All Angels, Mitcheldean

Name	St Michael's, parish church
Consecration	Before 1800
Erected	[Restored 1852–3 and 1890–1]
Endowment	Tithe £176. Glebe £12. OPE £5 5s. Fees £5. {Total £141}
Sittings	Free 12. Other 100. Total 112
Attend'ce 30 Mar.	Morning 110 + 75 SS. Total 185
	Afternoon 140 + 75 SS. Total 215
Avge attendance	I have no means of making an accurate return.
Remarks	From the gross endowment of £198 5s, sh'd be deducted for poor rates and other outgoings, on the endowm't charge on glebe house etc. etc. £71. [Total] £127 5s
Dated	31 March 1851
Signed	Edward Machen, rector [1847–57]
	Mitcheldean

[In 1810 when Henry Berkin began his Evangelical ministry at Mitcheldean there was a congregation of 20. This soon increased and every seat was occupied. He began a Sunday school in 1812 and by the following year there were 558 pupils. He was responsible for the erection of Holy Trinity, Harrow Hill (**6.6**): Nicholls 1863, 132–3.]

6.26 (26)   Independent, Mitcheldean

Name	Independent Chapel
Erected	Before 1800 [Rebuilt 1735, 1798 and 1822; altered 1850]
Building	Yes [separate and entire] Yes [exclusively as a place of worship]
Sittings	Free 102. Other 137. Total [239] Standing room for 50
Attend'ce 30 Mar.	Morning 95 + 57 SS. Total 152
	Evening 170. Total 170
Avge attendance	Morning 100 + 70 SS. Total 170
	Evening 230. Total 230
Dated	31 March 1851

Signed   Joseph Lander, minister [1850–73]
                Stinder's Cottage, Mitcheldean, Gloucestershire.
[Lander's predecessor John Horlick (1778–1858) was also the minister of Ruardean (**18.51**).]

6.27 (27)   **Wesleyan Methodist, Mitcheldean**
Name   Wesleyan Chapel
Erected   About 1812
Building   Yes [separate and entire] Yes [exclusively as a place of worship]
Sittings   All free 140. Total [140]
Attend'ce 30 Mar. Evening 25. Total [25]
Avge attendance [Not given]
Dated   31 March 1851
Signed   Samuel Wesley, minister
                Littledean, Woodside, Newnham, Gloucestershire
[Wesley was also the minister of Coleford (**18.31**), Flaxley (**6.22**), Joyford (**18.43**), Lydbrook (**18.41**) and Newnham (**6.11**). The chapel at Mitcheldean closed in 1855 and was re-opened the following year by Bible Christians who moved to a larger chapel in 1861.]

334.2   HUNTLEY SUB-DISTRICT

334.2.1 Parish of Blaisdon
Area 900 acres; 66 inhabited houses, 3 uninhabited. Population 299.
VCH 10, 6–11.

6.28 (28)   **Church of England, St Michael, Blaisdon**
Name   Consecrated to St Michael, and is an ancient parish church
Consecration   Before 1 Jany 1800 [14 June 1867]
Erected   [Apart from the tower rebuilt 1866–7]
Endowment   Tithe £190. *Glebe £20. OPE £15 [In 1860 total £210]
Sittings   Free 94. Other 12. Total 106
Attend'ce 30 Mar. Morning 28 + 37 SS. Total 65
                Afternoon 59 + 33 SS. Total 92
Avge attendance Morning 20 + 35 SS. Total 55
                Afternoon 60 + 35 SS. Total 95
Remarks   *The value of glebe house, as rated to the poor. I not quite certain as to
                the name given at the time of consecration.
Dated   31 March 1851
Signed   Robert Rochester Hurle MA, rector [1846–66]
                Blaisdon rectory, Longhope, Gloucester

334.2.2 Parish of Westbury-on-Severn
Area 8,695 acres; 470 inhabited houses, 6 uninhabited. Population 2,498.
The parish includes the tithing of Rodley. The Union workhouse situated within the parish had 74 inmates.
VCH 10, 79–102.

6.29 (29)   **Church of England, St Peter and St Paul, Westbury-on-Severn**
Name   St Peter's. Ancient parish church built in the year 1530
Consecration   [Not given]
Erected   [Restored 1861–2 and 1875–8]
Endowment   {Total £291}
Sittings   Free 800. Total 800

Attend'ce 30 Mar. [Not given] [Total 500]
Avge attendance [Not given] [Total 500]
Remarks Estimated number of persons attending the parish church on Sunday, 30 March 1851, including school children 500. Average number of congregation during the year 500.
Dated 31 March 1851
Signed Thomas May Wetherell, resident curate [1839–52]
Westbury upon Severn vicarage, nr Gloucester
[Incumbent Richard Wetherell 1798–1858]
[Wetherell (who was non-resident 1819–35) was also the incumbent of Notgrove (**14.9**).]

6.30 (30)   Independent, Adsett, Westbury-on-Severn
Name Ebenezer Chapel
Erected 1838
Building Yes [separate and entire] Yes [exclusively as a place of worship]
Sittings Free 170. Other 90. Total [260]
Attend'ce 30 Mar. Morning 62 + 38 SS. Total [100]
Evening 115. Total [115]
Avge attendance [Not given]
Remarks The average of the general morning congregation during the summer months is about 80, that of the evening of the same period 160. Owing to the children of the poor in this parish who attend any week day school chiefly going to the National [school], the teachers of which oblige them to attend there on the Sabbath also; the school in connexion with the above place of worship is much smaller than it was a few years back when this rule was not enforced.
Dated 31 March 1851
Signed Cyrus Hudson, minister [1849–59]
Chasehill, Westbury on Severn

6.31 (31)   Particular Baptist, Westbury-on-Severn
Name Marsh British School
Erected Abt 1821
Building Yes [separate and entire] No, lent on weekdays for British school.
Sittings Free abt 70. Others none. Total [70]
Attend'ce 30 Mar. Afternoon abt 40 + 35 SS. Total 75
Evening 40. Total 40
Avge attendance [Not given]
Remarks This place belongs to the Baptist church at Westbury Leigh [Wilts.] and is lent to be used during the week as a British school and occupied on Sabbaths by local preachers and Sunday school.
Dated 31 March 1851
Signed James Sherriff (MA), minister
Westbury Leigh, Wiltshire

6.32 (32)   Wesleyan Methodist, Westbury-on-Severn
Name Wesleyan Chapel
Erected 1822
Building Yes [separate and entire] Yes [exclusively as a place of worship]
Sittings Free 65. Other 60. Total [125]
Attend'ce 30 Mar. Morning 32 + 46 SS. Total 78

	Afternoon 75 + 45 SS. Total 120
Avge attendance	Morning 33 + 48 SS. Total 81
	Afternoon 90 + 48 SS. Total 138
Dated	30 March 1851
Signed	Hugh Bevan, local preacher [commercial traveller of provisions]
	72 Alvin Street, Gloucester

334.2.3 Parish of Minsterworth

Area 1,938 acres; 108 inhabited houses, 8 uninhabited. Population 494.
VCH 13 (forthcoming).

6.33 (33) (Summary form)	**Church of England, St Peter, Minsterworth**
Name	St Peter's
Erected	Unknown. Very ancient [Rebuilt 1869–70 and consecrated 22 Sept. 1870]
Building	Yes [separate and entire] Yes [exclusively as a place of worship]
[*Endowment*	Total £125]
Sittings	Free 300. Other 30. Total 330
Usual attend'ce	Morning 30. Total [30]
	Afternoon 100. Total [100]
	One service on Sunday: morning or afternoon, alternately.
	No Sunday school. The weekday school meets to attend the church services, but not for instruction.
Remarks	Additional note
	The above is an estimated return which I have obtained by making enquiries of the churchwarden, not being able to get any information from the clergyman or parish clerk. J. Constance
Signed	John Constance [registrar]
[*Incumbent*	Lort Mansel 1819–54]

[Mansel was a nephew of William Lort Mansel, the bishop of Bristol 1808–20: *ODNB* 'William Lort Mansel (1753–1820)'.]

6.34 (34)	**Wesleyan Methodist, Calcott's Green**
Name	Wesleyan Chapel
Erected	In 1845
Building	Yes [separate and entire] Yes [exclusively as a place of worship]
Sittings	Free about 80. Other about 80. Total [160] Standing room none.
Attend'ce 30 Mar.	Afternoon 3. Total [3] } SS
	Evening 7. Total [7] }none
Avge attend'ce (3m)	Morning 2. Total 2 } SS
	Afternoon 3. Total 3 }none
	Evening 5. Total 5
Remarks	Owing to the oppressive conduct of the Wesleyan preachers in expelling officers and members from the society on their own responsibility, the Society and congregation have left the chapel and worship in a room opened for that purpose of which a due return has been made (**6.35**).
Dated	5 April 1851
Signed	R. C. Stephens, trustee
	[Naight House], Minsterworth, Gloucestershire

6.35 (35)   **Wesleyan Reformers, Naight**
Name   Wesleyan Methodist (Reformers) preaching room
Erected   About the year 1825
Building   A separate building. Yes [exclusively as a place of worship]
Sittings   Free the whole 100. Other none. Total [100] Standing room none
Attend'ce 30 Mar.   Morning 8 SS. Total 8
                       Afternoon 45 + 14 SS. Total 59
                       Evening 51. Total 51
Avge attendance (3m) Morning 30 + 10 SS. Total 40
                       Afternoon 50 + 15 SS. Total 65
                       Evening 50. Total 50
Remarks   This room has not been occupied by the Wesleyan Methodist (Reformers)
                       more than three months, previous to that time it was a private building.
Dated   31 March 1851
Signed   R. C. Stephens, steward
                       [Naight House], Minsterworth, Gloucestershire

334.2.4 Parish of Churcham (part of which is in the Kingsholm sub-district 336.1.1–3).
Area 2,260 acres; 123 inhabited houses, 9 uninhabited. Population 610.
VCH 10, 11–29.

6.36 (36)   **Church of England, St Andrew, Churcham** (see also **8.1**)
Name   Church of St Andrew
Consecration   No records to show
Erected   [Chancel rebuilt 1859 and restored 1866–8. Rebuilt after a fire
                       1876–8]
Endowment   {Total £386}
Sittings   (All are free)
Attend'ce 30 Mar.   Afternoon 200. Total [200]
Avge attendance (3m) Morning 65. Total [65]
                       Afternoon 185. Total [185]
Remarks   The incumbent being absent from home on account of health, and this
                       paper having been forwarded to him, he has affixed his initials to these
                       queries, which his signature at the foot is meant to reply to or to certify,
                       and has requested the present officiating minister to certify the others.
Dated   27 March 1851
Signed   George Charles Hall, vicar [1837–95]
                       Churcham vicarage, Gloucester
[The benefice consisted of Churcham with Bulley (**6.38**). Within the parish Holy Innocents,
Highnam was consecrated 29 Apr. 1851.]

6.37 (37)   **Wesleyan Methodist, Birdwood**
Name   Birdwood Chapel
Erected   Before 1820
Building   Yes [separate and entire] Yes [exclusively as a place of worship]
Sittings   Free 150. Other 50. Total [200]
Attend'ce 30 Mar.   Morning 45 + 22 SS. Total 67
                       Afternoon 76. Total 76
                       No evening service
Avge attendance   [Not given]
Dated   31 March 1851

Signed	Richard Roberts, minister [1849–51]
	1 Worcester St, Gloucester

[The chapel was erected c.1805 for the Countess of Huntingdon's Connexion and sold to the Wesleyan Methodists c.1814.]

334.2.5 Parish of Bulley

Area 951 acres; 49 inhabited houses, 1 uninhabited. Population 241.
VCH 13 (forthcoming).

6.38 (38)	**Church of England, St Michael and All Angels, Bulley**
Name	St Andrew [That is the] ancient parish church [of Churcham]
Consecration	Unknown
Erected	Unknown [Restored and the chancel rebuilt 1886–7]
Endowment	Tithe £30 [See Churcham (**6.36**)]
Sittings	Free 126. Total 126
Attend'ce 30 Mar.	Morning 68. Total [68]
Avge attendance	[Not given]
Remarks	Additional note. The clergyman from home in consequence of his health. This schedule was left with the c[hurch]warden who says he does not possess the requisite information. I have therefore filled in the best information I can get. J. C. [John Constance, registrar]
Dated	31 March 1851
Signed	[Not given] ~~churchwarden~~
[*Incumbent*	George Charles Hall 1837–95]

[The benefice consisted of Churcham (**6.36**) with Bulley.]

334.2.6 Parish of Huntley

Area 1,409 acres; 119 inhabited houses, 6 uninhabited. Population 555.

6.39 (39)	**Church of England, St John the Baptist, Huntley**
Name	St John's
Consecration	Before 1800
Erected	[Apart from tower the church was rebuilt 1862–3]
Endowment	Tithe £241*. Glebe £50. OPE £32 [Total] £323. {Total £242}
Sittings	Free 163. Other 239. Total 402
Attend'ce 30 Mar.	Morning 82 + 95 SS. Total 177
	Afternoon 89 + 95 SS. Total 184
Avge attendance	Morning 100 + 110 SS. Total 210
	Afternoon 150 + 95 SS. Total 245
Remarks	*Deduct £35 for rates. £100 for curate, £60 for school, £5 for repairs of chancel, leaving a balance from the total value of the living of £123 to meet the repairs of the rectory and the charities of the parish, besides which there will be a reduction of from 20 to 30 per cent owing to the low price of corn. To which I should add £25 for collection of tithe and expenses.
Dated	31 March 1851
Signed	Daniel Capper, rector [1839–66]
	Huntley rectory, Gloucester

[Capper (1804–1886) was a wealthy Evangelical, the son and heir of Robert Capper (1768–1851), an early supporter of Thomas Snow (**16.23**) and involved with the opening of Portland Chapel, Cheltenham (**16.37**). He was distantly related to the Evangelical architect Samuel Sanders Teulon, who was engaged to rebuild St John the Baptist, Huntley (re-opened 1863). Teulon was also responsible for designing Huntley manor house and the Tyndale Monument at North Nibley: *ODNB* 'Samuel Sanders Teulon (1812–1873').]

334.2.7 Parish of Longhope
Area 3,070 acres; 131 inhabited houses, 3 uninhabited. Population 1,070.
VCH 12, 223–54.

6.40 (40)	**Church of England, All Saints, Longhope**
Name	All Saints. Parish church of Longhope
Consecration	[Not given]
Erected	[Restored 1858]
Endowment	Tithe £400. Glebe £19. Fees £2. Other sources none. {Total £384}
Sittings	Free 210. Other £140. Total 350
Attend'ce 30 Mar.	Morning 198 + 67 SS. Total 265
	Afternoon 100 + 66 SS. Total 166
Avge attendance (4m)	Morning 70 + 70 SS. Total 140
	Afternoon 120 + 70 SS. Total 190
Remarks	During a period previous to December last owing to the ill-health of the incumbent, recently deceased, the average attendance was scarcely more than 40 in the morning and 60 in the afternoon. Since that time the congregation has nearly doubled.
Dated	31 March 1851
Signed	William Henry Hill, curate
	Longhope, Gloucester
[*Incumbent*	Robert Napier Raikes 1828–51 (died 22 Mar. 1851)]

[Raikes had also been the incumbent of Old Sodbury (**3.12**)]. Hill was an Evangelical who had previously served as a curate of St Mary, Cheltenham 1837–8.]

6.41 (41)	**Baptist, Hopes Hill**
Name	Zion Baptist Chapel
Erected	1846
Building	Yes [separate and entire] with burial ground. The day and Sabbath schools are kept in the chapel.
Sittings	All the sittings are free 130. Total [130]
Attend'ce 30 Mar.	Morning 71 + 52 SS. Total 123
	Afternoon 84 + 49 SS. Total 133
	Evening 102. Total 102
Avge attendance	Congregations rather less than usual today
Remarks	We are much inconvenienced from being compelled to teach the Sunday and day schools in the chapel for want of a proper school room.
Dated	30 March 1851
Signed	Henry Clement Davies, Baptist minister
	Zion Cottage, Longhope, Gloucestershire

[The chapel was seeded by the congregation of Parker's Row, Gloucester (**8.26**)]

---

7. HO 129/335 NEWENT DISTRICT: 31 places of worship

335.1 NEWENT SUB-DISTRICT

335.1.1 Parish of Aston Ingham, Herefordshire
Area 2,378 acres; 142 inhabited houses, 9 uninhabited. Population 636.

7.1 (1)	***Church of England, St John the Baptist, Aston Ingham***
Name	*Parish church of Aston Ingham*
Consecration	*Years and years before 1800*
Erected	*[Apart from the tower mostly rebuilt in 1891]*
Endowment	*Tithe £350. Glebe (102 acres) £100. Fees vary from £2 to £5 per ann.*
	Easter offerings never received. Other sources nil. {Total £350}
Sittings	*Free aisle contains accommodation for more than 200 with the chancel.*
	Total [200]
Attend'ce 30 Mar.	*Morning 26 SS. Total [26]*
Avge attendance	*Morning 30 SS. Total [30]*
Remarks	*Tithe connected to a r[ent] charge of £50 allowed for rates leaving*
£300	*net subject to averages. Congregation averages from 100 to 150*
besides	*children, but I never counted the number. The church generally speaking*
	is nearly, if not quite full, tho' of late owing to the weather it has not been
	the case.
Dated	*31 March 1851*
Signed	*Henry Lawson Whatley, rector and minister [1835–73]*
	Newent, nr Gloucester

335.1.2 Parish of Linton, Herefordshire
Area 2,775 acres; 202 inhabited houses, 11 uninhabited. Population 952.

7.2 (2)	***Church of England, St Mary the Virgin, Linton***
(Summary form)	
Name	*Linton*
Erected	*Before 1800 [Restored 1878–9]*
[Endowment	*Total £479]*
Sittings	*[Not given]*
Usual attend'ce	*Morning 50 + about 14 SS. Total [64]*
	Afternoon 60 or 70. Total [60–70]
Signed	*Richard Lovett Bruton [registrar]*
	[Calvert Street, Newent]
[Incumbent	*Thomas Chandler Curteis 1841–65]*

7.3 (3)	**Baptist, Gorsley**
Name	Gorsley schoolroom licensed for public worship
Erected	1821 [Chapel opened 1852]
Building	Yes [separate and entire] No [not exclusively as a place of worship]
	for a day school
Sittings	All free 240. Other none. Total [240]
Attend'ce 30 Mar.	Morning 200. Total 200
	Afternoon 50 SS. Total 50
	Evening 200. Total 200

Avge attendance   Morning 200. Total 200
                    Afternoon 130 SS*. Total 130
                    Evening 250**. Total 250
Remarks   There is a good deal [of] sickness in the neighbourhood at this time among
                    the people, and measles very general among the children. This will account
                    for the small attendance today both of school and congregation.
                    *The school cannot assemble in the morning for want of room.
                    **The evening congregation embraces more than a hundred different
                    persons than the morning one.
Dated   [Not given]
Signed   John Hall, minister [1831–81]
                    Gorsley near Ross, Herefordshire

[Hall was also the minister of Kempley Green (**7.21**). Edward Goff (1739–1813) who made his
fortune in the coal trade, left £15,000 to establish free schools in Herefs., Shrops., Monmouths., and
Worcs. In each instance a schoolroom and a rent free school house was provided for the master
(who had to be a Baptist) and was paid £50 a year. Goff's School at Gorsley was built in 1821 and
the headteacher was also the pastor of a congregation. A chapel was opened in 1852. Hall began in
1831, remaining as headteacher until 1864 and then minister of the chapel until 1881.]

335.1.3 Parish of Oxenhall
Area 1,887 acres; 55 inhabited houses, 2 uninhabited. Population 288.
VCH 12, 254–81.

7.4 (4)   **Church of England, St Anne, Oxenhall**
Name   An ancient parish church of a distinct and separate parish dedicated to
                    St Ann
Consecration   Before 1800 [13 June 1867]
Erected   [Apart from the tower, rebuilt 1866–7]
Endowment   Land £1 9s 4d. Tithe £13 6s 8d. Glebe £30. OPE £32 10s. Fees £3
                    Total amount of income about £80. {Total £80}
Sittings   Free about 86. Other 55. Total 141
Attend'ce 30 Mar. Morning 54 + 9 SS. Total 63
Avge attendance   [Not given]
Dated   31 March 1851
Signed   Thomas Palling Little, perpetual curate [1848–83]
                    Newent, Gloucestershire

[Little was also the incumbent of Pauntley (**7.15**).]

335.1.4–8   Parish of Newent
Area 7,803 acres; 676 inhabited houses, 29 uninhabited. Population 3,306.
The parish includes the town of Newent and the tithings of Boulsdon and Killcott, Compton,
Cugley and Malswick. The Union workhouse situated within the parish had 73 inmates.
VCH 12, 7–94. *GNQ* 5, 189.

7.5 (5)   **Church of England, St Mary the Virgin, Newent**
(Summary form)
Name   Newent
Erected   Before 1800 [Restored 1880 and 1884]
[*Endowment*   Total £1,076]
Sittings   [Not given]
Usual attend'ce   Morning about 300. Total [300]
                    Afternoon about 150. Total [150]

Signed   Richard Lovett Bruton [registrar]
                     [Culvert Street, Newent]
[Incumbent   Arthur Andrew Onslow 1850–64]
[Onslow was the second son of Richard Francis Onslow, Archdeacon of Worcester 1815–49. In 1846 Reuben Partridge published a criticism of the Tractarian views expressed in a pastoral address to the parishioners of Newent by the then curate John Skally.]

7.6 (6)   **Independent, Broad Street**
Name   Newent Chapel
Erected   About 1844 [Opened 1846]
Building   Yes [separate and entire] Yes [exclusively as a place of worship]
Sittings   Free 150. Other 250. Total [400]
Attend'ce 30 Mar. Morning 37 + 60 SS. Total 97
                     Afternoon 56 + 75 SS. Total 131
                     Evening 73. Total 73
Avge attendance Morning 40 + 60 SS. Total 100
                     Afternoon 60 + 80 SS. Total 140
                     Evening 80. Total 80
Remarks   A day school has been taught in the vestry and will be soon re-established
Dated   30 March 1851
Signed   Joseph Chapman, minister [1851–3]
                     Newent, Gloucester

7.7 (8)   **Wesleyan Methodist, Glass House Hill**
Name   [Not given]
Erected   1810
Building   Yes [separate and entire] Only as a place of worship
Sittings   Free 100. Total [100]
Attend'ce 30 Mar. Morning 60. Total 60
                     Afternoon 80. Total 80
Avge attendance [Not given]
Dated   21 November 1851
Signed   Richard Lovett Bruton [registrar]
                     [Culvert Street, Newent]

7.8 (7)   **Wesleyan Methodist, Culver Street**
Name   Wesleyan Methodist Chapel
Erected   1815 [New chapel 1855]
Building   A separate and entire building. Yes [exclusively as a place of worship]
Sittings   Free 112. Other 90. Total [202] Standing room none
Attend'ce 30 Mar. Morning 19 + 27 SS. Total 46
                     Evening 56. Total [56]
Avge attendance Morning 20 + 40 SS. Total 60
                     Evening 60. Total 60
Remarks   Being mid-Lent Sunday many of the families are from home visiting elder friends.
Dated   31 March 1851
Signed   John Parsons, minister [1849–51]
                     Newent, Gloucestershire

335.1.9 Parish of Taynton

Area 2,501 acres; 143 inhabited houses, 5 uninhabited. Population 631.
VCH 12, 317–46.

7.9 (9)	**Church of England, St Lawrence, Taynton**
Name	Taynton. An ancient parish church. Date 1660
Consecration	[Not given]
Erected	[Altered 1825–6 and 1864–5; restored 1893–4]
Endowment	Tithe £450. Glebe £36. Fees £2 or £3. {Total £321}
Sittings	Free 207. Other about 130. Total 337
Attend'ce 30 Mar.	Morning between 80 and 90 + 39 SS. Total 124
	Afternoon supposed to be about 85 (as many as in the morning but not counted) + 37 SS. Total 122.
Avge attendance (3m)	Morning 70 or 80 + 35 SS. Total 110
	Afternoon 70 or 80 + 35 SS. Total 110
Dated	30 March 1851
Signed	William Hughes, curate of Taynton (1850–]
	Taynton, Gloucester
[*Incumbent*	Francis Jeune 1844–64]

[Jeune, 'a low churchman with Evangelical sympathies ... a determined opponent of Tractarianism' (Reynolds, 78, 173) was the master of Pembroke College, Oxford 1843–64 and bishop of Peterborough 1864–8: *ODNB* 'Francis Jeune (1806–1868)'. St Lawrence, Taynton was one of only about six Anglican churches and chapels erected in England during the Commonwealth period.]

7.10 (10)	**Wesleyan Methodist, Taynton**
Name	May Hill Chapel
Erected	1821
Building	Yes [separate and entire] Yes [exclusively as a place of worship]
Sittings	Free 140. Total [140]
Attend'ce 30 Mar.	Morning 54. Total 54
	Afternoon 57. Total 57
Avge attendance	Morning 65. Total 65
	Afternoon 60. Total 60
Dated	30 March 1851
Signed	Robert Hook [cider retailer]
	Thomas Catterick, Wesleyan minister [1850–1]
	Ledbury

[Catterick was also the minister of Redmarley D'Abitot (**7.25**).]

335.1.10 Parish of Tibberton

Area 1,400 acres; 74 inhabited houses, 4 uninhabited. Population 362.
VCH 13 (forthcoming).

7.11 (11)	**Church of England, Holy Trinity, Tibberton**
Name	Tibberton Church. Ancient parish church
Consecration	[Not given]
Erected	[Restored 1908]
Endowment	Tithe £327 10s. {Total £350}
Sittings	Free 154. Other 8. Total 162
Attend'ce 30 Mar.	Morning 39 + 25 SS. Total 64
	Afternoon 80 + 26 SS. Total 106
Avge attendance	Morning 50 + 26 SS. Total 76

	Afternoon 80 + 26 SS. Total 106
Remarks	The average number of the general congregation has perhaps been rather lower [?] than I have stated.
	Additional note [some words lost in page margins]
	The state of this parish with ... return is deplorable. I have held this living somewhat more ... . Before being instituted to it there had been no resident clergyman for 4[... years]
Dated	31 March 1851
Signed	William Lambert, rector [1849–52]
	Tibberton, Gloucestershire

7.12 (12)   **Wesleyan Methodist, Tibberton**

Name	Wesleyan Methodist Chapel
Erected	1839
Building	Yes [separate and entire] Yes [exclusively as a place of worship]
Sittings	Free 182. Other 30. Total [212]
Attend'ce 30 Mar.	Afternoon 45 + 38 SS. Total 83
	Evening 65. Total [65]
Avge attendance	~~Morning 50~~
Dated	31 March 1851
Signed	Charles Teague, steward [wheelwright]
	Tibberton, Gloucestershire

[Teague (1818–1914) was 'saved by grace and for over 60 years a sincere worshipper in this chapel. His Christian life won the affection and respect of all who knew him': tablet in the chapel.]

335.1.11–12 Parish of Rudford

Area 1,204 acres; 49 inhabited houses. 1 uninhabited. Population 232.
The parish includes the hamlet of Highleadon.
VCH 13 (forthcoming)

7.13 (13)   **Church of England, St Mary, Rudford**

(Summary form)

Name	Rudford
Erected	Before 1800 [Restored 1847–8 (chancel) and 1869–70]
[*Endowment*	Total £261]
Sittings	[Not given]
Usual attend'ce	Morning about 40 or 50. Total [40–50]
	There is service only one on the Sabbath excepting from January to September.
Signed	Richard Lovett Bruton [registrar]
	[Culvert Street, Newent]
[*Incumbent*	William Wilton Mutlow 1828–66]

335.1.13 Parish of Upleadon

Area 1,207 acres; 46 inhabited houses, 2 uninhabited. Population 275.
VCH 13 (forthcoming)

7.14 (14)   **Church of England, St Mary the Virgin, Upleadon**

Name	St Mary. An ancient parish church
Consecration	Before 1800
Erected	[Chancel rebuilt 1847–9; restored 1877–9 and 1966–9]
Endowment	Land £61 10s. OPE £16. {Total £80}

Sittings	Free 67. Other 52. Total 119
	[In pencil] 13 x 5 [65], 6 x 3 (18), 5 x 2 [10], 13 x 2 [26] [Total 119]
Attend'ce 30 Mar.	Morning 37 + 28 SS. Total 65
	Afternoon 21. Total 21
Avge attendance	Morning 40 + 30 SS. Total 70
	Afternoon 30. Total 30
Dated	31 March 1851
Signed	John Constable, curate [1850–5]
	Upleadon nr Newent, Gloucestershire
[*Incumbent*	Andrew Sayers 1835–70]

[Constable became vice-principal of Clapham Grammar School 1856–9 and principal of the Royal Agricultural College, Cirencester 1859–80. Sayers was also the incumbent of St Mary de Crypt, Gloucester (**8.34**).]

335.1.14 Parish of Pauntley

Area 1,967 acres; 52 inhabited houses, 5 uninhabited. Population 256.
VCH 12, 281–301

7.15 (15)   Church of England, St John, Pauntley

Name	An ancient parish church of a distinct and separate parish dedicated to St John the Baptist
Consecration	Before 1800
Erected	[Restored 1846–8]
Endowment	Tithe £13 6s 8d. Glebe £44. OPE £20 10s. Fees £2. Total amount of income about £80. {Total £80}
Sittings	Free 92. Other 42. Total 134
Attend'ce 30 Mar.	Morning none
	Afternoon about 65. Total 65
	Evening none
Avge attendance	[Not given]
Dated	31 March 1851
Signed	Thomas Palling Little, perpetual curate [1848–83]
	Newent, Gloucestershire

[Little was also the incumbent of Oxenhall (**7.4**).]

7.16 (16)   Wesleyan Methodist, Poolhill

Name	Wesleyan Methodist Chapel or Poolhill Chapel
Erected	1814
Building	Yes [separate and entire] Yes [exclusively as a place of worship]
Sittings	Free 104. Other 100. Total [204] Standing room for 65
Attend'ce 30 Mar.	Morning 17. Total 17
	Afternoon 65 + 66 SS. Total 131
	Evening 25. Total 25
Avge attendance	Morning 80 SS. Total 80
	Afternoon 60 + 80 SS. Total 140
	Evening 60. Total 60
Dated	31 March 1851
Signed	Richard Merrett, leader [wheelwright]
	Upleadon, Newent, Gloucestershire

335.2 R<small>EDMARLEY</small> S<small>UB</small>-<small>DISTRICT</small>

335.2.1 Parish of Dymock
Area 6,875 acres; 360 inhabited houses, 14 uninhabited. Population 1,771.
VCH 12, 122–174.

7.17 (17)	**Church of England, St Mary, Dymock**
Name	An ancient parish church dedicated to St Mary
Consecration	Before 1800
Erected	[Restored 1869–71 and 1879–80]
Endowment	Land ([Queen Anne's] Bounty) £30. Tithe (in lieu of) £60 (Originally endowed with vicaral tithes, now withheld). Fees £10 {Total £104}
Sittings	Free 300. Other 300. Total 600
Attend'ce 30 Mar.	Morning 182 + 98 SS. Total 280
	Afternoon 60 + 80 SS. Total 140
Avge attendance (6m)	Morning 250 + 95 SS. Total 345
	Afternoon 100 + 50 SS. Total 150
Remarks	The parish contains 7,000 acres. Hundreds of the people are from two to three and a half miles from from their own church, while there are seven parish churches within half or one mile from them; and consequently many of them attend worship in one or other of those churches.
Dated	31 March 1851
Signed	John Simons, vicar [1827–66]
	Dymock, near Ledbury

[After Simons, the patron (Frederick Lygon, the sixth Earl of Beauchamp) appointed a succession of Anglo-Catholics to the parish. The ritualist William Charles Edmund Newbolt 1870–6 'faced strong opposition' from his parishioners (*VCH* 12, 173). In 1887 he became the principal of Ely Theological College and in 1890 a canon of St Paul's Cathedral: *ODNB* 'William Charles Edmund Newbolt (1844–1930)'.]

7.18 (19)	**Wesleyan Methodist, Bromsberrow Heath**
Name	Wesleyan Meeting House
Erected	1847
Building	Yes [separate and entire] Yes [exclusively as a place of worship]
Sittings	Free 50. Total [50] Standing room none
Attend'ce 30 Mar.	Evening 50. Total 50
Avge attendance	Evening 35. Total 35
Dated	31 March 1851
Signed	James Underwood, proprietor [carpenter]
	Bromsberrow Heath, Dymock, Gloucestershire

['Between 1834 and 1844 eight nonconformist places [of worship] were registered' in the area: *VCH* 12, 172. By 1876 the Wesleyan Methodists assembled in a room at the George Inn.]

7.19 (18)	**Bible Christian, Broom's Green**
Name	Broom's Green Chapel
Erected	1837
Building	Separate and entire building. Exclusively as a place of worship.
Sittings	All free 55. Total [55]
Attend'ce 30 Mar.	Afternoon 26. Total 26
	Evening 40. Total [40]
Avge attendance	[Not given]
Dated	31 March 1851

Signed   Joseph Holden, steward
                  James Brooks [minister]
                  Drybrook, Mitcheldean, Forest of Dean
[Brooks was also the minister of Quarry Hill (**6.13**) and Drybrook (**6.14**). The chapel was opened by the Moravians in 1837, transferred to the Bible Christians in 1840, and passed to the Primitive Methodists in 1875.]

335.2.2 Parish of Kempley
Area 1,564 acres; 67 inhabited houses, 3 uninhabited. Population 305.
VCH 12, 196–222

7.20 (20)   Church of England, St Mary, Kempley
Name   Parish church
Consecration   Before 1800
Erected   [Restored 1912–3]
Endowment   Tithe £216. Glebe £7. {Total £204}
Sittings   Free 80. Other 30. Total 110
Attend'ce 30 Mar. Under sequestration
Avge attendance (6m) Morning 40 + 11 SS. Total 51
                  Afternoon 30. Total 30
Dated   7 April 1851
Signed   John Brooke, churchwarden [farmer of 43 acres]
                  Kempley, Ledbury
[*Incumbent*   William Servante 1839–71]
[Servante's three successors were Anglo-Catholics and in 1898 Edward Denny was forced to resign from the living following opposition from his parishioners. St Mary's church was declared redundant in 1975 and transferred to English Heritage in 1990. The present parish church dedicated to St Edward the Confessor was built 1902–3 as a chapel of ease and consecrated 26 Dec. 1903.]

7.21 (21)   Baptist, Kempley Green
Name   Kempley Green Chapel
Erected   1850
Building   Yes [separate and entire] Yes [exclusively as a place of worship]
Sittings   Free 70. Other none. Total [70]
Attend'ce 30 Mar. Afternoon 66. Total 66
Avge attendance (6m) Afternoon 40. Total [40]
Dated   30 March 1851
Signed   John Hall, minister
                  Linton, near Ross, Hereford
[Hall was also the minister of Gorsley (**7.3**).]

335.2.3 Parish of Preston
Area 884 acres; 12 inhabited houses, 2 uninhabited. Population 80.

7.22 (22)   Church of England, St John the Baptist, Preston
Name   Name unknown. Ancient parish church
Consecration   Before 1800
Erected   [Restored 1859–60 and the chancel in 1885]
Endowment   Tithe £98. Glebe £30. Aggregate £128. {Total £128}
Sittings   Free 70. Other 30. Total 100
Attend'ce 30 Mar. [Not given]
Avge attendance Morning 54½ + 13 SS. Total 67½
                  Afternoon 54½ + 13 SS. Total 67½

Remarks	The church is situated near several outlying hamlets belonging to other parishes which increases the congregation. The children from the same cause belong to other parishes.
Dated	31 March 1851
Signed	William John Morrish, curate [1846–]
	Ledbury, Herefordshire
[*Incumbent*	Charles Bryan 1820–59]

[Bryan was also the incumbent of Woolaston (**18.6**) with Alvington (**18.10**) and Lancaut (**18.6**). Before 1863 the dedication was to St Matthew, then to St John the Baptist.]

335.2.4 Parish of Bromsberrow
Area 1,803 acres; 53 inhabited houses. Population 260.
VCH 12, 95–122.

7.23 (23)	**Church of England, St Mary, Bromsberrow**
Name	I believe the church is dedicated to St Mary, but have no document at hand to enable me to speak with certainly. It is an ancient parish church.
Consecration	Before 1800
Erected	[Restored 1857–8]
Endowment	[The income is derived from] tithe, glebe and fees. {Total £339}
Sittings	Free 64. Other 82. Total 146. Benches for scholars 31. Total 177
Attend'ce 30 Mar.	Morning 70 + 40 SS. Total 110
	Evening 20. Total 20
Avge attendance	Morning 90 + 40 SS. Total 130
	Evening 50. Total 50
	I suppose this to be about the numbers, but I do not give it as positively accurate.
Dated	31 March 1851
Signed	Charles Hill, rector [1823–56]
	Bromsberrow rectory, Ledbury, Herefordshire

[Hall was also the incumbent of Madresfield 1832–56. He was succeeded at Bromsberrow by his son Reginald Pyndar Hill 1856–87: Lloyd, 95–153.]

335.2.5 Parish of Redmarley D'Abitot, Worcestershire [transferred to Glos. 1931]
Area 3,778 acres; 247 inhabited houses, 15 uninhabited. Population 1,192.
In ten years the population had increased by 211 by the erection of cottages at Snigs End and Lowbands by the Chartist Association called the National Cooperative Land Company (1846–51).
VCH (Worcs.) 3, 481–6.

7.24 (24)	**Church of England, St Bartholomew, Redmarley D'Abitot**
Name	Redmarley parish church
Consecration	Before 1800
Erected	[Apart from the tower rebuilt in 1855–6]
Endowment	Tithe (commuted) £900. Glebe £104. Fees £3. {Total £900}
Sittings	Free 82. Other 58. Total 140
Attend'ce 30 Mar.	Morning 124 + 62 SS. Total 186
	Afternoon 99 + 56 SS. Total 155
Avge attendance	Morning 120 + 60 SS. Total 180
	Afternoon 92 + 54 SS. Total 146
Remarks	The benefice is returned at its gross value. The net value = £700.
Dated	30 March 1851

Signed   James Commeline, rector [1837–53]
                    Redmarley, Ledbury
[Commeline was 'burned to death whilst reading in bed, 26 January 1853, aged 63': Venn.]

7.25a (25)   Wesleyan Methodist, Redmarley D'Abitot
Name   Dury Lane, 'Chappel'
Erected   Since 1810
Building   Separate building [Exclusively as a] place of worship
Sittings   Free 70. Total [70]
Attend'ce 30 Mar. Afternoon 71. Total 71
                    Evening 32. Total 32
Avge attendance   Afternoon 70. Total [70]
                    Evening 35. Total [35]
Dated   4 April 1851
Signed   John Colwell, 'tennant and chappel steward' [cooper]
                    Rock, Redmarley D'Abitot, Ledbury

7.25b (26)   Wesleyan Methodist, Redmarley D'Abitot
Name   'Dure' Lane Chapel or Meeting House
Erected   Have not been able to learn. It was once occupied as a school.
Building   Yes [separate and entire] Yes [exclusively as a place of worship]
Sittings   Free 80. Total [80] Standing room for 10 or 12
Attend'ce 30 Mar. Afternoon 79. Total 79
                    Evening 32. Total 32
Avge attendance   Afternoon 70. Total 70
                    Evening 30. Total 30
Remarks   I forward this lest there were not a proper return made for this place.
                    In this room we have had worship for about 25 years. T. C.
Dated   21 April 1851
Signed   Thomas Catterick, Wesleyan minister [1850–1]
                    Ledbury, Herefordshire
[Catterick was also the minister of Taynton (**7.10**).]

335.2.6 Parish of Staunton, Worcestershire [transferred to Glos. 1931]
Area 1,447 acres; 115 inhabited houses, 17 uninhabited. Population 559.
In ten years the population had increased by 157 by the erection of cottages at Snigs End and Lowbands by the Chartist Association called the National Cooperative Land Company (1846–51).

7.26 (27)   Church of England, St James the Great, Staunton
Name   Staunton parish church, dedicated to St James the Greater
Consecration   Unknown. Before 1800
Erected   [Restored 1860]
Endowment   Tithe £381. OPE £90. Gross amount about £471. Fees average £2
                    {Total £404}
Sittings   Free 85. Other 60. Total 145
Attend'ce 30 Mar. Morning 40 + 34 SS. Total 74
                    Afternoon 65 + 32 SS. Total 97
Avge attendance   [Not given]
Remarks   It is almost impossible to make a general average, so much depends upon
                    the weather, which likewise makes one Sunday a bad criterion. The day
                    was fine, but mid-Lent Sunday is hereabouts a Festival, when the people go

out to visit their friends, which has a risible effect upon the numbers especially at those in service.

Additional note. The congregation at the morn. and afternoon services, with few exceptions, consists of different persons, except, of course, the children.

Dated	31 March 1851
Signed	George Tribb, curate
	Staunton, Gloucester
[*Incumbent*	Thomas Hill 1799–61]

335.2.7 Parish of Corse

Area 2,190 acres; 127 inhabited houses, 12 uninhabited. Population 586.

In ten years the population had increased by 104 by the erection of cottages at Snigs End and Lowbands by the Chartist Association called the National Cooperative Land Company (1846–51).

VCH 8, 271–81

7.27 (28)	**Church of England, St Margaret, Corse**
Name	Corse parish church.
Consecration	[Not given]
Erected	[Restored 1851]
Endowment	Land, tithe and glebe about £450. OPE none. Pew rents, fees and dues no[ne] Easter offerings and other sources none. {Total £443}
Sittings	Free 40. Other 60. Total 100
Attend'ce 30 Mar.	Morning 60 + 35 SS. Total 95
	Afternoon 100 + 30 SS. Total 130
Avge attendance	Morning 70 + 35 SS. Total 105
	Afternoon 100 + 35 SS. Total 135
Dated	31 March 1851
Signed	Henry Malpas MA, curate [1850–]
	Corse, Gloucester
[*Incumbent*	Henry Knowles Creed 1828–55]

7.28 (29)	**Wesleyan Methodist, Corse**
Name	Wesleyan Chapel
Erected	1838
Building	Yes [separate and entire] Yes [exclusively as a place of worship]
Sittings	Free 120. Other 30. Total [150] Standing room none
Attend'ce 30 Mar.	Afternoon 52 + 60 SS. Total 112
	Evening 45. Total 45
Avge attendance	Afternoon 50 + 50 SS. Total 100
	Evening 50. Total 50
Dated	31 March 1851
Signed	Joseph Chandler, steward
	Red House, Corse, Gloucestershire

335.2.8 Parish of Hartpury

Area 3,618 acres; 176 inhabited houses, 10 uninhabited. Population 884.

VCH 13 (forthcoming)

7.29 (30)	**Church of England, St Mary, Hartpury**
(On a nonconformist form)	
Name	Hartpury Church

Erected	About twelve hundred and fifty [Restored 1881–2]
Building	Entire building. Exclusively [used] for worship
[*Endowment*	Total £196]
Sittings	Free 187. Other 147. Total [334] Standing room [in] aisles [and] belfrey
Attend'ce 30 Mar.	~~Morning and afternoon unable to obtain~~
	Morning 26 SS. Total 26
	Afternoon 26 SS. Total 26
Avge attendance	Morning few
	Afternoon full church
Remarks	This the best information I can obtain as the church is so inconveniently situated for the main of the parish.
Dated	30 December 1851
Signed	Richard Hill, registrar
	Hartpury church, Lentridge, Dymock
[*Incumbent*	Charles Crawley 1838–56]

[Crawley was also a minor canon of Gloucester cathedral (**8.22**), a magistrate and a deputy lieutenant of the county.]

7.30 (31)   **Wesleyan Methodist, Hartpury**

Name	Hartpury Chapel
Erected	In the year 1828 [New chapel 1887]
Building	Yes [separate and entire] Yes [exclusively as a place of worship]
Sittings	Free 120. Other 30. Total [150]
Attend'ce 30 Mar.	Morning 20 SS. Total 20
	Afternoon 44 + 11 SS. Total 55
	Evening 31. Total 31
Avge attendance	Afternoon 80. Total 80
	Evening 80. Total 80
Dated	1 April 1851
Signed	John Smedley, superintendent minister [1849–51]
	Gloucester

[Smedley was also the minister of Northgate Street Chapel, Gloucester (**8.30**) and Hucclecote **8.14**).]

7.31 (32)   **Roman Catholic, St Mary, Hartpury**

(On an Anglican summary form)

Name	Roman Catholic Chapel
Erected	Eighteen hundred and thirty [Restored 1936]
Sittings	From eighty to one hundred may be accommodated in the whole, but service performed only once a quarter since the Nuns left the parish. From the best information I can gain there may be present about six at such time.
Usual attend'ce	[Not given]
Signed	Richard Hill, [registrar]

[From 1794 Hartpury Court was occupied by English Dominican nuns who had fled from the French Revolution. They left in 1839 and opened a convent at Atherstone, Warwicks., sold in turn to Benedictines in 1858.]

8. HO 129/336 GLOUCESTER DISTRICT: 51 places of worship

VCH 4, 1–381

336.1.   KINGSHOLM SUB-DISTRICT

336.1.1–3 Parish of Churcham (most of which is in Westbury-on-Severn district, 334.2.4). Area 2,004 acres; 68 inhabited houses, 1 uninhabited. Population in the three hamlets of Higham, Linton and Over: 415 (includes 31 persons on sea-going vessels).

Request for information. Will you have the goodness to furnish information respecting the undermentioned churches, congregations including Sunday scholars.

8.1 (1)	**Church of England, St Andrew, Churcham** (see also **6.36**)
Sittings	Free all. Other none
Morning	250
Afternoon	SS 60
Evening	400

8.2 (1)	**Church of England, St Giles, Maisemore**

[Request for information. Will you have the goodness to furnish information respecting the undermentioned churches, congregations including Sunday scholars.]
VCH 13 (forthcoming)

[*Erected*	Chancel restored 1851, nave rebuilt 1868–9]
[*Endowment*	Total £89]
Sittings	Free all. Other none
Morning	110
Afternoon	250
Evening	SS 45
[*Incumbent*	Charles Herbert Martin 1829–57]
Dated	22 July 1852
Signed	John Bishop [registrar]

336.1.4 Parish of Lassington
Area 535 acres; 10 inhabited houses, 1 uninhabited. Population 80.
VCH 13 (forthcoming).

8.3 (2)	**Church of England, St Oswald, Lassington**
Name	Name unknown. Church of England
Consecration	Before 1800
Erected	[Nave and chancel 1875. All but the tower demolished in 1975.]
Endowment	Tithe £119. Glebe £12. {Total £120}
Sittings	Free 80. Other 30. Total 110
Attend'ce 30 Mar.	Morning 75 + 40 SS. Total [115]
	Afternoon 40 SS [Total [40]
	Evening no evening service
Avge attendance	Morning ditto
	Afternoon ditto
	Evening ditto
Dated	31 March 1851

Signed   William Dent, minister [1830–67]
                Beaumont House, Gloucester

[On the Census day, Dent was staying at a lodging house at 7 College Green, Gloucester. The church tower is now under the care of the Churches Conservation Trust.]

336.1.5 Parish of Maisemore

Area 1,930 acres; 103 inhabited houses. Population 471.
[For the Maisemore returns see **8.2**]

336.1.6 Parish of Ashleworth

Area 1,710 acres; 121 inhabited houses, 1 uninhabited. Population 590.
VCH 13 (forthcoming)

8.4 (3)   **Church of England, St Andrew and St Bartholomew, Ashleworth**
Name   An ancient parish church. Dedicated to St Andrew
Consecration   Before 1800
Erected   [Restored and enlarged 1869]
Endowment   Land in lieu of tithe £250. OPE house and land adjoining (3 acres)
                    Fees £2. {Total £187}
Sittings   Free 160. Other 100. Total 260
Attend'ce 30 Mar. Morning 40 + 45 SS. Total 85. Private school 15. Total 100
                    Afternoon 120 + 45. Total 165. Private school 15. Total 180
Avge attendance   [Not given]
Remarks   The number of individuals attending services throughout the day were
                    150, of the 'general congregation' as only 10 [people] attended twice.
Dated   31 March 1851
Signed   James Augustus Williams, curate [1847–54]
                    Ashleworth vicarage, Gloucester
[*Incumbent*   Henry Adams Sergison Atwood 1839–77]

[For the year 1850–1 Atwood was absent. As well as serving as curate, Williams taught 15 residential pupils aged 9 to 12 years, among them David Ricardo (see **10.62**).]

[Request for information. Will you have the goodness to furnish information respecting the undermentioned churches, congregations including Sunday scholars.]

8.5 (4)   **Church of England, St Lawrence, Sandhurst**
[*Erected*   Mostly rebuilt 1857–8]
[*Endowment*   Total £209]
Sittings   Free 160. Other 120. Total [280]
Morning   60
Afternoon   260
SS   64
[*Incumbent*   Thomas Evans 1844–54]

[Evans was under-master of King's School, Gloucester 1826–41, and on the death of his uncle, Arthur Benoni Evans, succeeded him as headmaster 1841–54. He was also chaplain to the Gloucester lunatic asylum. The rectory was occupied by a non-clerical family and the vicarage by the curate, Edmund Percy Brett, the vicar 1854–79: *VCH* 13 (forthcoming).]

8.6 (4)   **Church of England, St Lawrence, Barnwood** (336.1.16)
The clergyman objects to give any information.
[*Erected*   Chancel mostly rebuilt c.1860, restored 1873–4]
[*Endowment*   Total £195]
[*Incumbent*   George Sweet Escott 1844–71]

Attend'ce 30 Mar. Morning 237. Total [237]
                     Afternoon 237. Total [237]
Avge attendance   [Not given]
Dated   8 April 1851
Signed   John Francis Israel Herschell, chaplain [1851–7]
                     County Prison, Gloucester

[The prison was erected 1787–91 and extended in 1826 and 1844–50. In 1851 there were 251 prisoners.]

336.2   ST NICHOLAS SUB-DISTRICT

Combined area of the two sub-districts of St Nicholas and St John the Baptist: 680 acres.

336.2.1–2 Parish of St Nicholas, Gloucester

(St Nicholas with College Precincts) with 462 inhabited houses, 19 uninhabited. Population 3,117.

8.18 (15)   Church of England, St Nicholas, Westgate Street

Name   St Nicholas, Gloucester
Consecration   About 13th century. I know not [when]
Erected   I know not. [Restored 1865]
Endowment   Land £87. OPE Queen Anne Bounty £15. Pew rents uncertain. {Total
                     £116}
Sittings   Free 750. Other 32. Total 782
Attend'ce 30 Mar. Morning 300 + 140 SS. Total 440
                     Evening 500. Total 500
Avge attendance   Morning 300 + 140 SS. Total 440
                     Evening 500. Total 500
Remarks   As yesterday, 30 March, was a customary holiday and a time of visiting
                     and feasting; and as the assizes are being at present held in the city, the
                     average attendance at the churches was lessened and afforded   no correct
                     criterion of the usual congregations.
Dated   31 March 1851
Signed   William Elliott, incumbent [1843–52]
                     Gloucester

[The benefice consisted of St Nicholas with St Bartholomew: Medland, 109–28. The church is now under the care of the Churches Conservation Trust.]

8.19 (16)   Independent or Congregational, Levy's Yard

Name   Island School Room
Erected   About 1844 ['By 1833': *VCH* 4, 324]
Building   No, used also as a daily infants' school. No [not exclusively as a place
                     of worship]
Sittings   Free 80. Other none. Total [80]
Attend'ce 30 Mar. Evening 25. Total [25]
Avge attend'ce (6m) Evening 30. Total [30]
Dated   31 March 1851
Signed   Charles March, deacon of [the] Independent chapel with which this
                     schoolroom is connected
                     Gloucester

[The school was supported by the congregation of the Southgate Street chapel (**8.35**).]

336.2.3–5   Parish of St Mary de Lode with Holy Trinity, Gloucester

Area 3,510 acres; 475 inhabited houses, 19 uninhabited. Population 2,667.

Part of the parish of St Mary de Lode was in the Kingsholm district and in the South Hamlet district. St Mary de Lode includes Pool Meadow.

8.20 (17)   **Church of England, St Mary de Lode with Holy Trinity**
Name   St Mary de Lode with Holy Trinity
Consecration   Before 1800
Erected   [Nave and vestry rebuilt 1825–6, chancel restored by 1850; general restoration 1895–6]
Endowment   {Total £284}
Sittings   Free 180. Other 450. Total 630
Attend'ce 30 Mar.   Morning 460 + 120 SS. Total 580
                       Afternoon 250 + 139 SS. Total 389
                       Evening no service
Avge attendance   Morning 400 + 150 SS. Total 550
                       Afternoon 300 + 150 SS. Total 450
                       Evening no service
Remarks   I have returned the estimated number of persons who attended divine services yesterday and the average attendances for the last twelve months to the best of my ability. Yesterday being the Assize Sunday and also mid-Lent is an uncertain criterion.
Dated   31 March 1851
Signed   William Lucius Coghlan, vicar of St Mary de Lode [1843–62]
                       Gloucester

[From 1778 the livings of St Mary de Lode and Holy Trinity were jointly held and by 1838 were united as a benefice. Coghlan was also the curate of St Catherine.]

8.21 (18)   **Countess of Huntingdon, St Mary's Square**
Denomination   Protestant dissenters of the Connexion of the Countess of Huntingdon
Name   Countess of Huntingdon's Chapel or St Mary's Chapel
Erected   Before 1800 (i.e. 1788)
Building   Yes [separate and entire] Yes [exclusively as a place of worship]
Sittings   Free about 150. Other about 250. Total [about 400]
Attend'ce 30 Mar.   Morning 200 + 83 SS. Total [283]
                       Evening 400 + 40 SS. Total [440]
Avge attendance   [Not given]
Dated   31 March 1851
Signed   John Reynolds, minister [1849–51]
                       Wotton Lodge, near Glo'ster

[The chapel closed in 1869 and from 1870–6 it was a Congregational chapel. The formal association with the Countess of Huntingdon's Connexion ceased in 1877.]

8.22 (19)   **Church of England, Gloucester Cathedral**
Name   Gloucester Cathedral [dedicated to the Holy and Undivided Trinity]
Consecration   [Not given]
Erected   [Restored 1847–8, 1855–62 and 1868–81]
Sittings   All free. Total about 300
Attend'ce 30 Mar.   Morning 1,500 + 70 SS. Total 1,570
                       Afternoon 200 + 70 SS. Total 270
Avge attendance   Morning 150 + 70 SS. Total 220
                       Afternoon 200 + 70 SS. Total 270
Remarks   Sunday, 30 March was the assize Sunday which accounts for the increased numbers of attendants.

Dated   30 March 1851
Signed   Charles Crawley, senior minor canon [1841–56]
               Gloucester
[Crawley was also the incumbent of Hartpury (**7.29**).]

336.2.6–7 Parish of St Catherine, Gloucester

291 inhabited houses, 12 uninhabited. Population 1,922.
The parish includes the hamlet of Kingsholm in which was situated the Union workhouse
with 223 inmates.
[The original St Catherine's church, demolished in the 1650s, was in the north transept aisle of St
Oswald's priory. A new church of St Catherine (built near the priory ruins) was consecrated 13 Apr.
1868 and demolished in 1921, the parish church relocating to London Road. St Catharine [spelling
since 1886] was consecrated 21 June 1915.]

8.23 (20)	**Christian Brethren, Park Street**
Denomination	(I believe they are what is called the Plymouth Brethren)
Name	Park Street Chapel
Erected	I cannot say
Building	An entire building. Yes [exclusively as a place of worship]
Sittings	Free 65. Other all free. Total [65]
Attend'ce 30 Mar.	Morning 50. Total [50]
Avge attendance	[Not given]
Remarks	From what I have been able to ascertain from them the congregation numbers about from forty to fifty.
Dated	21 November 1851
Signed	William Whitehead, registrar of births and deaths [and an assistant overseer]
	4 College Court, Gloucester

336.3 St John the Baptist sub-district

Combined area of the two sub-districts of St Nicholas and St John the Baptist: 680 acres.

336.3.1 Parish of St Mary de Grace, Gloucester

With 44 inhabited houses. Population 296.
[In 1648 united with St Michael and St Mary de Grace was demolished in the 1650s]

336.3.2 Parish of St Aldate, Gloucester

With 144 inhabited houses, 2 uninhabited. Population 816.

8.24 (21)	**Church of England, St Aldate**
Name	St Aldate. An ancient parish church dilapidated in 1656, and rebuilt on a smaller scale in the year 1755
Consecration	In the year 1756
Erected	[Restored 1876]
Endowment	... acres deducting ... rates and taxes about £110. Glebe none. Fees greatly fluctuating average [about] £12. {Total £154}
Sittings	Free 30. Other 220. Other 250
Attend'ce 30 Mar.	Afternoon 150 + 86 SS. Total 249 [*recte* 236]
Avge attendance	[Not given]
Remarks	The living of St Aldate's and that of the adjacent parish of St John the Baptist were conjoined ninety five years ago, on account of the small population of the one and the poverty of the other, or rather of both.
Dated	31 March 1851

Signed   Francis Turner Bayly, perpetual curate [1804–54]
                  Gloucester

[Bayly was also the incumbent of St John the Baptist (**8.28**) and chaplain of the workhouse. He was the father of Francis Turner James Bayly, incumbent of Brookthorpe with Whaddon (**8.48**, **9.4**). In 1928 the church became the parish hall and was demolished in 1963. A temporary timber building was used until it was replaced by a new St Aldate's in Finlay Road, consecrated 13 June 1964.]

336.3.3 Parish of St Michael, Gloucester
With 214 inhabited houses, 1 uninhabited. Population 1,331.
The parish includes the hamlet of Barton St Michael (336.4.1)

8.25 (22)   **Church of England, St Michael, Eastgate Street**
Name   St Michael. The ancient parish church built under the 40th Section of an
                       Act of Parliament and passed in the 59 year of Geo. 3rd. c.134 [1819]
Consecration   To be consecrated on the 28 April 1851
Erected   [Apart from the tower, rebuilt and enlarged in 1849–50; demolished 1955]
Endowment   {Total £231}
Sittings   Free 108. Other 281. Total 389
Attend'ce 30 Mar.   [Not given]
Avge attendance   [Not given]
Dated   31 March 1851
Signed   Charles Hardwick, rector [1839–74]
                       St Michael's rectory, Gloucestershire

[The former incumbent, John Kempthorne (1775–1838) was an Evangelical and minor hymn-writer, who had previously served as the curate to bishop Henry Ryder and later as his chaplain when he was bishop of Lichfield and Coventry. He was in his parish 'for 22 years, with unsparing self-devotion, publicly, and from house to house, preaching Christ's gospel (his only hope). He laboured to promote God's glory in the salvation of man, and to maintain inviolate the principles and privileges of the Church of England' [monument, Gloucester cathedral]. While incumbent of St Michael's, Kempthorne was responsible for the erection of the chapel of ease of St James (**8.36**).]

8.26 (23)   **Baptist, Parker's Row** [later called Brunswick Road]
Name   Baptist Chapel
Erected   [In 1848 on the site of a smaller chapel opened on 8 May 1821.
                       [Enlarged and rebuilt 1872–3]
Building   Separate [and entire] Yes [exclusively as a place of worship]
Sittings   Free about 700*
Attend'ce 30 Mar.   Morning 500** + 54 SS. Total 554
                       Afternoon 111 SS. Total 111
                       Evening 630 ** Total 630
Avge attendance (9m) Morning 500 + 90 SS. Total 590
                       Afternoon 100 SS. Total 100
                       Evening 600. Total 600
Remarks   * Those who subscribe towards the support of the ministry, whether or
                       no known to be [able?] much or little, have seats or sittings appropriated to
                       them. Others are accommodated in any part of the chapel where there is
                       room, without distinction.
                       ** In consequence of the Independent chapel (**8.35**) being now rebuilding,
                       the congregation is at present united with us. Our average congregation
                       was previously about 450.
Dated   31 March 1851
Signed   Joseph Sims, deacon [builder and timber merchant]

[London Road]
George Woodrow, Baptist minister (absent from home on 30 March)
[1846–52]
Gloucester

[From this chapel the area outside the city was evangelised and chapels were established at Barton End, Longhope (**6.41**), Little Witcombe and Matson.]

8.27 (24)   Unitarian, Barton Street

Name	Barton Street Chapel
Erected	1699 [Restored 1867]
Building	Yes [separate and entire] Yes [exclusively as a place of worship]
Sittings	Free 50. Other 200. Total [250]
Attend'ce 30 Mar.	Morning 60 + 34 SS. Total 94
	Evening 80. Total 80
Avge attendance	[Not given]
Remarks	Unitarian since 1727–8
Dated	31 March 1851
Signed	Joseph Henry Hutton, minister [1849–52]
	[Wotton Parade], Wotton Hill, Gloucester

[Originally Presbyterian, by 1751 the congregation was Unitarian. Seceders from Barton Street Chapel established the Independent Southgate Chapel (**8.35**). Hutton, who became disillusioned with Unitarianism, became an Anglican, was ordained in 1876, and served as curate of Holy Trinity, Clifton 1876–8 (**2.3**).]

336.3.4 Parish of St John the Baptist, Gloucester
With 713 inhabited houses, 11 uninhabited. Population 4,081.

8.28 (25)   Church of England, St John the Baptist, Northgate Street

Name	St John the Baptist. An ancient parish church
Consecration	Before 1800 [1734]
Erected	[Rebuilt 1732–4, and restored 1874, 1880 and 1882]
Endowment	Land, rates and leases on 26 acres .. income about £96. OPE none
	Fees rec[eive]d last year £33. Other sources (grant per an[num] from the
	Ecclesiastical Commissioners) £40. {Total £150}
Sittings	Free 90. Other (for which no pew rents are paid) 560. Total 650
Attend'ce 30 Mar.	Morning ab[out] 300 + 99 SS. Total 399
	Evening between 500 and 600. Total 500–600
Avge attendance	[Not given]
Remarks	The answers respecting the income are supplied by the rector.
Dated	31 March 1851
Signed	Barry Charles Browne, curate [1849–54]
	10 Worcester Place, Gloucester
[*Incumbent*	Francis Turner Bayly 1804–54]

[Bayly was also incumbent of St Aldate (**8.24**) and chaplain of the workhouse. He was the father of Francis Turner James Bayly, incumbent of Brookthorpe with Whaddon (**8.48, 9.4**). After being declared redundant in 1972, the building became St John's Methodist Church.]

8.29 (26)   Church of England, St Mark, Kingsholm Road

Name	St Mark's church. A new parish under Sir Robert Peel's Act [6 and 7
	Vic. c.37, (1843)]
Consecration	31 August 1847, [as] an additional church
Erected	Erected by voluntary contributions
Endowment	[£200 from the Queen Anne's Bounty; and £500 each from the Bishop

of Gloucester and the Warneford's Trustees] {Total £150}

Sittings	Free 541. Total 541
Attend'ce 30 Mar.	[Not given]
Avge attendance	[Not given]
Remarks	All the Sunday scholars returned in another paper. The other averages are not ascertained.
Dated	31 March 1851
Signed	John James Barlow, perpetual curate [1846–68] Gloucester

[Barlow was also minister of St Margaret (**8.16**) and chaplain to the workhouse.]

8.30 (28)   **Wesleyan Methodist, Northgate Street**

Name	Northgate Street Chapel
Erected	Before the year 1800 [1787, enlarged 1839–40; replaced by a new chapel opened in 1878]
Building	Separate and entire building. Used exclusively as a place of worship.
Sittings	Free 240. Other 800 [?]
Attend'ce 30 Mar.	Morning 450 + 100 SS. Total [550] Afternoon 160 SS. Total [160] Evening 650. Total [650]
Avge attendance	Morning 500 + 120 SS. Total [620] Afternoon 180. Total [180] Evening 700. Total [700]
Dated	31 March 1851
Signed	John Smedley, superintendent minister [1849–51] Gloucester

[Smedley was also minister of Hartpury (**7.30**) and Hucclecote (**8.14**). 'The chapel became the head of a circuit which covered the north part of Gloucestershire': *VCH* 4, 326.]

8.31 (30)   **Christian Brethren, Worcester Street**

Name	Circular Room
Erected	[1836] Not erected for worship. Now used temporarily
Building	Separate building. Yes, except for occasional lectures on temperance.
Sittings	Free 450. Other none. Total [450] Standing room for 255
Attend'ce 30 Mar.	Morning 170. [SS] none. Total 170 Evening 276. [SS] none. Total 276
Avge attendance (6m)	Morning 250. Total [250] Evening 450. Total [450]
Remarks	The society of Christian Brethren are for the most part persons who were lately in the society known as the Wesleyan Methodist Connexion.
Dated	31 March 1851
Signed	William Manning, superintendent minister [cork cutter] 21 Westgate Street, Gloucester

[Manning was also the minister of Ebenezer Chapel (**8.38**).]

8.32 (29)   **Roman Catholic, St Peter ad Vincula, London Road**

Name	St Peter's Catholic Church
Erected	[Registered in] 1792 [Demolished in 1859 and replaced by a new church opened 22 Mar. 1860 and consecrated 8 Oct. 1868]
Building	Yes [separate and entire] Yes [exclusively as a place of worship]
Sittings	Free 70. Other 80. Total [150]
Attend'ce 30 Mar.	Morning 130. Total 130

Afternoon 40*. Total 40
Evening 140. Total 140

*Avge attendance (4m**)*   Morning 110. Total 110
Afternoon 30. Total 30
Evening 130. Total 130

Remarks   * instructions for the children
** I have only been the pastor four months.
Dated   31 March 1851
Signed   Leonard Calderbank, Catholic pastor [1850–64]
Catholic Chapel, London Road, Gloucester

8.33 (27)   Society of Friends, Greyfriars
Erected   [previous Meeting House 1678–1834, then sold] In the year 1834 or 1835
Building   Yes [separate and entire] Yes, excepted in a few instances for peace
and slavery and other Christian meetings ... [unclear]
Floor area   1,596 [square feet] No gallery except the ministry platform
Sittings   For 300. Total [300]
Attend'ce 30 Mar. Morning 36. Total [36]
Dated   First day of the 4 month (April) 1851
Signed   Thomas M. Savage [corn dealer]
[Barton Street], Gloucester

336.3.5 Parish of St Mary de Crypt, Gloucester
With 150 inhabited houses, 5 uninhabited. Population 1,042.

8.34 (31)   Church of England, St Mary de Crypt, Southgate Street
Name   St Mary de Crypt
Consecration   Before 1800
Erected   [Restored 1845, 1866, 1876 and 1905]
Endowment   {Total £120}
Sittings   Free 200. Other 450. Total 650
Attend'ce 30 Mar. [Not given]
Avge attend'ce (6m) Morning 350 + 95 SS. Total 445
Evening 500. Total 500
Dated   31 March 1851
Signed   Andrew Sayers, rector [1841–70]
Gloucester

[The benefice was St Mary de Crypt with All Saints and St Owen. Sayers was also the incumbent of Upleadon (**7.14**). A week after he was ordained in Gloucester cathedral George Whitefield preached his first sermon in St Mary de Crypt on 27 June 1736. He recorded that there was a large congregation. 'A few mocked, but most for the present seemed struck; and I have since heard that a complaint has been made to the bishop that I drove fifteen mad. The worthy prelate, as I am informed, wished that the madness might not be forgotten before next Sunday.' (Tyerman 1890 1, 50). His sermon, on 'The necessity and benefit of religious society' was the first of an estimated 18,000 preached during his lifetime: *ODNB* 'George Whitefield (1714–1770)'.]

8.35 (32)   Independent, Southgate Street
Name   Southgate Chapel
Erected   100 years ago [1730, enlarged 1830, replaced by a new chapel in 1851
and demolished in 1981]
Building   Yes [separate and entire] Yes [exclusively as a place of worship]
Sittings   Total 600
Attend'ce 30 Mar. [Not given]

Avge attendance 550. Total [550]
Remarks   The Independent chapel, Southgate St erected more than 100 year ago
              after several enlargements contained sittings for about 600 persons. It
              was taken down in 1850. The average attendance for 15 years had been
              550. A new Independent chapel has been erected on the same ground
              and will be opened 16 April 1851. It will accommodate 1,000 persons.
              [During the erection of the building the congregation joined the Baptists
              in Parker's Row (**8.26**)]
Dated   31 March 1851
Signed   Joseph Hyatt, minister [1832–57]
              [2] Brunswick Sq., Gloucester
[The congregation was established c.1715 by seceders from the Barton Street Chapel (**8.27**). The
chapel supported missions in outlying villages reaching as far as Newnham, Lydney and the Forest
of Dean. A school in The Island was supported by the congregation (**8.19**).]

336.3.6 Parish of St Owen
With 103 inhabited houses. Population 948. Church demolished 1643.
The parish contained the hamlet of Littleworth, and within the parish was the Gloucester
Infirmary (with 158 patients) and the city prison (with 25 prisoners). There were also 218
persons in ships and boats.
[After the church was demolished the parishioners were served by the incumbents of St
Mary de Crypt (**8.34**) until the benefices were united in the 18th century]

336.4   SOUTH HAMLET SUB-DISTRICT

336.4.1 Hamlet of Barton St Michael (part of the parish of St Michael 336.3.3)
Area 500 acres; 336 inhabited houses, 5 uninhabited. Population 1,744.

8.36 (33)   Church of England, St James, Upton Street
Name   St James' church. Church of a district under provisions of 1 and 2 Will.
               IV c.38 (1831)
Consecration 20 April 1841. Consecrated as an additional church, to which a district
               has been assigned. [As a chapel of ease to St Michael (**8.25**)]
Erected   By voluntary contributions [of] £2,500. Total cost £2,500 [Enlarged 1879]
Endowment   OPE £100. Pew rents £45. Fees £12. {Total £150}
Sittings   Free 400. Other 260. Total 660
Attend'ce 30 Mar. Morning 160 + 120 SS. Total 280
               Afternoon 210 + 100 SS. Total 310
               Evening no service
Avge attendance [Not given]
Remarks   The pew rents and fees fluctuate: the above is a fair average. The
               congregations are generally somewhat larger, but not much.
Dated   31 March 1851
Signed   John Emeris, perpetual curate [1848–72]
               Gloucester
[The church was erected by John Kempthorne, the incumbent of St Michael, Eastgate Street (**8.25**).]

8.37 (34)   Wesleyan Methodist, Victoria Street, Barton
Name   Victoria Street Chapel
Erected   1847
Building   Yes [separate and entire] Yes [exclusively as a place of worship]
Sittings   Free 150. Other 60. Total [210]
Attend'ce 30 Mar. [Not given]

Avge attendance	Morning 50. Total [50]
	Evening 100. Total [100]
Dated	31 March 1851
Signed	Thomas Yates, leader, steward and trustee
	2 Victoria Street [Gloucester]
[*Minister*	Charles Tucker 1851–3]

8.38 (35)   **Christian Brethren, Ryecroft**

Name	Ebenezer Chapel
Erected	Feby 1851
Building	Yes [separate and entire] Yes [exclusively as a place of worship]
Sittings	Free 160. Other none. Total [160] Standing room none
Attend'ce 30 Mar.	Afternoon 33 + 95 SS. Total 128
	Evening 50. Total 50
Avge attendance (2m)	Afternoon 33 + 101 SS. Total 134
	Evening 50. Total 50
Remarks	The society of Christian Brethren are for the most part, persons who were lately in the society known as the Wesleyan Methodist Connexion.
Dated	30 March 1851
Signed	William Manning, superintendent minister [cork-cutter]
	21 Westgate St, Glo'ster

[Manning was also the minister of the Circular Room (**8.31**). Wrongly identified in *VCH* 4, 330 as a congregation of Primitive Methodists.]

336.4.4–5   Parish of Hempsted

Area 1,311 acres (including South Hamlet), with 51 inhabited houses, 4 uninhabited. Population 251.
VCH 4, 420–29

8.39 (36)   **Church of England, St Swithin, Hempsted**

Name	Supposed to be Swithin, an ancient parish church
Consecration	Before 1800
Erected	[Restored 1885]
Endowment	{Total £449}
Sittings	Free 90. Other 110. Total 200
Attend'ce 30 Mar.	Morning 60 + 13 SS. Total 73
	Afternoon 44 + 12 SS. Total 56
Avge attendance	Morning 50 + 17 SS. Total 67
	Afternoon 75 + 17 SS. Total 92
Dated	31 March 1851.
Signed	Thomas Jones AM, clerk, ~~rector~~ minister [1826–67]
	Hempsted rectory, near Gloucester

[For much of his incumbency Jones was absent through ill-health.]

336.4.5 Extra-parochial South Hamlet

With 285 inhabited houses, 2 uninhabited. Population 1,739.
In twenty years the population had increased by 905 persons due to the erection of buildings and the presence of a mineral spring that attracted numerous visitors.

8.40 (37)   **Church of England, Christ Church, Brunswick Square**

Name	Christ Church in South Hamlet which is extra parochial. No district has without been assigned to the church with cure of souls.

Consecration	[8 April] 1823. Consecrated for the spiritual benefit of an increasing population in South Hamlet and Littleworth – both of them extra parochial.
Erected	By proprietary shares [of] £3,900. Total cost £3,900
	[Chancel enlarged 1865 and 1899–1900 and restored 1883–4]
Endowment	No land, tithe and glebe. OPE £9 (from £300 in 3 per cent). Pew rents £111*
	Fees £15**. No dues, Easter offerings and other sources. {Total £135}
Sittings	Free 70 (permitted). Other 430. Total 500
Attend'ce 30 Mar.	Morning 270 + 50 SS. Total 320
	Evening 305. Total 305
Avge attendance	Very uncertain return
	Morning probably 320 + 60 SS. Total 380
	Evening probably 380. Total 380
Remarks	* The sum of £111 depends on the letting of the pews to that amount.
	** The fees are of course uncertain, but they average about £15 a year.
Dated	31 March 1851
Signed	Robert Bartholomew Holmes, perpetual curate [1830–68]
	3 Brunswick Square, Gloucester

[This proprietary chapel was built by residents of the Spa to which a parish was attached in 1877.]

8.41 (38)   Church of England, St Luke, High Orchard, Hempsted (Sudbrook)

Name	St Luke's Church hereafter to be constituted a district church, but the assignment of a district is suspended for the present under peculiar circumstances with the sanction of the bishop of the diocese.
Consecration	21 April 1841, in consequence of the increased population in the vicinity of the docks
Erected	By private benefaction of the Reverend Samuel Lysons MA, of Hempsted Court near Gloucester, £3,000. Total cost £3,000
Endowment	OPE £1,000 consols [given by Samuel Lysons] Pew rents £50. Fees £15
Sittings	Free 160. Other 340. Total 500
Attend'ce 30 Mar.	Morning 110 + 48 SS. Total 158
	Afternoon 158 + 47 SS. Total 205
Avge attendance	Morning 250 + 66 SS. Total 306
	Afternoon 350 + 56 SS. Total 406
Remarks	On Sunday, 30 March, many of the congregation were kept away from church on the three following grounds:
	1. The fact of its being mid-Lent Sunday when the lower orders usually attend family members at home.
	2. It is the Sunday of the assize sermon at the cathedral which draws away the congregation of other churches.
	3. The prevalence of measles among the children of the hamlet.
Dated	31 March 1851
Signed	Samuel Lysons MA, perpetual curate [1841–77]
	Hempsted Court, near Gloucester

[Lysons, the noted historian and antiquary, was the wealthy incumbent of Rodmarton (**12.25**); he officiated at St Luke without a stipend. In 1843 he inherited family estates at Hempsted and Longney, and made considerable improvements to High Orchard at his own expense: *ODNB* 'Samuel Lysons (1806–1877)'. 'High Orchard, where the church has been erected was tenanted by people living in houses little better than huts ... since that time the whole character of the neighbourhood has changed. The hut-like dwellings were removed, and decent streets and manufactories have taken their place': *GNQ* 2, 515.]

8.42 (39)   **Church of England, The Mariners' Chapel, Gloucester Docks**

Name   The Mariners' Chapel

Licensed   29 January 1849, as an additional chapel [within South Hamlet]

Erected   By private benefaction or subscription, [of] between £500 to £600. Total cost between £500 and £600

Endowment   A grant of [£75] per annum from Church Pastoral Aid Society and private contribution

Sittings   Free 230. Total 230

Attend'ce 30 Mar. Morning 120. Total [120]
                  Evening 240 or 250. Total [240–250]

Avge attendance   Morning 140. Total [140]
                  Evening 260. Total [260]

Remarks   I should think on Sunday evenings 30 or 40 persons more than the chapel would seat are in attendance.

Dated   31 March 1851

Signed   James Hollins, chaplain [1849–55]
                  10 Hillfield Parade, Gloucester

['There are generally 1,000 mariners and boatmen at the port, and about 40,000 pass through in the year': CPAS, *Report of the Committee read at the Annual Meeting* (London) 1852, list of the Society's grants.]

336.4.7 Parish of Matson

Area 450 acres; 8 inhabited houses. Population 53.
VCH 4, 438–48

8.43 (40)   **Church of England, St Katherine, Matson**

Name   [Not given]

Consecration   [Not given]

Erected   [Rebuilt 1739; chancel rebuilt 1851–2 and nave 1893–4]

Endowment   Land £160. OPE £35. {Total £184}

Sittings   Free 12. Other 50. Total 62

Attend'ce 30 Mar. Morning 27. Total [27]
                  Afternoon 40. Total [40]

Avge attendance   [Not given]

Dated   31 March 1851

Signed   Robert Anwyl Prichard, rector [1850–64]
                  The Paddock, Gloucester

336.4.8 Parish of Upton St Leonards

Area 2,975 acres; 224 inhabited houses, 2 uninhabited. Population 1,124.

8.44 (41)   **Church of England, St Leonard, Upton St Leonards**

Name   A parish church dedicated to S. Leonard

Consecration   Before AD 1800

Erected   [Enlarged 1835, chancel rebuilt 1849–50, restored 1889]

Endowment   Land, tithe, glebe and OPE £83. Fees and dues £10. {Total £105}

Sittings   Free (unappropriated) 367. Free (appropriated) 142. Total 509

Attend'ce 30 Mar. Morning 150 + 70 SS. Total 220
                  Afternoon 330. Total 330

Avge attendance   [Not given]

Dated   31 March 1851

Signed	Jacob Clements MA, incumbent [1846–59]
	The Parsonage, Upton St Leonards, nr Gloucester

8.45 (42)   Wesleyan Methodist, Upton St Leonards

Name	Wesleyan Chapel
Erected	[1770] 1809
Building	Yes [separate and entire] Yes [exclusively as a place of worship]
Sittings	Free 100. Other 30. Total [130]
Attend'ce 30 Mar.	Afternoon 25. Total [25]
	Evening 30. Total [30]
Avge attendance	Afternoon 30. Total [30]
	Evening 50. Total [50]
Dated	31 March 1851
Signed	James Brown, leader (shoemaker)
	Upton St Leonards, nr Gloucester

[John Wesley recorded 'I preached in the new room, which is just finished at Upton': *Journal*, 14 Mar. 1770.]

336.4.10   Parish of Brockworth
Area 1,847 acres; 91 inhabited houses, 7 uninhabited. Population 425.

8.46 (43)   Church of England, St George, Brockworth
(Summary form)

Name	Brockworth Parish Church
Erected	[Restored 1846–7]
[*Endowment*	Total £150]
Sittings	Free about 100. Other about 100. Total 200
Usual attend'ce	Morning about 100 + about 40 SS. Total about 140]
	Afternoon about 100 + about 40 SS. Total [about 140]
Remarks	NB. The above information was obtained from a farmer 'liveing' in the parish of Brockworth.
Signed	Samuel Haycock
[*Incumbent*	George Watts 1847–64]

8.47 (44)   Particular Baptist, Brockworth

Name	Cooper's Hill Chapel
Erected	1850
Building	Yes [separate and entire] Yes [exclusively as a place of worship]
Sittings	Free 50. Other 21. Total [71]
Attend'ce 30 Mar.	Afternoon 40. Total [40]
	Evening 70. Total [70]
Avge attendance	[Not given]
Remarks	30 March afternoon 21. Evening ~~50~~ None
Dated	30 March 1851
Signed	Isaac Hopkins, deacon (quarryman)
	Birdlip Hill, Gloucestershire

336.4.11   Parish of Whaddon
Area 727 acres; 25 inhabited houses. Population 120.

8.48 (45)   Church of England, St Margaret of Scotland, Whaddon

Name	S. Margaret, Whaddon, commonly called Whaddon Church
	The ancient parish church

Consecration	Something before the year of our Lord 1300
Erected	[The nave restored 1854–5 and the chancel in 1880]
Endowment	Annual payment returned by Q[ueen] A[nne's] Bounty £20. Estimates £12 10s. Gov[ernors] of Q. A. Bounty £15 6s 2d ... £1 2s 6d. Land and tithe and glebe ... at the Reformation. Pew rents none. Fees about 7s 6d annually. Dues and Easter offerings none. Total £48 6s 2d. {Total £186}
Sittings	Free 90. Other for school children in chancel 60. Total 150
Attend'ce 30 Mar.	Afternoon about 75 or 80 + 35 SS. Total 115
Avge attendance	Morning 50 or 60 + 30 or 40 SS. Total 90
	Afternoon 80 + 30 or 40 SS. Total 110
Remarks	I furnish the above particulars as *voluntary* information, protesting against being compelled *legally* to answer a single question.
Dated	31 March 1851
Signed	Francis Turner James Bayly, clerk, perpetual curate [1839–83]
	Vicarage, Brockthorpe, Gloucester

[From 1840 the benefice consisted of Brookthorpe (**9.4**) with Whaddon. Bayly was the son of Francis Bayly the incumbent of St Aldate, Gloucester (**8.24**).]

336.4.12–3 Parish of Quedgeley

Area 1,453 acres; 64 inhabited houses, 1 uninhabited. Population 401.
The parish includes the hamlet of Woolstrop.
VCH 10, 215–24

8.49 (46)	**Church of England, St James, Quedgeley**
Name	St James, Quedgeley. Ancient parish church
Consecration	Previously to 1800
Erected	[Rebuilt and enlarged 1856–7]
Endowment	Tithe £232 12s 7d. Glebe 2 acres. Fees about £2. {Total £161}
Sittings	Free (including children's benches) 148. Other 29. Total 177
Attend'ce 30 Mar.	Morning 88 + 35 SS. Total 123
	Afternoon 137 + 35 SS. Total 172
Avge attendance	See remarks
Remarks	The congregation on 30 March 1851 *below average* owing to its being mid-Lent Sunday when all the young servants in this neighbourhood return to their several homes and their families are thus induced to be absent from church.
Dated	31 March 1851
Signed	William Frederick Erskine Knollys, rector [1843–61]
	Quedgeley rectory, Gloucester

336.4.14 Parish of Elmore

Area 1,486 acres; 75 inhabited houses, 4 uninhabited. Population 393.
VCH 13 (forthcoming)

8.50 (47)	**Church of England, St John the Baptist, Elmore**
Name	Elmore parish church. Ancient
Consecration	Before 1800
Erected	[Restored 1879–80]
Endowment	Land £74. Fees £1. {Total £73}
Sittings	Free 130. Other 30. Total 160
Attend'ce 30 Mar.	Morning 65 + 35 SS. Total [100]
Avge attendance	Morning 50. Total [50]

Afternoon 140. Total [140]
Dated   30 March 1851
Signed   Joseph Daniel, perpetual curate [1835–76]
                        Gloucester

[Daniel was also the incumbent of Longney (**9.1**). He was absent from his parishes and lived in Rodney Place, Cheltenham.]

8.51 (48)   Independent, Elmore
Name   None
Erected   Since 1800
Building   No [not separate and entire] No [not exclusively as a place of worship]
Sittings   Free 50. Total [50]
Attend'ce 30 Mar.   Afternoon 22. Total [22]
Avge attendance   [Not given]
Dated   31 March 1851
Signed   William Peters, superintendent (cordwainer) [shoemaker]
                        Elmore, near Gloucester, Gloucestershire

9. HO 129/337 WHEATENHURST DISTRICT: 23 places of worship

337.1   HARESFIELD SUB-DISTRICT

337.1.1 Parish of Longney

Area 1,070 acres; 109 inhabited houses, 10 uninhabited. Population 504.
VCH 10, 197–205

9.1 (1)	**Church of England, St Lawrence, Longney**
Name	Longney parish church. Of considerable antiquity
Consecration	Before 1800
Erected	[Restored 1873–4]
Endowment	Land, tithe and glebe £100. Fees uncertain £1 or £2. {Total £100}
Sittings	Free 186. Other 14. Total 200
Attend'ce 30 Mar.	Afternoon 90 + 32 SS. Total 122
Avge attendance	Morning 45 + 35 SS. Total [80]
	Afternoon 125 + 35 SS. Total [160]
Dated	30 March 1851
Signed	Joseph Daniel, vicar [1835–76]
	Gloucester

[Daniel was also the incumbent of Elmore (**8.50**). He was absent from his parishes and lived in Rodney Place, Cheltenham.]

9.2 (2)	**Independent, Churchend, Longney**
Name	Chapel
Erected	1839
Building	Yes [separate and entire] Yes exclusively [as a place of worship]
Sittings	Free 120*. Other 50. Total [170] Standing room for about 50
Attend'ce 30 Mar.	No minister on the 30 March
*Avge attend'ce***	Morning 30 + 20 SS. Total 50
	Afternoon 40 + 24 SS. Total 64
	Evening 90 + 12* SS. Total 102
Remarks	No minister at present or for the last twelve months
	* They are all free sittings except three for a minister. The chapel is supplied by lay preachers here for the last fifteen 15 months.
	**The exact number of attendants I could not give.
Dated	3 April 1851
Signed	William Longney, manager [farmer, brick-maker and barge-owner]
	Longney, Gloucester

[The previous minister was Joseph Lander 1846–50, who next served at Mitcheldean (**6.26**).]

337.1.2 Parish of Hardwicke

Area 2,378 acres; 108 inhabited houses, 2 uninhabited. Population 564.
VCH 10, 178–88

9.3 (3)	**Church of England, St Nicholas, Hardwicke**
Name	Church of the parish of Hardwicke, Gloucestershire
Consecration	Before 1800
Erected	[Restored 1843–5 and 1876–7]

Endowment	[See Standish (**9.7**)]
Sittings	Free 240. Other 30. Total 270
Attend'ce 30 Mar.	[Not given]
Avge attendance	[Not given]
Remarks	I never count the attendance at church: guess would be worse than nothing.
Dated	March 1851
Signed	Thomas Murray Browne, vicar [1839–64]
	Standish vicarage, nr Stroud

[The benefice consisted of Standish (**9.7**) with the chapel of ease of Hardwicke.]

337.1.3 Parish of Brookthorpe
Area 1,009 acres; 44 inhabited houses, 1 uninhabited. Population 191.

9.4 (4)   **Church of England, St Swithin, Brookthorpe**

Name	S. Swithin, Brookthorpe commonly called Brookthorpe Church. The ancient parish church
Consecration	About the year of our Lord 1250
Erected	[Restored and enlarged 1891–2]
Endowment	Land ... by Q[ueen] A[nne]'s Bounty £55. Tithe £84 16s. Glebe ... £2. OPE improprietor £11 13s 4d. Pew rents none. Fees averaging 10s 6d. Dues and Easter offerings none. Total £153 19s 10d. {Total £186}
Sittings	Free (but not unappropriated) 114. Other (for children) 70. Total 184
Attend'ce 30 Mar.	Morning 60 to 70 + 30 SS. Total 90–100
Avge attendance	Morning 55 to 65 + 30 to 45 SS. Total 85–110
	Afternoon 75 to 85 + 30 to 45 SS Total 105–130
Remarks	I have filled up the above schedule as a voluntary act, having no information to withhold, but distinctly protest against being legally obliged to answer a single one of the questions.
Dated	31 March 1851
Signed	Francis Turner James Bayly, cl[er]k, BA, Pemb. College, Oxon., vicar
	Vicarage, Brookthorpe, Gloucester [1839–83]

[From 1840 the benefice consisted of Brookthorpe with Whaddon (**8.48**). Bayly was the son of Francis Bayly the incumbent of St Aldate, Gloucester (**8.24**). The church is now under the care of the Churches Conservation Trust.]

337.1.4 Parish of Harescombe
Area 478 acres; 29 inhabited houses, 2 uninhabited. Population 147.

9.5 (5)   **Church of England, St John the Baptist, Harescombe**

Name	Harescombe church. Ancient parish church
Consecration	Before 1800
Erected	[Restored 1870–1]
Endowment	Land none. Tithe £85 16s. Glebe £30 17s. OPE ... are about £20 per annum and £21 to the governors of Queen Anne's Bounty, for interest an instalment of the loan advanced by them for the rebuilding of the rectory house. {Total £153}
Sittings	Free about 80. Other 50. Total 130
Attend'ce 30 Mar.	Afternoon 94. Total [94]
Avge attend'ce (6m)	Morning 45. Total [45]
	Afternoon 110. Total [110]
Remarks	The parish of Harescombe is united with Pitchcombe (**10.11**); consequently

the children of Harescombe attend (some of them) at Pitchcombe Sunday school and others at a neighbouring school in the parish of Brookthorpe (**9.4**), to which they are much nearer than either to Harescombe or Pitchcombe. There is a daily school at Brookthorpe supported chiefly by the lord of the Manor of Harescombe and Brookthorpe, and the children of Harescombe that attend the weekly school at Brookthorpe attend also on Sundays.

Dated	31 March 1851
Signed	Frederick Quarrington, curate [1839–51]
	Harescombe nr Gloucester
[*Incumbent*	Marlow Watts Wilkinson [1825–67]

[The benefice consisted of Harescombe with Pitchcombe (**10.11**). Wilkinson was also the incumbent of Uley (**5.16**) where he lived.]

337.1.5 Parish of Haresfield
Area 2,155 acres; 131 inhabited houses, 8 uninhabited. Population 627.
VCH 10, 188–97

9.6 (6)	**Church of England, St Peter, Haresfield**
Name	St Peter's. An ancient parish church
Consecration	Before 1800
Erected	Rebuilt by D[aniel] J[ohn] Niblett Esq. in 1842. Patron and lay improprietor, [and high sheriff of Gloucestershire 1816–7]
Endowment	Glebe £260. Fees £1 10s. {Total £221}
Sittings	Free 230. Other 20. Total 250*
Attend'ce 30 Mar.	Morning 67 + 31 SS. Total 98
	Afternoon 135 + 33 SS. Total 168
Avge attendance	Morning 70 + 40 SS. Total 110
	Afternoon 150 + 40 SS. Total 190
Remarks	* About 50 sittings originally intended for the school children in the gallery behind the organ are not now used.
Dated	31 March 1851
Signed	Edward Henry Niblett BA, vicar [1836–53]
	Haresfield, Glo'ster

[Preaching in August 1841, Niblett described the church as being 'the most unsightly building of those around ... lacking accommodation for the parishioners, unwholesome, uncomfortable and squalid in appearance': Hall, 337. Thomas Rudge, the incumbent 1780–1825, was also archdeacon of Gloucester 1814–25, and author of *The History of the County of Gloucester*, 1804: *ODNB* 'Thomas Rudge (1753–1825)'.]

337.1.6 Parish of Standish
Area 3,388 acres; 106 inhabited houses, 4 uninhabited. Population 534.
VCH 10, 230–42

9.7 (7)	**Church of England, St Nicholas, Standish**
Name	Standish Church
Consecration	Before 1800
Erected	[Restored 1867]
Endowment	{Total £527}
Sittings	Free 263. Other 10. Total 273
Attend'ce 30 Mar.	[Not given]

Avge attendance [Not given]
Remarks   I have never counted the congregation: guess would be worse than nothing.
Dated   March 1851
Signed   Thomas Murray Browne, vicar [1839–64]
                 Standish parsonage, nr Stroud
[The benefice consisted of Standish with Hardwicke (**9.3**). In July 1866 J. D. T. Niblett of Standish was the first Anglican Lay Reader to be admitted to the office in modern times.]

337.1.7 Parish of Moreton Valence
Area 1,432 acres; 71 inhabited houses, 4 uninhabited. Population 307.
VCH 10, 205–15

9.8a (8)   **Church of England, St Stephen, Moreton Valence**
Name   Moreton Valence
Erected   [Restored 1880]
Endowment   {Total £90}
Sittings   Mostly free. Total 250
Attend'ce 30 Mar.   [Not given]
Avge attendance   {Not given]
Remarks   No Sunday scholars. Children few and scattered attending neighbouring
                         church schools.
Dated   30 March 1851
Signed   John Fowell Jones [1830–77]
                         Saul Parsonage, Stroud
[Jones was also the incumbent of Saul (**9.12**) and of Gwernesney, Mon. 1830–71.]

9.8b (9)   **Church of England, St Stephen, Moreton Valence**
Name   Moreton Valence. An ancient church
Consecration   Before 1800
Erected   [Restored 1880]
Endowment   {Total £90}
Sittings   Free 21. Other 3. Total 24
Attend'ce 30 Mar.   Afternoon 50. Total 50
Avge attendance   Morning 40. Total 40
Dated   2 April 1851
Signed   George White, churchwarden [farmer]
                         [Court House], Moreton Valence, near Stroud, Gloucestershire

9.9 (10)   **Wesleyan Methodist, Moreton Valence**
Name   None
Erected   1840
Building   No [not separate and entire] No [not exclusively as a place of worship]
Sittings   Free 25. Total [25]
Attend'ce 30 Mar.   Morning 20. Total [20]
Avge attendance   [Not given]
Remarks   This house is open for prayer meetings [on] Sunday evenings. Average
                         attendance twenty persons.
Dated   31 March 1851
Signed   Joseph Jones, prayer leader [shop keeper]
                         Moreton Valence, Gloucestershire

337.1.8 Parish of Wheatenhurst (or Whitminster)
Area 1,247 acres; 87 inhabited houses, 7 uninhabited. Population 380.
VCH 10, 289–99

9.10 (11)	**Church of England, St Andrew, Wheatenhurst**
Name	Ancient parish church
Consecration	[Not given]
Erected	[Enlarged 1841–2 and restored 1884–5]
Endowment	Land £120. OPE £18. Fees £1 10s. {Total £135}
Sittings	Free 178. Other 86. Total 264
Attend'ce 30 Mar.	Morning 150 + 40 SS. Total 190
	Afternoon 195 + 35 SS. Total 230
Avge attendance	Morning 140 + 50 SS. Total 190
	Afternoon 185 + 45 SS. Total 230
Dated	31 April 1851
Signed	Anthony Ely, perpetual curate [1834–83]
	Wheatenhurst, Stroud

[Ely's son, Edwyn Anthony Ely, was the incumbent of Lassington 1867–83 (**8.3**).]

9.11 (12)	**Baptist, Wheatenhurst**
Name	Baptist [Chapel]
Erected	1830
Building	No [not separate and entire] No [not exclusively as a place of worship]
Sittings	Free 50. Total [50]
Attend'ce 30 Mar.	Morning [38] Total 38
	Afternoon 29. Total [29]
	Evening 9. Total [9]
Avge attendance	[Not given]
Dated	30 March 1851
Signed	William Barnfield, deacon (grocer)
	Wheatenhurst near Stroud

337.2   Frampton sub-district

337.2.1 Parish of Saul
Area 564 acres; 137 inhabited houses, 3 uninhabited. Population 550.
VCH 10, 155–69

9.12 (13)	**Church of England, St James, Saul**
Name	Saul.
Consecration	[Not given. 14 March 1865]
Erected	[Repaired and enlarged 1856 and rebuilt 1864–5]
Endowment	{Total £125}
Sittings	Free 188. Other 77. Also for school children 70. Total 335
Attend'ce 30 Mar.	[Not given]
Avge attendance	[Not given]
Dated	31 March 1851
Signed	John Fowell Jones, incumbent [1825–77]
	Saul Parsonage, Stroud

[Jones was also the incumbent of Moreton Valence (**9.8**); and of Gwernesney, Mon. 1830–71. Until 1839 Saul was a chapel of Standish and became a parish in 1866. Within the parish St Peter, Framilode was consecrated 21 Sept. 1854.]

9.13 (14)   **Wesleyan Methodist, Saul Corner, Saul**
Name   Saul Wesleyan Chapel
Erected   1809
Building   Yes [separate and entire] Yes [exclusively as a place of worship]
Sittings   Free 170. Other 100. Total [270]
Attend'ce 30 Mar.   Morning no services
                       Afternoon 7 + 17 SS. Total [24]
                       Evening no service
Avge attendance   [Not given]
Remarks   The conduct of the Wesleyan Conference preachers has been the means
                       of dividing nearly all the congregation away from the chapel. Otherwise
                       some five months ago there was a flourishing congregation attending this
                       place of worship. Their conduct therefore is the cause of the smallness of
                       the congregation this day. Those who formerly worshipped here hold
                       religious meetings in houses etc.
Dated   31 March 1851
Signed   William Williams, chapel steward [farmer of two acres]
                       Saul, near Stroud, Gloucestershire

[After the schism within Methodism nonconformity continued to flourish locally. There were
British schools (supported by nonconformists) at Saul and Framilode, and a Congregational chapel
(Saul Tabernacle) was erected in 1867.]

337.2.2 Parish of Arlingham
Area 3,225 acres; 156 inhabited houses, 8 uninhabited. Population 737.

9.14 (15)   **Church of England, St Mary, Arlingham**
Name   Arlingham parish church. An ancient church dedicated to St Mary
Consecration   Before 1800
Erected   [Restored 1867–8]
Endowment   Glebe £250. Fees £3. Easter offerings £3. {Total £193}
Sittings   Free 46. Other 287. Total 333
Attend'ce 30 Mar.   Morning 78 + 41 SS. Total 119
                       Afternoon 145 + 38 SS. Total 183
Avge attendance   [Not given]
Dated   [Not given]
Signed   Thomas Holmes Ravenhill, vicar [1848–93]
                       Arlingham nr Newnham, Gloucestershire

9.15 (16)   **Wesleyan Methodist, Arlingham**
Name   Ebenezer
Erected   1820
Building   Yes [separate and entire] Yes [exclusively as a place of worship]
Sittings   Free 100. Other 40. Total [140] Standing room none
Attend'ce 30 Mar.   Morning 15 + 12 SS. Total 27
                       Afternoon 12 SS. Total [12]
                       Evening 100. Total 100
Avge attendance   [Not given]
Dated   31 March 1851
Signed   Robert Chandler, steward [farmer]
                       Arlingham near Newnham, Gloucestershire

337. 2.3 Parish of Fretherne
Area 930 acres; 61 inhabited houses, 2 uninhabited. Population 267.
VCH 10, 155–69

9.16 (17)	**Church of England, St Mary, Fretherne**
(Summary form)	
Name	Fretherne parish church
Erected	Six years [ago] on an old site [Rebuilt 1846–7, consecrated 21 Oct. 1847; enlarged 1857–9 and 1866]
[*Endowment*	Total £282]
Sittings	Free 200. Total 200
Usual attend'ce	Morning about 30 SS. Total [30]
	Afternoon unknown + about 30 SS
Signed	Thomas Spire, registrar
[*Incumbent*	Sir William Lionel Darell 1844–78]
	[Fretherne Court, Gloucester]

[Darell (1817–83) succeeded his brother as the 4th baronet in 1853. He died at his London residence in Upper Brook Street, Hanover Square, Westminster.]

337.2.4 Parish of Frampton-on-Severn
Area 2,720 acres; 213 inhabited houses, 5 uninhabited. Population 994.
VCH 10, 139–55.

9.17 (18)	**Church of England, St Mary the Virgin, Frampton-on-Severn**
Name	The parish church of Frampton on Severn, dedicated to St Mary in July 1315 by Walter de Maydenstone, then bishop of Worcester [1313–7]
Consecration	Before 1800 [re-consecrated 29 Sept. 1870]
Erected	[Restored 1850–2 and nave enlarged and chancel rebuilt 1868–9]
Endowment	Endowment for church – the clergy
	Income about £200 a year (net). {Total £330}
Sittings	Free 135. Other 363. Total 498
Attend'ce 30 Mar.	Morning 120 + 83 SS. Total 203
	Afternoon 270 + 82 SS. Total 352
	Evening no service. I have a service at Fromebridge in the evening.
Avge attendance	Morning 150 + 90 SS. Total 240
	Afternoon 300 + 90 SS. Total 390
	Evening no service. I have a service at Fromebridge in the evening.
Remarks	No reliance can be placed on the return from the dissenting place of worship in this parish. More than half of the congregation are collected from the parishes of Saul, Fretherne etc. and the very same persons attend elsewhere on the very same Census day to swell the ranks of dissent in other parishes.
Dated	31 March 1851
Signed	George Chute, vicar [1847–53]
	Frampton on Severn, Dursley

9.18 (20)	**Independent or Congregational, Frampton-on-Severn**
Name	Brethren Chapel
Erected	AD 1776 [Tablet: 1760. Schoolroom 'erected by voluntary contributions, June 1849']
Building	A separate and entire building. Used exclusively as a place of worship

Sittings   Free 114. Other 136. Total [250]
Attend'ce 30 Mar.   Morning 76 + 34 SS. Total 110
                      Evening 200. Total 200
Avge attendance   [Not given]
Remarks   Owing to causes which need not be specified the congregation was not
                      so large on Sunday, 30 March, as it usually is. Twelve may be added
                      to the morning and thirty to the evening congregation. A small vestry
                      in front of the chapel capable of accommodating twenty persons is
                      always available when required.
Dated   31 March 1851
Signed   William Lewis, minister [1846–64]
                      [Luke House], Frampton on Severn, Gloucestershire

[The chapel was opened in 1776 by Rowland Hill (**5.8**). From 1842–6 Lewis had been the co-pastor
to William Richardson 1799–1846.]

9.19 (19)   Non-denominational, Fromebridge Mills
(Summary form)
Name   Private meeting house (at the house of Jesse Park) [hand loom weaver]
Erected   In use about four or five 5 years
Sittings   Free 50. Total [50]
Usual attend'ce   Evening 50. Total [50]
Signed   Thomas Spire, registrar

337.2.5–6 Parish of Eastington
Area 2,042 acres; 368 inhabited houses, 11 uninhabited. Population 1,886.
The parish includes the tithings of Alkerton and Eastington. The Union workhouse,
situated within the parish had 59 inmates (of whom 28 were children).
VCH 10, 123–39.

9.20 (21)   Church of England, St Michael, Eastington
Name   Eastington parish church. An ancient edifice
Consecration   Before 1800
Erected   [Nave extended 1850–1. Restored 1885]
Endowment   Tithe £525. Glebe £85. Gross £610. Fees £5. Dues £2. Easter offerings
                      £2. Total £9. {Total £551}
Sittings   Free 210. Other 365. Total 575 (besides school)
Attend'ce 30 Mar.   Morning 305 + 150 SS. Total 455
                      Afternoon 435 + 150 SS. Total 585
Avge attendance   [Not given]
Dated   31 March 1851
Signed   Thomas Peters, rector [1837–83]
                      Eastington rectory, nr Stroud, Gloucestershire

9.21 (23)   Particular Baptist, Eastington
Name   Baptist Chapel
Erected   1824 [Rebuilt 1871]
Building   Yes [separate and entire] Yes [exclusively as a place of worship]
Sittings   Free 60 + 110. Total [170] Standing room none
Attend'ce 30 Mar.   Morning 64 + 85 SS. Total 149
                      Afternoon 89 SS. Total 89
                      Evening 90. Total 90

Avge attendance Morning 80 + 90 SS. Total 170
                   Afternoon 95 SS. Total 95
                   Evening 120. Total 120
Dated   31 March 1851
Signed   George Steele, deacon [cordwainer (shoemaker)]
                   Eastington, Glo'shire

[The chapel, which was located between Westend and Nupend, was built by the Primitive Methodists in 1824, and sold to the Baptists in 1831.]

9.22 (22)   **Wesleyan Methodist, Alkerton**
Name   Eastington Wesleyan Methodist Chapel
Erected   In the year 1803 [Rebuilt 1870]
Building   Yes [separate and entire] Yes [exclusively as a place of worship]
Sittings   Free 220. Other 180. Total [400]
Attend'ce 30 Mar. [Not given]
Avge attendance   Morning 100 + 100 SS. Total 200
                    Afternoon no service
                    Evening 250 + 50 SS. Total 300
Dated   31 March 1851
Signed   Charles Warner, steward [cordwainer (shoemaker)]
                    Eastington, near Stroud, Gloucestershire.

337.2.7 Parish of Frocester
Area 1,833 acres; 62 inhabited houses, 9 uninhabited. Population 299.
VCH 10, 170–8. *GNQ* 2, 283–4, 341; 5, 47–50.

9.23 (24)   **Church of England, St Andrew, Frocester**
Name   Chapel of Frocester. Built about 200 years ago for the convenience of
                    the parishioners
Consecration   Before 1800
Erected   [Built c.1680–90 and restored 1896–7]
Endowment   Present income about £250. Fees about £3 {Total £229}
Sittings   Free about 60. Other 190. Total 250
Attend'ce 30 Mar. Morning 69 + 25 SS. Total 94
                    Afternoon about 98 + 26 SS. Total 124
Avge attendance   I cannot state the average. The congregation varies from about 100 to
                    180 or even at times to 200. Average no. of Sunday scholars about 30.
Remarks   The parish church, St Peter's, has just been rebuilt, but not yet consecrated,
                    situated one mile from the village.
Dated   31 March 1851
Signed   Charles Powell Jones, minister [1837–69]
                    Frocester, Stroud

[By 1828 the medieval parish church of St Peter was in ruins, and St Andrew's chapel of ease (rebuilt in the 17th century) was used for services. Though the site was opposed by the vicar, the old church was rebuilt 1849–51 and consecrated 16 Jan. 1852, services being shared between both sites until the chapel fell into disrepair in 1873. It was restored 1896–7 and both buildings remained in use until in 1952, apart from the tower, St Peter's was demolished and the chapel became the parish church.]

10. HO 129/338 STROUD DISTRICT: 81 places of worship

338.1.   STONEHOUSE SUB-DISTRICT

338.1.1 Parish of Leonard Stanley
Area 1,070 acres; 189 inhabited houses, 13 uninhabited. Population 861.
VCH 10, 257–67

10.1 (1)	**Church of England, St Swithin, Leonard Stanley**
Name	St Swithin. Ancient [priory] parish church
Consecration	Before 1800
Erected	[Restored 1884–5 and 1913–4]
Endowment	Land £187. OPE £7 11s 10d (funded money). Fees £3 to £4 {Total £200}
Sittings	Free 12. Other 350. Total 362
Attend'ce 30 Mar.	Morning 140 + 100 SS. Total 240
	Afternoon 240 + 98 SS. Total 338
Avge attendance	Morning 140 + 100. Total 240
	Afternoon 200 + 90 SS. Total 290
Remarks	A plan is in contemplation for increasing the number of free sittings, the want of provision is now severely felt.
Dated	7 April 1851
Signed	David Jones, perpetual curate [1839–78]
	Stanley St Leonard's, Stroud, Gloucestershire

10.2 (2)	**Wesleyan Methodist, The Street**
Name	Wesleyan Methodist Chapel
Erected	In the year 1810
Building	Yes [separate and entire] Yes [exclusively as a place of worship]
Sittings	Free 130. Other 305. Total [435]
Attend'ce 30 Mar.	Morning 120 + 80 SS. Total 200
	Evening 150. Total 150
Avge attendance	[Not given]
Dated	31 March 1851
Signed	John Stock, chapel steward [tailor]
	Frocester, Gloucestershire

338.1.2–3 Parish of Stonehouse
Area 1,625 acres; 557 inhabited houses, 48 uninhabited. Population 2,598.
The parish includes the extra parochial area of Haywards Field.
VCH, 10, 267–89; *GNQ* 8, 8–11

10.3 (3)	**Church of England, St Cyr, Stonehouse**
(Summary form)	
Name	Parish church
Consecration	[Not given]
Erected	[Apart from the tower rebuilt 1853–4. Restored 1884]
Endowment	{Total £510}
Sittings	Free 127. Other 262. Total 389
Usual attend'ce	Morning about 100 + from 100 to 120 SS. Total [200–220]

Afternoon about 250. Total [250]
Signed   William Ruskin
[*Incumbent*   Henry Cripps 1826–61]
               [Preston, Cirencester]

[Cripps was also the incumbent of Preston (**12.45**). Between April and May 1737 George Whitefield spent two months at Stonehouse, preaching at the parish church at the invitation of Sampson Harris, incumbent 1728–63.]

10.4 (4)   Church of England, St Matthew, Cainscross
Name   St Matthew's district church, under the provisions of 1 & 2 Will. IV, c.38 [1831]
Consecration   19 January 1837, as an additional church [11 Oct. 1898]
Erected   By private subscription for £3,780. Total cost £3,780 [Restored and enlarged 1897–8]
Endowment   OPE £33. Pew rents £53. Fees £10. Easter offerings £18
Sittings   Free 300. Other 350. Total 650
Attend'ce 30 Mar. Morning 250 + 164 SS. Total 414
                 Afternoon 300 + 161 SS. Total 461
Avge attendance [Not given]
Remarks   The pew rents, fees and Easter offerings are taken at the average of the last five years.
Dated   31 March 1851
Signed   John Geale Uwins, perpetual curate [1841–92]
                 Cainscross parsonage, nr Stroud, Gloucestershire

['On the occasion of his [Uwin's] jubilee, his parishioners presented him with a purse of £200, which he handed to the churchwardens to be used for renewing the church': Venn.]

10.5 (5)   Congregational or Independent, Stonehouse
Name   Congregational Chapel
Erected   [1811, replaced by a new chapel in 1823 and again in] 1827
Building   Yes [separate and entire] Yes [exclusively as a place of worship]
Sittings   Free 50. Gallery for 100. Other 246 [Total 396]
Attend'ce 30 Mar. Morning 140 + 155 SS. Total 295
                 Afternoon 155 SS. Total 155
                 Evening 320. Total 320
Avge attendance Morning 140 + 155 SS. Total 295
                 Afternoon 155 SS. Total 155
                 Evening 320. Total 320
Dated   7 April 1851
Signed   Thomas Maund, independent minister [1837–63]
                 Stonehouse, Gloucestershire

[This chapel was seeded from Ebley Chapel (**10.7**). Thomas Maund also had oversight of the congregation at Randwick (**10.9**).]

338.1.4 Parish of Randwick
Area 1,260 acres; 222 inhabited houses, 8 uninhabited. Population 959.
Since 1831 the population had declined by 72 due to the decline of the clothing industry.
VCH 10, 224–30

10.6 (6)   Church of England, St John the Baptist, Randwick
Name   'Randwick Church' dedicated to St John. An ancient parish church separated from the mother church in the reign of Henry VIII being

	previously a chapelry to Standish (**9.7**)
Consecration	Before 1800
Erected	[Chancel rebuilt 1825; nave and chancel restored 1864–7; south aisle rebuilt 1893–6 as a memorial to the lengthy incumbency of John Elliott]
Endowment	Land £80 (gross part). Tithe 72 net £48. Glebe house [1844] OPE £8 8s. Fees £2 10s (average). Dues, Easter offerings, other sources none. {Total £124}
Sittings	Free about 400. Other about 104. Total 504. (Taken according to the area)
Attend'ce 30 Mar.	Morning 75 + 59 SS. Total 134
	Afternoon 260 + 71 SS. Total 331
Avge attendance	[Not given]
Remarks	The morning 'general congregation' was rather below and the afternoon ditto, either above its usual average.
Dated	31 March 1851
Signed	John Elliott, minister [1819–91]
	Randwick nr Stroud

[Once a house was provided in 1844 John Elliott was the first resident incumbent. In 1851 he had three resident pupils aged 13 to 18. He died in post aged 100. George Whitefield preached in Randwick church several times. On 1 July 1739 the window behind the pulpit was removed so that the 2,000 people in the churchyard could hear the sermon, and on 15 July there were 270 communicants: Tyerman 1890, 1, 256, 263. John Wesley recorded 'I preached at Randwick, seven miles from Gloucester. The church was much crowded, though 1,000 or upwards stayed in the churchyard': *Journal,* 7 Oct. 1739. Wesley preached there again on 27 June 1742.]

10.7 (7)   **Countess of Huntingdon, Ebley**

Name	Ebley Chapel
Erected	[Opened 10 April] 1798 [Enlarged 1811 and replaced by a new chapel opened in 1881]
Building	Yes [separate and entire] Yes [exclusively as a place of worship]
Sittings	Free 151. Other 454. Total [605] Standing room for 432
Attend'ce 30 Mar.	Morning 229 + 155 SS. Total 384
	Evening 300 + 35 SS. Total 335
Avge attendance (6m)	Morning 300 + 150 SS. Total 450
	Evening 450 + 70 SS. Total 520
Remarks	The congregation on 30 March was thin. The weather was threatening and this greatly affected the attendance as the chapel is rather isolated. The 30th also was mid-Lent Sunday, or as it is generally called 'Mothering Sunday' in this district, and numbers on that day go and visit their friends. Both morning and evening we were considerably below average. It should further be observed that several members of families are generally at home. The husband, for example, at home with the children, and let the wife come out, or the wife to let the husband come out. Many children also, and servants and infirm persons, are at home during a part or a whole of the day, so that the hearers must at least be one third greater than the general congregation.
Dated	31 March 1851
Signed	Benjamin Parsons, minister [1826–55]
	Ebley, Stroud, Gloucestershire

[Parsons was the editor of the Countess of Huntingdon's Connexion *New Magazine* 1850–1, and also the minister of Randwick Chapel (**10.8**). 'The Congregationalists were the most thriving dissenting group in the parish during the 19th century ... The chapel joined the Countess of

Huntingdon's Connexion but remained affiliated to the Congregational Union': *VCH* 10, 287.]

10.8 (9)   **Countess of Huntingdon, Randwick**
Name   Randwick Chapel
Erected   1836
Building   Yes [separate and entire] Yes [exclusively as a place of worship]
Sittings   Free 90. Total [90] Standing room for 60
Attend'ce 30 Mar.   Afternoon 37. Total 37
Avge attend'ce (6m) Afternoon 40. Total 40
Remarks   All the sittings in this little chapel are free. The chapel was formerly called the Primitive Methodist Chapel. There is no Sunday school.
Dated   31 March 1851
Signed   Benjamin Parsons, minister of Ebley Chapel [1826–55]
                      Ebley, Stroud, Gloucestershire
[Randwick Chapel opened as a Primitive Methodist chapel and by the mid century 'it was affiliated to the Countess of Huntingdon's Connexion and was served from Ebley Chapel (**10.7**), but it continued to be known as a Primitive Methodist chapel.' *VCH* 10, 229.]

10.9 (10)   **Congregational or Independent, Oxlinch**
Name   (Licensed) dwelling house
Erected   [Not given]
Building   Dwelling house. No [not exclusively as a place of worship]
Sittings   Free 25. Total [25]
Attend'ce 30 Mar.   Evening 20. Total 20
Avge attendance   Evening 24. Total 24
Dated   7 April 1851
Signed   Thomas Maund, minister of Stonehouse Chapel (**10.5**)
                      Stonehouse, Gloucestershire
[This was one of a number of dissenting groups worshipping in houses in the area: *VCH* 10, 229.]

10.10 (8)   **Wesleyan Methodist, Randwick**
Name   Randwick Chapel
Erected   In 1824 [Tablet: 'Randwick Chapel, built 1807, rebuilt 1824']
Building   Yes [separate and entire] An infant school held in the lower vestry of the chapel
Sittings   Free 60. Other 110. Total [170] Standing room for 100
Attend'ce 30 Mar.   Morning 60 + 50 SS. Total 110
                      Evening 200. Total 200
Avge attendance   Morning 60 + 50 SS. Total 110
                      Evening 195. Total 195
Dated   31 March 1851
Signed   William Knee, trustee
                      Centenary Cottage, Randwick, Gloucestershire
[Knee (1774–1857) established the Sunday and Day schools in the village; and even after moving to Cheltenham he walked to Randwick to teach and to lead the prayer meeting.]

338.2   PAINSWICK SUB-DISTRICT

338.2.1 Parish of Pitchcombe
Area 217 acres; 35 inhabited houses, 10 uninhabited. Population 145.
In ten years the population had dropped by 98 because of the decline in the clothing industry.

10.11 (1)   **Church of England, St John the Baptist, Pitchcombe**
Name   Pitchcombe Church (parish church)
Consecration   In the year 1819, in the room of the old parish church which was in a
                  dilapidated condition having been erected in the year 1376.
Erected   The new church was erected by voluntary contributions.
                  [Restored 1869–70; consecrated 10 June 1870]
Endowment   Tithe £47 18s 9d (the outgoings average £6 per ann.). Glebe £6 15s.
                  Fees £2 [See Harescombe (**9.5**)]
Sittings   Free 80. Other 120. Total 200
Attend'ce 30 Mar. Morning 72 + 49 SS. Total 121
                  Afternoon 54 SS. Total 54
Avge attendance Morning 70 + 50 SS. Total 120
                  Afternoon 120 + 50 SS. Total 170
Remarks   Harescombe and Pitchcombe being one incumb[enc]y, there is only one
                  service in each church; and the morning congregation in each church is
                  always much smaller than the afternoon.
Dated   31 March 1851
Signed   Frederick Quarrington, curate [1839–51]
                  Harescombe, Gloucester
[*Incumbent*   Marlow Watts Wilkinson 1825–67]
[The benefice consisted of Harescombe (**9.5**) with Pitchcombe. Wilkinson was also the incumbent of Uley (**5.16**) where he lived.]

10.12 (2)   **Independent, Pitchcombe**
Name   Pitchcombe Independent Chapel
Erected   1804
Building   [Yes] separate [and entire] Yes [exclusively as a place of worship]
Sittings   Free 50. Other 100. Total [150] Standing room for 50
Attend'ce 30 Mar. Afternoon 50. Total 50
                  Evening 100. Total 100
Avge attendance Afternoon 80 (no SS). Total 80
                  Evening 120. Total [120]
Dated   31 March 1851
Signed   Rev Alfred Gillman, minister [1833–]
                  Swan Street, Stroud, Gloucestershire

338.2.2–5 Parish of Painswick
Area 5,815 acres; 789 inhabited houses, 100 uninhabited. Population 3,464.
The parish includes the tithings of Edge, Sheepscombe, Spoonbed and Stroud End (which includes the chapelry of Slad). Since 1831 the population Edge had declined by 321 due to the decline in the cloth industry.
VCH 11, 56–87

10.13 (4)   **Church of England, St Mary, Painswick**
Name   Parish church of Painswick
Consecration   Before 1800
Erected   [Restored 1878–9 and 1883]
Endowment   {Total £449}
Sittings   Free 253 (exclusive of children's seats). Other 448. Total 701
Attend'ce 30 Mar. [Not given]
Avge attendance Morning 366 + 159 SS. Total 525

Afternoon 566 + 159 SS. Total 725

Remarks The average of the afternoon congregation exceeds the average of the morning congregation by 200, but the congregations do not consist of entirely different persons.

Dated 31 March 1851

Signed Robert Strong, vicar of Painswick [1823–56]
Painswick vicarage, Gloucestershire ·

[Strong was the last incumbent to be elected to office by the parishioners. He was active in supporting CMS and his brother Leonard was a missionary in British Guiana: Stunt 95–105. Within the parish St John, Sheepscombe (**10.14**) was consecrated 21 Feb. 1820; Holy Trinity, Slad (**10.15**) on 14 Oct. 1834 and St John the Baptist, Edge 9 June 1865.]

10.14 (8)   **Church of England, St John the Apostle, Sheepscombe**

Name St John's Chapel

Consecration [Erected] 1819 [consecrated 21 February 1820] for the relief of the population of the parish of Painswick. [29 November 1872]

Erected By the Rev S[trickland] C[harles] E[dward] Neville, then curate of Painswick. By general and subscriptions, total cost about £1,200. [Enlarged 1872]

Endowment Glebe ... a vicarage house is built and garden cost £300. OPE £22 from Queen Anne's Bounty and £15 from Eccles[iastical] Commiss[ioners] Pew rents £5. Fees £8. {Total £55}

Sittings Free 280. Other 75. Total 355

Attend'ce 30 Mar. [Not given]

Avge attend'ce (3m) Morning and afternoon about 230 generally + 50 SS. Total 280

Dated 31 March 1851

Signed Joseph Duncan Ostrehan, incumbent [1828–51]
Sheepscombe parsonage, Stroud, Gloucestershire

[Subscribers to the erection of the church included the well-known Evangelicals William Marsh, Hannah More, Charles Simeon, Abel Smith, Lady Olivia Sparrow, Nicholas Vansittart and William Wilberforce. Sheepscombe was a chapel of ease to Painswick until 1844 when it became a parish church. From 1816 Neville, who had been the curate in charge of Painswick, became the first of a number of Evangelical clergy at Sheepscombe. These included Hugh Stowell, who served a brief curacy 1823–4; Joseph Baylee, a noted linguist, scholar and controversialist who was the founder and first principal of St Aidan's College, Birkenhead 1856–68, was incumbent 1871–83; and John Charles Wilcox, incumbent 1895–1906, was also the chaplain to the Wickliffe Preachers and biographer of John Kensit, the founder of the Protestant Truth Society (1889): *ODNB* 'Hugh Stowell (1799–1865), 'Joseph Baylee (1807–1883)'.]

10.15 (5)   **Church of England, Holy Trinity, Slad**

Name Holy Trinity, commonly called The Slad. It is a district from the parish of Painswick under the provisions of 59 Geo. III, c.134 [1819]

Consecration In 1834 [14 Oct. 1834 and 1 Apr. 1869]

Erected By subscription and a grant from the Church Building Society. Total cost (I believe) £1,000. [Enlarged 1868–9]

Endowment Pew rents £14. Other sources £44. {Total £50}

Sittings Free 300. Other 80. Total 380

Attend'ce 30 Mar. Morning 68 + 43 SS. Total 111
Afternoon 98 + 40 SS. Total 138

Avge attendance [Not given]

Remarks The vicar of the mother parish [of Painswick (**10.13**)] has reserved marriages to himself and the other fees are not worth naming.

Dated   31 March 1851
Signed   Arthur Hill, incumbent [1835–53]
                     The Slad parsonage, nr Stoud

[Slad (as it now known) was a chapel of ease to Painswick until 1844 when it became a parish. All Saints, Uplands, consecrated 11 May 1910, became the parish church of Slad 19 Oct. 1934.]

10.16 (10)   Independent, Gloucester Street, Painswick
Name   Independent or Upper Chapel
Erected   Before 1800 [1705. New chapel opened 13 June 1804, remodelled 1892–3]
Building   Yes [separate and entire] Yes [exclusively as a place of worship]
Sittings   Free 100. Other 350. Total [450]
Attend'ce 30 Mar. Morning 150 + 120 SS. Total 270
                     Afternoon 75. Total 75
                     Evening 280. Total 280
Avge attendance (6m) Morning 140 + 100 SS. Total 240
                     Afternoon 60. Total 60
                     Evening 300. Total 300
Remarks   The chapel was rebuilt in 1803. The former chapel supposed to be erected about the year 1680, divine service having been held there from that time until the present. At present there is not any settled minister.
Dated   31 March 1851
Signed   John Colain Beavins, deacon [tailor]
                     High Street, Painswick, Gloucestershire

[Following the alterations of 1892–3 the chapel was renamed the Cornelius Winter Memorial Chapel. In the mid-1750s Winter (1742–1808) had been converted at George Whitefield's London Tabernacle. He became Whitefield's personal assistant and accompanied him on his final visit to Georgia in 1770. Winter rebuilt the Painswick chapel and was the minister 1788–1808.]

10.17 (7)   Independent, Edge
Name   None
Erected   [Chapel opened 1856]
Building   A cottage rented for the purpose. Yes [exclusively as a place of worship]
Sittings   Free 40. Total [40]
Attend'ce 30 Mar. Morning Sabbath scholars taught
                     Afternoon 20. Total 20
                     Evening none
Avge attendance Morning 20 + 12 SS. Total 32
Dated   30 March 1851
Signed   Samuel Pitt, minister
                     King's Stanley, Gloucestershire

10.18 (6)   Primitive Methodist, Vicarage Street, Painswick
Name   'Chappel'
Erected   1849 [Replaced by Ebenezer Chapel in Bisley Street 1854]
Building   Separate [and entire] Exclusively [as a place of worship]
Sittings   Free 30. Other 60. Total [90] Standing room for 20
Attend'ce 30 Mar. Morning none
                     Afternoon 35. Total [35]
                     Evening 43. Total [43]
Avge attendance Morning none
                     Afternoon 60. Total [60]

Dated	30 March 1851
Signed	Nathan Sutton, local preacher [agricultural labourer]
	Rodborough near Stroud, Gloucestershire

[Between 1742 and 1790 John Wesley made 15 visits to Painswick before a Wesleyan chapel was opened in 1806. The membership declined, and by 1831 the chapel was closed and sold to the Baptists.]

10.19 (3)   Society of Friends, Vicarage Lane, Painswick

Name	Vicarage Lane, in parish of Painswick
Erected	Before 1800 [1705–6, altered 1793–4]
Building	Yes [separate and entire] Yes [exclusively as a place of worship]
Sittings	Free 140. Total [140] 575 [sq. ft] No gallery
Attend'ce 30 Mar.	Morning 3
	Afternoon not open
	Evening not open
Dated	31 day of the 3rd mo. 1851
Signed	William G. Padbury [farmer]
	Painswick

10.20 (9)   Church of Jesus Christ of Latter Day Saints, Sheepscombe

Name	Meeting Room
Erected	20 January 1851
Building	Part of buildings. Yes. Used exclusively as a place of worship.
Sittings	All free 50. Total [50]
Attend'ce 30 Mar.	Morning 15. Total [15]
	Afternoon 35. Total [35]
	Evening 40. Total [40]
Avge attendance	[Not given]
Dated	31 March 1851
Signed	Charles Blackwell, minister [agricultural labourer]
	Cowley, nr Cheltenham, Gloucestershire

338.2.6 Parish of Cranham

Area 1,859 acres; 83 inhabited houses, 7 uninhabited. Population 354.
The parish includes the hamlet called the Potteries.
VCH 7, 199–210.

10.21 (11)   Church of England, St James the Great, Cranham

Name	An ancient parish church, consecrated to St James
Consecration	Before 1800 [4 Nov. 1896]
Erected	[Restored 1861–2, and mostly rebuilt and enlarged 1894–5]
Endowment	Tithe* £163 (gross). Glebe £2. OPE £5 [Total] £170. Fees nothing.
	Easter offerings given to [the] clerk. [See Brimpsfield (12.8)]
Sittings	Free 135. Other 45. Total 180
Attend'ce 30 Mar.	Morning 40 + 47 SS. Total 87
Avge attendance	Morning 60 + 40 SS. Total 100
	Afternoon 130 + 40 SS. Total 175 [recte 170]
Remarks	* The value of tithe is here given as fixed at commutation. It is now diminished and gradually decreasing. The glebe consists of a cottage and garden given to [the] school-mistress and the other £5 arises from augmentation money from Queen Ann's Bounty.
Dated	30 March 1851
Signed	William Moore, rector [1829–79]

Brimpsfield, near Painswick

[The benefice consisted of Brimpsfield (**12.8**) with Cranham. Moore was resident curate of Cranham 1822–9, then the incumbent. In 1873 he was 'old, feeble and miserably poor. He cannot be induced to resign': [Various] *Cranham: The History of a Cotswold Village* (Slad) 2005, 135. Anglo-Catholicism was introduced to Cranham by the incumbent Henry Rastrick Hanson 1892–1924.]

10.22 (12)   Particular Baptist, Cranham

Name	Baptist Chapel
Erected	December 1839
Building	Separate [and entire] Exclusively [as a place of worship]
Sittings	Free 100. Other none. Total [100] Standing room none
Attend'ce 30 Mar.	Morning 5. {Total
	Afternoon 8. {13
Avge attendance	Morning 120. No scholars. Total 120
Remarks	The church assembling is only a few and only meets once a month for divine service, and we have no pastor or minister being too poor to pay one.
Dated	30 March 1851
Signed	Samuel Bendall, deacon [contractor]
	[Battle Cottage], Clare Street, Cheltenham

338.2.7 Parish of Miserden

Area 2,434 acres; 109 inhabited houses, 4 uninhabited. Population 489.
The parish includes the hamlets of Camp and Sutgrove.
VCH 11, 47–56

10.23 (15)   Church of England, St Andrew, Miserden

Name	Miserden parish church
Consecration	Before 1800
Erected	[Tablet: 'This church was restored by voluntary contributions, AD1866. W. Y. Mills MA, rector; J. Rolt MA, H. Sadler, churchwardens']
Endowment	Tithe £410 (subect to rates). Glebe 86 acres poor land. OPE, pew rents, fees, Easter offerings, other sources none. The rates amount to between £50 and £60 per year besides ... {Total £335}
Sittings	Total 200. Might be made easily. Total [200]
Attend'ce 30 Mar.	Morning 53 + 30 SS. Total 83
	Afternoon 86 + 30 SS. Total about 116
Avge attendance	[Not given]
Remarks	This is like many other parishes in the Cotswold Hills, getting to it of the parish church and in bad weather the population are unable to attend.
Dated	30 March 1851
Signed	William Yarnton Mills, rector [1848–70]
	Miserden rectory, nr Cirencester

[Mills was the curate of Miserden 1842–8 to William Mills 1797–1848, the absentee incumbent who lived at Shellingford, Oxon.]

10.24a (14)   Baptist, Miserden

Name	Baptist Chapel
Erected	About the year 1833
Building	No [not separate and entire] Yes [exclusively as a place of worship]
Sittings	Free sittings 55. Total [55]
Attend'ce 30 Mar.	Afternoon 44. Total [44]
	Evening 37. Total [37]

Avge attendance [Not given]
Remarks   Mr Thomas Davis, minister. Resident at Chalford Lynch, parish of
                   Bisley, Gloucestershire
Dated   30 March 1851
Signed   Thomas Hinton, deacon (acting for the minister) [tailor]
                   Duntisbourne Abbots, Gloucestershire
[Hinton was also a deacon at Winstone Baptist chapel (**12.6**). For Davis see Coberley (**16.8**); he was also the minister at Winstone.]

10.24b (13)   **Baptist, Miserden**
Name   Camp
Erected   1830
Building   Yes [separate and entire] Yes [exclusively as a place of worship]
Sittings   All free 50. Total [50]
Attend'ce 30 Mar. Afternoon 35. Total [35]
                   Evening 42. Total [42]
Avge attendance [Not given]
Dated   28 December 1851
Signed   Thomas Davis, minister [1832–63]
                   France Lynch, Bisley, Gloucestershire

338.3   BISLEY SUB-DISTRICT

338.3.1 Parish of Bisley
Area 8,033 acres; 1,151 inhabited houses, 135 uninhabited. Population 4,801.
The parish includes the tithings of Avenis, Bidfield, Bisley, Bussage, Chalford, Oakridge, Steanbridge, Througham and Tunley. Since 1831 the population had decreased by 1,095 due to decline in the cloth industry.
VCH 11, 4–40

10.25 (16)   **Church of England, All Saints, Bisley**
(Summary form)
Name   All Saints
Erected   Date not known, supposed to be 600 years ago [Restored 1851 and 1860–2]
[Endowment   Total £527]
Sittings   Free 8. Other 500. Total 508
Usual attend'ce Morning about 300 + from 150 to 200. Total [450–500]
                   Afternoon about 500. Total about 500]
Signed   William Whiting, parish clerk [breeches maker]
[Incumbent   Thomas Keble 1827–73]
[Keble, younger brother of the well-known John Keble (**13.2**), was the leader of the 'Bisley-Fairford school' of conservative high churchmen and supporters of the Oxford Movement who influenced several assistant curates in the large parish of Bisley. Thomas Keble was succeeded by his son Thomas Keble 1873–1903: *ODNB* 'Thomas Keble (1793–1875)'. Within the parish France Lynch was consecrated 15 Sept. 1857.]

10.26 (17)   **Church of England, St Bartholomew, Oakridge**
Name   St Barthlomew, Oakridge. A district parish of Bisley
Consecration   St Bartholomew's Day 1836 [24 Aug.]
Erected   By private subscription aided by the Incorporated Society for Building
                   etc. Churches. [£350 from the Society]
Endowment   OPE £800. Pew rents £3 10s. Fees (for 1850) £3 6s*
Sittings   Free 350. Other 30. Total 380

Attend'ce 30 Mar. [Not given]

Avge attendance   Morning abt 80 + 105 SS. Total [185]

Afternoon between 200 and 300 + 105 SS. Total [305–405]

Remarks   *The district having only been constituted in August 1849, the average amount of fees cannot yet be ascertained.

Dated   31 March 1851

Signed   Hugh Hovel Baskerville Farmar, perpetual curate [1849–51]

Oakridge parsonage, Bisley, Gloucestershire

[Subscriptions to build the church were raised by the efforts of Thomas Keble (**10.25**) and George Prevost (**5.24**), who addressed their appeal to 'persons disposed to support the cause of sound religion and the apostolical institutions of the church': Jones, 18. There were gifts from Thomas Keble (£100), John Keble (£100), George Prevost (£100), Isaac Williams (£40) and Edward Pusey (£5): GA, D2962/36. The endowment consisted of '£800 consols standing in the names of Sir G. Prevost and Mr Keble "in trust for Oakridge Chapel." This produces annually £23 6s. There is also in the Savings Bank a sum of £170 (more of less) which is considered as "a repair fund".' Note on Oakridge church, 17 April 1849, inserted inside GA GDR A2/4, Survey of the Diocese. The architect was Robert Stokes of Cheltenham.]

10.27 (18)   Church of England, Christ Church, Chalford

Name   Christ Church, built by the inhabitants of Chalford AD 1725

Consecrated AD 1841 under 1 and 2 Will. IV [c.38 (1831). Made a parochial district in 1842

Consecration   15 Sep. 1841, to render it available as a parochial district church

Erected   The old part by inhabitants of Chalford AD 1725. The new part [an extended nave, a chancel and tower] by the Rev S Gompertz

Total cost of new part £1,000

Endowment   Glebe house. OPE £108. Pew rents and fees £40. {Total £150}

Sittings   Free 210. Other 500. Total 710

Attend'ce 30 Mar.   Morning about 600 + 146 SS. Total 746

Afternoon about 600 + 140 SS. Total 740

Avge attendance   [Not given]

Dated   March 1851

Signed   Solomon Gompertz, minister [1842–64]

Chalford, Gloucestershire

[For details of the endowment, see *GNQ* 1, 136–7.]

10.28 (19)   Church of England, St Michael and All Angels, Bussage

Name   'St Michael's church' chapelry district, assigned under 16th section of Act of Parliament passed 59 Geo. III, [c.134] entitled 'An Act to amend and render more effectual etc. etc. [1819]

Consecration   [6 Oct.] 1846 [On the day of the consecration 44 priests assembled in the Ram Inn and processed to the church]

Erected   By private benefaction. [The amount] not known. Total cost not known. [In 1854 a south aisle was erected to accommodate the female inmates of the House of Refuge]

Endowment   Land £56. {Total £30}

Sittings   Free 200. Other 30. Total 230

Attend'ce 30 Mar.   Morning 100 + 85 SS. Total 185

Afternoon 150 + 80 SS. Total 230

Evening 200. Total 200

Avge attendance   [Not given]

Dated   30 March 1851

Signed   Robert Alfred Suckling, incumbent [1848–51]
                        Bussage, Chalford.

[The Latin inscription of the foundation stone of the church when translated reads: 'To the honour of God, the Lord both of the dead and living, and in pious care for the poor in Christ, the foundation stone of this church is laid on the 21st day of November in the year of salvation, 1844. Built at the sole expense of twenty scholars of the University of Oxford. Unknown in this place, but known to God': Rudd, 345. During Suckling's incumbency Bussage became 'a model Tractarian parish': Jones, 116. In April 1851 the House of Refuge (later 'House of Mercy', a diocesan home for reformed prostitutes) founded by Suckling and John Armstrong (**18.1**), was opened at Kirby's Cottage, Bussage: *VCH* 11, 36.]

10.29 (24) Independent, France Lynch

Name   France [Meeting] [Old Vestry]
Erected   [Rebuilt in] 1819. New site. In lieu of a larger ... building
Building   Yes [separate and entire] Yes [exclusively as a place of worship]
Sittings   Free 150. Other 450. Total [600]
Attend'ce 30 Mar.   Morning 223 + 96 SS. Total 319
                        Afternoon 108 SS. Total 108
                        Evening 300. Total 300
Avge attendance (3m) Morning 230 + 100 SS. Total 330
                        Afternoon 120 SS. Total 120
                        Evening 350. Total 350
Dated   31 March 1851
Signed   Thomas Whitta, minister
                        Chalford near Stroud

10.30 (26) Baptist, Coppice Hill, Chalford

Name   Copse [Chapel or Chalford Chapel]
Erected   Before 1800 [c.1740, altered c.1810. Replaced by a nearby chapel in 1873–4]
Building   Yes [separate and entire] Yes [exclusively as a place of worship]
Sittings   Free 40. Other 260. Total [300]
Attend'ce 30 Mar.   Morning 166 + 73 SS. Total 239
                        Afternoon 175 + 73 SS. Total 248
                        Evening 198. Total 198
Avge attendance   [Not given]
Dated   31 March 1851
Signed   Robert White, Baptist minister
                        Chalford, Gloucestershire

10.31 (30) Particular Baptist, Eastcombe

Name   Eastcombe Chapel
Erected   [Opened 4 August] 1801 [Enlarged 1817 and 1860]
Building   Entirely set apart for religious worship. Yes exclusively [as a place of worship]
Sittings   Free 295. Other 455. Total [750]
Attend'ce 30 Mar.   Morning 100 + 98 SS. Total 198
                        Afternoon 375 + 90 SS. Total 465
                        Evening 150. Total 150*
Avge attendance   [Not given]
Remarks   The chapel and premises are freehold and vested in trust for the use of the church and congregation Sunday and day schools.

*No preaching last night. This the number on the preceding Sunday evening and the usual number.

Dated	31 March 1851
Signed	Stephen Packer, minister [1847–54]
	Eastcombe near Bisley, Gloucestershire

[This chapel established congregations at Colesborne (**12.13**) and Coberley (**16.8**). During Packer's ministry about 70 people were received into membership. He was also minister at Bussage (**10.32**).]

10.32 (29)   Particular Baptist, Bussage

Name	Bussage Chapel
Erected	It was opened for religious worship [23 Dec.] 1849*
	(In connection with the Baptist Chapel, Eastcombe) (**10.31**)
Building	Yes [separate and entire] Yes [exclusively as a place of worship]
Sittings	Free 240 (old place). Total [240]
Attend'ce 30 Mar.	[Not given]
Avge attendance (6m)	Evening 280 to 300. Total [280–300]
Remarks	* This place is closed, till the new chapel now building will be completed which we expect will be ready for opening about midsummer next.Used for an evening congregation only!
	(PS. This place of worship is private property being built at the sole expense of William Davis Esq. of Bussage [House]).
Dated	31 March 1851
Signed	Stephen Packer, evening preacher [1847–54]
	Eastcombe, near Bisley

[The congregation at Bussage included dissidents from Eastcombe (**10.31**), where a division had taken place in 1844, and the squire, William Davis, who opposed the Oxford Movement: Lambert and Shipman, 21. Robert Suckling, incumbent of Bussage, jealously referred to the chapel as 'a huge meeting house ... and perhaps [God] will defeat this scheme ere it be finished': Williams, 143.]

10.33 (20)   Wesleyan Methodist, Bisley

Name	None
Erected	In 1796 [Replaced by a new chapel 1863–4]
Building	Yes [separate and entire] Yes [exclusively as a place of worship]
Sittings	Free 40. Other 108. Total [148]
Attend'ce 30 Mar.	Morning 51. Total 51
	Evening 50. Total 50
Avge attendance	[Not given]
Dated	31 March 1851
Signed	Thomas Blanch, trustee [farmer]
	Bisley, Gloucestershire

10.34 (25)   Wesleyan Methodist, Oakridge

Name	Wesleyan Chapel
Erected	1797 [Enlarged 1836, and replaced by a new chapel 1874]
Building	Yes [separate and entire] Yes [exclusively as a place of worship]
Sittings	Free 40. Other 134. Total [174]
Attend'ce 30 Mar.	Afternoon 130 + 14 SS. Total 144
	Evening 147. Total 147
Avge attendance	Afternoon 110 + 16 SS. Total 126
	Evening 130. Total 130
Dated	31 March 1851
Signed	John Whiting, steward [tailor]

Oakridge, nr Chalford

10.35 (23)   **Wesleyan Methodist, Chalford**
Name   Ebenezer
Erected   1814
Building   Yes [separate and entire] Yes [exclusively as a place of worship]
Sittings   Free 50. Other 201. Total [251]
Attend'ce 30 Mar. Afternoon 91 + 51 SS. Total 142
                      Evening 117. Total 117
Avge attendance   [Not given]
Dated   31 March 1851
Signed   George Drew, steward (carpenter) [builder and contractor]
                      Chalford, Glo'shire.

10.36 (22)   **Wesleyan Methodist, Tunley**
Name   Tunley Chapel
Erected   September 1848
Building   Yes [separate and entire] Yes [exclusively as a place of worship]
Sittings   Free 20. Other 60. Total [80] Standing room none
Attend'ce 30 Mar. Afternoon 52 + 15 SS. Total 67
                      Evening 12. Total 12
Avge attendance   Afternoon 50 +15 SS. Total 65
                      Evening 10. Total 10
Dated   30 March 1851
Signed   William Bucknell, manager [shepherd]
                      Tunley near Bisley, Gloucestershire
[The chapel was built by Henry William Hancox of Tunley farm.]

10.37 (28)   **Primitive Methodist, Chalford Hill**
Name   Bethel Chapel
Erected   1824 [Tablet: 'Built AD 1823, rebuilt AD 1824']
Building   A entire building. Exclusively as a place of worship
Sittings   Free 50. Other 100. Total [150] Standing room enough for 40
Attend'ce 30 Mar. Morning 8. Total [8]
                      Afternoon 60. Total [60]
                      Evening 70. Total [70]
Avge attendance   Afternoon 65. Total [65]
Dated   31 March 1851
Signed   Joseph Daniels, trustee [baker]
                      Bourne nr Stroud, Gloucestershire

10.38 (21)   **Primitive Methodist, Custom Scrubs**
Name   Custom Scrubs
Erected   1840
Building   A chapel separate and entire. Used exclusively as a place of worship
Sittings   Free 40. Other 28. Total [68] Standing room none
Attend'ce 30 Mar. Morning 9 [at a] prayer meeting. Total [9]
                      Afternoon 36. Total [36]
                      Evening 38. Total [38]
Avge attendance   [Not given]
Dated   30 March 1851

Signed	William Davis, steward [miller]
	Downcourt, 'Gloucestershier'

10.39 (27)   **New Jerusalem Church, Chalford**

Name	Millswood Chapel
Erected	In the year 1845
Building	Yes [separate and entire] Yes [exclusively as a place of worship]
Sittings	Free 20 + 70 SS. Total [90] Standing room for 20
Attend'ce 30 Mar.	Morning 35. Total [35]
	Evening 32. Total [32]
Avge attendance	Morning 30. Total [30]
	Evening 40. Total [40]
Dated	31 March 1851
Signed	Henry Whittell [dissenting] minister
	Millswood, Chalford

[The New Jerusalem Church, founded in 1787, was based on the mystical and theosophical writings of Emanuel Swedenborg: see Introduction, 23.]

338.4   STROUD SUB-DISTRICT

338.4.1 Parish of Stroud

Area 3,810 acres; 1,837 inhabited houses, 111 uninhabited. Population 8,798.
The parish includes the tithings of Upper and Lower Lypiatt, Paganhill and Steanbridge.
The steady increase in the population was attributed to the improvement in the cloth industry. The Union workhouse situated in the parish had 295 inmates.
VCH 11, 99–145

10.40 (32)   **Church of England, St Lawrence, The Shambles, Stroud**

Name	St Lawrence. A parish church
Consecration	Before 1800
Erected	[Final service held 8 July 1866 and then, apart from the tower, the building was demolished and rebuilt 1866–8; consecrated 4 Aug. 1868]
Endowment	Land £80. OPE £44 10s. Fees £30. Easter offerings £76. Other sources £32 10s {Total £132}
Sittings	Free 254. Other 1,156. Total 1,410
Attend'ce 30 Mar.	[Not given]
Avge attendance	[Not given]
Remarks	Curate's stipend £100 per annum
Dated	31 March 1851
Signed	George Proctor, perpet[ua]l curate [1845–58]
	Stroud, Gloucestershire

[The first minister, Matthew Blaydon Hale 1839–45, was later bishop of Perth 1857–75, and Bishop of Brisbane 1875–95. 'Stroud might fairly claim to be considered a pleasant parish to work in. The population was about 8,000; mostly labouring people or mill-hands connected with the different woollen cloth manufactories. They were for the most part decently housed. The mill-owners, and other well-to-do people, were extremely warm-hearted and kind, and they desired to make things pleasant for their pastors': Kitchin, 68.]

10.41 (31)   **Church of England, Holy Trinity, Whitehall**

Name	Holy Trinity Church. A chapel of ease
Consecration	[15 Oct.] 1839, as an additional church
Erected	By subscriptions and by [a] grant from the Society for Building and repairing churches. [Restored 1882–3]

Endowment	OPE £4 per ann[um] Pew rents £26. Fees £2 [see St Lawrence (**10.40**)]
Sittings	Free 700. Other 300 appropriated. Total 1,000
Attend'ce 30 Mar.	[Not given]
Avge attendance	[Not given]
Remarks	There are annual expenses amounting on an average to £9.
Dated	31 March 1851
Signed	George Proctor, clergyman [1845–58]
	Stroud, Gloucestershire

[The first minister, Edward Harold Brown 1840–1, was later bishop of Ely 1864–73, and bishop of Winchester 1873–90: *ODNB* 'Edward Harold Brown (1811–1891)'; Kitchin, 66–9. Holy Trinity was a chapel of ease until 4 Mar. 1879 when it became a separate district church.]

10.42 (33)   **Church of England, St Paul, Whiteshill**

Name	St Paul's, Whiteshill. A district church in the parish of Stroud
Consecration	[22] April 1841
Erected	By private benefaction and subscription for about £1,500. Total cost £1,500 [Erected 1840–1; enlarged 1881]
Endowment	Land £6. Glebe £9. OPE £16 [from] Queen Anne's Bounty. Fees £1 10s (average). Other sources £30 from Eccles[iastical] Commiss[ioners] [Samuel Warneford (**19.20**) gave £700 towards the endowment] {Total £50}
Sittings	Free 500. Other 100. Total 600
Attend'ce 30 Mar.	Morning 100 + 110 SS. Total 210
	Afternoon 400 + 120 SS. Total 520
Avge attendance	Morning 150 + 110 SS. Total 260
	Afternoon 400 + 120 SS. Total 520
Dated	31 March 1851
Signed	William Harris Roach, incumbent [1846–71]
	Whiteshill, Stroud, Gloucestershire

[St Paul's became a separate district in 1844.]

10.43 (41)   **Church of England, Union Workhouse, Upper Lypiatt**

Request for information. Will you have the goodness to furnish the following information at your earliest convenience. Congregations including Sunday scholars.

Morning	205 [In 1851 295 inmates were enumerated]
Afternoon	None
Evening	None
Sittings	Free 429. Accommodation sittings in the Union workhouse chapel. Other none. Total [429]
Dated	23 June 1852
Signed	John Selby Howell [registrar, parish clerk and schoolmaster] [Bath Place, Stroud]

10.44 (36)   **Congregational, Chapel Street**

Name	Old Chapel [Old Meeting]
Erected	Before 1800 [1711, enlarged 1813, and remodelled 1844]
Building	Yes [separate and entire] Yes [exclusively as a place of worship]
Sittings	Free 150. Other 550. Total [700] Standing room none
Attend'ce 30 Mar.	Morning 402 + 109 SS. Total 511
	Evening 420 + 54 SS. Total 474
	These numbers are not given as strictly correct but as near the truth as possible.

Avge attendance [Not given]
Dated 31 March 1851
Signed Samuel Stephens Marling, deacon [manufacturer of woollen cloth]
Stroud, Glo'shire
[*Minister* David James Evans 1852–7]
[Originally Presbyterian, by 1811 the chapel had become Congregational. Marling (1810–83) was a cloth manufacturer and Liberal MP for Gloucestershire West 1868–74, and Stroud 1875–80; knighted in 1882. In Stroud he mostly paid for the remodelling of the Old Chapel in 1844 and gave £10,000 to establish a middle class school, opened as Marling School in 1891.]

10.45 (39)   Independent or Congregational, Ruscombe
Name Ruscombe Chapel
Erected About 1829
Building Yes [separate and entire] Yes [exclusively as a place of worship]
Sittings Free 84. Other 350. Total [434]
Attend'ce 30 Mar. Afternoon 196 + 95 SS. Total 291
Evening 172 + 62 SS. Total 234
Avge attendance [Not given]
Dated 30 March 1851
Signed Evan Jones, minister [1835–55]
Whiteshill, near Stroud, Gloucestershire

10.46 (40)   Independent, Paganhill
Name Paganhill Chapel
Erected 1835
Building Separate building. Only for worship
Sittings Free 65. Total [65]
Attend'ce 30 Mar. Morning 11. Total 11
Afternoon 24. Total 24
Evening 50. Total 50
Avge attendance [Not given]
Dated 30 March 1851
Signed Lot Pearce, preacher
Whiteshill nr Stroud, Gloucestershire

10.47 (34)   Independent, Bedford Street
Name Bedford Street Chapel [Union Chapel]
Erected [Opened 27 Sept.] 1837 [Additional galleries erected and the chapel re-opened in Feb. 1851]
Building Separate [and entire] Yes [exclusively as a place of worship]
Sittings Free 375. Other 525. Total [900] Standing room none
Attend'ce 30 Mar. Morning 270 + 212 SS. Total 482
Afternoon no service
Evening 493. Total 493
Avge attendance [Not given]
Remarks Sunday while children not collected in the evening but attend indiscrim-inately with the congregation - say about 100. Number not certain.
Dated 31 March 1851
Signed William Wheeler, minister [1843–73]
Rowcroft, Stroud, Gloucestershire

10.48 (35)   **Baptist, John Street**
Name   Baptist Chapel
Erected   1824 [Altered 1837]
Building   Yes [separate and entire] Yes [exclusively as a place of worship]
Sittings   Free 300. Other 700. Total [1,000] Standing room for 300
Attend'ce 30 Mar.   Morning 500. Total [500]
                        Afternoon 500. Total [500]
                        Evening 700. Total [700]
Avge attendance   Afternoon 700 + 267 SS. Total 967
Dated   31 March 1851
Signed   William Yates, minister
                        Stroud, Gloucestershire

10.49 (37)   **Wesleyan Methodist, Acre Street**
Name   Wesleyan Chapel
Erected   Before 1800 [1763 and enlarged in 1796. Replaced by a new chapel in
                        Castle Street, opened 27 Oct. 1876; from 1879 the chapel belonged to
                        the Salvation Army]
Building   It is [separate and entire] It is [exclusively as a place of worship]
Sittings   Free 158. Other 352. Total [510]
Attend'ce 30 Mar.   Morning 270 + 110 SS. Total 380
                        Evening 300 + 30 SS. Total 330
Avge attendance   [Not given]
Dated   31 March 1851
Signed   Benjamin Antill, chapel steward (grocer)
                        [Cross], Stroud, Gloucestershire
[Tablet: 'On this site the Rev John Wesley 1703–1791 preached from a butcher's block, 26 June 1742. "The best of all is, God is with us"' [Wesley's dying words]. Throughout his life John Wesley was a regular preacher in Stroud. After the new octagonal chapel had opened he reported, 'I rode to Stroud, and in the evening preached in the new house. But a considerable part of the congregation was obliged to stand without' (*Journal*, 18 March 1765). 'Nonconformity continued to flourish in the town in the late 19th century; c.1890 it was said that the Sunday schools of the six main chapels had a total attendance of over 1,400': *VCH* 11, 140.]

10.50 (38)   **Primitive Methodist, Parliament Street**
Name   Primitive Methodist Chapel
Erected   1836
Building   Yes [separate and entire] Yes [exclusively as a place of worship]
Sittings   Free 203. Other 102. Total [305] Standing room for 40
Attend'ce 30 Mar.   Morning 183. Total [183]
                        Afternoon 250. Total [250]
                        Evening 200. Total [200]
Avge attendance   [Not given]
Dated   30 March 1851
Signed   George Rowland, a teacher [carpenter]
                        Parliament Street, Stroud
[*Minister*   Thomas Hobson]
[The former chapel is now the Cotswold Playhouse]

338.5   RODBOROUGH SUB-DISTRICT

338.5.1 Parish of King's Stanley
Area 1,679 acres; 482 inhabited houses, 53 uninhabited. Population 2,095.
VCH 10, 242–57

10.51 [un-numbered] Church of England, St George, King's Stanley

Name	St George's. An ancient parish church
Consecration	Before 1800
Erected	[Enlarged 1823, further enlarged and restored 1874–6]
Endowment	Tithe £410. Glebe £200. Fees £2. {Total £312}
Sittings	Free 160. Other 400. Total 560
Attend'ce 30 Mar.	Morning 170 + 117 SS. Total 287
	Afternoon 340 + 110 SS. Total 450
Avge attendance	Morning 150 + 125 SS. Total 275
	Afternoon 340 + 120 SS. Total 460
Dated	30 March 1851
Signed	James Fisher, curate and officiating minister [1850–5]
	King's Stanley, Gloucestershire
[*Incumbent*	William Forge 1820–57]

[Forge and his wife both suffered from ill-health, and he was frequently absent. Within the parish All Saints, Selsley was consecrated 28 Nov. 1862, and the parish was divided the following year. In March 1743 when George Whitefield preached in the open air at King's Stanley, though the weather was unfavourable, he observed that 'I thought I was on the very suburbs of heaven': Tyerman 2, 53.]

10.52 (44)   Baptist, Middleyard

Name	Baptist Chapel [The Old Meeting]
Erected	1630 [Tablet: 'Baptist Church founded 1640]
	[Replaced by new chapel in Middleyard in 1824–5]
Building	Yes [separate and entire] Yes [exclusively as a place of worship]
Sittings	Free 70. Other 300. Total [370] Standing room none
Attend'ce 30 Mar.	Morning 250 + 150 SS. Total 400
	Afternoon 150 SS. Total 150
	Evening 300 + 50 SS. Total 350
Avge attendance	[Not given]
Remarks	It appears that the Baptist interest was established in King's Stanley thirty-two years before the Act of Uniformity [1662] was 'past'.
Dated	31 March 1851
Signed	John Alder, deacon [retired baker]
	King's Stanley
[*Minister*	John Lewis 1851–4]

[This was reputed to be the earliest Baptist congregation in Gloucestershire.]

10.53 (45)   Baptist, King's Stanley

Name	Woodside
Erected	About 1838
Building	Yes [separate and entire] Yes [exclusively as a place of worship]
Sittings	All free 50. Total [50]
Attend'ce 30 Mar.	Morning 9 SS. Total 9
	Afternoon 30 + 9 SS. Total 39
Avge attendance	[Not given]

Dated	31 March 1851
Signed	Henry Hopkins, manager [woollen cloth weaver]
	King's Stanley, Glo'shire

10.54 (42)   Primitive Methodist, Broad Street

Name	No particular name
Erected	Opened 27 years [Replaced by a new chapel in 1861]
Building	Dwelling house. Not [exclusively a a place of worship]
Sittings	All free to the extent of the building 35. Total [35]
Attend'ce 30 Mar.	Morning from 20 to 30. [Total 20–30]
	Evening 20. Total [20]
Avge attendance	Evening about 20. SS none. Total [20]
Dated	2 April 1851
Signed	Jacob Smith, class leader and 'lokel' preacher [bean seller]
	King's Court, Rodborough near Stroud, Gloucestershire

10.55 (43)   Christian Brethren, King's Stanley

Denomination	Christians (called by many Plymouth Brethren)
Name	A room
Erected	[Not given]
Building	A cottage for this purpose. Yes [exclusively as a place of worship]
Sittings	All free sittings for 50. Total [50] The room 12 feet by 13 feet, all free.
Attend'ce 30 Mar.	Morning SS none
	Evening SS none
Avge attend'ce (24m)	Morning 30. Total 30
Remarks	We meet simply in the name of our Lord Jesus Christ in dependence on the Holy Ghost. Consequently hold no [...] and holding to no denomination, but open to receive all who love our Lord Jesus Christ in sincerity and trust. Some call us Plymouth Brethren but it is not so, we desire to know no name but the name of Jesus.
Dated	31 March 1851
Signed	David Appleby
	The Room, Davidbridge Mills, Stroud, Gloucestershire

338.5.2. Parish of Woodchester

Area 1,203 acres; 195 inhabited houses, 13 uninhabited. Population 893.
VCH 11, 294–304

10.56 (46)   Church of England, St Mary, Woodchester

Name	The Parish Church of Woodchester in the county of Gloucestershire said to be dedicated to St Mary. A very antient structure where once stood a Roman pavilion, the tessellated pavement still remains in the churchyard.
Consecration	'Consecrated' time immemorial. It has a fine Norman arch between the church and chancel.
Erected	Unknown. It was enlarged in the year 1815. [Replaced by a new church on a nearby site and consecrated on 24 Sept. 1863. The ruins of the old church still remain.]
Endowment	Tithe commuted at ... poor rates and cem[etery] charges £265. Glebe £68. OPE house and lawn. Fees about £5. Easter offerings about £5. Other sources none. {Total £310}
Sittings	Free none except benches in the 'isles' occupied by the Sunday school. Other 346. Total 346

Attend'ce 30 Mar. Morning 223 + 81 SS. Total [304]
              Afternoon 236 + 81 SS. Total 317]
Avge attendance Morning and afternoon about the same
Remarks   Free seats are much needed. Large seats capable of accommodating ten
              adults are appropriated to mansions from which only three or four
              attend and sometimes less.
Dated   31 March 1851
Signed   John Williams DD, rector [1833–57]
              Woodchester rectory, near Stroud, Gloucestershire
[Tablet: 'sacred to the memory of the Rev John Williams DD, 28 years curate of this parish, and
afterwards 24 years rector of Woodchester'.]

10.57 (47)   Baptist, Atcombe Road
Name   Woodchester Chapel
Erected   1825
Building   Yes [separate and entire] Yes [exclusively as a place of worship]
Sittings   Free 100. Other 250. Total [350]
Attend'ce 30 Mar. Morning 120 + 68 SS. Total [188]
              Afternoon 69 SS. Total [69]
              Evening 180. Total [180]
Avge attendance [Not given]
Dated   31 March 1851
Signed   Henry Le Fevre, minister [1849–52]
              Woodchester, Stroud

10.58 (48)   Roman Catholic, Church of Our Lady of the Annunciation, St Mary's Hill
Name   St Mary of the Annunciation
Erected   [Consecrated 10 Oct.] 1849
Building   A separate and entire building. Used exclusively as a place of worship
Sittings   Free 493 + 28 SS. Total [521] Standing room for about 100
Attend'ce 30 Mar. Morning 114 [SS] included. Total 114
              Afternoon 192 [SS] included. Total 192
              Evening 112 [SS] included. Total 112
Avge attendance (6m) Morning about 120 + 15 SS. Total 135
Remarks   Several who came to the morning service attended also in the afternoon
              and evening. The scholars were either in the chancel as servers [at Mass],
              or elsewhere in the church with the rest of the congregation.
Dated   31 March 1851
Signed   Samuel Procter, Roman Catholic priest and pastor
              St Mary's Mount, Woodchester, Stroud
[The Passionist Fathers were involved with Woodchester from 1846; in 1850 the work was
transferred to the Dominicans. The church and monastery (completed 1853) was founded by the
wealthy Roman Catholic convert William Leigh (1802–73).]

338.5.3 Parish of Rodborough
Area 1,310 acres; 463 inhabited houses, 36 uninhabited. Population 2,208.
The parish is also connected ecclesiastically with Minchinhampton.
VCH 10, 218–34

10.59 (49)   Church of England, St Mary Magdalene, Rodborough
(Summary form)
Name   Rodborough

Erected	The later part of the 14 century and [mostly] rebuilt in the year 1843. [Chancel rebuilt and enlarged 1895 and consecrated 18 Apr. 1896]
Endowment	{Total £300}
Sittings	Free 313. Other 479. Total 792
Usual attend'ce	Morning 290 + 110 SS. Total [400]
	Afternoon 260 + 100 SS. Total [370]
	*Evening 210. Total [210]
Remarks	*There is an evening service at the church during the summer months viz from March to September at which service the Sunday scholars are not required to attend.
Signed	William Peyton [woollen cloth maker; hand loom weaver]
	Butterrow, Rodborough
[*Incumbent*	Thomas Glascott 1841–76]

[Glascott was curate of Rodborough 1818–40. On the singers' pew in the church see *GNQ* 2, 354–5. Rodborough was a chapel of ease to Minchinhampton (**10.62**) until 1841 when a parish was created.]

10.60 (50) Calvinistic Methodist, Rodborough

Name	Rodborough Tabernacle
Erected	Before 1800 [1750, remodelled and enlarged 1836–7]
Building	Yes [separate and entire] Yes [exclusively as a place of worship]
Sittings	Free 200. Other 520. Total [720] Standing room for 100
Attend'ce 30 Mar.	Morning abt 340 + 110 SS. Total 450
	Afternoon 300 + 126 SS. Total 426
Avge attendance	Morning 350 + 150 SS. Total 500
Remarks	The afternoon congregation at Rodborough is various in number, but mostly much larger than the morning, excepting when the weather is stormy, as was the case this day. We consider that 500 persons, of all ages, may be reckoned as belonging to the congregation. Samuel Thodey, minister.
Dated	30 March 1851
Signed	James Bizzey, secretary (draper)
	[King Street], Stroud
[*Minister*	Samuel Thodey 1849–58]

[Thomas Adams (1717–70) was responsible for the erection of the chapel at Rodborough where he served as the pastor until his death in 1770. He had been converted on hearing George Whitefield preach on Minchinhampton Common and became one of Whitefield's closest supporters. In 1743 Adams suffered much from the local mob who attacked him in his house. Outside Kingswood (**20.11**) 'the Tabernacle became the chief Whitefieldian meeting in the county and attracted a large membership': *VCH* 11, 232).]

10.61 (51) Calvinistic Methodist, Kingscourt, Rodborough

Name	[None]
Erected	1837
Building	[A] schoolroom. Used for a day school
Sittings	All free 70. Total [70]
Attend'ce 30 Mar.	Morning none
	Afternoon none
	Evening 65. Total [65]
Avge attendance	Morning 70 [crossed out] Total 70
	Evening 70. Total [70]
Dated	30 March 1851
Signed	Robert Lucas, [British] schoolmaster
	Kingscourt, Rodborough, Gloucestershire

338.6   MINCHINHAMPTON SUB-DISTRICT

338.6.1 Parish of Minchinhampton
Area 4,895 acres; 1,058 inhabited houses, 137 uninhabited. Population 4,469.
The parish includes the tithings of Chalford and Rodborough, that included the hamlets of Box, Forwood, Holcombe, Littleworth, Theescombe, Amberley, St Cloe, Chalford, Hyde, Burley, Brimscombe and Cowcombe; and part of the chapelry of Nailsworth. Since 1831 the population had decreased by 645 due to the decline in the clothing industry.
VCH 11, 184–207

10.62 (52)	**Church of England, Holy Trinity, Minchinhampton**
Name	Minchinhampton
Consecration	Before 1800
Erected	The entire body of the par[ish[church and the chancel were pulled down and rebuilt in the year 1842 by private subscription and benefaction at a total cost of about £3,500. [David Ricardo (Lord of the manor and MP for Stroud 1832–3)] gave £2,000, the rector, Charles Whately, £500 and £1,000 from subscribers. Chancel altered 1869–71]
Endowment	Tithe rent charge £432 19s 4d. Glebe etc. estimated at about £500, but not producing so much, and necessary outgoing greatly reducing such as rates etc. {Total £300}
Sittings	Free 401. Other 690. Total 1,091
Attend'ce 30 Mar.	Morning 299 + 273 SS. Total 572
	Afternoon 384 + 303 SS. Total 684 [*recte* 687]
	Evening 230 in a lecture not in the church. Total [230]
Avge attendance	[Not given]
Remarks	The parish was divided, ecclesiastically, in the year 1840 into three: the other ecclesiastical parishes being Amberley (**10.63**) and Brimscombe (**10.64**). These take off a large proportion both of the population and also of rent charge.
Dated	[Not given]
Signed	Charles Whately, rector [1841–65]
	Minchinhampton near Stroud

[Ricardo was the second son of the political economist David Ricardo, whose country seat was Gatcombe Park: *ODNB*, 'David Ricardo (1772–1823'.]

10.63 (53)	**Church of England, Holy Trinity, Amberley**
Name	Church of 'the Holy Trinity', Amberley. Built under 1 and 2 Will. IV, [c.38 (1831)] afterwards formed into a separate ecclesiastical parish and endowed by order [of the Privy Council]
Consecration	5 September 1836, consecrated as [an] additional church
Erected	Built at the sole expense of D[avid] Ricardo Esq. Private benefaction £2,818 16s 5¾d. Total cost £2,818 16s 5¾d
Endowment	Land £20. Tithe £284 11s 6d. OPE £40 15s ... houses. Fees £2 2s (average). {Total £300}
Sittings	Free 281. Other 332. Total 613
Attend'ce 30 Mar.	Morning about 200 + 236 SS. Total 436
	Evening 350 (pouring rain. Mid-Lent). Total [350]
Avge attendance	Morning 220 + 250 SS. Total 570
	Evening 370 + 180 SS. Total 550
Remarks	The church was built in 1836, and pew rents set apart as endowment under

1 and 2 Will. IV [c.38 (1831)] At the next residence of the mother church in 1841, the parish was divided by order of Privy Council and Amberley was endowed with tithe and became a perpetual curacy.

Dated   31 March 1851

Signed   Robert Edward Blackwell, minister (perpet. curate) [1841–72]
                Amberley, Nailsworth

[On Ricardo, see above (**10.62**). Amberley church, designed like Oakridge (**10.26**) by Robert Stokes of Cheltenham, was in part a thank-offering for the narrow escape of Ricardo's son in a riding accident in 1834. Amberley was assigned a district in 1840 and became a rectory in 1866.]

10.64 (54)   **Church of England, Holy Trinity, Brimscombe**

Name   Trinity Church. A distinct and separate parish

Consecration   [7] April 1840, [as] an additional church

Erected   Private benefaction and subscription. Total cost (about) £2,000
                [mostly given by David Ricardo of Gatcombe Park. Restored 1881]

Endowment   Land, tithe and glebe £300 net. {Total £300}

Sittings   Free 89. Other 411. Total 500

Attend'ce 30 Mar. [Not given]

Avge attendance Morning 200 + 175 SS. Total 375
                Evening 250 + 75 SS. Total 325

Dated   31 March 1851

Signed   Henry James Legge, perpetual curate [1841–73]
                Minchinhampton, Gloucestershire

[Ricardo was an opponent of the Oxford Movement, and this is evident in the position of the chancel at the west end (rather than the customary east end) of the building.]

10.65 (57)   **Baptist, Tetbury Street, Minchinhampton**

Name   Hampton Chapel

Erected   1834

Building   A separate and entire building. Exclusively as a place of worship

Sittings   Free 50. Other 700. Total [750]

Attend'ce 30 Mar. Morning 80 + 32 SS. Total [112]
                Afternoon 104. Total [104]
                Evening 85. Total [85]

Avge attend'ce (18m) Morning and afternoon from 150 to 200. Total [150–200]

Dated   30 March 1851

Signed   Isaac Jones, deacon [wool-spinner]
                Minchinhampton, Gloucestershire

10.66 (56)   **Wesleyan Methodist, Littleworth**

Name   Wesleyan Chapel

Erected   Before 1800 [Tablet: 'Built 1790 – Littleworth Wesleyan Chapel – renovated 1887']

Building   Yes [separate and entire] Yes [exclusively as a place of worship]

Sittings   Free 146. Other 209. Total [355]

Attend'ce 30 Mar. Morning 84 + 77 SS. Total 161
                Afternoon 132 + 71 SS. Total 203

Avge attendance Morning 90 + 85 SS. Total 175
                Afternoon 170 + 85 SS. Total 255

Dated   31 March 1851

Signed   Henry Mortimer, steward [shopkeeper]
                Littleworth, nr Stroud Water, Gloucestershire

10.67 (58)   **Wesleyan Methodist, Brimscombe**
Name   Wesleyan Chapel
Erected   1804
Building   Separate and entire [building] Exclusively [as a place of worship]
Sittings   Free 100. Other 240. Total [340]
Attend'ce 30 Mar.   Morning 170 + 102 SS. Total 272
                      Evening 190. Total 190
Avge attendance   [Not given]
Dated   31 March 1851
Signed   Charles Shaylor, steward [master tailor]
                      Swells Hill, nr Brimscombe, Minchinhampton, Gloucestershire

10.68 (59)   **Primitive Methodist, Brimscombe**
Name   [None]
Erected   1838
Building   Separate building. For a p[l]ace of worship and Sunday school
Sittings   Free 40. Other 60. Total [100]
Attend'ce 30 Mar.   Morning 40. Total [40]
                      Afternoon 100. Total [100]
                      Evening 120. Total [120]
Avge attendance   [Not given]
Dated   30 March 1851
Signed   Thomas Hill, steward [baker employing one man]
                      Rodborough, near Hampton, Gloucestershire

10.69 (55)   **Church of Jesus Christ of Latter-day Saints, Minchinhampton**
Name   None
Erected   [Not given]
Building   Part of the building. No [not exclusively as a place of worship]
Sittings   All free 60. Total [60]
Attend'ce 30 Mar.   Morning 13 + 11 SS. Total [24]
                      Afternoon 32 + 16 SS. Total [48]
                      Evening 28. Total [28]
Avge attendance   Morning 60 + 16 SS. Total [76]
Remarks   We as a people occupy only a part of the house for religious worship
                      (Sunday school for children)
Dated   31 March 1851
Signed   Joseph Stay, an elder [a travelling elder]
                      To me: Watledge nr Nailsworth, Glo's'shire.

338.7   HORSLEY SUB-DISTRICT

338.7.1 Parish of Avening
Area 4,428 acres; 522 inhabited houses, 30 uninhabited. Population 2,321.
The parish includes the hamlets of Aston, Forest Green, Freeholds, West End, Bell Street
and Windsors Edge and part of Nailsworth chapelry. Since 1831 the population had
declined by 75 due to emigration to the colonies and migration due to the decline in the
woollen industry.
VCH 11, 156–66, 207–18

10.70 (60)   **Church of England, Holy Cross** (or Holy Rood), **Avening**
Name   Avening Parish Church, St Mary's [*sic*]

Consecration	Before 1800
Erected	[Restored 1887–9 and 1902–6]
Endowment	Tithe rent charge £656. Glebe £99. Fees about £10. {Total £769}
Sittings	Free 226. Other 328. Total 554
Attend'ce 30 Mar.	Morning 135 + 120 SS. Total 255
	Afternoon 174 + 137 SS. Total 311
	Evening 124. Total 124
Avge attendance	Morning 155 + 135 SS. Total 290
	Afternoon 210 + 140 SS. Total 350
	Evening 135. Total 135
Remarks	The free sittings are supplied by the rector. First, by giving up the chancel for Sunday school children; and second, by paying rent annually to the owner of south transept which is private property.
Dated	31 March 1851
Signed	John Pritchard Mills, curate [1844–52]
	Avening, Stroud, Gloucestershire
[*Incumbent*	Thomas Richard Brooke 1836–57]

[Brooke suffered from ill-health and mostly lived abroad. The benefice consisted of Avening with Nailsworth. (**10.71**). Baddeley, 181–90. Within the parish All Saints, Shortwood, Nailsworth, was consecrated 26 May 1866.]

10.71 (61) **Church of England, St George, Nailsworth**

Name	Nailsworth Chapel
Consecration or licensed	Neither one nor the other
Erected	No means of discovering (how or by who erected). [Erected as an unconsecrated chapel and opened 19 Oct. 1794 by subscription. The final service was held 15 May 1898; foundation stone of the replacement chapel laid (with full Masonic ceremony) on 6 Oct. 1898. The chapel, which cost about £6,000 was consecrated 29 Nov. 1900, and after enlargement 1937–8 was re-consecrated 19 Feb. 1939.]
Endowment	Pew rents £60 [See Avening (**10.70**)]
Sittings	Free 50. Other 250. Total 300
Attend'ce 30 Mar.	Morning 200 + 85 SS. Total 285
	Afternoon 160 + 80 SS. Total 240
Avge attendance	[Not given]
Remarks	It is impossible to give the information required.
Dated	31 March 1851
Signed	John Betts, officiating minister [1846–56]
	Nailsworth, near Stroud
[*Incumbent*	Thomas Richard Brooke 1836–57]

[The benefice consisted of Avening (**10.70**) with Nailsworth. St George's chapel was built to counteract the strong nonconformist presence in the community.]

10.72 (63) **Congregational or Independent, Lower Forest Green, Nailsworth**

Name	Lower Forest Green Chapel
Erected	Before 1800 [1688. New chapel 1821]
Building	Yes [separate and entire] Yes [exclusively as a place of worship]
Sittings	Free 60. Other 740. Total [800]
Attend'ce 30 Mar.	Morning 425 + 173 SS. Total 598
	Afternoon 362 + 182 SS. Total 544
Avge attendance	[Not given]

Remarks	The evening service is at present denominated a prayer meeting, and the attendance not very large. Even during the greater part of the year we have a popular service in the evening, and the afternoon is dispensed with when the congregation is good.
Dated	31 March 1851
Signed	George William Clapham, minister [1849–51]
	The parsonage, Nailsworth, Gloucestershire

10.73 (65)   Independent, Upper Forest Green, Spring Hill, Nailsworth

Name	Upper Forest Green
Erected	1821
Building	[Separate and] entire. For worship and Sunday school
Sittings	Free *20*. Other 400. Total [420] Standing room for 50
Attend'ce 30 Mar.	Morning 90 + *50* SS. Total *140*
	Afternoon 160. Total [160]
	Evening 30. Total [30]
Avge attendance	Morning 240 + 80 SS. Total 320
	Afternoon *120*. Total [120]
	Evening *35*. Total [35]
Remarks	Some attend in morning and not at other times, some in afternoon and not at other times, so that the congregation and school varies as 'occation' may be. Nath. Hill
Dated	30 March 1851
Signed	[Nathaniel Hill], assistant preacher [master black]smith
	Swells Hill, nr Brimscombe, Gloucestershire

[Information in italics in another hand and with the initials 'ICT' = I. C. Tabram, registrar.]

10.74 (67)   Baptist, Shortwood, Nailsworth

Name	Shortwood Meeting House
Erected	Before 1800 [Built 1715, rebuilt 1837–8 and a new Shortwood Chapel was built in Newmarket Road in 1881]
Building	Separate and entire. Exclusively [as a place of worship]
Sittings	Free 150. Other 900 (this does not include the sittings for the Sunday school). Total [1,050]
Attend'ce 30 Mar.	Morning 500* + 265 SS. Total 765
	Afternoon 380 + 269 SS**. Total 649
Avge attendance	Morning 650 + 270 SS. Total 920. [Of these, the 920 are] not present at any one time, but present in the course of the day.
Remarks	*The weather being unfavourable this is a less no. than the average. Of the 380 present in the afternoon about half were not present in the morning.
	**The scholars do not attend public worship in the afternoon.
Dated	31 March 1851
Signed	Thomas Fox Newnam, minister [1832–64]
	Nailsworth, nr Stroud

[The congregation was formed by seceders from the Lower Forest Green Chapel (**10.72**). Shortwood Chapel seeded the chapel at Leighterton (**11.6**), and supplied preachers for the evening service. Newman was also minister of the Nailsworth Baptist Room (**10.79**). 'The Shortwood Baptist Chapel had emerged as the premier nonconformist community at Nailsworth and the largest of its persuasion outside London'; the membership peaked in 1844, at 712: Urdank, 303, 326.]

Additional note (**66**)

Shortwood Meeting House

The statistics supplied in the census paper furnish only an impoverish view, for the following reason: the congregation is widely scattered, so that generally not many more than about half of the persons who really belong to the congregation worshipping at Shortwood Meeting House are present at one and the same time.

The lowest number that can be fairly stated as comprising the church (i.e. communicants in fellowship) and congregation is 1,000, besides the Sunday school. Of this number the communicants, or church members, are about 500.

Thomas Fox Newman, minister

31 March 1851

10.75 (62)	**Baptist, Avening**
Name	Baptist Chapel
Erected	1805 [Tablet: 'This place of worship was erected 1805, enlarged 1821']
Building	A separate building. Used only for worship and Sunday school
Sittings	Free 95 beside the sitting of scholars. Other 122. Total [217]
	Standing room none
Attend'ce 30 Mar.	Morning 110 + 90 SS. Total 200
	[Also recorded Morning 140; Afternoon 170; Evening 80]
Avge attendance	Morning about 120 + 90 SS. Total 210
Dated	31 March 1851
Signed	Samuel Webley, Baptist minister
	[Tetbury Hill], Avening, near Stroud

10.76 (64)	**Christian Brethren, Spring Hill, Nailsworth**
Denomination	Brethren in Christ
Name	A room for worship on Spring Hill
Erected	1841
Building	A separate and entire building. Yes [exclusively as a place of worship]
Sittings	All free 150. Other none. Total [150] Sanding room none
Attend'ce 30 Mar.	Morning 50. Total [50]
	Evening 45. Total [45]
Avge attend'ce (3m)	Morning 50. Total [50]
Dated	30 March 1851
Signed	Thomas Millard, no official character but responsible guide
	Spring Hill Room, Nailsworth

338.7.2 Parish of Horsley

Area 4,082 acres; 683 inhabited houses, 119 uninhabited. Population 2,931.

The parish includes the hamlets of Barton End, Chavenage, Downend, Luther Edge, Newmarket, Rockness, Shortwood and Sugley and part of the chapelry of Nailsworth. In 20 years the population had decreased by 759 due to the decline of employment in the woollen industry.

VCH 11, 175–84

10.77 (69)	**Church of England, St Martin, Horsley**
Name	St Martin's. The parish church
Consecration	[Rebuilt (apart from the tower) and consecrated on] 16 October 1839, in lieu of the old parish church
Erected	By grant from Diocesan Church Building Society and 'private benefaction or subscription' [for] £3,213 3s 1½d. Total cost £3,213 3s 1½d

Endowment	Glebe £50. OPE £32 10s. [Total] £82 10s. Fees £9. Easter offerings £4 Other sources Ecc[lesiastical] Com[missioners] and QAB £45 19s 10d [with the £82 10s, a total of] £141 9s 10d. {Total £137}
Sittings	Free 536. Other 496. Total 1,052
Attend'ce 30 Mar.	Morning 158 + 183 SS. Total 341
	Afternoon 324 + 184 SS. Total 508
Avge attendance	[Not given]
Dated	31 March 1851
Signed	Edward Nangreave Mangin, minister [1849–61]
	Horsley, near Stroud

[Thomas Dudley Fosbrooke, historian of Gloucestershire, was curate of Horsley 1794–1810: *ODNB* 'Thomas Dudley Fosbrooke (1770–1842)'.]

10.78 (68)   Church of England, Chavenage

Name	Chavenage Chapel. A chapel on the private premises of Chavenage House, used as a chapel of ease for the hamlet of Chavenage
Consecration	Unknown. Before 1800 [First recorded in 1803 and in use as a chapel for the parish from 1819]
Erected	[Not given]
Endowment	Other sources £35. {Total £35}
Sittings	Free 50. Other 30. Total 80
Attend'ce 30 Mar.	Morning 12 + 5 SS. Total 17
Avge attendance	Morning 15 + 7 SS. Total 22
	Afternoon 20 + 7 SS. Total 27
Remarks	The income is a yearly stipend of £35 being a voluntary contribution raised by the Lord of the Manor and the tenants on his estate (i.e. the Chavenage estate).
Dated	31 March 1851
Signed	Charles Henry Davis, MA, chaplain [1846–51]
	Nailsworth, Gloucestershire

[Davis, an Evangelical, wrote on liturgical and ecclesiastical reform, and was chaplain to the Stroud workhouse 1851–75.]

10.79 (70)   Baptist, Nailsworth

Name	Nailsworth Baptist Room*. NB This is in connection with the Baptist Meeting House at Shortwood (**10.74**)]
Erected	Before 1800
Building	Separate and entire. Exclusively [as a place of worship]
Sittings	Free 300. Total [300]
Attend'ce 30 Mar.	Evening 280. Total [280]
Avge attendance	Evening from 260 to 300
Remarks	* None of the persons worshipping in this room in the evening, which is the only service, are attendants at Shortwood Meeting House during the day. Probably not more than forty, on an average, are present who are each reported as belonging to the Shortwood congregation.
Dated	31 March 1851
Signed	Thomas Fox Newman, minister [1832–64]
	Nailsworth, nr Stroud

[Newman was minister of the Shortwood Meeting House (**10.74**). This inter-denominational preaching room, opened in 1790, was acquired by the Shortwood Baptists in 1836 and was in use until replaced by the new Shortwood Chapel, opened in 1881.]

10.80 (71) **Wesleyan Methodist, Downend**
Name Downend Chapel
Erected 1820
Building Yes [separate and entire] Yes [exclusively as a place of worship]
Sittings Free 50. Other 250. Total [300] Standing room for 50
Attend'ce 30 Mar. Morning 100. Total [100]
  Afternoon 180. Total [180]
  Evening 200. Total [200]
Avge attendance [Not given]
Dated 31 March 1851
Signed George Ford, chapel steward [mealman]
  [Mill Bottom], Nailsworth, Gloucestershire

10.81 (72) **Society of Friends, Chestnut Hill, Nailsworth**
Erected Before 1800 [c.1680] [Altered 1807 and 1819]
Building Yes [separate and entire] Yes [exclusively as a place of worship]
Sittings Free 70. Total [70] [Additional space 45] Total 115
  Ground floor 480 [square feet] [Additional space] 240 [square feet]
  Total [720 square feet] (Part not used, but on extraordinary occasions
  separated off by shutters)
Attend'ce 30 Mar. Morning 6. Total [6]
  Afternoon 5. Total [5]
  Evening not open
Dated 31 day of third month 1851
Signed Anthony R. Fewster [miller]
  Nailsworth

11. HO 129/339 TETBURY DISTRICT: 23 places of worship

339.1   DIDMARTON SUB-DISTRICT

339.1.1 Parish of Kingscote
Area 1,810 acres; 62 inhabited houses, 1 uninhabited. Population 297.

11.1a (1)	**Church of England, St John the Baptist, Kingscote**
Name	Saint John the Baptist. An ancient chapelry annexed to Beverston
Consecration	Before 1800
Erected	[Restored and enlarged 1851–6]
Endowment	Tithe rent charge £160. Glebe rented at £3. Fees about £2 [See **11.12** below]
Sittings	Free 85. Other 105. Total 190 (exclusive of Sunday scholars)
Attend'ce 30 Mar.	Morning no service
	Afternoon 128 + 72 SS. Total 200
	Evening no service
Avge attendance	Morning 90 + 70 SS. Total 160
	Afternoon 130 + 70 SS. Total 200
	Evening no service
Remarks	There is service at this chapel only once on the Sundays. Many persons attend at the second service at Bagpath Church. Several from Bagpath attend also at Kingscote.
Dated	31 March 1851
Signed	Alan Gardner Cornwall, rector [1839–72]
	Ashcroft House, Wotton-under-Edge

[The benefice consisted of Beverstone (**11.12**) with Kingscote. Cornwall, a chaplain to Queen Victoria, was also the rector of Newington Bagpath (**11.2**) with Owlpen (**5.11**).]

11.1b (2)	**Church of England, St John the Baptist, Kingscote**
(Summary form)	
Name	St John the Baptist
Erected	Probably temp. Henry VI or VII
Sittings	Free 85. Other 105. Total 190 (exclusive of Sunday scholars)
Usual attend'ce	Morning 90 + 70 SS. Total [160]
	Afternoon 130 + 70 SS. Total [200]
	Evening no service
Signed	Alan Gardner Cornwall, (rector) [1839–72]

339.1.2 Parish of Newington Bagpath
Area 2,131 acres; 62 inhabited houses, 1 uninhabited. Population 239.

11.2 (3)	**Church of England, St Bartholomew, Newington Bagpath**
Name	St Bartholomew. Ancient parish church
Consecration	Before 1800
Erected	[Chancel rebuilt 1858–9]
Endowment	Tithe rent charge £300. Glebe rented at £49. Fees about £2. {Total £319}
Sittings	Free 70. Other 126. Total 196 (exclusive of Sunday scholars)
Attend'ce 30 Mar.	Morning 96 + 87 SS. Total 183
	Afternoon no service

Evening no service
Avge attendance Morning 90 + 85 SS. Total 175
Afternoon 120 + 85 SS. Total 205
Evening no service
Remarks There is service once only on the Sunday, morning or afternoon alternately with that at the chapels of Owlpen and Kingscote. The congregation consists of persons from Kingscote as well as Bagpath. The schools from Kingscote attend as well as from Bagpath.
Dated 31 March 1851
Signed Alan Gardner Cornwall, rector [1827–72]
Ashcroft House, Wotton-under-Edge

[The benefice consisted of Newington Bagpath with Owlpen (**5.11**). Cornwall, a chaplain to Queen Victoria, was also the incumbent of Beverstone (**11.12**) with Kingscote (**11.1**). His son, Alan Kingscote Cornwall, who was the curate of Newington Bagpath 1858–72 succeeded him 1872–97.]

339.1.3 Parish of Ozleworth
Area 1,114 acres; 19 inhabited houses, 1 uninhabited. Population 88.

11.3 (20)   **Church of England, St Nicholas of Myra, Ozleworth** (333.3.1)
Name An ancient church
Consecration [Not given]
Erected [Restored and enlarged 1873–4]
Endowment Tithe £115. Glebe £23 4s. {Total £109}
Sittings [Not given]
Attend'ce 30 Mar. Morning 27. Total [27]
Afternoon alternate
Avge attendance Morning from 20 to 35. Total [20–35]
Afternoon from 25 to 30. Total [25–30]
Dated 31 March 1851
Signed Joseph Mayo, rector of Ozleworth [1821–51]
[The church is now under the care of the Churches Conservation Trust.]

339.1.4 Parish of Boxwell with Leighterton
Area 2,266 acres; 62. Population 285.

11.4 (4)   **Church of England, St Mary the Virgin, Boxwell**
(Summary form)
Name Boxwell
Erected [Restored 1900]
[Endowment Total £350]
Sittings Free 30
Usual attend'ce Morning 50 + 65 SS. Total [115]
Signed [Not given]
[Incumbent Richard Webster Huntley 1831–57]
[The benefice consisted of Boxwell with Leighterton (**11.5**). Huntley was also the vicar of Alberbury, Shropshire 1827–57.]

11.5 (5)   **Church of England, St Andrew, Leighterton**
(Summary form)
Name Leighterton
Erected [Restored 1876–7]

Endowment	[See Boxwell (**11.4**)]
Sittings	Free 32. Other 132. Total 164
Usual attend'ce	Morning 85 SS. Total [85]
Signed	[Not given]
[*Incumbent*	Richard Webster Huntley 1831–57]

[The benefice consisted of Boxwell (**11.4**) with Leighterton. On Huntley, see preceding entry. Leighterton was more populous, and the church there was used more than at Boxwell.]

11.6 (6)   Baptist, Leighterton

Name	Leighterton Baptist Chapel
Erected	1828
Building	A separate building. Yes, exclusively [as a place of worship]
Sittings	Free 150. Other none. Total [150] Standing room none
Attend'ce 30 Mar.	[Not given]
Avge attend'ce (3m)	Evening 50. Total 50
Remarks	This chapel was built by the Baptist Church at Shortwood (seven miles distant from Leighterton) and the pulpit is supplied on Sunday evenings chiefly by local preachers in connection with the Shortwood Church (**10.74**).
Dated	31 March 1851
Signed	Abraham Marsh Flint, one of the trustees [cloth manufacturer] Nailsworth nr Stroud, Gloucestershire

[Flint was the son of Thomas Flint, a previous minister of Shortwood Chapel 1799–1803.]

339.1.5 Parish of Oldbury-on-the-Hill

Area 1,342 acres; 101 inhabited houses, 2 uninhabited. Population 485.

11.7 (7)   Church of England, St Arild, Oldbury-on-the-Hill
(Summary form)

Name	Oldbury Church
Erected	[Chancel rebuilt 1761; most of the furnishings are mid-18th century.]
[*Endowment*	Total £250]
Sittings	Free 25. Other 120. Total 145
Usual attend'ce	Morning 60 + 90 SS. Total [150]
Signed	[Not given]
[*Incumbent*	Edward John Everard 1840–60]

[The benefice consisted of Oldbury-on-the-Hill with Didmarton (**11.9**). The church is now under the care of the Churches Conservation Trust.]

11.8 (9)   Independent and Baptist, Oldbury-on-the-Hill

Name	Union Chapel (Independent and Baptist united)
Erected	1843
Building	Yes [separate and entire] Yes [exclusively as a place of worship]
Sittings	Free 256. Other 54. Total [310] Standing room for 90
Attend'ce 30 Mar.	Morning 25 SS. Total 25
	Afternoon 70 + 23 SS. Total 93
	Evening 136. Total 136
Avge attendance	[Not given]
Remarks	The services of this chapel are conducted partly by local preachers. The Sabbath school is conducted in the morning without divine service.
Dated	31 March 1851
Signed	Daniel Best Sherry, minister [1844–59]

Sherston, near Malmesbury, Wilts.

339.1.6 Parish of Didmarton
Area 719 acres; 22 inhabited houses Population 101.

11.9 (8)   Church of England, St Lawrence, Didmarton
(Summary return)
Name	Didmarton
Erected	[Most of the furnishings date from the mid-18th century]
[Endowment	See Oldbury-on-the-Hill (**11.7**)]
Sittings	Fee 30. Other 120. Total 150
Usual attend'ce	Morning 60 + 90 SS. Total [150]
Signed	[Not given]
[Incumbent	Edward John Everard 1840–60]

[The benefice consisted of Oldbury-on-the-Hill (**11.7**) with Didmarton. When St Michael and All Angels was consecrated 8 Oct. 1872, Didmarton ceased to be the parish church, but became so once again after St Michael's was made redundant in 1991.]

339.2   TETBURY SUB-DISTRICT

339.2.1 Parish of Westonbirt with Lasborough
Area 1,904 acres; 41 inhabited houses. Population 234.
VCH 11, 283–94

11.10 (10)   Church of England, St Catherine, Westonbirt
Name	An ancient parish church
Consecration	[Not given]
Erected	[Restored 1840–41 and the chancel extended in 1878–9]
Endowment	Tithe commutation £113 5s. Glebe (87 acres 6 roods and 2 poles) £113 6s. OPE £24 8s (Queen Anne's Bounty). [Total] £250 19s. Fees £1. {Total £226}
Sittings	Free 150. Other 37. Total 187
Attend'ce 30 Mar.	Morning 68 + 30 SS. Total 98
	Afternoon 60 + 80 SS. Total 90
Avge attendance	Morning 60 + 25 SS. Total [85]
	Afternoon 60 + 25 SS. Total [85]
Dated	31 March 1851
Signed	Charles Norford, rector [1803–67]
	Tetbury, Gloucestershire

[Norford 'kept a night school for 60 years': Venn]

11.11 (11)   Church of England, St Mary, Lasborough
Name	Parish Church
Consecration	Before 1800
Erected	Unknown [Rebuilt 1860–1]
Endowment	Tithe £150
Sittings	Free 12. Other 45. Total 57
Attend'ce 30 Mar.	Afternoon 18 + 9 SS. Total [27]
Avge attendance	Afternoon 15 + 10 SS. Total [25]
Remarks	There is one service alternately, am and pm.
Dated	30 March 1851
Signed	Henry Goldney Randall, curate [1848–53]
[Incumbent	William Innes Baker 1805–59]

[Randall was the curate of St Peter, Bishopworth 1853–65, the incumbent of St Mary, Redcliffe, Bristol 1865–77, and archdeacon of Bristol 1873–81. Baker was non-resident and also the incumbent of Heyford Warden, Oxon., 1821–59.]

339.2.2 Parish of Beverston
Area 2,360 acres; 36 inhabited houses, 4 uninhabited. Population 199.

11.12 (12)   **Church of England, St Mary, Beverston**

Name	St Mary. An ancient parish church
Consecration	Before 1800
Erected	[Rebuilt 1844–5]
Endowment	Tithe commuted £396. Glebe £120. Fees £1. {Total £590}
Sittings	Free 100. Other 55. Total 155
Attend'ce 30 Mar.	Morning 49 + 20 SS. Total 69
	Afternoon 70 + 20 SS. Total 90
Avge attendance	[Not given]
Remarks	The tithes commuted [for corn rents] under a private Act.
Dated	31 March 1851
Signed	Alan Gardner Cornwall, rector [1839–72]
	Ashcroft House, Wotton-under-Edge

[The benefice consisted of Beverstone with Kingscote (**11.1**). Cornwall, a chaplain to Queen Victoria, was also the rector of Newington Bagpath (**11.2**) with Owlpen (**5.11**). His successor at Beverston (the first resident incumbent for 150 years) was the ecclesiastical historian and prolific theological writer John Henry Blunt (*ODNB* 'John Henry Blunt (1823–84)'.]

339.2.3 Parish of Cherington
Area 1,880 acres; 43 inhabited houses, 3 uninhabited. Population 220.
The parish includes the hamlet of Westrip.
VCH 11, 166–75

11.13 (13)   **Church of England, St Nicholas, Cherington**

Name	St Nicholas. An ancient parish church
Consecration	Before 1800
Erected	[Inscription, 'church repaired 1816; restored 1881]
Endowment	By land. {Total £176}
Sittings	Free 100. Other 6 faculty pews (50). Total about 150 exclusive of all the sittings for the school children
Attend'ce 30 Mar.	Morning 56 + 28 SS. Total [84]
	Afternoon 88 + 26 SS. Total [114]
Avge attendance	[Not given]
Dated	30 April 1851
Signed	Henry Cornelius Hart, curate [1850–3]
	Tetbury, Gloucestershire
[*Incumbent*	William George 1841–62]

[George was curate from 1829, then the incumbent. 'Between 1850 and 1855, when he was suspended for immorality, the living was served by curates': *VCH* 11, 174.]

339.2.4 Parish of Tetbury
Area 4,582 acres; 674 inhabited houses, 15 uninhabited. Population 3,325.
The parish includes the town of Tetbury and the tithings of Charlton, Doughton, Elmstree and Upton. The Union workhouse situated within the parish had 23 inmates.
VCH 11, 257–83

11.14 (14)   **Church of England, St Mary the Virgin, Tetbury**
Name   The church of St Mary the Virgin. A parish church
Consecration   [7] Oct. 1781. The old church having been taken down
Erected   [An Act to apply a certain sum of money arising by the sale of a house in
                    Tetbury, in the county of Gloucestershire, and by donations of several
                    persons, for rebuilding the parish church and chancel of Tetbury,
                    aforesaid, 5 Geo. III, c.52 (1765). Tower rebuilt 1890–3]
Endowment   Tithe £800. Glebe £150. Fees £15. Other sources £52. {Total £771}
Sittings   Free 336. Other 756. Total 1,092
Attend'ce 30 Mar. Morning 165 males, 164 females + 66 SS. Total 395
                    Evening 204 males, 247 females. Total 451
Avge attendance   [Not given]
Dated   30 March 1851
Signed   John Frampton, minister [1828–80]
                    Tetbury

[The benefice consisted of Tetbury with St Saviour's chapel of ease (**11.15**). The curate of Tetbury
1846–51 was Charles Fuge Lowder, who was later (as an extreme Anglo-Catholic) the incumbent
of St Peter, London Docks 1866–80. In 1855 he was the founder and first master of the Society of
the Holy Cross: *ODNB* 'Charles Fuge Lowder (1820–1880)'.]

11.15 (15)   **Church of England, St Saviour, New Church Street**
Name   The church of S. Saviour. A chapel of ease
Consecration   23 August 1848, as an additional church
Erected   By the vicar and churchwardens
                    [Cost defrayed by] societies, bank £300, benefactions, subscriptions and
                    other sources £3,700. Total cost £4,000
Endowment   Not endowed [See Tetbury, (**11.14**)]
Sittings   Free 400. Total 400
Attend'ce 30 Mar. Morning 27 m[ales], 42 f[emales] + 154 SS. Total 223
                    Afternoon 82 m[ales], 113 f[emales] + 72 SS. Total 267
Avge attendance   [Not given]
Dated   30 March 1851
Signed   John Frampton, minister [1828–80]
                    Tetbury

[By the 1960s the building had become a cemetery chapel and after being declared redundant in
1974, came under the care of the Churches Conservation Trust.]

11.16 (20)   **Independent, The Chipping**
Name   Independent Chapel [The Lower Meeting]
Erected   1700 [New chapel opened 1862]
Building   Yes [separate and entire] Yes [exclusively as a place of worship]
Sittings   Free 80. Other 160. Total [240]
Attend'ce 30 Mar. Morning ~~130 + 40 SS~~ Total [170]
                    Afternoon ~~100 + 40 SS~~ Total [140]
                    Evening ~~130~~ Total [130]
Avge attendance   130 + 40 SS. Total [170]
                    Afternoon 100 + 40 SS. Total [140]
                    Evening 130. Total [130]
Remarks   Calculated to hold between 350 and 400 persons
Dated   [Not given]

Signed   [Not given]
[*Minister*   Robert Collins 1841–54]

11.17 (16)   Particular Baptist, Church Street
Name   None
Erected   Before 1800 [1725, replaced by a new chapel 1779]
Building   Yes [separate and entire] Yes [exclusively as a place of worship]
Sittings   Free 50. Other 250. Total [300] Standing room none
Attend'ce 30 Mar. Morning 250 + 56 SS. Total 306
                    Afternoon 200 + 56 SS. Total 256
                    Evening 300. Total 300
Avge attendance   [Not given]
Dated   31 March 1851
Signed   George Davis, minister [1850–2]
                    Church Street, Tetbury, Gloucestershire
[Davis suffered from poor health and died aged 29. He had formerly been a Primitive Methodist and
was baptised by immersion at Lydney in 1846.]

11.18 (19)   Wesleyan Methodist, Gumstool Hill
Name   Methodist
Erected   1827
Building   Yes [separate and entire] Yes [exclusively as a place of worship]
Sittings   Free 9 x 54 [486] Other 15 x 6 [90] pews. Total [576]
Attend'ce 30 Mar. Afternoon 28. Total 28
                    Evening 29. Total 29
Avge attendance   [Not given]
Dated   1 April 1851
Signed   (Mrs) Elizabeth Tugwell, superintendent of school [grocer and draper]
                    Tetbury, Gloucestershire.
[The nucleus of the membership may have been former Tent Methodists, whose society was established
in Tetbury in 1823: Lander, 151.]

11.19 (18)   Christian Brethren, Bath Road
Denomination   *Catholic but not Roman
Name   The Arnold Room
Erected   1848
Building   Yes [separate and entire] Sunday and also a free day school for any poor
                    children.
Sittings   All free about 150. Total [150] Standing room about 200; area 18 feet by 40
Attend'ce 30 Mar. Morning 73. Total [73]
                    Afternoon schools
                    Evening 94. Total [94]
Avge attendance   Morning 50. Total 50
                    Afternoon 70 SS. Total 70
                    Evening 120. Total 120
Remarks   *Licensed as Protestant taking the word in the extended sense of considering
                    all human inventions in worship as popery, and all believers in the value
                    of the blood of Christ and of one body.
Dated   [Not given]
Signed   Frederick Withers, one of the body [wholesale and retail draper and mercer]
                    [Market Place], Tetbury

11.20 (17)   **Church of Jesus Christ of Latter-day Saints, Harper Street**
Name   Latter-day Saints
Erected   [Not given]
Building   Entire building. Dwelling house
Sittings   Free 70. Total [70]
Attend'ce 30 Mar. Morning 17. Total [17]
                  Afternoon 42. Total [42]
                  Evening 55. Total [55]
Avge attendance Morning 43. Total [43]
Dated   30 March 1851
Signed   Richard Russell [agricultural labourer]
                  Harper Street, Tetbury

339.2.5 Parish of Shipton Moyne
Area 2,298 acres; 79 inhabited houses, 2 uninhabited. Population 403.
VCH 11, 247–257.

11.21 (21)   **Church of England, St John the Baptist, Shipton Moyne**
Name   Shipton-le-Moyne Church. Antient parish church
Consecration   Before 1800
Erected   [Rebuilt 1864–5]
Endowment   Tithe (gross) £313 16s 4d. Glebe (gross) £115. OPE £5. Surplice fees £2.
                  {Total £442}
Sittings   Free 223. Other 100. Total 323
Attend'ce 30 Mar. Morning 123 + 64 SS. Total 187
                  Afternoon 130 + 64 SS. Total 194
Avge attendance [Not given]
Remarks   The endowment of the living is returned according to the gross amount
                  of the rent charge as originally fixed by the Tithe Commissioners, making
                  no deductions or allowances for necessary outgoings.
Dated   2 April 1851
Signed   Edmund William Estcourt, rector [1806–56]
                  [Long] Newnton, near Tetbury, Gloucestershire
[Estcourt was also the incumbent of Long Newton, Wiltshire (**11.22**). His second son, Edgar
Edmund Estcourt, after a curacy at Cirencester 1842–5 became a Roman Catholic. *ODNB* 'Edgar
Edmund Estcourt (1816–1884)'.]

339.2.6 Parish of Long Newnton, Wiltshire [transferred to Gloucestershire, 1930]
Area 2,289 acres; 60 inhabited houses. Population 294.

11.22 (22)   **Church of England, Holy Trinity, Long Newnton**
Name   Long Newton parish church, dedicated to the Holy Trinity. Date of tower,
                  about AD 1500. Body of church was rebuilt, on the old foundations 1841,
                  and in imitation of the former style (AD 1250) following as much as
                  possible of the pillars etc.
Consecration   Before AD 1800. Probably AD 1250
Erected   The body of the church was rebuilt in 1841, and new fittings put up; a
                  separate seat being allotted to each house in the parish. By private
                  benefactions or subscription £1,000. [North aisle 1870]
Endowment   Net income £370. Fees 15s. {Total £370}
Sittings   Free (appropriated, without charge) 312. Total 312

Attend'ce 30 Mar.   Morning 86 + 26 SS. Total 112
                      Afternoon 79 + 27 SS. Total 106
Avge attendance   Morning 80 + 30 SS. Total 110
                      Afternoon 80 + 30 SS. Total 110
                      Evening 80 + 30 SS. Total 110
Remarks   There is an evening service, but no afternoon service, in the summer;
                      afternoon, but no evening service in winter.
Dated   3 April 1851
Signed   Matthew Hale Estcourt, curate
                      Long Newnton rectory, Tetbury
[Incumbent   Edmund William Estcourt 1806–56]
[Estcourt was also the incumbent of Shipton Moyne (**11.21**). Matthew Hale Estcourt, his third son, was curate of Long Newnton, dying in 1858.]

339.2.7 Parish of Ashley, Wiltshire [transferred to Gloucestershire, 1930]
Area 946 acres; 18 inhabited houses. Population 84.

11.23 (23)   **Church of England, St James, Ashley**
Name   Ashley Church. It is the church of a distinct and separate parish built many
                      years before 1800
Consecration   Before 1800
Erected   [Restored 1858]
Endowment   Tithe £215. {Total £220}
Sittings   [Not given]
Attend'ce 30 Mar.   [Not given]
Avge attendance   Morning 40 + 14 SS. Total 54
                      Afternoon 58 + 14 SS. Total 72
Dated   31 March 1851
Signed   Henry Dwyer Shapter, curate [1850–4]
                      [Ashley] near Tetbury, Gloucestershire
[Incumbent   Edward Houlditch 1845–52]

12. HO 129/340 CIRENCESTER DISTRICT: 68 places of worship

340.1   COTSWOLD SUB-DISTRICT

341.1.1–2 Parish of Sapperton
Area 3,908 acres; 133 inhabited houses, 2 uninhabited. Population 646.
The parish includes the tithings of Sapperton and Frampton.
VCH 11, 87–99

12.1 (1)	**Church of England, St Kenelm, Sapperton**
Name	Sapperton Parish Church
Consecration	[Not given]
Erected	[Remodelled in the early 18th century and restored 1874]
Endowment	Tithe £67. Glebe £507. OPE by div: £12. {Total £367}
Sittings	Total 200
Attend'ce 30 Mar.	Morning 60 + 40 SS. Total 100
	Afternoon no service
	Evening no service
Avge attendance	Morning 65 + 45 SS. Total 110
	Afternoon 150 + 45 SS. Total 195
Dated	31 March 1851
Signed	Matthias Mawson Lamb, curate [1850–65]
	Sapperton, Cirencester
[*Incumbent*	William Pye 1833–78]

[The benefice consisted of Sapperton with Frampton Mansell (**12.2**). Lamb was the eldest son of John Lamb, the dean of Bristol 1837–50 and master of Corpus Christi College, Cambridge 1822–50. Pye resigned after a disagreement with members of the congregation and the living was sequestered for six years: *VCH* 11, 97.]

12.2 (2)	**Church of England, St Luke, Frampton Mansell**
Name	Frampton chapel of ease
Consecration	1841 [25 October 1844]
Erected	[By] Earl Bathurst [Restored 1983]
Endowment	[See Sapperton (**12.1**)]
Sittings	Free 150. Other 12. Total 162
Attend'ce 30 Mar.	Morning no service
	Afternoon 130 + 26 SS. Total 156
	Evening no service
Avge attendance	Morning 60 + 30 SS. Total 90
	Afternoon 125 + 30 SS. Total 155
Dated	31 March 1851
Signed	Matthias Mawson Lamb, curate [1850–65]
	Sapperton, Cirencester
[*Incumbent*	William Pye 1833–78]

[The benefice consisted of Sapperton (**12.1**) with Frampton Mansell.]

340.1.3 Parish of Edgeworth
Area 1,566 acres; 28 inhabited houses, 1 uninhabited. Population 148.
VCH 11, 41–7

12.3 (3)   **Church of England, St Mary, Edgeworth**

Name   Edgeworth. The ancient church of the distinct parish of Edgeworth
Consecration   Before 1800
Erected   [Restored 1869–72]
Endowment   Tithe commuted for £265. Glebe £40. OPE no other. Pew rents, fees,
                    dues, Easter offerings, other sources none. {Total £321}
Sittings   Free 7 small pews 53. 13 other pews 65. Total about 118
                    Part of chancel for Sunday school
Attend'ce 30 Mar. Morning 50 + 18 SS. Total 68
                    Evening 70 +18 SS. Total 88
Avge attendance   About the same for twelve months
Remarks   The parish of Edgeworth is very small, only 23 houses in the parish.
                    There is a day school open to all, attended now by about 14.
Dated   31 March 1851
Signed   Henry Prowse Jones, rector [1820–64]
                    Edgeworth, Cirencester, Gloucestershire
[Jones was also the incumbent of Haselton (**13.39**) with Yanworth (**13.40**).]

340.1.4–5 Parish of Duntisbourne Abbots
Area 3,290 acres; 73 inhabited houses, 2 uninhabited. Population 371.
The parish includes the tithing of Duntisborne Leer.

12.4 (4)   **Church of England, St Peter, Duntisbourne Abbots**
(Summary form)
Name   Duntisborne
Erected   Unknown [Restored 1871–2]
[Endowment   Total £300]
Sittings   Free 400. Total 400
Usual attend'ce   From 150 to 200
                    Morning from 100 to 150 + 40 SS. Total [140–190]
                    Afternoon 150 to 200 + 40 SS. Total [190–240]
Remarks   Clergyman refused to fill up this form.
Signed   O. J. Gibbins, registrar
[Incumbent   Richard Randall Suckling 1842–61]

340.1.6 Parish of Winstone
Area 1,437 acres; 53 inhabited houses, 3 uninhabited. Population 252.
VCH 11, 145–51. *GNQ* 1, 211.

12.5 (5)   **Church of England, St Bartholomew, Winstone**
Name   Parish church of Winstone. A rectory
Consecration   Before 1800. Ancient parish church
Erected   [Restored 1875–6]
Endowment   {Total £238}
Sittings   Free 60 + 50 SS. Total 110
Attend'ce 30 Mar. Morning 60 + 14 SS. Total 74
Avge attendance   Average afternoon attendance about 74. The morning attendance
                    generally small.
Dated   31 March 1851
Signed   Frederic Willam Hohler, rector [1839–71]
                    Winstone, Cirencester
[Hohler, the curate from 1835–9, was also the incumbent of Colesbourne (**12.12**).]

12.6 (6)   **Baptist, Winstone**

Name	Baptist Chapel
Erected	About the year 1817 [Chapel 1829]
Building	Yes [separate and entire] Yes [exclusively as a place of worship]
Sittings	Free 30. Other 20. Total [50]
Attend'ce 30 Mar.	Morning 27 + 6 SS. Total 33
	Afternoon 50 + 6 SS. Total 56
Avge attendance	[Not given]
Remarks	Mr Thomas Davis, minister, resident at Chalford Linch, parish of Bisley, Gloucestershire
	Thomas Hinton, deacon, acting for the minister
Dated	30 March 1851
Signed	Thomas Hinton, deacon [tailor]
	Duntisborne Abbots, Gloucestershire

[In 1816 a barn was registered for worship. Davis was also the minister of Coberley (**16.8**) and Miserden (**10.24**), while Hinton was also deacon at Miserden Baptist chapel (**10.24a**).]

340.1.7 Parish of Syde

Area 614 acres; 9 inhabited houses. Population 42.
VCH 7, 227–32

12.7 (7)   **Church of England, St Mary the Virgin, Syde**

Name	Syde Church. An antient parish church of a distinct and separate parish
Consecration	Unknown. But certainly before 1800
Erected	[Chancel rebuilt c.1850]
Endowment	Tithe rent charge £100. Glebe 30 acres. OPE none. Pew rents, Easter offerings and other sources, none. {Total £126}
Sittings	Free 44. Other 16. Total 60
Attend'ce 30 Mar.	Afternoon 14. Total [14]
Avge attendance	Morning from 30 to 35. Total [30–35]
	Afternoon from 30 to 35. Total [30–35]
Remarks	In consequence of illness only 14 assembled for worship on 30 March 1851, which I never knew before. The average attendance being from 30 to 35. The whole population is only 43.
Dated	31 March 1851
Signed	Jacob Wood, rector [1846–66]
	Stratton, near Cirencester

340.1.8 Parish of Brimpsfield

Area 2,611 acres; 96 inhabited houses, 4 uninhabited. Population 443.
The parish includes the hamlets of Birdlip and Caudle Green.
VCH 7, 140–9

12.8 (8)   **Church of England, St Michael, Brimpsfield**

Name	St Michael's, Brimpsfield. An ancient parish church
Consecration	Before 1800
Erected	[Restored 1883–4]
Endowment	Tithe gross £303. Glebe abt £30. OPE none [Total] £333. Fees trifling. Easter offerings given to clerk. {Total £410}
Sittings	Free 115. Other 80. Total 195 exclusive of school children
Attend'ce 30 Mar.	Afternoon 103 + 41 SS. Total 144
Avge attend'ce (6m)	Morning 80 + 45 SS. Total 125

	Afternoon 150 + 45 SS. Total 195
Remarks	The value of tithes is here given as fixed at commutation. It is now diminished and gradually decreasing. The glebe land is 31 acres exclusive of house.
Dated	30 March 1851
Signed	William Moore, rector [1829–79]
	Brimpsfield rectory, near Painswick

[From 1798 to 1892 the benefice consisted of Brimpsfield with Cranham (**10.21**): Butler, 73–97.]

12.9 (9)   Baptist, Birdlip
Name	Baptist [Moriah]
Erected	1841
Building	Separate [and entire] Yes [exclusively as a place of worship]
Sittings	Free 80. Other 20. Total [100]
Attend'ce 30 Mar.	Afternoon 26 + 17 SS. Total [43]
	Evening 30. Total [30]
Avge attendance	Morning 50. Total [50]
Dated	30 March 1851
Signed	Charles Sparkman, local preacher [plasterer]
	30 Portland Square, Cheltenham, Gloucestershire

12.10 (10)   Denomination not specified, and location not given
Name	[Not given]
Erected	[Not given]
Building	[Not given]
Sittings	Free 60. Total [60]
Attend'ce 30 Mar.	Morning 11 + 14 SS. Total [25]
	Afternoon 14 SS. Total [14]
Avge attendance	[Not given]
Dated	[Not given]
Signed	Philip Weaver, deacon

[Weaver was a deacon at the Baptist chapel at Coberley (**16.8**), so it is likely that this unnamed place of worship was also a Baptist chapel.]

340.1.9 Parish of Elkstone
Area 2,058 acres; 68 inhabited houses, 3 uninhabited. Population 336.
VCH 7, 210–8

12.11 (11)   Church of England, St John the Evangelist, Elkstone
Name	Parish church dedicated to St John Evangelist
Consecration	Before 1800
Erected	[Restored 1849–51 and 1894]
Endowment	Land, tithe, glebe and OPE. {Total £360}
Sittings	Free sufficient. Other sufficient
Attend'ce 30 Mar.	Morning small. Total about 36
	Afternoon full. Total 43
Avge attendance	Morning small
	Afternoon full
Dated	30 March 1851
Signed	Edward Ness, rector [1846–77]
	Elkstone, Cirencester

[Knowles, 187–200.]

340.1.10   Parish of Colesbourne
Area 2,200 acres; 46 inhabited houses, 2 uninhabited. Population 269.
VCH 7, 183–92

12.12 (12)	**Church of England, St James, Colesbourne**
Name	Parish Church of Colesbourne. Rectory ⅓ of great and small tithes paid to rector
Consecration	Ancient parish church
Erected	[Restored 1851–2]
Endowment	{Total £127}
Sittings	Free 60. Other 60. Total 120
Attend'ce 30 Mar.	Morning 80 + 35 SS. Total 115
Avge attendance	About the same as on 30 March 1851
Remarks	But one service
Dated	31 March 1851
Signed	Frederic William Hohler, rector [1838–71]
	Winstone, Cirencester

[Hohler was also the incumbent of Winstone (**12.5**) (where he lived); after 1855 he employed curates at Colesbourne.]

12.13 (13)	**Baptist, Colesbourne**
Name	Colesborne dwelling house
Erected	[Not given]
Building	[Not given]
Sittings	Free 50. Total [50]
Attend'ce 30 Mar.	Evening 40. Total [40]
Avge attendance	[Not given]
Dated	30 March 1851
Signed	John Smith, deacon [agricultural labourer]

340.1.11 Parish of Rendcomb
Area 2,532 acres; 41 inhabited houses. Population 264.
VCH 7, 218–27. *GNQ* 10, 34–41.

12.14 (14)	**Church of England, St Peter, Rendcomb**
Name	An ancient parish church
Consecration	Before 1800
Erected	[Restored 1895]
Endowment	Tithe £380. Glebe £20. {Total £373}
Sittings	Free 24. Other 14. Total 38 [38 x 5 = 190 sittings]
Attend'ce 30 Mar.	Morning 75 + 24 SS. Total 99
	Afternoon 75 + 24 SS. Total 99
Avge attend'ce (3m)	Morning 100 + 24 SS. Total 124
	Afternoon 100 + 24 SS. Total 124
Remarks	In making the above return respecting the sittings, I allude to the number of pews. Each pew wd contain 5 people. That is, make five sittings. J. P. rector.
Dated	31 March 1851
Signed	Joseph Pitt, rector [1844–87]
	Rendcomb rectory, near Cirencester, Gloucestershire

[Pitt had succeeded his father Cornelius Pitt (d. 1840) as rector, and was grandson of Joseph Pitt MP (1759–1842), who had acquired the right of presentation in 1798: Howes, 65.]

340.1.12 Parish of North Cerney

Area 4,158 acres; 144 inhabited houses, 2 uninhabited. Population 689.
The parish includes the tithings of Calmsden and Woodmancote.
VCH 7, 150–62; *GNQ* 1, 231–2; 3, 91–2

12.15 (15)	**Church of England, All Saints, North Cerney**
Name	North Cerney Church. Ancient parish church, four miles north of Cirencester
Consecration	Before 1800
Erected	[Restored 1877–8]
Endowment	Tithe rent charge £730. Glebe let at £95. Fees I receive no fees. {Total £654}
Sittings	Free 145. Other (35 pews appropriated to families and individuals [?]). 162 sittings. Total 307
Attend'ce 30 Mar.	Morning 165 + 65 SS. Total 230
	Afternoon 170 + 50 SS. Total 220
Avge attendance	[Not given]
Remarks	The land I occupy myself is rated at £47 9s 9d.
Dated	30 March 1851
Signed	Thomas Dawson Allen, rector [1827–75]
	North Cerney, Cirencester

[Allen was 'a supporter of the Evangelical party and advertised for a curate of similar views in 1866': *VCH* 7, 161.]

12.16 (16)	**Baptist, North Cerney**
Name	None
Erected	No [In 1816 a house was registered for worship]
Building	No [not separate and entire] No [not exclusively as a place of worship]
Sittings	Free 40. Other 30. Total [70]
Attend'ce 30 Mar.	[Not given]
Avge attendance	Afternoon 30. Total [30]
	Evening 50. Total [50]
Remarks	See le[tter]
Dated	[Not given]
Signed	William Peachy, deacon [tailor]
	Winstone, Cirencester

340.1.13 Parish of Bagendon (or Badgington)

Area 1,106 acres; 39 inhabited houses, 4 uninhabited. Population 183.

12.17 (17)	**Church of England, St Margaret of Antioch, Bagendon**
Name	Bagendon or Badgington, an ancient parish church
Erected	[Tower rebuilt 1832; restored 1889]
Endowment	Land £90. Tithe £190. Glebe £5. OPE £20. [Total] £305. {Total £191}
Sittings	Free 90. Other 60. Total 150
Attend'ce 30 Mar.	Morning 57 + 28 SS. Total 85
	Afternoon 78 + 28 SS. Total 106
Avge attendance	Morning 60 + 30 SS. Total 90
	Afternoon 90 + 30 SS. Total 120
Remarks	From the gross value of endowment (£305) as above, deduct the average annual amount of poor and highway rates etc., as well as interest on a mortgage from Queen Ann's Bounty for building parsonage. Average rates £25, interest £55 = £80
Dated	31 March 1851

Signed   Thomas Price, rector [1845–60]

340.1.14 Parish of Duntisborne Rouse

Area 1,730 acres; 30 inhabited houses, 2 uninhabited. Population 160.

12.18 (18)	**Church of England, St Michael and All Angels, Duntisborne Rouse**
Name	Ancient parish church, the name given on its consecration unknown
Consecrated	[Not given]
Erected	[Restored 1872 and 1936]
Endowment	Land £181 10s. Tithe £78 3s. Glebe £10. OPE none. Pew rents none. Fees £37. Dues none. Easter offerings 4d from each family. Other sources none. {Total £243}
Sittings	Free 80. Other none. Total 80
Attend'ce 30 Mar.	Morning 25 + 16 SS. Total 41
	Afternoon 36 + 16. Total 52
Avge attendance	[Not given]
Dated	31 March 1851
Signed	Henry Bubb, curate of the parish
	Duntisborne Rouse, Cirencester
[*Incumbent*	Vaughan Thomas 1811–58]

[Bubb had previously been the curate of Bagendon (**12.17**). He lived at Daglingworth House for 40 years, ten of them as curate of Daglingworth (**12.19**). Thomas, who lived in Oxford, was also the incumbent of Yarnton, Oxford 1803–58 and of Stoneleigh, Warwickshire 1804–58. 'Dr V. Thomas was a man well known to his generation as an able man of business ... [he] wrote voluminously in the public papers and during the epidemic of the cholera was most active in his suggestions': Stapleton, 227; *ODNB* 'Vaughan Thomas (1775–1858)'.]

340.1.15 Parish of Daglingworth

Area 1,884 acres; 73 inhabited houses, 3 uninhabited. Population 320.

12.19 (19)	**Church of England, Holy Rood, Daglingworth**
Name	The parish church, supposed to be Saxon
Consecration	Before 1800
Erected	[Restored 1845 and chancel and vestry rebuilt 1850–1]
Endowment	Tithe and glebe by both £290 to £300. {Total £266}
Sittings	Free between ~~30~~ and 40. Other about 120. Children 40
	Total ~~180~~ to 200
Attend'ce 30 Mar.	Morning 35 + 35 SS. Total 70
	Afternoon 90 + 34 SS. Total 124
Avge attendance	Morning 40 to 50 + 40 to 50 SS. Total 70 to 80 [*sic*]
	Afternoon 110 + 30 to 40 SS. Total 140 to 150
Remarks	Numbers lessened at church owing to an epidemic
Dated	30 March 1851
Signed	Henry Charles Raymond Barker, rector [1841–73]
	Daglingworth, Cirencester

[Henry Bubb, who lived at Daglingworth House for 40 years, served as the curate here and at Duntisbourne Rouse (**12.18**).]

340.2   CIRENCESTER SUB-DISTRICT

340.2.1 Parish of Baunton

Area 1,340 acres; 24 inhabited houses. Population 134.

12.20 (20)	**Church of England, St Mary Magdalene, Baunton**
Name	Baunton
Consecration	Before 1800
Erected	[Restored 1876]
Endowment	{Total £67}
Sittings	Free 53. Other 24. Total 77
Attend'ce 30 Mar.	Morning 23 + 46 SS. Total 69
	Afternoon 52 + 45 SS. Total 97
Avge attendance	[Not given]
Dated	31 March 1851
Signed	George Francis Master, perpet[ual] curate [1843–75]
	Baunton, Cirencester

[Master was also the incumbent of Stratton (**12.21**), where he lived.]

340.2.2 Parish of Stratton

Area 1,320 acres; 129 inhabited houses, 8 uninhabited. Population 622.
Since 1821 the population had increased by 351 due to the erection of more cottages.

12.21 (21)	**Church of England, St Peter, Stratton**
Name	St Peter's church
Consecration	Before 1800
Erected	[Enlarged and chancel rebuilt 1849–50]
Endowment	Glebe £330. {Total £336}
Sittings	Free 146. Other 162. Total 308
Attend'ce 30 Mar.	Morning 110 + 68 SS. Total 178
	Afternoon 200 + 70 SS. Total 270
Avge attendance	Morning 110. Total [110]
	Afternoon 200. Total [200]
Dated	31 March 1851
Signed	George Francis Master, rector [1844–75]
	Stratton, Cirencester

[Master was also the incumbent of Baunton (**12.20**).]

340.2.3 Parish of Coates

Area 2,330 acres; 78 inhabited houses, 1 uninhabited. Population 400.

12.22 (22)	**Church of England, St Matthew, Coates**
Name	Ancient parish church
Consecration	Before 1800
Erected	[Restored 1860–1]
Endowment	Land £420. {Total £369}
Sittings	Free 150. Other 50. Total 200
Attend'ce 30 Mar.	Morning 22 + 26 SS. Total 48
	Afternoon 45 + 26 SS. Total 71
Avge attendance	[Not given]
Remarks	As regards [the average attendance] I cannot vouch for full accuracy: it is however not far wrong. As to the average number of attendants at church it is difficult [to] define one. It differs as much in different seasons of the

year and according to weather.

Dated	30 March 1851
Signed	Thomas Crook Gibbs, rector of Coates [1848–1914]
	Coates rectory, Cirencester

[Gibbs had previously served as the curate 1846–8: Thorp, 301–24.]

12.23 (24) Wesleyan Methodist, Tarlton

Name	Tarlton Chapel
Erected	1827
Building	Yes [separate and entire] Yes [exclusively as a place of worship]
Sittings	Free 20. Other 63. Total [83]
Attend'ce 30 Mar.	Afternoon 35 + 20 SS. Total 55
	Evening 65. Total [65]
Avge attendance	Afternoon 40 + 17 SS. Total 57
	Evening 50. Total [50]
Dated	31 March 1851
Signed	Charles Bryne, steward
	Tarlton, Gloucestershire

12.24 (23) Primitive Methodist, Coates

Name	None
Erected	[Not given]
Building	No, only part of a dwelling house. No [not exclusively as a place of worship]
Sittings	Free 65. Total [65]
Attend'ce 30 Mar.	Afternoon 16. Total [16]
	Evening 50. Total [50]
Avge attendance	[Not given]
Remarks	The afternoon service is chiefly for the members when the class is not.
Dated	30 March 1851
Signed	John Bramble, class leader [agricultural labourer]
	Coates, near Cirencester, Gloucestershire

340.2.4 Parish of Rodmarton

Area 4,010 acres; 90 inhabited houses, 4 uninhabited. Population 416.
The parish includes the tithing of Calkerton.
VCH 11, 234–47. *GNQ* 3, 481–4; 2, 514–6, 533–5

12.25 (25) Church of England, St Peter, Rodmarton

Name	St Peter's church
Consecration	Before 1800
Erected	[Restored 1862 and 1883–4]
Endowment	Land £600. Fees £5. {Total £476}
Sittings	About 350. Total [about 350]
Attend'ce 30 Mar.	Morning 125 + 54 SS. Total [179]
	Afternoon 205 + 54 SS. Total [259]
Avge attendance	Morning 150 + 44 SS. Total 194
	Afternoon 250 + 44 SS. Total 294
Dated	31 March 1851
Signed	Rev Samuel Simm, curate of Rodmarton
	[Rodmarton Rectory], Cirencester
[Incumbent	Samuel Lysons 1833–77]

[Hempsted Court, Gloucester]

[From 1756–1893 successive generations of the Lysons family served as clergy at Rodmarton. Samuel Lysons, who was curate 1830–3, then incumbent, was non-resident from 1835. He was also the promoter and incumbent of St Luke's, High Orchard, Hempsted, Gloucester (**8.41**) where he officiated without a stipend: *ODNB* 'Samuel Lysons (1806–1877'.]

340.2.5 Parish of Kemble, Wiltshire [transferred to Gloucestershire, 1897]
Area 3,600 acres; 101 inhabited houses, 3 uninhabited. Population 496.
The parish includes the tithings of Ewen and Jervis Quarry.

12.26 (26)	**Church of England, All Saints, Kemble**
Name	'All Saints' an ancient parish church
Consecration	[Not given]
Erected	[Apart from the tower rebuilt 1872–3]
Endowment	Land £253. Tithe £7 15s. Fees sometimes £5 per annum. {Total £249}
Sittings	Free 100. Other 200. Total 300
Attend'ce 30 Mar.	Morning 66 + 52 SS. Total 118
	Afternoon 105 + 46 SS. Total 151
Avge attendance	Morning 120 + 58 SS. Total 178
	Afternoon 180 + 50 SS. Total 230
Remarks	A charity sermon was preached on the 31st with which the message lessened a congregation in an agricultural district; and the day besides very cold and stormy. Many persons have a great distance to come, and for that reason the congregation depends much upon the weather.
Dated	31 March 1851
Signed	William Sparriour Chapman, vicar [1844–61]
	Kemble, Cirencester

12.27 (27)	**Primitive Methodist, Kemble**
Name	None
Erected	1845
Building	No [not separate and entire] No [not exclusively as a place of worship]
Sittings	Free 60. Total [60]
Attend'ce 30 Mar.	Evening 60. Total 60
Avge attendance	Evening 50. Total 50
Dated	31 March 1851
Signed	Thomas Williams, Primitive Methodist minister
	Coxwell Street, Cirencester, Gloucestershire

[Williams was also the minister of Cirencester (**12.42**), Poole Keynes (**12.29**) Preston (**12.46**) and Somerford Keynes (**12.31**).]

340.2.6 Parish of Poole Keynes, Wiltshire [transferred to Gloucestershire, 1897]
Area 1,100 acres; 38 inhabited houses. Population 192.

12.28 (28)	**Church of England, St Michael and All Angels, Poole Keynes**
Name	St Michael. Ancient parish church
Consecration	Before 1800
Erected	[Rebuilt c.1770–5, altered 1845]
Endowment	Land (214 a[cres] 1 [rood] 18 [poles]). £383. Tithe £5 14s 4d. OPE £2 19s. [Total] £391 13s 4d. {Total £342}
Sittings	Free 104 (none legally appropriated, exclusive of the gallery erected for the children). Total 104
Attend'ce 30 Mar.	Morning 52 + 37 SS. Total 89

	Afternoon 63 + 37 SS. Total 100
Avge attendance	[Not given]
Remarks	On the 30 March the service was in the evening in consequence of the rector taking the duty in the adjoining parish. The no. of children is put at the same as that in the morning attendance as the invariable rule is that each child shall attend both services. The no. might have been less in the day ... from ... .
Dated	5 April 1851
Signed	Charles Avery Moore, rector [1845–54]
	Poole Keynes rectory, nr Cirencester

[Moore was later the incumbent of Sutterton, Lincs. 1859–75, and 'during the latter part of his incumbency was convinced that every sermon which he preached would be his last, and in consequence his discourses were of inordinate length': Venn.]

12.29 (29)   **Primitive Methodist, Poole Keynes**

Name	None
Erected	Not erected for the purpose of religious worship, but was dedicated to it in 1848
Building	No [not separate and entire] Yes [exclusively as a place of worship]
Sittings	Free 60. Total [60]
Attend'ce 30 Mar.	Evening 60. Total 60
Avge attendance (3m)	Evening 50. Total 50
Dated	31 March 1851
Signed	Thomas Williams, minister
	Coxwell Street, Cirencester, Gloucestershire

[Williams was also the minister of Cirencester (**12.42**), Kemble (**12.27**) Preston (**12.46**) and Somerford Keynes (**12.31**).]

340.2.7 Parish of Somerford Keynes, Wiltshire [transferred to Gloucestershire, 1897]
Area 1,640 acres; 80 inhabited houses, 3 uninhabited. Population 373.

12.30 (30)   **Church of England, All Saints, Somerford Keynes**

Name	Ancient parish church (All Saints)
Consecration	Not known
Erected	[Restored 1875–6]
Endowment	Tithe £142 (corn rent). Glebe 46 acres and house value £88. Total £230. {Total £261}
Sittings	Free 8. Other 176. Other 184
Attend'ce 30 Mar.	Afternoon 157. Total [157 including 41 children]
Avge attendance	Morning about 30. Total 30
	Afternoon no service till lately since 12 January
	Evening about 60. Total 60
Remarks	Since 12 January 1851 there has been only one service on the Sunday. The congregation 157 includes 41 children, 14 of whom belonged to the school.
Dated	31 March 1851
Signed	Nathaniel George Woodroofe AM, vicar [1803–51]
	Somerford Keynes, near Cirencester

12.31 (31)   **Primitive Methodist, Somerford Keynes**

Name	None
Erected	Since 1840
Building	No [not separate and entire] No [not exclusively as a place of worship]
Sittings	Free 60. Total [60] Standing room for 10

Attend'ce 30 Mar.   Afternoon 40. Total [40]
    Evening 70. Total [70]
Avge attendance   Afternoon 40. Total [40]
    Evening 70. Total [70]
Dated   [Not given]
Signed   Thomas Williams, Primitive Methodist minister
    Coxwell Street, Cirencester, Gloucestershire

[Williams was also the minister of Cirencester (**12.42**), Kemble (**12.27**) Poole Keynes (**12.29**) and Preston (**12.46**).]

340.2.8 Parish of Shorncote, Wiltshire [transferred to Gloucestershire, 1897]
Area 485 acres; 6 inhabited houses. Population 29.

12.32 (32)   **Church of England, All Saints, Shorncote**
Name   Shorncote church. Dedicated to All Saints. An ancient church of a distinct and separate parish
Consecration   Before AD 1800
Erected   [Restored 1882–3]
Endowment   Tithe £90. Glebe £60. {Total £130}
Sittings   Free 24. Other 16. Total 40
Attend'ce 30 Mar.   Afternoon 22. Total [22]
Avge attendance   [Not given]
Remarks   The population in round numbers is 30 and at present there is no school, it having been discontinued five years. Divine service always once every Sunday and sometimes twice.
Dated   31 March 1851
Signed   Edmund Wood MA, curate [1849–53]
    Oaksey near Cirencester
[Incumbent   John Greenly 1834–62]

[Greenly was also the headmaster of the cathedral school, Salisbury, a minor canon of the cathedral and incumbent of St Thomas, Salisbury. As a chaplain on HMS *Revenge*, he saw action at Trafalgar.]

340.2.9 Parish of South Cerney
Area 3,100 acres; 237 inhabited houses, 23 uninhabited. Population 1,103.

12.33 (33)   **Church of England, All Hallows, South Cerney**
Name   Very old church. Dedicated to All Hallows
Consecration   Before 1800
Erected   [Restored 1861–2]
Endowment   Land £180. Tithe 259 [acres] at £190. Easter offerings £4. {Total £231}
Sittings   Free 339. Other 299. Total 638
Attend'ce 30 Mar.   Morning 120 + 135 SS. Total 255
    Afternoon 270 + 135 SS. Total 405
Avge attendance   [Not given]
Remarks   The parish is under a lay rector. Land £180 and tithe £190 and vicar tithe £290 and Easter offerings £4.
Dated   31 March 1851
Signed   Joseph Wood, churchwarden
    South Cerney, near Cirencester
[Incumbent   Richard Wilbraham Ford 1807–62]

[The benefice consisted of South Cerney with Cerney Wick (**12.34**). Ford was also the incumbent of Little Rissington (**14.5**) (where he lived) and of Stourpaine, Dorset 1810–54.]

12.34 (34)   **Church of England, Holy Trinity, Cerney Wick**

Name	New chapel of ease [to] the mother church South Cerney. Dedicated to the Holy Trinity
Consecration	The 18 [*recte* 24] Augt. 1848, as a chapel of ease to the mother church
Erected	By private benefaction and the societies named. Incorporated Church Building Society £60. Cooperative Church Building Society £20. Bristol Church Diocesan £200. Private benefaction or subscription £480 Total cost £766
Endowment	Land £30 [See South Cerney (**12.33**)]
Sittings	Free 108. Total 108
Attend'ce 30 Mar.	Morning 60. Total [60]
Avge attendance	[Not given]
Remarks	Service is performed at this chapel once every Sunday only; morning and evening alternately.
Dated	31 March 1851
Signed	Joseph Wood, churchwarden South Cerney, near Cirencester
[*Incumbent*	Richard Wilbraham Ford 1807–64]

[The benefice consisted of South Cerney (**12.33**) with Cerney Wick. On Ford, see preceding entry.]

12.35 (35)   **Primitive Methodist, Cerney Wick**

Name	Independent Chapel
Erected	1815
Building	Private chapel. Yes [exclusively as a place of worship]
Sittings	Free 50. Other 30. Total [80] Standing room for 20
Attend'ce 30 Mar.	Afternoon 40 + 20 SS. Total [60] Evening 90. Total [90]
Avge attendance	[Not given]
Dated	31 March 1851
Signed	William Ricketts, steward [labourer] [South Cerney]

340.2.10   Parish of Siddington

Area 1,950 acres; 114 inhabited houses. Population 502.

12.36 (36)   **Church of England, St Peter, Siddington**

Name	St Peter's. An ancient parish church from the parish church of the consolidated parishes of St Peter and St Mary
Consecration	Before 1800
Erected	[Restored 1864]
Endowment	{Total £429}
Sittings	Free 170. Other 50. Total 220
Attend'ce 30 Mar.	Morning 65 + 54 SS. Total 119 Afternoon 99 + 54 SS. Total 153
Avge attendance	Morning 65 + 60 SS. Total 125 Afternoon 110 + 60 SS. Total 170
Dated	31 March 1851
Signed	N. N. C. [?] Hayward, off[iciatin]g minister Siddington rectory, Cirencester
[*Incumbent*	Henry John Bolland 1842–55]

[Under the Inclosure Act of 1778 St Mary, Upper Siddington and St Peter, Lower Siddington were united and St Mary's was demolished.]

340.2.11   Parish of Cirencester

Area 5,000 acres; 1,211 inhabited houses, 41 uninhabited. Population 6,096.
The parish includes the tithings of Barton, Chesterton, Oakley, Spirringate and Wiggold.
The Union workhouse situated in the parish had 257 inmates.

12.37 (37)   **Church of England, St John the Baptist, Cirencester**

Name	Saint John the Baptist. Ancient parish church
Consecration	Before 1800
Erected	A chapel of ease is awaiting consecration... Total cost £7,000 [Restored 1865–7]
Endowment	{Total £443}
Sittings	Total 1,500. In chapel to be consecrated ~~450~~
Attend'ce 30 Mar.	No account
Avge attendance	No account
Dated	[Not given]
Signed	[Not given]
[Incumbent	William Frederick Powell 1839–69]

[The benefice consisted of Cirencester with Watermoor. Holy Trinity, Watermoor was consecrated 6 Nov. 1851. Powell was an unpopular Anglo-Catholic who referred to the taunts of those who followed him in the street, 'hooting, yelling and jeering' at him: Welsford 2010.]

12.38 (39)   **Independent, Sheep Street**

Name	Independent or Congregational Chapel
Erected	1833 [New chapel opened in Dyer Street in 1887]
Building	Yes [separate and entire] Yes [exclusively as a place of worship]
Sittings	Free 120. Other 341. Total [461]
Attend'ce 30 Mar.	Morning 180 + 80 SS. Total 260
	Evening 280. Total 280
Avge attendance	[Not given]
Dated	31 March 1851
Signed	Edward Bewlay, minister [1840–51]
	Cirencester

12.39 (38)   **Baptist, Coxwell Street**

Name	Coxwell Street Chapel
Erected	Before 1800 [1709] [Rebuilt 1856–7]
Building	Yes [separate and entire] Yes [exclusively as a place of worship]
Sittings	Free 170. Other 230. Total [400]
Attend'ce 30 Mar.	Morning 136 + 70 SS. Total 206
	Evening 183. Total 183
Avge attendance	[Not given]
Dated	31 March 1851
Signed	John M. Stephens, minister
	Sheep Street, Cirencester

[Stephens had served as the co-pastor to his predecessor, Daniel White 1894–53. In May 1854 seceders from the chapel opened a Strict Baptist Chapel in Park Street.]

12.40 (43)   **Baptist, Watermoor**

Name	None
Erected	[Not given]
Building	No [not separate and entire] No [not exclusively as a place of worship]
Sittings	Free from 30 to 40. Other none. Total [30–40] Standing room none

Attend'ce 30 Mar.	Afternoon 20. Total [20]
Avge attendance	Afternoon 25. Total [25]
Remarks	This place of worship is a large room in a respectable cottage, nearly a mile from the church and other chapels. The congregation would have been more numerous on 30 March but for the stormy weather.
Dated	31 March 1851
Signed	Charles Darkin, minister [1841–52]
	Cirencester

12.41 (42)   Wesleyan Methodist, Gloucester Street

Name	Wesleyan Methodist Chapel
Erected	1808 [altered 1887]
Building	Yes [separate and entire] Yes [exclusively as a place of worship]
Sittings	Free 60. Other 188. Total [248] Standing room none
Attend'ce 30 Mar.	Morning 62 + 18 SS. Total 80
	Evening 130. Total 130
Avge attendance {6m)	Morning [80] Total 80
	Evening [150] Total 150
Remarks	The free sittings to the number they require, are occupied by the Sunday scholars, on the Lord's Day morning.
Dated	31 March 1851
Signed	Enoch Buttwell, deacon [shopkeeper]
	Gloucester Street, Cirencester

12.42 (40)   Primitive Methodist, Coxwell Street

Name	None
Erected	Used first for preaching about 1849 [A small chapel opened in Lewis Lane in 1851 and in 1896 it was replaced by a larger chapel in Ashcroft Road]
Building	No [not separate and entire] Yes [exclusively as a place of worship]
Sittings	Free 160. Total [160]
Attend'ce 30 Mar.	Afternoon 100. Total 100
	Evening 110. Total 110
Avge attendance	Afternoon 120. Total 120
	Evening 140. Total 140
Dated	31 March 1851
Signed	Thomas Williams, Primitive Methodist minister
	Coxwell Street, Cirencester, Gloucestershire

[Williams was also minister of Kemble (**12.27**), Poole Keynes (**12.29**), Preston (**12.46**) and Somerford Keynes (**12.31**).]

12.43 (46)   Society of Friends, Thomas Street

Erected	Before 1800 [1673, altered 1726 and enlarged 1810–1]
Building	Yes [separate and entire] Yes [exclusively as a place of worship]
Sittings	Ground floor 1,716 [square feet] 480 sittings
	Gallery 156 [square feet] 70 sittings
	Total 1,872 [square feet] 550 sittings
Attend'ce 30 Mar.	Morning 50. Total [50]
	Afternoon 37. Total [37]
	Evening not open
Dated	31 day of the 3rd mo. 1851
Signed	Thomas Brewin [corn merchant and seedsman]

Cirencester

12.44 (41)   **Unitarian, Gosditch Street**
Name   Presbyterian Meeting
Erected   Before 1800 [c.1750. Restored and re-opened 15 Jan. 1891]
Building   Separate and entire building. Yes [exclusively as a place of worship]
Sittings   All free sittings 50. Total [50]
Attend'ce 30 Mar. Morning 30. Total [30]
                  Afternoon 40. Total [40]
Avge attendance Morning 50. Total [50]
Remarks   (See letter)
Dated   31 March 1851
Signed   Frederick Horsfield, minister [1820–60]
                  Gosditch Street, Cirencester, Gloucestershire
[Founded 1662 as a Presbyterian congregation, by the 19th century it had become Unitarian.]

340.2.12   **Parish of Preston**
Area 2,190 acres; 44 inhabited houses. Population 218.

12.45 (44)   **Church of England, All Saints, Preston**
Name   All Saints. It is small with a chapel on the north and another on the south
                  side, a low stone tower at the west end in which are four bells.
Consecration   Before 1800
Erected   [Restored 1862]
Endowment   Land in lieu of tithes. {Total £128}
Sittings   Free 80. Other 60. Total 140
Attend'ce 30 Mar. Morning 45 + 29 SS. Total 74
                  Afternoon 80 + 28 SS. Total 108
Avge attendance [Not given]
Dated   [Not given]
Signed   [Not given]
[Incumbent   Henry Cripps 1817–61]
                  [Preston, Cirencester]
[Cripps was also the incumbent of Stonehouse (**10.3**).]

12.46 (45)   **Primitive Methodist, Preston**
Name   None
Erected   About 1836
Building   No [not separate and entire] No [not exclusively as a place of worship]
Sittings   Free 30. Total [30] Standing room for 20
Attend'ce 30 Mar. Evening 65. Total 65
Avge attendance Evening 40. Total 40
Dated   31 March 1851
Signed   Thomas Williams, Primitive Methodist minister
                  [Coxwell Street], Cirencester, Gloucestershire
[Williams was also minister of Cirencester (**12.42**), Kemble (**12.27**), Poole Keynes (**12.29**) and Somerford Keynes (**12.31**).]

340.2.13   Parish of Harnhill
Area 689 acres; 16 inhabited houses, 1 uninhabited. Population 77.

12.47 (47)   **Church of England, St Michael and All Angels, Harnhill**
Name   St Michael. An ancient parish church

Consecration	Before 1800
Erected	[Restored 1909]
Endowment	With £120 rent charge and 23 acres of glebe. Land (see glebe). Tithe £120. Glebe 23 acres. OPE and pew rents none. Fees sometimes a few shillings. Dues, Easter offerings and other sources none. {Total £155}
Sittings	Free 24. Other 38. Total 62
Attend'ce 30 Mar.	Morning 20 + 23 SS. Total 43
Avge attendance	[Not given]
Dated	31 March 1851
Signed	Thomas Maurice, rector [1840–81]
	Harnhill rectory, near Cirencester

[Maurice was also the incumbent of Driffield (**12.48**).]

340.2.14   Parish of Driffield

Area 1,310 acres; 33 inhabited houses, 3 uninhabited. Population 161.

12.48 (48)   Church of England, St Mary, Driffield

Name	St Mary. An ancient parish church, rebuilt about 1745
Consecration	Before 1800
Erected	[Restored 1737 and 1863]
Endowment	Endowed with 180 acres of land in lieu of tithe by Act of Parliament. Land £186 an[nuall]y. Tithe none. Glebe (see land). OPE and pew rents none. Fees sometimes a few shillings. Dues, Easter offerings and other sources none. {Total £270}
Sittings	Free 44. Other 48. Total 92
Attend'ce 30 Mar.	Afternoon 50 + 24 SS. Total 74
Avge attendance	[Not given]
Dated	31 March 1851
Signed	Thomas Maurice, vicar [1840–81]
	Harnhill rectory, near Cirencester

[Maurice was also the incumbent of Harnhill (**12.47**), where he lived.]

340.3   FAIRFORD SUB-DISTRICT

340.3.1   Parish of Barnsley

Area 2,090 acres; 66 inhabited houses. Population 322.
VCH 7, 13–21

12.49 (49)   Church of England, St Mary, Barnsley

Name	Barnsley Church. Dedication said to be in honour of 'St Mary'
Consecration	[Not given]
Erected	[Restored 1843–7]
Endowment	{Total £320}
Sittings	Free 155. Other 65. Total 220
Attend'ce 30 Mar.	Morning about 90 + 39 SS. Total 129
	Afternoon 92 + 39 SS. Total 131
Avge attendance	Morning about 130 + 40 SS. Total 170
	Afternoon 150 + 40 SS. Total 190
Dated	31 March 1851
Signed	George Ernest Howman, rector [1841–74]
	Barnsley, Cirencester

[Howman had been incumbent of Sonning, Berks. 1822–41; for much of his incumbency at Barnsley he was also master of St Nicholas' Hospital, Salisbury: *VCH* (Wilts.) 3, 354.]

340.3.2   Parish of Ampney Crucis

Area 2,660 acres; 138 inhabited houses, 2 uninhabited. Population 662.
The parish includes the hamlet of Alcott End.

12.50 (50)	**Church of England, Holy Rood, Ampney Crucis**
Name	Ampney Crucis. An ancient parish church
Consecration	Before 1800
Erected	[Restored 1854–5, 1870–3 and 1902]
Endowment	Glebe by £100 a year. {Total £84}
Sittings	Free 150. Other 150. Total 300
Attend'ce 30 Mar.	Morning 60 + 84 SS. Total 144
	Afternoon 125 + 94 SS. Total 219
Avge attendance	[Not given]
Dated	31 March 1851
Signed	Edward Andrew Daubeny, minister [1829–77]
	Ampney, near Cirencester, Gloucestershire

[Daubeny was also the incumbent of Ampney St Peter (**12.51**) (where he lived), and of Hampnett (**13.42**) and Stowell (**13.41**). His son Thomas was the curate 1856–64.]

340.3.3 Parish of Ampney St Peter

Area 533 acres; 44 inhabited houses, 3 uninhabited. Population 206.

12.51 (51)	**Church of England, Ampney St Peter**
Name	Ampney St Peter
Consecration	Before 1800
Erected	[Restored and enlarged 1878–9]
Endowment	Land £23 2s. OPE (Queen Anne's Bounty) £39. {Total £60}
Sittings	Free 34. Other 68. Total 102 (not including benches for the children)
Attend'ce 30 Mar.	Afternoon 84 + 32 SS. Total 116
Avge attendance	[Not given]
Dated	31 March 1851
Signed	Edward Andrew Daubeny, minister [1811–77]
	Ampney St Peter, Cirencester, Gloucestershire

[Daubeny was also the incumbent of Ampney Crucis (**12.50**), Hampnett (**13.42**) and Stowell (**13.41**). On his death the benefices of St Peter and St Mary Ampney were united and he was succeeded by his son Thomas.]

340.3.4 Parish of Ampney St Mary (also Ashbrook)

Area 1,170 acres; 28 inhabited houses, 2 uninhabited. Population 125.

12.52 (52)	**Church of England, Ampney St Mary**
Name	Ampney St Mary or Ashbrook Church. A parish church at least 150 years since
Consecration	Before 1800
Erected	[From 1879 the church was no longer used. In 1907 the chancel was restored and the nave 1913–4]
Endowment	Land £70. {Total £71}
Sittings	Free 100. Other 50. Total 150
Attend'ce 30 Mar.	Morning 58. Total [58]
Avge attendance	Morning 72. Total [72]
	Afternoon 120. Total [120]
	Evening 130. Total [130]

Remarks	The church is situate a mile from the village.
Dated	30 March 1851
Signed	Lawrence Latham, perpetual curate [1833–73]
	Quenington rectory, nr Fairford

[Latham was also the incumbent of Quenington (**12.63**).]

340.3.5 Parish of Poulton [transferred from Wiltshire, 1844]
Area 1,580 acres; 91 inhabited houses, 2 uninhabited. Population 408.

12.53 (53)   Church of England, St Michael and All Angels, Poulton
(Summary form)

Name	Not known
Erected	[Rebuilt on another site 1873–4]
[Endowment	Total £43]
Sittings	Free 60. Other 60. Total 120
Usual attend'ce	Morning 60 + 25 SS. Total [85]
	Afternoon 80 + 25 SS. Total [105]
	Evening none
Signed	Richard Adams [registrar], from inquiries
[Incumbent	Thomas Bowstead 1849–57]

[The medieval priory church of St Mary was used as the parish church until it was demolished and replaced by the new church dedicated to St Michael and All Angels.]

340.3.6 Parish of Down Ampney
Area 2,510 acres; 83 inhabited houses, 3 uninhabited. Population 443.

12.54 (54)   Church of England, All Saints, Down Ampney
Request for information. Will you be so good as to furnish the following information at your earliest convenience. Congregations including Sunday scholars.

[Erected	Restored 1863]
[Endowment	Total £116]
Morning	120
Afternoon	140
Evening	None
Sittings	Free 40. Other 200. Total 240
Dated	24 June 1852
Signed	Richard Adams
[Incumbent	Greville Phillimore 1851–67]

[Phillimore was the joint editor, with Hyde Wyndham Beadon and James Russell Woodford (**1.10**) of *The Parish Hymn Book* (1863): *ODNB* 'Greville Phillimore (1821–1884)'.]

340.3.7 Parish of Meysey Hampton
Area 1,920 acres; 80 inhabited houses, 4 uninhabited. Population 376.

No return   Church of England, St Mary the Virgin, Meysey Hampton

[Erected	Restored 1872–4]
[Endowment	Total £604]
[Incumbent	Frederick William Holme 1810–53]

[Holme's second son Myrick Holme was the incumbent of Marston Meysey (**12.56**).]

12.55 (55)   Baptist, Meysey Hampton

Name	Chapel
Erected	[Opened 26 Sept.] 1833 [Previously the congregation met in a private house]

Building	Yes [separate and entire] Yes [exclusively as a place of worship]
Sittings	Free 120. Total [120]
Attend'ce 30 Mar.	Afternoon 50 + 35 SS. Total 85
	Evening 30. Total [30]
Avge attendance	Morning 65 + 35 SS. Total 100
Remarks	Evening congregation has been lately thinned by the overbearing and unscrupulous restraints impos'd upon the people by certain individuals of the established sect. There being there no evening service. The result is plainly seen in the abuse and great desecration of the Sabbath evening and in the increased drunkenness, bad neighbourhood, and general disorder of the people.
Dated	31 March 1851
Signed	William Thomas, minister
	Fairford, Gloucestershire

340.3.8 Parish of Marston Meysey, Wiltshire
Area 1,276 acres; 52 inhabited houses, 1 uninhabited. Population 237.

12.56 (56)	**Church of England, St James, Marston Meysey**
Name	St James
Consecration	[Not given]
Erected	[Rebuilt 1874–6]
Endowment	Land 26 acres. OPE Queen Anne's Bounty stipend of £200. Other sources £14 added by Ecclesiastical Com[missioner]s. {Total £76}
Sittings	Free 40. Other 26. Total 66
Attend'ce 30 Mar.	[Not given]
Avge attendance	[Not given]
Dated	[Not given]
Signed	Myrick Holme [1840–72]
	Maisey Hampton, Cricklade

[Holme was the second son of Frederick William Holme, incumbent of Meysey Hampton, above.]

340.3.9 Parish of Kempsford
Area 4,790 acres; 221 inhabited houses, 7 uninhabited. Population 1,003.
The parish includes the hamlets of Dunfield, Horcott and Whelford.
VCH 7, 96–105

12.57 (57)	**Church of England, St Mary the Virgin, Kempsford**
(Summary form)	
Name	Saint Martin [sic]
Erected	[Restored 1856–8, 1885–7 and 1889–91]
[*Endowment*	Total £604 [By 1910 it had declined to £160]
Sittings	Free 80. Other 120. Total 200
Usual attend'ce	Morning 90 + 40 SS. Total [130]
	Afternoon 130 + 40 SS. Total [170]
	Evening none
Signed	Richard Adams [registrar], from inquiries
[*Incumbent*	Thomas Huntingford 1810–55]

[Huntingford (the nephew of George Isaac Huntingford, bishop of Gloucester 1802–15, translated to Hereford 1815–32) was also the precentor of Hereford cathedral 1817–55, and the incumbent of Weston under Penyard, Herefs., 1831–55. Within the parish, the chapel of ease dedicated to St Anne, at Whelford was consecrated 4 June 1864.]

13. HO 129/341 NORTHLEACH DISTRICT: 47 places of worship

341.1   BIBURY SUB-DISTRICT

341.1.1 Parish of Southrop
Area 1,453 acres; 86 inhabited houses. Population 425.
VCH 7, 129–36

13.1 (1)	**Church of England, St Peter, Southrop**
Name	St Peter's. An ancient parish church
Consecration	Before AD 1800
Erected	[Restored 1852 and 1895]
Endowment	Tithe (rent charge) £206. Glebe £47. Fees about £1. {Total £192}
Sittings	Free (Sunday school not included) 142. Other 8. Total 150
Attend'ce 30 Mar.	Morning 70 + 65 SS. Total 135
	Afternoon 135 + 65 SS. Total 200
Avge attendance	[Not given]
Dated	31 March 1851
Signed	Joseph Walker MA, vicar [1848–82]
	Lechlade, Gloucestershire

[Given the association with John Keble (**13.2**) it is suggested that 'Southrop should be a place of pilgrimage for all devout Anglo-Catholics': Verey and Brooks, 623.]

341.1.2 Parish of Eastleach Martin (or Bouthrop)
Area 1,960 acres; 43 inhabited houses. Population 197.
VCH 7, 55–61

13.2 (2)	**Church of England, St Michael and St Martin, Eastleach Martin**
Name	Eastleach Martin. Ancient country parish church
Consecration	Before 1800
Erected	[Restored 1865, 1881 and 1886]
Endowment	Tithe £133. Glebe £28. {Total £150}
Sittings	Free 90. Other 27. Total 117
Attend'ce 30 Mar.	Morning 65. Total [65]
Avge attendance	Morning 45. Total [45]
	Afternoon 80. Total [80]
Remarks	This parish church is situated only about 100 yards from the parish church of Eastleach Turville (**13.3**); and therefore there is but one service in each church, morning and evening, alternately.
Dated	31 March 1851
Signed	Rowland Helme Cooper, curate [1832–58]
	Eastleach, near Lechlade, Gloucestershire
[*Incumbent*	Hugh Pollard Willoughby 1827–58]

[Cooper was also the incumbent of Eastleach Turville (**13.3**). An earlier curate was the Tractarian leader John Keble, who although he had academic responsibilities at Oriel College, Oxford, held various Gloucestershire curacies: at Eastleach Martin and Eastleach Turville from 1815, Southrop (**13.1**) from 1823 and Coln St Aldwyns (**13.13**) 1826–35; and finally the incumbent of Hursley, Hampshire 1839–66. 'Mr Keble used to ride to and fro from Oxford, and on Sundays used to dine at a cottager's, for which he paid, and used to charge them not to provide anything extra for him; that was the stipulation': Coleridge, 1, 64; *ODNB* 'John Keble (1792–1866)'. Keble's younger brother

Thomas was the incumbent of Bisley (**10.25**). Willoughby was mostly non-resident and also the incumbent of Marsh Baldon, Oxon. 1831–58. In 1854 he was committed to Bedlam Hospital having been found not guilty (but insane) of shooting a barrister at the Old Bailey: www.oldbaileyonline.org. Eastleach Martin church is now under the care of the Churches Conservation Trust.]

341.1.3 Parish of Eastleach Turville
Area 2,670 acres; 103 inhabited houses, 4 uninhabited. Population 446.
VCH 7, 61–9

13.3 (3)	**Church of England, St Andrew, Eastleach Turville**
Name	Eastleach Turville. Ancient country parish church
Consecration	Before 1800
Erected	[Not given]
Endowment	OPE £30, and average value of 28 bush[e]l of wheat. {Total £66}
Sittings	Free 88. Other 29. Total 117
Attend'ce 30 Mar.	Afternoon 75. Total [75]
Avge attendance	Morning 40. Total [40]
	Afternoon 75. Total [75]
Remarks	Eastleach Turville and Eastleach Martin churches being within about 100 yards of each other, there is only one service in each, morning and afternoon alternately.
Dated	31 March 1851
Signed	Rowland Helme Cooper, perpetual curate [1851–8]
	Eastleach, near Lechlade, Gloucestershire

[Cooper was also the curate of Eastleach Martin (**13.2**).]

13.4 (4)	**Primitive Methodist, Eastleach Turville**
Name	None
Erected	1829 [Replaced by a new chapel opened in 1909]
Building	Yes [separate and entire] Yes [exclusively as a place of worship]
Sittings	Fee 80. Other [80] Total [160] Standing room for 30
Attend'ce 30 Mar.	Afternoon 90. Total [90]
	Evening 110. Total [110]
Avge attendance	[Not given]
Dated	31 March 1851
Signed	Richard Brown, steward [stonemason]
	Eastleach, Gloucestershire

341.1.4 Parish of Little Barrington
Area 925 acres; 30 inhabited houses, 1 uninhabited. Population 128.
In ten years the population had declined by 80 due to the demolition of some cottages.
VCH 6, 16–27

13.5 (5)	**Church of England, St Peter, Little Barrington**
Name	Little Barrington, an ancient parish church
Consecration	[Not given]
Erected	[Porch enlarged 1865]
Endowment	{Total £100}
Sittings	Free 94. Other 30. Total 124
Attend'ce 30 Mar.	Morning 24 + 26 SS. Total 50
	Afternoon 55 + 26 SS. Total 81
Avge attendance	Morning 30 + 26 SS. Total 56
	Afternoon 60 + 26 SS. Total 86

Remarks	Little Barrington is endowed with about 44 acres of glebe, with a modus for tithe: the aggregate annual amount is £95.
Dated	31 March 1851
Signed	Richard Hodges, vicar [1841–66]
	Burford, Oxon.

341.1.5 Parish of Windrush
Area 1,710 acres; 64 inhabited houses, 1 uninhabited. Population 332.
VCH 6, 178–84

13.6 (6)	**Church of England, St Peter, Windrush**
Name	Ancient parish church dedicated to St Peter
Consecration	Before 1800
Erected	[Chancel rebuilt 1873–4]
Endowment	Land [See Sherborne (**13.7**)]
Sittings	Free 210. Other 57. Total 267
Attend'ce 30 Mar.	Morning 50 + 40 SS. Total 90
	Afternoon 120 + 31 SS. Total 151
Avge attendance	Morning 50 + 45 SS. Total 95
	Afternoon 180 + 45 SS. Total 175
Dated	31 March 1851
Signed	Edward James Todd, vicar [1843–69]
	Nr Northleach, Gloucestershire

[The benefice consisted of Sherborne (**13.7**) with Windrush.]

341.1.6 Parish of Sherborne
Area 4,560 acres; 126 inhabited houses, 1 uninhabited. Population 674.
In 1831 the population was 767 and had increased during the rebuilding of Sherborne House and a model village.
VCH 6, 120–7

13.7 (7)	**Church of England, St Mary Magdalene, Sherborne**
Name	Ancient parish church of Sherborne, Gloucestershire, dedicated to St Mary Magdalene
Consecration	Before 1800
Erected	[New chancel 1750, chancel and nave rebuilt 1859]
Endowment	Land. {Total £194}
Sittings	All open seats. Total 353
Attend'ce 30 Mar.	Morning about 180 + 60 SS. Total 240
	Afternoon no service this Sunday
	Evening no service
Avge attendance	Morning about 150 + 60 SS. Total 210
	Afternoon about 280 + 60 SS. Total 340
	Evening no service
Remarks	The church contains sufficient room for the parishioners and is generally very full. The seats are open benches with the exception of two.
Dated	30 March 1851
Signed	Edward James Todd, vicar [1843–69]
	Nr Northleach, Gloucestershire

[The benefice consisted of Sherborne with Windrush (**13.6**).]

341.1.7 Parish of Farmington

Area 2,470 acres; 60 inhabited houses. Population 339.
VCH 9, 69–81

13.8 (8)	**Church of England, St Peter, Farmington**
Name	Old Parish Church
Consecration	[Not given]
Erected	[Restored 1890–1]
Endowment	Land ... some 1¼ acres. Tithe modus £120. {Total £120}
Sittings	Free about 150. Other about 40. Total 190 to 200
Attend'ce 30 Mar.	Morning: small congregation in morning
	Afternoon: church filled in afternoon
	SS about 50
Avge attendance	[Not given]
Remarks	It is presumed in case of an old country church to seating adequate to ye population of parish. The return as above ... sufficient.
Dated	24 March 1851
Signed	John Boudier, rector [1824–58]
	Farmington, Northleach

[Boudier was also the incumbent of St Mary's, Warwick 1815–72: Verey 1980, 72.]

341.1.8–9   Parish of Northleach

Area 3,460 acres; 272 inhabited houses, 4 uninhabited. Population 1,352.
The parish contains contains the tithing of Eastington where the Union workhouse was situated, and had 98 inmates.
VCH 9, 106–45. *GNQ* 3, 9–11, 559–62

13.9 (10)	**Church of England, St Peter and St Paul, Northleach**
Name	Northleach ancient parish church. NB The parish of Northleach and the adjoining parish or hamlet of Eastington are identical for all Ecclesiastical purposes.
Consecration	Before 1800
Erected	[Restored in 1884, 1897 and 1902]
Endowment	Land and tithe. [I do not] understand the distinction between land and glebe. F. A. Fees and dues: I decline stating the amount of income arising from such endowment. F. A. {Total £228}
Sittings	I can only answer this question in this way. Free sittings insufficient. Other sittings generally adequate for the accommodation required. Total about 700 or 750
Attend'ce 30 Mar.	It is submitted that this question should have been assigned to the church-wardens, certainly not to the clergyman. I had no time or opportunity for enumerating. But in truth the inclemency of the weather yesterday afforded no concession as to the number of persons usually attending divine service. F. A.
Avge attendance	Morning 200 + abt 150 to 180 SS. Total 350
	Afternoon 400 + abt 150 to 180 SS. Total 580
Dated	31 March 1851
Signed	Frederick Aston, vicar [1838–55]
	Vicarage, [Eastington], Northleach

[A chapel of ease at Eastington fell into disrepair and had been demolished by 1703; its ruins were still visible in 1750.]

13.10 (11)   **Independent, West End**
Name   Northleach Independent Chapel
Erected   About 1800 [1798 and replaced by a new chapel in 1860]
Building   Yes [separate and entire] Yes [exclusively as a place of worship]
Sittings   Free 100. Total [100]
Attend'ce 30 Mar.   Evening 90. Total 90
Avge attendance (3m) Evening 80. Total 80
Dated   30 March 1851.
Signed   Daniel Cornish, minister [1851–3]
                      Halham Cottage, Chedworth, nr Andoversford, Gloucestershire

13.11 (12)   **Wesleyan Methodist, Mill End**
Name   Wesleyan Methodist Chapel
Erected   1826
Building   Yes [separate and entire] Yes [exclusively as a place of worship]
Sittings   Free 70. Other 96. Total [186]
Attend'ce 30 Mar.   Afternoon 79 + 21 SS. Total 100
                      Evening 114. Total 114
Avge attendance   [Not given]
Dated   31 March 1851
Signed   William Henry Cornforth, minister [1849–51]
                      22 Gt Norwood St, Cheltenham

[Cornforth was also the minister of Charlton Kings (**16.4**), Cheltenham (**16.31, 33**), Golden Valley
(**16.32**), Arle (**16.34**), Turkdean (**13.45**) and Withington (**13.29**).]

341.1.10   Parish of Aldsworth

Area 3,460 acres; 77 inhabited houses, 1 uninhabited. Population 379.
VCH 7, 5–13

13.12 (13)   **Church of England, St Peter** (now St Bartholomew)**, Aldsworth**
Name   St Peter's of the ancient parish of 'Aldisworth'
Consecration   Before 1800
Erected   [Restored 1842–3, and the chancel and vestry rebuilt in 1877]
Endowment   {Total £66}
Sittings   Free about 250. Other 60. Total 310
Attend'ce 30 Mar.   [Not given]
Avge attendance   [Not given]
Remarks   Re [the] question is invidious: for the number attendant on divine service
                      on any given Sunday (liable to a variety of influences as well seasonal
                      as religious and political, and none more than these generated by this
                      confusing document) can hardly present to any reasonable disinterested
                      person, competent ground for any ... clear conclusion on a statistical
                      point [very unclear handwriting]
Dated   29 March 1851
Signed   John George Bellingham, incumbent [1839–65]
                      [4 Holles Place, Brompton, London]

[From 1745 the dedication was sometimes St Peter. Between 1852–6 Bellingham was unwell and
until he left the parish in 1865 it was served by curates.]

341.1.11 Parish of Coln St Aldwyns

Area 3,420 acres; 98 inhabited houses, 2 uninhabited. Population 492.
VCH 7, 44–55

13.13 (14)   **Church of England, St John the Baptist, Coln St Aldwyns**

Name	The parish church of Coln St Aldwyns
Consecration	Before 1800
Erected	[Restored 1818, 1853, 1868 and 1897–9]
Endowment	Land £69. OPE £30. Fees £3. Easter offerings £2. {Total £103}
Sittings	Free 51. Other 194. Total 245
Attend'ce 30 Mar.	Morning 75 + 49 SS. Total 124
	Afternoon 130 + 49 SS. Total 179
Avge attendance	Morning 100 + 45 SS. Total 145
	Afternoon 140 + 45 SS. Total 185
	Evening no service
Dated	31 March 1851
Signed	Charles Gore Gambier Gambier, vicar [1848–51]
	Coln St Aldwyns, Fairford

[A former incumbent Thomas Keble 1782–1835 lived at the family home (Court House, later renamed Keble House) at Fairford. From 1826, and until his death in 1835, his son the Tractarian leader John Keble, (**13.2**) was his curate.]

341.1.12–14   Parish of Bibury

Area 2,190 acres; 127 inhabited houses, 12 uninhabited. Population 586.
The parish includes the chapelry of Winson (**13.16**) and the tithings of Ablington and Arlington.
VCH 7, 21–44

13.14 (15)   **Church of England, St Mary, Bibury** [see sketch above, p 264]

Name	Bibury Church
Consecration	Before 1800
Erected	[Restored 1863 and 1895–1900]
Endowment	Tithe commuted at £320 8s 6d. Glebe (27 acres) £364 5s. [Total] £684 13s 6d. {Total £1,023}
Sittings	Free for adults 333. Sittings for school 80. Total 413
Attend'ce 30 Mar.	Morning 80 + 71 SS. Total 151
	Afternoon 134 + 81 SS. Total 215
Avge attendance	[Not given]
Remarks	It should be remarked that many of the 333 sittings, entered as free, are appropriated, more or less, by contest, by instructions, to certain families, but the general congregation, are by no means restricted from the use of them as may require No faculty pews exist nor is any exclusive claims of use permitted.
Dated	31 March 1851
Signed	Henry Snow, vicar [1843–74]
	Bibury, Fairford

[The benefice consisted of Bibury with Winson (**13.16**). At a confirmation service in 1850 there were 121 candidates (58 males and 63 females): GA, A2/5]

13.15 (16)   **Baptist, Arlington**

Name	Arlington Chapel
Erected	Before 1800 [1754, rebuilt 1833]
Building	Yes [separate and entire] Yes [exclusively as a place of worship]
Sittings	All free 240.* Total [240]
Attend'ce 30 Mar.	Morning 139 + 80 SS. Total 219
	Afternoon 150 + 72 SS. Total 222

Avge attendance [Not given]
Remarks * There is no charge for sittings, but families who regularly attend have their own seats usually, for convenience sake. The second service is alternately in the afternoon and evening. On the Sunday in which there is no preaching, a sermon being read.
Dated 31 March 1851
Signed Richard Hall, minister
Arlington, nr Fairford, Gloucestershire
[Hall was also the minister of Coln Rogers (**13.19**).]

341.2 CHEDWORTH SUB-DISTRICT

341.2.1 Chapelry of Winson (within the parish of Bibury)
Area 1,190 acres; 34 inhabited houses, 1 uninhabited. Population 170.

13.16 (17) **Church of England, St Michael, Winson**
Name Winson Chapel
Consecration Before 1800
Erected [Restored c.1882]
Endowment Tithe commuted at £330 10s. [See Bibury (**13.15**)]
Sittings Free 90. Total 90
Attend'ce 30 Mar. Morning 26 + 54 SS.* Total 80
Afternoon 51 + 46 SS.* Total 97
Avge attendance [Not given]
Remarks * It should be here commented that about one half of the above entered numbers of Sunday scholars belong to and come from the neighbouring village of Coln Rogers, many of whom attend the Sunday school at Winson are dismissed in time for divine service at their own parish church of Coln Rogers (**13.18**).
Dated 31 March 1851
Signed Henry Snow, vicar [1843–74]
Bibury, Fairford
[The benefice consisted of Bibury (**13.14**) with Winson.]

13.17 (18) **Primitive Methodist, Winson**
Name None
Erected Before 1800
Building No, a part of a dwelling house. No [not exclusively as a place of worship]
Sittings Free 40. Other none. Total [40] Standing room for 10
Attend'ce 30 Mar. Afternoon 32. Total [32]
Avge attendance Afternoon 35. Total [35]
Dated 31 March 1851
Signed William Sparrow, manager
Winson, Glouc'shire, near Northleach

341.2.2 Parish of Coln Rogers
Area 1,508 acres; 27 inhabited houses. Population 156.
VCH 9, 21–30

13.18 (19) **Church of England, St Andrew, Coln Rogers**
Name St Andrew's church. Ancient parish church of a distinct and separate parish
Consecration Before 1800
Erected [Restored 1844–5 and 1888–92]

Endowment	Tithe £248. Glebe £28. {Total £225}
Sittings	Free 110. Other for children 28. Total 138
Attend'ce 30 Mar.	Morning 38 + 12 SS. Total 50
	Afternoon 48 + 22 SS. Total 70
Avge attendance	[Not given]
Remarks	The average net income of the benefice for the last ten years is £190.
Dated	31 March 1851
Signed	Henry Brookes Forster, rector [1841–79]
	Andoversford, near Cheltenham

13.19 (20)   Baptist and Independent, Coln Rogers

Name	Coln Rogers Chapel
Erected	About the year 1820
Building	Yes [separate and entire] Yes [exclusively as a place of worship]
Sittings	Free 100. Other none. Total [100]
Attend'ce 30 Mar.	Evening 91. Total 91
Avge attendance	Evening 100. Total 100
Remarks	This place of worship is supplied on alternate Sunday evenings by the Baptist minister of Arlington (**13.15**) and the Independent minister of Chedworth (**13.22**).
Dated	30 March 1851
Signed	Richard Hall, minister
	Arlington, nr Fairford, Gloucestershire

[Richard Hall was also the minister of Arlington (**13.15**). The place of worship may well have been a barn: *VCH* 9, 30.]

341.2.3 Parish of Coln St Denys

Area 2,430 acres; 44 inhabited houses. Population 229.
VCH 8, 28–34

13.20 (21)   Church of England, St James the Great, Coln St Denys

Name	The parish church
Consecration	A very ancient church, consecrated long before 1800
Erected	[Restored 1848 and 1891–2, and the tower rebuilt 1904–5]
Endowment	Tithe £295. Glebe £100. {Total £450}
Sittings	All free [150] Total 150
Attend'ce 30 Mar.	Morning 35 + 35 SS. Total 70
	Afternoon 57 + 35 SS. Total 92
Avge attendance	Morning 50 + 35 SS. Total 85
	Afternoon 100 + 35 SS. Total 135
Remarks	Sunday, 30 March, the weather being very wet and stormy the congregations were unusually small.
Dated	31 March 1851
Signed	William Price, rector [1810–60]
	Coln St Denis, Northleach, Gloucestershire.

[Price was also the incumbent of Farnborough, Hants., 1815–60, where the curate was his son William Henry Price.]

341.2.4 Parish of Chedworth

Area 4,689 acres; 224 inhabited houses, 17 uninhabited. Population 963.
In 20 years the population had declined by 63.
VCH 7, 163–74

13.21 (22)	**Church of England, St Andrew, Chedworth**
Name	Chedworth. Ancient parish church
Consecration	From dates engraven on the walls, it seems to have been built in the 15th century.
Erected	Probably by the Neville family of Warwick who held the manor for many centuries and lost it in H[enry] VII's reign. [Restored and enlarged 1882–3]
Endowment	Tithe rent charge£275. Glebe £100. Fees £3. Dues (pension) £1 6s 8d. {Total £302}
Sittings	Free 268. Other 143. Total 411*
Attend'ce 30 Mar.	Morning 77 + 64 SS. Total 141
	Afternoon 185 + 59 SS. Total 244
Avge attendance	[Not given]
Remarks	*18 inches for each person. I have measured the seats three times, with a slightly different result each time. Say 411 more or less.
Dated	31 March 1851
Signed	Arthur Gibson, vicar [1828–78]
	Chedworth, near Andoversford

Further remarks (**13.21a**).

Church

The sums set down in answer to section V (how endowed) represent the gross value of the living of Chedworth. There are serious deductions. The chief deduction being for rates (gross and high vary) and income amount to about £40 a year on the average.

School

The difference between the number in the books and the actual attendance, is accounted for very imperfectly, thus that the absentees are employed in some agricultural work or others for which they earn a few pence per day from 4d to 7d according to their ages. They begin to be on the something seven years of age, and in large families, the children are such employed, bring in more than their father. [E.g.] Williams, labourer has three sons who attend school on Sundays, but not on week days now, though two of them did attend in entire. They earn as under:

The youngest, aged seven, 4d a day.

The next, aged nine, 5d

The oldest, aged eleven to twelve, 7d

This is 8s a week, and I suppose on the pattern varies to be no more than 7s; for 8s is high and exceptional this winter.

Public worship

The numbers stated as in church yesterday in answer to question VII [on attendance] are actual and careful numeration. The congregation was below average, by reason of weather and influenza, but I cannot say what the average attendance is. In good weather the church is nearly full in the afternoon.

13.22 (24)	**Independent, Pancake Hill, Lower Chedworth**
Name	Chedworth Independent Chapel
Erected	1804 [Tablet: 'Erected AD 1752 and re-erected AD 1804']
Building	Yes [separate and entire] No (used for a day school)
Sittings	Free 116. Other 106. Total [222]
Attend'ce 30 Mar.	Morning 76 + 50 SS. Total 126
	Afternoon 139 + 56 SS. Total 195
	Evening 70. Total 70

Avge attendance   Morning 80 + 50 SS. Total 130
                     Afternoon 150 + 56 SS. Total 206
                     Evening 80. Total 80
Remarks   The consequence of the unfavourable weather on the 30th the attendance
                     being less than usual, the average number of attendants during twelve
                     months is stated.
Dated   31 March 1851
Signed   Joseph Stratford, minister [1847–52]
                     Chedworth, Andoversford, Gloucestershire
[Stratford was also the minister of Upper End chapel, Chedworth (**13.23**), and officiated at evening
services at Coln Rogers (**13.19**).]

13.23 (23)   Independent, Upper End, Chedworth
Name   None
Erected   First used for public religious worship 1847
Building   No [not separate and entire] No [not exclusively as a place of worship]
Sittings   Free 10. Other 50. Total 60. Standing room for 65
Attend'ce 30 Mar. Evening 75. Total [75]
Avge attendance (6m) Evening 70. Total [70]
Dated   31 March 1851
Signed   Joseph Stratford, minister [1847–52]
                    Chedworth, Andoversford, Gloucestershire
[Stratford was also the minister of Lower Chedworth chapel (**13.22**).]

341.2.5 Parish of Compton Abdale
Area 2,215 acres; 52 inhabited houses, 2 uninhabited. Population 256.
VCH 9, 31–41

13.24 (25)   Church of England, St Oswald, Compton Abdale
Name   Compton Abdale parish church
Consecration   [Not given]
Erected   [Restored 1883 and 1904–5]
Endowment   Land £80. {Total £81}
Sittings   Free 25. Total 25
Attend'ce 30 Mar. Afternoon 55 + 10 SS. Total 65
Avge attendance Morning 30 + 10 SS. Total 40
                   Afternoon 60 + 12 SS. Total 72
Dated   30 March 1851
Signed   Edward William Garrow, perpetual curate [1847–67]
                   Compton Abdale, Northleach, Gloucestershire
[On the day of the Census Garrow conducted services at Sevenhampton (**13.32**). One of his
successors at Compton Abdale, Edmund Lowndes (who had previously served eight curacies
between 1917–37) 'was in dispute with his parishioners for much of his incumbency', so alternative
services were held in a barn and were conducted by a [lay] Reader from Cheltenham: *VCH* 9, 40.]

13.25 (27)   Particular Baptist, Compton Abdale
Name   Compton Baptist Chapel
Erected   1830
Building   Yes [separate and entire] For religious worship only
Sittings   Free 90. Total [90]
Attend'ce 30 Mar. Afternoon 24. Total [24]
                   Evening 51. Total [51]

Avge attendance Afternoon 35. Total [35]
  Evening 50. Total [50]
Dated 31 March 1851
Signed Jacob Short, deacon
  25 Exmouth St, Cheltenham, Gloucestershire
[Short was also deacon of Foxcote (**13.28**) and Shipton Oliffe (**13.37**).]

13.26 (26) **Church of Jesus Christ of Latter-day Saints, Compton Abdale**
Name None
Erected 1841
Building [A] dwelling house. No [not exclusively as a place of worship]
Sittings Free 50. Total [50]
Attend'ce 30 Mar. Afternoon 28. Total } Total 68
  Evening 40. Total }
Avge attendance Afternoon 28. Total } Total 40 [*sic*]
  Evening 32. Total }
Dated [Not given]
Signed Henry Lovesy, elder [agricultural labourer]
  Compton Abdale

341.2.6 Parish of Withington
Area 5,830 acres; 165 inhabited houses, 7 uninhabited. Population 823.
VCH 9, 248–79

13.27 (28) **Church of England, St Michael, Withington**
Name Parish church
Consecration Before 1800
Erected [Restored 1871–3]
Endowment Glebe [of over 1,000 acres] £591. {Total £686} [During the agricultural depression of 1897, glebe income fell to £288 [*VCH* 9, 271]
Sittings Free 150. Other 150. Total 300
Attend'ce 30 Mar. Morning 200 + 70 SS. Total 270
  Afternoon 200 + 70 SS. Total 270
Avge attendance Morning 200 + 70 SS. Total 270
  Afternoon 200 + 70 SS. Total 270
Dated 31 [March] 1851
Signed [Hon.] George Gustavus Chetwynd Talbot, rector [1834–96]
  Withington, Andoversford
[The incumbent was the fifth son of the Earl of Shrewsbury. 'The interior is disappointing, scraped and largely spoiled during the restoration in 1871–3': (Verey and Brooks, 740).]

13.28 (30) **Particular Baptist, Foxcote**
Name 'Foxcoatte' Chapel
Erected In the year 1831
Building Yes [separate and entire] Yes [exclusively as a place of worship]
Sittings Free 110. Total [110]
Attend'ce 30 Mar. Afternoon 60. Total [60]
  Evening 62. Total [62]
Avge attendance Morning 55 SS. Total [55]
  Afternoon 45. Total [45]
  Evening 60. Total [60]
Dated 31 March 1851

Signed   Jacob Short, deacon
                  25 Exmouth St, Cheltenham
[Short was also deacon of Compton Abdale (**13.25**) and Shipton Oliffe (**13.37**).]

13.29 (29)   Wesleyan Methodist, Brockwell End
Name   Ebenezer Chapel
Erected   1841 [Enlarged in 1848]
Building   Yes [separate and entire] Yes [exclusively as a place of worship]
Sittings   Free 80. Other 40. Total [120]
Attend'ce 30 Mar. Afternoon 32 + 16 SS. Total 48
                  Evening 80. Total 80
Avge attendance [Not given]
Remarks   We have supplied preaching regularly for about 25 years previous to the
                  erection of the chapel.
Dated   31 May 1851
Signed   William Henry Cornforth, minister [1849–51]
                  22 Gt Norwood Street, Cheltenham
[Cornforth was also minister of Charlton Kings (**16.4**), Cheltenham (**16.31, 33**), Golden Valley
(**16.32**), Arle (**16.34**), Northleach (**13.11**) and Turkdean (**13.45**).]

341.2.7 Parish of Dowdeswell
Area 2,246 acres; 49 inhabited houses, 2 uninhabited. Population 304.
The parish includes the village of Andoversford.
VCH 9, 43–69

13.30 (31)   Church of England, St Michael and All Angels, Dowdeswell
Name   Dowdeswell Church. An ancient parish church
Consecration   Before 1800
Erected   [Restored c.1840]
Endowment   Glebe £41. Fees given away. Easter offerings £1. {Total £402}
Sittings   Free 134. Other 70. Total 204
Attend'ce 30 Mar. Morning abt 60 + 30 SS. Total 90
                  Afternoon abt 150 + 25 SS. Total 175
Avge attendance Morning 65 + 30 SS. Total 95
                  Afternoon 175 + 25 SS. Total 200
Remarks   30 March, being very stormy in afternoon reduced the afternoon
                  congregation below the usual average.
Dated   William Rogers Coxwell, curate or minister [1834–54, then incumbent
                  1854–94]
                  Whithorn House, Charlton Kings, Gloucestershire
[*Incumbent*   Charles Coxwell 1826–54]
[Coxwell was brother-in-law of Hester Rogers, the lady of the manor. In 1854 he assumed the name
Coxwell-Rogers; he was succeeded by his son William 1845–94 and grandson Richard 1894–1908.]

341.2.8 Parish of Whittington
Area 1,422 acres; 47 inhabited houses. Population 233.
VCH 9, 233–48

13.31 (32)   Church of England, St Bartholomew, Whittington
Name   Known as Whittington church. An ancient parish church for centuries
                  exterior that formed the church of an ancient chapelry, I apprehend.
Consecration   Before 1800
Erected   [Restored 1872]

Endowment	Tithe £276 10s. Glebe £61. OPE none. Pew rents none. Fees £1. Other sources none. {Total £279}
Sittings	Free 47. Other 78. Total 125
Attend'ce 30 Mar.	Morning 45 + 13 SS. Total 58
	Afternoon 44 + 7 SS. Total 51
Avge attendance	[Not given]
Dated	30 March 1851
Signed	Thomas Charles Griffith, minister [1846–66]
	Whittington rectory, Cheltenham
[*Incumbent*	William Hicks 1811–66]

[Hicks was also incumbent of Coberley (**16.7**), where he lived.]

341.2.9 Parish of Sevenhampton

Area 2,600 acres; 107 inhabited houses, 10 uninhabited. Population 553.
VCH 9, 166–87

13.32 (33)   Church of England, St Andrew, Sevenhampton

Name	Parish church of Sevenhampton
Consecration	[Not given]
Erected	[Restored 1892–3]
Endowment	Land etc. £58. {Total £49}
Sittings	Free 56. Other 25. Total 81*
Attend'ce 30 Mar.	Morning 38 + 21 SS. Total 59
Avge attendance	Morning 40 + 40 SS. Total 80
	Afternoon 90 + 40 SS. Total 130
Remarks	*There are also open seats in the church for the accommodation of upwards of 50 persons.
Dated	30 March 1851
Signed	Edward William Garrow, off[iciating] minister
	Sevenhampton, Andoversford
[*Incumbent*	Edward Ellerton 1825–51]

[Garrow was the incumbent of Compton Abdale (**13.24**). Ellerton was also the incumbent of Theale, Berks. 1831–51.]

13.33 (35)   Baptist, Brockhampton

Name	Salem
Erected	1850
Building	Separate [and entire] Yes, exclusively [as a place of worship]
Sittings	Free 120. Other none. Total [120]
Attend'ce 30 Mar.	Morning no service
	Afternoon 36. Total [36]
	Evening 80. Total [80]
Avge attend'ce (10m)	Morning none
	Afternoon 45. Total 45
	Evening 100. Total 100
Remarks	About to form a Sabbath school
Dated	30 March 1851
Signed	John Lewis, local preacher [commercial clerk]
	2 Carlton Street, Cheltenham

13.34 (34)   **Particular Baptist, Brockhampton Quarry**

Name	[Bethel]
Erected	1834
Building	Yes [separate and entire] Yes [exclusively as a place of worship]
Sittings	All free 50. Other none. Total [50] Standing room for 250
Attend'ce 30 Mar.	Afternoon 28. Total [28]
	Evening 40. Total [40]
Avge attendance	Morning 43. Total [43]
Dated	30 March 1851
Signed	Richard Margells, minister [carpenter]
	Withington, Glo'stershire

341.2.10 Parish of Shipton Sollars (alternative spelling Shipton Solers).
Area 1,160 acres; 19 inhabited houses. Population 96.
VCH 9, 187–208

13.35 (36)   **Church of England, St Mary, Shipton Sollars**

Name	Shipton Sollars church. Ancient parish church
Consecration	Before 1800
Erected	[Restored 1884–5 and 1929–30]
Endowment	Land and farm £400. Glebe £8. Fees a few shillings for christenings and marriages. [See Shipton Oliffe (**13.36**)]
Sittings	All free 50. Other 12. Total 62
Attend'ce 30 Mar.	[Not given]
Avge attendance	Morning prayers occasionally in summer 20. Total [20]
Remarks	Shipton Sollars parish is united to Shipton Oliffe parish, and the population of the parish attends Shipton Oliffe church, which affords better accommodation. Christenings, burials and marriages all performed in the Shipton Oliffe church.
Dated	31 March 1851
Signed	William Peachy Mellersh, curate [1837–62]
	Shipton rectory, Andoversford, Gloucestershire
[*Incumbent*	Lawrence William Eliot 1817–62]

[Mellersh was also the incumbent of Salperton (**13.38**), where he lived. Eliot was also the incumbent of Peper Harow, Surrey 1801–62, where he lived. The benefice (united in 1776) consisted of Shipton Oliffe (**13.36**) with Shipton Sollars and the civil parishes were united in 1871. Soon after 1851 services ceased at Shipton Sollars and by 1883 the church was used as a cattle shed. In 1884 the new incumbent Charles Pugh reopened it for services. After again falling into disrepair, the church was restored 1929–30 and reopened for worship. Since declared redundant, it is now under the care of the Churches Conservation Trust.]

341.2.11 Parish of Shipton Oliffe
Area 1,050 acres; 49 inhabited houses, 4 uninhabited. Population 241.
VCH 9, 187–208

13.36 (38)   **Church of England, St Oswald, Shipton Oliffe**

Name	Shipton Oliffe church. Ancient parish church
Consecration	Before 1800
Erected	[Restored 1903–4]
Endowment	Land and farm at Shipton Sollars £400. Glebe £8. Fees a few shillings for christenings and marriages. {Total £430}
Sittings	Free 92. Other 120. Total 212

Attend'ce 30 Mar. Morning 64 + 25 SS. Total 89
Avge attendance (3m) Morning 70 + 25 SS. Total 95
                     Afternoon 130 + 25 SS. Total 155
Remarks   Shipton Oliffe parish and Shipton Sollars parish all consolidated. It is a
                     discharged rectory. In winter, morning and afternoon services altern-
                     ately. In summer two services alternately.
Dated   31 March 1851
Signed   William Peachy Mellersh, curate [1837–62]
                     Shipton rectory, Andoversford, Gloucestershire
[*Incumbent*   Lawrence William Eliot 1817–62]
[See note at precding entry.]

13.37 (37)   Strict Baptist, Shipton Oliffe
Name   No none
Erected   [Not given]
Building   Dwelling house. No [not exclusively as a place of worship]
Sittings   Free 35. Total [35]
Attend'ce 30 Mar. Morning 19. Total [19]
                  Evening 28. Total [28]
Avge attendance Morning 16. Total [16]
                  Evening 30. Total [30]
Dated   31 March 1851
Signed   Jacob Short, deacon
                  25 Exmouth St, Cheltenham, Glo'shire
[Short was also the deacon of Compton Abdale (**13.25**) and Foxcote (**13.28**).]

341.2.12   Parish of Salperton
Area 1,210 acres; 38 inhabited houses. Population 145.
VCH 9, 155–66; *GNQ* 5, 190

13.38 (39)   Church of England, All Saints, Salperton
Name   All Saints, Salperton church. Ancient parish church
Consecration   Before 1800
Erected   [Restored 1885–6]
Endowment   Land £79 7s 6d. OPE from patron £8. Queen Anne's Bounty £13
                  [Total] £100 7s 6d. {Total £107}
Sittings   Free 28. Other 94. Total 122
Attend'ce 30 Mar. Morning 35 + 17 SS. Total 52
                  Afternoon 70 + 17 SS. Total 87
Avge attendance Morning 45 + 17 SS. Total 62
                  Afternoon 80 + 17 SS. Total 97
Remarks   Morning and afternoon services alternately throughout the entire year.
                  No parsonage house in the parish.
Dated   [Not given]
Signed   William Peachy Mellersh, curate [i.e. the incumbent, 1840–84]
                  Shipton rectory, Andoversford, Gloucestershire
[Mellersh was also curate of the Shiptons (**13.35**, **36**).]

341.2.13–14   Parish of Hazleton
Area 2,530 acres; 64 inhabited houses, 2 uninhabited. Population 278.
The parish includes the chapelry of Yanworth.
VCH 9, 91–106

13.39 (40)   Church of England, St Andrew, Hazleton

Name	'Haselton' church. Ancient parish church
Consecration	[Not given]
Erected	Before 1800 [Restored and enlarged 1864–6]
Endowment	Land £240. {Total £383}
Sittings	Free 19. Other 5. Total 24
Attend'ce 30 Mar.	Morning 60 + 40 SS. Total 100
Avge attendance	Morning 60 + 40 SS. Total 100
	Afternoon 80 + 40 SS. Total 120
Remarks	Only one service, each Sunday, morning and afternoon alternately.
Dated	30 March 1851
Signed	Charles Edward Dighton, curate
	'Haselton', Northleach
[*Incumbent*	Henry Prowse Jones 1840–60]

[The benefice consisted of Haselton with Yanworth (**13.40**). Jones was also the incumbent of Edgeworth (**12.3**).]

13.40 (41)   Church of England, St Michael, Yanworth

Name	Yanworth Church
Consecration	Before 1800
Erected	[Restored 1899]
Endowment	Tithe £250 [See Haselton (**13.39**)]
Sittings	Free 25. Other 5. Total 30
Attend'ce 30 Mar.	Afternoon 50 + 18 SS. Total 68
Avge attendance	Morning 40 + 18 SS. Total 58
	Afternoon 60 + 18 SS. Total 78
Dated	30 March 1851
Signed	Charles Edward Dighton, curate
	Hasleton, Northleach
[*Incumbent*	Henry Prowse Jones 1840–60]

[See note at preceding entry]

341.2.15 Parish of Stowell

Area 823 acres; 6 inhabited houses. Population 28.
VCH 9, 208–17

13.41a (42)   Church of England, St Leonard, Stowell

Name	Is generally known by the name of Stowell chapel. Church of an ancient chapelry, united to Hampnett for nearly 200 years.
Consecration	Before 1800
Erected	[Restored 1898–9]
Endowment	Land none. By tithe. Glebe and OPE none. Pew rents none. Fees for marriages. Dues, Easter offerings and other sources none. [See Hampnett (**13.42**)]
Sittings	Free 16. Other 12. Total 28
Attend'ce 30 Mar.	Morning 8. Total 8
	Afternoon no service
	Evening no service
	We have no children or school. [The few children in the parish attended the Sunday school and National School at Hampnett]
Avge attendance	Morning 11. Total 11
	Afternoon 15. Total 15

	Evening no service
Dated	31 March 1851
Signed	Richard Gable Councer, chapel warden [farmer of 1,100 acres]
	Stowell Park, Northleach, Glo'shire
[*Incumbent*	Edward Andrew Daubeny 1819–71]

[The benefice consisted of Hampnett (**13.42**) and Stowell. Daubeny was also incumbent of Ampney St Peter (**12.51**) (where he lived) and Ampney Crucis (**12.50**). The congregation consisted of the family and servants of Stowell; and from 1782 to 1880 the farmhouse of a large farm, occupied by tenants (one of whom was Councer); house remodelled as a country seat 1885–90.]

13.41b (43)   **Church of England, St Leonard, Stowell**

Name	Stowell chapel. Annexed to Hampnett, I believe, in 1660, but whether a separate parish or not, previously, I do not know.
Consecration	Before 1800
Erected	[Restored 1898–9]
Endowment	Tithe. Fees [for] marriages
Sittings	Free 16. Other 12. Total 28
Attend'ce 30 Mar.	Morning 8. Total 8
	Afternoon no service
	Evening no service
	No children in the parish
Avge attendance	Morning 11. Total 11
	Afternoon 15. Total 15
	Evening no service
	No school or children in the parish
Remarks	This chapel is little more than a private place of worship for one farmer and his servants. The farm house was once a noble mansion. A service alternately in the morning and afternoon. It is, however, called a distinct parish, but they bury at Hampnett.
Dated	30 March 1851
Signed	Richard Rice, curate [1849–56]
	Hampnett, Northleach

[Rice was the curate of Hampnett (**13.42**) and Stowell and the second master of Northleach Grammar School 1849–68; he lived at Hampnett rectory.]

341.2.16   Parish of Hampnett

Area 1,406 acres; 31 inhabited houses. Population 211.
Within the parish was the Northleach House of Correction (**13.43**).
VCH 9, 81–91

13.42 (44)   **Church of England, St George, Hampnett**

Name	Hampnett church. An ancient parish church
Consecration	Before 1800
Erected	[Restored 1868]
Endowment	By land. By tithe. By glebe. Fees marriages etc. Easter offerings 4d per cottage. {Total £475}
Sittings	Free 44. Other 30. Total 74
Attend'ce 30 Mar.	Morning no service
	Afternoon 53 + 17 SS. Total 70
	Evening no service
Avge attendance	Morning 26 + 18 SS. Total 44
	Afternoon 53 or thereabouts + 18 SS. Total 71

Remarks	The service is alternately w[ith] Stowell, in the morning and afternoon. In the summer there is an evening service, when the church is attended by more people than there are sittings.
Dated	30 March 1851
Signed	Richard Rice, curate [1849–56]
	Hampnett, Northleach
[*Incumbent*	Edward Andrew Daubeny 1819–71]

[The benefice consisted of Hampnett and Stowell (**13.41**). Daubeny was also incumbent of Ampney St Peter (**12.51**) (where he lived) and Ampney Crucis (**12.50**). Rice was curate of Hampnett and Stowell (**13.41**) and second master of Northleach Grammar School 1849–68; he lived at Hampnett rectory.]

13.43 (341.1.9)   Church of England, House of Correction, Northleach

Name	Northleach House of Correction in Hampnett parish
Erected	[1792, courtroom erected 1834]
Sittings	Pews, seats and forms all free
Attend'ce 30 Mar.	Morning 66. Total [66]
	Afternoon 66. Total [66]
Avge attendance	Morning 57. Total [57]
	Afternoon 57. Total [57]
Remarks	There is no chapel as a distinct building from this House of Correction. What is used as a place for celebrating divine worship is a large room, neither consecrated nor licensed by the bishop of the diocese, fitted up with a pulpit only, containing two pews for the governor [Christopher Reeves] and matron, three seats for the turnkeys and fixed forms for the prisoners.
Dated	31 March 1851
Signed	Charles Thorp, chaplain [1847–55]
	Northleach, Gloucestershire

[In 1851 Northleach housed 68 male prisoners (aged from 10 to 50), mostly agricultural labourers and errand boys. Now the Cotswold Heritage Centre. Other Houses of Correction at this time were at Horsley, Littledean, and Lawford's Gate, Bristol.]

341.2.17   Parish of Turkdean

Area 1,890 acres; 58 inhabited houses, 4 uninhabited. Population 278.
VCH 9, 217–33; *GNQ* 10, 33–42

13.44 (45)   Church of England, All Saints, Turkdean

Name	Ancient parish church. Dedicated to All Saints
Consecration	Before 1800
Erected	[Restored 1839, 1859 and 1897]
Endowment	{Total £208}
Sittings	Free 92. School children 48. Other 78. Total 218
Attend'ce 30 Mar.	[Not given]
Avge attendance	[Not given]
Dated	31 March 1851
Signed	Frederick Biscoe, vicar [1837–80]
	Turkdean vicarage, Northleach

['In the 1850s parts of the church's fabric and fittings were described as unecclesiastical and unsightly': *VCH* 9, 232.]

13.45 (46)   Wesleyan Methodist, Turkdean

Name	None
Erected	Not known

Building	No [not separate and entire] No [not exclusively as a place of worship. A house was used for worship]
Sittings	Free 60. Total [60]
Attend'ce 30 Mar.	Afternoon 32 + 13 SS. Total 45
	Evening 34. Total 34
Avge attendance	[Not given]
Remarks	We have regularly supplied teaching from 1836.
Dated	31 March 1851
Signed	William Henry Cornforth, minister [1849–51]
	22 Gt Norwood Street, Cheltenham

[Cornforth was also the minister of Charlton Kings (**16.4**), Cheltenham (**16.31, 33**), Golden Valley (**16.32**), Arle (**16.34**), Northleach (**13.11**) and Withington (**13.29**).]

341.2.18 Parish of Cold Aston (or Aston Blank)
Area 2,250 acres; 64 inhabited houses, 2 uninhabited. Population 310.
VCH 9, 9–20

13.46 (47)	**Church of England, St Andrew, Cold Aston**
Name	St Andrew. An ancient parish church
Consecration	Before 1800
Erected	[Restored 1875–6]
Endowment	Land £24. Tithe £18 17s. Glebe £156. {Total £186}
Sittings	Total 180
Attend'ce 30 Mar.	Morning 45 + 85 SS. Total [130]
	Afternoon 100 + 140 SS. Total [240]
	Evening 100. Total [100]
Avge attendance	[Not given]
Dated	31 March 1851
Signed	Thomas Townsend, vicar [1845–88]
	Aston Blank, Stow-on-the-Wold

[From 1972 the name of the parish reverted to the medieval usage, Cold Aston.]

13.47 (48)	**Particular Baptist, Cold Aston**
Name	Cold Aston Baptist Chapel
Erected	About 1840
Building	Yes [separate and entire] Yes [exclusively as a place of worship]
Sittings	All free 90. Total [90]
Attend'ce 30 Mar.	Morning none
	Afternoon none
	Evening 50. Total [50]
Avge attendance	Evening from 60 to 80. Total [60–80] SS none
Remarks	It is supplied by local preachers from the Baptist church at Bourton on the Water (**14.8**). All seats are free. No Sunday school is connected with us. Service only in the evening.
Dated	31 March 1851
Signed	Rev John Statham, superintendent minister [1849–55]
	Bourton-on-the-Water, Gloucestershire

[Statham was also the minister of Bourton-on-the-Water (**14.8**), Clapton (**14.2**), Little Rissington (**14.6**) and Lower Slaughter (**14.15**).]

14. HO 129/342 STOW-ON-THE-WOLD DISTRICT: 38 places of worship

342. 1 BOURTON-ON-THE-WATER SUB-DISTRICT

342.1.1 Parish of Clapton-on-the-Hill
Area 783 acres; 26 inhabited houses. Population 112.
VCH 6, 59–63

14.1 (1)   **Church of England, St James, Clapton-on-the-Hill**
(Summary form)
Name   Not known
Erected   Not known [Restored 1670 and 1951–2]
[Endowment   See Bourton-on-the-Water (**14.7**)]
Sittings   About 100
Usual attend'ce   Morning sometimes 30 + about 15 SS. Total [45]
                    Afternoon sometimes 40 or more. Total [40]
                    Evening service alternate morning ... .
Signed   Thomas Boggis, curate [1848–55]
[Incumbent   Robert Waller 1836–71]
[Boggis was an active Freemason: Venn. The benefice consisted of Bourton-on-the-Water (**14.7**) with Lower Slaughter (**14.14**) and Clapton-on-the-Hill. In 1736 Holy Communion was administered once a year and by 1825 three times a year: *VCH* 6, 62.]

14.2 (2)   **Particular Baptist, Clapton-on-the-Hill**
Name   The cottage occupied by John Gladwin
Erected   [1797 and replaced by a new chapel in 1908]
Building   A cottage licensed for worship. No, a dwelling house [not exclusively
                    as a place of worship]
Sittings   About 50 seats. Total [50]
Attend'ce 30 Mar. Morning none
                    Evening 40. Total [40]
Avge attendance   Evening 38. Total [38]
Dated   31 March 1851
Signed   John Statham, superintendent minister [1849–52]
                    Bourton on the Water
[Statham was also the minister of Bourton-on-the-Water (**14.8**), Cold Aston (**13.47**), Little Rissington (**14.6**) and Lower Slaughter (**14.15**).]

342.1.2 Parish of Great Barrington [part transferred from Berkshire, 1844]
Area 2,983 acres; 108 inhabited houses, 1 uninhabited. Population 545.
VCH 6, 16–27.

14.3 (3)   **Church of England, St Mary, Great Barrington**
Name   The ancient parish church
Consecration   Before 1800
Erected   [Restored 1880]
Endowment   {Total £221}
Sittings   Free 220. Other 148. Total 368
Attend'ce 30 Mar. [Not given]
Avge attendance   [Not given]

Dated	30 August 1851
Signed	Thomas Lewes, vicar [1820–73]
	Taynton, Burford, Oxfordshire

[Lewes was also the incumbent of Taynton, Oxon. 1819–73, where he lived.]

342.1.3 Parish of Great Rissington

Area 2,420 acres; 102 inhabited houses, 2 uninhabited. Population 493.
VCH 6, 98–106

14.4 (4)   Church of England, St John the Baptist, Great Rissington
(Summary form)

Name	Not known
Erected	An Norman structure [Rebuilt 1873]
[*Endowment*	Total £647]
Sittings	Free 300. Other about 50. Total 350
Usual attend'ce	Morning 200 + 40 SS. Total [240]
	Afternoon 300. Total [300]
Signed	William Gunter Williams, curate
[*Incumbent*	Edward Rice 1810–56]

[Rice was also dean of Gloucester 1825–62 and from 1802 precentor of York Minster. At Great Rissington he was succeeded by his son, the hon. Henry Rice 1856–96. Another son, Francis William, was the incumbent of Fairfird (**12.60**): Verey 1908, 83]

342.1.4 Parish of Little Rissington

Area 1,300 acres; 57 inhabited houses, 3 uninhabited. Population 279.
VCH 6, 106–13

14.5 (6)   Church of England, St Peter, Little Rissington

Name	Little Rissington parish church
Consecration	Built, repaired and consecrated for seven centuries, probably
Erected	Unknown, but enlarged, restored and beautified by Mr [John] Bennett, 1850. [Restored 1845–50 and 1882–3]
Endowment	Land £100. Tithe £10. Glebe £100. Fees 5s. {Total £294}
Sittings	Free 100. Other 59. School room 90. Total 249
Attend'ce 30 Mar.	Morning 62 + 70 SS. Total 132
	Afternoon 98 + 70 SS. Total 168
Avge attendance	Morning 56 + 70 SS. Total 126
	Afternoon 108 + 70 SS. Total 178
Remarks	It is impossible to place any value on the land – tenants can't pay their rent.
Dated	31 March 1851
Signed	Richard Wilbraham Ford, rector [1811–62]
	Little Rissington, Burford, Oxfordshire

[Ford was also the incumbent of South Cerney (**12.33**) with Cerney Wick (**12.34**) and of Stourpaine, Dorset 1810–54. At a confirmation service in 1850 there were 163 candidates (78 males and 85 females): GA, A2/5.]

14.6 (7)   Particular Baptist, Little Rissington

Name	Baptist Chapel
Erected	About 1800
Building	Yes [separate and entire] Yes [exclusively as a place of worship]
Sittings	Free 90. Other none
Attend'ce 30 Mar.	Morning SS none
	Evening 40. Total [40]

Avge attendance Morning SS none
          Evening 38. Total [38]
Dated   31 March 1851
Signed   John Statham, superintending minister [1849–55]
          Bourton on the Water

[Statham was also the minister of Bourton-on-the-Water (**14.8**), Clapton (**14.2**), Cold Aston (**13.47**) and Lower Slaughter (**14.15**).]

342.1.5 Parish of Bourton-on-the-Water
Area 2,282 acres; 213 inhabited houses, 10 uninhabited. Population 1,040.
VCH 6, 33–49. *GNQ* 5, 513–5.

14.7 (8)   Church of England, St Lawrence, Bourton-on-the-Water
Name   Ancient parish, the church dedicated to St Lawrence
Consecration   Before 1800
Erected   [Rebuilt nave and tower 1784; restoration 1872–8; rebuilt nave 1889–91]
Endowment   Net income according to former lettings £450. {Total £475}
Sittings   All free and other. Total nearly 400
Attend'ce 30 Mar. [Not given]
Avge attendance   [Not given]
Remarks   I cannot give an average. The church is generally well attended in the
            afternoon.
Dated   31 March 1851
Signed   Robert Waller, rector [1836–71]
            Bourton on the Water, 'Stow in the Wold'

[The benefice consisted of Bourton-on-the-Water with Lower Slaughter (**14.14**) and Clapton-on-the-Hill (**14.1**).]

14.8 (9)   Particular Baptist, Bourton-on-the-Water
Name   Baptist Chapel
Erected   Before 1800 [Built 1701, enlarged 1748, rebuilt and reopened August
            1765. Replaced in by a new chapel on another site opened in 1876]
Building   Yes [separate and entire] Yes [exclusively as a place of worship]
Sittings   Free 190. Other 325. Total [515] Standing room only [in] the aisles
Attend'ce 30 Mar. Morning 266 + 87 SS. Total 353
            Evening 450. Total 450
Avge attendance   About the same as above
Dated   31 March 1851
Signed   John Statham, minister [1849–55]
            Bourton on the Water

[Statham was also the minister of Clapton (**14.2**), Cold Aston (**13.47**), Little Rissington (**14.6**) and Lower Slaughter (**14.15**). At Bourton-on-the-Water 'there is a handsome and commodious Baptist Chapel, which is well attended, a large proportion of the more wealthy inhabitants being dissenters': *Post Office Directory, 1856*, 232. 'Bourton has long had a strong tradition of religious nonconformity ... [and in the 17th century had] ... a far higher number of Protestant dissenters than anywhere else in the Stow deanery': *VCH* 6, 47. A former minister (1743–95) was the prolific hymn writer, scholar and preacher Benjamin Beddome, 'for many years one of the most respected Baptist ministers in the west of England': *ODNB* 'Benjamin Beddome (1717–1795).]

342.1.6 Parish of Notgrove
Area 1,530 acres; 40 inhabited houses. Population 195.
VCH 9, 145–55; *GNQ* 1, 365–9.

14.9a (10)   **Church of England, St Bartholomew, Notgrove**

Name	Parish church
Consecration	I suppose 900 or a 1,000 years ago
Erected	[Restored 1871–3]
Endowment*	Land £309 acres. Fees very trifling. Easter offerings perhaps £1
	{Total £256}
Sittings	Free 85. Other 15. Total 100
Attend'ce 30 Mar.	Morning 18 + 37 SS. Total 55
	Afternoon 50 + 35 SS. Total 85
Avge attendance (9m)	Morning 12 + 30 SS. Total 42
	Afternoon 50 + 30 SS. Total 80
Remarks	*The rector, the Rev Richard Wetherell, of Hawkhurst, Staplehurst, Kent, can best answer these questions. Many of the regular congregation were absent today in consequence of sickness, some are out visiting, it being mid-Lent Sunday, and others from various causes.
Dated	30 March 1851
Signed	Thomas Hill, curate [1828–53]
	Notgrove, Northleach
[*Incumbent*	Richard Wetherell 1810–58]

[Wetherell was also the incumbent of Westbury-on-Severn (**6.29**).]

14.9b (11)   **Church of England, St Bartholomew, Notgrove**

Name	Notgrove parish church
	Nearly the centre of the parish and at the end of the village
Consecration	900 or a 1,000 yrs ago
Erected	[Restored 1871–3]
Endowment*	£309 acres of land. Fees very trifling. Easter offerings perhaps £1
Sittings	Free 85. Other 15. Total 100
	These are independent of the forms used by the school children.
Attend'ce 30 Mar.	Morning 18 + 37 SS. Total 55
	Afternoon 50 + 35 SS. Total 85
Avge attendance	Morning 12 + 30 SS. Total 42
	Afternoon 50 + 30 SS. Total 80
Remarks	*The rector, the Rev Richard Wetherell, of Hawkhurst, Staplehurst, Kent, can best answer these questions. Many of the regular congregation were absent today in consequence of sickness, some out visiting, it being mid-Lent Sunday and others from various causes.
Dated	30 March 1851
Signed	Thomas Hill, curate [1828–53]
	Notgrove, Northleach

342.1.7   Parish of Naunton

Area 3,106 acres; 126 inhabited houses, 2 uninhabited. Population 568.
The parish includes the hamlet of Aylworth and the tithing of Harford.
VCH 6, 76–87

14.10 (12)   **Church of England, St Andrew, Naunton**

Name	The church of the parish of Naunton, Saint Andrew's, an ancient parish church
Consecration	Before 1800
Erected	[Nave and south porch rebuilt 1878. Restored 1899]

Endowment	Land £400. Tithe £100. Fees £1 10s. Easter offerings £1 5s 6d. {Total £504}
Sittings	Free 164. Other 152. Total 316
Attend'ce 30 Mar.	Morning 110 + 45 SS. Total 155
	Afternoon 125 + 41 SS. Total 166
Avge attendance	Morning 120 + 48 SS. Total 168
	Afternoon 135 + 43 SS. Total 178
Dated	31 March 1851
Signed	John Hurd, rector [1807–60]
	Naunton rectory, Stow-on-the-Wold

[Hurd was succeeded by the Evangelical theologian Edward Arthur Litton who was the vice-principal of St Edmund's Hall, Oxford 1851–54, incumbent of St Clement's, Oxford 1858–61 and rector of Naunton 1860–97: *ODNB* 'Edward Arthur Litton (1813–1897)'.]

14.11 (13)   Baptist, Naunton

Name	Naunton Chapel
Erected	[Opened 13 July 1800; rebuilt and opened 2 Aug.] 1850 [when 1,300 people were present]
Building	Yes [separate and entire] Yes [exclusively as a place of worship]
Sittings	Free 148. Other 152. Total [300] Standing room for 80 persons. Aisles and lobby are other space for standing.
Attend'ce 30 Mar.	Morning 210 (congregation) + 30 SS (children). Total 240
	Afternoon no service
	Evening 280 (no SS). Total 280
Avge attendance (8m)	Morning 220 + 30 SS. Total 250
	Afternoon no service
	Evening 260 (SS none). Total 260
Remarks	A former chapel was built in 1798 on land adjoining the new one: which chapel was taken down last year. Two vestries and a lecture room capable of accommodating 120 persons are attached to the chapel opening with folding doors, so as to admit of hearing the preacher if necessary.
Dated	31 March 1851
Signed	John Teall, Baptist minister
	Naunton, Stow-on-the-Wold, Gloucestershire

[Teall was also the minister of Lower Guiting (**15.8**). The two chapels had been united since 1828. During the years 1818–21 the Anglican seceder Thomas Snow (**16.23**) occasionally preached at Naunton. On 23 Sept. 1863 the Baptist leader Charles Spurgeon preached in a field near the chapel to a congregation of 2,000: *ODNB* 'Charles Haddon Spurgeon (1834–92)'.]

14.12 (14)   Wesleyan Methodist, Naunton Hill

Name	Naunton Hill
Erected	[Not given]
Building	No [not separate and entire] No [not exclusively as a place of worship]
Sittings	Free 30. Total [30]
Attend'ce 30 Mar.	Afternoon 20. Total [20]
Avge attendance	[Not given]
Dated	29 March 1851
Signed	Samuel Cooke, minister [1849–51]
	Chipping Norton, Oxfordshire

[Cooke was also minister of Bledington (**14.20**), Broadwell (**14.27**) and Stow-on-the-Wold (**14.32**).]

342.1.8 Parish of Eyford
Area 1,380 acres; 11 inhabited houses, 1 uninhabited. Population 48.
VCH 6, 72–6
[From the 16th century no church building existed.]

342.1.9 Parish of Upper Slaughter
Area 1,390 acres; 50 inhabited houses, 1 uninhabited. Population 218.
VCH 6, 134–42

14.13 (15)	**Church of England, St Peter, Upper Slaughter**
Name	Ancient parish church
Consecration	Before 1800
Erected	[Partial rebuilding 1822, and restored 1876–7]
Endowment	Land £203. Fees, dues and Easter offerings, small and uncertain. {Total £131}
Sittings	Free 110. Other 140. Total 250
Attend'ce 30 Mar.	Morning 47 + 20 SS. Total 67
	Afternoon 59 + 20 SS. Total 79
Avge attendance	[Not given]
Remarks	The general average of persons attending divine service exceeds the above return.
Dated	30 March 1851
Signed	Francis Edward Witts, rector [1808–54]
	Upper Slaughter, Stow-on-the-Wold

[The diarist Witts, who was also the incumbent of Stanway (**15.19**) and of East Lulworth, Dorset 1832–54, lived at Upper Slaughter. His son Edward Francis Witts was curate of Stanway 1839–54, then incumbent of Upper Slaughter 1854–86: Verey, 1980.]

342.1.10 Parish of Lower Slaughter
Area 1,140 acres; 48 inhabited houses, 3 uninhabited. Population 230.
VCH 6, 128–34

Request for information. Will you have the goodness to furnish the following information at your earliest convenience. Congregations including Sunday scholars.

14.14 (16)	**Church of England, St Mary, Lower Slaughter**
Name	Lower Slaughter Church
Erected	[Rebuilt 1866–7]
[*Endowment*	See Bourton-on-the-Water (**14.7**)]
Sittings	Sittings free. Gallery and 12 others
	Three large sittings private
Attendance	Service once daily (morning)
	Total 20, 30 and more attend services
	About 25 [S] scholars
[*Dated*	20 June 1852
Signed	William Wells, registrar of births and deaths
[*Incumbent*	Robert Waller 1836–71]

[The benefice consisted of Bourton-on-the-Water (**14.7**) with Lower Slaughter and Clapton-on-the-Hill (**14.1**).]

14.15 (17)	**Particular Baptist, Lower Slaughter**
Name	A licensed cottage occupied by William Bowl
Erected	[Not given]

Building	Cottage [separate and entire] Cottage [as a place of worship]
Sittings	Free 90. Total [90]
Attend'ce 30 Mar.	Afternoon 70. Total [70]
	Evening 74. Total [74]
Avge attendance	Afternoon 70. Total [70]
Dated	31 March 1851
Signed	John Statham, superintendent [1849–55]
	Bourton on the Water

[Statham was also the minister of Bourton-on-the-Water (**14.8**), Clapton (**14.2**), Cold Aston (**13.47**) and Little Rissington (**14.6**).]

342.1.11   Parish of Wyck Rissington
Area 1,140 acres; 43 inhabited houses. Population 219.
VCH 6, 114–20

14.16 (342.1.3)   **Church of England, St Lawrence, Wyck Rissington**

Name	St Peter's. Ancient parish church
Consecration	Unknown
Erected	Before 1800 [Enlarged 1822 and 1836; restored 1879]
Endowment	{Total £206}
Sittings	Free 40. Other 130. Total 170
Attend'ce 30 Mar.	Morning 50 + 31 SS. Total [81]
	Afternoon 50. Total [50]
Avge attendance	[Not given]
Dated	31 March 1851
Signed	William John Deane, curate [1849–52]
	Wyck Rissington, Stow-on-the-Wold, Gloucestershire
[*Incumbent*	George Leigh Cooke 1820–53]

[Cooke was a mathematician, the Sedleian Professor of Natural Philosophy at Oxford 1810–53 and also the incumbent of two Warwickshire parishes, Cubbington 1820–53 (where he lived) and Hunningham 1820–53. He was described as 'a zealous clergyman, a kind and benevolent landlord and an honourable gentleman': *ODNB* 'George Leigh Cooke (1779–1853)'. By the 17th century the church was known as St Peter's.]

342.1.12   Parish of Icomb [transferred from Worcestershire, 1844]
Area 970 acres; 34 inhabited houses. Population 140.
VCH (Worcs.) 3, 412–8; *GNQ* 1, 154–5; 3, 338–9

14.17 (18)   **Church of England, St Mary, Icomb**

Name	Icomb parish church. Church of England (ancient)
Consecration	Before 1800
Erected	Unknown [Restored 1870–1]
Endowment	Glebe 90 acres ... £100. {Total £149}
Sittings	Free 50. Other 50. Total 100
Attend'ce 30 Mar.	Morning 35 + 16 SS. Total 35 [51]
	Afternoon 70 + 20 SS. Total 70 [90]
Avge attendance	Morning 35 + 15 SS. Total 35 [50]
	Afternoon 70 + 20 SS. Total 70 [90]
Dated	31 March 1851
Signed	William Grasett Clarke, curate of the parish of Icomb [1846–]
	Icomb, Stow-on-the-Wold, Gloucestershire
[*Incumbent*	John Harward 1791–1856]

342.1.13 Parish of Westcote
Area 1,503 acres; 49 inhabited houses. Population 242.
VCH 6, 172–8

14.18 (19)	**Church of England, St Mary, Westcote**
Name	The parish church of Westcote is an ancient structure with the name of St Mary. No other place of worship in the parish.
Consecration	[Not given]
Erected	[Chancel and vestry rebuilt 1875–6 and nave and porch rebuilt 1886]
Endowment	The net annual value about £230. The fees ... the land three years under 10s per acre. The Easter offerings [are] about £1 collected by the parish clerk and by the rector's permission claimed by him. {Total £209}
Sittings	Free 130. Other 55. Total 185
Attend'ce 30 Mar.	[Not given]
Avge attendance	[Not given]
Remarks	I estimated the congregation at church on Sunday, 30 March 1851, as a fair average for the population, morning and evening: of course in the longer days of summer, the attendance is most inconsistent. The Sunday scholars about twenty.
Dated	31 March 1851
Signed	Thomas Pinder Pantin, rector [1828–66]
	Westcote rectory, Stow-on-the-Wold

[Pantin's nephew, John Wiclif Pantin, was his curate 1850–9, and successor 1866–97.]

342.1.14 Parish of Bledington
Area 1,110 acres; 81 inhabited houses, 12 uninhabited. Population 391.
VCH 6, 27–33

[Request for information. Will you have the goodness to furnish the following information at your earliest convenience. Congregations including Sunday scholars]

14.19 (16)	**Church of England, St Leonard, Bledington**
Name	'Bleddington' Church
Erected	[Restored 1881]
Endowment	{Total £88}
Sittings	Free 42. Other 22. Total [64]
Attendance	Morning about 40. Total [40]
	Afternoon [about] 60. Total [60]
Dated	20 June 1852
Signed	William Wells, registrar of births and deaths.
[*Incumbent*	John Oakley Hill 1843–71]

14.20a (21)	**Wesleyan Methodist, Bledington**
Name	Bledington
Erected	[1852 and enlarged 1889]
Building	No [not separate and entire] No [not exclusively as a place of worship]
Sittings	Free 60. Total [60]
Attend'ce 30 Mar.	Afternoon 80. Total [80]
Avge attendance	[Not given]
Dated	29 March 1851
Signed	Samuel Cooke, minister [1849–51]
	Chipping Newton, Oxfordshire

[Cooke was also minister of Naunton Hill (**14.12**), Broadwell (**14.27**) and Stow-on-the-Wold (**14.32**).]

14.20b (20)   Wesleyan Methodist, Bledington
Name   Meeting House
Erected   Before 1800
Building   No [not separate and entire] No [not exclusively as a place of worship]
Sittings   Free 80. Total [80] Standing room none
Attend'ce 30 Mar. Morning 20. Total [20]
                    Afternoon 80. Total [80] SS none
                    Evening 80. Total [80]
Avge attendance   Afternoon 70. Total [70]
Remarks   The evening services are held only a few times during the summer.
Dated   31 March 1851
Signed   Joseph Perry, one of the leaders of class
                    Kingham, near Chipping Norton

342.2   STOW-ON-THE-WOLD SUB-DISTRICT

342.2.1 Parish of Oddington
Area 1,660 acres; 128 inhabited houses, 7 uninhabited. Population 545.
VCH 6, 87–98

14.21 (22)   Church of England, St Nicholas, Oddington
Name   Ancient parish church, St Nicolas
Consecration   Before 1800
Erected   [Restored 1913]
Endowment   Land £260 (gross) £235 (net). Tithe £6 (gross) £5 (net). Glebe rent £105
                    (gross) £100 (net). [Total] £379 (gross) £340 (net).* I have maybe about
                    £1 10s or £1 from fees which add to the foregoing sum. {Total £344}
Sittings   Free 120. Other 132. Children 50. Total 302
Attend'ce 30 Mar. Morning 74 + 30 SS. Total 104
                    Afternoon 127 + 30 SS. Total 157
Avge attendance   Morning 90 + 50 SS. Total 140. Afternoon 150 + 50 SS. Total 200.
Remarks   On Sund[ay], 30 March our congregation was below the average in
                    consequence of unfavourable weather; also it is important to add that
                    at this particular time the families of the dean of Gloster (who usually
                    resides here), the rector and the squire were not resident.
Dated   31 March 1851
Signed   Henry Usher, curate [1849–56]
                    Oddington, Chipping Norton, Oxon.
[*Incumbent*   William Wiggin 1844–71]
[The dean at this time was Edward Rice: see **14.4**. Since St Nicholas' church was remote, a new church, Holy Ascension, was built between the two communities of Upper and Lower Oddington, and consecrated 26 Aug. 1852.]

342.2.2 Parish of Daylesford, Worcestershire [transferred to Gloucestershire, 1931]
Area 653 acres; 15 inhabited houses. Population 66.
VCH (Worcs.) 3, 334–8

14.22 (23)   Church of England, St Peter, Daylesford
Name   An ancient parish church dedicated to St Peter
Consecration   Before 1800
Erected   [Rebuilt 1860]

Endowment	Tithe commuted £200. Glebe £7. {Total £152}
Sittings	Free 30. Other 28. Total 58
Attend'ce 30 Mar.	Morning 28. Total 28
Avge attendance	Morning 27 + 8 SS. Total 35
	Afternoon 35 + 8 SS. Total 43
Dated	31 March 1851
Signed	Thomas Winter, minister [1825–72]
	Daylesford nr Chipping Norton

342.2.3 Parish of Adlestrop

Area 1,285 acres; 45 inhabited houses. Population 196.
VCH 6, 8–16

14.23a (24) Church of England, St Mary Magdalene, Adlestrop

Name	Adlestrop rectory, consolidated with Broadwell. Distinct parish
Consecration	Of olden consecration. Time of Queen Elizabeth as far as I know.
Erected	I believe in the time of Queen Elizabeth, by the Leigh family. [Rebuilt 1764–5, chancel altered 1824]
Endowment	Land by land. Tithe under revaluation. [See Broadwell (**14.26**)]
Sittings	Free 95. Other (including benches for choir and children) 140. Total 235
Attend'ce 30 Mar.	[Not given]
Avge attendance	[Not given]
Dated	28 March 1851
Signed	Lord Saye and Sele, rector [1825–52]
	Adlestrop, Chipping Norton

[The benefice consisted of Broadwell (**14.26**) with Adlestrop. Lord Saye and Sele was also the canon treasurer of Hereford cathedral.]

14.23b (25) Church of England, St Mary Magdalene, Adlestrop

Name	Aldestrop rectory
Consecration	Before 1800
Erected	[Not given]
Endowment	[Not given]
Sittings	Free 95. Other (including benches for choir and children) 140. Total 235
Attend'ce 30 Mar.	Morning 90 + 26 SS. Total 116
	Afternoon 94 + 26 SS. Total 120
Avge attend'ce (2m)	Morning 100 + 28 SS. Total 128
	Afternoon 110 + 28 SS. Total 138
Remarks	All the parishioners without exception are in the habit of attending either morning or afternoon service or both, who are not prevented by some bodily incapacity.
Dated	30 March 1851
Signed	Robert Trimmer MA, curate
	Aldestrop, nr Chipping Norton, Oxon.
[*Incumbent*	Lord Saye and Sele, rector 1825–52]

[Curates officiated at Adlestrop until 1852. Robert Trimmer was a fellow and tutor of Wadham College, Oxford 1846–52]

342.2.4 Parish of Evenlode, Worcestershire [transferred to Gloucestershire, 1931]
Area 1,563 acres; 65 inhabited houses, 3 uninhabited. Population 312.
VCH (Worcs.) 3, 347–52

14.24 (26)	**Church of England, St Edward, King and Martyr, Evenlode**
Name	Evenlode parish church
Consecration	Before 1800
Erected	[Restored 1879]
Endowment	Land £431. Tithe £54 11s. Glebe £5. {Total £396}
Sittings	Free 90. Other 60. Total 150
Attend'ce 30 Mar.	Morning 40 + 60 SS. Total 100
	Afternoon 80 + 58 SS. Total 138
Avge attendance	Morning 55 + 60 SS. Total 115
(over 6 months)	Afternoon 90 + 60 SS. Total 150
Dated	31 March 1851
Signed	Charles James, rector [1830–57]
	Evenlode, Moreton in Marsh

14.25 (27)	**Independent, Evenlode**
Name	None
Erected	First used for worship in 1849
Building	No [not separate and entire] No [not exclusively as a place of worship]
Sittings	Free 70. Total [70]
Attend'ce 30 Mar.	Evening 56. Total [56]
Avge attendance	[Not given]
Remarks	Besides this the undersigned has charge of three other places of worship, the principal of which is at his place of residence.
Dated	30 March 1851
Signed	Benjamin Harris Cowper, minister [1849–52]
	Moreton in Marsh, Gloucestershire

[Cowper was also the minister of Longborough (**14.37**) and Moreton-in-Marsh (**19.23**).]

342.2.5 Parish of Broadwell
Area 1,600 acres; 91 inhabited houses, 3 uninhabited. Population 388.
VCH 6, 49–59

14.26 (28)	**Church of England, St Paul, Broadwell**
Name	St Paul's church, Broadwell
Consecration	Before AD 1800
Erected	[Restored 1866]
Endowment	Fees 7s. {Total £643}
Sittings	Free 70.* Other 104. Total 174
Attend'ce 30 Mar.	Morning 63 + 49 SS. Total 112
	Afternoon 71 + 49 SS. Total 120
Avge attendance	Afternoon 80 + 50 SS. Total 130
Remarks	*The free sittings (70) do not include the benches for Sunday scholars. I do not know the rent of the glebe (336 acres) or the amount of tithe.
Dated	31 March 1851
Signed	Robert Potter, curate [1846–56]
	Broadwell, Stow-on-the-Wold
[*Incumbent*	Lord Saye and Sele 1825–52]

[The benefice consisted of Broadwell with Adlestrop (**14.23**). Lord Saye and Sele was also canon treasurer of Hereford cathedral. Within a 'few years a wider use of music and ritual in the form of service roused the opposition of at least two prominent (and eccentric) inhabitants': *VCH* 6, 57]

14.27a (30)   Wesleyan Methodist, Broadwell

Name	Broadwell
Erected	[Not given]
Building	No [not separate and entire] No [not exclusively as a place of worship]
Sittings	Free 40. Total [40]
Attend'ce 30 Mar.	Evening 40. Total [40]
Avge attendance	[Not given]
Dated	29 March 1851
Signed	Samuel Cooke, minister [1849–51]
	Chipping Norton, Oxfordshire

[Cooke was also minister of Naunton Hill (**14.12**), Bledington (**14.20**), and Stow-on-the-Wold (**14.32**).]

14.27b (29)   Wesleyan Methodist, Broadwell

Name	None
Erected	Before 1800
Building	No [not separate and entire] No [not exclusively as a place of worship]
Sittings	Free 10. Other none. Standing·room none
Attend'ce 30 Mar.	Evening 50. Total 50
Avge attendance	[Not given]
Dated	30 March 1851
Signed	George Hodgkins, manager [carpenter]
	Broadwell, Stow-on-the-Wold, Glo'shire

342.2.6–8   Parish of Stow-on-the-Wold

Area 3,130 acres; 474 inhabited houses, 26 uninhabited. Population 2,250.
The parish includes the hamlets of Donnington and Maugersbury. The Union workhouse situated at Maugersbury had 125 inmates.
VCH, 6, 142–65

14.28 (31)   Church of England, St Edward, Stow-on-the-Wold

Name	St Edward, an ancient church
Consecration	Before 1800
Erected	[Restored in the 1680s, 1846–7 and 1873]
Endowment	{Total £525}
Sittings	Free 370. Other 450. Total 820. See letter.
Attend'ce 30 Mar.	Morning 300. Total 300
Avge attendance	[Not given]
Dated	31 March 1851
Signed	Robert William Hippisley, rector [1844–98]
	Stow-on-the-Wold

[From the 1850s the rector was in sometimes violent dispute with most of the inhabitants. 'Factions grew up, and before he resigned in 1899 [sic] the townspeople had hanged the rector in effigy ... a curate was appointed and paid by a committee independent of the rector': *VCH*, 6, 151, 160–1.]

14.29 (34)   Baptist, Sheep Street, Stow-on-the-Wold

Name	Baptist Chapel
Erected	Before 1800 [1700, new chapel opened 10 August 1852]
Building	Separate [and entire] Yes [exclusively as a place of worship]
Sittings	Free 150. Other 50. Total [200] [Standing room] a vestry in which abt 20 many hear.

Attend'ce 30 Mar.   Morning 128 + 74 SS. Total 202
                       Afternoon 73 SS. Total 73
                       Evening 117. Total 117
Avge attendance   [Not given]
Dated   31 March 1851
Signed   Joseph Acock, minister [1845–59]
                     Maugersbury, Stow-on-the-Wold, Glo.

14.30 (36)   Baptist, Donnington
Name   Preaching room at Donnington
Erected   1845. [The room was later replaced by a chapel, opened 30 June 1883]
Building   A room in a dwelling house. Used exclusively for religious worship.
Sittings   All free 50. Total [50]
Attend'ce 30 Mar. Afternoon 40. Total [40]
Avge attendance   [Not given]
Dated   31 March 1851
Signed   Joseph Miles, Baptist minister [1843–75] [timber merchant]
                     [Donnington, Stow-on-the-Wold]

14.31 (37)   Particular Baptist, Maugersbury
Name   Ebenezer Chapel
Erected   Anno Domini 1840
Building   Separate [and entire] Exclusively as a place of worship
Sittings   Free 100. Total [100] Standing room for 20
Attend'ce 30 Mar. Morning 80. Total 80
Avge attendance   Morning 80 or 100. [Total 80–100]
Dated   31 March 1851
Signed   Robert Roff, minister [1842–62]
                     Stow-on-the-Wold, Glou'shire

14.32a (35)   Wesleyan Methodist, Sheep Street, Stow-on-the-Wold
Name   Stow-on-the-Wold
Erected   1814 [Enlarged 1868]
Building   Yes [separate and entire] Yes [exclusively as a place of worship]
Sittings   Free 64. Other 68. Total [132]
Attend'ce 30 Mar. Afternoon 40 + 60 SS. Total [100]
                     Evening 80. Total [80]
Avge attendance   [Not given]
Dated   29 March 1851
Signed   Samuel Cooke, minister [1849–51]
                     Chipping Norton, Gloucestershire

[Cooke was also the minister of Naunton Hill (**14.12**), Bledington (**14.20**) and Broadwell (**14.27**). John Wesley recorded: 'I preached at Stow-on-the-Wold, about ten, to a very dull, quiet congregation': *Journal*, 28 Aug. 1767.]

14.32b (33)   Wesleyan Methodist, Sheep Street, Stow-on-the-Wold
Name   Wesleyan Chapel
Erected   1814
Building   Separate [and entire] Exclusively [as a place of worship]
Sittings   Free 64. Other 136. Total [200]
Attend'ce 30 Mar. Morning 65 SS. Total 65
                     Afternoon 130 + 60 SS. Total 190

Evening 120. Total 120

Avge attendance	Morning 66 SS. Total 66
	Afternoon 150 + 66 SS. Total 216
	Evening 150. Total 150
Remarks	There is no free space or standing room.
Dated	31 March 1851
Signed	Samuel Portlow, steward [cordwainer]
	Sheep Street, Stow-on-the-Wold, Gloucestershire

14.33 (32) Society of Friends, off Market Square, Stow-on-the-Wold
(On a nonconformist form)

Name	Chapel of the Society of Friends
Erected	N[ot] k[nown] [1719]
Building	Separate and entire. Not in use [as a place of worship]
Sittings	[Not given]
Attend'ce 30 Mar.	[Not given]
Avge attendance	[Not given]
Remarks	This chapel has not been made use of as a place of worship for upwards of six months. It is quite shut up.
	Mr Richardson, with whom I left the form, returned it to me not filled up, when I considered it my duty to state all I knew. T. R.
Dated	31 March 1851
Signed	Thomas Rolf, enumerator [grocer]

342.2.9 Parish of Nether Swell (or Lower Swell)
Area 1,670 acres; 93 inhabited houses, 2 uninhabited. Population 431.
VCH, 6, 165–72

14.34 (38) Church of England, St Mary the Virgin, Nether Swell

Name	Name unknown. An ancient church of a distinct and separate parish
Consecration	Before AD 1800 [28 October 1870]
Erected	[Large north aisle 1851–2 which became the nave when a new chancel was built in 1870]
Endowment	Glebe not fixed. OPE £10 (Dr [Robert] South's benefaction). Fees not known (lately appointed to the living). {Total £100}
Sittings	Free 8. Other 142. Total 150
Attend'ce 30 Mar.	Morning 63 + 40 SS. Total 103
	Afternoon 125 + 41 SS. Total 166
Avge attendance (5m)	Morning 63 + 40 SS. Total 103
	Afternoon 125 + 41 SS. Total 166
Remarks	Church much too small, badly arranged and in a miserable condition.
Dated	30 March 1851
Signed	David Royce, vicar [1850–1902]
	Stow-on-the-Wold, Gloucestershire

[Royce described the church in *TBGAS* 7, 45–55. Robert South died in 1716.]

342.2.10 Parish of Upper Swell
Area 1,460 acres; 16 inhabited houses. Population 83.

14.35 (39) Church of England, St Mary, Upper Swell

Name	I can give no information as to the name or description of the church beyond its being the ancient church of the parish of Upper Swell.

Consecration   It is quite impossible for me to say when the church was consecrated. It must have been so many centuries back and I know of no documents to refer to for information.

Erected   This question cannot be answered for the same reasons as apply to [the previous question] No information can be given on this point [concerning the cost. Restored 1872]

Endowed   Glebe. Other sources modus. {Total £85}

Sittings   Free 70 + 35 SS. Total 105

Attend'ce 30 Mar.   Morning 39. Total 39

Avge attendance   [Not given]

Remarks   With regard to the average number of attendants during a given number of months preceding the 30 March, I am quite unable to give it with any accuracy: my attention not having been drawn to the fact as not anticipating such an enquiry would be made.

Dated   30 March 1851

Signed   Watson Buller van Notten Pole, rector [1828–81]
Stow-on-the-Wold

[Pole was also the incumbent of Condicote (**14.38**).]

342.2.11   Parish of Longborough

Area 2,770 acres; 151 inhabited houses, 5 uninhabited. Population 656.

14.36 (40)   Church of England, St James, Longborough

Name   Longborough parish church dedicated to St James. Ancient church. Norman period

Consecration   [Not given]

Erected   [Restored 1883–4]

Endowment   {Total £221}

Sittings   Free 113. Other pews 205. Children's galleries 75. Total 393

Attend'ce 30 Mar.   Morning 142 + 68 SS. Total 210
Afternoon 139 + 61 SS. Total 200

Avge attendance   [Not given]

Remarks   The morning service on the 30 March is a fair average of the year, the afternoon is under the mark.

Dated   31 March 1851

Signed   Archibald Charles Henry Morrison, vicar [1846–66]
Longborough vicarage, Stow-on-the-Wold

[The benefice consisted of Longborough with Sezincote (342.2.12). The north transept or Sezincote chapel, added in 1822–3, was the family pew and burial vault for the Cockerell family.]

14.37 (41)   Independent, Longborough

Name   Independent Chapel

Erected   In the year 1849, in lieu of a room previously employed for the purpose

Building   Yes [separate and entire] Yes [exclusively as a place of worship]

Sittings   Free 125. Total [125]

Attend'ce 30 Mar.   Afternoon 83 + 6 SS. Total 89
Evening 125. Total 125

Avge attendance   [Not given]

Remarks   This chapel is a branch chapel connected with that at Moreton in Marsh. Religious services have been held in the village by Independents since about 1800.

Dated   30 March 1851

Signed   Benjamin Harris Cowper, minister [1849–52]
                    Moreton in Marsh, Gloucestershire
[Cowper was also minister of Evenlode (**14.25**) and Moreton-in-Marsh (**19.23**).]

342.2.12 Parish of Sezincote
Area 1,413 acres; 13 inhabited houses. Population 111.
The parish of Sezincote is united with the parish of Longborough (**14.36**).
[St Bartholomew's church was demolished c.1712.]

342.2.13 Parish of Condicote
Area 890 acres; 39 inhabited houses. Population 174.
VCH 6, 63–72; *GNQ* 4, 316–7

14.38 (42)	**Church of England, St Nicholas, Condicote**
Name	I can give no account of the name of the church beyond it being the parish church of Condicote.
Consecration	It is quite impossible for me to say when the church was consecrated. It may have been so many centuries back and I know of no documents to refer to.
Erected	This question cannot be answered for the same reasons as apply to [the previous question] Cost: no information [can] be given on this point. [Restored 1888–9]
Endowment	By glebe. Other sources by modus. {Total £158}
Sittings	Free 58. Other 34. Total 92
	This number is exclusive of the Sunday scholars' seats.
Attend'ce 30 Mar.	Afternoon 57 + 33 SS. Total 90
Avge attendance	[Not given]
Remarks	With regard to the average number of attendants during a given number of months preceding the 30 March, I am quite unable to give it with any accuracy: my attention not having been drawn to the fact as not anticipating such an enquiry would be made.
Dated	30 March 1851
Signed	Watson Buller van Notten Pole, rector [1840–81] Stow-on-the-Wold.

[Pole was also the incumbent of Upper Swell (**14.35**).]

---

15. HO 129/343 WINCHCOMBE DISTRICT: 39 places of worship

343.1   GUITING SUB-DISTRICT

343.1.1 Parish of Cutsdean, Worcestershire [transferred to Gloucestershire, 1931]
Area 1,578 acres; 35 inhabited houses. Population 192.
The chapelry is in the parish of Bredon (345.2.7–8).
VCH (Worcs.) 3, 279–92

15.1 (1)	**Church of England, St Luke, Cutsdean**
Name	Cutsdean Chapel
Consecration	Not known. Ancient church
Erected	Not known [Apart from the tower rebuilt in 1863]
Endowment	Glebe – farm [See Bredon (**17.24**)]
Sittings	Total 190
Attend'ce 30 Mar.	Morning [70] + 53 SS. Total 123
	Afternoon 90 + 51 SS. Total 141
Avge attendance	Morning 70 + 55 SS. Total 125
	Afternoon 80 + 55 SS. Total 135
Dated	31 March 1851
Signed	Edward Duke, curate
	Cutsdean, Winchcomb
[Incumbent	Thomas Alfred Strickland 1837–52]

[The benefice consisted of Bredon (**17.24**) with Norton (**17.25**) and Cutsdean.]

15.2 (2)	**Particular Baptist, Cutsdean**
Name	Baptist
Erected	Opened for religious worship in 1838
Building	Separate [and entire] Yes [exclusively as a place of worship]
Sittings	Free 60. Other 30. Total [90] Standing room 20 feet by 3
Attend'ce 30 Mar.	Morning 46. Total [46]
	Afternoon none
	Evening 63. Total [63]
Avge attendance	[Not given]
Dated	31 March 1851
Signed	Daniel Ricketts, Baptist minister [1839–70]
	Cutsdean, Winchcomb, Gloucestershire

[Ricketts was also the minister of Stanton (**15.21**)]

343.1.2 Parish of Temple Guiting
Area 6,180 acres; 110 inhabited houses, 8 uninhabited. Population 525.
The parish includes the hamlets of Barton Ford and Kineton.

15.3 (3)	**Church of England, St Mary, Temple Guiting**
Name	Temple Guiting
Consecration	Ancient church. Not known
Erected	Not known [Restored 1884–5]
Endowment	Glebe £64. OPE £20 (Parliamentary grant). Fees £2. Easter offerings 16s.
	{Total £94}
Sittings	Free 40. Other 220. Total 260

Attend'ce 30 Mar. Morning 200. Total 200
                     Afternoon 300. Total 300
Avge attendance (3m) Morning 200 + 30 SS. Total 230
                     Afternoon 300. Total 300
Dated   29 March 1851
Signed   Edward Du Pré incumbent [1849–63]
                     Near Winchcomb, Gloucestershire

['The interior is disappointing because of the awful restoration in 1884 when the walls were scraped, and then and since then, anything possible seems to have been done to eradicate the Georgian restoration': Verey 1976, 110.]

343.1.3 Parish of Didbrook

Area 2,578 acres; 40 inhabited houses, 6 uninhabited. Population 178.
The parish includes the township of Pinnock and Hyde and the hamlets of Coscomb and Wormington Grange. The decrease in population of 146 since 1821 was due to the demolition of cottages.

15.4 (4)   Church of England, St George, Didbrook

(Summary form)
Name   St Paul [sic]
Erected   [Restored 1923]
[Endowment   Total £257]
Sittings   Total 200
Usual attend'ce   Afternoon 100 + 20 SS. Total [120]
Signed   James Lovesy [enumerator]
[Incumbent   William Whalley 1843–71]

[The benefice consisted of Didbrook with Pinnock and Hailes chapel (**15.18**). Whalley, who lived in Bath, was also the incumbent of Toddington (**15.27**) with Stanley Pontlarge (**15.34**) where he also failed to complete the returns.]

15.5 (5)   Wesleyan Methodist, Didbrook

Name   Wesleyan Chapel
Erected   In 1838
Building   Yes [separate and entire] Yes [exclusively as a place of worship]
Sittings   Free 53. Other 25. Total [78]
Attend'ce 30 Mar. Afternoon 45. Total 45
                     SS none
Avge attendance   Evening 35. Total 35
Remarks   There are usually two services on Sunday, but in consequence of local
                     circumstances there was no service in the evening of 30 March 1851.
Dated   31 March 1851
Signed   George Reeves, steward and trustee [wheelwright]
                     Didbrook, near Winchcomb, Gloucestershire

343.1.5 Parish of Guiting Power (or Lower Guiting)

Area 3,380 acres; 157 inhabited houses, 11 uninhabited. Population 690.
The parish includes the hamlets of Farmcote, Guiting Grange and Cartlet.

15.6 (7)   Church of England, St Michael and All Angels, Lower Guiting

Name   St Michael. Ancient parish church
Consecration   [Not given]
Erected   [Enlarged 1819–20 and 1843–4 and restored 1902–3]
Endowment   I cannot say. {Total £124}

Sittings   Free 180. Other 200. Total 380
Attend'ce 30 Mar. Morning about 180 + about 50 SS. Total 230
                     Afternoon about 220 + about 55 SS. Total 275
                     Evening about 160. Total 160 ·
Avge attendance [Not given]
Remarks   The parish is at present under peculiar circumstances, the vicar being
                     suspended. As the bishop's curate only, I am unable to supply any
                     accurate information relative to the value of the living.
Dated   25 March 1851
Signed   Joseph Green, bishop's curate [1849–51]
                     Stow-on-the-Wold, Gloucestershire
[Incumbent   John Walker Dolphin 1837–59]
[The benefice consisted of Lower Guiting with Farmcote (**15.7**). Dolphin was 'suspended for three
years from 25 November 1849': GA, GDR/A2/5.]

15.7 (6)   **Church of England, St Faith, Farmcote**
Name   Farmcote appended to the parish [of] Lower Guiting
Consecration   [Not given]
Erected   [Minor restoration 1890]
Endowment   [See Lower Guiting (**15.6**)]
Sittings   Free 12. Other 25. Total 37
Attend'ce 30 Mar. Afternoon 8. Total 8
Avge attendance [Not given]
Remarks   This is a small chapel. There are but two farmhouses: one of which is at
                     present unoccupied. It is distant 4½ miles from this place and duty is per-
                     formed there once every second Sunday by the minister of Lower Guiting.
Dated   28 March 1851
Signed   Joseph Green AM, bishop's curate for Farmcote
                     Stow-on-the-Wold, Gloucestershire
[Incumbent   John Walker Dolphin 1837–59]
[See preceding note.]

15.8 (8)   **Baptist, Lower Guiting**
Name   Baptist Chapel
Erected   1835 [Opened May 1836]
Building   Yes [separate and entire] Yes [exclusively as a place of worship]
Sittings   Free 135. Total [135] Standing room for 70 persons
Attend'ce 30 Mar. Morning no service
                     Afternoon 90 + 20 SS. Total 110
                     Evening no service
Avge attend'ce (6m) Afternoon 80 + 20 SS. Total 100
Dated   30 March 1851
Signed   John Teall, minister
                     Naunton, Stow-on-the-Wold, Gloucestershire
[Teall was also the minister of Naunton (**14.11**).]

343.1.6 Extra-parochial of Rowell
Area 1,640 acres; 2 inhabited houses. Population 12.

343.1.7 Parish of Hawling
Area 1,846 acres; 44 inhabited houses, 1 uninhabited. Population 212.

15.9 (9)   **Church of England, St Edward, Hawling**

Name   Hawling. Ancient parish church

Consecration   [Not given]

Erected   [Minor restoration 1868]

Endowment   Tithe from the patron £70. Glebe £30. OPE ... hamlet £30. Easter offerings 13s 4d. Total £102 3s 4d. {Total £100}

Sittings   All free, the parish being the property of H[enry] T[homas] Hope Esq., MP [for Gloucester 1833–41, 1847–52] Total sittings sufficient for the parishioners

Attend'ce 30 Mar. Morning 65 + 22 SS. Total 87
                    Afternoon alternate service
                    Evening lecture in the evening to about 20. Total [20]

Avge attendance   Morning and afternoon 100 + 30 SS. Total 130
                    Afternoon alternate service
                    Evening lecture to about 20. Total 20

Remarks   Wet morning which always diminishes the average number

Dated   31 March 1851

Signed   John Tucker, rector [1846–59]
                    Hawling rectory, Cheltenham

[Tucker was also the incumbent of Charlton Abbots (**15.11**).]

15.10 (10)   **Wesleyan Methodist, Hawling**

Name   Wesleyan Chapel

Erected   1837

Building   Yes [separate and entire] Yes [exclusively as a place of worship]

Sittings   Free 66 persons. Other 30 persons. Total [96]

Attend'ce 30 Mar. Morning 7 SS. Total [7]
                    Afternoon 44 + 7 SS. Total [51]
                    Evening 32. Total [32]

Avge attendance   [Not given]

Dated   1 April 1851

Signed   Charles Lodge, trustee [farmer of 210 acres]
                    Aston Blank, Bourton on the Water, Gloucestershire

343.1.8 Parish of Charlton Abbots

Area 2,190 acres; 20 inhabited houses. Population 112.

15.11 (11)   **Church of England, St Martin, Charlton Abbots**

Name   Charlton Abbots, ancient manor house church or chapel

Consecration   [Not given]

Erected   [Restored 1886]

Endowment   Land at Colesborne £18 8s 3d per annum. Tithe from the patron £10 per annum. OPE Queen Anne's Bounty funds £600; £18 18s 8d. Total £58 7s 10d. Other sources Q[ueen] A[nne's] B[ounty] land at Arle near Cheltenham £11 0s 11d. {Total £100}

Sittings   All free. All the parish belonging to one proprietor [Joseph] Chamberlyne Chamberlyne Esq., Stow-on-the-Wold. Total sittings sufficient for the parishioners.

Attend'ce 30 Mar. Morning and afternoon alternate 56
                    Morning 21 SS. Total 77

Avge attendance   Morning and afternoon average number 70. Total [70]

	Morning 30 SS. Total 100
Remarks	A wet Sunday causing a reduction in number of the congregation.
Dated	31 March 1851
Signed	John Tucker, perpetual curate [1831–59]
	Andoversford, Cheltenham

[Tucker was also the incumbent of Hawling 1846–59 (**15.9**). Chamberlyne (1791–1874) of Maugersbury Manor House gave £2,000 to provide fresh drinking water for Stow-on-the-Wold.]

343.1.9 Parish of Sudeley Manor

Area 2,622 acres; 14 inhabited houses. Population 77.

15.12 (12)   Church of England, St Mary, Sudeley Manor
(Summary form)

Name	[Not given]
Erected	[Rebuilt 1858–63 and consecrated 24 June 1863]
[*Endowment*	Total £45]
Sittings	Total 40
Usual attend'ce	Afternoon 20. Total 20 (usual number)
Signed	James Lovesy [enumerator]
[*Incumbent*	John Ridout Harvey 1834–71]

[The benefice consisted of Winchcombe (**15.13**) with Gretton (**15.14**) and Sudeley Manor.]

343.1.10 Parish of Winchcombe

Area 5,700 acres; 607 inhabited houses, 33 uninhabited. Population 2,824.
The parish includes the township of Winchcombe and the hamlets of Abbey Demesnes, Langley, Coates, Cockbury, Corndean, Greet, Gretton, Naunton, Frampton and Postlip. The Union workhouse situated within the parish had 91 inmates most of whom were agricultural labourers.

15.13 (13)   Church of England, St Peter, Winchcombe
Request for information. Would you be so good as to furnish the following information as speedily as possible. Congregations including Sunday scholars.

[*Erected*	Restored 1870–3]
[*Endowment*	Total £134]
Morning	500
Afternoon	No service
Evening	300
Sittings	Free 1,000. Other 80. Total 1,080
Dated	25 June 1852
Signed	James Lovesy [enumerator]
[*Incumbent*	John Ridout Harvey 1834–71]

[The benefice consisted of Winchcombe with Gretton (**15.14**) and Studley Manor (**15.12**). John Noake visiting the church in 1848 noted the 'clumsy gallery', and box pews 'at least five feet high, and look[ing] as gloomy as ancient closets. The ground beneath the pavement of the church is said to be full of dead bodies and the effluvia is occasionally most offensive.' The stone pulpit had a very narrow entrance, and so 'a very obese preacher' would have to be pushed in by the clerk. 'On a table in the chancel I observed some charity bread, and was informed that it is the custom here not to give away the loaves until the evening, in order to ascertain if the applicants have attended church twice in the day, without which they must expect no relief': Noake, 340, 349.]

15.14 (13)   Church of England, Christ Church, Gretton
[Request for information. Would you be so good as to furnish the following information as speedily as possible. Congregations including Sunday scholars]

Morning	{Service held alternately, the average
Afternoon	{number of attendants inclusive of
Evening	{Sunday school scholars would be about 100.
Sittings	Free 100. Other none. Total 200
Dated	28 June 1852
Signed	James Lovesy [enumerator]
[Incumbent	John Ridout Harvey 1834–71]

[The benefice consisted of Winchcombe (**15.13**) with Gretton and Studley Manor (**15.12**). Apart from the tower the church was demolished and replaced by Christ Church, Gretton (on another site) and consecrated 4 June 1868.]

15.15 (14) Baptist, High Street, Winchcombe

Name	Baptist Chapel
Erected	1811 [Tablet: 'Baptist Chapel, 1 Jan. 1811']
Building	Yes [separate and entire] Yes [exclusively as a place of worship]
Sittings	Free 80. Other 250. Total [330] Standing room for 80
Attend'ce 30 Mar.	Morning 100 + 90 SS. Total 190
	Afternoon 80 + 100 SS. Total 180
	Evening 250 + 30 SS. Total 280
Avge attendance	[Not given]
Dated	31 March 1851
Signed	Stephen Dunn, minister
	Winchcomb, Gloucestershire

15.16 (15) Wesleyan Methodist, Cold Lane, Winchcombe

Name	Wesleyan Chapel
Erected	Before 1800 [1789, new chapel 1810]
Building	Yes [separate and entire] Yes [exclusively as a place of worship]
Sittings	Free 120. Other 187. Total [307] Standing room none
Attend'ce 30 Mar.	Morning 106 + 52 SS. Total 158 }'Exact'
	Evening 161 [SS] none. Total 161 }
Avge attendance	Morning 120 + 55 SS. Total 175
	Evening 180 [SS] none. Total 180
Remarks	The congregations were unusually small owing to 30 March being the Sunday immediately following the High Sheriff's procession and Winchcomb Fair.
Dated	31 March 1851
Signed	William Edwards, minister [1848–51]
	Winchcomb, Gloucestershire.

15.17 (16) Wesleyan Methodist, Gretton

Name	Wesleyan Chapel
Erected	In 1815
Building	Yes [separate and entire] Yes [exclusively as a place of worship]
Sittings	Free 84. Other 48. Total [132]
Attend'ce 30 Mar.	Afternoon 11 SS. Total [11]
	Evening 11. Total [11]
Avge attendance	[Not given]
Dated	31 March 1851
Signed	Robert Greening, trustee [agricultural labourer]
	Gretton, Gloucestershire

[The Wesleyan Methodists of Gretton met in 'an old, dilapidated building' the residence of 'two rich old misers, bachelor brothers.' A Methodist minister 'took it into his head that these two old gentlemen possessed wealth enough to found a Methodist chapel, or at all events to repair the ancient domicile in which they were wont to assemble.' During the course of a service the minister, the Rev [James] Byron, prayed 'We beseech thee, O Lord, in thy tender mercy (among other things) to blow this old place down with the next wind, that we may have a better house to worship thee in ... The two brothers, who were far more attached to their purses than their religion, without waiting for the conclusion of the prayer, thrust the rev. gentleman out of the house, and never again admitted him': Noake, 344–5. Byron was a minister in the Cheltenham circuit 1815–7.]

343.1.11 Parish of Hailes

Area 1,520 acres; 18 inhabited houses, 3 uninhabited. Population 90.

15.18 (17)	**Church of England, Hailes Chapel, Hailes**
Name	Hailes Chapel
Consecration	Before 1800.
Erected	[Restored 1905]
Endowment	Not being [the] incumbent, I am unable to answer these questions. G. S. [See Didbrook (**15.4**)]
Sittings	Free 67. Other 7. Total 74
Attend'ce 30 Mar.	[Not given]
Avge attendance	Morning 15 to 25 + 10 to 12 SS. Total 25 to 37
	Afternoon 20 to 30 + 10 to 12 SS. Total 30 to 42
Remarks	Having been prevented by illness from being present in Hailes Chapel on 30 March 1851, I cannot ... estimate the number of persons present as requested.
Dated	5 April 1851
Signed	George Stott, curate [1843–52]
	Didbrook, Winchcomb
[Incumbent	William Whalley 1843–71]

[The benefice consisted of Didbrook (**15.4**) with Pinnock and Hailes chapel. Whalley, who lived in Bath, was also incumbent of Toddington (**15.27**) with Stanley Pontlarge (**15.34**). 'Interior little altered from 17th century' (British Listed Buildings); Chatfield, 38–40.]

343.1.12 Parish of Stanway

Area 3,390 acres; 78 inhabited houses, 2 uninhabited. Population 359.
The parish includes the hamlets of Taddington, Wood Stanway and Hornileazow.
VCH 6, 223–32

15.19 (18)	**Church of England, St Peter, Stanway**
Name	Stanway parish church
Consecration	Before 1800
Erected	[Rebuilt 1896–7]
Endowment	Land £188 10s. Fees £1 10s. {Total £220}
Sittings	Free 89. Other 133. Total 222
Attend'ce 30 Mar.	Morning 73 + 12 SS. Total 85
	Afternoon 87 + 12 SS. Total 99
Avge attendance	[Not given]
Remarks	The parish is divided into three hamlets, separated from each other. The inhabitants of one hamlet Taddington are two miles and upwards from their parish church and being within half a mile of Cutsdean Church (**15.1**) attend divine service at Cutsdean not at Stanway.
Dated	31 March 1851

Signed   Edward Francis Witts, curate [1839–54]
                    The vicarage, Wood Stanway, Winchcomb
[*Incumbent*   Francis Edward Witts 1814–54]
[Witts was also the incumbent of Upper Slaughter, where he lived (**14.13**), and of East Lulworth, Dorset 1832–54. His son Edward Francis Witts was the curate of Stanway 1839–54 then succeeded his father as incumbent of Upper Slaughter 1854–86: Verey, 1980.]

343.1.13   Parish of Stanton
Area 1,650 acres; 57 inhabited houses, 1 uninhabited. Population 307.

15.20 (19)   **Church of England, St Michael and All Angels, Stanton**
Name   St Michael's Church, Stanton. An ancient parish church
Consecration   Before 1800
Erected   [Chancel rebuilt 1874, aisles restored 1896–8]
Endowment   [Not given] {Total £377}
Sittings   Free 120. Other 70. Total 190
Attend'ce 30 Mar.   Morning 43 + 30 SS. Total 73
Avge attendance   Morning 50 +30 SS. Total 80
                        Afternoon 90 + 30 SS. Total 120
                        Evening 90 + 15 SS. Total 105
Remarks   During the winter months there is a morning service on one Sunday, and
                        an afternoon service on the next. During the summer there is an evening
                        service every other Sunday. Snowshill and Stanton form one benefice.
Dated   30 March 1851
Signed   William Henry Bloxsome, curate [1838–62]
                        Stanton, near Broadway
[Bloxsome was also the incumbent of Evesbatch, near Bromyard, Herefs., 1838–73. His son, also William Henry Bloxsome, was curate of Stanton with Snowshill 1862–8. The benefice consisted of Stanton and Snowshill (**15.22**).]

15.21 (20)   **Baptist, Stanton**
Name   Baptist Chapel
Erected   1842
Building   Separate [and entire] Yes, exclusively [as a place of worship]
Sittings   No sittings all free 50. Total [50] Standing room 14 feet by 2½
Attend'ce 30 Mar.   Morning 10 SS. Total 10
                        Afternoon 34 + 10 SS. Total 44
                        Evening none
Avge attendance   [Not given]
Dated   30 March 1851
Signed   Daniel Ricketts, Baptist minister
                        Cutsdean, Winchcombe, Gloucestershire
[Ricketts was also the minister of Cutsdean (**15.2**), where he lived.]

343.1.14 Parish of Snowshill
Area 2,294 acres; 59 inhabited houses. Population 303.

15.22 (21)   **Church of England, St Barnabas, Snowshill**
Name   An ancient parish chapelry assigned to the adjoining parish of Stanton
                        commonly known as Snowshill church. The name given at its consecration
                        is not now known.

Consecration	Before 1800 [re-consecrated 8 Oct. 1864]
Erected	[Rebuilt 1863–4]
Endowment	[See Stanton (**15.20**)]
Sittings	Free 120. Other 36. Total 156
Attend'ce 30 Mar.	Afternoon 51 + 42 SS. Total 93
Avge attendance	Morning 80. Total [80]
	Afternoon 120. Total [120]
Remarks	A single service one Sunday in the morning, the next in the afternoon.
Dated	30 March 1851
Signed	William Henry Bloxsome, curate [1838–62]
	Stanton, near Broadway

[See note at **15.20** above.]

15.23 (22)   Baptist, Snowshill

Name	None
Erected	Not known
Building	No [not separate and entire] No [not exclusively as a place of worship]
Sittings	All free 100. Total [100]
	20 ft by 15
Attend'ce 30 Mar.	Evening 37. Total [37]
Avge attendance	[Not given]
Dated	30 March 1851
Signed	George Jameson Smith, lay preacher
	Blockley nr Moreton in Marsh, Gloucestershire

343.2   CLEEVE SUB-DISTRICT

343.2.1 Parish of Buckland

Area 2,270 acres; 83 inhabited houses. Population 368.
The parish includes the hamlet of Laverton.
GNQ 3, 318–21

15.24 (23)   Church of England, St Michael, Buckland

Name	It is an ancient parish church dedicated to St Michael and commonly known as Buckland Church. It is reserved only for public worship. Built in the style of the 15th century.
Consecration	Before 1800
Erected	[Restored 1879–85]
Endowment	Dues 10s. {Total £222}
Sittings	Free 30. Other 6. Total 36
Attend'ce 30 Mar.	Morning 25 + 50 SS. Total 75
	Afternoon 76 + 38 SS. Total 114
Avge attendance	Morning 59 + 43 SS. Total 102
	Afternoon 105 + 45 SS. Total 150
Dated	30 March 1851
Signed	William Phillipps, minister [1848–77]
	Broadway, of Buckland, Gloucestershire

[Phillipps was the curate 1841–7, then the incumbent.]

343.2.2 Parish of Wormington
Area 560 acres; 15 inhabited houses, 2 uninhabited. Population 62.

15.25 (24)	**Church of England, St Catherine, Wormington**
Name	St Catherine's. Ancient parish church of a distinct and separate parish
Consecration	Before 1800
Erected	[Restored 1884–5 and 1926]
Endowment	OPE none. Pew rents none. Fees nominal. Dues, Easter offerings and other sources none. {Total £143}
Sittings	Free 40. Other 60. Total 100
Attend'ce 30 Mar.	Morning 26 + 10 SS. Total 36
Avge attendance	Morning 25 + 10 SS. Total 35
	Afternoon 30 + 10 SS. Total 40
Dated	31 March 1851
Signed	John Richard Frederick Billingsley, rector [1838–78]
	Wormington rectory, Evesham

343.2.3 Parish of Dumbleton
Area 2,100 acres; 89 inhabited houses, 1 uninhabited. Population 457.

15.26 (25)	**Church of England, St Peter, Dumbleton**
Name	Dumbleton. Ancient parish church
Consecration	Before 1800
Erected	[Restored 1862 (tablet: '13 May 1862'), 1872–3 and 1904–5]
Endowment	Tithe £210. Glebe £114. {Total £354}
Sittings	Free 120. Other 150. Total 270
Attend'ce 30 Mar.	Morning 70 + 42 SS. Total 112
	Afternoon 100 + 25 SS. Total 125
Avge attendance	[Not given]
Dated	30 March 1851
Signed	Robert Wedgewood, rector [1850–81]
	Dumbleton rectory, nr Evesham

343.2.4 Parish of Toddington
Area 1,857 acres; 46 inhabited houses, 5 uninhabited. Population 189.

15.27 (26)	**Church of England, St Andrew, Toddington**
Name	Toddington
Consecration	[3 Apr. 1877]
Erected	[Rebuilt 1723 and dedicated to St Andrew (in place of St Leonard) and rebuilt 1868–9]
Endowment	[Not given] {Total £200 in 1860}
Sittings	[Not given]
Attend'ce 30 Mar.	Morning 400. Total [400]
Avge attendance	[Not given]
Dated	[Not given]
Signed	[Not given]
[*Incumbent*	William Whalley 1843–71]

[Whalley, who lived in Bath, was also the incumbent of Didbrook (**15.4**) with Pinnock and Hailes chapel (**15.18**)] where he also failed to complete the returns. The benefice consisted of Toddington with Stanley Pontlarge (**15.34**).]

343.2.5 Parish of Alderton

Area 1,750 acres; 103 inhabited houses, 2 uninhabited. Population 486.
The parish include the hamlet of Dixton.
VCH 6, 189–97

15.28 (27)	**Church of England, St Margaret of Antioch, Alderton**
Name	Ancient parish church, St Margaret
Consecration	Before 1800
Erected	[Restored 1888–92]
Endowment	Lands in lieu of tithe for Alderton and by tithe [valued at £150] for the hamlet of Dixton. {Total £337}
Sittings	Free 250. Other 50. Total 300
Attend'ce 30 Mar.	Morning 54 + 36 SS. Total 90
	Afternoon 70 + 30 SS. Total 100
Avge attendance	[Not given]
Remarks	The weather cold and stormy and therefore unfavourable for persons leaving home.
Dated	31 March 1851
Signed	Charles Covey, rector [1842–75]
	Alderton rectory, Cheltenham

[Covey, who had been curate of Alderton from 1827, was also incumbent of Great Washbourne (**15.30**) was succeeded by his son Charles Rogers Covey at Alderton and Great Washbourne 1886–1915. In the parish the chapel of All Saints, Dixton was demolished in the early 19th century.]

15.29 (28)	**Wesleyan Methodist, Alderton**
Name	Wesleyan Chapel
Erected	In 1833 [Replaced by a new chapel in 1899]
Building	Yes [separate and entire. Other details not given]
Sittings	Free 86. Other 24. Total [110] Standing room none
Attend'ce 30 Mar.	Afternoon 60 + 26 SS. Total 86
Avge attendance	Afternoon 60 + 26 SS. Total 86
	Evening 65 (SS) none. Total 65
Remarks	'There whas no service in the evening of 30 March 1851.'
Dated	31 March 1851
Signed	James Timbrell, appointed by the minister [road labourer]
	Alderton near Beckford, Gloucestershire

343.2.6 Parish of Great Washbourne

Area 470 acres; 23 inhabited houses. Population 117.
VCH 6, 232–37

15.30 (29)	**Church of England, St Mary, Great Washbourne**
Name	Ancient parish church, St Mary
Consecration	Before 1800
Erected	[Restored 1961]
Endowment	Land [75 acres of a] smallholding in lieu of tithes ... by a payment from Queen Anne's Bounty in the whole amounting to about £60. {Total £59}
Sittings	Free 40. Other 36. Total 76
Attend'ce 30 Mar.	Morning 13 SS. Total 13
	Afternoon 30 + 13 SS. Total 43
Avge attendance	[Not given]
Remarks	The weather stormy and not favourable for persons leaving home.

Dated	31 March 1851
Signed	Charles Covey, rector [1837–75]
	Alderton rectory, Cheltenham

[Covey, who was also the incumbent of Alderton (**15.28**) was succeeded by his son Charles Rogers Covey at Alderton and Great Washbourne 1886–1915.]

343.2.7 Parish of Beckford [transferred to Worcestershire, 1931]
Area 2,650 acres; 95 inhabited houses, 4 uninhabited. Population 450.
The parish includes the hamlets of Bangrove, Didcote and Grafton.
VCH 8, 250–62

15.31 (30)	**Church of England, St John the Baptist, Beckford**
Name	Beckford, an ancient parish church dedicated to St John the Baptist
Consecration	Before 1800
Erected	[In the mid-19th century 'the church was restored at great expense',
	VCH 8, 261; and with a further restoration 1911–2]
Endowment	Tithe rent charge about £192. {Total £317}
Sittings	Free 242. Other 55. Total 297
Attend'ce 30 Mar.	Morning 174 + 29 SS. Total 203
Avge attendance	[Not given]
Dated	31 March 1851
Signed	John Timbrill, vicar [1797–1865]
	Beckford near Tewkesbury

[John Timbrill (who changed his name to Trimberell) was also the incumbent of Dursley (**5.20**) with Woodmancote (**5.21**) and of Bretforton, Worcs. 1816–65, and archdeacon of Gloucester 1825–65. The benefice consisted of Beckford with Ashton under Hill (**19.26**).]

343.2.8–9 Parish of Overbury (see 345.2.3–5)
Area 2,190 acres; 127 inhabited houses, 12 uninhabited. Population 586.
Most of the parish of Overbury is in the sub-district of Overbury (345.2) and contains the hamlets of Little Washbourne and Alston (both transferred from Worcestershire to Gloucestershire in 1844).

15.32 (31)	**Church of England, St Mary the Virgin, Little Washbourne**
Name	Little Washbourne Chapel, a chapel of ease
Consecration	Before 1800
Erected	[Not restored]
Endowment	Land £117 14s 10d. [See Overbury (**17.18**)]
Sittings	Free 24. Other 40. Other 64
Attend'ce 30 Mar.	[Not given]
Avge attendance	Morning 12. Total [12]
	Afternoon 12. Total [12]
Dated	31 March 1851
Signed	William Cloudesley Faulkner, curate [1847–78]
	Beckford, Tewkesbury, Gloucestershire
[*Incumbent*	William Smith 1839–76]

[The benefice consisted of Overbury (**17.18**) with Alstone (**15.33**) and the chapelries of Teddington (**17.19**) and Little Washbourne: Chatfield, 41–3; *VCH (Worcs.)* 3, 477–8. The church is now under the care of the Churches Conservation Trust.]

15.33 (32)	**Church of England, Alstone**
Name	Alston Chapel, a chapel of ease
Consecration	Before 1800

Erected	[Restored 1880]
Endowment	Land £17 10s. [See Overbury (**17.18**)]
Sittings	Free 42. Other 20. Total 62
Attend'ce 30 Mar.	[Not given]
Avge attendance	Morning 14. Total [14]
	Afternoon 25 to 30. Total [25–30]
Dated	31 March 1851
Signed	William Cloudesley Faulkner, curate [1847–78]
	Beckford, Tewkesbury, Gloucestershire
[*Incumbent*	William Smith 1839–76]

[The benefice consisted of Overbury (**17.18**) with Alstone and the chapelries of Teddington (**17.19**) and Little Washbourne (**15.32**).]

343.2.10   Parish of Stanley Pontlarge

Area 960 acres; 10 inhabited houses, 2 uninhabited. Population 66.

15.34 (33)   **Church of England,** [unknown dedication] **Stanley Pontlarge**

Name	Chapel of ease, Stanley
Consecration	[Not given]
Erected	[Restored 1860–1]
Endowment	[Not given]
Sittings	[Not given]
Attend'ce 30 Mar.	Morning 25. Total [25]
Avge attendance	[Not given]
Remarks	This paper has been forwarded by me to the officiating minister, the Rev W[illiam] Whalley of Toddington – who declines filling it up.
Dated	[Not dated]
Signed	James Lovesy, [e]numerator
[*Incumbent*	William Whalley 1843–71]

[Whalley, who lived in Bath, was also the incumbent of Toddington (**15.27**) with Stanley Pontlarge and of Didbrook (**15.4**) with Pinnock and Hailes Chapel (**15.18**)]

343.2.11   Extra parochial Prescott

Area 430 acres; 12 inhabited houses, 2 uninhabited. Population 51.
VCH 6, 220–23

[By the 16th century the chapel at Prescott was no longer in use and thereafter the parishioners worshipped at Stanley Pontlarge (**10.34**)]

343.2.12–15   Parish of Bishop's Cleeve

Area 8,150 acres; 457 inhabited houses, 24 uninhabited. Population 2,117.
The parish includes the township of Bishop's Cleeve and the hamlets of Gotherington, Woodmancote, Southam and Brockhampton, together with Stoke Orchard.
VCH 8, 2–25

15.35 (35)   **Church of England, St Michael and All Angels, Bishop's Cleeve**

Name	Bishop's Cleeve. An ancient parish church
Consecration	Before 1800
Erected	[Restorations in 1886, 1896–7 and 1900]
Endowment	[240 acres of glebe] {Total £1,574}
Sittings	Free about 100. Other about 250. Total 350
Attend'ce 30 Mar.	Morning 80 + 63 SS. Total [143]
	Afternoon 166 + 35 SS. Total [201]
	(Wet Sunday – stormy – accounts for the smallness of congregation)

Avge attendance	Morning 70 + 70 SS. Total [140]
	Afternoon 250. Total [250]
Remarks	I believe this benefice is worth about £1,600 per annum, but your informant has no accurate knowledge on this point.
Dated	31 March 1851
Signed	Henry Palmer, curate [1845–51]
	Bishop's Cleeve, rectory
[*Incumbent*	William Lawrence Townsend 1830–83]

[Townsend, who had also been the incumbent of Alderton 1830–42 (**15.28**), suffered from ill-health. Mostly non-resident, he was criticised in the press for neglecting his parochial duties: *Bristol Mercury,* 26 Jan. 1839. See also Aldred, 190–2. 'In 1871 the people of Cleeve protested against ritualistic innovations by the curate': *VCH* 8, 21. The benefice consisted of Bishop's Cleeve with Stoke Orchard (345.1.14). There were two ancient chapels within the parish – St James the Great, Stoke Orchard (**15.36**) and The Ascension, Southam (a medieval building, formerly a church and later a barn, restored 1861–2).]

15.36 (34)   Church of England, St James the Great, Stoke Orchard

Name	Chapel of ease
Consecration	Before 1800
Erected	[Restored 1862]
Endowment	[See Bishop's Cleeve (**18.35**)]
Sittings	Free 100. Total 100
Attend'ce 30 Mar.	Morning 50 + 27 SS. Total 77
Avge attendance	Morning 46 + 30 SS. Total 76
	Afternoon 86 + 30 SS. Total 116
Remarks	Stoke Orchard is a chapel of ease belonging to Bishop's Cleeve and forms a portion of the Bishop's Cleeve benefice. There is a single duty at the chapel alternating morning and evening.
Dated	31 March 1851
Signed	Henry Palmer, curate [1845–51]
	Bishop's Cleeve, Cheltenham
[*Incumbent*	William Lawrence Townsend [1830–83]

[The benefice consisted of Bishop's Cleeve (**15.35**) with Stoke Orchard.]

15.37 (37)   Countess of Huntingdon's Connexion, Woodmancote

Name	Woodmancote chapel
Erected	1825 [Replaced by a new chapel, opened 6 June 1854]
Building	Yes [separate and entire] Yes [exclusively as a place of worship]
Sittings	Free 100. Total [100] Standing room 30 feet long, 20 wide, 14 high
Attend'ce 30 Mar.	Morning 50 SS. Total [50]
	Afternoon 55 + 24 SS. Total [79]
	Evening 42. Total [42]
Avge attendance	Morning 45 SS. Total [45]
	Afternoon 55 + 20 SS. Total [75]
	Evening 50. Total [50]
Dated	30 March 1851
Signed	James Downing, manager [draper employing three men]
	135 High St, Cheltenham

[Downing was also associated with the chapel at Bishop's Cleeve (**15.39**).]

15.38 (36)   Countess of Huntingdon's Connexion, Gotherington

Denomination	The late Selina, Countess of Huntingdon's Connexion
Name	Gotherington chapel
Erected	1833
Building	Yes [separate and entire] Yes, except as a Sunday school.
Sittings	Free 168. Total [168] Standing room for about 32 including the vestry
Attend'ce 30 Mar.	Morning 45 SS. Total 45
	Afternoon 57 + 32 SS. Total 89
	Evening 30 + 6 SS. Total 36
Avge attendance	Morning 65 SS. Total 65
	Afternoon 90 + 40 SS. Total 130
	Evening 50 + 10 SS. Total 60
Dated	31 March 1851
Signed	William Jackson, one of the trustees [farmer]
	Brick House Farm, Gotherington

15.39 (38)   Countess of Huntingdon's Connexion, Bishop's Cleeve

Name	Cleeve chapel
Erected	1844
Building	Yes [separate and entire] Yes [exclusively as a place of worship]
Sittings	Free 250. Total [250] Standing room length 32 feet, width 20 feet, height 18 feet
Attend'ce 30 Mar.	Morning 12 + 38 SS. Total [50]
	Afternoon 50 SS. Total [50]
	Evening 60. Total [60]
Avge attendance (6m)	Morning 12 + 40 SS. Total [52]
	Afternoon 50 SS. Total [50]
	Evening 30 + 20 SS. Total [50]
Dated	30 March 1851
Signed	James Downing, manager [draper employing three men]
	135 High St, Cheltenham

[Downing was also associated with the chapel at Woodmancote (**15.37**).]

---

16. HO 129/344 CHELTENHAM DISTRICT: 42 places of worship

344.1 CHARLTON KINGS SUB-DISTRICT

344.1.1 Hamlet of Uckington, Elmstone Hardwicke
Area of the hamlet 880 acres; 41 inhabited houses. Population 173.
Part of the parish of Elmstone Hardwicke (345.1.1).

344.1.2 Parish of Swindon
Area 721 acres; 47 inhabited houses, 4 uninhabited. Population 221.

16.1 (2)	**Church of England, St Lawrence, Swindon**
Name	An ancient parish church of Norman date. Dedicated to St Lawrence
Consecration	Before 1800
Erected	[Mostly rebuilt 1844–6]
Endowment	Tithe £230. Glebe £100. Fees £60. {Total £339}
Sittings	Free 224. Total 224
Attend'ce 30 Mar.	Morning 98 + 34 SS. Total 132
	Afternoon 137 + 36 SS. Total 173
Avge attendance	[Not given]
Dated	31 March 1851
Signed	Samuel Raymond, rector [1829–51]
	Cheltenham

344.3 Parish of Prestbury
Area 3,022 acres; 259 inhabited houses, 15 uninhabited. Population 1,314.
VCH 8, 67–81

16.2 (3)	**Church of England, St Mary, Prestbury**
Name	An ancient parish church. Name given at consecration not known
Consecration	[Not given]
Erected	[Restored 1864–8]
Endowment	Land about £27. Tithe about £220. Fees about £20. Easter offerings about £3. {Total £234}
Sittings	Free 50. Other 280. Children's 90. Total 420
Attend'ce 30 Mar.	Morning 264 + 62 SS. Total 326
	Afternoon 198 + 42 SS. Total 240
Avge attendance	Morning 290 + 75 SS. Total 370 [*recte* 365]
	Afternoon 290 + 70 SS. Total 370 [*recte* 360]
Dated	31 March 1851
Signed	John Edwards, vicar [1825–60]
	Prestbury, near Cheltenham

[His son, also John Edwards (later known as Baghot de la Bere), and incumbent from 1860, was an extreme Anglo-Catholic. Suspended in 1878 for illegal ritualistic practices, he was deprived of the living in 1881 but remained as curate until resigning in 1884, and moved to Sussex. He was curate of St Paul, Brighton 1884–90, and vicar of St Mary, Buxted 1890–8: Yates 1999, 250–2.]

344.4 Parish of Charlton Kings
Area 3,170 acres; 649 inhabited houses, 35 uninhabited. Population 3,174.
Since 1821 the increase in population of 1,567 was due to the proximity of Cheltenham.

16.3 (4)   **Church of England, St Mary, Charlton Kings**

Name   I believe, St Mary's, officially a chapelry of Cheltenham. Long since a parish church

Consecration   I am not aware that any record of this exists. But long before the Reformation.

Erected   [Mostly rebuilt 1877–8]

Endowment   Land none. Tithe none. Glebe and house £35. OPE ... paid by ... £40. Queen Anne's Bounty £24 6s 2d. Pew rents none. Fees very variable. Dues and Easter offerings none. There is a subscription made about Easter for a second service. {Total £177}

Sittings   Free 150. Other 531. Children's 100. Total 781

Attend'ce 30 Mar.   Morning 444 + 126 SS. Total 570
Afternoon 381 + 116 SS. Total 497
Evening 164. Total 164

Avge attendance   Morning 400 + 120 SS. Total 520
Afternoon 320 + 100 SS. Total 420
Evening 130. Total 130
This is little more than a guess.

Remarks   The congregation of yesterday as counted enables me to estimate more correctly the average as above.

Dated   31 March 1851

Signed   James Frederic Secretan Gabb, perpetual curate [1834–75]
[The Parsonage], Charlton Kings, nr Cheltenham.

[Within the parish Holy Apostles opened for worship 5 June 1871 but was not consecrated until 2 June 1885, because of theological differences between the Evangelical promoter and the Anglo-Catholic incumbent of St Mary's. A separate parish was created 22 Sept. 1885.]

16.4 (5)   **Wesleyan Methodist, Charlton Kings**

Name   Wesleyan Chapel

Erected   1838

Building   Yes [separate and entire] Yes [exclusively as a place of worship]

Sittings   Free 92. Other 82. Total [174]

Attend'ce 30 Mar.   Afternoon 17 + 36 SS. Total 53
Evening 65. Total 65

Avge attendance   [Not given]

Dated   31 March 1851

Signed   William Henry Cornforth, minister [1849–51]
22 Gt Norwood Street, Cheltenham

[Cornforth was also minister at Cheltenham (**16.31, 33**), Golden Valley (**16.32**), Arle (**16.34**), Northleach (**13.11**) Turkdean (**13.45**) and Withington (**13.29**).]

344.1.5 Parish of Leckhampton

Area 1,330 acres; 400 inhabited houses, 9 uninhabited. Population 2,149.
Since 1821 the increase in population of 1,831 was due to the proximity of Cheltenham.

16.5 (7)   **Church of England, St Peter, Leckhampton**

Name   Parish church

Consecration   Before 1800

Erected   [Rebuilt and enlarged 1865–6]

Endowment   Glebe £350. {Total £356}

Sittings   Free 142. Other 176. Total 318

Attend'ce 30 Mar.   [Not given]

Avge attendance   Morning 100 + 65 SS. Total 165

Afternoon 160 + 65 SS. Total 225

Dated   31 March 1851
Signed   Charles Brandon Trye, rector [1830–84]
[Trye was succeeded by his son Reginald Trye 1884–1912.]

16.6 (6)   Church of England, St Philip and St James, Grafton Road
Name   St Philip and St James, proprietary church or chapel, under the Act 5 Geo.
                  IV [c.103 (1824)]
Consecration   1 May 1840, as an additional church. [As a chapel of ease to St Peter,
                  Leckhampton. Rebuilt 1879–82 and consecrated 13 Apr. 1882]
Erected   Partly by subscription and partly by money advanced by proprietors. The
                  site having been presented by a private benefactor. Money advanced by
                  proprietors about £2,000. Private benefaction and subscription about
                  £2,000. Total cost about £4,000
Endowment   The income is very precarious; a portion of the pew rents is the private
                  property of the proprietors; other pew rents ditto go to the minister.
                  The whole proceeds are voluntary and the property is private.
Sittings   Free 350. Other 480. Total 830
                  This is the number by measurement, but many of the sittings are incon-
                  venient and practically useless.
Attend'ce 30 Mar. Morning 507 + 150 SS. Total 657
                  Afternoon 510 + 150 SS. Total 660
                  Evening. NB in the evening some members of this congregation attend
                  other churches.
Avge attendance (6m) Morning 510 + 150. Total 660
                  Afternoon 510 + 150 SS. Total 660
Remarks   Some persons attend divine service in the morning who do not in the
                  afternoon, and vice versa. I reckon that about 800 attend once at least
                  every Sunday. (As far as I think it right to make a return).
Dated   31 March 1851
Signed   Joseph Esmond Riddle, minister [1840–59]
                  Cheltenham
[A memorial in the church referred to Riddle's 'simplicity of character, his integrity, and his
kindness of heart'. He was 'a painstaking and laborious scholar, a vigorous defender of Evangelical
principles against the Tractarian movement, and an earnest but unimpassioned preacher': *ODNB* 'Joseph
Esmond Riddle (1804–1859)'. The parish of St Philip and St James was created 14 May 1869.]

344.1.6 Parish of Coberley
Area 3,421 acres; 51 inhabited houses. Population 243.
VCH 7, 174–83

16.7 (8)   Church of England, St Giles, Coberley
Name   Coberley Church. Dedicated to St Giles. Ancient parish church
Consecration   Before 1800
Erected   [Rebuilt (apart from the tower and porch) 1868–71]
Endowment   Land not any. Tithe rent charge £424. Glebe (17 acres) £12. OPE not
                  any. [Total] £436. Pew rents not any. Fees £1. Dues, Easter offerings,
                  other sources not any. {Total £320}
Sittings   Free 80. Other 100. Total 180
Attend'ce 30 Mar. Morning 36 + 16 SS. Total 52
                  Afternoon 51 + 16 SS. Total 67
Avge attendance [Not given]

Remarks	The sittings of the Sunday scholars are not included! The day has been wet: especially the afternoon!
Dated	31 March 1851
Signed	William Hicks, rector [1816–66]
	Coberley rectory, Cheltenham

[Hicks was also the incumbent of Whittington (**13.31**) and from 1853 he appointed curates who lived in or near Cheltenham.]

16.8 (9)   **Baptist, Coberley**

Name	Coberley Chapel [Ebenezer Chapel]
Erected	1826
Building	Yes [separate and entire] Yes [exclusively as a place of worship]
Sittings	Free 150. Other 40. Total [190] Standing room 30 feet long, 20 wide and gallery 30 by 10
Attend'ce 30 Mar.	Morning 76 + 20 SS. Total [96]
	Afternoon 110 + 20 SS. Total [130]
Avge attendance	Morning 69 + 24 SS. Total 29 [*recte* 93]
	Afternoon 70 + 20 SS. Total [90]
Dated	30 March 1851
Signed	Philip Weaver, deacon
	Hatherley Lane, Cheltenham
[*Minister*	Thomas Davis 1832–63]

[Weaver, who succeeded Davis, was also a deacon at the chapel in the parish of Brimpsfield (**12.10**). Davis was an evangelist, setting up preaching stations at Birdlip (**12.9**), Colesbourne (**12.13**), Compton Abdale (**13.25**), Cowley (**16.8**), Cranham (**10.22**), Elkstone, Foxcote (**13.28**), Haselton, Shipton Oliffe (**13.37**) and Withington. He was also minister of Miserden (**10.24**) and Winstone (**12.6**). Attempts to preach at Whittington were abandoned because of opposition: Oliver, 110–2.]

344.1.7 Parish of Cowley

Area 1,834 acres; 68 inhabited houses, 3 uninhabited. Population 317.
VCH 7, 192–9

16.9 (10)   **Church of England, St Mary, Cowley**

Name	Dedicated to St Mary. Commonly known by the name of Cowley church. Ancient parish church
Consecration	Before 1800
Erected	[Restored 1871–2]
Endowment	Land £81 10s. Tithe £231. {Total £322}
Sittings	Free 60. Other 80. Total 140
Attend'ce 30 Mar.	Morning 35 + 16 SS. Total 51
	Afternoon 60 + 12 SS. Total 72
Avge attendance	[Not given]
Dated	31 March 1851
Signed	John Colborne, minister [curate 1846–54]
	Cheltenham
[*Incumbent*	Robert Smith 1837–70]

[Smith lived in or near Gloucester and employed curates.]

16.10 (11)   **Baptist, Cowley**

Name	None [Moriah Chapel]
Erected	[1841]
Building	Dwelling house [separate and entire]

Sittings	Free 50. Total [50] Standing room for 45
Attend'ce 30 Mar.	Evening [41] Total 41
Avge attendance	[Not given]
Dated	31 March 1851
Signed	William Greening, deacon [agricultural labourer]
	Cowley, Glo'shire

344.1.8 Parish of Great Witcombe

Area 918 acres; 34 inhabited houses, 1 uninhabited. Population 167.

16.11 (12) **Church of England, St Mary, Great Witcombe**

Name	Parish Church
Consecration	Before 1800
Erected	[1750–2 and restored 1889–90]
Endowment	Tithe £130. {Total £97}
Sittings	Total 100, and benches for the school children
Attend'ce 30 Mar.	Morning 38 + 22 SS. Total 60
	Afternoon 75 + 23 SS. Total 98
Avge attendance	Morning 50 + 30 SS. Total 80
	Afternoon 90 + 30 SS. Total 120
Remarks	The gross estimate value of the living is stated as fixed by the commutation of tithes in the year 1838, without deducting rates etc. which would considerably reduce it.
Dated	31 March 1851
Signed	John Rawlin Trye, minister [1845–80]
	Witcombe, Gloucester

344.1.9 Parish of Badgeworth

Area 3,927 acres; 191 inhabited houses, 9 uninhabited. Population 874.
The parish includes the hamlets of Badgeworth, Bentham, Little Shurdington and Little Witcombe.

16.12 (13) **Church of England, Holy Trinity, Badgeworth**

Name	Badgeworth Church. Ancient parish church
Consecration	[Not given]
Erected	[Restored 1868–9]
Endowment	Land £47. Tithe £300. Fees £4. {Total £295}
Sittings	Free 80. Other 120. Total 200
Attend'ce 30 Mar.	Morning 120 + 27 SS. Total 147
	Afternoon 150 + 27 SS. Total 177
Avge attendance	[Not given]
Remarks	The average has not been computed and the return of congregation is hardly anything to be depended on, as it is very irregular owing to the population being scattered and affected by the weather and the employment of boys and men in bird tending and cattle leading at different seasons.
Dated	31 March 1851
Signed	Alfred William Ellis Viner, vicar [1849–1903]
	Vicarage, Badgeworth, Cheltenham

[The benefice consisted of Badgeworth with Great Shurdington (**16.13**). Within the parish the chapel of ease of St Peter, Bentham was consecrated 29 June 1889.]

344.1.10 Parish of Great Shurdington
Area 383 acres; 39 inhabited houses, 2 uninhabited. Population 173.

16.13 (14)	**Church of England, St Paul, Great Shurdington**
Name	Believed to be dedicated to S. Paul. Church of an ancient chapelry annexed to Badgeworth, but of a distinct and separate parish.
Consecration	[Not given]
Erected	[Restored and enlarged 1851–2]
Endowment	Tithe £40 [See Badegeworth (**16.12**)]
Sittings	Free 56. Other 130. Total 186
Attend'ce 30 Mar.	[Not given]
Avge attendance	Morning 80 + 50 SS. Total 130
	Afternoon 120 + 50 SS. Total 170
Remarks	Under 'total sittings' is not included the space allotted to Sunday scholars.
Dated	31 March 1851
Signed	Harry Wright, stipendiary curate [1849–59]
	Cheltenham
[*Incumbent*	Alfred William Ellis Viner 1849–1903]

[The benefice consisted of Badgeworth (**16.12**) with Great Shurdington.]

16.14 (15)	**Independent, Great Shurdington**
Name	None
Erected	[Not given]
Building	No, a cottage. No [not exclusively as a place of worship]
Sittings	Free 60. Total [60]
Attend'ce 30 Mar.	No Sunday school
Avge attendance	Evening 15. Total [15]
Remarks	The service is held only in the evening, and this evening there happened to be no service.
Dated	31 March 1851
Signed	Baynham Nathaniel Coopley [wheelwright and blacksmith] (attendant on the evening of 30th).
	The Post Office, Shurdington
	For Thomas Holiday, Winchcombe

344.1.11 Parish of Up Hatherley
Area 810 acres; 10 inhabited houses, 1 uninhabited. Population 50.
[St Philip and St James, Up Hatherley was consecrated 27 April 1886]

344.1.12 Parish of Staverton
Area 720 acres; 60 inhabited houses, 12 uninhabited. Population 278.
VCH 8, 89–95

16.15 (16)	**Church of England, St Catherine, Staverton**
(Summary form)	
Name	Staverton
Erected	[Restored 1871–2 and 1896–7]
[*Endowment*	Total £436]
Sittings	Free about 50. Other about 25. Total about 75
Usual attend'ce	Morning 30 to 40 + 30 to 40 SS. Total [60–80]
	Afternoon 70 to 100 + 30 to 40 SS. Total [100–140]
Signed	Thomas Purnell, vicar [1841–92]

[Boddington Manor]
[The benefice consisted of Staverton with Boddington (345.1.2). From 1889 Robert Hughes Wilkinson Purnell was curate to his father and succeeded him 1892–8.]

344.2   CHELTENHAM SUB-DISTRICT

344.2   Parish of Cheltenham

Area 3,740 acres; 6,356 inhabited houses, 612 uninhabited. Population 35,051.
The parish includes the township of Cheltenham, the tithings of Alstone and Arle and the hamlets of Naunton, Westall and Sandford. The Union Workhouse situated in the parish had 537 inmates. 'The increase of population [from 3,076 in 1801 to 35,051 in 1851] is attributed to the resort of visitors to the mineral springs, and to the number of families who have become permanently resident in the town and its vicinity': Civil Census.]

16.16a (18)   **Church of England, St Mary, High Street**

Name	[Not given]
Consecration	Some 1,000 years since
Erected	[Restored 1859–61 and 1875–7]
Endowment	Land, tithe, glebe none. OPE £40 per an[num] by Henry VIII. Pew rents none. Fees say £350 (uncertain). Dues none. Easter offerings £500 per an[num] Other sources none. {Total £688}
Sittings	Free 400. Other 1,200. Total 1,600
Attend'ce 30 Mar.	Morning 1,600 + 120 SS. Total 1,720
	Afternoon 1,000. Total 1,000
	Evening 2,000. Total 2,000
Avge attendance	Always full and crowded
Dated	31 March 1851
Signed	Francis Close, incumbent [1826–56]
	[The Grange, Lansdown Terrace], Cheltenham

[Close was the curate of Holy Trinity (**16.17**) 1824–6; perpetual curate of St Mary 1826–56; and dean of Carlisle 1856–81. His Evangelical preaching attracted many residents and visitors. Within the parish he was responsible for the erection of St Paul (**16.18**), Christ Church (**16.20**), St Peter (**16.21**) and St Luke, consecrated 7 Nov. 1854. St Matthew, the chapel of ease to St Mary, was consecrated 17 Apr. 1879. Close, a noted controversialist and opponent of the Oxford Movement, was responsible for making Cheltenham an important educational centre: *ODNB* 'Francis Close (1797–1882)'. When Joseph Leech attended a service at the parish church the building was almost full. 'I never before saw such a congregation in my life, for the size of the building: it seemed as though they were piled on each other's heads – tier upon tier, they sat with their eyes intent upon the reading desk, until the vicar (sic), making his appearance from the vestry, occupied his place': Leech 1847, 256. On 3 Feb. 2013 St Mary's became Cheltenham Minster.]

16.16b (21)   **Church of England, St Mary, High Street**
(Summary form)

Name	St Mary's parish church, Cheltenham
Erected	Antient
Sittings	Free 320. Other 1,500. Total 1,820
Usual attend'ce	Morning, afternoon and evening always crowded
	SS 130 girls. Exclusive of the day school of boys which attend – 130 also.
Signed	Francis Close, incumbent

16.17 (17)   **Church of England, Holy Trinity, Portland Street**

Name	Holy Trinity, Cheltenham
Consecration	11 April 1823
Erected	By subscription [as a proprietary chapel] Supposed total cost £16,000

Endowment	Land grounds. Pew rents £267 1s 8d. Dues [unclear] {Total £305}
Sittings	Free 444. Other 906. Total 1,350
Attend'ce 30 Mar.	Morning 1,056. Total [1,056]
	Afternoon 738. Total [738]
Avge attendance	Morning 1,100. Total [1,100]
	Afternoon 780. Total [780]
Remarks	Those persons in attendance on divine service 30 March were counted. The number was apparently below the usual average.
Dated	31 March 1851
Signed	John Browne, curate [1828–57]
	East Hayes, [Pittville Circus Road], Cheltenham

[Browne (1794–1857), who 'acquired fame as a preacher' (Venn) was second to Close in the Anglican hierarchy of Cheltenham. Holy Trinity was a chapel of ease to St Mary's until 1898 when it became a parish church.]

16.18 (19)   Church of England, St Paul, St Paul's Road

Name	St Paul's Church. District parish, Cheltenham
Consecration	In 1830 [12 July 1830] An additional church. Constituted a separate district in 1845, under the provisions of a late Act for churches whose rites [sic] are conveyed to the Church Commissioners.
Erected	By private benefaction and grant from Church Commissioners
Endowment	Pew rents £300. Deduct expenses £110. Collections to nearest pound £190. Expenses £60. [Total] £250. Fees etc. are paid to the incumbent of St Mary's during his incumbency. {Total £150}
Sittings	Free 700. Other 700. Total 1,400
Attend'ce 30 Mar.	Morning 700 + 200 SS. Total 900*
	Evening 1,200. Total 1,200
Avge attendance	[Not given]
Remarks	*The numbers were actually counted in the gross. There was accidentally a larger than average evening congregation by one third. Pew rents amount to about £300 from which are taken £110 for annual expenses.
Dated	31 March 1851
Signed	Charles Henry Bromby, incumbent [1843–64]
	[Training College], Cheltenham

[Bromby was minister of St Paul's and from 1847 the first principal of Cheltenham Training College. He was bishop of Tasmania 1864–82, and on returning to England served in the dioceses of Lichfield and Bath and Wells: *ODNB* 'Charles Henry Bromby (1814–1907)'.]

16.19 (23)   Church of England, St James, Suffolk Square

Name	St James Church, Suffolk Square, Cheltenham. Proprietary church
Consecration	5 Oct. 1830, as a church built by proprietors, but never endowed.
Erected	Present bishop of Glo'ster and Bristol. Private benefaction £9,000. Total cost £9,000 [Erected under 5 Geo. IV, c.103 (1824)]
Endowment	Pew rents £250 (ministers), £700 (ten proprietors). {Total £250}
Sittings	Free 350. Other 1,400. Total 1,750
Attend'ce 30 Mar.	Morning 1,400 + 200 SS. Total 1,600
	Afternoon 600 + 200 SS. Total 800
Avge attendance	The attendance seldom or never varies.
Dated	31 March 1851
Signed	Francis Duncan Gilby, incumbent [1843–66]
	[Cockington House, Lansdown], Cheltenham

16.20 (22)	**Church of England, Christ Church, Malvern Road**
Name	Christ Church, Cheltenham built under the provisions of 5 Geo. IV, c.103 [1824]
Consecration	On 26 January 1840 [*recte* 21 Jan. 1840]
Erected	By certain proprietors. Total cost (by shares) £18,000. [Internally remodelled 1888–9 and 1893]
Endowment	OPE ... £285. Pew rents £150 to £200. {Total £400}
Sittings	Free 434. Other 1,401. Total 1,835
Attend'ce 30 Mar.	Morning 1,460. Total [1,460]
	Afternoon 800. Total [800]
Avge attendance	[Not given]
Dated	26 March 1851
Signed	Archibald Boyd, incumbent [1842–59]
	[11] Hatherley Place, Cheltenham

[Boyd was the moderate Evangelical incumbent of Christ Church, then of St James', Paddington 1859–67; and dean of Exeter 1867–83: *ODNB* 'Archibald Boyd (1803–1883)'. Within the parish St Mark's church was consecrated 8 Jan. 1862, and St Stephen's chapel of ease 20 Dec. 1883.]

16.21 (20)	**Church of England, St Peter, Tewkesbury Road**
Name	The church of the new parish of St Peter, in the borough of Cheltenham
Consecration	22 March 1849, as the church for the new parish constituted by Order of Council under 6 and 7 Vict. c.37 [1843]
Erected	Entirely by private subscriptions £4,500. Total cost £4,500
Endowment	{Total £150}
Sittings	Free 700. Other 350. Total 1,050
Attend'ce 30 Mar.	[Not given]
Avge attendance	[Not given]
Dated	31 March 1851
Signed	William Hodgson, perpetual curate [1845–66]
	Nash Cottage, [North Place], Cheltenham

[From 1844 to 1849 the congregation of 350 people had assembled in the infant schoolroom in Waterloo Place. A district was created in 1845, and a parish in 1868.]

16.22 (28)	**Independent, Albion Street**
Name	Albion Street Congregational Chapel
Erected	1835 as a Methodist chapel. Became an Independent chapel 1828
Building	Yes [separate and entire] Yes [exclusively as a place of worship]
Sittings	Free 80. Other 200. Total [280] Standing room none
Attend'ce 30 Mar.	Morning 54 + 69 SS. Total 123
	Evening 100. Total 100
Avge attendance	Morning 70 + 66 SS. Total 136
	Afternoon 70 SS. Total [70]
	Evening 140. Total 140
Dated	31 March 1851
Signed	Edward Minton, minister [1848–52]
	17 Queen's Retreat, [Gloucester Road], Cheltenham

16.23 (24)	**Congregational or Independent, Grosvenor Street**
Name	Highbury Chapel [Snow's Chapel]
Erected	About 1801. First used as a Congregational Chapel 1827
Building	Yes [separate and entire] Yes [exclusively as a place of worship]
Sittings	Free 150. Other 600. Total [750]

Attend'ce 30 Mar.   Morning 466 + 174 SS. Total 640
                       Evening 470. Total 470
Avge attendance   Morning 500 + 150 SS. Total 650
                       Evening 750. Total 750
Remarks   This chapel was built by a lady [Harriet Wall] for the Rev Mr [Thomas]
                       Snow, a seceder from the established church who afterwards returned to
                       the Church [of England], and after passing through several hands, was
                       purchased for a Congregational Chapel and opened in connexion with
                       this denomination in 1827 [as Highbury Chapel]
Dated   31 March 1851
Signed   Andrew Morton Brown LLD, minister [1843–79]
                       1 Oxford Street, Cheltenham
                       (This is incorrect of my own knowledge. J. Scott).
[The minister of Highbury Chapel also had oversight of the congregation at Oxenton (**17.17**). In
1822 after Snow left the chapel it was purchased by Charles Simeon, but there being no
endowment, and the bishop unwilling to consecrate, it was auctioned for £1,200. The purchaser then
sold it to the Congregationalists for £1,300 (£1,200 of this was given by the wealthy Congregational
benefactor Thomas Wilson who lived at Highbury Place, London and was treasurer of Highbury
College): Munden 1999, 321–7; Munden 2009, 57–63; *ODNB* 'Thomas Wilson (1764–1843)'. The
chapel was named after this Highbury connection. It closed in 1852, was replaced by Highbury
Congregational Chapel in Winchcombe Street (demolished 1932), in turn replaced by a new
Highbury Chapel opened in Priory Terrace in 1934. Brown (1812–1879) 'was a popular preacher,
although perhaps not in the same league of popularity as Francis Close': Aldred 2012, 55.]

16.24 (31)   **Independent or Congregational, St George's Square**
Name   Cheltenham Chapel [St George's Chapel]
Erected   [Opened 2 August] 1809 [Tablet: 'Cheltenham Chapel, 1809']
Building   Yes [separate and entire] Yes [exclusively as a place of worship]
Sittings   Free 250. Other 550. Total [800] Standing room none
Attend'ce 30 Mar.   Morning 163 + 55 SS. Total 218
                        Evening 174. Total 174
Avge attendance (4m) Morning 200 + 55 SS. Total 255
                        Evening 220. Total [220]
Remarks   About 100 sittings are let. The chapel will seat 800 persons.
Dated   31 March 1851
Signed   John Rawlinson, minister [1850–4]
                        Northfield Cottage, North Place, Cheltenham.
[Cheltenham Chapel was opened by Rowland Hill (see **5.8**), and some of the early ministers were
from the Countess of Huntingdon's Connexion. The chapel closed in 1857 and was then occupied by
Presbyterians 1858–86, who then relocated to St Andrew's Presbyterian church, Fauconberg Road.]

16.25 (44)   **Congregational, Upper Bath Street**
(Summary form)
Name   Upper Bath Street Chapel
Erected   About 1822
Building   Yes [separate and entire] Yes [exclusively as a place of worship]
Sittings   Free 200. Total [200]
Usual attend'ce   Morning 42 + 30 SS. Total 72
                        Afternoon 27 + 30 SS. Total 57
                        Evening 56. Total 56
Signed   Caleb Parker [dyer]
                        Suffolk Road, [Cheltenham]

Sittings	100
	Ground floor 26 ft by 30 ft. No gallery
Attend'ce 30 Mar.	Morning 21. Total [21]
	Afternoon 9. Total [9]
Dated	31 day of the 3rd month 1851
Signed	John Matthews [farmer, of 33 acres]
	Urban Lodge, Oxford Street, Cheltenham

16.40 (43)   Unitarian, Chapel Walk

Name	Bays Hill Chapel
Erected	[Opened 5 Apr.] 1844
Building	Yes [separate and entire] Yes [exclusively as a place of worship]
Sittings	All free. Other 300
Attend'ce 30 Mar.	Morning 60 + 12 SS. Total 72
	Evening 35. Total 35
Avge attendance	Morning 50 + 14 SS. Total [64]
Dated	3 April 1851
Signed	Thomas Bartlett Shenton, secretary [printer and stationer]
	90 Winchcombe Street, Cheltenham
[*Minister*	Henry Solly 1847–51]

[Solly was involved in many radical causes, including 'universal suffrage and education, anti-corn law agitation, the co-operative movement, early closing for shops and Sunday opening of museums, anti-slavery and much else.' He was sympathetic towards Chartism; by denomination a Unitarian, he 'always disliked the Unitarian label'. In June 1862 he founded the Working Men's Club and Institute Union and became the first secretary in the following year: *ODNB* 'Henry Solly (1813–1903)'. He was highly critical of Francis Close whom he described as 'a most earnest, bigoted, devout and bitter opponent of heresy in every form, but especially of Unitarianism': Solly, 2, 33]

16.41 (34)   Synagogue, St James' Square

Name	Jewish Synagogue
Erected	Fourteen years [Opened 14 May 1839]
Building	Yes [separate and entire] Yes [exclusively as a place of worship]
Sittings	Free 15. Other 70. Total [85]
Attend'ce 30 Mar.	Morning 16. Total 16
Avge attendance (6m)	Morning 20. Total 20
Remarks	Service held on Saturdays
Dated	30 March 1851
Signed	Hertz Karo. Samuel Sternberg [pawn-broker] Montague Alex, sec'y [surgeon-dentist]
	21 Rodney Terrace, Cheltenham [Alex's surgery]
[*Reader*	Raphael Jacobsohn]

[A Jewish congregation existed in Cheltenham by 1823, and originally worshipped in a room in St George's Place. Outgrowing this, they purchased the synagogue site in Dec. 1834, and building began in 1837: Blake, 32; Torode, 39]

16.42 (33)   Church of Jesus Christ of Latter-day Saints, Clare Street

Name	Tabernacle Chapel
Erected	About 1837 [Closed 1860]
Building	Yes [separate and entire] Yes [exclusively as a place of worship]
Sittings	All free 630. Total [630]
Attend'ce 30 Mar.	Morning 150. Total [150]
	Afternoon 300. Total [300]

	Evening 500. Total [500]
Avge attendance	[Not given]
Remarks	230 joined members. 230 to 300 more generally attend. The Tabernacle Chapel was rented by this body on the 8 March 1851, formerly occupied Zoar Chapel, Manchester Walk, Cheltenham.
Dated	31 March 1851
Signed	James A. Ross, president of Cheltenham conference
	15 Townsend Street, Cheltenham

[The chapel was opened by Baptists in 1836, who moved in 1843 to Ebenezer Chapel (**16.28**). Occupied by the Mormons 1843–60; then the St Luke's Mission Room 1860–1933.]

17. HO 129/345 TEWKESBURY DISTRICT: 37 places of worship

345.1   DEERHURST SUB-DISTRICT

345.1.1 Parish of Elmstone Hardwicke
Area 2,610 acres; 97 inhabited houses, 3 uninhabited. Population 391.
The parish includes the hamlets of Uckington (344.1.1) and Hardwicke.
VCH 8, 50–60

17.1a (1)	**Church of England, St Mary Magdalene, Elmstone Hardwicke**
Name	Ancient parish church of Elmstone Hardwicke
Consecration	Before 1800
Erected	[Mostly rebuilt 1871–8]
Endowment	Tithe vicarial £219 10s. Glebe £13 12s. {Total £233}
Sittings	Free 52. Other 159. Total 211
Attend'ce 6 Apr.	Morning 63 + 21 SS. Total 84
	Afternoon 110 + 21 SS. Total 131
Avge attendance	[Not given]
Remarks	Elmstone Hardwicke comprises two hamlets, Uckington and Hardwicke, the former in Cheltenham Union the latter in that of Tewkesbury, the two hamlets are also in different registrar's districts.
Dated	7 April 1851
Signed	John Byron, vicar [1833–79]
	Moor Place, near Cheltenhem, Gloucestershire

17.1b (344.1.1)	**Church of England, St Mary Magdalene, Elmstone Hardwicke**
(Summary form)	
Name	Elmstone Hardwicke
Erected	Ancient
Sittings	Free 52. Other 159. Total 211
Usual attend'ce	Morning 50 + 21 SS. Total [71]
	Afternoon 100. Total [100]
Signed	John Byron, vicar [1833–79]

345.1.2 Parish of Boddington
Area 930 acres; 91 inhabited houses, 4 uninhabited. Population 443.
VCH 8, 188–96

No return	**Church of England, St Mary Magdalene, Boddington**
[*Erected*	Restored 1876 and 1891]
[*Endowment*	See Staverton (**16.15**)]
[*Incumbent*	Thomas Purnell 1841–92]
[The benefice consisted of Staverton (**16.15**) with Boddington.]	

17.2 (2)	**Protestant Free Church, Boddington**
Name	Preaching room
Erected	June 1850
Building	Separate building. Yes [exclusively as a place of worship]
Sittings	Free 80. Total [80] Standing room for 20

Attend'ce 30 Mar.   Morning 45 SS. Total [45]
                      Evening 80. Total [80]
Avge attendance   [Not given]
Dated   31 March 1851
Signed   John Blagdon, owner [lord of the manor and magistrate]
           Boddington Manor, nr Cheltenham

345.1.3 Parish of The Leigh

Area 1,720 acres; 88 inhabited houses, 2 uninhabited. Population 470.
The parish includes the hamlet of Evington.
VCH 8, 60–7; *GNQ* 5, 189–90

17.3 (3)   **Church of England, St Catherine, The Leigh**
Name   [Not given]
Consecration   Before 1800.
Erected   [Restored 1884–5]
Endowment   Land (130 acres) £240. {Total £247}
Sittings   Free 100. Other 100. For children in chancel 50. Total 250
Attend'ce 30 Mar.   Morning 33 + 15 SS. Total [48]
                      Afternoon 82 + 18 SS. Total [100]
Avge attendance   Morning 20 + 12 SS. Total [32]
                    Afternoon 50 + 20 SS. Total [70]
Remarks   The net income of the benefice will not, I expect, at present be more than
            £200. Having been appointed to the living of Leigh only a short time and
            not having resided in the parish, I know little about it. I hope that the
            congregations will soon increase in numbers and the Sunday scholars
            also and that a weekly school will be established. J. S. Austin.
Dated   30 March 1851
Signed   John Southgate Austin, vicar [1851–82]
           Leigh vicarage, near Gloucester
[In the 1840s only about 30 people attended the parish church – but at the same time the Methodist
chapel was increasing in numbers: *VCH* 8, 66.]

345.1.4 Parish of Hasfield

Area 1,460 acres; 69 inhabited houses, 5 uninhabited. Population 300.
VCH 8, 282–90

17.4 (4)   **Church of England, St Mary, Hasfield**
Name   Hasfield Church. An ancient parish church
Consecration   Before 1800
Erected   [Restored 1849–50 and 1895]
Endowment   Land, tithe and glebe about £350. {Total £378}
Sittings   Free 75. [Free for] children 60. Other 75. Total 210
Attend'ce 30 Mar.   No service in the church but [SS] held in the licensed schoolroom.
Avge attendance   No reliable return can be made. The building has been closed for several
                    months, as well for necessary repairs after enlargement.
Dated   31 March 1851
Signed   James Sevier, rector [1833–81]
           Hasfield rectory, near Gloucester
[Sevier 'became a considerable landowner in the parish': *VCH* 8, 289.]

345.1.5 Parish of Tirley

Area 1,850 acres; 111 inhabited houses, 6 uninhabited. Population 526.

The parish includes the hamlet of Haw.
VCH 8, 95–105

17.5 (5)	**Church of England, St Matthew, Tirley**
Name	An ancient church, dedicated to St Matthew
Consecration	Before 1800
Erected	[Restored 1892–4]
Endowment	Glebe £362. Fees say £3. {Total £375}
Sittings	Free 66. Other 118. Total 184. In addition sittings for about 30 children in belfry 30. Total 214
Attend'ce 30 Mar.	Morning 35 + 29 SS. Total 64
	Afternoon 150 + 32 SS. Total 182
Avge attendance	Morning 40 + 35 SS. Total 75
	Afternoon 120 + 40 SS. Total 160
Dated	31 March 1851
Signed	Arthur Frederick Forde, curate [1849–54]
	Tirley, Tewkesbury, Glo'ster
[*Incumbent*	Joseph Frederic Hone 1827–88]

[From the early 19th century the church was known as St Matthew, but by the 1890s it had reverted to the 18th century usage, St Michael.]

17.6 (6)	**Wesleyan Methodist, Tirley**
Name	Upper Chapel
Erected	1821 [New chapel built 1887]
Building	Separate building. Exclusively [as a place of worship]
Sittings	Free 100. Other none. Total [100] Standing room for 200
Attend'ce 30 Mar.	Morning about 16. Total [16]
	Evening about 40. Total [40]
Avge attendance	Morning 60. Total [60]
Dated	31 March 1851
Signed	John Watts, manager (farmer) [of 135 acres]
	Tirley, Gloucestershire

17.7 (7)	**Bible Christian, Tirley**
Name	Lower Chapel
Erected	About 1839
Building	A separate building. Exclusively as a place of worship
Sittings	Free about 40. Other none. Total [40]
Attend'ce 30 Mar.	Afternoon 10. Total [10]
	Evening 30. Total [30]
Avge attend'ce (6m)	Morning 35. Total [35]
Dated	31 March 1851
Signed	Richard Hogg, manager (farmer) [of 214 acres]
	[Great House], Hasfield, Gloucestershire.

345.1.6 Parish of Chaceley, Worcestershire [transferred to Gloucestershire, 1931]
Area 1,725 acres; 67 inhabited houses, 2 uninhabited. Population 348.
VCH (Worcs.) 4, 55–6

17.8 (8)	**Church of England, St John the Baptist, Chaceley**
Name	St John the Baptist. An ancient chapeltry [of Longdon]
Consecration	Consecrated

Erected   [Restored 1881–2]
Endowment   Tithe £177. Glebe £7. Fees £2. {Total £134}
Sittings   Free 200. Other 150. Total 350
Attend'ce 30 Mar. Morning no service
                  Afternoon 100 + 15 SS. Total 115
Avge attendance   Morning 150 + 30 SS. Total 180
                  Afternoon 150 + 30 SS. Total 180
                  Evening 150. Total 150
Dated   30 March 1851
Signed   Samuel Stanley Paris, minister [1847–97]
                  Forthampton House, Forthampton, Tewkesbury

345.1.7   Parish of Pendock, Worcestershire
Area 1,163 acres; 70 inhabited houses, 3 uninhabited. Population 302.
VCH (Worcs.) 3, 478–81

17.9 (9)   **Church of England** *[dedication unknown],* **Pendock**
Name   *Pendock Church*
Consecration   *Before 1800*
Erected   *[Not given]*
Endowment   *Tithe £280 net. Glebe 24 acres. Fees £2. {Total £280}*
Sittings   *Free 52. Other 38. Total 90*
Attend'ce 30 Mar. *Morning 81 + 27 SS. Total 108*
                    Afternoon 11 + 27 SS. Total 38
Avge attendance   *Morning 45 to 90 + 20 to 30 SS. Total 65 to 120*
                    Afternoon 15 to 30 + 20 to 30 SS. Total [35–60]
Remarks   *Sunday school children sit with teachers in the belfry independent of the*
                    other sittings. Poor rates on tithes average from £30 to £40 per an.,
                    land tax £8. There is a rectory house and garden!
Dated   *31 March 1851*
Signed   *William Samuel Symonds, rector and patron [1845–87]*
                    Tewkesbury
[The church is now under the care of the Churches Conservation Trust.]

17.10 (10)   **Wesleyan Methodist, Pendock**
Name   *Wesleyan Chapel*
Erected   *In 1824. The old or previous chapel before 1810*
Building   *Yes [separate and entire] Yes [exclusively as a place of worship]*
Sittings   *Free 60. Other 90. Total [150] Standing room none*
Attend'ce 30 Mar. *Morning 40. Total 40*
Avge attendance   *Morning 80. Total 80*
                    Evening 60. Total 60
Remarks   *Unfavourable circumstances being the cause of the congregation being*
                    so thin in the morning and no evening service.
Dated   *31 March 1851*
Signed   *Thomas Weston, chapel steward [master tailor]*
                    [Cromer Green], Pendock, near Ledbury

345.1.8 Parish of Forthampton
Area 2,440 acres; 94 inhabited houses. Population 468.
VCH 8, 196–208

17.11 (11)   **Church of England, St Mary the Virgin, Forthampton**
Name   Parish Church. Dedicated to St Mary. A perpetual curacy
Consecration   Before 1800
Erected   [Restored 1788; enlarged 1847–8; restored 1864–6 and 1869–72]
Endowment   Tithe £139. Fees about £5. {Total £138}.
Sittings   Free 150. Other 168. Total 318
Attend'ce 30 Mar.   [Not given]
Avge attendance   Morning 100 + 60 SS. Total 160
                        Afternoon 80 + 60 SS. Total 140
Dated   31 March 1851
Signed   Francis Henry Laing, curate [1848–56]
                        Forthampton, nr Tewkesbury
[*Incumbent*   Robert Bathurst Plumptre 1819–56]
[Plumptre (the third son of John Plumptre, the dean of Gloucester 1808–25), had poor health and
employed curates during periods of absence from his parish. He was succeeded by Francis Henry
Laing 1856–63, who in 1864 assumed the surname Wolryche-Whitmore.]

345.1.9–12 Parish of Deerhurst
Area 2,930 acres; 196 inhabited houses, 6 uninhabited. Population 892.
The parish includes the hamlets of Deerhurst, Apperley with Whitefield and Deerhurst
Walton.
VCH 8, 34–49

17.12 (12)   **Church of England, St Mary, Deerhurst**
Name   Ancient parish church
Consecration   Before 1800
Erected   [Restored 1861–2]
Endowment   Land £30. OPE £71. {Total £182}
Sittings   Free about 115. Other about 250. Total 365
Attend'ce 30 Mar.   [Not given]
Avge attendance   Morning 50 + 20 SS. Total [70]
                        Afternoon 130 + 20 SS. Total [150]
Dated   31 March 1851
Signed   William George Sinclair Addison, minister [1846–56]
                        Coombe Hill, Cheltenham
[Within the parish the chapel of ease of Holy Trinity, Apperley was consecrated 29 July 1857. The
Saxon church of Odda's Chapel was discovered in 1865 and restored 1885. It is now under the care
of English Heritage: Gilbert, 73–114.]

17.13 (13)   **Wesleyan Methodist, Apperley**
Name   Wesleyan 'Chappel'
Erected   Before 1800 [1750] [Replaced by a nearby chapel in 1904]
Building   Yes [separate and entire] Yes [exclusively as a place of worship]
Sittings   All free 150. Total [150] Standing room for 150
Attend'ce 30 Mar.   Afternoon 60 + 60 SS. Total 120
                        Evening 60. Total 60
Avge attendance   Afternoon 60 + 60 SS. Total 120
                        Evening 60. Total 60
Dated   30 March 1851
Signed   Thomas Croft, local preacher [brickmaker]
                        [Upper Brick Works], Mythe Hook, nr Tewkesbury, Gloucestershire

[The chapel was opened by the Moravians but by 1792 it was no longer used by them; from 1799 it was leased to the Wesleyan Methodists and purchased by them in 1845. It is one of the few surviving Moravian chapels in the county.]

345.1.13 Parish of Tredington
Area 870 acres; 31 inhabited houses, 1 uninhabited. Population 143.
VCH 8, 228–36

17.14 (14)	**Church of England, St John the Baptist, Tredington**
Name	Tredington Church of St John the Baptist
Consecration	Most probably in 11th century
Erected	[Restored 1845 and 1880s]
Endowment	Together not exceeding £60 per annum. {Total £51}
Sittings	Total 104
Attend'ce 30 Mar.	[Not given]
Avge attendance	Afternoon 60 to 70. Total [60–70]
Remarks	Population about 130
Dated	30 March 1851
Signed	John Surman, churchwarden [landed proprietor, farmer of 230 acres; captain Royal South Glosters; deputy lieutenant and JP] Tredington Court, nr Tewkesbury
[Incumbent	Robert Hepworth 1829–56]

[Hepworth lived in Cheltenham and the parish was served by curates. On the Surman family of Tredington Court, see *VCH* 8, 230–1.]

345.1.14 Parish of Bishop's Cleeve
The parish includes the hamlet of Stoke Orchard (**15.35, 36**).

345.2   OVERBURY SUB-DISTRICT

345.2.1 Parish of Woolstone
Area 787 acres; 20 inhabited houses, 1 uninhabited. Population 86.
VCH 8, 105–9

17.15 (15)	**Church of England, St Martin de Tours, Woolstone**
Name	Woolstone Church
Consecration	An old parish church
Erected	[Restored 1871–3]
Endowment	Tithe about £200 per annum. OPE in the whole. {Total £193}
Sittings	Total about 100.
Attend'ce 30 Mar.	Morning 36. Total [36]
	Afternoon 55 + 8 SS. Total [63]
Avge attendance	Morning 14 + 8 SS. Total [22]
	Afternoon 25. Total [25]
Remarks	The rector of this parish being only lately deceased, I have filled up the above to the best of my ability as churchwarden.
Dated	31 March 1851
Signed	Richard Williams, churchwarden Gotherington, nr Cheltenham

[*Previous incumbent* Alexander Luders 1829–51, who died a week before the enumeration.]

345.2.2 Parish of Oxenton
Area 1,050 acres; 29 inhabited houses, 1 uninhabited. Population 139.
VCH 8, 220–8

17.16 (16)	**Church of England, St John the Baptist, Oxenton**
Name	'Saint Faith'. An old Saxon church and the only one in the parish
Consecration	Before 1800
Erected	[Restored 1904–5]
Endowment	Tithe ... £6. OPE £78 by Queen Anne's Bounty. {Total £68}
Sittings	Free 150. Other 50. Total 200
Attend'ce 30 Mar.	[Not given]
Avge attendance	Morning 45 + 7 SS. Total 52
	Afternoon 75 + 7 SS. Total 82
Remarks	Service alternate. The larger congregation in the afternoon
Dated	31 March 1851
Signed	George Richard Port, perpetual curate [1838–55]
	Oxenton, Tewkesbury

17.17 (17)	**Non-denominational, Oxenton**
Denomination	No particular denomination [in another hand, 'Independent']
Name	Dissenting Chapel
Erected	1837
Building	Yes [separate and entire] Yes [exclusively as a place of worship]
Sittings	Free 150. Other none. Total [150]
Attend'ce 30 Mar.	Morning SS none
	Afternoon 60. Total [60]
	Evening 80. Total [80]
Avge attendance	[Not given]
Remarks	The service is conducted by ministers of different denominations.
Dated	30 March 1851
Signed	Thomas Barnett, manager [farmer of 347 acres]
	Overbury, nr Tewkesbury, Gloucestershire

['In 1865 a chapel was built at Oxenton and served from Highbury Congregational Church, Cheltenham (**16.23**). In the 1870s the community met with opposition from the Anglican incumbent, who tried to dissuade children from attending the chapel': *VCH* 8, 227.]

345.2.3–5   **Parish of Overbury, Worcestershire** (see 343.2.8–9)
Area 2,760 acres; 199 inhabited houses, 9 uninhabited. Population 956.
The parish includes the hamlets of Little Washbourne (**15.32**) and Alstone (**15.33**), both transferred to Gloucestershire in 1844; and Conderton and Teddington (**17.19**), transferred to Gloucestershire in 1931.
VCH (Worcs.) 3, 468–78

17.18 (18)	*Church of England, St Faith, Overbury*
(Summary form)	
Name	*St Faith's episcopal church. Rev W. Smith*
Consecration	*About the year 1100*
Erected	*[Restored 1879–80]*
[Endowment	*Total £421]*
Sittings	*Free abt 100. Other abt 130. Total 230*
	About 300 from the present arrangement of seats (but capable of holding many more)
Usual attendance	*Morning about 30 + about 68 SS. Total [98]*
	Afternoon about 50. Total [50]
Signed	*Elizabeth Jukes, Sunday school teacher [schoolmistress (aged 22)]*

Overbury
[*Incumbent*   *William Smith 1839–76*]
[*The benefice consisted of Overbury with Alstone (15.33) and the chapelries of Teddington (17.19) and Little Washbourne (15.32)*]

17.19 (19)   Church of England, St Nicholas, Teddington

Name	Teddington Chapel. A chapel of ease [to Overbury (**17.18**)]
Consecration	Before 1800
Erected	[Not given]
Endowment	Land £39 11s 2d
Sittings	Free 56 + 26 SS. Total 82
Attend'ce 30 Mar.	[Not given]
Avge attendance	Morning 18. Total [18]
	Afternoon 45. Total [45]
Dated	31 March 1851
Signed	William Cloudesley Faulkner, curate [1847–78]
	Beckford, Tewkesbury, Gloucestershire
[*Incumbent*	William Smith 1839–76]

[Faulkner was also curate of Alstone (**15.33**), Teddington and Little Washbourne (**15.32**). The benefice consisted of Overbury (**17.18**) with Alstone and the chapelries of Teddington and Little Washbourne (**15.32**).]

17.20 (20)   Independent, Teddington

Name	None
Erected	[Not given]
Building	No [not separate and entire] No [not exclusively as a place of worship]
Sittings	Free 50. Total [50]
Attend'ce 30 Mar.	Morning 33 + 8 SS. Total 41
	Evening 32 + 3 SS. Total 35
Avge attendance	Morning 30 + 12 SS. Total 42
	Evening 45 + 5 SS. Total 50
Dated	31 March 1851
Signed	Richard Flock, inhabitant [shopkeeper]
	Teddington, near Tewkesbury

345.2.6   Parish of Kemerton [transferred to Worcestershire, 1931]
Area 1,590 acres; 128 inhabited houses, 9 uninhabited. Population 528.
VCH 8, 209–20

17.21 (21)   Church of England, St Nicholas, Kemerton

Name	Parish church. Anciently dedicated to St Nicholas, and rebuilt and reconsecrated, 1847
Consecrated	19 October 1847. The old church, ruinous, rebuilt (all but the tower [restored in 1879]) and enlarged. [North aisle 1849]
Erected	Not 'an additional church' but with additional room
	Parochial rate under £400. Private benefaction or subscription over £4,000. Total cost about £4,400. This large expense, in addition to the desire to do the work well, on the part of those who undertook to complete it, was principally caused by opposition made to the restoration at first, and consequent legal expenses.
Endowment	Land, tithe and glebe £520. Pew rents, fees, dues, Easter offerings and other sources.* {Total £560}

Sittings	Free about 50. Other 324 (in the nave, 300; in the chancel for clergy and choir, 24). Total 374.** (The church will hold, and has held, 500)
Attend'ce 30 Mar.	Morning 80 + 30 SS. Total 110
	Afternoon 180 + 30 SS. Total 210
*Avge attendance****	Morning 100 + 40 SS. Total 140
	Afternoon 230 + 40 SS. Total 270
Remarks	* The parish having been put to some expense in connexion with the re-building of the church, the present incumbent has not hitherto demanded the dues etc. to which he is entitled, and the fees in like manner have not been worth recording, not exceeding a few shillings.
	** Strictly speaking, there are no appropriated sittings. There is room for all the parish, and whoever wants a seat, will obtain it on application to the churchwardens, agreeably to the rule of the church.
	*** I cannot make this return with anything like certainty, nor have I been able to find any who can. We are not in the habit of counting our congreg-ations. I have made the nearest approach I can to the truth, and as I believe, under the mark.
Dated	3 April 1851
Signed	Thomas Thorp, rector [1839–77]
	Kemerton, Tewkesbury

[Thorp was archdeacon and chancellor of Bristol 1836–73, and president of the Cambridge Camden Society. He supported the Oxford Movement, Kemerton becoming one of the earliest churches to have a surpliced choir. Later, the congregation was unhappy when an Evangelical, George Mallet, was appointed incumbent, and the widow of the previous Anglo-Catholic incumbent bought the living in 1902: *ODNB* 'Thomas Thorp (1797–1877)'; Herbert, 192–215; Mercier, 24–40.]

17.22 (23)   Wesleyan Methodist, Kemerton

Name	Wesleyan Methodist Chapel
Erected	1819 [on land adjacent to the house of William Mumford]
Building	Yes [separate and entire] Yes [exclusively as a place of worship]
Sittings	Free 100. Other 36. Total [136] Sanding room for 20
Attend'ce 30 Mar.	Morning 63 + 25 SS. Total [88] }Total
	Evening 83. Total [83] }171
Avge attendance	[Not given]
Dated	31 March 1851
Signed	George Mumford, local preacher and class leader [a landed proprietor] acting under the authority of the superintending minister
	Kemerton, Gloucestershire

17.23 (22)   Roman Catholic, Kemerton

Name	St Benet's
Erected	In the year 1843 [Opened 19 July 1843]
Building	Yes [separate and entire] Yes [exclusively as a place of worship]
Sittings	Free 170. Total [170] Standing room for 40 or 50
Attend'ce 30 Mar.	Morning 140. Total 140
	Afternoon 90. Total 90
Avge attendance	[Not given]
Dated	31 March 1851
Signed	Peter Ridgway, Roman Catholic priest [1848–96]
	Kemerton, Tewkesbury

345.2.7–8   Parish of Bredon, Worcestershire

Area 5,818 acres; 363 inhabited houses, 9 uninhabited. Population 1,661.
The parish includes the village of Bredon and the hamlets of Norton by Bredon, Hardwick with Mitton, Kinsham and Westmancote; the chapelry of Cutsdean (**15.1**) is in the return for the Winchcombe district (343.1.1).
VCH (Worcs.) 3, 279–92

17.24 (24)   Church of England, St Giles, Bredon

Name	*St Giles. An ancient parish church.*
Consecration	*[Not given]*
Erected	*[Restored c.1843]*
Endowment	*Land £2,000. {Total £1,498}*
Sittings	*Free 300. Total 300*
Attend'ce 30 Mar.	*Morning, afternoon and evening. Unknown*
Avge attendance	~~*Morning and afternoon about 300. SS about 90 when all are assembled*~~
Remarks	*The church will accommodate about 350 persons including children and the places are generally occupied.*
Dated	*31 March 1851*
Signed	*Thomas Alfred Strickland, rector [1837–52]*
	Bredon, near Tewkesbury

[The benefice consisted of Bredon with Norton (17.25) and Cutsdean (15.1). Noake, 151–61.]

17.25 (27)   Church of England, St Giles, Norton

Name	*Norton Chapel. Chapel of ease to Bredon*
Consecration	*Not known [under the circumstances of the consecration]*
Erected	*[Nave rebuilt 1877 and chancel in 1883]*
Endowment	*Not separately endowed [See Bredon (17.24)]*
Sittings	*Free 100. Total 100*
Attend'ce 30 Mar.	*Morning, afternoon and evening not known*
Avge attendance	*Morning, afternoon and evening not known*
Remarks	*There is insufficient room in the chapel for the present population.*
Dated	*31 March 1851*
Signed	*Thomas Alfred Strickland, rector [1837–52]*
	Bredon, near Tewkesbury

[The benefice consisted of Bredon (17.24) with Norton and Cutsdean (15.1)]

17.26 (26)   Particular Baptist, Westmancote

Name	*Westmancote Chapel*
Erected	*Before the year 1800 [1779]*
Building	*Separate and entire building. Used exclusively as a place of worship*
Sittings	*Free 170. Other 80. Total [250] Standing room none*
Attend'ce 30 Mar.	*Morning 230 + 34 SS. Total 264*
	Afternoon 200 [+ 34 SS] Total 234
Avge attendance	*[Not given]*
Dated	*31 March 1851*
Signed	*John Francis, Baptist minister [1842–]*
	Westmancote, near Tewkesbury, Worcestershire

[Francis was also the minister of Kinsham (17.27) and Natton (17.29).]

17.27 (25)   Particular Baptist, Kinsham

Name	*Kinsham Chapel*
Erected	*The year 1848*

Building	Separate and entire building. Used exclusively as a place of worship, except for a Sunday school
Sittings	Free sittings to hold 120 persons. Other none. Total [120] Standing room none
Attend'ce 30 Mar.	Evening 100 + 28 SS. Total 128
Avge attendance	[Not given]
Dated	31 March 1851
Signed	John Francis, Baptist minister [1842–]
	Westmancote, Tewkesbury, Worcestershire.

[Francis was also the minister of Westmancote (**17.26**) and Natton (**17.29**)]

345.3 TEWKESBURY SUB-DISTRICT

345.3.1 Parish of Ashchurch

Area 4,201 acres; 154 inhabited houses, 7 uninhabited. Population 786.
The parish includes the tithings of Pamington, Fiddington, Natton, Aston on Carrant, Northway and Newton.
VCH 8, 172–88

17.28 (29) Church of England, St Nicholas, Ashchurch

Name	Ashchurch
Consecration	[Not given]
Erected	[Restored 1888–9 and 1930–1]
Endowment	Land £150. Tithe £40. Fees £1. {Total £270}
Sittings	Free 200. Other 150. Total 350
Attend'ce 30 Mar.	Morning 50. Total 50
	Afternoon 80. Total [80]
Avge attendance	Morning 100. Total [100]
	Afternoon 150. Total [150]
Dated	31 March 1851
Signed	John Askew, perpetual curate [1844–63]
	Ashchurch, Tewkesbury

17.29 (28) Seventh Day Baptists, Natton

Denomination	Seventh-day Baptists or the Sabbath-keeping church
Name	Natton Chapel
Erected	Licensed for divine worship 1748
Building	Separate and entire building. Exclusively for a place of worship
Sittings	Free 90. Total [90] Standing room for 10
Attend'ce 30 Mar.	Attendance 12. Total [12]
	No Sunday school afternoon
Avge attendance	[Not given]
Dated	25 March 1851
Signed	John Francis, minister [1846–67]
	Westmancote, Tewkesbury

[Francis was also minister of Kinsham (**17.27**) and Westmancote (**17.26**). Seventh Day Baptists, who assembled for worship on Saturday, had met in Oxenton (**345.2.2**) in c.1718. In 1871 the Natton congregation divided and a chapel opened at Kinsham, Worcs.; by the 1880s Natton was the only Seventh Day Baptist chapel outside London. At one time it 'attracted members from as far afield as Upton upon Severn, Bishop's Cleeve and Cheltenham': Ritchie, 159–66; Perry, 105–29; *GNQ* 2, 354.]

17.30 (30) Wesleyan Methodist, Aston on Carrant

Name	Wesleyan Chapel. Ebenezer Chapel

Erected	1845
Building	Yes [separate and entire] Yes [exclusively as a place of worship]
Sittings	Free 96. Other 20. Total [116]
Attend'ce 30 Mar.	Afternoon 45. Total 45
	Evening 45. Total 45
Avge attendance	Afternoon 45. Total 45
Dated	30 March 1851
Signed	Thomas Smith, steward [blacksmith]
	Aston on Carrant, near Tewkesbury

345.3.5 Parish of Walton Cardiff

Area 650 acres; 13 inhabited houses, 2 uninhabited. Population 60.
VCH 8, 236–42

17.31 (31)   Church of England, St James, Walton Cardiff

Name	The church of Walton 'Cardiffe', dedicated to St James. The church of a very ancient chapelry, long constituted a separate parish
Consecration	Ages before 1800, as an adjunct or chapel in connection with the monastery of Tewkesbury
Erected	[1658. A new church was rebuilt on the same site in 1869]
Endowment	Land £18. Tithe £48 [tithe commuted in 1848] {Total £53}
Sittings	Free 95. Total 95
Attend'ce 30 Mar.	Morning 16. Total [16]
Avge attendance	Morning 16. Total [16]
	Afternoon 40. Total [40]
Remarks	There is only one service here in the week. The morning congregation is always smaller than the afternoon, as it interferes less with their agricultural employments.
Dated	31 March 1851
Signed	George Pruen Griffiths, curate [1850–2]
	Church Street, Tewkesbury
[*Incumbent*	Charles Greenhall Davies 1847–77]

[Davies was also the incumbent of St Mary the Virgin, Tewkesbury (**17.32**).]

345.3.6 Parish of Tewkesbury

Area 2,333 acres; 1,274 inhabited houses, 81 uninhabited. Population 5,878.
The parish includes the borough of Tewkesbury and the hamlets of Mythe and Southwick with Park. The Union workhouse situated within the parish had 98 inmates.
VCH 8, 110–69; GNQ 1, 195–7, 304–6

17.32 (33)   Church of England, St Mary the Virgin, Tewkesbury

Name	The abbey church of Tewkesbury, dedicated to St Mary the Virgin
Consecration	The ancient abbey was built in the reign of Henry I.
Erected	[Repairs 1824–30 and restored 1874–9]
Endowment	Land in lieu of tithe £260. Tithe £67. OPE £5 3s 6d. Fees £38. Easter offerings £14. {Total £313}
Sittings	There are no appropriated sittings in the abbey. The churchwardens locate the congregation. Total about 1,400
Attend'ce 30 Mar.	Morning about 500 + 92 SS. Total 592
	Afternoon about 250 + 86 SS. Total 336
	Evening about 500. Total 500
Avge attendance	~~Vide infra~~

Remarks	I would observe that during the spring, summer and autumnal months the attendance in the abbey is far greater than during the winter months, e.g. on a Sunday in June the congregation would be three times larger than on a wet and cold Sunday in the beginning of March.
Dated	31 March 1851
Signed	George Pruen Griffiths, curate [1850–2]
	Church Street, Tewkesbury
[*Incumbent*	Charles Greenhall Davies 1846–77]

[Davies was also incumbent of Walton Cardiff (**17.31**); Petit, 70–85.]

17.33 (32)   Church of England, Holy Trinity, Tewkesbury

Name	Holy Trinity, Tewkesbury
Consecration	30 Aug. 1837, as an additional church under 5 Geo. IV, c.103 [1824]
Erected	By neighbouring gentry and clergy. Private benefaction, subscriptions etc. £4,047 1s 4d. Total cost £4,047 1s 4d
Endowment	OPE £5,200 principal.* Pew rents £100 per an[num] Fees about 10s. Dues and Easter offerings none. Other sources subscription for lecture £20 {Total £140}
Sittings	Free nearly 400. Other nearly 450. Total 850
Attend'ce 30 Mar.	Morning 250 + 181 SS. Total 431
	Afternoon no service
	Evening 700 (SS not known). Total 700
Avge attendance	The attendance on 30 March is a good average.
Remarks	*This is principal, but the interest of £4,000 thereof is, by stipulation, paid to the gentleman who provided that part of the endowment during his life, and as from the pew rents, many of the attendants and of the church are paid, the net income of the minister is at present about £140. A curate is kept and the incumbent is resident.
Dated	31 March 1851
Signed	Francis John Scott BA, incumbent [1849–57]
	[High Street], Tewkesbury

[The parish was created in 1893.]

17.34 (34)   Independent, Barton Street

Name	Independent Chapel [Upper Meeting]
Erected	Before 1800 [c.1719, enlarged 1828, 1836 and 1840]
Building	Yes [separate and entire] Yes [exclusively as a place of worship]
Sittings	Free 200. Other 400. Total [600] Standing room for 50
Attend'ce 30 Mar.	Morning 300 + 150 SS. Total 450
	Afternoon 180 SS. Total 180
	Evening 400. Total 400
Avge attendance	Morning 350 + 180 SS. Total 530
	Afternoon 200 SS. Total 200
	Evening 450. Total 450
Remarks	The congregation was smaller and fewer children were at the Sunday school on the 30 March on account of the many cases of measles in the town. H. W.
Dated	31 March 1851
Signed	Henry Welsford, minister [1819–69]
	Barton Street, Tewkesbury

['Tewkesbury has a long history and a strong tradition of religious dissent': *VCH* 8, 163. In 1676 it was said that three-quarters of the inhabitants of the town were nonconformists. From 1712–24 there was a nonconformist academy in Tewkesbury and it was described as being 'most flourishing, famed for as much learning as any one seminary among the nonconformists': McLachlan, 127.]

17.35 (35)   Particular Baptist, Barton Street

Name	Baptist Chapel
Erected	1804 or 1805 [Opened 21 June 1805, replacing the 17th century Baptist Chapel, in an alley off Church Street]
Building	Separate building. Exclusively as a place of worship
Sittings	Free 250. Other 260. Total [510]
Attend'ce 30 Mar.	Morning 320. Total [320]
	Afternoon 40. Total [40]
	Evening 350. Total [350]
Avge attendance	[Not given]
Dated	31 March 1851
Signed	Joseph Potter, deacon [retired cabinet maker]
	67 Barton Street, Tewkesbury
[Ministers	John Berg 1843–51; Thomas Wilkinson 1851–6]

17.36 (36)   Wesleyan Methodist, Tolzey Lane

Name	Wesleyan Methodist Chapel
Erected	Before 1800 [1777. A chapel on the same site was opened 16 Oct. 1814, and replaced by a new chapel in 1878]
Building	Yes [separate and entire] Yes [exclusively as a place of worship]
Sittings	Free 144. Other 320. Total [464] Standing room nil
Attend'ce 30 Mar.	Morning 144 + 120 SS. Total 264
	Evening 259. Total 259
Avge attendance	Morning 146 + 120 SS. Total 266
	Evening 265. Total 265
Dated	31 March 1851
Signed	Thomas Collins, trustees steward [statuary, mason and builder]
	The Cross, Tewkesbury

345.3.7 Parish of Twyning
Area 3,155 acres; 215 inhabited houses, 9 uninhabited. Population 1,011.
VCH 13 (forthcoming)

17.37 (37)   Church of England, St Mary Magdalene, Twyning

Name	Twyning
Consecration	[Not given]
Erected	[Mostly rebuilt 1867–70]
Endowment	{Total £180}
Sittings	[Not given]
Attend'ce 30 Mar.	[Not given]
Avge attendance	Morning 300. Total 300
	Afternoon 200. Total 200
Dated	[Not given]
Signed	R. [registrar?]
[Incumbent	Henry Goodwin 1844–1908]

[By 1863 Goodwin was no longer resident, the parish being served by curates. He was declared bankrupt in 1864, and again in 1882. From 1880 to 1908 he was chaplain of the Watford Union workhouse, Herts.: *London Gazette* 1864, 1882; *Cheltenham Chronicle,* 29 Feb. 1908.]

18. HO 129/576, 577, 347 'FOREST OF DEAN': 52 places of worship

HO 129/576 CHEPSTOW DISTRICT (MONMOUTHSHIRE)

576.2 CHEPSTOW SUB-DISTRICT

576.2.10 Parish of Tidenham

Area 9,527 acres; 324 inhabited houses, 5 uninhabited. Population 1,753.
The parish includes Beachley, Bishton, Church End, Sedbury, Stoat and Webden; and the chapelry of Lancaut (attached to Woolaston). In 1851 about 60 additional persons were resident in the parish, mostly labourers employed in the construction of the railway.
VCH 10, 50–79

18.1 (52)   **Church of England, St Mary, Tidenham**

Name	St Peter. Old parish church
Consecration	Before 1800
Erected	[Restored 1857–8]
Endowment	Land £10. Tithe £399. Glebe £9. OPE £12. Fees £10. {Total £441}
Sittings	Total 350
Attend'ce 30 Mar.	Morning 240. Total [240]
	Afternoon 76. Total [76]
Avge attendance	Morning 250. Total [250]
	Afternoon 80. Total [80]
Dated	25 March 1851
Signed	John Armstrong, vicar [1845–53]
	Tidenham vicarage, Chepstow

[When Armstrong came to Tidenham he found that the parish was in 'a very disturbed state' over the changes that his predecessor (James Henry Scudamore Burr) had introduced into the church services. Both Burr and Armstrong supported the Oxford Movement. During Armstrong's ministry 'the afternoon services at the church consisted of prayer and catechising'. He was a gifted preacher and committed to education and social justice. Elsewhere he was the originator of the penitentiary movement and supported the establishment of the House of Mercy at Bussage (**10.28**): Carter, 109–93. Though in poor health Armstrong became first bishop of Grahamstown (1853–6): *ODNB* 'John Armstrong (1813–1856)'. Within the parish St John, Beachley (**18.3**) was consecrated 10 Sept. 1833; St Luke, Tutshill 12 Aug. 1853; and St Michael and All Angels, Tidenham Chase 5 Apr. 1888. Within the parish of Tidenham was St James, Lancaut (**18.6**).]

18.2a (51)   **Church of England, Licensed schoolroom, Tutshill**

Name	Schoolroom licensed for public worship classes
Licensed	~~1848~~ 1850. Licensed as an addition to the church until a chapel of ease can be buil[t]
Erected	By subscription. From private and other sources £120
	Total cost £120
Sittings	Free 100. Total 100
Attend'ce 30 Mar.	Afternoon 82. Total [82]
Avge attendance	Afternoon 80 + 15 SS. Total 95
Dated	25 March 1851
Signed	John Armstrong, vicar [1845–53]
	Tidenham vicarage, Chepstow

[There were three schoolrooms in the parish; Sunday services were held at Tutshill and Tidenham

Chase. St Luke, Tutshill was consecrated 12 Aug. 1853, and enlarged 1872.]

18.2b (53)   Church of England, Licensed schoolroom, Tutshill

Name	Schoolroom licensed for public worship, Tutshill
Licensed	1849. Licensed in addition to the old church till a chapel of ease can be built.
Erected	By subscription. From private and other sources £250. Total cost £250
Sittings	Free 120. Total 120
Attend'ce 30 Mar.	Afternoon 89. Total [89]
Avge attendance	Afternoon 80 + 25 SS. Total 105
Dated	25 March 1851
Signed	John Armstrong, vicar [1845–53]
	Tidenham vicarage, Chepstow.

18.3 (54)   Church of England, St John, Beachley

Name	St John's Church. District chapelry
Consecration	10 September 1833. Consecrated as a chapel of ease, and since made a district chapelry and perpetual curacy by an Order in Council, 14 October 1850
Erected	By a grant from the Church Building Society (£110) and by private contributions (£619 4s 5d). Total cost £729 4s 5d
Endowment	OPE £10 3s 11d. (... 300 3% consols). Average of three years – pew rents £9. Fees £1 12s. Total £20 15s 4d
Sittings	Free 100. Other 74. Total 174
Attend'ce 30 Mar.	Morning 50 + 41 SS. Total 91
	Afternoon 60 + 42 SS. Total 102
Avge attendance (3m)	Morning 45 + 45 SS. Total 90
	Afternoon 55 + 40 SS. Total 95
Dated	31 March 1851
Signed	Charles Augustus Morgan MA, perpetual curate [1833–53]
	Tidenham House, nr Chepstow

[Morgan was also the incumbent of Machen, Newport 1831–73; chancellor of Llandaff cathedral 1851, chaplain in ordinary to the Queen 1829.]

18.4 (56)   Baptist and others, Woodcroft

Name	Reading Room
Erected	1843
Building	Separate and entire. Yes [exclusively as a place of worship]
Sittings	Free 110. Total [110]
Attend'ce 30 Mar.	Afternoon 74. Total [74]
Avge attendance	Afternoon 90. Total [90]
Remarks	Services only Sab[bath] afternoons and on Tuesday evenings when about half the average Sab[bath] attendance may be present generally.
Dated	31 March 1851
Signed	Thomas Jones, minister
	7 Mount Pleasant, Chepstow

[Jones was also minister of the Baptist Church, Chepstow 1833–70. He was elected president of the Monmouthshire Baptist Association.]

18.5 (55)   Wesleyan Methodist, Tidenham

Name	Boughspring Chapel
Erected	1836
Building	Yes [separate and entire] Yes [exclusively as a place of worship]

Sittings	Free 100. Other 20. Total [120]
Attend'ce 30 Mar.	Evening 43. Total [43]
Avge attendance	Evening 45. Total [45]
Dated	30 March 1851
Signed	John Hathins, trustee of Boughspring
	'Chaple', Tidenham Chase

HO 129/576 CHEPSTOW DISTRICT (MONMOUTHSHIRE)

576.3 LYDNEY SUB-DISTRICT

576.3.1 Parish of Woolaston
Area 5,416 acres; 228 inhabited houses, 4 uninhabited. Population 1,110.
VCH 10, 102–18

18.6 (57) Church of England, St Andrew, Woolaston
Name	Woolastone. An ancient parish church
Consecration	[Not given]
Erected	[Mostly rebuilt 1859]
Endowment	Glebe and rent charges. Tithe £335. Glebe 46 ac[res] odd. OPE none. {Total £446}
Sittings	Free 180 (when children sit). Other 400. Others 50. Total [630]
Attend'ce 30 Mar.	Morning 100 + 73 SS. (Distinct from more). Total 173
	Afternoon 200 + 73 SS. (Distinct from more). Total 298 [*recte* 273]
Avge attendance	The average attend at [morning] and afternoon between 300 and 400. Sunday school [70?]
Dated	31 March 1851
Signed	Charles Bryan, rector [1813–59]
	'Woolastone, Lidney'

[Bryan was also incumbent of Preston (**7.22**). The benefice consisted of Woolaston with Alvington (**18.10**) and Lancaut. By c.1865 services at St James, Lancaut (in the parish of Tidenham) were discontinued and by 1885 the building had become a ruin: Wood, 207–18; Parry, 53–103.]

18.7 (59) Particular Baptist, Park Hill, Woolaston
Name	Park Hill Chapel
Erected	In 1835
Building	Separate and entire. Used exclusively as a place of worship except for Sunday school
Sittings	All free sittings, no exceptions. On particular occasions we have had more than 100 [persons] sitting and standing.
Attend'ce 30 Mar.	Morning 19. Total [19]
	Afternoon 35. Total [35]
Avge attendance	Morning 100 to 120 [Total 100–120]
	Afternoon about 30
	(SS 20)
Dated	26 March 1851
Signed	John Lewis, minister [1839–55]
	Park Hill Cottage [Woolaston]

18.8 (60) Church of the United Brethren, Brockweir, Woolaston
(Summary form)	
Name	Moravian Episcopal Chapel. (The United Brethren or Moravian). Brockweir in the extreme NW corner of Woolastone parish. The village is in Hewelsfield parish.

Erected	1832
Building	The clergyman's house adjoins. Used exclusively as a place of worship
Sittings	All free 200. It might hold 300 if crowded. [Total 200–300]
Usual attend'ce	Morning 60 + 60 SS. Total 120
	Afternoon no service
	Evening 120 + 40 SS. Total 160
Signed	Lewis West, [minister 1832–70]
	Brockweir, nr Chepstow

18.9 (58)   Bible Christians, Woodside, Woolaston

Name	Woodside Chapel
Erected	1836
Building	Yes [separate and entire] Yes [exclusively as a place of worship]
Sittings	Free 40. Other 70. Total [110] Standing room none
Attend'ce 30 Mar.	Morning 43 SS. Total 43
	Afternoon 120 + 45 SS. Total 165
	Evening 100. Total 100
Avge attendance	[Not given]
Dated	31 March 1851
Signed	Thomas James, chapel steward
	Brookend, Newnham, Gloucestershire

[This was 'the first Bible Christian chapel in west Gloucestershire': *VCH* 10, 117.]

576.3.2 Parish of Alvington
Area 2,553 acres; 73 inhabited houses. Population 370.
VCH 5, 5–14

18.10 (61)   Church of England, St Andrew, Alvington

Name	An ancient parish church
Consecration	Before 1800
Erected	[Restored 1857–8]
Endowment	[See Woolaston (**18.6**)]
Sittings	Free 25. Other 275. Total 300
Attend'ce 30 Mar.	Morning 50 + 27 SS. Total 77
Avge attendance	[Not given]
Remarks	The annual amount of the endowment must be obtained from the incumbent.
Dated	31 March 1851
Signed	Stephen Morgan White, minister [1850–2]
	Alvington, Newnham
[*Incumbent*	Charles Bryan 1813–59]

[The benefice consisted of Woolaston (**18.6**) with Alvington and Lancaut (**18.6**).]

576.3.3–4   Parish of Lydney
Area 8,073 acres; 389 inhabited houses, 7 uninhabited. Population 2,577.
The parish includes the village of Newarne, and the tithings of Alaxton, Aylburton, Nass and Purton.
VCH 5, 46–84; *GNQ* 2, 501–2

18.11 (62)   Church of England, St Mary, Lydney

Name	St Mary's. Ancient parish church
Consecration	N[ot] k[nown]

Erected	N[ot] k[nown] Cost n[ot] k[nown] [Restored 1849–52]
Endowment	{Total £737}
Sittings	Free kneelings 30. Other kneelings 324. Total kneeling 354. In the nave and aisles 354. The singers and children are in the chancel crowded.
Attend'ce 30 Mar.	Morning 280 + 122 SS. Total 402
	Evening (6 o'clock) 211. Total 211
Avge attendance	Morning 240 + 90 SS. Total 330
	Evening 200. Total 200
Remarks	The children assemble in the schools morning and afternoon on Sunday, but many of them live at distant parts of the parish and only attend church in the morning. The schools are daily school. We want £500 to re-pew the church, and we should have double the number in the congregation, if you will send us [what is] required. The present pews are awkward double exclusive pews.
Dated	31 March 1851
Signed	Charles Taylor, vicar [1838–59]
	'Lidney', Gloucester

[The benefice consisted of Lydney with Aylburton (**18.12**), St Briavels (**18.18**) and Hewelsfield (**18.16**).]

18.12 (66)   Church of England, St Mary, Aylburton

Name	'Ailburton Chapel attached to Lidney'
Consecration	[Not given]
Erected	[Rebuilt 1855–6]
Endowment	[See Lydney (**18.11**)]
Sittings	Free 30. Other 100. Total 130
Attend'ce 30 Mar.	Afternoon 60. Total [60]
Avge attendance	[Not given]
Remarks	The services here are alternate morning and afternoon. Average number in the morning about 50.
Dated	31 March 1851
Signed	Charles Taylor, vicar of Lidney with its chapelries [1838–59]
	'Lidney', Gloucester

18.13 (63)   Baptist, Lydney

Name	Baptist Meeting House
Erected	1836 [Enlarged 1876]
Building	Yes [separate and entire] Yes [exclusively as a place of worship]
Sittings	Free 130. Other 120. Total [250] (including vestry). Standing room none, except the aisles
Attend'ce 30 Mar.	Morning 140. Total [140]
	Afternoon 150 SS. Total [150]
	Evening 150. Total [150]
Avge attendance	Morning 140. Total [140]
	Afternoon 150. Total [150]
	Evening 180. Total [180]
Remarks	The chapel is occupied by teachers and the Sunday scholars attends only in the afternoon.
Dated	30 March 1851
Signed	Thomas Nicholson, deacon [colliery proprietor]
	Lydney, Gloucestershire

18.14 (64)   Wesleyan Methodist, Newarne, Lydney

Name	'Wesleyan Methodist Chapple'
Erected	Septr. 1850
Building	Yes [separate and entire] Yes [exclusively as a place of worship]
Sittings	Free 130. Total [130] Standing room for 40
Attend'ce 30 Mar.	Afternoon 70. Total [70]
	Evening 110. Total [110]
Avge attendance	Morning 100 + 20 SS. Total [120]
Dated	31 March 1851
Signed	D. L. Watts, general manager (and John Jones)
	Lydney, Gloucestershire

18.15 (65)   Primitive Methodist, Lydney

Name	None
Erected	In the year of our Lord, 1850 [Replaced in 1869 by Ebenezer Chapel]
Building	A separate building. Exclusively for worship. [Consisted of two cottages converted into a chapel]
Sittings	Free 100. Other none. Total [100] Standing room for 40
Attend'ce 30 Mar.	Morning 60. Total [60]
	Afternoon 100. Total [100]
	Evening 140. Total [140]
	Total [during the day] 300
Avge attendance (2m)	Afternoon 100. Total [100]
	Evening 100. Total [100]
Dated	31 March 1851
Signed	Thomas Peters, trustee [shoemaker]
	Lydney, Gloucestershire

576.3.5 Parish of Hewelsfield

Area 1,189 acres; 107 inhabited houses, 6 uninhabited. Population 497.
The parish includes part of the extra-parochial community of Hudnolls.
VCH 5, 150–9

18.16 (67)   Church of England, St Mary Magdalene, Hewelsfield

Name	St Mary, Magdalene
Consecration	Before 1800
Erected	[Restored 1863–7]
Endowment	[See Lydney (**18.11**)]
Sittings	Free about 20. Other 121. Total 141
Attend'ce 30 Mar.	Morning about 60 + about 50 and 60 SS. Total 111 [*recte* 110–120]
Avge. attendance	[Not given]
Remarks	There is only alternate service in this church. On the 30 of March there was morning service. The afternoon averages between 200 and 300.
Dated	30 March 1851
Signed	Charles Taylor, vicar of the above chapelry [1838–59]
	Hewelsfield, near Coleford, Gloucestershire

[The benefice also included Lydney (**18.11**) with Aylburton (**18.12**), and St Briavels (**18.18**).]

18.17 (69)   Independent, Hewelsfield

Name	Zion
Erected	1822
Building	Yes [separate and entire] Yes [exclusively as a place of worship]

Sittings	Free 130. Other none. Total [130] Standing room none
Attend'ce 30 Mar.	Morning SS none
	Evening 33. Total 33
Avge attendance	Morning SS none
	Evening 45. Total 45
Remarks	A Sunday school and day school had been held for years in connexion with the chapel. Both are broke up and the children now are taken up by the church school both week days and Sundays.
Dated	30 March 1851
Signed	John Baker, member [labourer]
	Hewelsfield village, near Coleford, Gloucestershire

576.3.6 Parish of St Briavels

Area 5,104 acres; 267 inhabited houses, 21 uninhabited. Population 1,194.
The parish includes the extra-parochial communities of Hudnolls (part in Hewelsfield), The Fence, The Bearse and Mawkins Hazell.
VCH 5, 247–71

18.18 (68)	**Church of England, St Mary, St Briavels**
Name	St Mary's church – ancient – vicarage
Consecration	Before 1800
Erected	[New tower 1830–1; restored 1861]
Endowment	[See Lydney (**18.11**)]
Sittings	Free 6. Other 354. Total 360
Attend'ce 30 Mar.	Morning 175 + 48 SS. Total 223
	Afternoon 160 + 46 SS. Total 206
Avge attendance	[Not given]
Dated	31 March 1851
Signed	John Lewis, curate [1847–53]
	St Briavels, Coleford
[*Incumbent*	Charles Taylor 1838–59]

[The benefice also included Lydney (**18.11**) with Aylburton (**18.12**), and Hewelsfield (**18.16**).]

18.19 (70)	**Wesleyan Methodist, Brockweir Common**
(Summary form)	
Name	Brockweir Common Chapel
Erected	About the year 1818
Building	A separate building. Exclusively a place of worship
Sittings	Can accommodate 80. The sittings are all free. No other sittings
	Total [80]
Usual attendance	Morning 12 to 18. No [Sunday] school. Total [12–18]
	Afternoon 30 to 40. Total [30–40]
	Evening no service
Signed	John Teague [farmer of 14 acres]
	St Briavels Common, St Briavels, nr Coleford

HO 129/577 Monmouth district

577.1   Coleford sub-district

577.1.1–4   Parish of Newland

Area 8,743 acres; 925 inhabited houses, 20 uninhabited. Population 4,417.
The parish includes the tithings of Bream, Clearwell, Newland and Coleford. The other

part of the parish (in Herefordshire) includes the tithing of Lea Bailey (347.2.5).
VCH 5, 117–38, 195–231

18.20 (6)   **Church of England, All Saints, Newland**

Name	All Saints
Consecration	Before 1800
Erected	[Restored 1861–2]
Endowment	Tithe £525. Fees £20 annum. {Total £525}
Sittings	Free 124. Other 700. Total 824
Attend'ce 30 Mar.	Morning 156 + 56 SS. Total 212
	Afternoon 166. Total 166
Avge attendance	Morning 250 + 60 SS. Total 310
	Afternoon 150. Total 150
	[The Sunday school was held in the vestry]
Remarks	Newland Church was built for the whole parish. Now there are five chapels of ease in different hamlets for the accommodation of the inhabitants. The morning congregation is ⅓ more than the afternoon, about 250 children besides. I have no means of ascertaining the attendance during the last twelve months with accuracy.
Dated	31 March 1851
Signed	George Ridout, vicar of Newland [1832–71]
	Newland, nr Monmouth

[Before 1842 All Saints was the unofficial parish church for the Forest of Dean; Christ Church, Berry Hill (**18.37**) was opened by the incumbent Payler Matthew Procter 1803–22: Nicolls 1863, 161–71. From 1813 George Ridout was lecturer (i.e. an assistant minister) at Newland and then incumbent. The benefice consisted of Newland with Clearwell (**18.23**) and Redbrook (**18.24**), Bream (**18.22**) and Coleford (**18.21**).]

18.21 (10)   **Church of England, St John the Evangelist, Coleford**

Name	St John's church erected upon the site of an old chapel of ease to Newland. [Known as the New Chapel]
Consecration	[18] January 1821. In lieu of an old chapel of ease to Newland. [15 May 1880]
Erected	[Replaced by a larger building on another site]
Endowment	Land £109 10s. OPE £41 10s. [See Newland (**18.20**)]
Sittings	Free 440. Other 672. Total 1,112
Attend'ce 30 Mar.	Morning 260 + 75 SS. Total 335
	Evening 480 + 70 SS. Total 550
Avge attendance	[Not given]
Remarks	Having been only three weeks in residence I cannot make the return so accurate as I should wish.
Dated	31 March 1851
Signed	John Bayldon, minister [1851–61]
	Coleford, Gloucestershire
[*Incumbent*	Joseph Lawson Sisson [DD] 1843–86]

[Sisson, who was at odds with his congregation, was forced into appointing assistant curates in his place. Bayldon, who served at least six curacies, never became an incumbent. The benefice consisted of Newland with Clearwell (**18.23**) and Redbrook (**18.24**), Bream (**18.22**) and Coleford. A separate parish of Coleford was created in 1872.]

18.22 (1)   **Church of England, St James, Bream**

Name	St James Chapel in Bream. An old chapel, but newly re-built in the year

	1824
Consecration	Re-consecrated 1 April 1825. An old chapel having been newly rebuilt.
Erected	Unknown. Originally by voluntary contributions. Total cost £700 [Mostly rebuilt 1860–1 and enlarged 1891]
Endowment	Land rent £18. Tithe and glebe none. OPE (bequest) £32. Pew rents none. Fees 15s (average). Dues, Easter offerings, other sources none. [See Newland (**18.20**)]
Sittings	Free 80. Other 170. Total 250
Attend'ce 30 Mar.	Morning none Afternoon 135 + 65 SS. Total 200
Avge attendance	Afternoon 200 + 70 SS. Total 270
Dated	31 March 1851
Signed	Henry Poole, minister [1819–57] Parkend, near Lydney, Gloucestershire

[Poole was also the minister of Parkend (**18.36**). The benefice consisted of Newland (**18.20**) with Clearwell (**18.23**) and Redbrook (**18.24**), Bream and Coleford (**18.21**). The district of Bream was created in June 1854. Nicholls 1863, 152–60.]

18.23 (4) Church of England, St Peter, Clearwell

Name	St Peter's Chapel, Clearwell in the parish of Newland
Consecration	[6 Jan.] 1830, as a chapel of ease for the hamlet of Clearwell
Erected	[By] the Rev Henry Douglas [and] the Rev George Ridout. Church Building Soc. £400. Private and other sources £950. Total £1,350 [Replaced by a new church on another site; consecrated 5 April 1866]
Endowment	Land £15 4s. Fees 12s [See Newland (**18.20**)]
Sittings	Free 400. Other 80. Total 480
Attend'ce 30 Mar.	Afternoon 125 + 51 SS. Total 176
Avge attendance	[Not given]
Remarks	The service is every alternate Sunday afternoon. On other Sunday morning and evening with a lecture weekly (the usual attendance is about 200 besides children. A funeral took off a third of the congregation).
Dated	30 March 1851
Signed	George Ridout, minister [1832–71] Newland, nr Monmouth

[The benefice consisted of Newland (**18.20**) with Clearwell and Redbrook (**18.24**), Bream (**18.22**) and Coleford (**18.21**). In 1866 Clearwell became a consolidated chapelry.]

18.24 (5) Church of England, Licensed Room, Lower Redbrook

Name	Redbrook licensed room. [For a day and Sunday school]
Licensed	1825. For the benefit of the hamlet of Redbrook
Erected	[Not given]
Sittings	Free 80. Other 70. Total 150
Attend'ce 30 Mar.	Afternoon 45. Total [45]
Avge attendance	[Not given]
Remarks	One service each Sunday alternate after[noon] and ev[ening] The afternoon service always much less than evening.
Dated	30 March 1851
Signed	Charles William Grove, curate of Newland [1843–] Newland, nr Monmouth
[*Incumbent*	George Ridout 1832–71]

[The benefice consisted of Newland (**18.20**) with Clearwell (**18.23**) and Redbrook, Bream (**18.22**) and Coleford (**18.21**). The chapel of ease of St Saviour, Redbrook was consecrated 14 Aug. 1873.]

18.25 (9)	**Church of England, Scowles**
Name	Scowles Chapel
Licensed	1850. For the benefit of the inhabitants of the hamlet called the 'Scowles'
Erected	[In 1849 by] Charles Wm Grove. By private subscription Total cost £140
Endowment	[See Newland (**18.20**)]
Sittings	Free 100. Other none. Total 100
Attend'ce 30 Mar.	Evening 70. Total [70]
Avge attendance	[Not given]
Remarks	There is but one service at this chapel on the Sunday, and always at 6 pm of that day.
Dated	30 March 1851
Signed	Charles William Grove, curate of Newland [1843–] Newland, nr Monmouth
[*Incumbent*	George Ridout 1832–71]

[The benefice consisted of Newland (**18.20**) with Clearwell (**18.23**) and Redbrook (**18.24**), Bream (**18.22**) and Coleford (**18.21**).]

18.26 (13)	**Baptist, Coleford** (see also **18.47b**)
Name	Coleford Baptist Chapel
Erected	About 1799 [Enlarged 1828 and replaced by a new chapel 1858]
Building	Yes [separate and entire] Yes [exclusively as a place of worship]
Sittings	Free 190. Other 310. Total 500
Attend'ce 30 Mar.	Morning 350 + 200 SS. Total 550 Afternoon 271 SS. Total 271 Evening 480. Total 480
Avge attendance	Morning 350 + 220 SS. Total 570 Afternoon 250 SS. Total 250 Evening 480. Total 480
Remarks	The calculation under [sittings] is made for adults: children sit closer than adults. Hence the apparent discrepancy between [the number of sittings and the morning attendance on 30 March] Morning congregation lessened by its being mid-Lent Sunday.
Dated	31 March 1851
Signed	John Penny, minister Coleford, Gloucestershire

[Penny was also the minister of the mission stations of Lane End (**18.27**), Little Drybrook (**18.28**) and Milkwall (**18.39**).]

18.27 (11)	**Baptist, Lane End, Coleford**
Name	Lane End School
Erected	[Not given]
Building	Yes [separate and entire] A day school
Sittings	Free 80. Total [80]
Attend'ce 30 Mar.	Afternoon 35. Total 35
Avge attendance	Afternoon 40. Total 40
Remarks	This is merely a sub-station of the Baptist church of Coleford, and its services are conducted chiefly by laymen. I sign as minister in virtue of a general superintendence. Attendance very varied.
Dated	31 March 1851

Signed   John Penny, minister
                   Coleford, Gloucestershire
[Penny was also the minister of Coleford (**18.26**) and of the mission stations at Lane End, Little Drybrook (**18.28**) and Milkwall (**18.39**).]

18.28 (12)   Baptist, Little Drybrook, near Coleford
Name   [None]
Erected   [Not given]
Building   No [not separate and entire] No [not exclusively as a place of worship]
Sittings   Free 50. Total [50]
Attend'ce 30 Mar. Afternoon 25. Total 25
Avge attendance Afternoon 25. Total 25
Remarks   This is a sub-station of the Baptist church at Coleford, and its services
                   are conducted chiefly by laymen. I sign as minister in virtue of a general
                   superintendence.
Dated   31 March 1851
Signed   John Penny, minister
                   Coleford, Gloucestershire
[Penny was also the minister of Coleford (**18.26**) and of the mission stations at Lane End (**18.27**), Little Drybrook and Milkwall (**18.39**).]

18.29 (7)   Baptist, Redbrook
Name   Baptist Meeting Room
Erected   [Not given]
Building   No [not separate and entire] No [not exclusively as a place of worship]
Sittings   Free 80. Total [80]
Attend'ce 30 Mar. Afternoon 62. Total [62]
Avge attendance Afternoon 60. Total [60]
Dated   7 April 1851
Signed   Henry Clark, minister
                   Monmouth
[Clark was the minister of Monnow Street Baptist Chapel, Monmouth.]

18.30 (8)   Wesleyan Methodist, Redbrook
Name   [None]
Erected   About 1830
Building   Yes [separate and entire] Yes [exclusively as a place of worship]
Sittings   Free 155. Other 45. Total [200] Standing room none are permanently
Attend'ce 30 Mar. Morning 80. Total [80]
                   Afternoon 40 SS. Total [40]
                   Evening 150. Total [150]
Avge attendance Morning 80. Total 80
                   Afternoon 40 SS. Total 40
                   Evening 150. Total 150
Dated   7 April 1851
Signed   Charles Herbert, steward (maltster)
                   Redbrook, Monmouth

18.31 (15)   Wesleyan Methodist, Coleford
Name   Magistrates' Room
Erected   About 1840
Building   No [not separate and entire] No [not exclusively as a place of worship]

Sittings   Free 120. Total [120]
Attend'ce 30 Mar.   Morning 30. Total [30]
                      Evening 70. Total [70]
Avge attendance   [Not given]
Dated   31 March 1851
Signed   Samuel Wesley, minister [1850–1]
                      Little Dean, Woodside, Newnham, Gloucestershire
[Wesley was also the minister of Flaxley (**6.22**), Joyford (**18.43**), Lydbrook (**18.41**), Newnham (**6.11**) and Mitcheldean (**6.27**). John Wesley, who had frequently preached in Coleford, referred to it as 'our other Kingswood': *Journal,* 30 Sept. 1754.]

18.32 (16)   **Wesleyan Methodist, Worral Hill, Coleford** (see also **18.47a**)
(Summary form)
Name   Worral Hill Chapel
Erected   Since 1800
Building   Yes [separate and entire] Yes [exclusively as a place of worship]
Sittings   All free
Usual attend'ce   Morning 40 + 10 SS. Total 50
                      Afternoon 60 + 10 SS. Total 70
Remarks   This chapel is out of my district but I have endeavoured to procure correct
                      information
Signed   H. B. Messenger.
                      Coleford, Gloucester

18.33 (2)   **Wesleyan Methodist, Bream**
Name   None
Erected   [Not given]
Building   No [not separate and entire] No [not exclusively as a place of worship]
                      [An] inhabited house
Sittings   [Not given]
Attend'ce 30 Mar.   Evening 90. Total 90
Avge attendance   Evening 100. Total 100
Dated   31 March 1851
Signed   Richard Tilby Haybury, society steward
                      Bream, nr Lydney, Gloucestershire

18.34 (3)   **Primitive Methodist, Clearwell**
Name   Primitive Methodist. Preaching room
Erected   1836
Building   No [not separate and entire] No [not exclusively as a place of worship]
Sittings   Free 90. Other none. Total [90] Standing room none
Attend'ce 30 Mar.   Morning 30. Total 30
                      Afternoon 70. Total 70
                      Evening 64. Total 64
Avge attendance   Morning 40. Total [40]
                      Afternoon 64. Total [64]
                      Evening 80. Total [80]
Dated   31 March 1851
Signed   George Gripp, minister
                      Dry Bridge Street, Monmouth

18.35 (14)	**Wesleyan Reformers, Coleford**
Name	Wesleyan Reform Chapel
Erected	Before 1800
Building	Yes [separate and entire] Yes, excepting that it is now temporarily used as a British School
Sittings	Free 130. Other 72. Total [202]
Attend'ce 30 Mar.	Morning 35. Total 35
	Evening 60. Total 60
Avge attendance (6m)	Morning 30. Total 30
	Evening 75. Total 75
Remarks	In consequence of a secession the congregation is not at present quite equal to ⅔ of what it was until the last six months.
Dated	31 March 1851
Signed	William Woods, manager and steward [schoolmaster]
	[Market Street], Coleford, Gloucestershire

[The building was a former Countess of Huntingdon's Chapel 1789–1819, and was later used as a National school and a British and Foreign school.]

577.5–8 Township of West Dean

Area 10,035 acres; 1,256 inhabited houses, 42 uninhabited. Population 6,084.
In 1842 under the Dean Forest Ecclesiastical Districts Act (5 and 6 Vict. c.65) the Forest was divided into four ecclesiastical districts, irrespective of the previous division into the township of East Dean and West Dean. The four churches were: Christ Church, Berry Hill (**18.37**), Holy Trinity, Harrow Hill (**6.6**), St Paul, Parkend (**18.36**) and St John the Evangelist, Cinderford (**6.8**).
[For the creation of parishes in the Forest of Dean, see Snell 2006, 448–51.]

18.36 (17)	**Church of England, St Paul, Parkend**
Name	St Paul's Church. Of a new and distinct district
Consecration	2 May 1822. A new church and district
Erected	By aid from the Society for the Promoting the Building and Enlargement of Churches and Chapels; from the Board of Woods etc. and chiefly from private subscriptions. Aforesaid Society's grant £250. By grant from Board of Woods etc. £250. Private and other sources £2,200 [from QAB] Total £2,700 [Restored 1898]
Endowment	Land and tithe none. Glebe £5. OPE £150 (from Queen Anne's Bounty and Parliamentary grant). Pew rents none. Fees £5 (average). Dues and Easter offerings none. {Total £150}
Sittings	Free 500. Other 100. Total 600 [The benches were free and the pews were for the Forest officials, colliery masters and agents: *VCH* 5, 394]
Attend'ce 30 Mar.	Morning 190 + 122 SS. Total 312
	Afternoon 134 + 100 SS. Total 234
	Evening no service
Avge attendance	Morning 300 + 150 SS. Total 450
	Afternoon 350 + 135 SS. Total 485
	Evening none
Dated	31 March 1851
Signed	Henry Poole, minister (perpetual curate) [1822–57]
	Parkend near Lydney, Gloucestershire

[Poole was also minister of Bream (**18.22**). From 1829 he lived with his sister at Parkend. 'Before I began the building of my parsonage my own means were entirely exhausted, having expended full

£1,000 of my own in the erection of three churches, two schoolhouses, cottages to each', and now he needed a further £300 to pay off debts on building the parsonage. 'He sacrificed literally all he possessed, and his poor sister did the same': Nicholls 1863, 159–60; *VCH* 5, 394. Within the parish All Saints, Viney Hill was consecrated 25 April 1867.]

18.37 (18)   Church of England, Christ Church, Berry Hill

Name	Christ Church. *A district church by authority of an Act of Parl. made [5 and] 6 Vict. c.65 entitled an Act to divide the Forest of Dean into Ecclesiastical Districts [1842]
Consecration	[7 July 1816]
Erected	By private subscription [Restored 1913]
Endowment	Land £107. Glebe £15. OPE £33 19s 10d [Endowment of £2,000 from] (Queen Anne's Bounty Fund). Surplice fees about £8. {Total £150}
Sittings	Free 275.** Other 130 (for children of ch[urch] school). All free Total 400
Attend'ce 30 Mar.	Morning 185 + 105 SS. Total 290
	Afternoon 300 + 95 SS. Total 395
Avge attendance	Morning 190 + 103 SS. Total 293
	Afternoon 270 + 90 SS. Total 360
Remarks	*The church was built much earlier. [Opened 6 Jan. 1813 as a chapel-schoolroom that became the north aisle of the new church. A district was assigned in 1844.]
	** There are 275 free sittings (reckoning ten grown persons to occupy 18 feet) but many more contrive to find room. This is independent of the Sunday scholars for whom there are seats for 120 or 130.
Dated	30 March 1851
Signed	James Banks MA, perp. curate [1847–52]
	Christ Church parsonage, near Coleford, Gloucestershire

[Before 1842, All Saints Newland (**18.20**) had been considered the unofficial parish church of the Forest of Dean. The incumbent Payler Matthew Procter 1803–22 erected Christ Church, the first of many new places of worship to be opened in the Forest. It doubled as a schoolroom and when it opened attracted 300 children. Subscribers to the church included the well-known Evangelicals Lady Olivia Sparrow and Nicholas Vansittart. An appeal to provide an endowment was launched in June 1813, requesting 'assistance to place amongst these people a clergyman who would not only publicly preach, but reside, privately visit their cottages, disseminate the scriptures and assist the master of the National school in impressing upon the minds of the children the principles of the Christian faith': Nicholls 1863, 168. 'Christ Church in the Forest of Dean will remain for ages a lasting monument of the pious worth and religious zeal of its benevolent and truly Christian founder': *Gentleman's Magazine* (1822), 92, 570. A parish was created in 1844: *VCH* 5, 390–1. Banks was headmaster of Ludlow Grammar School 1852–7 and a diocesan inspector of schools. In 1858 on inheriting Moor Court, Hereford from his great uncle James Davies, he assumed that surname himself, and combined 'the functions of squire, clergyman and banker, becoming a partner in his brother's bank'. He was a distinguished classical scholar and author: *ODNB* 'James Davies (formerly Banks) (1820–1883)'. His immediate predecessor at Christ Church was Thomas Rock Garnsley 1824–47, who in 1820–1 had served as a chaplain in Sierra Leone; returning home through poor health, he was a deputation speaker for CMS 1821–4: Nicholls 1863, 148–51.]

18.38 (19)   Church of England, schoolroom, Upper Lydbrook

Name	Licensed school house
Licensed	[January] 1822. Licensed for divine service there being no church
Erected	By subscription under Rev Mr [Henry] Berkin late incumb[en]t of Holy Trinity, [Harrow Hill] (**6.6**). Restored 1910–2]
Sittings	[Not given]

Attend'ce 30 Mar.	Morning 70 + 104 SS. Total 174
	Afternoon 350. Total 350
Avge attendance	[Not given] [400]
Remarks	There is a church in course of erection.
Dated	31 March 1851
Signed	William Watkins Deering, official minister [1851–2]
	Welsh Bicknor, Ross, Herefordshire

[On the background to the opening of the schoolroom by Henry Berkin, see Nicholls 1863, 140. The 'church in course of erection' was Holy Jesus, consecrated 4 Dec. 1851: *VCH* 5, 391–2.]

18.39 (21) Baptist, Milkwall, near Coleford

Name	[None]
Erected	[Not given]
Building	No [not separate and entire] No [not exclusively as a place of worship]
Sittings	Free 50. Total [50]
Attend'ce 30 Mar.	Afternoon 22. Total 22
Avge attendance	Afternoon 20. Total 22 [*sic*]
Remarks	This is merely a sub-station of the Baptist Church at Coleford, and its services are conducted chiefly by laymen. I sign as minister in virtue of a general superintendence.
Dated	31 March 1851
Signed	John Penny, minister
	Coleford, Gloucestershire

[Penny was also minister of Coleford (**18.26**) and of the mission stations at Lane End (**18.27**) and Little Drybrook (**18.28**).]

18.40 (22) (347.2.7) Baptist, Lower Lydbrook
(On an Anglican form)

Name	Baptist Chapel
Licensed	In the year of our Lord, 1812. Licensed as 'scool room' and preaching house [Replaced by a new chapel in 1864]
Erected	Subscription by Mr Boyce. Private sources £200. Total cost £200
Sittings	Free 100. Total 100
Attend'ce 30 Mar.	Morning 38 + 20 SS. Total 58
	Afternoon 35 SS. Total [35]
	Evening 79. Total [79]
Avge attendance	Morning 30 + 24 SS. Total 54
	Afternoon 30 SS. Total [30]
	Evening 100. Total [100]
Remarks	No minister
Dated	30 March 1851
Signed	William Cole, 'clark of the chapel'
	Lydbrook, near Ross, Gloster shire

[Early on the chapel received financial support from the Edward Goff charity (**7.3**).]

18.41 (20) Wesleyan Methodist, Lydbrook

Name	None
Erected	About 1800
Building	No [not separate and entire] No [not exclusively as a place of worship]
Sittings	Free 50. Total [50]

Attend'ce 30 Mar. Afternoon 50. Total [50]

Evening 34. Total [34]

Avge attendance [Not given]

Dated Samuel Wesley, minister [1850–1]

Signed Little Dean, Woodside, Newnham, Gloucestershire

[Wesley was also the minister of Coleford (**18.31**), Flaxley (**6.22**), Joyford (**18.43**), Newnham (**6.11**) and Mitcheldean (**6.27**).]

18.42 (23)   **Wesleyan Methodist, West Dean**

Name Whitecroft

Erected 1823 [Replaced by a larger chapel 1874]

Building Yes [separate and entire] Yes [exclusively as a place of worship]

Sittings Free 200. Total [200]

Attend'ce 30 Mar. Morning 40 + 40 SS. Total 80

Afternoon 60. Total 60

Avge attendance [Not given]

Dated 30 March 1851

Signed William Baker, minister [1850–1]

St James's Street, Monmouth

[In 1859 half of the congregation left the chapel and became Wesleyan Reformers.]

18.43 (25)   **Wesleyan Methodist, Joyford**

Name Wesleyan Chapel

Erected 1825

Building Yes [separate and entire] Yes [exclusively as a place of worship]

Sittings Free 140. Total [140]

Attend'ce 30 Mar. Afternoon 100. Total [100]

Avge attendance Morning 120. Total [120]

Dated 31 March 1851

Signed Samuel Wesley, minister [1850–1]

Little Dean, Woodside, Newnham, Gloucestershire.

[Wesley was also the minister of Coleford (**18.31**), Flaxley (**6.22**), Lydbrook (**18.41**), Newnham (**6.11**) and Mitcheldean (**6.27**).]

18.44 (27)   **Primitive Methodist, Upper Lydbrook**

Name Primitive Methodist 'Chapple'

Erected 1828 [Rebuilt 1852 as Ebenezer Chapel]

Building Separate [and entire] Exclusively as a place of worship

Sittings Free 56. Other 45. Total [101]

Attend'ce 30 Mar. Morning 52. Total [52]

Evening 62. Total [62]

Avge attendance [Not given]

Dated 31 March 1851

Signed Robert Wall, steward [tin plate maker]

[Lydbrook Hill], Lydbrook, Gloucestershire

['In 1868 the Primitive Methodists had 13 meetings and 339 members in the Forest': *VCH* 5, 402.]

18.45 (22)   **Primitive Methodist, West Dean**

Name Pillowell Chapel

Erected 1835 [Replaced by a new chapel erected elsewhere in 1885]

Building	Yes [separate and entire] Yes [exclusively as a place of worship]
Sittings	Free 246 [sic]. Total 144
Attend'ce 30 Mar.	Morning 78 SS. Total 78
	Afternoon 90 + 50 SS. Total 140
	Evening 124. Total 124
Avge attendance	Morning 70 SS. Total 70
	Afternoon 100 + 70 SS. Total 170
	Evening 150. Total 150
Dated	31 March 1851
Signed	Samuel Jordan, local preacher [labourer]
	Yorkley, near Lydney, Gloucestershire

18.46 (24)   Primitive Methodist, Ellwood, West Dean

Name	Ellwood Primitive Methodist Chapel
Erected	1841 [Replaced by a new chapel in 1876]
Building	Yes [separate and entire] Yes [exclusively as a place of worship]
Sittings	Free 170. Other none. Total [170] Standing room for 30. Size 30 ft by 24
Attend'ce 30 Mar.	Morning 50 + 52 SS. Total 102
	Afternoon 48 SS. Total 48
	Evening 120. Total 120
Avge attendance	Morning 60 + 50 SS. Total 111 [*recte* 110]
	Afternoon 56 SS. Total 56
	Evening 110. Total 110
Dated	31 March 1851
Signed	Jonas Smith, trustee [coal miner]
	Ellwood, near Coleford, Gloucestershire

18.47 (26)   Summary sheet

Coleford, Monmouth.

S. C.   577.1.1.27
3 May 1853   577.1.1. 28 duplicate of 13
                                       577.1.1 31

Will you be so good as to supply the following information at your earliest convenience.

a)   **Coleford Wesleyan Methodist (18.32)**

Free seats	64
Other [seats]	90
Total	154
Congregation including SS	
Morning	50
Evening	70

b)   **Coleford Baptist Chapel (18.26)**

Free seats	220
Other [seats]	280
Total	500
Congregations including SS	
Morning	550
Evening	450

c)   **Symonds Yat Rock Baptist**
Free seats   40
Total   40
Congregations including SS
Afternoon   80

Dated   13 September 1852
Signed   H. B. Messenger

557.1.9 Parish of Staunton
Area 1,517 acres; 48 inhabited houses, 3 uninhabited. Population 211.
The parish includes the extra parochial community of Coal Pit Hill.
VCH 5, 272–84

18.48 (28)	**Church of England, All Saints, Staunton**
Name	All Saints. The ancient parish church of Staunton
Consecration	Before 1800
Erected	[Restored 1871–2 and 1903–7]
Endowment	Tithe £149 5s 2d. Glebe £11 18s. Fees £2 2s. {Total £241}
Sittings	Free 60. Other 120. Total 180
Attend'ce 30 Mar.	Morning 53 + 30 SS. Total 83
	Afternoon 66 + 30 SS. Total 96
Avge attendance	Morning 50 + 35 SS. Total 85
	Afternoon 65 + 35 SS. Total 100
Remarks	In addition to the above stated endowment the Crown pays to the present incumbent a compensation for loss of tithes consequent on arable land being turned into woods.
Dated	31 March 1851
Signed	Richard Davies, rector [1833–57]
	Staunton, near Coleford, Gloucestershire

[Davies, a lifelong friend of Edward Field (**18.49**), preached the sermon at his consecration as a bishop in Lambeth Palace chapel 28 Apr. 1844.]

577.1.10   Parish of English Bicknor
Area 2,377 acres; 111 inhabited houses, 5 uninhabited. Population 584.
In 1842 under Act of 5 and 6 Vict. c.48, the two extra parochial communities of Mailscot and New Weir were annexed to English Bicknor.
VCH 5, 101–17

18.49 (29)	**Church of England, St Mary the Virgin, English Bicknor**
Name	English Bicknor
Consecration	An old parish church
Erected	[Partially rebuilt 1839; restored 1894]
Endowment	Tithe commuted at £377. Glebe about 22 acres. Fees about £3 10s. {Total £300}
Sittings	Free 190. Other 172. Total 362
Attend'ce 30 Mar.	Morning 80 + 60 SS. Total [140]
	Afternoon 70 + 50 SS. Total [120]
Avge attend'ce (6m)	Morning and afternoon
	About the same as on 30 March
Remarks	The numbers attending are merely guessed at. They have not been counted.

Dated   31 March 1851
Signed   John Burdon, rector [1844–77]
             Coleford

[Burdon was also the incumbent of Welsh Bicknor 1850–68. The previous rector of English Bicknor was the high churchman Edward Field 1834–44, later bishop of Newfoundland 1844–76. Field erected schools in the parish and restored the church. 'The state of society at English Bicknor, when Field came to the parish, was at a very low ebb. There were two or three disreputable public houses, and the noisy contention of drunken men in the streets was by no means uncommon. The farmers did not generally set a good example – the ringers and singers were a troublesome lot': Tucker, 11–6, 21–2, 32, 48, 252–3, 267; *ODNB* 'Edward Field (1801–1876)'.]

HO 129/347 ROSS DISTRICT (HEREFORDSHIRE)

347.2.   ROSS SUB-DISTRICT

347.2.7   Parish of Ruardean
Area 1,590 acres; 226 inhabited houses, 10 uninhabited. Population 1,033.
VCH 5, 231–47

18. 50 (21)   **Church of England, St John the Baptist, Ruardean**
Name   St Luke [sic]. An ancient parish church
Consecration   Before 1800
Erected   [In serious disrepair by the mid-19th century. Restored 1866–7 and rebuilt 1889–90]
Endowment   Tithe £100. {Total £100}
Sittings   Free 134. Other 347. Total 481
Attend'ce 30 Mar. Morning 100 + 67 SS. Total 167
             Afternoon 300 + 67 SS. Total 367
Avge attendance [Not given]
Dated   31 March 1851
Signed   Joseph Terrett, churchwarden [butcher]
             Mitcheldean, Gloucestershire
[*Incumbent*   William Penfold 1851–81]

[In 1842 the chapelry of Ruardean (formerly attached to Walford, Herefordshire) became a separate parish. The historian, antiquary and Freemason Thomas Dudley Fosbrooke was first curate then incumbent of Walford with Ruardean 1810–42: *ODNB* 'Thomas Dudley Fosbrooke (1770–1842)'. His successor Henry Formby, who supported the Oxford Movement, became unpopular with his parishioners, resigned in 1845 and the following year became a Roman Catholic. Later William Penfold was also an unpopular incumbent: Maclean, 124–48.]

18.51 (23)   **Independent, Ruardean**
Name   Chapel
Erected   Before 1800 [1798 and enlarged 1813]
Building   Yes [separate and entire] Yes [exclusively as a place of worship]
Sittings   Free 150. Total [150] Standing room for 50
Attend'ce 30 Mar. Morning 164. Total [164]
             Evening 110. Total [110]
Avge attendance Morning 130 + 40 SS. Total 170
Dated   31 March 1851
Signed   John Horlick, Independent minister [1801–58]
             [No address given]
[Horlick was also the minister of Mitcheldean 1801–50 (**6.26**). When he opened a Sunday school

c.1814, he found that 'very few of the population could read. Of the old Foresters few can write, even as much as their names.' (from his extensive testimony to the Children's Employment Commission, 1842).]

18.52 (24)   **Bible Christian, Crookend End, Ruardean**
Name   Ebenezer
Erected   1828 [Enlarged 1873]
Building   Yes [separate and entire] Yes [exclusively as a place of worship]
Sittings   Free 70. Other 35. Total [105]
Attend'ce 30 Mar.   Morning 40 + 52 SS. Total [92]
                      Afternoon 51 SS. Total [51]
                      Evening 80. Total [80]
Avge attendance   [Not given]
Dated   31 March 1851
Signed   James Brooks, minister
                      Drybrook, Mitcheldean, Gloucestershire
[Brooks was also minister of Broom's Green (**7.19**), and Drybrook (**6.13–14**).]

> **19. HO 129/404, 406, 389 'NORTH GLOUCESTERSHIRE'**: 40 places of worship

HO 129/404 STRATFORD ON AVON DISTRICT (WARWICKSHIRE)

404.3.3 STRATFORD ON AVON SUB-DISTRICT

404.3.3 Parish of Clifford Chambers [transferred to Warwickshire, 1931]
Area 2,500 acres; 71 inhabited houses, 2 uninhabited. Population 305.
VCH 6, 207–16

19.1 (28)	**Church of England, St Helen, Clifford Chambers**
Name	St Helen's
Consecration	Before 1800. Registers begin 1538. [rec-consecrated 4 June 1887]
Erected	[Rebuilt and enlarged 1886–7]
Endowment	Tithe £51. Glebe £112. OPE £2 11s. Easter offerings and other £10. {Total £172}
Sittings	Total 140
Attend'ce 30 Mar.	Morning 70 + 40 SS. Total 110
	Afternoon 51 + 38 SS. Total 89
Avge attendance	Morning 60 + 38 SS. Total 98
	Afternoon 70 + 36 SS. Total 106
Dated	30 March 1851
Signed	Francis Annesley, rector [1845–79]
	Stratford on Avon, Warwickshire

404.3.5 Parish of Preston-on-Stour [transferred to Warwickshire, 1931]
Area 1,990 acres; 88 inhabited houses, 1 uninhabited. Population 421.
VCH 8, 81–9

19.2 (30)	**Church of England, St Mary Magdalene, Preston-on-Stour**
Name	Ancient church dedicated to St Mary Magdalene
Consecration	Before 1800
Erected	[Restored 1904]
Endowment	OPE modus of £8. Queen Anne's Bounty £47 9s 6d. Fees 10s. {Total £55}
Sittings	Free 189. Other 122. Total 311
Attend'ce 30 Mar.	Afternoon 151 + 79 SS. Total 230
Avge attendance	[Not given]
Dated	31 March 1851
Signed	William Barrett, perpetual curate [1839–51]
	Stratford upon Avon, Warwick

[Barrett was soon to become the incumbent of Saintbury (**19.36**).]

HO 129/404 STRATFORD ON AVON DISTRICT (WARWICKSHIRE)

404.4 OLD STRATFORD SUB-DISTRICT

404.4.1 Parish of Marston Sicca (or Long Marston) [transferred to Warwickshire 1931].
Area 1,680 acres; 72 inhabited houses, 2 uninhabited. Population 332.

19.3 (33)	**Church of England, St James the Great, Marston Sicca**
Name	No name. An ancient parish church

Consecration	Not known. Before 1800
Erected	[Not given]
Endowment	{Total £253}
Sittings	Free 70. Other 10. Total [80]
Attend'ce 30 Mar.	Morning 50 SS. Total [50]
	Evening 25 SS. Total [25]
Avge attendance	Morning 50 SS. Total [50]
	Afternoon 50 SS. Total [50]
Remarks	The above church is very old, date of erection not known. There is a stone [?] for [... ...] near the chancel dated 1661.
Dated	[Day not given] March 1851.
Signed	William Frederick Kerr, rector [1839–78]
	Stratford on Avon, Warwickshire

19.4 (34)   **Wesleyan Methodist, Long Marston**

Name	None
Erected	[Not given]
Building	No [not separate and entire] No [not exclusively as a place of worship]
Sittings	[Not given]
Attend'ce 30 Mar.	[Not given]
Avge attendance	Evening 50. Total [50]
Dated	31 March 1851
Signed	Thomas Gibbs, steward
	[No address]

404.4.2 Parish of Dorsington [transferred to Warwickshire, 1931]
Area 910 acres; 28 inhabited houses, 2 uninhabited. Population 115.

19.5 (35)   **Church of England, St Peter, Dorsington**

Name	St Peter's, Dorsington. An ancient parish church
Consecration	Before 1800
Erected	[Rebuilt 1754]
Endowment	Glebe appropriated about £200. Easter offerings none received. {Total £199}
Sittings	Free 53. Other 52. Total 105
Attend'ce 30 Mar.	Afternoon 42 + 14 SS. Total 56
Avge attendance	Morning 40 + 20 SS. Total 60
	Afternoon 50 + 20 SS. Total 70
Remarks	The usual services in the church are morning and afternoon; but the morning service was omitted on Sunday, 30 March owing to the absence of the officiating minister of Dorsington, and the afternoon duty performed by a substitute.
Dated	31 March 1851
Signed	Henry Sharp, churchwarden
	Dorsington near Bidford, Stratford on Avon
[*Incumbent*	Robert Lawrence 1838–51]

[Lawrence's daughter Caroline Frances married Thomas Pownall Boultbee, curate of St Mary's Cheltenham 1849–53 and theological tutor of Cheltenham College 1853–63: *ODNB* 'Thomas Pownall Boultbee 1818–84'.]

404.4.3–4   Parish of Weston-on-Avon [transferred to Warwickshire, 1931]
Area 1,540 acres; 25 inhabited houses. Population 115.

The parish includes Milcote (partly in Gloucestershire and partly in Warwickshire).

No return   Church of England, All Saints, Weston-on-Avon
[*Endowment*   Total £84]
[*Incumbent*   James Davenport 1849–1904]
[Davenport, the son of Charles Davenport, was his curate and successor at Welford-on-Avon (**19.6**).]

404.4.5–6 Parish of Welford-on-Avon [transferred to Warwickshire, 1931]
Area 3,550 acres; 160 inhabited houses, 12 uninhabited. Population 605.
The parish includes the hamlets of Bickmarsh and Little Dorsington.

19.6 (39)   Church of England, St Peter, Welford-on-Avon
(Summary form)
Name   St James [sic] church
Consecration   Before 1540
Erected   [Restored 1866–7]
[*Endowment*   Total £442]
Sittings   Free 64. Other 236. Total 300
Usual attend'ce   From 60 to 80 besides Sunday scholars
               Morning (as above) + 94 SS*
               Afternoon (as above)
               Evening nil
Remarks   * The above scholars are taught by the Wesleyan Methodists in their
               chapel, and was returned at the time the Census was taken at their school.
               The Rev Charles Davenport preaches a sermon and has a collection for
               them in his church once in the year, and pays the amount over to the
               Wesleyan teachers. They in return agree to teach the children the church
               catechism, and take them every Sabbath morning to his church.
Signed   Robert Hirst
[*Incumbent*   Charles Davenport 1820–64]
[Davenport was succeeded by his son James Davenport 1864–1904.]

19.7 (36)   Wesleyan Methodist, Welford-on-Avon
Name   Wesleyan Chapel
Erected   In the year 1801 [Opened 1802; enlarged 1913]
Building   Yes [separate and entire] Yes [exclusively as a place of worship]
Sittings   Free 113. Other 65. Total [178]
Attend'ce 30 Mar. Evening 150. Total 150
Avge attendance   [Not given]
Remarks   The service being only in the evening the Sunday scholars attend not as
               a body at that time.
Dated   3 April 1851
Signed   Henry Hopkins, chapel steward [master boot and shoemaker]
               Welford, near Stratford on Avon, Warwickshire

19.8 (37)   Primitive Methodist, Welford-on-Avon
Name   None
Erected   [Not given]
Building   No [not separate and entire] No [not exclusively as a place of worship]
Sittings   Free 11 Other 30. Total [41]
Attend'ce 30 Mar. Afternoon 14. Total [14]
Avge attendance   [Not given]

Dated	[Not given]
Signed	James Symmonds, minister
	Birmingham Road, Stratford upon Avon, Warwickshire

19.9 (38)   Church of Jesus Christ of Latter-day Saints, Welford-on-Avon

Name	None
Erected	Before 1800
Building	No [not separate and entire] Yes [exclusively as a place of worship]
Sittings	Standing room for 60
Attend'ce 30 Mar.	Afternoon 17. Total 17
	Evening 14. Total 14
Avge attendance	Afternoon 18. Total 18
	Evening 16. Total 16
Dated	30 March 1851
Signed	Cotterell Ballard, elder of the Church of Jesus Christ [agricultural labourer]
	Welford, near Stratford on Avon

HO 129/406 SHIPSTON-ON-STOUR DISTRICT (WARWICKSHIRE)

406.1 CAMPDEN SUB-DISTRICT

406.1.1 Parish of Quinton [transferred to Warwickshire, 1935]
Area 4,800 acres; 137 inhabited houses, 11 uninhabited. Population 587.
The parish includes Upper and Lower Quinton and the hamlet of Admington.

19.10 (1)   Church of England, All Saints, Quinton

Name	All Saints. Ancient church
Consecration	Before 1800
Erected	[Restored 1899]
Endowment	Glebe. OPE money payment. Easter offering 10s 6d. Other sources about £80 a year. {Total £70}
Sittings	Free 150. Other 250. Total about 400
Attend'ce 30 Mar.	Morning 134 + 48 SS. Total 182
Avge attendance	Morning 170 + 50 SS. Total 220
	Afternoon 300 + 50 SS. Total 350
Dated	27 March 1851
Signed	James Fowle, vicar [1826–75]
	Quinton, Ch[ipping] Campden, Gloucestershire

[Fowle was also the incumbent of Pebworth 1825–75 (**19.30**).]

406.1.3–4 Parish of Ilmington, Warwickshire
Area 4,000 acres; 206 inhabited houses, 12 uninhabited. Population 985.
The parish includes the hamlet of Lark Stoke in Gloucestershire. Population 13.

406.1.5–6 Parish of Mickleton
Area 3,766 acres; 163 inhabited houses, 1 uninhabited. Population 829.
The parish includes the hamlet of Hidcote Bartrim.

19.11 (3)   Church of England, St Lawrence, Mickleton

Name	St Lawrence. Ancient parish church
Consecration	Before 1800
Erected	[Restored 1868–70]
Endowment	Land £76. Tithe commuted rent charge £105. Glebe and house £15.
	Fees £5 12s. Easter offerings £1. Other sources annual sermon 10s.

	{Total £299}
Sittings	Free 200. Other 300. Total 500
Attend'ce 30 Mar.	Morning 160. Total [160]
	Afternoon 226. Total [226]
Avge attendance	Morning 180. Total [180]
	Afternoon 300. Total [300]
Remarks	200 free sittings. [There] are three galleries, one for school boys, one for school girls, and the other for men and for singers.
Dated	30 March 1851
Signed	Richard Gascoyne, curate [1840–56]
	Mickleton vicarage, nr Campden, Gloucestershire
[*Incumbent*	William Thomas Hadow 1834–65]

[The benefice consisted of Mickleton with Ebrington (**19.13**). Hadow was also the incumbent of Haseley near Warwick 1827–65.]

19.12 (4)   Wesleyan Methodist, Mickleton

Name	Wesleyan Preaching Room
Erected	Occupied since the year 1837 [A chapel was erected in 1891]
Building	Part of an house. Yes [exclusively as a place of worship]
Sittings	Free 44. Total [44]
Attend'ce 30 Mar.	Evening 33. Total [33]
Avge attendance	Evening 30. Total [30]
Dated	30 March 1851
Signed	William Luckett, steward [agricultural labourer]
	Mickleton, Gloucestershire

406.1.7 Parish of Ebrington

Area 2,960 acres; 116 inhabited houses, 3 uninhabited. Population 594.
The parish includes the hamlet of Hidcote Boyce.

19.13 (5)   Church of England, St Eadburgha, Ebrington

Name	'St Eadburgh'. Ancient parish church
Consecration	Before 1800
Erected	[Restored 1875–6]
Endowment	Land with house about £100. Tithe rent charge £10 6s. OPE £10.
	Fees about £5. Easter offerings about £2 10s. [See Mickleton (**19.11**)]
Sittings	Free about 186. Other about 142. Total 328.*
Attend'ce 30 Mar.	Morning 123 + 66 SS. Total 189
	Afternoon 176 + 62 SS. Total 238
Avge attendance	[Not given]
Remarks	*There are besides the 328 sittings, benches placed in the chancel for 100 children.
Dated	31 March 1851
Signed	William Annesley, minister
	Ebrington, Campden, Gloucestershire
[*Incumbent*	William Thomas Hadow 1834–65]

[Hadow was also incumbent of Haseley, near Warwick 1827–65. His son, William Elliot Hadow, was curate of Ebrington from 1858 and incumbent 1865–7. He was 'a zealous Freemason': Venn. The benefice consisted of Mickleton (**19.11**) with Ebrington.]

406.1.9–12 Parish of Chipping Campden

Area 4,660 acres; 490 inhabited houses, 10 uninhabited. Population 2,351, including 265 working on railway construction.

The parish includes the hamlets of Berrington, Broad Campden and Westington with Combe.

19.14 (6) **Church of England, St James, Chipping Campden**

Name	Campden parish church. Dedicated to St James
Consecration	Before 1800
Erected	[Restored 1875–6]
Endowment	Land and tithe £640 (net). {Total £640}
Sittings	Free 322. Other 918. Total 1,240
Attend'ce 30 Mar.	Morning 335 + 143 SS. Total 478
	Afternoon 246 + 146 SS. Total 392
Avge attendance	[Not given]
Remarks	The stormy character of the weather would operate to diminish the attendance especially of the schools, which (together) are often as many or more than 200. This would make the whole greater by 110 than is given above and would make the total to be 1,258 instead of 1,148.
Dated	[Not given]
Signed	Charles Edward Kennaway, vicar [1832–73]
	Campden, Gloucestershire

[Kennaway was also the minister of Christ Church, Cheltenham 1840–3 (**16.20**), and of Holy Trinity Chapel, Brighton 1843–7 (and was succeeded by Frederick William Robertson 1847–53, previously curate of Christ Church, Cheltenham 1842–7). He was 'a very amiable pious man, bred up among the Evangelical clergy, but moderate, and now disposed I should say to keep a middle course between that party and the High Church section owing Pusey and Newman as their leaders, and at present exercising no small influence – probably to good – in the church': Verey 1978, 146. Within the parish were the chapels of ease at Westington, opened 28 Dec. 1855 and St Michael and All Angels, opened 15 Oct. 1868: *GNQ* 5, 188.]

19.15 (10) **Church of England, Broad Campden**

Name	Broad Camden Chapel
Consecration	Has been desecrated since the Reformation till about six years since.
Erected	Unknown
Endowment	None [See Chipping Campden (**19.14**)]
Sittings	Free about 100. Other none. Total about 100
Attendance 28 Mar.	(Friday). Evening about 50. Total about 50
Avge attend'ce (4m)	Evening 50. Total 50
Remarks	There is week day service performed only, and that only for about eight months in the year.
Dated	28 March 1851
Signed	George Branson Dodwell, curate of Campden [1850–9]
	Curate of Campden, Campden, Gloucestershire
[*Incumbent*	Charles Edward Kennaway 1832–73]

[Dodwell was headmaster of Chipping Campden Grammar School 1855–62. Previously he had served in two parishes in Nova Scotia (and taught divinity at Bishops College, Lennoxville); he returned to Canada after leaving the Grammar School.]

19.16 (7) **Baptist, High Street, Chipping Campden**

Name	Baptist Chapel
Erected	Before 1800 [1724 and rebuilt 1872]
Building	Separate building. Exclusively as a place of worship
Sittings	Free 80. Other 150. Total [230] Standing room for 50
Attend'ce 30 Mar.	Morning 50 + 32 SS. Total 82

Evening 60. Total 60

Avge attendance	Morning 70 + 40 SS. Total 110
	Evening 70. Total 70
Dated	1 April 1851
Signed	Eli Amery, minister
	Campden, Gloucestershire

[The chapel was opened by the Presbyterians in 1724 and acquired by the Baptists in 1785.]

19.17 (8)   Wesleyan Methodist, Chipping Campden

Name	Wesleyan Chapel
Erected	1841 [Former tablet: 'Wesleyan Chapel, 1841']
Building	Yes [separate and entire] Yes [exclusively as a place of worship]
Sittings	Free 150. Other 60. Total [210] Standing room none
Attend'ce 30 Mar.	Afternoon 150 + 35 SS. Total 185
	Evening 110. Total 110
Avge attendance	Afternoon 180 + 35 SS. Total 215
	Evening 120. Total 120
Dated	31 March 1851
Signed	John Long, chapel steward [silk throwster employing 58 people]
	Campden, Glo'shire.

[In 1841 Robert Miles sold his house to the Methodists for their use as a chapel.]

19.18 (9)   Primitive Methodist, Chipping Campden

Denomination	~~Primitive Methodist Preaching House~~
Name	None
Erected	[Not given]
Building	No [not separate and entire] No [not exclusively as a place of worship]
Sittings	Free 40. Other none. Total [40] Standing room for 20
Attend'ce 30 Mar.	Morning none
	Afternoon none
	Evening 60. Total [60]
Avge attendance	[Not given]
Remarks	Service only in the evening
Dated	6 April 1851
Signed	Richard James, class leader [labourer on the turnpike road]
	Sheep St, Campden, Gloucestershire

19.19 (11)   Society of Friends, Broad Campden

Erected	Before 1800 [Built 1663, enlarged 1677]
Building	Yes [separate and entire] Yes [exclusively as a place of worship]
Floor area	Ground floor: 40 ft x 16 ft = 640 [sq. ft] Seats for 300
	Gallery: 15½ ft x 12 ft = 186 [sq. ft] Seats for 80
	Total 826 [square feet] Total seats 360
Attend'ce 30 Mar.	Morning 4. Total [4]
	Afternoon no meeting
	Evening no meeting
Remarks	There is a small stable attached which has not been measured as never used.
Dated	30th day of 3rd month 1851
Signed	George S. Gillett [machinist clerk]
	Brailes, near Shipston-on-Stour

406.2.   MORETON SUB-DISTRICT

406.2.2 Parish of Bourton-on-the-Hill
Area 2,960 acres; 115 inhabited houses, 10 uninhabited. Population 550.
VCH 6, 197–205; GNQ, 2, 484–8

19.20 (18)	**Church of England, St Lawrence, Bourton-on-the-Hill**
Name	Bourton on the Hill. A parish church
Consecration	[Not given]
Erected	A very antient parish church. Unknown when erected. [Chancel restored 1889]
Endowment	Pew rents none. Fees, dues, Easter offerings and other sources. To the offering I know not. {Total £675}
Sittings	[Not given]
Attend'ce 30 Mar.	[Not given]
Avge attendance	[Not given]
Remarks	Sufficient room and accommodation for both the poor and the rich. About ½ of the inhabitants of the parish are considered to attend.
Dated	26 March 1851
Signed	Samuel Wilson Warneford, rector [1810–55] [No address given]

[Warneford was a generous philanthropist who funded hospitals in Birmingham, Leamington Spa, London and Oxford; the Clergy Orphan School (from 1897 St Edmund's School), Canterbury. Within the diocese of Gloucester the Warneford Ecclesiastical Charity for the building, rebuilding, enlarging and repairing of churches, chapels and parsonages, and the Warneford Clerical Trust supporting clergy widows and orphans: ODNB 'Samuel Warneford (1763–1855)'. The benefice consisted of of Bourton-on-the-Hill with Moreton in the Marsh (**19.22**).]

406.2.3 Parish of Batsford
Area 932 acres; 19 inhabited houses. Population 107.

19.21 (19)	**Church of England, St Mary, Batsford**
Name	St Mary. Parish church
Consecration	Consecrated
Erected	Church rebuilt, not the chancel, by second Lord Redesdale, since 1800 Private benefactor [Rebuilt 1860–2]
Endowment	Tithe and glebe yes. {Total £370}
Sittings	Free between 60 and 70. Other between 80 and 90. [In another hand: free 65, other 85] Total 150
Attend'ce 30 Mar.	Morning perhaps 40 + 12 SS. Total 52 Afternoon 12 + 12 SS. Total 24
Avge attendance	Morning 60 or 70 + 12 SS. Total 80 or 90 Afternoon 30 odd + 12 SS. Total 52
Dated	31 April 1851
Signed	Cyril George Hutchinson, incumbent [1842–52] Batsford rectory, Moreton in Marsh, Gloucestershire

[Lord Redesdale was also bore the whole cost of the erection of St John, Aston Magna, Blockley, consecrated 29 Oct. 1846. On Redesdale, see ODNB 'John Thomas Freeman-Milford (1805–86)'.]

406.2.4 Parish of Moreton-in-Marsh
Area 900 acres; 296 inhabited houses, 6 uninhabited. Population 1,512.
VCH 6, 240–50.

19.22 (21)   **Church of England, St David, Moreton-in-Marsh**

Name	Parish church, Moreton in Marsh
Consecration	[Not given]
Erected	Ancient. Date unknown. [Rebuilt 1858–9 and enlarged 1891–2]
Endowment	[See Bourton-on-the-Hill (**19.20**)]
Sittings	[Not given]
Attend'ce 30 Mar.	[Not given]
Avge attendance	[Not given]
Remarks	Sufficient accommodation for the parishioners rich and poor. Services attended by one half of the population.
Dated	30 March 1851
Signed	Henry Mellish Stowers, minister [1846–]
	Moreton in Marsh, Gloucestershire
[Incumbent	Samuel Wilson Warneford 1810–55]

[The benefice consisted of of Bourton-on-the-Hill (**19.20**) with Moreton-in-Marsh.]

19.23 (22)   **Independent, Oxford Street, Moreton-in-Marsh**

Name	Independent Chapel
Erected	In 1817 in lieu of a previous building. [Founded 1796. New chapel opened 1861]
Building	Yes [separate and entire] Yes [exclusively as a place of worship]
Sittings	Free 180. Other 150. Total [330]
Attend'ce 30 Mar.	Morning 150 + 125 SS. Total 275
	Evening 180 + 50 SS. Total 230
Avge attendance	Evening 250 + 50 SS. Total 300
Remarks	The general average is so much higher than actual attendance on 30 March in consequence of an evening service held at the parish church on Sunday evenings during Lent, which draws off a large number of the general congregation.
Dated	31 March 1851
Signed	Benjamin Harris Cowper, minister [1849–52]
	Moreton in Marsh, Gloucestershire

[Cowper was also the minister of Evenlode (**14.25**) and Longborough (**14.37**).]

406.2.5 Parish of Lower Lemington

Area 855 acres; 14 inhabited houses. Population 58.
VCH 6, 216–20

19.24 (23)   **Church of England, St Leonard, Lower Lemington**

Name	An ancient chapel
Consecration	[Not given]
Erected	[Restored 1880]
Endowment	{Total £27}
Sittings	Free 45. Other 15. Total 60
Attend'ce 30 Mar.	Evening 40. Total [40]
Avge attendance	[Not given]
Remarks	[Situated] in archdeaconry of Gloucester and in the Campden ecclesiastical division. It is a sole parish.
Dated	31 March 1851
Signed	Charles Dudley, perpetual curate [1849–55]
	Shipston-on-Stour, Co. of Worcester

406.2.8 Parish of Todenham
Area 2,477 acres; 98 inhabited houses, 3 uninhabited. Population 462.
VCH 6, 250–8; *GNQ* 1, 257–8

19.25 (25)	**Church of England, St Thomas of Canterbury, Todenham**
Name	Todenham parish church
Consecration	[Not given]
Erected	[Restored 1879]
Endowment	Land £2 10s. Tithe £149. Glebe £246. OPE £26 9s 10d.
	Total £417 19s 10d. Individual rate and church rate £53. Pew rents
	none. Fees £1 14s 6d. {Total £254}
Sittings	Free 66. Other 134. Total 200
Attend'ce 30 Mar.	Morning 80 + 69 SS. Total 149
	Afternoon 82 + 67 SS. Total 149
Avge attendance	Morning 100 + 74 SS. Total 174
	Afternoon 100 + 74 SS. Total 174
Remarks	Average number of attendants of which are stated about 100 at each
	service, but the average of attendance once each Sunday, 150. The
	Sunday school children sit in the chancel.
Dated	31 March 1851
Signed	Gilbert Malcolm, rector [1812–55]
	Todenham, Moreton in Marsh.

[Malcolm was the brother of Sir John Malcolm, the governor of Bombay 1827–31 and MP for Launceston 1831–2; his statue is in Westminster Abbey: *ODNB* 'John Malcolm (1769–1833)'.]

HO 129/389 EVESHAM DISTRICT (WORCESTERSHIRE)

389.1 EVESHAM SUB-DISTRICT

389.1.1 Parish of Ashton under Hill [transferred to Worcestershire, 1931]
Area 1,300 acres; 88 inhabited houses, 1 uninhabited. Population 396.
VCH 8, 245–50

19.26 (2)	**Church of England, St Barbara, Ashton under Hill**
Name	Ashton under Hill. Chapel [of ease] dedicated to St Barbara
Consecration	Before 1800
Erected	[Alterations 1834–6, restored 1867 and 1913]
Endowment	Tithe rent charge of £110 [See Beckford (**15.31**)]
Sittings	Free 150. Other 73. Total 223
Attend'ce 30 Mar.	[Not given]
Avge attend'ce (2m)	Afternoon 126. SS 28. Total 154
Remarks	I could not number them on Sunday last.
Dated	31 March 1851
Signed	John Timbrill, minister [1797–1865]
	Beckford near Tewkesbury

[Timbrill was the incumbent of Beckford (**15.31**), of Dursley (**5.20**) with Woodmancote (**5.21**) and of Bretforton, Worcs. 1816–65. He was also the archdeacon of Gloucester 1825–65. The benefice consisted of Beckford (**15.31**) with Ashton under Hill.]

19.27 (3)	**Wesleyan Methodist, Ashton under Hill**
Name	None
Erected	In 1849
Building	No [not separate and entire] Yes [exclusively as a place of worship]

Sittings	Free 60. Other none. Total [60] Standing room for 40
Attend'ce 30 Mar.	Morning 32. SS none. Total [32]
	Evening 63. SS none. Total [63]
Avge attendance	Morning 25. SS none. Total [25]
	Evening 60. SS none. Total [60]
Remarks	The date [1849] is that of the commencement of the services.
Dated	31 March 1851
Signed	Charles Garrett, steward
	Ashton under Hill, near Beckford, Gloucestershire

389.1.3 Parish of Hinton-on-the-Green [transferred to Worcestershire, 1931]
Area 2,259 acres; 35 inhabited houses, 2 uninhabited. Population 192.
VCH 8, 262–8

19.28 (6)	**Church of England, St Peter, Hinton-on-the-Green**
Name	It is an ancient parish church, but what name was given to it on its consecration I cannot ascertain.
Consecration	Before 1800
Erected	[Restored 1862–3; new chancel 1894–5]
Endowment	{Total £200}
Sittings	Free 80. Other 50. Total 130
Attend'ce 30 Mar.	Morning 36 + 28 SS. Total 64
	Afternoon 41 + 28 SS. Total 69
Avge attendance	[Not given]
Dated	31 March 1851
Signed	Edmund Goldsmith, rector [1849–69]
	Hinton rectory, Evesham

[Goldsmith's successor Robert James Baker 1869–77 'introduced changes in ritual, including a choral communion service and the use of a surpliced choir': *VCH* 8, 267.]

389.1.4 Parish of Aston Somerville [transferred to Worcestershire, 1931]
Area 993 acres; 15 inhabited houses, 5 uninhabited. Population 89.

19.29 (7)	**Church of England, St Mary, Aston Somerville**
Name	It is the ancient parish church of the distinct and separate parish of Aston Somerville.
Consecration	Before 1800
Erected	[Modest restoration 1908]
Endowment	Tithe £230. Glebe £23. Total £253. {Total £272}
Sittings	Free 72. Other (three pews of eight sittings each) i.e. 24. Total 96
Attend'ce 30 Mar.	Morning 10 + 7 SS. Total 17
	Afternoon 23 + 8 SS. Total 31
	Evening there is none
Avge attendance	Morning 10 + 8 SS. Total 18
	Afternoon 25 + 8 SS. Total 33
	Evening no service
Dated	30 March 1851
Signed	George Head, rector [1848–93]
	Aston Somerville, Evesham

389.2   BROADWAY SUB-DISTRICT

389.2.1 Parish of Pebworth [transferred to Worcestershire, 1931]
Area 3,050 acres; 157 inhabited houses, 7 uninhabited. Population 737.
The parish includes the hamlet of Broad Marston.

19.30 (24)	**Church of England, St Peter, Pebworth**
Name	St Peter's. Ancient church
Consecration	Before 1800
Erected	[No 19th century restoration]
Endowment	Glebe. OPE modus about £100 per annum. Easter offerings. Other sources. Parliamentary grant fund. {Total £98}
Sittings	Free 100. Other 200. Total about 300
Attend'ce 30 Mar.	Afternoon 180 + 40 SS. Total 220
Avge attendance	Morning 100 + 60 SS. Total 160
	Afternoon 200 + 60 SS. Total 260
Dated	[Not given]
Signed	James Fowle, vicar [1825–75]
	Pebworth, Chipping Campden, Gloucestershire

[Fowle was also the incumbent of Quinton (**19.10**).]

19.31 (25)	**Wesleyan Methodist, Pebworth**
Name	Wesleyan Chapel
Erected	1840
Building	Yes [separate and entire] Yes [exclusively as a place of worship]
Sittings	Free 82. Other 79. Total [161]
Attend'ce 30 Mar.	Morning 65. Total [65]
	Evening 75. Total [75]
Avge attendance	Morning 150. Total [150]
Dated	30 March 1851
Signed	Samuel Rastall, steward [master baker employing one man]
	Pebworth, Gloucestershire

389.2.10 Parish of Cow Honeybourne
Area 1,360 acres; 80 inhabited houses, 8 uninhabited. Population 343.
Transferred in 1931 from Gloucestershire to Worcestershire, and in 1953 amalgamated with the adjoining parish of Church Honeybourne (which had always been in Worcestershire).

[The benefice consisted of the parish church of St Ecgwin, Church Honeybourne with the chapel (unknown dedication) of Cow Honeybourne. By the 19th century the church at Cow Honeybourne had fallen into disrepair and had been converted into tenements. It was restored 1861–2 and used as a chapel until closed in 1975 and converted into apartments. The incumbent of both parishes was the wealthy William Baldwin Banaker 1817–65, against whom an unsuccessful case was brought in 1828 by a churchwarden of Church Honeybourne, for neglect and irregularities in the parish.]

19.32 (34)	**Wesleyan Methodist, Cow Honeybourne**
Name	Wesleyan Chapel
Erected	About 1815 [Rebuilt 1864]
Building	Yes [separate and entire] Yes [exclusively as a place of worship]
Sittings	Free 60. Other 50. Total [110] Standing room none
Attend'ce 30 Mar.	Afternoon 50 + 46 SS. Total [96]
	Evening [60] + 4 SS. Total 64
Avge attendance	Morning 40 + 40 SS. Total [80]
	Afternoon 50 + 40 SS. Total [90]

	Evening 60 + 6 SS. Total [66]
Dated	30 March 1851
Signed	Edward Leadbetter, Wesleyan local preacher [tailor]
	William Hemming. Broadway, Worcestershire

[The Church of England at Cow Honeybourne was in ruins 'and now a Wesleyan Chapel stands on the other side of the road, which is filled to repletion': Noake, 228.]

389.2.11 Parish of Aston-sub-Edge

Area 755 acres; 33 inhabited houses, 1 uninhabited. Population 132.

19.33 (35)	**Church of England, St Andrew, Aston-sub-Edge**
Name	Aston-sub-Edge church
Consecration	Before 1800
Erected	[Rebuilt in 1796–7 following a fire]
Endowment	Glebe £200. {Total £204}
Sittings	Free 71. Other 32. Total 103
Attend'ce 30 Mar.	Morning 26 + 16 SS. Total 42
	Evening 37 + 17 SS. Total 54
Avge attendance	Morning 36 + 20 SS. Total 56
	Afternoon 60 + 22 SS. Total 82
	Evening 50 + 12 SS. Total 62
Dated	31 March 1851
Signed	Henry Cooper, curate [1839–57]
	Willersey rectory, nr Broadway
[*Incumbent*	John Besly 1831–68]

[Besly was also the incumbent of St Bartholomew, Longbenton, Northumberland 1830–68 where he lived. Cooper was also the incumbent of Willersey (**19.37**). At an afternoon service in the 1840s the parishioners seemed 'united and happy amongst themselves, and most respectful towards their minister. I was delighted in observing the cordiality with which they touched their hat, or curtsied, or extended the friendly hand and exchanged the word of greeting as he passed; and there were the churchwardens at their posts, ready to open the seats or to assist the clergyman; a quiet, breathing devotion seemed to settle down upon the services, and the very atmosphere itself felt warmer than at the icy region of Church Honeybourne. How immense is the power of a church clergyman for good or for evil! There are about twenty-five children in the Sunday school ...': Noake, 230–1.]

389.2.12 Parish of Weston-sub-Edge

Area 2,632 acres; 75 inhabited houses, 7 uninhabited. Population 358.

19.34 (36)	**Church of England, St Lawrence, Weston-sub-Edge**
Name	An ancient parish church, dedicated to St John the Baptist
Consecration	Before 1800
Erected	[Restored 1853–61]
Endowment	Tithe £775. Glebe £75. Fees £1 10s. {Total £811}
Sittings	Free 125. Other (including children) 175. Total 300
Attend'ce 30 Mar.	Morning 38 + 43 SS. Total 81
	Afternoon 65 + 51 SS. Total 116
Avge attendance	[Not given]
Dated	31 March 1851
Signed	George Drinkwater Bourne, rector [1846–1905]
	C[hipping] Campden, Gloucestershire

[In the early 20th century the dedication was changed to St Lawrence.]

19.35 (37)	**Wesleyan Methodist, Weston-sub-Edge**

Name	Wesleyan Chapel
Erected	1836 [Now Vale Cottage]
Building	Separate [and entire] Yes [exclusively as a place of worship]
Sittings	Free 120. Total 120. Standing room for about 50 or upwards
Attend'ce 30 Mar.	Afternoon 15. Total 15
	Evening 35. Total 35
Avge attend'ce (3m)	Morning 35. Total 35
Dated	30 March 1851
Signed	The **+** mark of John Steel, steward
	Weston-sub-Edge, Gloucestershire

389.2.13   Parish of Saintbury
Area 1,336 acres; 31 inhabited houses, 2 uninhabited. Population 138.

19.36 (38)   Church of England, St Nicholas, Saintbury
(Summary sheet)

Name	St Nicholas
Consecration	Before 1800
[*Erected*	Restored 1842 and 1902]
[*Endowment*	Total £415]
Sittings	Free 80. Other 60. Total 140
Usual attend'ce	Total 135
	Morning 50 + 15 SS. Total [65]
	Afternoon 60 + 10 SS. Total [70]
Signed	William Barrett, rector [1851–73]

[Barrett had previously been the incumbent of Preston-on-Stour (**19.2**). The church is now under the care of the Churches Conservation Trust.]

389.2.14   Parish of Willersey
Area 1,344 acres; 81 inhabited houses, 3 uninhabited. Population 372.

19.37 (39)   Church of England, St Peter, Willersey

Name	Willersey Church
Consecration	Before 1800
Erected	[Restored 1866–72]
Endowment	Tithe 15s. OPE £170. Fees £2 2s. Easter offerings 15s. {Total £162}
Sittings	Free 154. Other 187. Total 341
Attend'ce 30 Mar.	Afternoon 138 + 22 SS. Total 160
Avge attendance	Morning 65 + 22 SS. Total 87
	Afternoon 150 + 22 SS. Total 172
	Evening 145 + 12 SS. Total 157
Remarks	Altho' not obliged by law to make this return and although considering it in the matter of income as requested ... that a lay person would all furnish it, yet hoping it may have been sent for a good purpose, I have filled it up. H. C.
Dated	31 March 1851
Signed	Henry Cooper, rector [1840–57]
	Willersey rectory, near Broadway

[Cooper was also the curate of Aston sub-Edge (**19.33**). John Noake observed: 'The Rev H. Cooper, the rector, performed the whole services, and preached a good sermon in defence of the church ordinances, discipline and rubric, and in proof of the spirituality of our branch of the church. The choir at this place consisted of a bass-viol, flute and several voices. The old man with the flute took upon himself the leadership; and now and then, where he deemed it necessary to interpret certain passages with unusual emphasis, he would sing in one of the richest nasal twangs I ever heard, at the same time using his flute as a baton, and flourishing it about to the imminent danger of the eyes and noses of his compeers. The number of scholars in the Sunday school here is about 22 boys and 33 girls': Noake, 231.]

389.2.16 Parish of Childswickham [transferred to Worcestershire, 1931]
Area 2,040 acres; 94 inhabited houses, 2 uninhabited. Population 466.
The parish includes the hamlet of Murcott.

19.38 (44)	**Church of England, St Mary the Virgin, Childswickham**
Name	Wickham church. An ancient parish church
Consecration	Before 1800
Erected	[Restored 1874]
Endowment	Glebe £146. OPE £6 5s. Fees £1 10s. Easter offerings 15s. Other sources £1 8s. {Total £105}
Sittings	Free 240. Total 240
Attend'ce 30 Mar.	Morning 28 + 40 SS. Total 68
	Afternoon 60 + 40 SS. Total 100
Avge attendance	Morning 25 + 50 SS. Total 75
	Afternoon 70 + 50 SS. Total 120
Dated	31 March 1851
Signed	Thomas Marsden, minister [1843–55]
	Childswickham, Broadway, Gloucester

19.39 (45)	**Independent, Childswickham**
Name	Ebenezer Chapel
Erected	AD 1842
Building	Yes [separate and entire] Yes [exclusively as a place of worship]
Sittings	Free 100. Other none. Total [100]
Attend'ce 30 Mar.	Morning 28 SS. Total [28]
	Afternoon 29 SS. Total [29]
	Evening 70. Total [70]
Avge attendance	Morning 60 to one service. 35 [SS] on the books. Total 95
Remarks	This chapel is in connection with the Congregational chapel, Broadway, and is supplied by a member and the minister of that place. The service is held on the afternoon of one Sabbath and the evening of the next.
Dated	31 March 1851
Signed	Joseph Hooper, minister [1850–4]
	Broadway, Worcestershire

[Hooper was also the minister of Broadway (389.2.15).]

19.40 (46)	**Wesleyan Methodist Preaching Place, Childswickham**
Name	Wesleyan Preaching Place
Erected	[Not given]
Building	Part of a dwelling house. No [not used exclusively for worship]
Sittings	Free 65. Total [65]
Attend'ce 30 Mar.	Afternoon 45. Total [45]
Avge attendance	Morning [50] Total 50
	Afternoon 50. Total [50]
Dated	31 March 1851
Signed	Thomas Saunders, occupier [of the place of worship]

20. HO 129/327–8 'SOUTH BRISTOL': 49 places of worship

HO 129/327   KEYNSHAM DISTRICT (SOMERSET)

327.1   BITTON SUB-DISTRICT

327.1.3–4 Parish of Bitton
Area 4,567 acres; 760 inhabited houses, 51 uninhabited. Population 3.575.
The parish includes the chapelry of Hanham and the hamlet of Oldland (327.2.2).

20.1 (3)	**Church of England, St Mary, Bitton**
Name	St Mary's. An ancient parish church
Consecration	Before 1800
Erected	[Restored throughout the 19th century]
Endowment	Tithe £265. Pew rents nil. Fees £30. Easter offerings nil. {Total £200}
Sittings	Free 268. Other 398. Total 666
	[At Bitton there were separate free seats for men and women: Leech 2004, 264.]
Attend'ce 30 Mar.	Morning 150 + 50 SS. Total [200]
	Afternoon 200 + 50 SS. Total [250]
Avge attendance	[Not given]
Dated	31 March 1851
Signed	Henry Nicholson Ellacombe, vicar [1850–1916]
	Bitton vicarage, Bristol

[The benefice consisted of Bitton with Hanham (**20.2**) and Oldland (**20.28**). Inside the church Joseph Leech spotted a notice: 'If any Camdenian, Antiquarian, or member of an Architectural Society should visit this church, the vicar begs he will do him the favour to call at the vicarage': Leech 2004, 267. This referred to Henry Thomas Ellacombe, curate 1817–35 and incumbent 1835–50, who rebuilt St Anne, Siston (**20.22**), and erected Christ Church, Hanham (**20.3**) and Holy Trinity, Kingswood (**20.27**). His son Henry Nicholson had been his curate 1848–50 and was, like his father, a renowned gardener; he remained at Bitton the rest of his life: *ODNB* 'Henry Thomas Ellacombe (1790–1885)'; 'Henry Nicholson Ellacombe (1822–1916)'.]

20.2 (9)	**Church of England, St George, Hanham Abbots**
Name	Hanham Abbots church, formerly an ancient chapel of ease to Bitton, but constituted the parish church of the eccles[iastica]l district of Hanham, under 1 & 2 Vict. c.106 [1838] in 1844.
Consecration	Before 1800
Erected	[Mostly rebuilt 1854; restored 1909]
Endowment	Land and house £20. Tithe £45. OPE £40. {Total £45}
Sittings	Free 120. Other 120. Total 240
Attend'ce 30 Mar.	Afternoon 54. Total 54
Avge attendance	[Not given]
Dated	31 March 1851
Signed	William Fry, perpetual curate [1845–94]
	Hanham parsonage, nr Bristol

20.3 (10)	**Church of England, Christ Church, Jefferies Hill, Hanham**
Name	Christ Church, chapel of ease to ecclesiastical parish church of Hanham.
Consecration	18 October 1842, as an additional church

Erected	[By] private subscription for £2,143 10s 5d. Total cost £2,143 10s 5d.
Endowment	Unendowed, being chapel of ease to [St George], Hanham (**20.2**)
Sittings	Free 540. Other 100. Total 640
Attend'ce 30 Mar.	Morning 94 + 144 SS. Total 238
	Evening 239. Total 239
Avge attendance	[Not given]
Dated	31 March 1851
Signed	William Fry, perpetual curate [1845–94]
	Hanham parsonage, nr Bristol

[On 4 March 1844 Christ Church Hanham became a parish and the ancient chapel of Hanham Abbots (**20.2**) a chapel of ease to Christ Church. Subscribers to the erection of the church included Edward Bouverie Pusey, John Keble (**13.2**), George Anthony Denison and Samuel Warneford (**19.20**). For a poem on the erection of Christ Church, see Ellacombe, 223.]

20.4 (5)	**Independent, Bitton**
Name	Oldland Common Tabernacle
Erected	1811
Building	Yes [separate and entire] Yes [exclusively as a place of worship]
Sittings	Free 256. Other 94. Total [350]
Attend'ce 30 Mar.	Morning 100 + 85 SS. Total 185
	Afternoon no service or Sunday school
Avge attendance	Morning 120 + 130 SS. Total 250
	Evening 300.* Total 300
Remarks	* The Sabbath school children do not attend the evening service as a body. Many of them come with their parents but the number cannot be ascertained. This chapel is supplied with preachers by the Bristol Itinerant Society connected with the Independent churches of Bristol.
Dated	30 March 1851
Signed	George Short, senior deacon
	Oldland Common, near Bristol

[The Bristol Itinerant Society provided pastoral support for about 14 Independent chapels, including Knowle (**20.40**), Mangotsfield (**20.29**), Marshfield (**3.24**), Oldland, Rodford (**3.4**) and Wick (**3.19**).]

20.5 (4)	**Independent, Upton Cheyney, Bitton**
Name	Upton Chapel
Erected	1834
Building	Separate from a school. Exclusively as a place of worship
Sittings	Free 104. Other 52. Total [156] Standing room none
Attend'ce 30 Mar.	Morning 73 + 20 SS. Total 93
	Evening 106. SS none. Total 106
Avge attendance	Morning 70 + 24 SS. Total 94
	Evening 115. Total 115
Dated	30 March 1851
Signed	Thomas Page, minister [1850–7]
	Longwells Green near Hanham, Gloucestershire

[Page was also the minister of Oldland (**20.12**).]

20.6 (7)	**Wesleyan Methodist, Bitton**
Name	Wesleyan Methodist Chapel
Erected	[Not given]
Building	Yes [separate and entire] Yes [exclusively as a place of worship]
Sittings	Free 48. Other 50. Total [98]

Attend'ce 30 Mar. No service
Avge attendance Afternoon 12. Total 12
                  Evening 12. Total 12
Remarks   It is in consequence of a secession that there is no service at present.
Dated   31 March 1851
Signed   Charles Clay, minister [1850–1]
                  Kingswood, near Bristol
[Clay was also the minister of Hanham Street (**20.7**), Cock Road (**20.14**), Kingswood (**20.16**), Longwell Green (**20.17**), Soundwell (**20.33**) and St George (**2.26**).]

20.7 (11)   Wesleyan Methodist, Hanham Street, Bitton
Name   Wesleyan Methodist Chapel
Erected   1827
Building   Yes [separate and entire] Yes [exclusively as a place of worship]
Sittings   Free 300. Other 100. Total [400]
Attend'ce 30 Mar. Morning 152 SS. Total 152
                  Afternoon 20. Total 20
Avge attendance Morning 200 SS. Total 200
                  Afternoon 150. Total 150
                  Evening 150. Total 150
Remarks   The present number of hearers is below the average in consequence of a secession.
Dated   31 March 1851
Signed   Charles Clay, minister [1850–1]
                  Kingswood near Bristol
[See note to preceding entry.]

20.8 (12)   Wesleyan Methodist, Hanham Green
Name   None
Erected   [Not given]
Building   No. A dwelling house. No [not exclusively as a place of worship]
Sittings   Free 60. Total [60]
Attend'ce 30 Mar. [Not given]
Avge attendance [Not given]
Dated   31 March 1851
Signed   Ann Bartlett [wife of an agricultural labourer]
                  Hanham Green

20.9 (8)   Primitive Methodist, North Common, Bitton
Name   None
Erected   [Not given]
Building   No [not separate and entire] No [not exclusively as a place of worship]
Sittings   Free 40. Total [40]
Attend'ce 30 Mar. Evening 40. Total [40]
Avge attendance [Not given]
Dated   31 March 1851
Signed   Edward Hosey, minister
                  Upper Eastern, Bristol, Gloucestershire
[Hosey was also the minister of the chapel at Oldland Common (**20.18**).]

20.10 (6)   Methodist Reformers, Bitton
Name   Methodist

Erected	Don't know
Building	No [not separate and entire] No [not exclusively as a place of worship] A dwelling house
Sittings	Free 60. Other None. Total [60] Standing room none
Attend'ce 30 Mar.	SS none Evening 35. Total [35]
Avge attend'ce (4m)	General congregation 45. Total [45]
Dated	31 March 1851
Signed	James Swain, steward Bitton, nr Bristol

327.2   Oldland sub-district

327.2.2 Hamlet of Oldland

Area 2,589 acres; 1,181 inhabited houses, 69 uninhabited. Population 5,877.
The hamlet of Oldland is part of the parish of Bitton (327.1.3–4) and includes the village of Kingswood.

20.11 (28)   **Independent, Park Road, Oldland**

Name	Kingswood Tabernacle and sometimes Whitefield's Tabernacle.
Erected	In the year 1742 by Rev George Whitefield [Enlarged 1802 and 1830; adjacent chapel opened 1852]
Building	Separate [and entire] Yes [exclusively as a place of worship]
Sittings	Total 1,200
Attend'ce 30 Mar.	Morning 640 + 225 SS. Total 865 Afternoon 796 + 118 SS. Total 914 Evening 660. Total 660
Avge attendance	Morning 650 + 280 SS. Total 930 Afternoon 860 + 130 SS. Total 990 Evening 680. Total 680
Remarks	This place of worship will be left in June and used for schools and classrooms. A larger chapel is nearly finished on the same property capable of seating 1,470 persons.
Dated	31 March 1851
Signed	John Glanville, minister [1833–55] Kingswood Hill, Bristol

[Glanville also superintended the chapel at Warmley (**20.23**). Former tablet: 'This building was erected by George Whitefield BA and John Cennick AD 1741. It is Whitefield's first tabernacle, the oldest existing memorial to his great share in the 18th century revival'.]

20.12 (33)   **Independent, Oldland**

Name	Tabernacle
Erected	1822. Purchased by the Independent denomination in 1840
Building	Yes [separate and entire] Yes [exclusively as a place of worship]
Sittings	Free 190. Other 46. Total [236] Standing room none
Attend'ce 30 Mar.	Morning 49 + 50 SS. Total 99 Afternoon 69 SS. Total 69 Evening 142. Total 142
Avge attendance	Morning 49 + 50 SS. Total 99 Afternoon 80 SS. Total 80 Evening 142. Total 142
Dated	31 March 1851

Signed   Thomas Page, minister [1850–7]
                  Longwells Green, nr Hanham, Gloucestershire
[Page was also the minister of Upton Cheney (**20.5**).]

20.13 (35)   Baptist, Oldland
Name   Hanham Meeting
Erected   January 1650 [New chapel 1714; enlarged 1802]
Building   Yes [separate and entire] Yes [exclusively as a place of worship]
Sittings   Free 490. Other 10. Total [500]
Attend'ce 30 Mar. Morning 50 + 20 SS. Total 70
                  Afternoon 350 + 16 SS. Total 366
                  Evening 40 + 8 SS. Total 48
Avge attendance Morning 18 SS. Total 18
                  Afternoon 200 + 20 SS. Total 220
                  Evening 30 + 10 SS. Total 40
Dated   31 March 1851
Signed   John Ody, deacon [furrier]
                  Herring Lane, Hanham, near Bristol

20.14 (36)   Wesleyan Methodist, Cock Road, Bitton
Name   Cock Road day and Sunday school
Erected   [Not given]
Building   Yes [separate and entire] No, used also as a day school
Sittings   Free 170. Total [170]
Attend'ce 30 Mar. Morning 93 SS. Total 93
                  Evening 23. Total 23
Avge attendance Morning 110 SS. Total 110
                  Evening 60. Total 60
Dated   31 March 1851
Signed   Charles Clay, minister [1850–1]
                  Kingswood, near Bristol
[Clay was also the minister of Bitton (**20.6**), Hanham Street (**20.7**), Kingswood (**20.16**), Longwell Green (**20.17**), Soundwell (**20.33**) and St George (**2.26**).]

20.15 (37)   Wesleyan Methodist, The Batch, Oldland
Name   Wesleyan Chapel
Erected   1833
Building   Separate and entire. Yes [exclusively as a place of worship]
Sittings   Free 250. Other 350. Total [600]
Attend'ce 30 Mar. [Not given]
Avge attendance Morning 200 + 240 SS. Total 440
                  Evening 450 + 100 SS. Total 550
Dated   31 March 1851
Signed   James Meadmore, minister [1850–1]
                  Downend, nr Bristol
[Meadmore was also the minister of Downend (**20.31**), Iron Acton (**3.53**), Mangotsfield (**20.32**), Rangeworthy (**4.31**) and Wick (**3.20**).]

20.16 (32)   Wesleyan Methodist, Kingswood
Name   Wesleyan Methodist Chapel
Erected   1844
Building   Separate and entire building. Used exclusively as a place of worship

Sittings	Free 600. Other 600. Total [1,200]
Attend'ce 30 Mar.	Morning 231 + 32 SS. Total 263
	Evening 180. Total 180
Avge attendance	Morning 670 + 200 SS. Total 970 [*recte* 870]
	Afternoon 30. Total 30
	Evening 670. Total 670
Remarks	The number of hearers is below the average in consequence of a secession.
Dated	31 March 1851
Signed	Charles Clay, minister [1850–1]
	Kingswood, near Bristol

[Clay was also the minister of Bitton (**20.6**), Hanham Street (**20.7**), Cock Road (**20.14**), Longwell Green (**20.17**), Soundwell (**20.33**) and St George (**2.26**). Early in his field preaching, John Wesley recorded: 'The places in Kingswood where I now usually preached were these: once a fortnight, a little above Cotham, a village on the south side of the wood; on Sunday morning, near Hanham Mount; once a fortnight, at the schoolhouse, in the middle of Kingswood; on Sunday, in the evening at Rose Green; and once a fortnight, near the Fishponds, on the north side of the wood': *Journal*, 29 June 1739.]

20.17 (38)   Wesleyan Methodist, Longwell Green, Bitton

Name	Wesleyan Methodist Chapel
Erected	About 1845
Building	Sunday school room attached. Yes [exclusively as a place of worship]
Sittings	Free 100 + 50 SS. Total [150]
Attend'ce 30 Mar.	No service
Avge attendance	Afternoon 50. Total 50
	Evening 50. Total 50
Remarks	No hearers at present in consequence of a secession.
Dated	31 March 1851
Signed	Charles Clay, minister [1850–1]
	Kingswood, near Bristol

[On Clay, see preceding note.]

20.18 (29)   Primitive Methodist, Oldland Common

Name	None
Erected	[Not given]
Building	No [not separate and entire] No [not exclusively as a place of worship]
Sittings	Free 70. Total [70]
Attend'ce 30 Mar.	Afternoon 70. Total [70]
Avge attendance	[Not given]
Dated	31 March 1851
Signed	Edward Hosey, minister
	Upper Easton, Bristol, Gloucestershire

[Hosey was also the minister of North Common (**20.9**).]

20.19 (30)   Wesleyan Reformers, Oldland Common

Name	Oldland British School
Erected	1844
Building	Yes [separate and entire] No [not exclusively as a place of worship]
Sittings	Free 500. Other none. Total [500]
Attend'ce 30 Mar.	Afternoon 400. Total 400
	Evening 250. Total 250
Avge attendance	[Not given]
Remarks	Opened for religious worship on Sunday, 30 March 1851

Dated	31 March 1851
Signed	Samuel Long, steward
	Oldland Common, near Bristol

20.20 (31)   Wesleyan Reformers, Kingswood Hill

Name	Ebenezer
Erected	A house opened for religious worship 1851
Building	Yes [separate and entire] Yes [exclusively as a place of worship]
Sittings	Free 230. Other none. Total [230] Standing room none
Attend'ce 30 Mar.	Morning 104 + 54 SS. Total 158
	Afternoon 81 SS. Total 81
	Evening 92. Total 92
Avge attendance	[Not given]
Dated	31 March 1851
Signed	Joseph Golding, steward
	Kingswood Hill, nr Bristol

20.21 (34)   Church of the United Brethren, Regent Street, Kingswood Hill

Name	Moravian Chapel
Erected	1757 [Replaced by new chapel on adjacent site, opened 22 June 1857]
Building	Yes [separate and entire] Yes [exclusively as a place of worship]
Sittings	Free 180. Total [180] Standing room none
Attend'ce 30 Mar.	Morning 43 + 37 SS. Total 80*
	Afternoon 68 + 38 SS. Total 106*
	Evening no service in the winter
Avge attendance	[Not given]
Remarks	*These numbers expressed the average attendance.
Dated	30 March 1851
Signed	Peter Cornelius West, minister
	Kingswood Hill, Bristol

327.1   BITTON SUB-DISTRICT

327.1.5 Parish of Siston

Area 1,827 acres; 201 inhabited houses, 16 uninhabited. Population 926.
The population had declined by 88 in the decade before 1851, due to the depressed state of the spelter [zinc] works.

20.22 (13)   Church of England, St Anne, Siston

Name	[Not given]
Consecration	An old church [A] parish church
Erected	[South transept dated 1796; restored 1887]
Endowment	With tithes and glebe land. {Total £323}
Sittings	Free 280. Other 40. Total 320
Attend'ce 30 Mar.	[Not given]
Avge attendance	[Not given]
Remarks	A return of numbers attending divine service on Sunday, 30 March, I give no certain [...] from of a table listed return of the character desired to be made. The usual congregation is dependant upon [the] weather, being distant from the church.
Dated	4 April 1851
Signed	Thomas Boys Croome, incumbent [1847–77]

Siston rect[ory], Bristol
[Within the parish, St Barnabas, Warmley was consecrated on 23 Apr. 1851.]

20.23 (15)   Independent, Warmley

Name	Warmley Chapel
Erected	1846
Building	Separate [and entire] Used only for a Sunday school and chapel
Sittings	Free 170. Other 30. Total [200]
Attend'ce 30 Mar.	Morning no service. 70 SS. Total [70]
	Afternoon no service. 78 SS. Total [78]
	Evening 100. Total [100]
Avge attendance	Evening 160. Total [160] (Owing to local circumstances, attendance on 30 March remarkably similar)
Remarks	This place of worship is attached to Kingswood Tabernacle (**20.11**) of which the Rev John Glanville is minister and it is under his care. The village of Warmley has no other place of worship (except one room and that only on afternoons) in it at present. The chapel is presently used as a Sunday school. (Service is only held in the chapel in the evening. Sunday school in the morning and afternoon.)
Dated	31 March 1851
Signed	Alfred Davidson, trustee
	Warmley, near Bristol
[*Minister*	John Glanville 1833–55]
	[Kingswood Hill, Bristol]

[Glanville was the minister of Kingswood Tabernacle (**20.11**).]

20.24 (14)   Wesleyan Reformers, Warmley

Name	Ebenezer Chapel
Erected	About 1801. Since closed but now opened
Building	A separate building. Used as a place of worship and Sunday school.
Sittings	Free 210. Other 100. Total [310] Standing room for about 40 persons
Attend'ce 30 Mar.	Morning 300. Total [300]
	Evening 400. Total [400]
Avge attendance	Morning 300 + 200 SS. Total 500
Remarks	This place was opened for public worship in consequence, as we conceive, of the unrighteous proceedings of the Wesleyan Conference in 1849–50.
Dated	7 April 1851
Signed	Isaac Hicks, sec[retar]y and steward [grocer's shopman]
	Oldland Com[mo]n, Bitton, near Bristol

327.2   OLDLAND SUB-DISTRICT

327.2.1 Parish of Mangotsfield

Area 2,591 acres; 871 inhabited houses, 45 uninhabited. Population 3,967.

20.25 (17)   Church of England, St James, Mangotsfield

Name	Church of St James'. The parish church of Mangotsfield
Consecration	Before 1800
Erected	[Restored 1849–51]
Endowment	Land let at £50. OPE £13 (from patron). £35 13s 10d (Queen Anne's Bounty). Fees £18 (average). Easter offerings abt £20. Gross income £136 13s 10d.* {Total £136}

Sittings	Free 50. Other 300. Total 350
Attend'ce 30 Mar.	Morning 80 + 45 SS. Total 125**
	Afternoon 300 + 45 SS. Total 345**
Avge attendance	[Not given]
Remarks	* These are the gross amounts of income, without deducting charges, losses of rent, a curate's stipend.
	** An average attendance.
Dated	31 March 1851
Signed	Robert Brodie MA, perpetual curate [1822–59]
	Mangotsfield, near Bristol

[The benefice consisted of Mangotsfield with Downend (**20.26**). The curate of Mangotsfield 1842–54 (later incumbent of Christ Church, Downend 1874–8) was the wealthy Alfred Peache. Besides major benefactions to the London College of Divinity (opened 1863) and Huron College, London, Ontario, in 1877 he established the Peache Trust to appoint Evangelical clergy to livings in his gift: *ODNB* 'Alfred Peache (1818–1900)'.]

20.26 (16)   Church of England, Christ Church, Downend

Name	Christ Church, Downend, being a chapel of ease to the parish church of Mangotsfield
Consecration	[28] October 1831. Consecrated as a chapel of ease additional to the ~~ancient~~ parish church of Mangotsfield.
Erected	By public subscription aided by the Incorporated Society for Building etc. Churches and Chapels (£1,000) and by Diocesan Society for the same (£200). Private subscriptions about £1,800. Total cost £3,000 [Chancel rebuilt 1913]
Endowment	OPE (interest of £100) £3 12s 4d. Pew rents £45 (uncertain).* [See Mangotsfield (**20.25**)]
Sittings	Free 777. Other 247. Total 1,024
Attend'ce 30 Mar.	Morning 200 + 150 SS. Total 350
	Evening 600. Total 600
Avge attendance	Same as [above]
Remarks	*Income very uncertain and liable to curates' stipend and clerk's ditto. There is no separate cure of souls at Downend. The chapel is as described, as a chapel of ease dependant on the mother church of Mangotsfield. It is desirable that Downend should be made a parish, and this chapel, if an endowment could be obtained, to be made its parish church.
Dated	31 March 1851
Signed	Robert Brodie MA, perpetual curate [1831–59]
	Mangotsfield, near Bristol

[A hymn was specially composed for the occasion of the laying of the foundation stone 15 Apr. 1830. The benefice consisted of Mangotsfield (**20.25**) with Downend. On 12 May 1874 Downend became a perpetual curacy.]

20.27 (18)   Church of England, Holy Trinity, Kingswood

Name	Holy Trinity. A district parish church
Consecration	[11 Sept.] 1821. It was consecrated as an additional church to the parish church of Bitton (**20.1**).
Erected	By voluntary contributions assisted by a parliamentary grant. Total cost £4,112 10s 2d.* [Restored 1898–1900]
Endowment	{Total £150}
Sittings	Free 870. Other 130. Total 1,000
Attend'ce 30 Mar.	[Not given]

Avge attendance [Not given]
Remarks   * The above stated sum of £4,112 10s 2d, the entire amount for which
                   the church was built, consisted of the parliamentary grant and voluntary
                   subscriptions, but in what proportion, I have no means of ascertaining.
Dated   21 April 1851
Signed   Charles Maunder, incumbent [1845–54]
                   Kingswood parsonage, nr Bristol

[The church was erected to bring improvement the lot of the local people: 'The wickedness and gross immorality of the inhabitants of Kingswood Forest, have been for years proverbially notorious. It has been a matter of much surprise, that within so short a distance of the two populous towns of Bath and Bristol, a people should exist very little removed from a state of barbarism' (*The Christian Remembrancer*, Jan. 1822, 4, No 37, 8). Joseph Ditcher, the first minister of Holy Trinity 1821–35, became prominent in the mid-1850s when as incumbent of South Brent, Somerset, he brought a case against the Anglo-Catholic archdeacon of Taunton (George Anthony Denison) over his belief in the real presence in the Eucharist.]

20.28 (19) Church of England, St Anne, Oldland
(Summary form)
Name   Oldland Chapel
Consecration   Re-erected about 25 years [Opened 14 November 1830]
[Endowment   See Bitton (**20.1**)]
Sittings   Free about 350. Other about 50. Total 400
Usual attend'ce General congregation average about 60 or 70. SS about 80. Total [140–150]
Remarks   The incumbent refused to make a return.
Signed   William Mills Grace, registrar
[Incumbent   Henry Nicholson Ellacombe, vicar 1850–1916]

[The benefice consisted of Bitton (**20.1**) with Hanham (**20.2**) and Oldland. The district of Oldland was created on 26 June 1861.]

20.29 (27) Independent, Cossham Street, Mangotsfield
Name   'Non'
Erected   1827 [Enlarged 1857]
Building   A separate and entire building. Used exclusively as a place of worship.
Sittings   Free 120. Other 25. Total [145] Standing room 'non'
Attend'ce 30 Mar. Morning 35 + 80 SS. Total 115
                   Afternoon 100 SS. Total 100
                   Evening 60. Total 60
Avge attendance Morning 40 + 80 SS. Total 120
                   Afternoon 100 SS. Total 100
                   Evening 60. Total 60
Remarks   This chapel is supplied by agents from the Bristol Itinerant Society free
                   of expense.
Dated   30 March 1851
Signed   William Moon, minister for the day
                   Sussex Street, St Phillips, Bristol

[The Bristol Itinerant Society provided pastoral support for about 14 Independent chapels, including Knowle (**20.40**), Mangotsfield, Marshfield (**3.24**), Oldland (**20.4**), Rodford (**3.4**) and Wick (**3.19**).]

20.30 (24) Baptist, Salisbury Road, Downend
Name   Baptist Chapel
Erected   About the year 1790 [1786]
Building   Yes [separate and entire] Yes [exclusively as a place of worship]

Sittings   Free 250. Total [250]
Attend'ce 30 Mar. Morning 140. Total [140]
                    Afternoon 90 SS. Total [90]
                    Evening 200. Total [200]
Avge attendance   [Not given]
Remarks   Dimensions of the chapel: 48 feet by 36 feet. Sittings nearly two thirds
                    of the chapel.
Dated   31 March 1851
Signed   Joseph Mitchell, pastor
                    Downend, near Bristol

[The chapel was founded by Caleb Evans, founder of the Bristol Education Society, and pastor of the Broadmead Baptist Chapel, Bristol (**1.32**). In May 1841, 15 members left the chapel and began holding services at the lunatic asylum at Fishponds (**2.81**).]

20.31 (23)   Wesleyan Methodist, Downend
Name   Bethel
Erected   1805
Building   Separate and entire] Yes [exclusively as a place of worship]
Sittings   Free 200. Other 150. Total [350]
Attend'ce 30 Mar. Morning 100. Total 100
                    Evening 110. Total 110
Avge attendance   Morning 150. Total 150
                    Evening 200. Total 200
Dated   31 March 1851
Signed   James Meadmore, minister
                    Downend, nr Bristol

[Meadmore was also the minister of Iron Acton (**3.53**), Mangotsfield (**20.32**), Oldland (**20.15**), Rangeworthy (**4.31**) and Wick (**3.20**).]

20.32 (20)   Wesleyan Methodist, Staple Hill, Mangotsfield
Name   Wesleyan Chapel
Erected   1846
Building   Separate and entire. Yes [exclusively as a place of worship]
Sittings   Free 160. Other 70. Total [230]
Attend'ce 30 Mar. [Not given]
Avge attendance   Afternoon 100 + 100 SS. Total 200
                    Evening 150 + 100 SS. Total 250
Dated   31 March 1851
Signed   James Meadmore, minister
                    Downend, nr Bristol

[On Meadmore, see preceding note. John Wesley described Mangotsfield as 'a place famous for all manner of wickedness, and the only one in the neighbourhood of Kingswood which we had totally neglected. But on a sudden light is sprung up even in this thick darkness': *Journal*, 20 Sept. 1781.]

20.33 (21)   Wesleyan Methodist, Soundwell, Mangotsfield
Name   Wesleyan Methodist Chapel
Erected   [1843]
Building   Yes [separate and entire] Yes [exclusively as a place of worship]
Sittings   Free 34. Other 36. Total [70]
Attend'ce 30 Mar. No service
Avge attendance   Afternoon 60. Total 60
                    Evening 40. Total 40

Remarks	No service conducted at present in consequence of a secession.
Dated	31 March 1851
Signed	Charles Clay, minister [1850–1]
	Kingswood, near Bristol

[Clay was also the minister of Bitton (**20.6**), Hanham Street (**20.7**), Cock Road (**20.14**), Kingswood (**20.16**), Longwell Green (**20.17**) and St George (**2.26**).]

20.34 (26)   Primitive Methodist, Mangotsfield

Name	Primitive Chapel
Erected	1836
Building	An entire building. As a place of worship
Sittings	Free 70 available for worship. Other 20 sittings let. Total [90]
	Standing room only an entrance
Attend'ce 30 Mar.	Morning [100] Total 100
Avge attendance	Afternoon [80] Total 80
Remarks	No 80
Dated	30 March 1851
Signed	Charles Watkins, local preacher
	Mangotsfield, near Bristol

20.35 (22)   Methodist Reformers, Mangotsfield

Name	[None]
Erected	[Not given]
Building	Private building. No [not exclusively as a place of worship]
Sittings	Free 100. Total [100] Standing room for 90
Attend'ce 30 Mar.	Morning no service
	Afternoon 45. Total [45]
	Evening no service
Avge attend'ce (6m)	Morning no service
	Afternoon 86. Total [86]
	Evening no service
Dated	30 March 1851
Signed	Hannah Gains, sextoness
	Mangotsfield, nr Bristol

20.36 (25)   Methodist Reformers, Mangotsfield

Name	A private room
Erected	[Not given]
Building	No [not separate and entire] No [not exclusively as a place of worship]
Sittings	[Not given]
Attend'ce 30 Mar.	[Not given]
Avge attendance	[Not given]
Remarks	The preaching was in a small room holding from 12 to 30 [people]
Dated	20 December 1851
Signed	William Mills Grace, registrar
	Downend, nr Bristol

HO 129/328   BEDMINSTER DISTRICT (SOMERSET)

328.1.   BEDMINSTER SUB-DISTRICT

328.1.1 Parish of Bedminster

Area 4,161 acres; 3,396 inhabited houses, 191 uninhabited. Pop. 19,424. The parish includes the tithings of Bishoport and Knowle. The civil parish of Bedminster was transferred to Bristol in 1837 and the ecclesiastical parish to the diocese of Gloucester and Bristol in 1845. Within the parish was Bristol prison, in which there were 184 prisoners.

20.37 (68)   Church of England, St John the Baptist, Bedminster
(Summary form)

Name	St Johns
Erected	Not known [Demolished 1854. Rebuilt; new church consecrated 30 Oct. 1855]
Endowment	{Total £400}
Sittings	Total 500
Usual attend'ce	Morning 100 + 50 SS. Total [150]
	Afternoon 100. Total [100]
	Evening no service
Signed	Charles Ring [registrar?]
[*Incumbent*	Martin Richard Whish 1806–52]

[The benefice consisted of St John, Bedminster with St Mary, Redcliffe (**1.12**), St Thomas (**1.20**) and Abbots Leigh. Within the parish St Paul was consecrated 24 Oct. 1831; St Peter 22 Apr. 1843 (**20.38**); St Luke 22 Jan. 1861 and Holy Nativity, Knowle, 4 June 1883. (Consecration of the new church of St John the Baptist, delayed by protests concerning the reredos, was 30 Oct. 1855: *Bristol Mercury*, 30 June to 3 Nov. 1855. After the wartime destruction of St John's, St Paul's became the parish church of Bedminster. Whish's curate 1839–44 was his son Martin Henry Whish. The ritualist Henry Eland was minister of St Paul's church 1838–52 and the incumbent of St John the Baptist 1852–82; on his death it was said that 'his life during the last 40 years in Bedminster parish has been synonymous with the history of the Oxford Movement in Bristol': Cobb, 11; Leech 2004, 129–33.]

20.38 (67)   Church of England, St Peter, Bishopsworth

Name	St Peter's. Chapel of ease with district attached
Consecration	[22 Apr.] 1843. As a chapel of ease to an outlying district of the parish of Bedminster
Erected	By private contributions and a grant from the Church Building Society. Total £1,200
Endowment	Tithe rent charge or small tithe £40. OPE (Ecc[lesiastica]l Com[mission]ers) £30. Fees about £1. {Total £125}
Sittings	Free 400. Total 400
Attend'ce 30 Mar.	Morning [not given] + 44 SS. Total [44 SS]
	Afternoon [not given] + 46 SS. Total [46 SS]
Avge attendance	Morning [not given] + 45 to 50 SS. Total [45–50 SS]
	Afternoon [not given] + 45 to 50 SS. Total [45–50]
Remarks	I object to answer the first part of [attendance on 30 March] because the information can be of no statistical value unless all the circumstances of each case are fully explained, as well as the difficulties with which the clergymen may have to contend.
Dated	30 March 1851
Signed	Henry Branckner, clerk, MA, perpetual curate [1847–57]
	Clifton, Bristol

[St Peter's was a chapel of ease to St John's, Bedminister until made a parish in 1853.]

20.39 (78)   **Independent, Bishoport**

Name	Bishoport Chapel
Erected	1828
Building	An entire building. Yes [exclusively as a place of worship]
Sittings	Free 90. Other 30. Total [120]
Attend'ce 30 Mar.	Morning 30 + 40 SS. Total 70
	Afternoon 43 SS. Total 43
	Evening 70. Total 70
Avge attendance	[Not given]
Dated	30 March 1851
Signed	William Hicks, deacon [pawnbroker]
	18 Horse Fair, Bristol

20.40 (77)   **Independent, Knowle**

Name	Knowle Chapel
Erected	1832
Building	Yes [separate and entire] Yes [exclusively as a place of worship]
Sittings	Free 150. Other none. Total [150]
Attend'ce 30 Mar.	[Not given]
Avge attendance	Afternoon 25. Total [25]
Remarks	The school is held in the morning only. Divine service in the afternoon only. The Bristol Itinerant Society supplies the pulpit gratuitously.
Dated	31 March 1851
Signed	John Bond, superintendent
	37 Temple Street, Bristol

[The Bristol Itinerant Society provided pastoral support for about 14 Independent chapels. including Knowle, Mangotsfield (**20.29**), Marshfield (**3.24**), Oldland (**20.4**), Rodford (**3.4**) and Wick (**3.19**).]

20.41 (74)   **Independent, Park Street**

Name	Park Street Chapel
Erected	In the year 1842
Building	Yes [separate and entire] Yes [exclusively as a place of worship]
Sittings	Free 130. Total [130]
Attend'ce 30 Mar.	Afternoon 45. Total 45
	Evening 94. Total 94
Avge attendance	Afternoon 50. Total 50
	Evening 110. Total 110
Remarks	This chapel is situated in a very poor neighbourhood and has service out of the labours of the Bristol City Mission Society. There is service regularly held in it every Wednesday
Dated	31 March 1851
Signed	Henry Kingdom, city missionary and minister
	Victoria Place, Bedminster, Bristol

[Kingdom was also involved with the Sargeant Street chapel (**20.42**). In 1851 there were eight Bristol City Mission (**1.48**) places of worship (including **2.8, 41–42**; **20.41–42**).]

20.42 (73)   **Independent, Sargeant Street**

Name	Sargeant Street Chapel
Erected	Opened for divine worship in September 1850
Building	Yes [separate and entire] Yes [exclusively as a place of worship]

Sittings   Free 300. Total [300]
Attend'ce 30 Mar.   Afternoon 150. Total 150
                       Evening 300. Total [300]
*Avge attend'ce (6 m)*Afternoon 150. Total 150
                       Evening 300. Total 300
Remarks   This place of worship is situated in the midst of a poor and very populous
                       neighbourhood and has service out of the labours of the Bristol City
                       Mission Society. Sunday nights it is always crowded with an attentive
                       congregation. There are also three services held in it on other days of
                       the week.
Dated   31 March 1851
Signed   Henry Kingdom, city missionary and minister
                       Victoria Place, Bedminster, Bristol

[Kingdom was also involved with the Park Street Chapel (**20.41**). In 1851 there were eight Bristol
City Mission (**1.48**) places of worship (including **2.8, 41–42**; **20.41–42**).]

20.43 (70)   Baptist, West Street
Name   Bedminster Baptist Chapel
Erected   Before 1800
Building   Yes, separate [and entire] Yes [exclusively as a place of worship]
Sittings   Free 160. Other 40. Total [200] Standing room 50
Attend'ce 30 Mar.   Morning 60 + 30 SS. Total 90
                       Afternoon Sunday School
                       Evening 35 + 15 SS. Total 50
Avge attendance   Morning 40 + 30 SS. Total [70]
                       Evening 70 + 20 SS. Total [90]
Dated   31 March 1851
Signed   Henry Bennett, manager [proprietor of coal mines]
                       Rock Cottages, nr Turnpike, West Street, Bedminster, Bristol

20.44 (76)   Wesleyan Methodist, Bedminster
Name   Wesleyan Chapel
Erected   Since 1800
Building   Yes [separate and entire] Yes [exclusively as a place of worship]
Sittings   Free 250. Other 450. Total [700]
Attend'ce 30 Mar.   Morning 100 + 55 SS. Total 155
                       Evening 130. Total 130
Avge attendance   [Not given]
Remarks   Recent agitations in the body have for the moment diminished the
                       attendance.
Dated   31 March 1851
Signed   Charles Westlake, Wesleyan minister [1850–2]
                       15 Somerset Square, Bristol

[Westlake was also the minister of Langton Street (**20.45**).]

20.45 (71)   Wesleyan Methodist, Langton Street
Name   Langton Street Chapel
Erected   About 20 years ago [Opened 19 June 1828, replacing the chapel in Guinea
                       Street opened by John Wesley 29 Sept. 1779]
Building   Yes [separate and entire] Yes [exclusively as a place of worship]
Sittings   Free 500. Other 1,000. Total [1,500]

Attend'ce 30 Mar. Morning 600 + 110 SS. Total 710
                                Afternoon no service
                                Evening 800. Total 800
Avge attendance [Not given]
Dated 31 March 1851
Signed Charles Westlake, Wesleyan minister [1850–2]
                                15 Somerset Square, Bristol
[Westlake was also the minister of Bedminster (**20.44**). John Wesley recorded, 'I preached at Pill. On Wednesday I opened the new chapel in Guinea Street': *Journal*, 27 Sept. 1779.]

20.46 (79) **Wesleyan Methodist, Bedminster**
Name Wesleyan Chapel
Erected 1836 [Replaced by the adjacent Ebenezer Chapel opened in 1886]
Building Yes [separate and entire] Yes [exclusively as a place of worship]
Sittings Free 300. Other 400. Total [700]
Attend'ce 30 Mar. Morning 100 + 80 SS. Total 180
                                Afternoon 80 SS. Total 80
                                Evening 140. Total 140
Avge attendance [Not given]
Remarks The congregation has recently been greatly reduced by division.
Dated 10 December 1851
Signed William Hessell, minister [1850–2]
                                19 Somerset Square, Bristol

20.47 (75) **Bible Christian, Bedminster**
Name None
Erected Before 1800
Building No [not separate and entire] Yes [exclusively as a place of worship]
Sittings Free 80. Other none. Total [80] Standing room none
Attend'ce 30 Mar. Morning 30. Total 30
                                Evening 50. Total 50
Avge attendance Morning 30. Total 30
                                Evening 50. Total 50
Dated 30 March 1851
Signed Henry Howell, steward [warehouseman at a soap factory]
                                49 Castle Street, Bristol

20.48 (69) **Wesleyan Reformers, Back Lane**
Name British School Rooms
Erected 1847 (Temporary. Occupied for religious worship by the Reform
                                Wesleyans) [Hebron Chapel opened 1854]
Building Yes [separate and entire] Used for British School during the days of
                                the week
Sittings Free 750. Total [750]
Attend'ce 30 Mar. Morning 500. Total 500
                                Afternoon 300 SS. Total 300
                                Evening 600. Total 600
Avge attendance Not given
Remarks These schoolrooms are only temporary occupied for religious worship
                                by the Reform Wesleyans having them let to them for that purpose by
                                the school committee.

Dated	31 March 1851
Signed	Jesse Peters, steward
	East Street, Bedminster, Bristol

20.49 (72)   Wesleyan Reformers, Baynton's Buildings, Ashton Gate

Name	Ashton Gate Preaching Room
Erected	August 1849
Building	Yes, a separate and entire building. Used for a place of worship and Sunday school.
Sittings	Free 22. Other none. Total [22] Standing room none
Attend'ce 30 Mar.	Morning school 72 SS. Total 72
	Afternoon 40 to 50. Total 40–50
	Evening 70 to 80. Total 70–80
Avge attendance	Not given
Remarks	Number of scholars in the back of the school. ~~Total 99~~
Dated	31 March 1851
Signed	Luke Holbeck, Wesleyan Reform
	Baynton's Buildings, Ashton Gate, [Bedminster]

APPENDIX 1:
STATISTICAL SUMMARIES BY REGISTRATION DISTRICT, WITH KEY TO MAIN ENTRIES

1   HO 129/329 Bristol district   Serial in this edition

Church of England churches	22	*25*	**1.1–22**
Independent chapels	9	*11*	**1.23–31**
Baptist			
General chapels	4	*6*	**1.32–5**
Welsh chapel	1		**1.36**
Methodist			
Wesleyan chapels	3	*3*	**1.37–9**
Primitive chapels	2		**1.40–1**
Wesleyan Reformers chapel	1	*6*	**1.42**
Calvinistic chapel	1	*1*	**1.43**
United Brethren (Moravian) chapel	1	*1*	**1.44**
Countess of Huntingdon's chapel	1		**1.45**
Christian Brethren chapels	2	*1*	**1.46–7**
Non-denominational	2		**1.48–9**
Roman Catholic churches	3	*3*	**1.50–2**
Society of Friends (Quakers)	1	*1*	**1.53**
New Jerusalem Church (Swedenborgian)	1		**1 54**
Unitarian chapel	1	*2*	**1.55**
Synagogue	1	*1*	**1.56**
Latter-day Saints (Mormons)		*1*	
Others		*6*	
Total	56	*68*	

Note: 68 is the total given in the 1851 published report. The discrepancy between this and the 56 arising from the reconstruction in this edition can largely be eliminated by including here the 13 returns for Bedminster (see section **20**).

2   HO 129/330 Clifton district

Church of England churches	25	**2.1–5, 16–20, 22, 35–8, 54–6, 64, 67, 69, 71, 75–7**
Independent chapels	10	**2.6–8, 23, 39–42, 78–9**
Baptist		
General chapels	7	**2.24, 43–44, 57, 65, 80–1**
Particular chapel	1	**2.9**
Methodist		
Wesleyan chapels	18	**2.10–13, 25–8, 45–6, 58–60, 68, 70, 72, 82–3**
Primitive chapels	4	**2.29–30, 47, 73**
Wesleyan Association chapel	1	**2.31**
Wesleyan Reformers chapels	12	**2.21, 32–4, 48–9, 61–2, 74, 84–6**
Christian Brethren chapels	2	**2.50–1**

Roman Catholic churches	4	**2.14–5, 52, 63**
Society of Friends (Quakers)	2	**2.66, 88**
Unitarian chapel	1	**2.87**
Latter-day Saints (Mormons)	1	**2.53**
Total	88	

3   HO129/331 Chipping Sodbury district

Church of England churches	25	**3.1, 3, 5, 8, 12, 14–5, 17–8, 21–3, 28–30, 32–6, 43–4, 47–8, 51**
Church of England schoolroom	1	**3.37**
Independent chapels	10	**3.2, 4, 6, 16, 19, 24, 38, 45, 49, 52**
Baptist		
General chapels	4	**3.9, 13, 31, 39**
Particular chapel	1	**3.40**
Methodist		
Wesleyan chapels	5	**3.20, 41, 46, 50, 53**
Primitive chapels	3	**3.7, 25, 42**
Non-denominational	1	**3.26**
Roman Catholic church	1	**3.10**
Society of Friends (Quakers)	1	**3.11**
Unitarian chapel	1	**3.27**
Total	53	

4   HO 129/332 Thornbury district

Church of England churches	19	**4.1, 4, 7, 13–4, 16–7, 19–22, 33, 35, 37–40, 46, 48**
Independent chapels	9	**4.23–26, 41–43, 47, 49**
Baptist		
General chapels	3	**4.27–8, 34**
Methodist		
Wesleyan chapels	13	**4.2–3, 5, 8–10, 18, 29–32, 44–5**
Calvinistic chapel	1	**4.36**
Wesleyan Reformers chapels	3	**4.6, 11, 15**
Society of Friends (Quakers)	1	**4.12**
Total	49	

5   HO 129/333 Dursley district

Church of England churches	13	**5.1, 3, 7, 11–2, 14, 16, 20–1, 24–6, 29**
Independent chapels	8	**5.2, 4–5, 8, 17, 22, 27, 30**
Baptist		
General chapels	3	**5.13, 18, 31**
Particular chapel	1	**5.9**
Methodist		
Wesleyan chapels	7	**5.6, 10, 15, 19, 23, 28, 32**
Total	32	

6   HO 129/334 Westbury-on-Severn district

Church of England churches	16	**6.1–2, 5–6, 8, 16, 21, 24–5, 28–9, 33, 36, 38–40**
Church of England licensed room	1	**6.7**
Independent chapels	7	**6.3, 9, 17–19, 26, 30**
Baptist		
General chapels	3	**6.4, 10, 41**
Particular chapel	1	**6.31**
Methodist		
Wesleyan chapels	7	**6.11–2, 22, 27, 32, 34, 37**
Bible Christian chapels	3	**6.13–15**
Wesleyan Reformers chapels	3	**6.20, 23, 35**
Total	41	

7   HO 129/335 Newent district

Church of England churches	13	**7.4–5, 9, 11, 13–5, 17, 20, 22–3, 27, 29**
Independent chapel	1	**7.6**
Baptist		
General chapels	2	**7.3, 21**
Methodist		
Wesleyan chapels	8	**7.7–8, 10, 12, 16, 18, 28, 30**
Bible Christian chapel	1	**7.19**
Roman Catholic church	1	**7.31**
Total	26	(+ 2 in Herefs., 3 in Worcs.)

8   HO 129/336 Gloucester district

Church of England churches	32	**8.1–8, 10–1, 13, 16–8, 20, 22, 24–5, 28–9, 34, 36, 39–44, 46, 48–50**
Independent chapels	3	**8.19, 35, 51**
Baptist		
General chapel	1	**8.26**
Particular chapel	1	**8.47**
Methodist		
Wesleyan chapels	5	**8.9, 14, 30, 37, 45**
Countess of Huntingdon's chapel	1	**8.21**
Christian Brethren chapels	4	**8.15, 23, 31, 38**
Non-denominational	1	**8.12**
Roman Catholic church	1	**8.32**
Society of Friends (Quakers)	1	**8.33**
Unitarian chapel	1	**8.27**
Total	51	

9   HO 129/337 Wheatenhurst district

Church of England churches	14	**9.1, 3–8, 10, 12, 14, 16–7, 20, 23**
Independent chapels	2	**9.2, 18**
Baptist		

General chapel	1	**9.11**
Particular chapel	1	**9.21**
Methodist		
Wesleyan chapels	4	**9.9, 13, 15, 22**
Non-denominational	1	**9.19**
Total	23	

10   HO 129/338 Stroud district

Church of England churches	28	**10.1, 3–4, 6, 11, 13–15, 21, 23, 25–8, 40–3, 51, 56, 59, 62–4, 70–1, 77–8**
Independent chapels	12	**10.5, 9, 12, 16–7, 29, 44–7, 72–3**
Baptist		
General chapels	10	**10.24, 30, 48, 52–3, 57, 65, 74–5, 79**
Particular chapels	3	**10.22, 31–2**
Methodist		
Wesleyan chapels	10	**10.2, 10, 33–6, 49, 66–7, 80**
Primitive chapels	6	**10.18, 37–8, 50, 54, 68**
Calvinistic chapels	2	**10.60–1**
Countess of Huntingdon's chapels	2	**10.7–8**
Christian Brethren chapels	2	**10.55, 76**
Roman Catholic church	1	**10.58**
Society of Friends (Quakers)	2	**10.19, 81**
New Jerusalem Church (Swedenborgian)	1	**10.39**
Latter-day Saints (Mormons)	2	**10.20, 69**
Total	81	

11   HO 129/339 Tetbury district

Church of England churches	14	**11.1–5, 7, 9–15, 21**
Independent chapel	1	**11.16**
Independent and Baptist chapel	1	**11.8**
Baptist		
General chapel	1	**11.6**
Particular chapel	1	**11.17**
Methodist		
Wesleyan chapel	1	**11.18**
Christian Brethren chapel	1	**11.19**
Latter-day Saints (Mormons)	1	**11.20**
Total	21	(+ 2 in Wilts.)

12   HO 129/340 Cirencester district

Church of England churches	36	**12.1–5, 7–8, 11–2, 14–5, 17–22, 25, 33–4, 36–7, 45, 47–54, 57, 60, 63, 65–6**
Independent chapels	3	**12.38, 61, 67**
Baptist		

General chapels	11	**12.6, 9, 13, 16, 39–40, 55, 58, 62, 64, 68**
Methodist		
Wesleyan chapels	2	**12.23, 41**
Primitive chapels	4	**12.24, 35, 42, 46**
Unclear	1	**12.10**
Roman Catholic church	1	**12.59**
Society of Friends (Quakers)	1	**12.43**
Unitarian chapel	1	**12.44**
Total	60	(+ 8 in Wilts.)

13   HO 129/341 Northleach district

Church of England churches	30	**13.1–3, 5–9, 12–4, 16, 18, 20–1, 24, 27, 30–2, 35–6, 38–44, 46**
Independent chapels	3	**13.10, 22–23**
Baptist		
General chapels	2	**13.15, 33**
Particular chapels	4	**13.25, 28, 34, 47**
Strict chapel	1	**13.37**
Baptist and Independent chapel	1	**13.19**
Methodist		
Wesleyan chapels	3	**13.11, 29, 45**
Primitive chapels	2	**13.4, 17**
Latter-day Saints (Mormons)	1	**13.26**
Total	47	

14   HO 129/342 Stow-on-the-Wold district

Church of England churches	21	**14.1, 3–5, 7, 9–10, 13–4, 16–9, 21, 23, 26, 28, 34–6, 38**
Independent chapel	1	**14.37**
Baptist		
General chapels	3	**14.11, 29–30**
Particular chapels	5	**14.2, 6, 8, 15, 31**
Methodist		
Wesleyan chapels	4	**14.12, 20, 27, 32**
Society of Friends (Quakers)	1	**14.33**
Total	35	(+ 3 in Worcs.)

15   HO 129/343 Winchcombe district

Church of England churches	25	**15.3–4, 6–7, 9, 11–4, 18–20, 22, 24–8, 30–6**
Baptist		
General chapels	4	**15.8, 15, 21, 23**
Methodist		
Wesleyan chapels	5	**15.5, 10, 16–17, 29**
Countess of Huntingdon's chapels	3	**15.37–39**
Total	37	(+ 2 in Worcs.)

16   HO 129/344 Cheltenham district

Church of England churches	17	**16.1–3, 5–7, 9, 11–3, 15–21**
Independent chapels	5	**16.14, 22–5**
Baptist		
General chapels	5	**16.8, 10, 28–30**
Particular chapel	1	**16.27**
Methodist		
Wesleyan chapels	5	**16.4, 31–4**
Wesleyan Association chapels	2	**16.35–6**
Countess of Huntingdon's chapel	1	**16.37**
Non-denominational	1	**16.26**
Roman Catholic church	1	**16.38**
Society of Friends (Quakers)	1	**16.39**
Unitarian chapel	1	**16.40**
Synagogue	1	**16.41**
Latter-day Saints (Mormons)	1	**16.42**
Total	42	

17   HO 129/345 Tewkesbury district

Church of England churches	15	**17.1, 3–5, 11–2, 14–6, 21, 28, 31–3, 37**
Independent chapel	1	**17.34**
Baptist		
Particular chapel	1	**17.35**
Seventh-day chapel	1	**17.29**
Methodist		
Wesleyan chapels	5	**17.6, 13, 22, 30, 36**
Bible Christian chapel	1	**17.7**
Non-denominational	2	**17.2, 17**
Roman Catholic church	1	**17.23**
Total	27	(+ 10 in Worcs.)

18   HO 129/576, 577 'Forest of Dean'

Church of England churches	18	**18.1, 3, 6, 10–2, 16, 18, 20–3, 25, 36–7, 48–50**
Church of England schoolrooms	3	**18.2, 24, 38**
Independent chapels	2	**18.17, 51**
Baptist		
General chapels	9	**18.4, 13, 26–29, 39–40, 47c**
Particular chapel	1	**18.7**
Methodist		
Wesleyan chapels	10	**18.5, 14, 19, 30–3, 41–3**
Primitive chapels	5	**18.15, 34, 44–6**
Bible Christian chapels	2	**18.9, 52**
Wesleyan Reformers chapel	1	**18.35**
United Brethren (Moravians)	1	**18.8**
Total	52	

19   HO 129/389, 404, 406 'North Gloucestershire'

Church of England churches	24	**19.1–3, 5–6, 10–1, 13–5, 20–2, 24–6, 28–30, 33–4, 36–8**
Independent chapels	2	**19.23, 39**
Baptist		
General chapel	1	**19.16**
Methodist		
Wesleyan chapels	9	**19.4, 7, 12, 17, 27, 31–32, 35, 40**
Primitive chapels	2	**19.8, 18**
Society of Friends (Quakers)	1	**19.19**
Latter-day Saints (Mormons)	1	**19.9**
Total	40	

20   HO 129/327 'South Bristol'

Church of England churches	10	**20.1–3, 22, 25–8, 37–8**
Independent chapels	10	**20.4–5, 11–12, 23, 29, 39–42**
Baptist		
General chapels	3	**20.13, 30, 43**
Methodist		
Wesleyan chapels	13	**20.6–8, 14–7, 31–3, 44–6**
Primitive chapels	3	**20.9, 18, 34**
Bible Christian chapel	1	**20.47**
Wesleyan Reformers chapels	8	**20.10, 19–20, 24, 35–6, 48–9**
Church of United Brethren (Moravians)	1	**20.21**
Total	49	(13 of which are in Bedminster)

APPENDIX 2:
SUMMARY TOTALS, BY DENOMINATION

Denomination	Glos. (Sections 2–20)	Bristol & Bedminster	Total	No returns	Published report (p. ccxlii)
Church of England	398	24	422	9	433
Independent	71	13	84	5	96
Independent and Baptist	2	-	2	-	-
Baptist	73	5	78	{4	1
Particular Baptist	22	-	22	{	83
Strict Baptist	1	-	1	{	{17
Welsh Baptist	-	1	1	{	{
Seventh Day Baptist	1	-	1	{	{
Wesleyan Methodist	131	6	137	8	144
Primitive Methodist	29	2	31	6	30
Bible Christian	7	1	8	1	7
Wesleyan Association	3	-	3	-	3
Wesleyan Reformers	25	3	28	6	30
Calvinistic Methodist	3	1	4	-	-
United Brethren (Moravians)	2	1	3	-	3
Countess of Huntingdon	7	1	8	-	11
Christian Brethren	9	2	11	-	8
Roman Catholic	11	3	14	2	14
Society of Friends (Quakers)	10	1	11	2	12
New Jerusalem Church (Swedenborgian)	1	1	2	-	1
Unitarian	5	1	6	-	7
Synagogues	1	1	2	-	2
Latter-day Saints (Mormons)	6	-	6	1	9
Others	7	2	9	-	16
Total	825	69	894	44	928

APPENDIX 3:
PLACES OF WORSHIP IN BRISTOL AND GLOUCESTERSHIRE, 1851: NUMERICAL STRENGTH BY DENOMINATION

Church of England	422
Methodist	211
Baptist	103
Independent	84
Roman Catholic	14
Christian Brethren	11
Society of Friends (Quakers)	10
Other	9
Countess of Huntingdon	8
Latter-day Saints (Mormons)	7
Unitarian	6
United Brethren (Moravians)	3
Independent and Baptist	2
New Jerusalem Church (Swedenborgians)	2
Synagogues	2
Total	894

As a summary figure the Religious Census report also recorded that within the diocese of Gloucester and Bristol there were in all 1,135 places of worship, of which 523 were Church of England and 612 other denominations. *Religious Worship in England and Wales,* 112.

APPENDIX 4:
SUMMARY TOTALS FOR BRISTOL

While, as already noted, the individual returns for the five City sub-districts are missing, the published report of the 1851 Census provides summary totals of places of worship, as follows:

The 1851 Religious Census for Bristol (population 65,716)   68 places of worship

| | | Number of sittings | | | 30 March 1851 | | |
		free	appropr-iated	total	morning	afternoon	evening
Church of England	25	5,711	8,956	16,017	9,545	804	7,269
Independent	11	2,817	4,957	7,774	4,112	25	4,084
Baptist	6	1,180	2,186	4,166	2,858	150	2,228
Wesleyan Methodist	3	1,190	1,740	2,930	584	90	590
Wesleyan Reformers	6	2,940	480	3,420	1,777	70	2,822
Calvinistic Methodist	1	340	810	1,150	702	-	725
United Brethren (Moravian)	1	400	-	400	262	-	147
Christian Brethren	1	170	-	170	70	-	76
Roman Catholic	3	916	334	1,250	1,560	580	850
Society of Friends	1	600	-	600	455	-	200
Unitarian	2	320	670	990	690	-	320
Synagogue	1	80	180	260	95	17	126
Latter-day Saints (Mormons)	1	-	-	-	-	-	-
Others	6	2,900	150	3,050	1,122	550	1,552

'The return omits to state the number of sittings in one place of worship belonging to the established church, attended by a maximum number of 14 persons at a service. The number of attendants is not given in the case of three places of worship belonging to the established church containing 1,786 persons. Neither sittings nor attendants are given in the case of one place of worship belonging to the Wesleyan Methodists; one place of worship belonging to the Wesleyan Reformers; and one place of worship belonging to the Latter-day Saints.' *Religious Worship in England and Wales,* 63.

APPENDIX 5:
PLACES OF WORSHIP NOT LISTED IN THE RELIGIOUS CENSUS

Some of the following are clear omissions from the Religious Census, but others are more tentative since they are taken from post-1851 county directories. It is likely that further places of worship, in private homes and known only to the worshippers, escaped the attention of the enumerators.

Church of England
St Lawrence, Barnwood
St Paul, Bedminster
St Mary Magdalene, Boddington
St John's, Cheltenham
St Mary the Virgin, Meysey Hampton
Holy Trinity, Stapleton
St Peter, Wapley cum Codrington
Sandford District National schoolroom,
    Cheltenham (St Luke's)
All Saints, Weston-on-Avon

Independent
Zion Chapel, Bedminster
Boxwell
Brockworth
Gas Green, Cheltenham
Coleford
Siddington

Baptist
Charlton Kings
Fishponds
Painswick
Woodford

Wesleyan Methodist
Bourton-on-the-Water
Coombe Hill, The Leigh
Hamfallow, Halmore
Horsley
Oldbury-on-the-Hill
Old Sodbury
Painswick
Westcote

Primitive Methodist
Alveston
Russell Street, Cheltenham
Duntisborne Abbots
Great Rissington

Jacksons Green, Painswick
Church Street, Tewkesbury

Bible Christian
Upper Sudley

Methodist Reformers
Bristol
    Broadmead
    Jacob Street
    Limehouse Lane
    Pyle Hill
    Thomas Street
    York Street, St Paul's

Roman Catholic
Bedminster
Nympsfield
Painswick

Society of Friends (**Quakers**)
Nailsworth
Tewkesbury

Latter-day Saints (**Mormons**)
Gloucester

APPENDIX 6:
THE LETTER TO CLERGY AND MINISTERS

Census of Great Britain, 1851
Instructions for filling up the schedule on the adjoining page.
(Prepared under the direction of Her Majesty's Principal Secretaries of State).

I	**Where situated**
	Describe accurately:
1	The locality of the building; and if it is situated in a town, the name of the street or other place.
2	The county.
3	The superintendent registrar's district or poor law union.

II   When erected

If the building was erected *before* the year 1800, or, if it has been erected since 1830 on the site or in lieu of one which existed before that year, in either of those cases write 'before 1800'. It it was erected *in* the year 1800, or has been erected *since,* on the site or in lieu of a previously existing building, insert as nearly as can be ascertained the precise year in which it was built, 'in the year 1800', or, 'about the year 1801' according to the fact of the case.

III   Whether a separate and entire building

As contra-distinguished from a mere room or part of a building. Insert in this column 'yes' or 'no' as the case may be.

IV   Whether exclusively a place of worship

Write also in this column 'yes' or 'no' according to the fact.

V   Space available for worship

4   In calculating the extent of the floor area, that space should be included which, being divided off by moveable shutter, is occasionally made use of for the purpose of divine worship, but no distinct room exclusively or chiefly used for meetings for discipline. If the building contains no gallery (the minsters' gallery' excepted), write across the column marked (5) the words 'no gallery', immediately opposite the words 'in the galleries'.

5   The annexed diagram is designed as an illustration of the mode in which the admeasurement of the area of a building of irregular shape may be taken; bearing in mind, however, that complete accuracy of mensuration is not essential, and that a near approximation to it is all that is desired.

VI   Number of attendants

If from any cause it be difficult to ascertain the number in attendance, the person making the return is at liberty to state the estimated *average* number of attendants on Sunday during the twelve calendar months preceding 30 March 1851, or during such portion of that period as the building has been open for public worship, stating in the column for 'remarks' the exact period, in months, for which the additional return is made.

And if, in consequence of repairs, or from other temporary cause, the building should not be open for public worship, on 30 March 1851, he will write he words 'no meeting', and insert the average number who are supposed to have attended on Sundays during twelve months next preceding the Sunday on which the meeting was last held.

VII   Remarks
Any observations which it may be deemed requisite to make in explanation of the return may be inserted in this column; or, if the column should not contain sufficient space for the purpose, may be written on a separate paper, and appended to the return.

VII   Signature etc.
The return should be signed by some member of the society, especially appointed for the purpose by the monthly meeting to which the meeting house belongs.

(Signed) George Graham, registrar general.

Approved (signed) G. Grey

Whitehall, 28 January 1851.

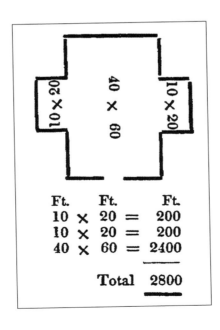

APPENDIX 7:
THE CONSECRATION OF ANGLICAN CHURCHES AND CHAPELS

The dioceses of Gloucester and Bristol were united in October 1836. The first bishop of the united diocese was James Henry Monk 1836–56 (who had been bishop of Gloucester from 1830); consecrations up to the end of his tenure are listed here. He was succeeded by Charles Baring 1856–61, William Thomson 1861–3 and Charles John Ellicott 1863–97. From January 1898 the dioceses were divided again.

1820–1827	**John Kaye (Bishop of Bristol – translated to Lincoln 1827–53)**	
31.08.1821	St Mary the Virgin, Fishponds (**2.71**)	
12.08.1822	St Andrew, Clifton (**2.1**)	
23.09.1823	St George, Brandon Hill, Bristol (**1.6**)	

1827–1834	**Robert Gray (Bishop of Bristol)**	
10.11.1830	Holy Trinity, Hotwells, Bristol (**2.3**)	(Bp of Llandaff)
14.11.1830	St Anne, Oldham (**20.28**)	
24.10.1831	St Paul, Bedminster (No return)	(Bp of Bath and Wells)
28.10.1831	Christ Church, Downend (**20.26**)	
17.02.1832	Holy Trinity, St Philips, Bristol (**2.35**)	
21.08.1834	St John the Baptist, Frenchay (**2.77**)	(Bp of Bath and Wells)

1834–1836	**Joseph Allen (Bishop of Bristol – translated to Ely 1836–45)**	
23.04.1835	St Matthew, Kingsdown, Bristol (**2.18**)	(Bp of Lichfield & Coventry)

1815–1824	**Henry Ryder (Bishop of Gloucester - translated to Lichfield and Coventry 1824–36)**	
07.07.1816	Christ Church, Berry Hill (**18.37**)	
26.06.1817	Holy Trinity, Harrow Hill (**6.6**)	
1819	St John the Baptist, Pitchcombe (**10.11**)	
21.02.1820	St John the Apostle, Sheepscombe (**10.14**)	
1820	All Saints, Blakeney (**6.2**)	
18.01.1821	St John the Evangelist, Coleford (**18.21**)	Replaced 15.05.1880
11.09.1821	Holy Trinity, Kingswood (**20.27**)	
02.05.1822	St Paul, Parkend (**18.36**)	
08.04.1823	Christ Church, Brunswick Square, Gloucester (**8.40**)	
11.04.1823	Holy Trinity, Cheltenham (**16.17**)	

1824–1830	**Christopher Bethell (Bishop of Gloucester – translated to Exeter 1830 then Bangor 1830–59)**	
01.04.1825	St James, Bream (**18.22**)	
22.01.1829	St John, Cheltenham (no return)	
06.01.1830	St Peter, Clearwell (**18.23**)	Replaced 05.04.1866

1830–1836	**James Henry Monk (Bishop of Gloucester)**	
05.10.1830	St James, Cheltenham (**16.19**)	
12.07.1831	St Paul, Cheltenham (**16.18**)	
10.09.1833	St John, Beachley (**18.3**)	
14.10.1834	Holy Trinity, Slad (**10.15**)	

1836–1856   James Henry Monk (Bishop of Gloucester and Bristol)

05.09.1836	Holy Trinity, Amberley (**10.63**)
19.01.1837	St Matthew, Cainscross (**10.4**)
24.08.1837	St Bartholomew, Oakridge (**10.26**)
30.08.1837	Holy Trinity, Tewkesbury (**17.33**)
20.11.1838	Blind Asylum Chapel, Bristol (**1.3**)
15.10.1839	Holy Trinity, Whiteshill, Stroud (**10.41**)
16.10.1839	St Martin, Horsley (**10.77**)
21.01.1840	Christ Church, Cheltenham (**16.20**)
07.04.1840	Holy Trinity, Brimscombe (**10.64**)
01.05.1840	St Philip and St James, Leckhampton (**16.6**) Replaced 13.04.1882
20.04.1841	St James, Gloucester (**8.36**)
21.04.1841	St Luke, Hempsted (**8.41**)
22.04.1841	St Paul, Whiteshill, Stroud (**10.42**)
27.04.1841	St John the Evangelist, Clifton (**2.4**)
15.09.1841	Christ Church, Chalford (**10.27**) Erected 1725
01.03.1842	Northwick Episcopal Chapel, Henbury (**4.13**)
07.10.1842	St Matthew, Twigworth (**8.11**)
18.10.1842	Christ Church, Jeffries Hill, Hanham (**20.3**)
22.04.1843	St Peter, Bishopsworth, Bedminster (**20.38**) (Bp of Salisbury)
12.09.1843	St Barnabas, Ashley Road, Bristol (**2.19**)
20.09.1843	St Luke, Barton Hill, Bristol (**2.36**)
16.04.1844	St Mark, Woodmancote (**5.21**)
24.08.1844	St Bartholomew, Lower Cam (**5.26**)
08.10.1844	Christ Church, Clifton (**2.5**)
22.10.1844	St John the Evangelist, Cinderford (**6.8**)
25.10.1844	St Luke, Frampton Mansell (**12.2**)
31.01.1845	St Andrew, Montpelier, Bristol (**2.16**)
09.10.1845	St Saviour Coalpit Heath (**3.3**)
24.02.1846	Bishops Chapel in his residence in Stapleton
06.10.1846	St Michael and All Angels, Bussage (**10.28**)
31.08.1847	St Mark, Kingsholm, Gloucester (**8.29**)
19.10.1847	St Nicholas, Kemerton (**17.21**)
21.10.1847	St Mary, Fretherne (**9.16**)
21.12.1847	St Simon the Apostle, Baptist Mills, Bristol (**2.37**)
22.12.1847	Holy Trinity, Horfield (**2.20**)
18.05.1848	St Mark, Lower Easton, Bristol (**1.10**)
22.08.1848	St Michael the Archangel, Two Mile Hill, Bristol (**1.14**)
23.08.1848	St Saviour, Tetbury (**11.15**)
24.08.1848	Holy Trinity, Cerney Wick (**12.34**)
29.01.1849	The Mariner's Chapel, Gloucester (**8.42**) Licensed but not consecrated
22.03.1849	St Peter, Cheltenham (**16.21**)
31.06.1849	St Jude the Apostle, The Dings, Bristol (**2.38**)
03.04.1850	St Bartholomew, Wick (**3.18**)
23.04.1851	St Barnabas, Warmley, Siston (**20.22**)
28.04.1851	St Michael, Gloucester (**8.25**)
29.04.1851	Holy Innocents, Highnam (**6.36**)
30.06.1851	St Philip and St James, Hucclecote (**8.7, 13**)
06.11.1851	Holy Trinity, Watermoor, Cirencester (**12.37**) (Bp of Llandaff)

25.11.1851	St Matthias on the Weir, Bristol	(Bp of Jamaica)
27.11.1851	St Giles, Hillesley (**3.35**)	
04.12.1851	Holy Jesus, Lydbrook (**18.38**)	(Bp of Llandaff)
16.01.1852	St Peter, Frocester (**9.23**)	Rebuilt
12.08.1853	St Luke, Tutshill (**18.2**)	
26.08.1852	Holy Ascension, Oddington (**14.21**)	
23.02.1854	St Matthias chapel, Fishponds	
21.09.1854	St Peter, Framilode (**9.12**)	
25.09.1854	St John the Baptist, Hallen (**2.64**)	
07.11.1854	St Luke, Cheltenham (**16.16**)	New chancel 03.01.1866
08.11.1854	St Paul, Clifton (**2.1**)	Rebuilt 29.09.1868
24.04.1855	St Clement, Newfoundland Road, Bristol (**1.16**)	
26.07.1855	St Cyr, Stinchcombe (**5.24**)	Rebuilt
09.08.1855	St Peter, Pilning (**4.4**)	
10.08.1855	St Peter, Clifton Wood, Bristol (**2.1**)	Replaced 26.09.1882
30.10.1855	St John, Bedminster (**20.37**)	Rebuilt

INDEX OF PERSONS

Most references are in the form *14.29* and relate to entry numbers in the body of the edition. Other references are to page numbers.

Frise, John 12.62
Finzil, Conrad 1.46

GABB, James Frederic Secretan 16.3
Gains, Hannah 20.35
Gambier, Charles Gore Gambier 13.13
Gamsley, Thomas 18.37
Garraway, James 2.7
Garrett, Charles 19.27
Garrow, Edward William 13.24, 13.32
Gascoyne, Richard 19.11
Gazard, Andrew 5.27
George, William 7, 11.13
Gibbins, O. J. 12.4
Gibbs, Thomas 19.4; Thomas Crook 12.22
Gibbons, J. 16.35
Gibson, Arthur 13.21
Gilby, Francis Duncan 16.19
Giles, James 2.62
Gill, Robin 37
Gillett, George S. 19.19
Gillman, Alfred 10.12
Glanville, John 20.11, 23
Glascott, Thomas 10.59
Glenorchy, Willielma 18, 2.6
'Goddard, Mrs' 24
Godwin, John 3.2; William 12.59
Goff, Edward 7.3; 18.40
Gompertz, Solomon 10.27
Golding, Joseph 20.20
Goldsmith, Edmund 19.28
Goodwin, Henry 7, 17.37
Grace, William Mills 20.28, 20.36
Grant, Charles 2.36
Gray, Henry 4.4; Robert 4.4, 411
Grey, Mrs 2.20
Green, Aaron 1.56
Green Joseph 15.6–7
Greening, Robert 15.17
Greening, William 16.10
Greenly, John 12.32
Gregory, Robert 32; William 2.6
Greswell, Clement 4.46
Griffiths, George Pruen 17.31–2; Thomas Charles 13.31
Gripp, George 18.34
Grove, Charles William 18.24–5

HADOW, William Elliot 19.13; William Thomas 19.11, 19.13
Hadley, Joseph L. 5.32
Hale, Matthew Blaydon 10.40

Hall, George Charles 6.36, 6.38; John 7.3, 7.21; Richard 13.15, 13.19
Ham, James Panton 1.31
Hancox, Henry William 10.36
Hands, Francis 4.44
Hanson, Henry 10.21
Hathins, John 18.5
Hardwick, Charles 8.25
Hardy, Thomas 34
Harris, Charles T. 1.40; Sampson 16, 10.3
Hart, Henry Cornelius 11.13; Richard 26
Harvey, George Ludford 3.47
Harvey, Henry 4.7; John Ridout 15.12–4; Ludford 3.47
Harward, John 14.17
Hasluck, James George Edward 3.8, 3.33
Haybury, Richard Tilbey 18.33
Haycock, Samuel 8.46
Haycroft, Nathaniel 1.32
Hayward, George Christopher 5.12; N. C. 12.36
Hazlitt, William 3.27
Head, George 19.29
Hemming, William 19.32
Hensman, John 18, 27, 2.1–2, 2.36
Hepworth, Robert 17.14
Herbert, Charles 18.30
Herrett, Joseph H. 3.52
Herschell, John Francis Israel 8.17
Hessell, William 20.46
Hicks, Isaac 20.24; John 4.13, 4.22; John Champion 4.22; William 13.31; 16.7, 20.39
Higgs, Charles 8.15
Hill, Arthur 10.15; Charles 7.23; John Oakley 14.19; Nathaniel 10.73; Reginald Pyndar 7.23; Richard 7.29, 7.31; Rowland 15, 18–9, 26, 30, 2.78; 4.36, 4.42; 5.8, 5.22; 6.3; 9.18; 16.24; Thomas 7.26, 10.68, 14.9–10; William Henry 6.40
Hinleath, Hugh 3.29
Hinton, Thomas 10.24a; 12.6
Hippisley, Robert 14.28
Hirst, John 6.20, 23
Hitchman, William 3.39
Hobbs, George 2.25
Hobson, Thomas 10.50
Hodges, Henry 2.21; Richard 13.5
Hodgkins, George 14.27b
Hodgson, William 16.21
Hogg, Richard 17.7
Hohler, Frederic William 12.5, 12.12

Roleston, Francis Hammond 3.9
Rolf, Thomas 14.33
Rolt, J. 10.23
Ross, James A. 16.42
Rossiter, William 2.27
Rowland, George 10.50
Royce, David 14.34
Rudge, Thomas 9.6
Riskin, William 10.3
Russell, Richard 11.20
Ryder, Henry 27, 29, 8.25, 411

SADLER, H. 10.23
Sage, Daniel 4.8b
Salt, George 2.22
Salter, John 3.51
Sargent, Isaac 4.10
Saunders, Thomas 19.40
Savage, Thomas 8.33
Sayce, Henry Samuel 2.56
Saye and Sele 14.23a, 26
Sayers, Andrew 7.14; 8.34
Sayres, Edward 3.22
Scott, Francis John 17.33
Servante, William 7.20
Seton-Karr, John 4.39
Sevier, James 17.4
Shadrack, Eliakim Lloyd 5.22
Shapter, Henry Dwyer 11.23
Sharp, Henry 19.5
Shaylor, Charles 10.67
Shelton, John 5.13
Shenton, Thomas Bartlett 16.40
Sherer, George 3.23
Sherry, Daniel Best 11.8
Sherwood, Thomas Moulden 8.7
Sherriff, James 6.31
Ship, Charles 40
Short, George 20.4; Jacob 13.25, 13.28, 13.37
Simeon, Charles 18, 27–8, 2.1; 10.14; 16.23
Simm, Samuel 12.25
Simons, John 7.17
Sims, Joseph 8.26
Sisson, Joseph Lawson 3.48; 18.21
Skally, John 7.5
Slatterie, John 4.41
Slay, Joseph 10.69
Smedley, John 7.30; 8.14, 30
Smith, Abel 10.14; George 3.13, 3.39;
    George Jameson 15.23; Isaac 2.73; Jacob
    10.54; James Ben 2.50; John 12.13,
    16.29; Jonas 18.46; Joseph 26; Robert

8.13, 16.9; Thomas 3.8, 17.30; William
    15.32–3; 17.18–9
Smythies, Thomas Gosselin 6.8
Snow, Henry 13.14, 13.16; Thomas 30, 6.39,
    14.11, 16.23, 16.37
Solly, Henry 16.40
Southcott, Joanna 23–4; Joseph 23
Sparkman, Charles 12.9
Sparks, Enos 2.80
Sparrow, Olivia 10.14; 18.37; William 13.17
Spencer, William 3.19
Spire, Thomas 9.16, 9.19
Sprod, Sidney 2.48
Spurgeon, Charles Haddon 14.11
Statham, John 13.47; 14.2, 14.6, 14.8, 14.15
Stay, Joseph 10.69
Sternberg, Samuel 16.41
Stock, John 10.2
Steel, John 42, 19.35
Steele, George 9.21
Stephens, John M. 12.39; Maurice 4.19–21;
    R. 6.34–5
Sternberg, Samuel 16.41
Stock, Thomas 22
Stokes, Robert 10.26, 10.63
Stott, George 15.18
Strange, William, 3.11
Stratford, Joseph 13.22–3
Stratton, Mr 2.70
Strickland, John 1.4; Thomas Alfred 15.1;
    17.24–5
Strong, Leonard 10.13
Strong, Robert 10.13
Stowers, Henry 19.22
Stowell, Hugh 2.3; 10.14
Stowers, Henry Mellish 19.22
Sturge, Edward 4.12a–b
Suckling, Richard Randall 12.4; Robert
    Alfred 32, 10.28, 10.32
Surman, John 17.14
Sutton, Nathan 10.18
Swain, James 20.10
Swedenborg, Emmanuel 1.54
Symonds, William Samuel 17.9
Symmonds, James 19.8

TABRAM, I. C. 10.73
Tait, Archibald Campbell 1.13
Taylor, Charles 18.11–2, 18.16, 18.18
Talbot, George Gustavus Chetwynd 13.27
Taylor, James 2.39; John Brain 4.26; Richard
    8.9; 15.8; Samuel 26

INDEX OF PLACES

Most references are in the form *6.24* and are to entry numbers in the body of the edition. Remaining references are to pages in the Introduction. Unless otherwise indicated, all places are now or were once in Bristol or Gloucestershire.

ABENHALL 31, 6.24
Abson 3.17
Acton Turville 3.30–1
Adlestrop 14.23
Adsett 11
Alderley 3.43
Alderton 15.28–9
Aldsworth 13.12
Alkerton 9.22
Almondsbury 4.4–5
Alston 15.33
Alveston 4.1–3
Alvington 18.10
Amberley 10.63
America 15–6, 26
Ampney Crucis 12.50
Ampney St Mary 12.52
Ampney St Peter 12.51
Apperley 22, 17.13
Arlingham 9.14–5
Arlington 13.15
Ashbrook *see* Ampney St Mary
Ashchurch 17.28
Ashleworth 9, 8.4
Ashley (Bristol) 2.16–21
Ashley (Glos.) 11.23
Aston Blank 13.46–7
Aston Ingham (Herefs.) 7.1
Aston Somerville 19.29
Aston-sub-Edge 19.33
Ashton under Hill 19.26–7
Aston on Carrant 17.30
Aust 4.14
Avening 11, 10.70, 10.75
Awre 6.1
Aylburton 18.12

BADGEWORTH 16.12
Badminton, Great 3.32
Bagendon 12.17
Barnsley 12.49
Barnwood 8.6, (16)
Barrington, Great 14.3
Barrington, Little 13.5

Barrow Gurney, Som. 15
Barton End, Gloucester 14
Bath (Som.) 16
Batsford 19.21
Baunton 12.20
Beachley 18.3
Beckford 15.31
Bedminster 20.37, 20.41–9
Berkeley 1, 7, 10, 20, 23–4, 31, 4.39, 4.41, 4.44
Berry Hill 18.37
Beverston 11.12
Bibury 13.14–5
Birdlip 12.9
Birdwood 18
Bishoport 20.39
Bishop's Cleeve 12, 18, 15.35, 15.39; 20.38
Bishopworth 11.11
Bisley 6, 32–3, 10.25, 10.33
Bitton 10, 31, 34, 20.1, 20.4–7, 20.9–10, 20.14, 20.17
Blackfriars, London 19
Blackwell, Som. 15
Blagdon, Som. 15
Blaisdon 6.28
Blakeney 19, 30, 6.2, 6.3–4
Bledington 14.19–21
Blockley 8, 24
Boddington 17.2
Bourton on the Hill 10, 19.20
Bourton-on-the-Water 13, 14.7–8
Bouthrop (Eastleach Martin) 13.2
Boxwell 11.4
Bradley Greenfield 14, 5.5
Bradley Hill 6.15
Bream 28, 18.22, 18.33
Bredon 17.24
Breech Hill, Som. 15
Brimpsfield 12.8, 12.10
Brimscombe 10.64, 10.67–8
Bristol 4, 6, 8, 11–3, 16–8, 22–6, 29–31, 36; sections 1, 2 and 20 *passim*
Broad Campden 19.15, 19.19
Broadmead 14, 18